This rich volume with its useful and original focus on teaching makes me wish I were teaching Arabic literature again. Including chapters by experts on all the major and many minor genres, the highly stimulating collection will be fruitfully read by teachers and students of Arabic and world literature.

Geert Jan van Gelder, Laudian Professor of Arabic emeritus, University of Oxford

This critically acute and pedagogically canny collection offers a host of ways to bring Arabic literature more fully into comparative and world literature classrooms, as well as in more specifically Middle Eastern courses. These essays offer new pathways into a wide range of classic and modern texts, in illuminating discussions that will be full of interest for teachers, scholars, and general readers alike.

David Damrosch, Ernest Bernbaum Professor and Chair, Department of Comparative Literature, Harvard University

In this fine addition to a growing corpus of such materials, Muhsin al-Musawi and his colleagues have brought to bear on the teaching of Arabic literature a wide-ranging, high quality and apposite set of texts, insights, and best practices, designed to guide both novices and seasoned experts alike.

Shawkat M. Toorawa, Professor of Arabic Literature, Yale University

ARABIC LITERATURE FOR THE CLASSROOM

Arabic Literature for the Classroom argues for a more visible presence of Arabic within the humanities and social sciences, stressing the need to make Arabic literature available as a world literature, without damaging its own distinctive characteristics.

The 19 chapters that make up this book broach theoretical and methodical cultural concerns in teaching literatures from non-American cultures, along with issues of cross-cultural communication, cultural competency and translation. While some chapters bring out the fascinating and ever tantalizing connections between Arabic and the literatures of medieval Europe, others employ specific approaches to teaching particular texts, potential methodologies, themes and a variety of topics that can place Arabic widely in a vast swath of academic application and learning. Topics that are explored include gender, race, class, trauma, exile, dislocation, love, rape, humor, and cinema, as well as issues that relate to writers and poets, women's writing and the so-called *nahḍah* (revival) movement in the nineteenth century.

The comparative framework and multi-disciplinary approach mean that this book injects new life into the field of Arabic Literature. It will therefore be an essential resource for students, scholars and teachers of Arabic Literature, as well as for anyone with an interest in learning more about Arabic culture.

Muhsin J. al-Musawi is Professor of Arabic and Comparative Literature at Columbia University and the author of many books in English and Arabic, including *Arabic Poetry*. His publications cover theory, postcolonial discourse, the Arabic novel, poetry, medieval Islamic knowledge and modern Arabic poetics.

ARABIC LITERATURE FOR THE CLASSROOM

Teaching Methods, Theories, Themes and Texts

Edited by Muhsin J. al-Musawi

LONDON AND NEW YORK

First published 2017
by Routledge
2 Park Square, Milton Park, Abingdon, Oxon OX14 4RN

and by Routledge
605 Third Avenue, New York, NY 10017

Routledge is an imprint of the Taylor & Francis Group, an informa business

British Library Cataloguing in Publication Data
A catalogue record for this book is available from the British Library

Library of Congress Cataloging in Publication Data
Names: al-Musawi, Muhsin J., editor.
Title: Arabic literature for the classroom : teaching methods, theories, themes and texts / edited by Muhsin J. al-Musawi.
Description: Abingdon, Oxon; New York, NY : Routledge, 2017. | Includes bibliographical references and index.
Identifiers: LCCN 2016049451| ISBN 9781138211964 (hardback) | ISBN 9781138211971 (pbk.) | ISBN 9781315451657 (ebook)
Subjects: LCSH: Arabic literature–Study and teaching.
Classification: LCC PJ7505 .A73 2017 | DDC 892.7/071–dc23
LC record available at https://lccn.loc.gov/2016049451

ISBN: 978-1-138-21196-4 (hbk)
ISBN: 978-1-138-21197-1 (pbk)
ISBN: 978-1-315-45165-7 (ebk)

Typeset in Bembo
by Taylor & Francis Books

CONTENTS

FIGURES

CONTRIBUTORS

Roger Allen retired in June 2011 after serving for 43 years as Professor of Arabic and Comparative Literature at the University of Pennsylvania. In 2009–10 he was President of the Middle East Studies Association of North America. He is the author of numerous studies in book and article form devoted to the Arabic literary tradition, and is also a translator of numerous contributions to the tradition of both modern and pre-modern Arabic narrative.

Muhsin J. al-Musawi is Professor of Arabic and Comparative Literature, Columbia University. The editor since 2002 of the *Journal of Arabic Literature*, he is also the recipient of the Owais Award in literary criticism. His publications cover theory, postcolonial discourse, the Arabic novel, and poetry, Orientalism, the *Arabian Nights*, medieval Islamic knowledge, and modern Arabic poetics. Author of numerous books in Arabic, and also five novels, his books in English include: *Scheherazade in England*; *Anglo-Orient*; *The Postcolonial Arabic Novel*; *Islam on the Street*; *The Medieval Islamic Republic of Letters*; *Arabic Poetry: Trajectories of Modernity and Tradition*; *The Islamic Context of the Thousand and One Nights*; and *Reading Iraq: Culture and Power in Conflict.*

Hanadi Al-Samman is Associate Professor of Arabic Language and Literature in the Department of Middle Eastern and South Asian Languages and Cultures at the University of Virginia. Her research focuses on contemporary Arabic literature, diaspora and sexuality studies, as well as transnational and Islamic feminism(s). She published several articles in *Journal of Arabic Literature*, *Women's Studies International Forum*, *Alif: Journal of Comparative Poetics*. She is the co-editor of an *International Journal of Middle East Studies*' special issue "Queer Affects," *The Beloved in Middle Eastern Literature: The Culture of Love and Languishing*, and author of *Anxiety of Erasure: Trauma, Authorship, and the Diaspora in Arab Women's Writings*.

Taoufik Ben Amor is Gordon Gray Jr. Senior Lecturer in Arabic Studies. He has published three textbooks, including *Advanced Writing Skills in Arabic* (Routledge, 2013), and a number of papers on teaching Arabic as a foreign language, language, music and identity. He is an active musician and music producer.

miriam cooke is Braxton Craven Distinguished Professor of Arab Cultures. She is the author of several books about war, gender and Arab women writers, Islamic feminism, Muslim networks and Syrian culture. Her most recent publication is *Dancing in Damascus: Creativity, Resilience and the Syrian Revolution* (2017).

Terri DeYoung is Professor of Arabic Language and Literature at the University of Washington. She received her BA from Princeton University (1977), her MA from the American University in Cairo (1981), and her PhD from the University of California, Berkeley (1988). She is the author of a number of articles and studies on modern and medieval Arabic literature. Her monographs include *Placing the Poet: Badr Shakir al-Sayyab and Postcolonial Iraq* (1998), and *Mahmud Sami al-Barudi: Reconfiguring Society and the Self* (2015).

Tarek El-Ariss is Associate Professor of Arabic and Comparative Literature at the University of Texas at Austin, and Associate Editor of the *Journal of Arabic Literature.* He was the EUME postdoctoral fellow at the Forum for Transregional Studies, Berlin (2012–13). He is author of *Trials of Arab Modernity: Literary Affects and the New Political* (Fordham, 2013), and editor of *The Arab Renaissance: A Bilingual Anthology of Nahda Literature and Culture (1707–1937)* (Modern Language Association, 2016).

Hoda El Shakry is Assistant Professor of Comparative Literature at Pennsylvania State University, where she specializes in modern Arab/ic and African literatures. Her research and publications explore literature and visual culture of the Middle East and North Africa, Islamic philosophy, postcolonial studies and critical theory. Her current book project investigates literary engagements with Islamic thought in twentieth-century Arabophone and Francophone literature of the Maghreb.

Nathaniel Greenberg is Assistant Professor of Arabic at George Mason University and author of *The Aesthetic of Revolution in the Film and Literature of Naguib Mahfouz (1952–1967).* His research and teaching interests focus on modern Arabic cultural production, including film and literature. He serves currently as the book review editor for the *Journal of Arabic Literature.*

Ghenwa Hayek is Assistant Professor of Modern Arabic Literature in the Department of Near Eastern Languages and Civilizations at the University of Chicago. She is the author of *Beirut, Imagining the City: Space and Place in Lebanese Literature* (I.B. Tauris, 2015).

Nizar F. Hermes is Advanced Assistant Professor of Classical Arabic Literature at the University of Virginia. His book *The [European] Other in Medieval Arabic Literature and Culture Ninth–Twelfth Century AD* appeared in 2012, and he is currently co-editing a volume with Gretchen Head entitled *The City in Arabic Literature: Classical and Modern Perspectives* (forthcoming from Edinburgh University Press).

Elizabeth M. Holt is Assistant Professor of Arabic in the Division of Languages and Literature at Bard College, and Associate Editor of the *Journal of Arabic Literature.* She is the author of *Fictitious Capital: Silk, Cotton, and the Rise of the Arabic Novel* (Fordham University Press, 2017), and is finishing a second monograph on cultural cold war in the Arab world.

Boutheina Khaldi is Associate Professor at the American University of Sharjah, and author of *Egypt Awakening in the Early Twentieth Century* and a number of other books in Arabic. She has co-edited textbooks for the AUS.

Brinda J. Mehta is the Germaine Thompson Professor of French and Francophone Studies at Mills College in Oakland, California. She is the author of five books: *Dissident Writings of Arab Women: Voices Against Violence* (2014); *Notions of Identity, Diaspora and Gender in Caribbean Women's Writing* (2009); *Rituals of Memory in Contemporary Arab Women's Writing* (2007); *Diasporic (Dis)locations: Indo-Caribbean Women Writers Negotiate the Kala Pani* (2004, winner of the Frantz Fanon Award for Caribbean Thought); and *Corps infirme, corps infâme: la femme dans le roman balzacien* (1992).

James T. Monroe is Emeritus Professor of Arabic and Comparative Literature at the University of California, Berkeley, focusing on classical Arabic literature and Hispano-Arabic literature. His books include *The Art of Badi'u al-Zaman al-Hamadhani as Picaresque Narrative*; *Hispano-Arabic Strophic Songs in the Modern Oral Tradition*, co-authored with Benjamin M. Liu; *Hispano-Arabic Poetry. A Student Anthology*; *Islam and the Arabs in Spanish Scholarship (Sixteenth Century to the Present)*; and *Al-Maqamat al-Luzumiyah, by Abu-l-Tahir Muhammad ibn Yusuf al-Tamimi al-Saraqusti ibn al-Astarkuwi.*

Jeffrey Sacks is Associate Professor of Arabic and Comparative Literature at the University of California, Riverside. He is the author of *Iterations of Loss: Mutilation and Aesthetic Form, al-Shidyaq to Darwish* (Fordham University Press, 2015), and has translated Mahmud Darwish's *Why Did You Leave the Horse Alone?* (Archipelago, 2006).

Jocelyn Sharlet is Associate Professor of Comparative Literature at the University of California, Davis, where she teaches courses on Middle Eastern literature, world literature and Arabic. She has published *Patronage and Poetry in the Islamic World: Social Mobility and Status in the Medieval Middle East and Central Asia* (I.B. Tauris, 2011), and articles in a range of journals, including the *Journal of Arabic Literature,*

Middle Eastern Literatures and the *Journal of Persianate Studies*, as well as chapters in several edited volumes.

Jaroslav Stetkevych is Chicago University Emeritus Professor and a prominent classical scholar, and author of a number of books, especially *The Zephyrs of Najd*, and *The Golden Bough of Muhammad.*

Shaden M. Tageldin is Associate Professor of Cultural Studies and Comparative Literature and Director of the African Studies Initiative at the University of Minnesota. Her book, *Disarming Words: Empire and the Seductions of Translation in Egypt* (University of California Press), was awarded Honorable Mention for the 2013 Harry Levin Prize of the American Comparative Literature Association. She is working on her second book, provisionally titled *Toward a Transcontinental Theory of Modern Comparative Literature.*

ACKNOWLEDGEMENTS

This book is no ordinary edited volume or the outcome of a simple "call for papers." Rather, it has stemmed from a series of invitations to participate in four conferences on teaching Arabic that were held at Columbia University and the New School. Contributions to this volume are thus the outcome of several years of conversations, reflections, feedback, and a rigorous vetting and editing process at the end. Thanks are due to Columbia University's Arabic Studies Seminar, the Department of Middle Eastern, South Asian, and African Studies (MESAAS), and Middle East Institute (MEI) for their generous funding of these conferences. I also thank the Dean of Arts and Sciences at the New School, and also Nargis Virani, who hosted the first conference. I am grateful to Veli Yashin and Yasmine Khayyat for their help in organizing the first three conferences. I am lucky to have with me Elizabeth Holt and Tarek El-Ariss who offered great help at a later stage. Sahar Ullah Ishtiaqi deserves such thanks for her work, and so does Joscelyn Shawn Ganjhara Jurich.

Ample thanks should go to Riad El-Rayyes Books, and to Riyad and Fatima specifically, for granting me the rights to reproduce and translate works by the late Mahmud Darwish. Similar thanks go to the director of the Cairo-based Women and Memory Forum, Hoda Elsadda, for permission to reproduce Nabawiyya Musa's letter to Dunlop. I thank profusely Nawal al-Sa'dawi for permission to republish her letter to President Husni Mubarak. To Margaret Obank, editor of *Banipal*, go warm thanks for permission to reproduce Qasim Haddad's "The Poets." To my dear friend, the great artist and prominent Iraqi painter Dia al-Azzawi, goes my sincere appreciation and gratitude for the volume's cover art.

Editing an anthology with many contributors necessarily incurs further debts: I thank warmly Terri DeYoung, Roger Allen, Tarek El-Ariss, and my former student and colleague Nizar Hermes; they did their best to cope with many difficulties during the editing process. Due thanks should go to all contributors for their patience and commitment to the project throughout. Due thanks go to the anonymous reviewers for their insightful comments and also to my great colleagues Geert Jan van Gelder, Shawkat Toorawa, and David Damrosch for their endorsements. To Joe Whiting and his assistant Emma Tyce, and Ruth Bradley at Routledge goes my sincere gratitude for very professional and friendly support throughout.

INTRODUCTION

Arabic Literature for the Classroom: Teaching Methods, Theories, Themes and Texts

Muhsin J. al-Musawi

This edited book argues for a more visible presence of Arabic within the humanities and social sciences. While focusing on Arabic literature for the classroom, it places the discussion within the broad concept of *adab*,[1] as a comprehensive endeavor albeit with thorough grounding in Arabic sciences. It purports to lead learners and teachers neatly and nicely into fields that have remained outside modern European conceptualization of literature as pure literariness. It presents therefore not only multiple readings of Arabic literature and language to learners and teachers of Arabic within various academic contexts, but also interdisciplinary approaches and thematic pursuits to students and scholars in the broad fields of knowledge.

The book engages with the transgeneric, the extraterritorial, and the broad cultural terrain to explore gender, race, class, trauma, exile, dislocation, love, rape, humor, and cinema, along with issues that relate to writers and poets, movements, women's writing, and specific but enduring narratives like the *Arabian Nights* and the *maqāmāt.* These are pursued, discussed, and presented not only in terms of translation, transference, and appropriation, but also in view of a *realpolitik* that gives meaning to Mahmud Darwish's act of reading, for example, and which makes a text like the *Story of Zahra* a classroom ideal. Almost nothing that every learner or scholar desires is left out, for topics, themes, texts, movements, and people appear lively and in dialogue with issues that cut across disciplines and fit well into world literature. In sum, while the book is specifically tailored for the classroom, it aspires to invigorate it as a dynamic space for interaction and knowledge acquisition. It provides instructors with perspectives and topics that serve planning and designing new courses while accommodating already existing programs and courses.

Its comparative framework and multi-disciplinary approach thus place it appropriately within the field of comparative and world literature, and also associate it with the pedagogical goals of other literature departments like English and French.

It even goes beyond the goals and demands of university-based programs and presents an appeal to those interested in the broad realms of Arab culture. Its uniqueness, however, derives from its focus on teaching methods that incorporate studies of such topics as critical pedagogy, popular narratives such as the *Thousand and One Nights*, frametales, humor, trauma, love, urban life, the Maghreb region, Arab Spring cinema, and renowned figures such as the Palestinian poet Mahmud Darwish.

The 19 studies that make up this book broach theoretical and methodical cultural concerns in teaching literatures from non-American cultures along with issues of cross-cultural communication, cultural competency and translation. While some studies bring out the fascinating and ever-tantalizing connections between Arabic and the literatures of medieval Europe, other articles employ specific approaches to teaching particular texts, potential methodologies, themes and a variety of topics that can place Arabic widely in a vast swath of academic application and learning.

However, as mentioned above, the significance and uniqueness of the book are not confined to Arabic pedagogy and literary fields, and not only to the teaching and learning of Arabic, but also to its conversations and interactions with other disciplines and programs devoted to other literary cultures. Along with its primary focus on the classroom learning experience, it also discusses objectives that will enable instructors and their like to prepare their teaching plans easily and efficiently. It takes into account the needs of students who are majoring in Arabic, and provides information and advice that will lead both instructors and learners toward the broader goals of in-depth learning and teaching methodology.

The contributors come from different academic ranks, but all are involved in teaching Arabic and comparative literature, along with such topics as women's writing, Francophone literature, humor and urban studies. All these scholars are able to come up with a number of perspectives that enhance and valorize the teaching/learning spectrum. The book is, after all, the outcome of four conferences – three of them held at Columbia University over the years 2008–12, and one in co-coordination with the New School in New York. After passing through conference discussions, these contributions underwent a rigorous vetting process which gives space to nonconformist opinions that are powerfully argued.

The book is planned in its present form as a coherent and sustained project. Under Part I, Theory and Method, there are seven essays, each with a specific focus that nevertheless reflects on the rest, albeit with its own argument. In "Proxidistant reading: Toward a critical pedagogy of the *nahḍah* in US comparative literary studies," Shaden M. Tageldin follows her intricate way of resistance to either/or discussions of *nahḍah*,[2] situating the argument in this in-betweenness that presents acts and pursuits in a proxidistant reading that assumes neither equivalence nor non-relation between the modifiers Arabic, Western, and world.

Her navigation to bring together secondary sources and others from outside literariness to read *nahḍah*, is well pursued in the next chapter, "Teaching Arab women's letters," by Boutheina Khaldi. By showing the power and richness of this epistolary art, Khaldi brings a new dimension to our reading of the so-called Arab renaissance at the turn of the nineteenth century. These letters can endow curricula with richness and depth beyond the limits that circumscribe *nahḍah,* as male endeavor.

This is also the point that miriam cooke would like to demonstrate in her chapter "Arab women writers 1980–2010," but not through epistolary art. She addresses this period to update our knowledge of women's writing, and hence to enhance understanding of this writing as a mainstream in culture industry.

Brinda Mehta is more concerned with Algerian women's writing in her "Teaching Francophone Algerian women's literature in a bilingual French-English context: Creative voices, dissident texts." The article takes us to these texts and writers and discusses them as classroom material that is bound to incite interest and discussion from a number of perspectives, especially the feminist and the postcolonial.

Jocelyn Sharlet leads us back to an early period that, in one way or another, laid the ground for the previous discussions. She rather addresses the classical period in her "Approaches to teaching classical Arabic literature in English translation," which she presents as necessarily transferable in world literature through translation, hence faring easily in comparative literature, humanities and social sciences.

This is what Nizar Hermes stretches further in his "Classical and medieval Arabic literary delights: Towards teaching the humanistic literature of the Arabs," to argue humor in classical *adab* as the most viable means of engaging comparatists and other humanists in search of a common ground among cultures. As he draws on his experience in teaching these "delights," he shows how such texts and anecdotes work in an active classroom.

This certainly dovetails with the next chapter, which shows how literary texts work in teaching language. In "Language through literature," Taoufik Ben Amor uses his experience in teaching to emphasize the urgent need to bring more literature into the classroom. By bringing together theories and teaching methods, these seven essays uniquely demonstrate the significance of new visions and practices to inject the classroom with vitality and appeal which should be in keeping with the increasing interest in Arabic.

With the chapters in Part II, on Theme, learners, teachers and scholars are well prepared to explore thematic issues that range from identity to humor as pacifier, to trauma, urban life under war, and issues of reading poetry, cinema and narrative. This thematic range does not hang on topics, though these can be found there, but rather on problems that may confront the student of Arab culture.

In her "Lessons from the Maghreb," Hoda El Shakry examines the Maghreb as "an imagined and geopolitical site." The Maghreb's ethno-linguistic diversity and geopolitical location have contributed to the development of a semiotically and culturally unstable model of national and supranational identity. Although this surmise may sound difficult to sustain, the essay argues its case rigorously and challenges other projections and stipulations.

In confrontation with a *realpolitik,* with issues of enforced proclamations and settlements, humor comes forward as one way of laying bare the trampling on human life. Such is the significant engagement of Tarek El-Ariss with "Teaching humor in Arabic literature and film," where humor in, and for, modern debacles operates as a classroom venue, simple but powerful.

Hanadi al-Samman brings methodologies and thematics together from a different angle in "The art of teaching Arab traumas triumphantly," whereby a pedagogy that goes beyond historical facts and into trauma reenactments is presented. Students will engage with Arab pain and suffering through texts and thematic concerns.

The presentation of this traumatic experience finds further elucidation and examination in Ghenwa Hayek's "The urban gateway: Teaching the city in modern Arabic literature." In her endeavor to exercise "a city-based approach," Hayek argues its viability to bring to light new, intersectional readings of familiar texts and contexts, in situations like the Lebanese civil war.

If the traumatic is only an outcome of dislocation, enforced eviction, and destruction, then Hayek's discussion of Darwish's narrative of Beirut under siege only prepares us for Jeff Sacks's impressive undertaking, "Teaching Mahmud Darwish," for here Sacks problematizes critical-theoretical engagements with loss and with the question of Palestine, and argues how Darwish offers lessons in reading poetry. Darwish's language unsettles common understanding and reading of poetry and poetics.

It is this concern with "Teaching the modernist Arabic poem in translation" that becomes the main issue of the next chapter, by Muhsin al-Musawi. The chapter takes a number of poems in translation, especially by Darwish, to pose another problem, that of the discourse of space against erasure. However, to teach Darwish, especially his "Birwa Ode," requires an engagement with an Arab poetics that the poet unearths, re-reads, and presents anew to cope with hard realities.

No less concerned with art, poetry, narrative, and performing art is Nathaniel Greenberg's "The politics of perception in post-revolutionary Egyptian cinema." Here he discusses the censorship code in Egypt, representations of the public sphere, and also the ever-changing consciousness in these narrative representations.

These thematic engagements rest on texts and art that make up Part III of this volume, Text. Roger Allen's "Teaching the *maqâmât* in translation" draws the possibilities of course designs that cover this major participant in pre-modern narrative in Arabic. This chapter, which builds up strong conversational lines with other essays in this volume (Chapters 5, 6, 13 and 18), shows how this narrative art has sustained a presence throughout Arab culture to pursue generic, transgeneric, and also political and social concerns. Its practitioners and writers raise questions that relate to authors and writers as significant actors.

Indeed, this is what makes Terri DeYoung's "Ibn Ḥazm: Friendship, love and the quest for justice" of so much importance. In raising the case of this Andalusian intellectual, essayist, poet, jurist, and political figure, DeYoung focuses on how Andalusian literature fits into a schema of Arabic literary periodization, and how it makes itself relevant to a European (specifically early modern) literary context.

The texts and their writer lead us to a similar but modern case. Elizabeth Holt's "*The Story of Zahra* and its critics: Feminism and agency at war" acquaints us with how the writer Hanan al-Shaykh would like us to read her narrative which other critics look at from different angles like war, sex, struggle, pain, trauma, rape, and death – topics that can unsettle any definitive interpretation. Where should the classroom stand, with a writer's reading or with that of critics who are of different views and perspectives?

The last two chapters are by James Monroe, "The Arabic frametale and two European offspring," and Muhsin al-Musawi, "Teaching the *Arabian Nights.*" Monroe's essay is thoroughly researched to demonstrate the impact of the frametale on Andalusian and medieval European literature. Monroe proposes some theological dimension to the appearance, growth and appropriation of some frametales. This is not what Muhsin al-Musawi is after. The reception and multiple translations or abridgements and appropriations relate to a history of translation in dialogue with and response to power relations, a case that should draw a line between a history of Arabic manuscripts and that of European translations. These last chapters can work well for a full-semester course.

In sum, these contributions build up a conversation among them which can generate further ideas and suggestions among teachers, learners, and educators. Indeed, they inject a new life into the field and bring it much closer to other domains of knowledge while inviting other disciplines to engage more with *adab* as a comprehensive pursuit.

Notes

1 *Adab* is an inclusive term for knowledge, including prose and poetry, genres, subgenres and prosimetrum.
2 *Nahḍah* is an umbrella term for late nineteenth- to early twentieth-century engagement with issues of modernity and nation building.

PART I

Theory and method

1

PROXIDISTANT READING

Toward a critical pedagogy of the *nahḍah* in US comparative literary studies

Shaden M. Tageldin

Courses that teach modern Arabic literature, particularly those that address non-specialists, often focus on relatively recent exemplars of the canon. Most engage texts that hail from the mid- to late twentieth century – a period in which the fate of "new" narrative genres (for example, the novel) is well established – rather than those that evoke a time when the boundaries between "tradition" and "modernity" were in flux. Yet a critical pedagogy of the nineteenth- and early twentieth-century Arab "renaissance" (*nahḍah*) could bring modern Arabic literature more squarely into the fold of empire and postcolonial studies, critical translation theory, and world and comparative literature. This essay reflects on both the theoretical importance and the practical experience of teaching the dynamics of early Arab literary modernity to non-specialist audiences – undergraduate and graduate – in comparative literature. Two problems emerge in this context: first, the self-Orientalism of *nahḍah* texts, which often uphold a thesis of post-Ottoman "decline" and post-European "awakening" and thus reinforce Orientalist views of Arab-Islamic culture in a post-9/11 era of anti-Arab and Islamophobic sentiment; and second, a relative dearth (to date) of high-quality, in-print, and affordable English translations.

Conjoining comparatist methods of "close" and "distant" reading, I propose a twofold praxis of *proxidistant reading* to address these problems of world, time, and access: a praxis that connects modern Arabic literature to modern Western and world literatures in ways that assume neither easy equivalence nor absolute non-relation between *adab* and *literature*, and the modifiers *Arabic*, *Western*, *world*. First, while *nahḍah* intellectuals reengineered the Arab-Islamic idea of *adab* – once coterminous with knowledge itself – to translate the modern Western idea of *literature*, premodern *adab* and its modern Arabic "nemesis" share more than *nahḍah* ideology concedes: both can be narrowly "literary" or radically transdisciplinary, belletristic or "lowbrow," formal (*fuṣḥā*) or dialectal (*'āmmiyyah*). Thus I propose that we read *nahḍah* texts as testimonies to the *discontinuous continuity* – or *continuity in death* – of premodernity and modernity, "Wests" and "Easts," interrogating conceptions of world and time that exaggerate either the proximity or the distance of literary-cultural epistemes, genres, and modes of expression across these postulated divides. Second, I propose that we read translations of *nahḍah* "literature" both up close to and afar from original texts and from the imagined purview of the "literary."

To impart a prismatic vision of the *nahḍah* to students who must rely on limited English translations, I suggest *peri-literary* approaches – "time travel" to the *nahḍah* through secondary sources, as well as primary sources (e.g. novels) set in the era yet composed in later periods – and *para-literary* readings that place the many forms that *nahḍah* "literature" actually took (historical, sociopolitical, scientific, popular) alongside those that fit its belletristic theoretical mold. By teaching an earlier "modern" than the "modern Arabic literature" comparatists typically teach, and by comparing the *nahḍah* with similar "renaissances" elsewhere in the non-Western world, we can help students understand Arabic-speaking cultures not as objects of global modernity but as complex *subjects* thereof – and develop a complementary (or contestatory) vision of the rise of world and comparative literatures usually imputed to nineteenth-century Europe.

This proposition challenges a prevailing US view of the Arab world and Islam as anti-European and premodern, already explored in Edward Said's *Orientalism*: a view that accepts Samuel Huntington's "clash of civilizations" thesis and posits a "medieval," unchanging Arab-Islamic world.[1] (Witness a *Washington Post* news story of 10 April 2010, reporting the political foment in Egypt on the eve of the 2011 presidential elections. Its headline, "Political Stirrings in Egypt, a Land of Little Change," compounds the absurdity of its lead: "'Change' is not a word often associated with Egypt."[2] Not long after this article appeared, the revolution of 25 January 2011 would topple Egyptian President Ḥusnī Mubārak.) The fact that the *nahḍah* took place, then, contests the Orientalist logic of Eastern stasis. Yet the prevailing intellectual mood of the *nahḍah* itself – read closely – is steeped in Orientalism. If teaching the modern Arab "renaissance" forces students in the US academy to collapse the Occident/Orient binary assumed by Orientalist thought – to replace the post-9/11 question "Why do they hate us so?" with the question "Why did they once love us so, and perhaps do still?" – the textual corpus of the "renaissance" itself too often reifies Orientalist binaries.

Indeed, throughout late nineteenth- and especially early twentieth-century Arabic literary history and criticism, the scholar of the *nahḍah* encounters Arab self-murder. The Arab must die to awaken. In his *Tārīkh ādāb al-lughah al-'arabiyyah*, often considered the first modern Arab foray into literary historiography, Jurjī Zaydān dates the beginning of the modern Arab renaissance – what he calls "*al-nahḍah al-akhīrah*" ("the latest renaissance"), in one of the earliest conscious uses of the term – to the French retreat from Egypt in 1801.[3] While Zaydān concedes that the French invasion of Egypt in 1798 "rattled the nerves" of the East ("*ihtazzat lahu a'ṣābuhu*"), he ignores the possibility that the theses of pre-1798 "decline" and post-1798 "renaissance" that so permeate his historical account of Arab literary modernity might issue from what Jean-Paul Sartre (prefacing Frantz Fanon) dubbed the "nervous condition" of the colonized native.[4] Zaydān insists that eighteenth-century Ottoman Egypt and Syria languished in "backwardness and corruption" ("*al-ta'akhkhuri wa-l-fasādi*") punctuated only by "*nūran ḍa'īlan*" ("faint light") from the intellectual labors of Syrian Christian monastic orders.[5] (Even the latter are described only to be dismissed: "Yet this [activity … was] not enough to illuminate this darkened atmosphere," presumably because it was primarily "religious" – non-secular, hence non-"scientific" and non-"modern."[6]) To prove the Arab-Islamic world's "backwardness" in the centuries just prior to its first encounter with modern imperial Europe, Zaydān turns to the testimony of "French philosopher," historian, and Orientalist Constantin-François de Chasseboeuf, comte de Volney (1757–1820) in his two-volume travelogue *Voyage en Syrie et en Égypte*.[7] Twice he gives Volney the final word on pre-nineteenth-century Arab cultural and material production, authorizing as "truth" the Frenchman's ascription of "ignorance" and inferiority to both Ottoman Egypt and Syria and his concomitant valorization of Europe: the presumed catalyst of "that blessed spark" of Arab renewal.[8] To his credit, Zaydān makes it clear that this European-inspired *nahḍah* is neither unique nor absolute, but only the latest such "renaissance" in Arab-Islamic history. He also suggests that Europe is not the only source of Arab literary modernity; although modern Arab writers had translated "countless" European novels by 1913 and had imitated the European novel form in their fiction, Zaydān argues, the Arabs had possessed the form "earlier."[9] Still, he makes it clear that this "latest renaissance" is also the first in a long time – since the heyday of the 'Abbāsid period (750–1258) in the ninth to eleventh centuries. Between the 'Abbāsid world of Hārūn al-Rashīd, on the one hand, and the nineteenth-century world of Bashīr al-Shihābī in Syria and of the Khedives Ismā'īl and 'Abbās Ḥilmī II in Egypt, on the other, yawns an abyss of near-inertia.[10] Abdelfattah Kilito captures the time warp well: as modern Arabic literature, he maintains, "jumped from its own calendar to another, alien one [the European], memory lost its bearings and plunged into another memory and another time frame."[11] What develops from this darkroom of forgetting and "rememory" (after Toni Morrison) is the image of an Arab-Islamic world roused by Europe from long, deathlike "sleep."

Zaydān's view typifies the dominant psychology of the modern Arab renaissance. Echoes of his logic sound in the later work of Aḥmad Amīn (1886–1954), a leading Egyptian Muslim intellectual of the twentieth century. Certainly Amīn's *Zu'amā' al-iṣlāḥ fī al-'aṣr al-ḥadīth* (Leaders of Reform in the Modern Era, 1948), a study of ten major Muslim reformists of the nineteenth century that culminates in a biography of Muḥammad 'Abduh, takes a more critical view of the European-Arab encounter. Amīn is keenly aware that the political pressures of European colonialism drove the selective adoption of Western civilization, in its material (*māddiyyah*) and its spiritual (*ma'nawiyyah*) forms, by Muslim reformists from India to Egypt and Turkey to Tunisia.[12] Yet this awareness does not extend to an epistemological critique of the decline/renaissance thesis. Like Zaydān, Amīn cites Volney's account to certify an Arab-Islamic "death" that demands "rebirth" through Europe.[13] If, as Said has argued, the repetition of *idées reçues* about the Arab-Islamic Orient masquerades as objective "truth" in much modern European Orientalist scholarship, Amīn enacts a native repetition of foreign Orientalism by citing Volney's impression as fact, taking the European's dim view of the Orient as his own.[14] Amīn dubs the pre-nineteenth-century Islamic world a "decrepit old man whom the events [of history, especially the Crusades] had destroyed," comparing this deteriorating subject to a Europe that "had begun … to awaken since the Crusades and to create a new civilization for itself."[15] So radical is the European-inspired "awakening" of the nineteenth-century Arabic-speaking world, contends Amīn, that "the difference between sons and fathers in the nineteenth century was wider than the difference between the people of the eighteenth century and [those] of the fifteenth."[16] If Amīn tacitly imputes the "renaissance" of Western Christendom (from supposed "Dark Ages" of its own) to its transformative encounter with Arab-Islamic cultures during the Crusades, he overtly ascribes the "awakening" of the "East" to the pressures of European conquest.

Other *nahḍah* intellectuals would judge Arabic even less generously. Writing in 1928, the Egyptian Muslim literary critic Aḥmad Ḥasan al-Zayyāt – later editor of the Cairo periodical *al-Risālah* (The Message) – describes Arabic literature (virtually from its inception) as a "brackish creek," stagnant water over which "gnats buzz."[17] This "death" awaits Western rejuvenation; the young Arab, al-Zayyāt maintains, drinks the (presumably fresh) water and "luscious fruits" of European literature because it speaks to life, his life in the present.[18] Al-Zayyāt paints Arabic literature as a still birth, arguing that its linguistic heterogeneity (first dialectal, later translingual) from pre-Islamic times onward has doomed it to "chaos" and to failure as "literature."[19] Zaydān, at least, ascribed other "renaissances" to earlier ages of Arabic literature and gave a nod to indigenous as well as foreign precursors of literary modernity; Amīn, intimating the impact of colonial power on the modern Arab renaissance, unwittingly invites his reader to denaturalize the ideas of "decline" and "renaissance" and to reinterpret both as ideological constructs. Al-Zayyāt's self-Orientalization is more absolute.

Teaching such texts in comparative literature, we might reinforce the "truth" of Zaydān's, Amīn's, and al-Zayyāt's assumptions – shared by many of their time – that the Arab-Islamic world was in "decline" and needed Europe to resurrect it.[20] Such a pedagogical prospect is all the more ethically troubling at a time when global Islamophobia is ever more strident. One risks ratifying mainstream Western media and popular culture, which ceaselessly represent the Arab-Islamic world as a "backward" threat to the "progressive" West. That those like al-Zayyāt often ventriloquize, rather than speak in their own voice, Orientalist assumptions of Muslim decline and regeneration is a nuance subtle enough to get lost in the classroom.[21] In teaching the *nahḍah*, we risk upholding Orientalism even as we undo it.

To counter this problem, we might assign primary sources that encourage students to construct a thick description of the impact of European colonialism on nineteenth-century Arab and Muslim self-understanding. Such sources might help students see that "renaissance" functions here as an ideologically motivated and translational term – translingual, transcultural, and transhistorical. Recovering Greco-Roman antiquity, the European Renaissance assimilated a once-rejected "pagan" literature to a Christian worldview, thereby forging a new humanism – at once sacred and secular – that prefigured the more radical rationalism of the European Enlightenment. The nineteenth-century Arab renaissance less often recouped forgotten antecedents from its own past. Rather, it reoriginated the Arab-Islamic present in the past that *Europe* had recently reclaimed. To ideologues of the *nahḍah*, Islam once had represented a symbiosis of reason and faith and had incarnated a range of powers – epistemic, scientific, military, economic – now associated with European modernity. Consequently, they hoped that by rewiring Arab-Islamic time through the circuitry of European time, a rationalist Islam might skirt its anti-rationalist double and become coeval with post-Enlightenment Europe. If many sixth- and seventh-century Arabs saw Islam as an enlightened end to the pre-Islamic era's presumed *Jāhiliyyah* ("Age of Ignorance") of faith, many nineteenth- and early twentieth-century Arabs apprehended European modernity as an enlightened end to a second *Jāhiliyyah*: the presumed loss of scientific reason that had engulfed the Arab-Islamic world since its invasions by European Crusaders in the eleventh through thirteenth centuries (1095–1291), by Mongols in the thirteenth (1258–60), and by Ottomans in the sixteenth (1516–17).

That the term *nahḍah* also translates as "awakening" compounds its translational instability. Certainly "awakening" skirts the direct comparison to European history that "renaissance" – a periodization freighted with European historical assumptions and cultural politics – implies. Yet within the nineteenth- and early twentieth-century geopolitical context in which Arabic-speaking intellectuals were called to reimagine themselves in the shadow of Western power, "awakening" still conjures forth a sleepy Arab-Islamic world to which Europe has just offered a jolt of civilizational caffeine. Some intellectuals of the period understood that "awakening," too, demands translation, as Roger Allen has noted, citing Mīkhā'īl Nu'aymah's interrogation of the concept.[22] How can one measure, Nu'aymah asks, the precise angle of a culture's sleep or wakefulness, progress or regression, or even homeostasis? By what standard does one compare? Implicit here is a critique of the use of European measures to evaluate Arab-Islamic world and time.

Embracing Nu'aymah's critique, we might undercut the self-Orientalism of *nahḍah* discourse by teaching against the periodization of the *nahḍah* itself – and the walls that periodization throws up between disciplines and genres. A rejection of the binarism of *inḥiṭāṭ* (decline) and its antithesis (anti-decline) might unearth more non-Eurocentric precedents for Arab literary modernity and thus also more continuities between medieval/modern *adab* than the reigning ideology of the *nahḍah* allows. As I argue elsewhere, the logic of the *nahḍah* originates in the affirmation of self-value rather than the assertion of self-lack: in a persistent tendency to forge *equivalence* between the increasingly threatened self and the increasingly empowered European, to apprehend the imperial European subject as an incarnation (hence also a death-defying survival) of precolonial Arab-Islamic sovereignty, to take the European for the self, indeed – and this is crucial – for one's *best* self.[23] This illusion of equivalence underwrites the passion with which intellectuals of the *nahḍah* flung themselves into translation. The dissonance between that self-validating illusion and geopolitical reality engenders the perception of self-lack that lurks in even the earliest texts of the *nahḍah* and which comes to dominate *nahḍah* discourse by the early twentieth century. Thus the *nahḍah* at once issues from an ideological continuity – the proposition that the Arab-Islamic world can resurrect its erstwhile glory *through* the eye/*I* of Europe, whose Orientalist fascination is thought to confirm the potency of Arab-Islamic culture – and imposes two interrelated ideological breaks: between "premodern" and "modern" genealogies of Arab-Islamic intellectual history, on the one hand, and between the Arab-Islamic "dead" and the "living nations" of Europe, on the other. How, then, to distinguish the forms of pre/postcolonial continuity our pedagogy might excavate from those assumed by the *nahḍah*'s traffic in equivalences between a precolonial Arab-Islamic world and an imperial European modern world order, equivalences that ultimately (and paradoxically) feed an ideology of intractable difference between the two? By recalling the fact that "modern Arabic literature" stands in no easy continuity with what precedes it or with modern European literature, but in a relation of discontinuous continuity – or continuity in death – with both. By proposing that "modern Arabic literature" is neither inherently "the same as" nor inherently "different from" its premodern incarnations or its European contemporaries but always contingently same/different, always proxidistant. Rather than uphold facile equivalences or non-equivalences between spaces and times, a critical pedagogy of the *nahḍah* would replace its dominant paradigm of decline/awakening with tensile *proxidistances*: the first between "Eastern" and "Western" strains of intellectual history; the second between "premodern" and "modern" strains of Arab-Islamic intellectual production.

We might begin by undoing the assumption that the idea of Arab-Islamic "decline," which always shadows the notions of awakening or renaissance, originates in European discourse alone. Writing in 1957, Albert Hourani observed that historians of the Ottoman Empire "tend to think of the Empire of Suleiman the Magnificent as the 'true' Empire" and to dub "what came after sheer decline." By espousing the decline thesis, he maintained, "we are indeed only reflecting what the Ottomans themselves believed, or at least what they were in the habit of saying."[24] Hourani implies that the ideology of Arab-Islamic "decline" emerges not only from the nineteenth-century Arab encounter with the imperial West and from modern Western Orientalist scholarship, but also from longstanding perspectives in Ottoman imperial historiography, which viewed the "golden age" of Süleyman's reign (1520–66) as the pride that preceded the fall. To my mind, the importance of Hourani's argument lies beyond his interrogation of the decline thesis (which, arguably, he was the first to challenge). It lies in the fact that Hourani calls us to reimagine the decline thesis itself anti-Eurocentrically, to root its postlapsarian logic in Ottoman as well as European provenance. We see that imperial triumphalism, Eastern or Western, generates decline as its necessary obverse. Such a recognition helps us decolonize the idea of empire itself, acknowledging the impact of pre-European imperial formations and thus breaking the equation "empire = Europe," and reinterpret the awakening/decline binary as an ideological creature of empires West and East. In pursuing that reinterpretation, however, we should be careful *not* to assume equivalence between the meanings and locations of *decline* in Ottoman and European imperial discourses on the Arab-Islamic world. Acknowledging the forked tongue of the decline thesis need not mean reinforcing the facile comparative periodizations "'like Europe, the Middle East also,' or 'this happened in the Middle East even before it did in Europe.'"[25] As Dana Sajdi observes, such "anti-decline" logics, like the decline thesis they oppose, would fail to decenter the West.[26] Listen, instead, for the variable pitch, tenor, and resonance of the forked tongue of *decline*.

Were we so to listen, we might hear a counterpoint to the view that the modern Arab "renaissance" ushered in an unprecedented simplification of Arabic, an opening of *fuṣḥā* to colloquial registers and other modes of vernacularization. These claims index nineteenth-century transformations in the Arab-Islamic world to a Western European Renaissance/Reformation/Enlightenment model. In shedding classical *fuṣḥā* for a modernized, truer-to-"life" literary Arabic (if not necessarily dialect itself) as Renaissance Europe shed "dead" Latin for vernaculars, the story goes, the Arabic-speaking world also shed the ossified religious orthodoxy of clerical Islam as Western Europe shed the monologic authority of the Roman Catholic Church, paving the way for a rationalist regime of progress in the Arab-Islamic context akin to that of the European Enlightenment.

Yet that thesis may not hold water if we peer over the edge of the supposed watershed of 1798 and Napoleon's invasion of Egypt. Sajdi's scholarship reveals that as early as the sixteenth century, soldiers began to produce chronicles in Egypt, and by the eighteenth century, barbers, farmers, soldiers, and priests produced such texts in Syria. *Tārīkh* (hence perhaps also *adab*?) ceased to be the province of scholars alone. Pre-print knowledge production, she suggests, was thus potentially more democratic than that of the ensuing age of print.[27] The entry of non-elite writers into historical – and literary – production invariably also brought colloquial registers of Arabic to the written page, intermixing these with "literary" *fuṣḥā*. Even the *'ulamā'* of the eighteenth century did not always write a grammatically correct or "pure" Arabic. We find 'Abd al-Raḥmān al-Jabartī, in his 1798 *Tārīkh muddat al-Faransīs bi-Miṣr* (History of the Period of the French in Egypt), composed in the thick of the Napoleonic invasion, writing a prose peppered with colloquialisms and Ottomanisms: a style not so different from that of Mikhāyil Mishāqah (1800–88), whose 1873 *al-Jawāb 'alā iqtirāḥ al-aḥbāb* (Response to a Suggestion by Loved Ones) – a searing account of Ottoman dominion and Christian, Muslim, and Druze relations in Mount Lebanon and Damascus during the late eighteenth and nineteenth centuries, culminating in the 1860 massacres of Christians by Muslim and Druze factions – is said to be a *nahḍah*-era departure from "premodern" historiography.[28] If we turn our eye to historiographies like al-Jabartī's or Mishāqah's, the lines between pre- and post-*nahḍah* literary styles blur.

In Yūsuf al-Shirbīnī's *Kitāb hazz al-quḥūf bi-sharḥ qaṣīd Abī Shādūf* (translated as *Brains Confounded by the Ode of Abū Shādūf Expounded*), a seventeenth-century text, we find a wickedly irreverent indulgence in the most vulgar – vernacular *and* coarse – forms of Egyptian colloquial expression to "represent" (and attack) rural life.[29] Indeed, al-Shirbīnī's text offends both the ethical and belletristic sensibilities of *adab*, presaging many of the "breaks" with tradition that contact with European literature supposedly would usher into modern Arabic literature in the mid-nineteenth century. We might read al-Shirbīnī's romps in ungrammaticality and questionable morality – undertaken, of course, in the name of conventional grammar and morality – as precursors of the linguistic and social play of Fāris al-Shidyāq's mid-nineteenth-century fiction *al-Sāq 'alā al-sāq* (Crossed Legs, 1855), a pivotal work by a major Syro-Lebanese intellectual of the *nahḍah*.[30] Yet al-Shidyāq's *Sāq*, in unrhymed and rhymed prose (*saj'*) intercut with poetry, was a printed text composed largely in *fuṣḥā*. Remarking the concluding chapter of *al-Sāq*, Stephen Sheehi notes that here al-Shidyāq "even mixes colloquial into his classical language."[31] What laces al-Shirbīnī's pre-print *Hazz al-Quḥūf* now graces only the ending of al-Shidyāq's 700-page tome. Does the fact that this paradigmatic text of the *nahḍah* is *less* colloquial than its seventeenth-century Egyptian forebear testify to what Sajdi suggests is a print-driven standardization of modern Arabic?[32]

Reading al-Jabartī with Mishāqah and al-Shirbīnī with al-Shidyāq helps us see how a redefinition of *adab* is already afoot before Arab contact with modern European "literature." Attention to such texts in the US comparative literature classroom – all four are available in English translation, although Mishāqah is not yet readily so – also would help us better gauge *what* changes during the long nineteenth century. If, for instance, a text like al-Shidyāq's *Sāq* is innovative, it may be so – as Sheehi suggests – "not because of its narrative continuity, stylistic diversity, humor, and linguistic force but because it forges and animates a new type of hero," in dialogue with the narrator and embodying his literary-political "unconscious," busily renegotiating the terms of Arab selfhood in the shadow of Western colonialism.[33]

For to assume, as *nahḍah* discourse often does, both an inherent difference between Arab-Islamic and Western Enlightenment discourses and their inherent translatability may make it too easy to exaggerate, on the one hand, the opposition of "Europe" to "Islam" and too easy to substitute, on the other, a European for an Arab-Islamic genealogy or destiny. We must remember that the break that nineteenth-century Arabic-speaking intellectuals installed between "old" and "new" regimes of knowledge was not natural. Rather, it was a construct that accrued a life of its own. It interrupted one reality – the possibility of proxidistance between Eastern and Western, premodern and modern ways of knowing – and interposed itself as a reality in turn, *effecting* the division it imagined between East and West, premodernity and modernity. Thus we find less difference than we imagine between pre-/postcolonial *adab* (or that category and its Western analogue, *literature*) – and yet, some difference still. How the *nahḍah* styles itself comes to *make* that difference.

The decline thesis is inherently comparative – just as incommensurability always haunts the production of "equivalents" in translation, incomparability (positive or negative) always tugs at the seams of comparability. Both decline and its corollary, the *nahḍah*, are crises of comparison. In teaching the *nahḍah* in the US comparative literature classroom, we might interrupt empiricist history with the productive ambiguity of the literary, and also disrupt a tendency in literary studies to over-privilege texts, to ignore political and social praxes that not only circle and subtend the textual but at times even contravene it.[34] Interrupting history with literature and literature with political economy, we can better unravel the tautological relation between "equivalence" and "difference," recognize how it is that Arab-Islamic thought came to substitute Europe for itself – its best self.

The problem of access: peri-literary and para-literary circumnavigations

I turn now to a second problem of teaching the *nahḍah* in the comparative literature classroom, where one cannot presuppose that all students can read original texts in Arabic. In such a pedagogical context, the availability, quality, and affordability of English translations often dictate the Arabic texts that one can teach. Histories are reasonably well represented. By contrast, the archive of early *nahḍah* imaginative literature – prose fiction, poetry, drama – in English translation is uneven. Scattered poems appear in various anthologies (some aging), and translations of literary criticism are rare: most are excerpted in scholarly monographs. When translations of book-length works are available, their cost is often prohibitive. Until recently, we could count English translations, some out of print, of a few novels: Muḥammad al-Muwayliḥī's *Ḥadīth 'Īsā ibn Hishām* (1898–1902, 1907, 1927; *A Period of Time*), Maḥmūd Ḥaqqī's *'Adhrā' Dinshawāy* (1906; *The Maiden of Dinshway*), and Muḥammad Ḥusayn Haykal's *Zaynab* (1913).[35] Among autobiographies, we find in translation Zaydān's *Mudhakkirāt Jurjī Zaydān* (The Memoirs of Jurjī Zaydān) and, from a later period, Ṭāhā Ḥusayn's *al-Ayyām* (The Days).[36] Other translations appear in excerpts, either in anthologies or embedded in published scholarship; more recent examples include 'Ā'ishah al-Taymūriyyah's *Natā'ij al-aḥwāl fī al-aqwāl wa-l-af'āl* (1888; Conclusions Foregone in What Is Said and Done), arguably the first modern Arabic novel by a female writer; al-Shidyāq's comparison, penned from the hybrid contact zone of Malta, of Arab and European musics; and neoclassical odes by the Egyptian poet Aḥmad Shawqī (1868–1932) and by the Iraqi poet Ma'rūf al-Ruṣāfī (1875–1945).[37]

We are on the cusp of a sea change. Humphrey Davies has published a magisterial four-volume English translation of al-Shidyāq's *al-Sāq 'alā al-sāq*, a text that the late Egyptian scholar and novelist Raḍwā 'Āshūr dubbed the "first" modern Arabic novel.[38] Six English translations of Zaydān's pioneering historical novels also recently have appeared. One, *Tree of Pearls, Queen of Egypt*, a translation by Samah Selim of Zaydān's final novel, *Shajarat al-Durr: Riwāyah tārīkhiyyah gharāmiyyah* (Shajarat al-Durr: A Historical Love Story, 1914), has been published to critical acclaim.[39] Alongside Selim's translation, five others – by Roger Allen, Issa J. Boullata,

Michael Cooperson, William Granara, and Paul Starkey – afford a rich snapshot of Zaydān's corpus.[40] Finally, Tarek El-Ariss's edited volume, *The Arab Renaissance: A Bilingual Anthology of the* Nahda, is forthcoming from the Modern Language Association.

Still, many key texts of the *nahḍah* remain untranslated, among these the Egyptian reformist 'Alī Mubārak's *'Alam al-Dīn*, published in Alexandria in 1882 and often (if erroneously) dubbed the "first" modern Arabic novel. Further, we need not just more translations of primary texts, but also translations of translations. The modern Arab renaissance was, after all, intricately bound up with translation. Some 804 works – mostly in European languages and spanning military science, history, literature, philosophy, sociology, the natural sciences – were translated (mostly into Arabic) and published in Egypt in the nineteenth century alone.[41]

I work around this uneven availability of translations by deploying a pedagogical method that I would call *peri-literary*. Where necessary, I teach *around* the literature of the modern Arab renaissance. Wary as I am of Franco Moretti's suggestion that we jettison close reading for distant reading, I use (1) research studies of the kind Moretti employs to distill patterns or tendencies within a period, and (2) primary sources from later periods that afford a telescope through which my students and I can time-travel to the *nahḍah*.[42]

Five such texts have impressed my students: Ahdaf Soueif's *Map of Love*; Abdelfattah Kilito's *Lan tatakallam lughatī* (*Thou Shalt Not Speak My Language*); Samah Selim's study of popular fiction and the *nahḍah*; Yaḥyā Ḥaqqī's *Qindīl Umm Hāshim* (twice translated, as *The Saint's Lamp* and as *The Lamp of Umm Hashim*); and al-Ṭayyib Ṣāliḥ's *Mawsim al-hijrah ilā al-shamāl* (*Season of Migration to the North*).[43] Soueif's English-language novel enfolds the history of the Egyptian *nahḍah* – with nods to figures from the greater Syrian context, as the plot involves (for one) the Palestinian intellectual Rūḥī al-Khālidī – in a fictional form palatable to non-specialists. The novel calls into question the assumed antagonism of the colonial signifier (English) to the native one (Arabic), reminding us that the latter entered into an ideological love affair with the former through translation – and produced a modern standard Arabic seemingly unbroken (purely "native") but in effect a (legalized?) illegitimate child.[44] At first discomfited by Kilito's apparent injunctions against bilingualism and translation, my graduate students came to appreciate his deft readings of the epistemological turn Arabic literature took in the nineteenth century. Through Kilito, they could grasp the struggle of *nahḍah* literati like al-Shidyāq and al-Manfalūṭī to write in Arabic but be heard in two languages, European and Arab: a struggle buried in the "unchanging" face of Arabic. Time and again, my students returned to al-Shidyāq's fear (as reported by Kilito) that the acquisition of a second language might subtract knowledge of the first. Some resisted the notion that bilingualism is a loss; others understood that al-Shidyāq is writing of bilingualism under politically unequal conditions of exchange, in which learning the terms of the "new" – of colonial modernity – often demanded that one abandon "old" words: the terms of a native order seen as "lack," a minus whose subtraction in fact would be a plus. The involution of *adab* is one example. From

Selim's essay on popular fiction and the *nahḍah*, in turn, my undergraduate students grasped what Moretti calls the great "unread" – the 90 percent of literary production, usually popular, omitted from the theoretical generalizations made in a given period's name. Selim suggests that our view of the *nahḍah* is premised on high-culture assumptions, shackled by the prejudices of the period elites who circumscribed "literature" in a narrow frame.

Selim's analysis might help us engage the generic hybridity of a text like Ḥaqqī's *The Lamp of Umm Hashim* (1944), which I have taught in a freshman seminar on education and empire in literature, history, and culture. My eagle-eyed freshmen recognized that the text – a novella – also reads as a traditional folktale and moral or religious parable. I seized this observation as a pedagogical opportunity, inviting them to consider how Ḥaqqī's crossing (and recrossing) of the boundaries separating "traditional" Arabic genres from "modern" European ones might embody – at the level of form – the crux of the tale: protagonist Ismā'īl's uneasy negotiation of modern European medicine and the traditional folk cures of popular Egyptian Islam, the Europhile ideology of the *nahḍah* and the resurrection of a rationalist-mysticist Islam as anti-colonial episteme. In an undergraduate course on colonial and postcolonial theory, I used Ṣāliḥ's *Season of Migration to the North* (1966) to explore ontological and epistemological quandaries of the *nahḍah* intellectual, whose mind is stocked, like Muṣṭafā Sa'īd's locked library, with English books – receiving even the Qur'ān (a text traditionally deemed "untranslatable," incomparable, inimitable by believing Muslims) in English.[45] One student, inspired by Saree Makdisi's and Waïl Hassan's research, became fascinated by the role of the *nahḍah* in shaping the intellectual consciousness Muṣṭafā Sa'īd represents.[46] She critiqued the form in which Ṣāliḥ chose to wage *his* critique. While I pointed out that Ṣāliḥ combines oral storytelling conventions with novelistic technique, she noted his thoroughgoing assimilation of the former to the latter. If Ṣāliḥ wants to question the Europeanization of Arab-African intellectual production, she asked, why write a novel to do it? Why not write in a form less "indebted" to the West? These are probing, critical questions – precisely the ones we want students to ask.

I come now to a final observation on teaching the modern Arab renaissance. If my pedagogical praxis is at times *peri-literary*, the objects I teach are occasionally *para-literary*. The modern Arabic "literature" emerging at the turn of the twentieth century exceeds poetry and prose fiction. I see the literature of the *nahḍah*, in fact, as *para-literature: adab* sits alongside literature, but also in adjacency to, analogy to, even beyond literature "proper." To capture the generic and thematic complexity of the *nahḍah* for our students, we need to include texts that do not always present as literature "proper," yet engage poetry and imaginative prose in the articulation of social, cultural, or political theory. To that end, I have taught excerpts from Rifā'ah Rāfi' al-Ṭahṭāwī's *Takhlīṣ al-ibrīz fī talkhīṣ Bārīz* (Extracting Pure Gold to Render Paris, Briefly Told), an account of five years of study in Paris, first published in Egypt in 1834.[47] Al-Ṭahṭāwī, a nineteenth-century Egyptian intellectual reformer, often is regarded as "father" of the *nahḍah*, and this text as its inaugural gesture. Thanks to Daniel Newman's English translation, published in 2004 as *An*

Imam in Paris, I introduced it in my comparative literature courses.[48] Twice I did so in graduate seminars on "(post)colonial translation," once in an undergraduate course on reading literary movements. My experience captures the value of teaching a text that encapsulates the para-literary tendencies of the *nahḍah*.

Our discussions focused on the section "Fī al-kalam 'alā ahl Bārīs" (On the People of Paris), which crystallizes the (re)construction of religion, gender and sexuality, and race in the Egyptian nineteenth century. First, we examined how al-Ṭahṭāwī reinforces deep-seated notions of Christian–Muslim difference yet articulates Christian alterity on the modern ground of secular knowledge, not the traditional ground of theological truth or falsehood. This alterity he invokes negatively, in the case of local Christians like the Copts, who are imagined to "display a natural tendency towards ignorance and stupidity," and positively, in the case of distant Christians like the Parisians, who are said to "distinguish themselves from many Christians by their keen intelligence, profound perceptiveness and depth of mind."[49] We compared al-Ṭahṭāwī's separation of the French from Christianity with Napoleon's similar maneuver in his first Arabic proclamation to the people of Egypt (2 July 1798) and his negotiations of religion and reason with those of the nineteenth-century Bengal renaissance intellectuals Bankim Chandra Chattopadhyay (Bankimchandra Chatterji), Rabindranath Tagore, and Swami Vivekananda, whose writings betray similar anxieties about the place of Hindu traditions in a British-inflected modernity.[50]

Second, we considered al-Ṭahṭāwī's prismatic engagement with Arab-Islamic and European patriarchies and heteronormativities. Remarking his citation of a poem that counsels men, "[b]e disobedient to women, for this is rightly guided obedience," students argued his misogyny; after all, the cited text tacitly pronounces female power wrongheaded and female subordination "rightly guided," thereby legitimating sexism in pseudo-Islamic terms.[51] Yet al-Ṭahṭāwī also quotes "one" Frenchman as saying that "in Eastern countries [women] are like furniture, whereas the Franks treat them like spoilt children."[52] To what extent is al-Ṭahṭāwī seeing women's "proper" status through a French gaze too? To students weaned on media representations of oppressed Muslim women, I noted that French as well as Arabic sources underpin al-Ṭahtāwī's misogyny – that European Orientalist literature informs his understanding of "Eastern" and "Western" views of women, one objectifying, the other infantilizing, both pernicious.

Similarly, al-Ṭahtāwī's text compelled students to question assumptions that the West is the eternal standard-bearer of sexual "freedom," the East an eternal site of sexual "repression." Al-Ṭahṭāwī remarks, for instance, that "[a]mong the good qualities of … [the] language and poetry [of the French] is that they refuse to extol homosexual love. Indeed, in French it is highly inappropriate for a man to say, 'I fell in love with a boy.' This would be considered repugnant and troublesome. As a result, when one of them translates one of our books, he changes the words, rendering this sentence by 'I fell in love with a girl,' or 'a soul,' in order to avoid this."[53] As one student noted, the passage marks Egypt's migration to a nineteenth-century French order (as described by Michel Foucault in his *History of Sexuality*) that re-encodes hetero- and homosexuality as fixed identities rather than diffuse eroticisms.[54] I suggested two ways of understanding this shift. While al-Ṭahṭāwī might well uphold French heterosexism for its coincidence with Qur'ānic doctrines, in which acts of same-sex physical desire are ostensibly punishable by law, he also might do so because to permit the Muslim to think sexuality outside European norms would be to exclude the Muslim from modernity – increasingly identified with Europe. The latter explains al-Ṭahṭāwī's puzzling assertion that "[o]ne of the praiseworthy aspects of … [the] nature [of the French], and *one they truly have in common with the Arabs*, is the fact that they do not have any propensity towards the love of boys or the celebration of its pursuit": an assertion complicated, if not refuted, by the very erotic conventions of Arabic poetry he goes on to cite.[55] At stake here is a translation of Arabic toward *common ground with France.*

Turning to race, we explored how al-Ṭahṭāwī tacitly correlates the inability of the French to countenance the love of men for "boys" as well as "girls" with their rejection of interracial desire. Noting that the French "consider that Blacks can never have any beauty at all," al-Ṭahṭāwī concludes, "they do not have two directions in love."[56] Arab male poets, by contrast, celebrate the beauty and erotic allure of black women (and men!) as often as they deny these. Thus *Takhlīṣ* also may mark the migration of Egypt to modern Western conceptions of race, grafted on prejudices old. Might we view gender and race in modernity as terms in translation between (Muslim) "East" and (French) "West," in which – as Lydia Liu has argued in the context of Qing dynasty China – European and non-European terms are thrown together into "super-signs" that point meaning toward the more geopolitically powerful of the two parties in translation, usually the European, *inflecting* a supposedly common ground of translational "equivalence"?[57]

In a graduate context, this discussion led us to examine al-Ṭahṭāwī's theory of translational equivalence and its insistent construction of radical exchangeability between languages, despite its astute recognition of the stubborn incommensurability that must haunt any such exchange. We compared al-Ṭahṭāwī's views of translatability with those of the German-Jewish intellectual Walter Benjamin in "Die Aufgabe des Übersetzers" (1923, "The Task of the Translator"); the Bengali intellectual Rabindranath Tagore in "Sabhapatir Abhibhashan" (1923), his presidential address to the Bengali Literary Convention of North India; and the Chinese intellectual Lu Xun in "'Yingyi' yu 'wenxue de jiejixing'" (1930, "'Hard Translation' and 'The Class Character of Literature'").[58] While al-Ṭahṭāwī concedes that one language may know "more than" what another implies – and that even within one language, the particularity of a signifier shades and shapes a signified all too easily taken as universal (not "every Muḥammad [is] the messenger of God") – he submerges the incommensurability (hence supplementarity) of languages in translation in a deep kinship between their intentions. Ultimately, he argues, "[i]f a person were to delve deeply into any given language, he would be, perforce, a scholar of another tongue."[59] We explored possible echoes of al-Ṭahṭāwī's view in Benjamin, who concedes that the words of different languages (their "modes of intention") exclude one another yet posits their translatability in a "suprahistorical kinship of languages [that] rests in the intentions underlying each language as a whole – an intention … realized only by the totality of their intentions supplementing each other."[60] Al-Ṭahṭāwī and Benjamin share a similar tendency to stage translation in rarefied linguistic terms, bracketing the ways in which history and geopolitics might attach unequal weight to languages in translation.[61]

Writing, like Benjamin, in 1923 – nearly a century after al-Ṭahṭāwī and more than 150 years after the onset of British imperialism in Bengal – Tagore could better grasp and resist the colonial perils of translation. "[T]he French language will not answer the needs of your soul once you uproot it from the nature of French life," Tagore writes. "I can use a lion's hide to make a rug or drape the wall, but I cannot swap my skin for his."[62] Where al-Ṭahṭāwī strategically ignores the difference between the lion's hide and his own skin, preferring to entertain the illusion that French and Arabic might share common depths, Tagore insists that a signifying skin not only clothes but clings tightly to meaning – too tightly to admit the separation that a Ṭahṭāwīan-Benjaminian reading of translation demands. Detached from the original historical, political, and sociocultural sphere that gives it life, the foreign signifier can be put to instrumental use in another context ("to make a rug or drape the wall") but loses exchange value: it cannot be *swapped* for a native signifier – that is, reattached to new life. Although Tagore here sounds strangely like Benjamin, who declares that "content and language form a certain unity in the original, like a fruit and its skin," while "the language of a translation envelops its content like a royal robe with ample folds," the difference lies in Tagore's refusal to give the transplanted skin any content.[63] It lies flat on a floor or against a wall; it cannot enrobe, even loosely, a human body and soul. Decrying the established hegemony of English and the emerging hegemony of Hindi in India, Tagore is keenly aware that British imperialism and international domination inflect the relation between Bangla and those languages. So long as languages are geopolitically unequal, they cannot enter a purified zone of translatability. Thus he declares that "no good comes out of a vocation founded on begging. It is simpler to master a foreign tongue by paying from your own language for everything you get."[64] Even in this schema, however, we wondered whether geopolitical inequality might not intrude on "equal" exchange. How does one know if what one gets is commensurate with what one pays? Might this trade too not spawn a deficit in the native tongue? Recalling the observation Kilito attributes to al-Shidyāq – that whoever learns a foreign language *subtracts* an equal measure of knowledge from the native tongue – we reconsidered al-Ṭahṭāwī.[65] Al-Ṭahṭāwī asks, "can counterfeit tinsel mimic pure gold?" ("*hal dhahabun ṣirfun yuḥākīhi bahrajun*[?]"), wondering if French can compare with an Arabic long presumed to be the gold standard.[66] He may begin his ruminations in a sphere of (imagined) equal exchange, paying for French with Arabic, measure for measure, yet ultimately he decides to sell Arabic's gold standard to French, for French becomes the *measure* of valuation, the "pure gold" (*ibrīz*) of Paris to which his book's title refers.

Teaching the modern Arab renaissance outside specialist contexts may help students read the Arab world, Islam, the West, and points elsewhere at once up close and at a distance, recognizing that the predicaments that haunt Arab modernity – the question of translatability; the valorization of the secular and diminution of the sacred; the novelization of world literary space; the foreclosure of alternative regimes of race, gender, and sexuality; the reification of sameness or difference between the West and the so-called Rest, especially Islam – are not coincidentally the core questions driving the study of world and comparative literature today, and the articulation of local politics in the shadow of the global.

Notes

* This essay is an abridged and revised version of an earlier one by the same title in *Journal of Arabic Literature* 43.2–3 (2012): 227–268, reprinted by permission from Brill. Unless otherwise indicated, all translations are mine.

1 See Samuel P. Huntington, *The Clash of Civilizations and the Remaking of World Order* (New York: Simon & Schuster, 1998); and Bernard Lewis, *What Went Wrong? The Clash Between Islam and Modernity in the Middle East* (New York: Oxford University Press, 2002).

2 Janine Zacharia, "Political Stirrings in Egypt, a Land of Little Change," *The Washington Post*, Saturday 10 April 2010, A11, www.washingtonpost.com/wp-dyn/content/article/2010/04/09/AR2010040905163_pf.html, accessed 15 April 2010.

3 Jurjī Zaydān, *Tārīkh ādāb al-lughah al-ʿarabiyyah*, vol. 4, new edn, ed. Shawqī Ḍayf (Cairo: Dār al-Hilāl, n.d. [1910–13]), 6. Nadia Al-Bagdadi notes that Zaydān published parts of his *Tārīkh* as early as 1894 in the Cairo-based journal *al-Hilāl*, which he edited, and "credit[ed] himself with having coined … the notion and new concept of literary history." See Nadia Al-Bagdadi, "Registers of Arabic Literary History," *New Literary History* 39.3 (Summer 2008): 437–61; references to 445, 460 nn24–26.

4 See Zaydān, *Tārīkh*, 4:11, and Jean-Paul Sartre, preface to Frantz Fanon, *The Wretched of the Earth*, trans. Constance Farrington (New York: Grove Press, 1963), 7–31; quotation from 20.

5 Zaydān, *Tārīkh*, 4:7, 8. Zaydān discusses three clerics of seventeenth- and eighteenth-century Aleppo and names seven others (ibid., 4:8–11).

6 Ibid., 4:11, 8.

7 Ibid., 4:7, 11. See also C.-F. Volney [Constantin-François de Chasseboeuf, comte de Volney], *Voyage en Syrie et en Égypte, pendant les années 1783, 1784, et 1785* (Paris, 1787). The first English translation is C.-F. [Constantin-François] Volney, *Travels through Syria and Egypt in the Years 1783, 1784, and 1785* (London, 1788).

8 Zaydān, *Tārīkh*, 4:6.

9 Ibid., 4:209.

10 Ibid.

11 Abdelfattah Kilito, *Thou Shalt Not Speak My Language*, trans. and introd. Waïl S. Hassan (Syracuse, NY: Syracuse University Press, 2008), 9.

12 Aḥmad Amīn, *Zuʿamāʾ al-iṣlāḥ fī al-ʿaṣr al-ḥadīth* (Cairo: Maṭbaʿat Lajnat al-Taʾlīf wa-l-Tarjamah wa-l-Nashr, 1965 [1948]), 338–41.

13 Ibid., 6–7.

14 On the "textual attitude" of European Orientalism toward its object, see Said, *Orientalism*, 92–94, 166.

15 Amīn, *Zuʿamāʾ*, 8.

16 Ibid., 339–40.

17 Aḥmad Ḥasan al-Zayyāt, "Fī al-adab al-ʿarabī," *al-Jadīd* 1.2 (6 February 1928): 19–20; quotations from 19.

18 Ibid., 19–20.

19 Ibid., 19.

20 Harvard University's Widener Library holds a typescript translation of Amīn's *Zu'amā' al-iṣlāḥ*; see Aḥmad Amīn, *Leaders of Religious and Political Reform in the Eighteenth and Nineteenth Century Islamic World* (n.p., n.d.).
21 On ventriloquy, see Waïl S. Hassan, "Translator's Introduction," in Abdelfattah Kilito, *Thou Shalt Not Speak My Language* (Syracuse, NY: Syracuse University Press, 2008), xii.
22 See Roger Allen, "The Post-Classical Period: Parameters and Preliminaries," in *Arabic Literature in the Post-Classical Period*, ed. Roger Allen and D.S. Richards (Cambridge: Cambridge University Press, 2006), 15; and "Mīkhā'īl Nu'aymah, al-'Udw fī 'al-Rābiṭāh al-Qalamiyyah'" (Mīkhā'īl Nu'aymah, Member of the Society of the Pen), in *Fatāwā kibār al-kuttāb wa-l-udabā'* (Cairo: Idārat al-Hilāl, 1923), 65–71, esp. 65.
23 See Shaden M. Tageldin, *Disarming Words: Empire and the Seductions of Translation in Egypt* (Berkeley: University of California Press, 2011).
24 See Albert Hourani, "The Changing Face of the Fertile Crescent in the XVIIIth Century," *Studia Islamica* 8 (1957): 89–122, quotation from 91; and Dana Sajdi, "Decline, Its Discontents and Ottoman Cultural History: By Way of Introduction," in *Ottoman Tulips, Ottoman Coffee: Leisure and Lifestyle in the Eighteenth Century*, ed. Dana Sajdi (London: I.B. Tauris, 2007), 1–40, esp. 7–9.
25 Sajdi, "Decline," 39.
26 On the dialectic relation of decline/anti-decline, see ibid., 25–27, 39–40.
27 See Dana Sajdi, "Print and Its Discontents: A Case for Pre-print Journalism and Other Sundry Print Matters," *The Translator* 15.1 (2009): 105–38, esp. 114, 128.
28 For a bilingual edition of al-Jabartī's text, see 'Abd al-Raḥmān al-Jabartī, *Al-Jabartī's Chronicle of the First Seven Months of the French Occupation of Egypt, 15 June–December 1798, Muḥarram–Rajab 1213/Tārīkh muddat al-Faransīs bi-Miṣr, Muḥarram–Rajab A.H. 1213, 15 Yūnyū–Dīsimbir A.D. 1798*, ed. and trans. S[hmuel]. Moreh (Leiden: E.J. Brill, 1975). Mishāqah's narrative, *al-Jawāb 'alā iqtirāḥ al-aḥbāb*, appears in English as Mikhāyil Mishāqa, *Murder, Mayhem, Pillage, and Plunder: The History of the Lebanon in the 18th and 19th Centuries*, trans. and introd. W[heeler]. M. Thackston, Jr. (Albany: State University of New York Press, 1988).
29 See Yūsuf al-Shirbīnī's *Kitāb Hazz al-Quḥūf bi-Sharḥ Qaṣīd Abī Shādūf* (*Brains Confounded by the Ode of Abū Shādūf Expounded), Volume 1: Arabic Text*, ed. and introd. Humphrey Davies (Leuven: Peeters, 2005).
30 See Fāris ibn Yūsuf al-Shidyāq, *al-Sāq 'alā al-sāq, fī mā huwa al-Fāriyāq, aw Ayyām wa shuhūr wa a'wām fī 'ujm* [or *'ajm*] *al-'Arab wa-l-A'jām* (Paris, 1855).
31 Stephen Sheehi, *Foundations of Modern Arab Identity* (Gainesville: University Press of Florida, 2004), 123.
32 That the *nahḍah* scholar felt compelled to standardize the Arabic of earlier, pre-print texts is borne out, Sajdi notes, by the example of the Damascene *'ālim* Muḥammad Sa'īd al-Qāsimī (d. 1900), whose print edition of an eighteenth-century Damascene barber's chronicle sought to "*refine (the language), correcting it to the extent possible*" ("Print," 132, italics in the original).
33 Sheehi, *Foundations*, 124.
34 On questions of text, context and theory in Arabic and comparative literary studies, see Elliott Colla, "Field Construction," *International Journal of Middle East Studies* 43.4 (November 2011): 722–24; Hosam Aboul-Ela, "Our Theory Split," *International Journal of Middle East Studies* 43.4 (November 2011): 725–27; Shaden M. Tageldin, "The Returns of Theory," *International Journal of Middle East Studies* 43.4 (November 2011): 728–30; Mohamed-Salah Omri, "Notes on the Traffic between Theory and Arabic Literature," *International Journal of Middle East Studies* 43.4 (November 2011): 731–33; and Samah Selim, "Toward a New Literary History," *International Journal of Middle East Studies* 43.4 (November 2011): 734–36.
35 For an English translation see, *A Period of Time: A Study and Translation of Hadith 'Isa ibn Hisham by Muhammad al-Muwaylihi*, trans. and introd. Roger Allen (Reading: Ithaca Press, 1992). See also Maḥmūd Ṭāhir Ḥaqqī, *'Adhrā' Dinshawāy*, introd. Yaḥyā Ḥaqqī (Cairo: al-Dār al-Qawmiyyah li-l-Ṭibā'ah wa-l-Nashr, 1964 [1906]); the English

translation is *The Maiden of Dinshway*, in *Three Pioneering Egyptian Novels*, trans. and introd. Saad El-Gabalawy (Fredericton, NB: York Press, 1986), 17–48. Finally, for a translation of Muḥammad Ḥusayn Haykal's *Zaynab: Manāẓir wa akhlāq rīfiyyah, bi-qalam Miṣrī Fallāḥ* (Cairo, 1913), see Mohammed Hussein Haikal, *Zainab: The First Egyptian Novel*, trans. John Mohammed Grinsted (London: Darf, 1989).

36 For the English translation of Jurjī Zaydān's *Mudhakkirāt* see Thomas Philipp, *Ǧurǧī Zaidān: His Life and Thought* (Wiesbaden, Germany: Steiner Verlag, 1979). On Zaydān's autobiography as a cue to the changing epistemes and political economy of the *nahḍah*, see Sheehi, *Foundations*, 191–94. See also Ṭāhā Ḥusayn, *al-Ayyām*, vols. 1–3 (Cairo: Dār al-Ma'ārif, [2003–04 (1929, 1940, 1967)]). The English translation is Taha Hussein, *The Days: His Autobiography in Three Parts*, 2nd edn, trans. E.H. Paxton, Hilary Wayment and Kenneth Cragg (New York: American University in Cairo Press, 2001).

37 See Aisha Ismat al-Taimuriya, "Introduction to *The Results of Circumstances in Words and Deeds* (1887/88)," trans. Marilyn Booth, in *Opening the Gates: A Century of Arab Feminist Writing*, ed. Margot Badran and miriam cooke (Bloomington: Indiana University Press, 1990), 126–28.

38 See Raḍwā 'Āshūr, *al-Ḥadāthah al-mumkinah: al-Shidyāq wa-l-Sāq 'alā al-Sāq, al-Riwāyah al-ūlā fī al-adab al-'arabī al-ḥadīth* (Cairo: Dār al-Shurūq, 2009); and [Aḥmad] Fāris al-Shidyāq, *Leg Over Leg, or the Turtle in the Tree, Concerning the Fāriyāq, What Manner of Creature Might He Be*, ed. and trans. Humphrey Davies, vols. 1–4 (New York: New York University Press, 2013–14).

39 For *Shajarat al-Durr* in English, see Jurji Zaydan, *Tree of Pearls, Queen of Egypt*, trans. Samah Selim (Syracuse, NY: Syracuse University Press, 2012).

40 For Jurjī Zaydān's novels in translation, see bibliography.

41 'Āyidah Ibrāhīm Nuṣayr, *Ḥarakat nashr al-kutub fī Miṣr fī al-qarn al-tāsi' 'ashar* (Cairo: al-Hay'ah al-Miṣriyyah al-'Āmmah li-l-Kitāb, 1994), 276, 287.

42 On distant reading, see Franco Moretti, "Conjectures on World Literature," in *Debating World Literature*, ed. Christopher Prendergast (New York: Verso, 2004), 148–62.

43 See Ahdaf Soueif, *The Map of Love* (New York: Anchor, 2000 [1999]); 'Abd al-Fattāḥ Kīlīṭū, *Lan tatakallam lughatī* (Beirut: Dār al-Ṭalī'ah li-l-Ṭibā'ah wa-l-Nashr, 2002); and Kilito, *Thou Shalt Not*; Samah Selim, "The People's Entertainments: Translation, Popular Fiction, and the *Nahdah* in Egypt," in *Other Renaissances: A New Approach to World Literature*, ed. Brenda Deen Schildgen, Gang Zhou and Sander L. Gilman (New York: Palgrave Macmillan, 2006), 35–58; Yaḥyā Ḥaqqī, *Qindīl Umm Hāshim* (Cairo: Dār al-Ma'ārif, 1944); Yahya Haqqi, *The Saint's Lamp and Other Stories*, trans. M.M. Badawi (Leiden: E.J. Brill, 1973); and Yahya Hakki, *The Lamp of Umm Hashim and Other Stories*, trans. Denys Johnson-Davies (New York: American University in Cairo Press, 2004); and al-Ṭayyib Ṣāliḥ, *Mawsim al-hijrah ilā al-shamāl* (Beirut: Dār al-'Awdah, 1967), first published in 1966 in the journal *Ḥiwār*; and Tayeb Salih, *Season of Migration to the North*, trans. Denys Johnson-Davies, introd. Laila Lalami (New York: New York Review of Books, 2009 [1969]).

44 See Shaden M. Tageldin, "The Incestuous (Post)Colonial: Soueif's *Map of Love* and the Second Birth of the Egyptian Novel in English," in *The Edinburgh Companion to the Arab Novel in English: The Politics of Anglo Arab and Arab American Literature and Culture*, ed. Nouri Gana (Edinburgh: Edinburgh University Press, 2013), 82–105.

45 On this point, see Aamir R. Mufti, "Global Comparativism," *Critical Inquiry* 31.2 (Winter 2005): 472–89, esp. 479–82; and Saree S. Makdisi, "The Empire Renarrated: *Season of Migration to the North* and the Reinvention of the Present," *Critical Inquiry* 18.4 (Summer 1992): 804–20, esp. 812–13.

46 See Makdisi, "The Empire Renarrated"; and Wail S. Hassan, *Tayeb Salih: Ideology and the Craft of Fiction* (Syracuse, NY: Syracuse University Press, 2003).

47 Rifā'ah Badawī Rāfi' al-Ṭahṭāwī, *Takhlīṣ al-ibrīz fī talkhīṣ Bārīz*, ed. Mahdī 'Allām, Aḥmad Aḥmad Badawī and Anwar Lūqā (Cairo: Muṣṭafā al-Bābī al-Ḥalabī, 1958 [1834; 1849]). Another nineteenth-century Arabic travelogue teachable to this end is that of Muḥammad ibn 'Abd Allāh al-Ṣaffār, translated as *Disorienting Encounters: Travels of a*

Moroccan Scholar in France in 1845–1846: The Voyage of Muḥammad aṣ-Ṣaffār, trans. and ed. Susan Gilson Miller (Berkeley: University of California Press, 1992). Gilson's translation is based on the original Arabic manuscript (MS 113) at the Bibliothèque Royale in Rabat. Al-Ṣaffār read al-Ṭahṭāwī; taken together, their accounts invite comparison of early to mid-nineteenth-century responses to Europe in the Mashriq and the Maghrib.

48 Rifā'a[h] Rāfi' al-Ṭahṭāwī, *An Imam in Paris: Account of a Stay in France by an Egyptian Cleric (1826–1831): (Takhlīṣ al-ibrīz fī talkhīṣ Bārīz aw al-Dīwān al-nafīs bi-īwān Bārīs)*, trans. and introd. Daniel L. Newman (London: Saqi, 2004). A second edition appeared in 2011.

49 Al-Ṭahṭāwī, *An Imam*, 173.

50 On Bankim Chandra Chattopadhyay (Bankimchandra Chatterji) and Swami Vivekananda, see Tapan Raychaudhuri, *Europe Reconsidered: Perceptions of the West in Nineteenth-Century Bengal*, 2nd edn (New York: Oxford University Press, 2002). Vivekananda's travelogue is especially interesting to read alongside al-Ṭahṭāwī's.

51 Al-Ṭahṭāwī, *An Imam*, 173.

52 Ibid., 177.

53 Ibid., 178.

54 For a similar argument, see Joseph A. Massad, *Desiring Arabs* (Chicago, IL: University of Chicago Press, 2007), 31–35.

55 Al-Ṭahṭāwī, *An Imam*, 178 (emphasis mine).

56 Ibid., 180.

57 Lydia H. Liu, *The Clash of Empires: The Invention of China in Modern World Making* (Cambridge, MA: Harvard University Press, 2004), 13–14.

58 See Rabindranath Tagore, "Presidential Address at the Bengali Literary Convention of North India, 3 March 1923," trans. Swapan Chakravorty, in *Rabindranath Tagore: Selected Writings on Literature and Language*, ed. Sisir Kumar Das and Sukanta Chaudhuri (New Delhi: Oxford University Press, 2001), 310–19; and Lu Xun, "'Hard Translation' and 'The Class Character of Literature'," trans. Yang Xianyi and Gladys Yang, in *Lu Xun: Selected Works*, 3rd edn, vol. 3 (Beijing: Foreign Languages Press, 1980), 75–96. For the original Bangla and Chinese, respectively, see Rabindranath Tagore, "Sabhapatir Abhibhashan," *Shantiniketan* (Jyaistha 1330 [May–June 1923]), and Lu Xun, "'Yingyi' yu 'wenxue de jiejixing,'" in *Lu Xun quanji* [The Complete Works of Lu Xun], vol. 4 (Beijing: Renmin wenxue chubanshe, 2005), 199–227.

59 Al-Ṭahṭāwī, *Takhlīṣ*, 128.

60 Walter Benjamin, "The Task of the Translator: An Introduction to the Translation of Baudelaire's *Tableaux parisiens*," in *Illuminations*, trans. Harry Zohn (New York: Schocken Books, 1969), 74.

61 On al-Ṭahṭāwī's theory of translation and its relation to that of Walter Benjamin, see Tageldin, *Disarming Words*, 132–36.

62 Tagore, "Presidential Address," 315.

63 Benjamin, "The Task," 75.

64 Tagore, "Presidential Address," 316.

65 See Kilito, *Thou Shalt Not*, 71.

66 Al-Ṭahṭāwī, *Takhlīṣ*, 129.

Bibliography

Aboul-Ela, Hosam. "Our Theory Split." *International Journal of Middle East Studies* 43.4 (2011): 725–727.

Al-Bagdadi, Nadia. "Registers of Arabic Literary History." *New Literary History* 39.3 (Summer 2008): 437–461.

al-Jabartī, 'Abd al-Raḥmān. *Al-Jabartī's Chronicle of the First Seven Months of the French Occupation of Egypt, 15 June–December 1798*. Ed. and trans. S[hmuel]. Moreh. Leiden: E.J. Brill, 1975.

Allen, Roger. "The Post-Classical Period: Parameters and Preliminaries." In *Arabic Literature in the Post-Classical Period*. Ed. Roger Allen and D.S. Richards. Cambridge: Cambridge University Press, 2006. 1–21.

al-Muwayliḥī, Muḥammad. *A Period of Time: A Study and Translation of Hadith 'Isa ibn Hisham*. Trans. and introduction Roger Allen. Reading: Ithaca Press, 1992.

al-Shidyāq, [Aḥmad] Fāris. *Leg Over Leg, or the Turtle in the Tree, Concerning the Fāriyāq, What Manner of Creature Might He Be*. Ed. and trans. Humphrey Davies. Vols 1–4. New York: New York University Press, 2013–2014.

al-Ṭahṭāwī, Rifā'a[h] Rāfi'. *An Imam in Paris: Account of a Stay in France by an Egyptian Cleric (1826–1831): (Takhlīṣ al-ibrīz fī talkhīṣ Bārīz aw al-Dīwān al-nafīs bi-īwān Bārīs)*. Trans. and introd. Daniel L. Newman. London: Saqi, 2004. 2nd edn, 2011.

al-Taimuriya, Aisha Ismat ['Ā'ishah 'Iṣmat al-Taymūriyyah]. "Introduction to the Results of Circumstances in Words and Deeds (1887/88)." Trans. Marilyn Booth. In *Opening the Gates: A Century of Arab Feminist Writing*. Ed. Margot Badran and miriam cooke. Bloomington: Indiana University Press, 1990. 126–128.

Badran, Margot, and miriam cooke, eds. *Opening the Gates: An Anthology of Arab Feminist Writing*. Bloomington: Indiana University Press, 2004.

Benjamin, Walter. "The Task of the Translator: An Introduction to the Translation of Baudelaire's *Tableaux parisiens*." In *Illuminations*. Trans. Harry Zohn. New York: Schocken Books, 1969. 69–82.

Cachia, Pierre. "A 19th Century Arab's Observations on European Music." *Ethnomusicology* 17.1 (January 1973): 41–51.

Colla, Elliott. "Field Construction." *International Journal of Middle East Studies* 43.4 (November 2011): 722–724.

Davies, Humphrey. "Introduction." In Yūsuf al-Shirbīnī's *Brains Confounded by the Ode of Abū Shādūf Expounded (Kitāb Hazz al-Quḥūf bi-Sharḥ Qaṣīd Abī Shādūf), Volume 2. English translation, introduction and notes*, by Yūsuf ibn Muḥammad ibn 'Abd al-Jawād ibn Khiḍr al-Shirbīnī. Trans. and introd. Humphrey Davies. Leuven: Peeters, 2007. xv–lxxiv.

El-Ariss, Tarek, ed., *The Arab Renaissance: A Bilingual Anthology of the* Nahda. New York: Modern Language Association, forthcoming 2017.

Haikal, Mohammed Hussein. *Zainab: The First Egyptian Novel*. Trans. John Mohammed Grinsted. London: Darf, 1989.

Hakki, Yahya. *The Lamp of Umm Hashim and Other Stories*. Trans. Denys Johnson-Davies. New York: American University in Cairo Press, 2004.

Ḥaqqî, Maḥmūd Ṭāhir. "The Maiden of Dinshway." In *Three Pioneering Egyptian Novels*. Trans. and introd. Saad El-Gabalawy. Fredericton, NB: York Press, 1986. 17–48.

Haqqi, Yahya. *The Saint's Lamp and Other Stories*. Trans. M.M. Badawi. Leiden: E.J. Brill, 1973.

Hassan, Waïl S. *Tayeb Salih: Ideology and the Craft of Fiction*. Syracuse, NY: Syracuse University Press, 2003.

Hassan, Waïl S. "Translator's Introduction." In *Thou Shalt Not Speak My Language*, by Abdelfattah Kilito. Trans. Waïl S. Hassan. Syracuse, NY: Syracuse University Press, 2008. vii–xxvi.

Hourani, Albert. "The Changing Face of the Fertile Crescent in the XVIIIth Century." *Studia Islamica* 8 (1957): 89–122.

Huntington, Samuel P. *The Clash of Civilizations and the Remaking of World Order*. New York: Simon & Schuster, 1998.

Hussein, Taha. *The Days: His Autobiography in Three Parts*. 2nd edn. Trans. E.H. Paxton, Hilary Wayment and Kenneth Cragg. New York: American University in Cairo Press, 2001.

Jessup, Henry Harris. *The Women of the Arabs*. New York: Dodd and Mead, 1873.

Kilito, Abdelfattah. *Thou Shalt Not Speak My Language*. Trans. and introd. Waïl S. Hassan. Syracuse, NY: Syracuse University Press, 2008.

Lewis, Bernard. *What Went Wrong? The Clash Between Islam and Modernity in the Middle East*. New York: Oxford University Press, 2002.

Liu, Lydia H. *The Clash of Empires: The Invention of China in Modern World Making*. Cambridge, MA: Harvard University Press, 2004.

Lu Xun. "'Hard Translation' and 'The Class Character of Literature'." Trans. Yang Xianyi and Gladys Yang. In Lu Xun, *Selected Works*. 3rd edn. Vol. 3. Beijing: Foreign Languages Press, 1980. 75–96.

Lu Xun. "'Yingyi' yu 'wenxue de jiejixing.'" In *Lu Xun quanji* [*The Complete Works of Lu Xun*]. Vol. 4. Beijing: Renmin wenxue chubanshe, 2005. 199–227.

Makdisi, Saree S. "The Empire Renarrated: *Season of Migration to the North* and the Reinvention of the Present." *Critical Inquiry* 18.4 (Summer 1992): 804–820.

Massad, Joseph A. *Desiring Arabs*. Chicago, IL: University of Chicago Press, 2007.

Mishāqa[h], Mikhāyil. *Murder, Mayhem, Pillage, and Plunder: The History of the Lebanon in the 18th and 19th Centuries*. Trans. and introd. W[heeler]. M. Thackston, Jr. Albany: State University of New York Press, 1988.

Moretti, Franco. "Conjectures on World Literature." In *Debating World Literature*. Ed. Christopher Prendergast. New York: Verso, 2004. 148–162.

Mufti, Aamir R. "Global Comparativism." *Critical Inquiry* 31.2 (Winter 2005): 472–489.

Omri, Mohamed-Salah. "Notes on the Traffic between Theory and Arabic Literature." *International Journal of Middle East Studies* 43.4 (November 2011): 734–36.

Philipp, Thomas. *The Autobiography of Jurji Zaidan, Including Four Letters to His Son*. Washington, DC: Three Continents Press, 1990.

Philipp, Thomas. *Ǧurǧī Zaidān: His Life and Thought*. Wiesbaden: Steiner Verlag, 1979.

Rastegar, Kamran. "Literary Modernity between Arabic and Persian Prose: Jurji Zaydan's *Riwayat* in Persian Translation." *Comparative Critical Studies* 4.3 (2007a): 359–378.

Rastegar, Kamran. *Literary Modernity between the Middle East and Europe: Textual Transactions in Nineteenth-Century Arabic, English, and Persian Literatures*. London: Routledge, 2007b.

Raychaudhuri, Tapan. *Europe Reconsidered: Perceptions of the West in Nineteenth-Century Bengal*. 2nd edn. New York: Oxford University Press, 2002.

Said, Edward W. *Orientalism*. New York: Vintage, 1979 [1978].

Sajdi, Dana. "Decline, Its Discontents and Ottoman Cultural History: By Way of Introduction." In *Ottoman Tulips, Ottoman Coffee: Leisure and Lifestyle in the Eighteenth Century*. Ed. Dana Sajdi. London: I.B. Tauris, 2007. 1–40.

Sajdi, Dana. "Print and Its Discontents: A Case for Pre-print Journalism and Other Sundry Print Matters." *The Translator* 15.1 (2009): 105–138.

Salih, Tayeb. *Season of Migration to the North*. Trans. Denys Johnson-Davies. Introd. Laila Lalami. New York: New York Review of Books, 2009 [1969].

Sartre, Jean-Paul. "Preface." In *The Wretched of the Earth*, by Frantz Fanon. Trans. Constance Farrington. New York: Grove Press, 1963. 7–31.

Selim, Samah. "The People's Entertainments: Translation, Popular Fiction, and the *Nahdah* in Egypt." In *Other Renaissances: A New Approach to World Literature*. Ed. Brenda Deen Schildgen, Gang Zhou and Sander L. Gilman. New York: Palgrave Macmillan, 2006. 35–58.

Selim, Samah. "Toward a New Literary History." *International Journal of Middle East Studies* 43.4 (November 2011): 734–736.

Sheehi, Stephen. *Foundations of Modern Arab Identity*. Gainesville: University Press of Florida, 2004.

Soueif, Ahdaf. *The Map of Love*. New York: Anchor, 2000 [1999].
Spivak, Gayatri Chakravorty. *Death of a Discipline*. New York: Columbia University Press, 2003.
Stetkevych, Suzanne Pinckney. *The Mantle Odes: Arabic Praise Poems to the Prophet Muḥammad*. Bloomington: Indiana University Press, 2010.
Tageldin, Shaden M. *Disarming Words: Empire and the Seductions of Translation in Egypt*. Berkeley: University of California Press, 2011a.
Tageldin, Shaden M. "The Returns of Theory." *International Journal of Middle East Studies* 43.4 (November 2011b): 728–730.
Tageldin, Shaden M. "Proxidistant Reading: Toward a Critical Pedagogy of the *Nahḍah* in U.S. Comparative Literary Studies." *Journal of Arabic Literature* 43.2–3 (2012): 227–268.
Tageldin, Shaden M. "The Incestuous (Post)Colonial: Soueif's *Map of Love* and the Second Birth of the Egyptian Novel in English." In *The Edinburgh Companion to the Arab Novel in English: The Politics of Anglo Arab and Arab American Literature and Culture*. Ed. Nouri Gana. Edinburgh: Edinburgh University Press, 2013. 82–105.
Tagore, Rabindranath. "Sabhapatir Abhibhashan." *Shantiniketan* (Jyaistha 1330 [May–June 1923]).
Tagore, Rabindranath. "Presidential Address at the Bengali Literary Convention of North India, 3 March 1923." Trans. Swapan Chakravorty. In *Rabindranath Tagore: Selected Writings on Literature and Language*. Ed. Sisir Kumar Das and Sukanta Chaudhuri. New Delhi: Oxford University Press, 2001. 310–319.
Thackston, W[heeler]. M., Jr. "Introduction." In *Murder, Mayhem, Pillage, and Plunder: The History of the Lebanon in the 18th and 19th Centuries*, by Mikhāyil Mishāqa. Trans. and introd. W[heeler]. M. Thackston, Jr. Albany: State University of New York Press, 1988. 1–8.
Volney, C.-F. [Constantin-François de Chasseboeuf, comte de Volney]. *Voyage en Syrie et en Égypte, pendant les années 1783, 1784, et 1785*. Paris, 1787.
Volney, C.-F. [Constantin-François]. *Travels through Syria and Egypt in the Years 1783, 1784, and 1785*. London, 1788.
Zacharia, Janine. "Political Stirrings in Egypt, a Land of Little Change." *The Washington Post*. Saturday 10 April 2010. A11. www.washingtonpost.com/wp-dyn/content/article/2010/04/09/AR2010040905163_pf.html (accessed 15 April 2010).
Zaidan, Jurji. *The Caliph's Sister: Harun al-Rashid and the Fall of the Persians*. Trans. Issa J. Boullata. Bethesda, MD: Zaidan Foundation, 2010a.
Zaidan, Jurji. *The Conquest of Andalusia*. Trans. Roger Allen. Bethesda, MD: Zaidan Foundation, 2010b.
Zaidan, Jurji. *The Battle of Poitiers: Charles Martel and 'Abd al-Rahman*. Trans. William Granara. Bethesda, MD: Zaidan Foundation, 2011a.
Zaidan, Jurji. *The Caliph's Heirs: Brothers at War: The Fall of Baghdad*. Trans. Michael Cooperson. Bethesda, MD: Zaidan Foundation, 2011b.
Zaidan, Jurji. *Saladin and the Assassins*. Trans. Paul Starkey. Bethesda, MD: Zaidan Foundation, 2011c.
Zaidan, Jurji. *Tree of Pearls, Queen of Egypt*. Trans. Samah Selim. Syracuse, NY: Syracuse University Press, 2012.

2

TEACHING ARAB WOMEN'S LETTERS

Boutheina Khaldi

In spite of the existence of a large corpus of Arab women's biographies, novels, memoirs, essays, and poetry, coupled with critical studies, very little has been written on women's letter-writing as an art in its own right.[1] Thus this genre has never been part of a school curriculum. It has suffered absolute neglect and hence has generated no interest. This chapter argues that Arab women's letter-writing can be a very interesting teaching subject, and not only because it enriches curricula on Arabic literature, women's studies, and comparative literature, but also because of its engagement with the Arab *nahḍah*.[2] This chapter will also discuss the pedagogy of how to teach Arab women's letters.

One might begin by drawing attention to two short articles in Arabic penned by the prominent Arab woman writer, Mayy Ziyādah (d. 1941), who left an abiding mark on *nahḍah* thought.[3] In the first article entitled "Our Epistolary Art: Yesterday and Today,"[4] written in 1915, she refers to a long-established epistolary tradition. She points out how specific letters in the classical Arabic tradition have received acclaim for their clarity and brevity and she criticizes those that are characterized by their ornateness and floridity. She also draws a comparison between the Arab and eighteenth-century French epistolary art. The comparative framework draws attention to the importance of this art to the public sphere where the reciprocal exchange of ideas sets up an egalitarian base that challenges claims of superiority, hierarchy and absolutism. In the second article, entitled "Madame de Sévigné wa 'Aṣruhā"[5] (Mme de Sevigné and her Time), which appeared in *al-Muqtaṭaf* (July 1918), Mayy Ziyādah highlights the centrality of epistolarity to the salon. While her salon gathered together a cadre of the most distinguished members of the *nahḍah élite*, epistolarity served to tie the *literati* together regardless of distance and time. In a succinct reading of letter-writing in eighteenth-century France Dena Goodman concludes: "if the salons were the heart of the Enlightenment, letters circulated through them [i.e. salons] like its life blood."[6]

Whether we refer to a pre-print or post-print age, the epistolary art is worth including in university curricula because it held *une importance grandissante* in Arab literary and political history. The Umayyad secretary (kātib) 'Abd al-Ḥamīd (d. 750), celebrates it as the most needed art in a rising empire.[7] The claim hardly seems like an exaggeration on his part in that the ensuing centuries witnessed the preparation and compilation of one manual for secretaries after another, culminating in al-Qādī Shihāb al-Dīn Aḥmad al-Qalqashandī's (d. 1418) voluminous compendium, *Ṣubḥ al-A'shā fī Ṣinā'at al-Inshā'* (Dawn for the Benighted Regarding Chancery Craft).[8]

Combining a mastery of fine writing, Arabic language and its sciences, calligraphy, statecraft, and communicative skills, the epistolary art has over the ages secured for itself a high acclaim as a symptom of Arabic erudition. In Europe, it accrued recognition in the seventeenth century as an integrating dynamic that brought together the citizens of the Republic of Letters across Europe. In Dena Goodman's study of the French Enlightenment, epistolary writing was central: "The Republic of Letters had begun among men who were spread out across Europe and held together by an epistolary network."[9] Notwithstanding the presence of other means of communication, the epistolary art was, according to Dibon, "the primary means of coordinating the life of the *República Literaria*, of making its activities known to its citizens, of heralding the appearance of books … and of spreading news about research in progress."[10] In salons and literary assemblies the letter began to acquire so much significance that theorists of communicative action and the public sphere such as Jürgen Habermas credit it with the potential of shaping, coordinating and systematizing intellectual dialogue. Habermas, for one, argues: "If conversation shaped the discursive space within the salon, the letter moved the Enlightenment out of the private world of the salon into the public world beyond it." Letters were used as such "to bridge the gap between the private circles in which they gathered and the public arena that they sought to shape and conquer."[11]

These preliminary remarks with respect to the function and literary significance of letter-writing should pave the way for the classroom audience to perceive its formative impact in the makeup of *élite* culture. In the pre-*nahḍah* era the letter had long been a cultural dynamic, and not only as a venue for autobiographical communication much utilized by biographers like Yāqūt al-Ḥamawī (d. 1229) in his voluminous *Mu'jam al-Udabā'* (Dictionary of Writers, 1226) and Ibn Khallakān (d. 1282) in his multi-volume *Wafayāt al-A'yān* (Obituaries of Eminent Men, 1256–74), but also as a means of communication among writers across Islamic territories. With the rise and development of official correspondence, a distinguished writer like Abū al-Qāsim Ibn 'Alī al-Ḥarīrī (d. 1122), was commissioned as an officer in the Postal Service (*Ṣāḥib al-Barīd*). In his massive tenth-century compendium, *Kitāb al-Aghānī* (The Book of Songs), the polymath and litterateur Abū al-Faraj al-Iṣfahānī (d. 967) cites and reproduces correspondences among writers in order to enable the reader to see through their wit, irony, and humor. As is appropriate given the title of his work, these letters often include short poems that raise them to the efficacy and compactness of songs. The process of translating them might well stimulate students to engage more actively with the course.[12]

With the advent of the *nahḍah* as a movement generated by a number of factors, including colonial incursions and the rise of urban societies, the letter underwent further expansion and circulation. Transportation, the press, and the telephone only served to enhance such a role. Before mapping out Arab women's letter-writing typologies, it may be appropriate to identify some of the multiple functions of the letter. In addition to working as an annex to both café and salon that carries the conversation further, the letter can also stimulate other lines of conversation that reveal each writer's self-image as a public intellectual. We can adduce as an example the letter sent by the *nahḍah* intellectual, Fu'ād Ṣarrūf (d. 1985), in which he expresses the need to seek the opinion of a brilliant and critical mind like Mayy Ziyādah about the lecture he is planning to deliver in Palestine. He asks her to listen as he rehearses it. In her response dated 24 October 1934, Mayy Ziyādah thanks him for privileging her with that role: "It is truly nice of you to accept me as your preliminary public."[13] Comparable to a practice that was common in Europe, especially in the eighteenth century, this mode of trial is a recurrent mark in letter-writing and subsequent conversations. Habermas draws attention to the significance of this practice in the formation of ideas. He claims that it is almost a given to have prominent eighteenth-century European writers test their ideas "in lectures [or letters] before the *academies* and especially in the *salons*"[14] before submitting them for publication. However, the multiple functions of letters extend even beyond ideas.

The personal in the letter is usually quite conspicuous even when it presumably argues a certain position or disputes an issue. It is this personal touch that gives epistolarity its spontaneity, and hence its captivating appeal. At times it verges on confession, a disclosure that brings it closer to narrative. It is not out of place here to associate the rise of letter-writing in the *nahḍah* period with the concomitant rise of the Arabic novel, a point that can provide a springboard for an exciting classroom discussion in which narrative forms, authorship, and polyphony are addressed. As the epistolary art is recognizably formative in the rise of fiction, the comparison between correspondence and loquacity can evolve into further discussions.[15] As a revelation of the "imprint of the soul," letter exchange enhanced and prompted other narrative forms and, in Habermas's view, "explained the origin of the typical genre [of the diary] and authentic literary achievement of the century: the domestic novel, the psychological description in autobiographical form."[16] With the rising tide of studies devoted by women academics to the writings of women during the *nahḍah* period,[17] a course on epistolary art can thereby grow into a multi-dimensional spectrum that navigates widely but connectively to explore women's literary achievements in comparison with their male counterparts.

This last intersectional cultural space should not be underestimated, particularly in a classroom that aspires to promote vibrant discussion. The case is worthy of investigation, not only because of its complexity, its navigational nature between an interiorization of male discourse and a claimed opposition to it, as traced in

Malak Ḥifnī Nāṣif's (d. 1918) articles and letter exchange with Mayy Ziyādah,[18] but also because it constitutes a space in which women writers employed diplomacy to win over the best *nahḍah* minds to their sociable and intellectual space: the salon. As argued elsewhere, the woman writer as *salonnière* was capable of playing the role of critic and social broker by reconciling opponents and generating rational debates.[19] In matters pertaining to this role, for instance, we have more than one example in which Hudā Sha'rāwī (d. 1947) and Mayy Ziyādah addressed political leaders and intellectuals whose actions fell short of expectations: Hudā Sha'rāwī critiqued the Egyptian national leader Sa'd Zaghlūl (d. 1927), and Mayy Ziyādah the leading intellectual and editor of the influential daily *al-Jarīdah*, Aḥmad Luṭfī al-Sayyid (d. 1963).[20]

Women's letter typologies

Women's letters constitute a particularly rich ground for the expression of their ideas and thus deserve to be studied more fully, especially if we bear in mind the recent attention to epistolary writing worldwide. The Book Culture chain, near Columbia University (113 and Broadway, New York) posted on its website its Sunday "Tea and Letters" sessions throughout March 2014, a kind of salon or retreat where participants could practice writing letters to each other or to friends and families. Book Culture defines the exercise as "fun." However, the avowed "fun" has already been in practice for some time. College and secondary school teachers have made extensive use of this practice, not only to promote and polish students' writing skills, but also, I argue, to enable self-expression in an autobiographical vein that is much needed nowadays in order to provide some kind of balance to the heavily theorized curriculum. The practice is symptomatic of two directions: a reaction against mundane and stifling realities in a post-mechanical age; and a resurgence of individualism. The classroom can serve as the ground for both directions which in combination can foster a vibrant classroom discussion.

However, this practice is not only symptomatic of this age and era. It was practiced, for example, by Madame de Staël (d. 1817) and her salon attendees. A fictitious practice was carried out among them, as if to liberate them from personal or social constraints through confessions and self-expression. Habermas stipulates that Madame de Staël "cultivated to excess that social game in which after dinner everyone withdrew to write letters to one another."[21] He explains how this feigned practice brought into effect fictional and realistic writing. Madame de Staël "became aware that the persons themselves became *sujets de fiction* for themselves and the others."[22]

Although letters can be classified as both personal and public, we often come across some that elude this classification, such as those of the educator and advocate of women's rights, Nabawiyyah Mūsā (d. 1951), whose letter to the British consultant to the Egyptian Ministry of Education, Douglas Dunlop (1888–1919), is dated 1916. In the letter Nabawiyyah Mūsā tenders her resignation as deputy director of Būlāq School for Girls, accusing Dunlop of corrupting the educational system and describing him as "worse than the Germans, for the Germans exploit the right of a warrior but he exploits the right of a peaceful person; he has confiscated my right after I had entrusted him with it."[23] She adds: "He is worse than a thief because the thief robs people of money that comes and goes, whereas he robs people of their morals which cannot be regained once they are lost."[24] The letter highlights the damage the British administration inflicted. Instead of ending with a plea for reform, it comes up with resignation as the only suitable response to the British colonial policy.

Nawāl al-Saʿdāwī's personal letter to the former President of Egypt, Ḥusnī Mubārak, dated 1981,[25] is another example of a personal letter turned into a public event. The letter was sent from prison, where, as a political prisoner, the writer was detained without trial or access to lawyers. The accusation leveled by the state against a number of prisoners involved "subversive activity" and "conspiracy to overthrow the regime."[26] Nawāl al-Saʿdāwī's letter is a response to the President's claim in a press conference that the detention does not involve imprisonment or even detention, but rather "*taḥaffuẓ*," literally "preservation" or "keeping something under lock and key."[27] For al-Saʿdāwī and the other prison inmates it is in fact an endless incarceration, unpredictable, and an act of dispossession played out by the state against political prisoners and writers. This kind of letter combines self-expression with political commitment. It makes use of the inauguration speech which the new president has given as a way of interrogating a statist discourse that is intended to obfuscate real issues, debunk human rights, and retain political prisoners as a state property to be managed and controlled at will. The letter succeeds in disclosing this dissimulation and camouflage on the part of the state security apparatus and in exposing its black holes. The personal and public are intertwined, and what has started as a personal response now becomes a public statement with considerable bearing on Egyptian politics.

Another example of a personal letter is by none other than Mayy Ziyādah, dated 14 July 1918, to her mentor, the prominent intellectual and editor of *al-Muqtaṭaf*, Yaʿqūb Ṣarrūf (d. 1927). It is an answer to his uncompromising preference for her letters, as better, and more expressive, than her articles. Her response touches on the role and effect of letter-writing. A personal letter is self-expressive, and hence it requires no dictionaries or reference material: "But when I intend to address you, there are no dictionaries nor are there languages. I push my books aside, clean my desk, touch my pen playfully, then take a deep breath. That makes me laugh as I imagine you standing in front of me, either smiling or sarcastic."[28] Mayy Ziyādah explains how, when she writes, she is her "real self," something that is different from her "adopted one" that appears in public: "I write not as one who writes, but as 'one who thinks aloud,' as our friend Mme de Sevigné used to say."[29]

The use of Mayy Ziyādah's letters can be a rewarding experience in the classroom because of her multiple interests and sharp mindedness, and it is thus worthwhile to cite another of her personal letters, this one to Jibrān Khalīl Jibrān (d. 1931). However, since this involves correspondence between two writers, there is always the implication that it is readership-oriented. If preserved, it will find its way to the press sooner or later. Known in America as Kahlil Gibran, the writings of this poet, novelist, and painter can enliven class discussion. In a letter dated 12 May 1912, Mayy Ziyādah firmly criticizes his support of extramarital relationships in his novel *al-Ajniḥah al-Mutakassirah* (Broken Wings, 1912). She interrogates his worldview, its social, religious and personal implications, and expounds on the customs and social codes which are binding and normative in the Arab region. She states:

> I disagree with you with respect to marriage. I respect your ideas and honor your convictions because I know that you are sincere in fostering them and loyal in defending them. I agree with you with respect to women's freedom. Women must have the freedom to choose their husbands and follow their predilections and not that of their relatives and neighbors. If they themselves select their partners, they will be totally bound by the obligations of that partnership. You call these "heavy chains" forged by generations, and I respond: "yes, heavy chains, but they are forged by nature which made a woman 'what she is'." Even if the mind succeeds in breaking the chains of conventions, it will not succeed in breaking the chains of nature because the laws of nature are immutable … I feel very strongly the shackles by which women are chained, but, if we allow Salmā Karāmah, the protagonist of the novel or any woman that resembles her to meet a selfless and noble friend, is it right to allow every woman who does not find in marriage the happiness that she dreamt of when she was young to choose a male friend other than her husband and to meet with him without the knowledge of her husband?[30]

In a classroom, a letter like this can lead to a series of discussions that raise serious questions about the current use of the term "feminism" that has been transplanted from the West. Mayy Ziyādah, and even more so Hudā Sha'rāwī, strongly support women's rights but also recognize the particularity of their social and religious milieu.

As the purpose in women's letter-writing throughout is to communicate a message or express a feeling, these letters build up a shared code that addresses women's expectations and needs. The sense of bonding that genealogically connects these women writers to each other is so strong that a woman writer like Zaynab Fawwāz (d. 1914) restrains herself from attacking Hanā Hūrānī (d.?) because of this bond.[31] This sisterhood takes on a broader scope, however, when a writer decides to be anonymous, especially when there are social obstacles and self-censorship that deter her from disclosing her identity. Thus we find the Palestinian poet Fadwā Ṭūqān (d. 2003), for instance, appropriating the pen name Danānīr (after the Abbasid slave singer and poet). As a mask, the name enables her to escape censure, but it also connects her genealogically to another poet and singer from the past.[32]

Sisterhood is more conspicuous in Mayy Ziyādah's letter exchange with Malak Ḥifnī Nāṣif. The correspondence between the two conveys how both adopt different approaches to male discourse. Mayy Ziyādah resorts to reconciliation, since man is "a father, a brother, a friend, a fiancé, and a husband. If he falls, we fall with him; if he rises, we rise with him."[33] Malak Ḥifnī Nāṣif, on the other hand, deconstructs male discourse as being heavily entrenched in segregation and a misunderstanding of women's natural, social, and political rights. No less important is the "psychodynamics of female bonding," to borrow Elaine Showalter's phrase, that binds sisterhood together. Mayy Ziyādah writes in 1902: "yesterday I felt the presence of your soul, and while going through your ideas, I found out how deep your wounds were, and I wanted very much to have my soul embrace and kiss yours."[34]

Another example of sisterhood can be seen in the "epistolary poem,"[35] as Marilyn Booth calls it, written by the Arab poet Wardah al-Yāzijī (d. 1924) to the Turkish poet Wardah al-Turk (d.?) in 1867:

> O Rose of the Turks, I am Rose of the Arabs
> Between us we have found the closest of kinships.
> ... A precious friend whose news delights my hearing,
> and yet she has disappeared from sight, secluded by veils.[36]

In this epistolary poem we glean a strong sense of sisterhood, one that transcends ethnic and national boundaries and establishes a genealogy based on gender and shared concerns. A discussion of this female bonding can serve as a spark for interesting classroom experience.

The personal letter that has one specific addressee in mind can be more telling, in that it is usually written with the passion of "the heart's blood."[37] For this very reason it conveys not only the character of *l'expéditeur* (sender) or that of *le destinataire* (recipient), as filtered through the former's eyes, but also social and cultural issues that, in the case of Malak Ḥifnī Nāṣif and Mayy Ziyādah, pertain to the makeup of the Arab *élite* at the turn of the last century.

Let me first consider two letters from Mayy Ziyādah to Ya'qūb Ṣarrūf that take us to the issue of linguistic competence and translational transaction in each Arab woman writer's style. This is an explosive terrain. It can provide a springboard for many other issues with respect to identitarian politics and poetics. Seductive and distancing, Mayy Ziyādah's multilingual competence is an inviting topic, intriguing, problematic, and culturally rich. The more competent a person is in a number of languages, the more susceptible to slippage and transference s/he becomes. Often lured by the selection of one expression over another and drawn to variables in syntax and vocables, Mayy Ziyādah's style may seem peculiar to many. Hence the significance of the letter exchange between her and Ya'qūb Ṣarrūf on the difference between her personal correspondence and her articles. Mayy Ziyādah's letter of 14 July 1918, is very much in response to his Wednesday letter that criticized her articles and hence informed her response, and not "yesterday's" comforting letter that comes perhaps as a move on Ya'qūb Ṣarrūf's part to please her: "The letter you sent me on Wednesday hurt me because your letters were always very friendly."[38]

The same response questions mentorship as a practice followed among a community of writers: what she would like to communicate is her need for his guidance as a mentor, and not his harsh rebuttal that comes as a surprise. In a classroom, one can explore the implications within this context of gender, class, and race. Can a feminist grow out of this institution as a self-produced agent? Or is she bound to be contaminated by her mentor's discourse and method? What if the mentor turns into a patriarch? Let us go back to the letter again. Instead of the "friend I know," she writes, "I found only a master rebuking the lowest employee in his office."[39] Hence, the feminist in her revolt against that rebuke, but with the understanding that she can overlook it because it comes from Ya'qūb Ṣarrūf. The twist in this part of the letter, its navigation between accommodation and revolt, can be problematized further as a stage in Arab women's feminism. She writes: "Although I refuse the blame and rebuke from anyone, no matter how great this person is, my respect for an erudite and noble man like you has made me accept your reproach even if it was harsh."[40]

Another point that can make women's letter-writing, as a multi-faceted undertaking, an interesting subject for classroom discussion is Mayy Ziyādah's tactful, though apparently genuine, conciliatory tone to defer to his judgment and hence preserve his personal letters, even when they include a harsh letter composed on a Wednesday: "You said in yesterday's letter, 'Burn my letter and throw its dust to the four winds.' How can I do that? It is your hand that wrote it and your mind that dictated it, just as you chose your expressions and ideas at will … Any letter you write is dear to me. It has a beautiful life of its own."[41]

Mayy Ziyādah's letter of 1920 to Ya'qūb Ṣarrūf takes a different direction: he had already accused her of thinking "in a foreign language before expressing herself in Arabic," an accusation which, she argues, can apply to all people familiar with other languages.[42] She nevertheless takes the accusation further, placing it in the context of issues of expressiveness. She seems to suggest that excessive objectification and depersonalization will lead to a dry language. She explains: "Whenever I read an article by the so-called 'greatest writers' and 'outstanding poets,' my knowledge of foreign languages leads me to ask myself where is the personality of these leading figures, of which I find no trace in their writings?"[43] This intersection can be read on a number of levels. It indirectly places her in a higher position than other "greatest writers." It insists on the need to be familiar with foreign languages. It also highlights expressiveness as a stylistic merit that can be rightly claimed by women writers. These features can also generate interesting classroom discussions.

The personal letter as a public phenomenon is more challenging: an address to a leader or president, such as Nawāl al-Sa'dāwī's letter, is bound to find its way to the press. The same applies to Hudā Sha'rāwī's letter, undersigned the Wafdist Women's Central Committee, to Sa'd Zaghūl (12 December 1920). In this letter she writes:

> We are surprised and shocked by the way we have been treated recently, in contrast to previous treatment and certainly contrary to what we expect from

> you. You supported us when we created our committee. Your congratulatory telegrams expressed the finest hopes and most noble sentiments. What makes us all the more indignant is that by disregarding us the Wafd [its proposed charter for independence that secured the consultation of male organizations only] has caused foreigners to disparage the renaissance of women. They claim that our participation in the nationalist movement was merely a play to dupe civilized nations into believing in the advancement of Egypt and its ability to govern itself.[44]

Left out of the political discussion with the British, the Wafdist Women's Central Committee led by the woman president Hudā Sha'rāwī, was indignant. Even though the Wafd leader Sa'd Zaghūl has hailed her as *ra'īsah* (president), she has not been consulted. In her response she lampoons male politics for taking advantage of women's participation in demonstrations and protests to showcase for the British the advancement of Egypt and its ability to govern itself. This seems to Hudā Sha'rāwī a short-lived opportunist tactic.

Arab women's letters in the classroom

As a new and challenging classroom experience, "teachability" of this genre demands a systematic methodology, one that examines and classifies letters not only under the main categories of the personal and the public, but also as a repertoire of social and political engagement. Each letter can occupy one class session, prompt the discussion of a number of issues, and bring students closer to the writer and her culture.

In order to build up methodologies for this kind of venture, one also needs to benefit from other educators' efforts. Although there are many methodologies that have been practiced and applied as specific teaching models,[45] I will make use of Renate A. Schulz's, as it offers practical guidelines that can be modified and tested in the classroom.

Schulz lays emphasis on the classroom experience as one of transition from "literary appreciation" to "literary interpretation," or what she calls the movement from "learning to read" to "reading to learn."[46] As Arab women's letters invoke multiple concerns, they necessarily reflect on this two-fold process. Learning to read these letters requires a rearrangement of a cultural script or schema. The experience of reading and interpreting letters can grow into a comprehensive educational exercise. Understanding, through analysis and interrogation, places the classroom at the intersection of successful teaching methodologies. These skills require a number of approaches. In differentiating between learning skills, Paul Ricoeur stipulates: "Explanation is more directed toward the analytic structure of the text," whereas "understanding is more directed toward the intentional unity of discourse."[47] While the instructor can approach a specific letter as a viable text for analysis and understanding, that same analysis can direct the discussion toward a collective classroom experience conducive to interpretation as both a collective and individual appropriation. Outcomes are commensurate with each individual's response and appropriation.

However, this comprehensive experience cannot be achieved without preparations that involve both instructor and student. Schema theorists stress the interconnectedness between a worldview constructed by each student and knowledge of a particular text. Their understanding of, and response to, a letter relies on these schemata. Students often come equipped with ready knowledge that will require revision in view of the new material, viz., the letter, its cultural script and its author's background. The instructor is not only a learning guide, but also the provider of material and critical tools that help students build up a cultural script and schema.

Students have to acquire some understanding of Arab women's writers, their lives and cultural milieu.[48] I suggest that this preparation be placed alongside the text of the letter. By drawing on this combination, students can be led smoothly into the intricacies and allusions of the text. As they reflect on each other, background material and textual analysis can engage students in cognitive tasks that can turn the whole experience of reading and comprehension into a detective search for hidden implications. The letter is often a web of reflections and allusions.

In the main, however, the instructor can follow Benjamin Bloom's taxonomy of thinking processes that help him understand the types of cognitive tasks he assigns to his students.[49] These models have the following learning objectives: "lower-order thinking skills" like knowledge, comprehension, and application that ultimately lead to the "higher-order thinking skills" that include analysis, synthesis, and assessment.[50]

In order to pursue this application while laying more emphasis on what is deemed necessary to engage with letter-writing, let us take as an example a letter by Mayy Ziyādah to Ya'qūb Ṣarrūf. In this letter she accepts the role of the novice addressing the mentor who has been taken seriously by the Syrian and Egyptian intellectual *élite* as the philosopher and authoritative scholar of his own time.[51] A brief but succinct selection of background material can provide students with an understanding of the cultural and historical nature of these figures, especially as both happened to impact culture at the turn of the last century. Indeed, even other letters by Mayy Ziyādah can broaden this understanding of the period under consideration, especially when she inserts her own coquettish reflections on the "emperor," as she calls Ya'qūb Ṣarrūf.[52] These coquettish comments and reflections can draw students further into this correspondence and involve them in the more personal side of the letter. The instructor can use visual images of both Mayy Ziyādah and Ya'qūb Ṣarrūf, along with Ya'qūb Ṣarrūf's journal *al-Muqtaṭaf*. At this stage quotes from other writers who reminisced on how intimidated they were in their prime by seeing him can strengthen students' knowledge and consolidate a "cultural schema."[53] This will add to the students' knowledge of the cultural milieu and the nature of the literary production. They will be able to "personalize" these public figures and draw them closer to their sympathetic understanding and reflection. In other words, instructors can draw on the background material neatly in order to prepare students to read the text of the letter, probe its intricacy, and discern the overt and covert strategies used by women writers.

This underused genre can provide a lively discussion in the classroom, not only of the intimate moments in the careers of these women writers, but also of their engagement with social and political issues that make up the history of the *nahḍah*, or Arab modernity, at the turn of the nineteenth century onwards.

Appendix A: A letter from Nabawiyyah Mūsā to Douglas Dunlop, 1916

The Honorable Consultant,

I would like to confess to you what is in my mind. However, I am worried that if I do, you will think I am crazy and that I underestimate your mighty power. I would like to let you know that I know well that you are the consultant to the Ministry of Education, i.e., its actual minister; you are capable of dismissing me from work with no reason, and that no one can dispute your decision. You can even do more than that; you are capable of preventing me from getting a job in any provincial council. You are even capable of stopping me from getting any job with the help of your supporters, who are many. Moreover, you are one of the British whose word is heard in a country where martial law reigns. A word from you can put an end to my life.

In other words, I fully recognize your power, and yet I would like to do you a favor by telling you what is being said behind your back, since a mighty man does not know what is being said about him. He might benefit if he knew. With due respect, I would like to tell you that, whenever I am in my bedroom and I have closed its windows and doors and made sure nobody will hear me, I would say:

This consultant is worse than the Germans, for the Germans exploit the right of a warrior but he exploits the right of a peaceful person; he has confiscated my right after I had entrusted him with it. When I entered this school, I found that people have no morals. They do not work for work's sake, but only for money, something that they consider everything in their life. I have been surprised how these people have agreed to disregard morality and ignore it altogether.

As for me, I used to work for work's sake, but no sooner had I started working than I became like my other colleagues who only work for money. So where are my morals? Who has robbed me of them? It is the consultant who has robbed both me and others of their morals. He is worse than a thief because the thief robs people of money that comes and goes, whereas he robs people of their morals which cannot be regained once they are lost. I want to tell you frankly that I would like to regain my morals. So consider this letter as one month's notice of my resignation.

Yours faithfully,
Nabawiyyah Mūsā

Nabawiyyah Mūsā, Tārīkhī bi Qalamī [Writing My Own History] *(Cairo: Multaqā al-Mar'ahwal-Dhākirah, 1999), 208.*

Appendix B: A letter from Nawāl al-Sa'dāwī to Ḥusnī Mubārak, 1981

Dear Ḥusnī Mubārak, the President of the Republic,
Greetings,

While behind bars in al-Qanāṭir prison, I heard your public statement about the cutting edge of law that does not differentiate between one person and another. There are two crimes perpetrated against me: The first is putting me behind bars since 6/9/1981 for no other crime than my declared position and my statements published in newspapers in defense of freedom of speech and basic human rights for Egyptian people. To be sure of what I am saying, you can examine the investigation report that the public prosecutor conducted with me.

The second crime involves slandering my national and literary reputation while defenseless behind bars. On its first page dated 23/11/1981 *Al-Aḥrār* newspaper published information that tarnishes my very clean national name by leading public opinion to believe that the accusation raised against me involves participation in the execution of a Soviet plan to create chaos in the country, an accusation that neither the Intelligence Department nor the Bureau of Investigation have dared to raise against me.

What makes these two crimes weigh heavily on me is that the same words that people compete to write in today's newspapers are the very same words for which I was condemned and imprisoned. All this has been happening while I am still in prison waiting to be released. My release, however, does not only involve leaving the prison, but also living up to the promise you made, especially when you have confirmed that you do not promise something you fail to comply with.

You have promised that the cutting edge of law would not differentiate between one person and another. So will a legal action be taken against all those who have participated in the two above-mentioned crimes? Will you be able to restore my legal, human, moral, and literary rights that have been missing for days, weeks, and months?

Indeed, my national reputation and literary respect are the equal of my very life. I did not inherit them. They were not given to me by a sovereign power or an office. I have built them throughout these years with my struggle and perseverance. They have made the name Nawāl al-Sa'dāwī, the Egyptian writer known for her free thought and courageous sound judgment in Egypt and all over the world.

So can you keep your promise? I hope so. Thanks.

Greetings,

Nawāl al-Saʿdāwī

Nawāl al-Saʿdāwī, Mudhakkirātī fī Sijn al-Nisāʾ [My Prison Memoirs] *(Beirut: Dār al-Ādāb, 2000), 189–190.*

Notes

1 See Boutheina Khaldi, "Epistolarity in a Nahḍah Climate: The Role of Mayy Ziyādah's Letter Writing," *Journal of Arabic Literature* 40 (2009): 1–36.

2 The term *Nahḍah* (awakening) denotes a break with transmitted tradition and the application of imported Western ideas within a revivalist recovery of both Islamic-Arab rationalism and the European Enlightenment legacy. For more on the *Nahḍah* and its problematic, see J. Brugman, *An Introduction to the History of Modern Arabic Literature* (Leiden: E.J. Brill, 1984), 8–13; Muhsin al-Musawi, *Islam on the Street* (Lanham, MD: Rowman & Littlefield, 2010); Shaden M. Tageldin, *Disarming Words: Empire and the Seductions of Translation in Egypt* (Berkeley: University of California Press, 2011); and Tarek El-Ariss, *Trials of Modernity: Literary Affects and the New Political* (New York: Fordham University Press, 2013).

3 See Marilyn Booth, "Mayy Ziyada and the Feminist Perspective, 1908–1931," BA thesis, Harvard University, 1978; Marilyn Booth, "Biography and Feminist Rhetoric in Early Twentieth Century Egypt: Mayy Ziyada's Studies of Three Women's Lives," *Journal of Women's History* 3:1 (1991): 38–64; Boutheina Khaldi, *Egypt Awakening in the Early Twentieth Century: Mayy Ziyādah's Intellectual Circles* (London and New York: Palgrave Macmillan, 2012).

4 For more on this point and the above-mentioned article, see Khaldi, "Epistolarity in a Nahḍah Climate," 15, fn. 55.

5 Ibid., 3, fn. 5.

6 Dena Goodman, "Enlightenment Salons: The Convergence of Female and Philosophic Ambitions," *French Revolution in Culture*, spec. issue of *Eighteenth-Century Studies* 22:3 (spring, 1989), 340.

7 See Roger Allen, *Introduction to Arabic Literature* (Cambridge: Cambridge University Press, 2007), 139–140; Muhsin al-Musawi, "Pre-Modern Belletristic Prose," *The Cambridge History of Arabic Literature: Literature in the Post-Classical Period*, eds. Roger Allen and D.S. Richards (Cambridge: Cambridge University Press, 2006), 101–133; Wadād al-Qāḍī, "The Impact of the Qur'ān on the Epistolography of ʿAbd al-Ḥamīd," *Approaches to the Qur'ān*, eds. G.R. Hawting, Abdul-Kader A. Shareef (London and New York: Routledge, 1993), 285–313.

8 Muhsin al-Musawi, "Vindicating a Profession or a Personal Career? Al-Qalqashandī's Maqāmah in Context," *Journal of Mamluk Studies* 7 (Chicago Div. Jan. 2003): 111–135. For more on the shift towards epistolary art, see Muhsin al-Musawi, *The Medieval Islamic Republic of Letters: Arabic Knowledge Construction* (Notre Dame, IN: Notre Dame University Press, 2015), 135, 161, 179, 198–200, 308.

9 Dena Goodman, *The Republic of Letters: A Cultural History of the French Enlightenment* (Ithaca, NY and London: Cornell University Press, 1994), 28.

10 Ibid., 17; cited in Khaldi, "Epistolarity in a Nahḍah Climate," 17.

11 Jürgen Habermas, *The Structural Transformation of the Public Sphere: An Inquiry into the Category of Bourgeois Society*, trans. Thomas Burger with the assistance of Frederick Lawrence (Cambridge, MA: MIT Press, 1989), 340.
12 For more on Abū al-Faraj al-Iṣfahānī, see Hilary Kilpatrick, *Making the Great Book of Songs: Compilation and the Author's Craft in Abū al-Faraj al-Iṣfahānī's Kitāb al-Aghānī* (New York and Canada: Routledge, 2010).
13 Cited in Khaldi, "Epistolarity in a Nahḍah Climate," 6–7.
14 Habermas, *The Structural Transformation of the Public Sphere*, 35.
15 On the epistolary novel, see Janet Gurkin Altman, *Epistolarity: Approaches to a Form* (Columbus: Ohio State University Press, 1982); on loquacity, see T. Todorov, *Poetics of Prose*, trans. Richard Howard (London: Blackwell Publishers, 1977); on Todorov's "narrative men," see Muhsin al-Musawi, "The Growth of Scholarly Interest in the Arabian Nights," *Muslim World* (Hartford, CT) LXX (1981): 196–212.
16 Habermas, *The Structural Transformation of the Public Sphere*, 49.
17 Booth, "Mayy Ziyada and the Feminist Perspective, 1908–1931"; Booth, "Biography and Feminist Rhetoric in Early Twentieth Century Egypt: Mayy Ziyada's Studies of Three Women's Lives"; Marilyn Booth, *May Her Likes be Multiplied: Biography and Gender Politics in Egypt* (Berkeley: University of California Press, 2001); Khaldi, *Egypt Awakening in the Early Twentieth Century*; and Margot Badran and Miriam Cooke, eds, *Opening the Gates: An Anthology of Arab Feminist Writing* (Bloomington and Indianapolis: Indiana University Press, 2004).
18 See Khaldi, *Egypt Awakening in the Early Twentieth Century*, appendices E, F, G, H, 165–173.
19 Ibid., 62–70.
20 See Huda Shaarawi, *Harem Years: The Memoirs of an Egyptian Feminist (1879–1924)*, trans. Margot Badran (New York: The Feminist Press, 1986), 122; Khaldi, "Epistolarity in a Nahḍah Climate," 25–27.
21 Habermas, *The Structural Transformation of the Public Sphere*, 50.
22 Ibid.
23 Nabawiyyah Mūsā, *Tārīkhī bi Qalamī* [Writing My Own History] (Cairo: Multaqā al-Mar'ahwal-Dhākirah, 1999), 208. For a full translation of the letter, see Appendix A.
24 Ibid.
25 Nawāl al-Sa'dāwī, *Mudhakkirātī fī Sijn al-Nisā'* [My Prison Memoirs] (Beirut: Dār al-Ādāb, 2000), 189–190. For a full translation of the letter, see Appendix B.
26 Ibid.
27 Ibid., 285.
28 See Khaldi, "Epistolarity in a Nahḍah Climate,"13. For a full translation of Ziyādah's letter, see Khaldi, *Egypt Awakening in the Early Twentieth Century*, Appendix B, 160–162.
29 Ibid.
30 Khaldi, "Epistolarity in a Nahḍah Climate," 18.
31 Zaynab Fawwāz, *al-Rasā'il al-Zaynabiyyah* [Zaynab's Letters] (Cairo: Al-Hay'ah al-Miṣriyyah al-'Āmmah lil Kitāb, 2007), 71.
32 See Fadwa Tuqan, *A Mountainous Journey: A Poet's Autobiography*, trans. Olive E. Kenny and Naomi Shihab Nye (Saint Paul, MN: Graywolf Press, 1990), 73; Radwa Ashour and Ferial Ghazoul, eds, *Arab Women Writers: A Critical Reference Guide, 1873–1999* (Cairo: The American University in Cairo Press, 2008), 210.
33 Khaldi, *Egypt Awakening in the Early Twentieth Century*, Appendix E, 166.
34 Ibid., Appendix G, 170.
35 Badran and Cooke, *Opening the Gates*, 22.
36 Ibid.
37 Habermas, *The Structural Transformation of the Public Sphere*, 49.
38 Khaldi, *Egypt Awakening in the Early Twentieth Century*, Appendix B, 160.
39 Ibid., 161.
40 Ibid.
41 Ibid.

42 Ibid., 163.
43 Ibid.
44 Shaarawi, *Harem Years*, 122.
45 See for instance Benjamin S. Bloom, ed., *Taxonomy of Educational Objectives: Handbook I: Cognitive Domain* (New York: David McKay. Part Two, 1956), 62–197.
46 Renate A. Schulz, "Literature and Readability: Bridging the Gap in Foreign Language Reading," *The Modern Language Journal* 65 (1981): 43.
47 Paul Ricoeur, *Interpretation Theory: Discourse and the Surplus of Meaning* (Fort Worth: Texas Christian University Press, 1976), 74; see also Norman H. Holland, *The Dynamics of Literary Response* (New York: Oxford University Press, 1968); Wolfgang Iser, *The Act of Reading: A Theory of Aesthetic Response* (Baltimore, MD: Johns Hopkins University Press, 1978).
48 The following books can provide a good background material for the study of Arab women writers: Roger M.A. Allen, ed., *Essays in Arabic Literary Biography, 1850–1950* (Wiesbaden: Otto Harrassowitz Verlag, 2010); Ashour and Ghazoul, *Arab Women Writers*; Badran and Cooke, *Opening the Gates.*
49 Bloom, *Taxonomy of Educational Objectives.*
50 Anita Jones Vogely, "Introductory Spanish Literature Courses: An Instructional Model," *Hispania* 80:2 (May 1997): 244.
51 Khaldi, *Egypt Awakening in the Early Twentieth Century*, 61.
52 Some of the correspondence has been translated into English. See ibid., appendices B, C and D.
53 Jeanne M. Yanes, "Comprehensible Input via Culture-Schema: Preparation and Inspiration for Literary Study," *Hispania* 75: 1348–1354.

Bibliography

Allen, Roger. *Essays in Arabic Literary Biography, 1850–1950.* Wiesbaden: Otto Harrassowitz Verlag, 2010.

Al-Musawi, Muhsin. "The Growth of Scholarly Interest in the Arabian Nights." *Muslim World* (Hartford, CT) LXX (1981): 196–212.

Al-Musawi, Muhsin. "Vindicating a Profession or a Personal Career? Al-Qalqashandī's Maqāmah in Context." *Journal of Mamluk Studies* 7 (Chicago, IL Div. Jan. 2003): 111–135.

Al-Musawi, Muhsin. "Pre-Modern Belletristic Prose." In *The Cambridge History of Arabic Literature: Literature in the Post-Classical Period.* Eds Roger Allen and D.S. Richards. Cambridge: Cambridge University Press, 2006.

Al-Musawi, Muhsin. *Islam on the Street.* Lanham, MD: Rowman & Littlefield, 2010.

Al-Musawi, Muhsin. *The Medieval Islamic Republic of Letters: Arabic Knowledge Construction.* Notre Dame, IN: Notre Dame University Press, 2015.

Al-Qāḍī, Wadād. "The Impact of the Qur'ān on the Epistolography of 'Abd al-Ḥamīd." In *Approaches to the Qur'ān.* Eds G.R. Hawting, Abdul-Kader A. Shareef. London and New York: Routledge, 1993. 285–313.

Al-Sa'dāwī, Nawāl. *Mudhakkirātī fī Sijn al-Nisā'* [My Prison Memoirs]. Beirut: Dār al-Ādāb, 2000.

Altman, Janet Gurkin. *Epistolarity: Approaches to a Form.* Columbus: Ohio State University Press, 1982.

Ashour, Radwa and Ferial Ghazoul, eds. *Arab Women Writers: A Critical Reference Guide, 1873–1999.* Cairo: The American University in Cairo Press, 2008.

Badran, Margot and Miriam Cooke, eds. *Opening the Gates: An Anthology of Arab Feminist Writing.* Bloomington and Indianapolis: Indiana University Press, 2004.

Bloom, S. Benjamin, ed. *Taxonomy of Educational Objectives: Handbook I: Cognitive Domain.* New York: David McKay. Part Two, 1956.

Booth, Marilyn. "Mayy Ziyada and the Feminist Perspective, 1908–1931." BA thesis. Harvard University, 1978.

Booth, Marilyn. "Biography and Feminist Rhetoric in Early Twentieth Century Egypt: Mayy Ziyada's Studies of Three Women's Lives." *Journal of Women's History* 3:1 (1991): 38–64.

Booth, Marilyn. *May Her Likes be Multiplied: Biography and Gender Politics in Egypt*. Berkeley: University of California Press, 2001.

Brugman, J. *An Introduction to the History of Modern Arabic Literature*. Leiden: E.J. Brill, 1984.

El-Ariss, Tarek. *Trials of Modernity: Literary Affects and the New Political*. New York: Fordham University Press, 2013.

Fawwāz, Zaynab. *al-Rasā'il al-Zaynabiyyah* [Zaynab's Letters]. Cairo: Al-Hay'ah al-Miṣriyyah al-'Āmmah lil Kitāb, 2007.

Goodman, Dena. *The Republic of Letters: A Cultural History of the French Enlightenment*. Ithaca, NY and London: Cornell University Press, 1994.

Habermas, Jürgen. *The Structural Transformation of the Public Sphere: An Inquiry into the Category of Bourgeois Society*. Trans. Thomas Burger with the assistance of Frederick Lawrence. Cambridge, MA: MIT Press, 1989.

Holland, Norman H. *The Dynamics of Literary Response*. New York: Oxford University Press, 1968.

Iser, Wolfgang. *The Act of Reading: A Theory of Aesthetic Response*. Baltimore, MD: Johns Hopkins University Press, 1978.

Khaldi, Boutheina. "Epistolarity in a Nahḍah Climate: The Role of Mayy Ziyādah's Letter Writing." *Journal of Arabic Literature* 40 (2009): 1–36.

Khaldi, Boutheina. *Egypt Awakening in the Early Twentieth Century: Mayy Ziyādah's Intellectual Circles*. London and New York: Palgrave Macmillan, 2012.

Kilpatrick, Hilary. *Making the Great Book of Songs: Compilation and the Author's Craft in Abū al-Faraj al-Iṣfahānī's Kitāb al-Aghānī*. New York and Canada: Routledge, 2010.

Mūsā, Nabawiyyah. *Tārīkhī bi Qalamī* [Writing My Own History]. Cairo: Multaqā al-Mar'ahwal-Dhākirah, 1999.

Ricoeur, Paul. *Interpretation Theory: Discourse and the Surplus of Meaning*. Fort Worth: Texas Christian University Press, 1976.

Schulz, Renate A. "Literature and Readability: Bridging the Gap in Foreign Language Reading." *The Modern Language Journal* 65 (1981): 43–53.

Shaarawi, Huda. *Harem Years: The Memoirs of an Egyptian Feminist (1879–1924)*. Trans. Margot Badran. New York: The Feminist Press, 1986.

Tageldin, Shaden M. *Disarming Words: Empire and the Seductions of Translation in Egypt*. California: University of California Press, 2011.

Todorov, T. *Poetics of Prose*. Trans. Richard Howard. London: Blackwell Publishers, 1977.

Tuqan, Fadwa. *A Mountainous Journey: A Poet's Autobiography*. Trans. Olive E. Kenny and Naomi Shihab Nye. Saint Paul, MN: Graywolf Press, 1990.

Vogely, Anita Jones. "Introductory Spanish Literature Courses: An Instructional Model." *Hispania* 80(2) (May 1997): 244–254.

Yanes, Jeanne M. "Comprehensible Input via Culture-Schema: Preparation and Inspiration for Literary Study." *Hispania* 75.5 (1992): 1348–1354.

3

ARAB WOMEN WRITERS 1980–2010

miriam cooke

Modern Arabic literature has undergone a feminist revolution. A mere 30 years ago there were virtually no women in the canon and, therefore, in English translation.[1] Various independence movements from British and French colonizers, Algerian liberation movements, the rise of the left in the Arab world in the 1950s–60s, and the Lebanese civil war, all have given rise to women's increased literary participation. The first generation trail-blazers such as Zeinab Fawwaz (1846–1914), Labibah Hashim (1880–1952), Alice Butrus al-Bustani in Lebanon, and 'A'isha al-Taymuriyyah (1840–1902) in Egypt suffered from oblivion. The second generation of women writers such as the Iraqi Nazik al-Mala'ika (1923–2007) and 'Atika al-Khazraji (1927–97), the Syrian Ulfa al-Idlbi (1912–2007), Colette Khuri (b. 1937), and Ghada Samman (b. 1942), the Palestinian Fadwa Tuqan (1917–2003), the Lebanese Layla al-Baalabaki (b. 1934) and Emily Nasrallah (b. 1931), the Egyptians Latifah al-Zayyat (b. 1923), Alifa Rifaat (1930–96), and Nawal El Saadawi (b. 1930), all achieved Arab recognition which, with the exception of El Saadawi, was rarely augmented as a result of widespread Western translations. Today the Arab women writers of the third and fourth generations such as Hanan al-Shaykh, Hoda Barakat, Sahar Khalifeh, Radwa Ashur, Evelyne Accad, Etel Adnan, Raja 'Alim, Samar Yazbek, Fadia Faqir, Miral al-Tahawy, and Ahdaf Soueif dominate the scene. Although there are still very few pre-modern translations of women's writings, hundreds of twentieth-century Arabic poems, novels, short stories and memoirs penned by Arab women are now available in English translation as publishers compete with each other for publication rights to the works of women writers. Moreover, Arab women who live outside their birth countries are writing in English and expanding the canon of Arab women's literature.

What has happened to transform the status and perception of Arab women writers in the American academy? I would propose three answers: (1) the emergence of women's studies has drawn attention to the erasure of women throughout history; (2) wars in the region that have engaged the American government and military have brought the Arab world closer to the American reader; and (3) the crisis in academic publishing has challenged conventional notions of what counted as appropriate classroom texts; novels are being used in place of textbooks.

Women's studies

During the 1980s, there were lively debates about the place of women's studies in American education. Feminists were divided: some insisted that the study of women had to be mainstreamed; others believed that a separate institutional base was essential. For the former, a women's studies center or department might provide administrations with the excuse to do no more than fund a minor, ancillary project and allow campus life to go on as usual. For the latter, that institutional project was far from minor. By virtue of the name alone, a freestanding women's studies program would compel constant attention to a new field of enquiry that questioned the modus operandi of most disciplines. Tertiary institutions went both ways.

By the 1990s, women's studies were part of the American academic landscape just as women writers across centuries and continents were becoming a significant part of their literary canons. The impetus for establishing women's studies began with a focus on Euro-American women and gender issues, but during the 1980s scholarly interest turned to Asian and African women and eventually to Arab women. Edward Said's *Orientalism*, published in 1977, had indicted much of the scholarship on the Middle East and other colonized regions as being inextricably involved with colonial politics. Scholars could counteract this charge of bias only by becoming aware of and open about their own identity and positioning when they wrote about Arabs. Men and women from post-independence countries who studied and taught in American universities brought a postcolonial consciousness to their classrooms. In her 1988 game-changing essay "Under Western Eyes: Feminist Scholarship and Colonial Discourses," Chandra Talpade Mohanty contested the representation of women from countries outside the Euro-American fold as uniformly victimized. She demanded that cross-cultural feminist work attend to local contexts and global imperial designs. During the 1990s, Arab women began to be seen as something other than the odalisques of Orientalist painters like Delacroix or the veiled chattel of travel literature. It was no longer unthinkable that they might write books.

War

The role of war and civil conflict in the cultural life of the Middle East and of Arabs in America cannot be overestimated. War figures prominently in many Arabic novels, short stories and poems. Each Arab–Israeli confrontation has echoed around the Arab world and also in the communities of Arabs in an America traditionally allied with Israel. Each war served to accentuate rifts between Arab immigrants and their American neighbors. For many, it was the Gulf War of 1991 that created a new ethnic identity: the Arab-American. With the 1999 publication of Munir Akash and Khaled Mattawa's *Post Gibran: Anthology of New Arab American Writing*, Arabs in America joined hyphenated others in producing a specific segment of American ethnic literature. Other anthologies highlighted women's role, particularly the value of keeping alive the connection to the ancestral line of mothers and grandmothers, in harmonizing this hyphenated identity as in Joanna Kadi's *Food for Our Grandmothers: Writings by Arab-American and Arab-Canadian Feminists* (1994). It is important to note that their literature is not only American or Canadian; it is also Arab.

While war was pervading the lives and works of Arabs in and outside the Arab world, it was also attracting the interest of American readers. They were curious to know more about the people with whom their government was becoming involved. Who was this Saddam Hussein who had invaded neighboring Kuwait in 1990 and drawn America and its allies into the region? Did women suffer as much as their men did when they went to the front to fight? How could women tolerate the "intolerable conditions" that Islam imposed on them? Would American women marines based in the Arabian Peninsula after the Gulf War teach Saudi women a thing or two about their rights as women? The questions were mostly shaped by negative stereotypes, but they reflected a growing awareness of a part of the world that previously had been dismissed.

The events of 9/11 sharpened this interest. Questions like "Why do they hate us so much?" in some cases gave way to a real curiosity about Muslims and Arabs. Muslim and Arab denunciation of the Arab Islamists who had declared war on the West opened a chink in the iron carapace surrounding knowledge of the Arab world. Arab women and men writing about themselves and for each other provided new vistas on to the mysterious Orient, the land of Scheherazade. Vilashini Cooppan discusses the teaching of *A Thousand and One Nights* after the American invasion of Iraq in 2003 when students could compare the Baghdad of CNN with the opulent capital of the ninth-century Caliph Harun al-Rashid and thereby "recode a place we knew only in the Manichaean modalities of war" (Cooppan 2009, 35). Moreover, students can read directly about Iraqis' experiences in the several war novels and memoirs, many by women. The impact of 9/11 on Arab and Muslim women writers was recognized in anthologies edited by women writers, such as Fawzia Afzal-Khan's *Shattering the Stereotypes: Muslim Women Speak Out* (2005), a collection that was foreworded by the leading Egyptian feminist novelist Nawal El Saadawi.

Academic publishing

This enhanced interest in Arabs and their cultures coincided with the 1990s crisis in scholarly publishing. Academic presses could no longer afford to publish highly specialized, often abstruse works that trade publishers would not consider. Even the traditional textbook market for the humanities began to dry up. That did not mean that professors were not assigning textbooks. Rather it meant that they were looking for different kinds of textbooks. Discovering the heuristic efficacy of fiction and poetry, professors in a wide variety of Middle East courses, including the social sciences, are now assigning literary texts. Anthologies, short story collections and novels are replacing the potted surveys that had been the mainstay of Arabic literature courses. Reynold Alleyne Nicholson's (1907) *A Literary History of the Arabs*, republished 15 times, is no longer a choice. New names, particularly women's names, are constantly being added to syllabi. The explosion of literary production by Arab women and the growth of general reader interest in Arab women and their literary works have created a new market. Consequently, the translation process has become less arbitrary and dependent on translators' interests and whims. Since 9/11, reader interest has led to a different attitude toward translation of literary texts from the Arab world and attempts are being made to systematize the flow of Arabic literature into English.

State of the field

Foremothers?

Myth had it that the first women to write fiction in Arabic were the Syrian Colette Khuri and Lebanese Layla al-Ba'albakki.[2] However, other than al-Ba'albakki's "Spaceship of Tenderness to the Moon" (1964), anthologized by Fernea and Bezirgan (1977), their novels and short stories were not translated, and so passing reference to these two women was deemed sufficient in modern Arabic literature courses.[3] Then in 1983 Zed Press in London translated Nawal El Saadawi's *Woman at Point Zero*. A star was born!

Two events in 1986 changed the fortunes of Arab women writers and internationalized their works. During the first International Women's Book Fair in London, Quartet Books launched Lebanese Hanan al-Shaykh with her *Story of Zahra* (Arabic, 1980) and Egyptian Alifa Rifaat with *Distant View of a Minaret*, a collection of short stories that were first published in this English edition. Two more stars were born. In each case, women were shown to have led unfulfilled or oppressed lives against which they ultimately rebelled. During that same year, Palestinian critic Joseph Zeidan published his *Masadir al-adab al-nisa'i* (Sources of Women's Literature) and it seemed impossible that there might be 486 women writers in the modern Arab world.[4] Today, however, this is not surprising.

Critics began to turn their attention to Arab women writers collectively and individually. In my 1987 *War's Other Voices*, I grouped over 50 women who had written about their struggle and survival in the Lebanese arena of violence prior to the Israeli invasion of 1982 into a literary school that I called the Beirut Decentrists. I challenged the notion that in war men are the warriors and women the civilians; that men write about war and women about the home. *Women and the War Story* (1997) returned to the topic of war and gender with an analysis of the war writings of Algerian, Iraqi, Palestinian and post-1982 Lebanese women. The notion that

Lebanese women had been exceptional in writing about war gave way to an understanding that women are not sheltered from the effects of their countries' wars and that many of them, especially in the era of postmodern warfare, have written about this supposedly male-only arena. The list of women's novels and short stories about wars in the Arab world is long and in the Internet age this list has been supplemented by many blogs and online stories.

Feminist literature?

The question that many asked during the 1980s was: are these women writing from a feminist perspective? Some resisted the label feminist because it was said to be too Western and imported, and reminiscent of the colonial project to save Arab women from their men. Others embraced the term because of its rich history of women's empowerment.

In 1990, with historian Margot Badran, I published *Opening the Gates: A Century of Arab Feminist Writing*. The anthology brought together expository and literary selections from a wide range of women's works that we considered feminist. We insisted on the attribute "feminist," because it indicated the writers' awareness of gender injustice, their rejection of it and their determination to do something to change their circumstances. The anthology was thus more than a collection of Arab women's writings; it emphasized women's ways of knowing and asserting themselves. Above all, it made available to English-language readers a taste of the feast of Arab women's written expression dating back to the nineteenth century. Zeidan's *Arab Women Novelists* (1995) signaled an important stage in Arab women's literary history: there were enough practitioners of a single genre, the novel, to warrant devoting an entire monograph to their oeuvre.

Islam

Towards the end of the last century, Islam preoccupied several Arab women writers (cooke 2001). After the success of the Iranian Revolution that brought Ayatollah Khomeini's Shiite Islam into conflict with the Saudis' Sunni Islam, political Islam became a dominant trend in the Middle East and a literary topos. While Islamists had been active since the 1930s, with the Muslim Brothers calling for reform in society and the establishment of an Islamic state, they did not write literature or even memoirs until the 1970s, after those who had been in prison were released. Both men and women had spent time in Jamal Abd al-Nasir's prisons and described the ordeals they underwent there. Among these writers was Zaynab al-Ghazali, the leader of the Association of Muslim Ladies. Her 1970s prison memoirs, *Days from my Life* (translated as *Return of the Pharaoh: Memoir in Nasser's Prison*) celebrated this woman's ability to survive the worst tortures and to be stronger in her political and religious resistance than her male colleagues. During the 1990s several women addressed Islamic topics, among them Algerian Assia Djebar and Egyptian Nawal El Saadawi. Djebar's 1987 *Far from Medina* told the stories (some true, some not) of powerful women who interacted with the Prophet Muhammad in the seventh century. El Saadawi devoted several novels, including *Fall of the Imam* (1987) and *Innocence of the Devil* (1993), to exposing the misogyny of monotheistic religions. Egyptian Miral al-Tahawy's 1998 *Blue Aubergine* probed the secluded life of a girl from a tribal family who experiments with conservative Islam as a way to participate in modern society. In 1998 also, the Algerian journalist Baya Gacemi published *I, Nadia, Wife of a Terrorist*. She had recorded and transcribed the life of an Algerian peasant woman who married a leader of GIA, or the Groupe Islamique Armée. This Algerian Islamist organization terrorized cities, towns and countryside in the wake of the annulment of the 1992 election that briefly brought the Islamists to power.

Teaching strategies

In 1980, my first year of teaching at Duke University, the only writings available in English were snippets from famous Arab women like the sixth–seventh-century Arabian poet Tumadir bint 'Amr, aka al-Khansa', and the eighth-century Iraqi mystic Rabi'a al-'Adawiya which were scattered in anthologies of Arabic literature. To teach a class on Arab women writers I had to produce supplementary materials. Since I was at the beginning of a new project about the women who had lived through and creatively engaged with their experiences of the Lebanese civil war (1975–90), I had translated a few of their stories. I added them to the syllabus, but they were still too few to constitute an entire course. I therefore included men's writings about women and the course became an "images of Arab women" class. The class was small, and the students had enrolled out of curiosity; they had not known that Arab women were literate, let alone authors. They were intrigued by the defiance and courage that they read, but they remained skeptical about these women who were clearly exceptions to the rule of Arab women's silence, especially literary silence. I could and did show my students shelves of books by Lebanese, Palestinian, Egyptian, Iraqi, Jordanian, Kuwaiti, Moroccan and Algerian women, but since none of the students could read Arabic and they did not understand that the French texts might be Arab, their doubts were not allayed.

Today, however, because the range of Arab women's works translated into and written directly in English has increased exponentially, professors have bewildering choices and challenges. New questions confront the instructor: to what extent should coverage be attempted? How much attention should be drawn to cultural and linguistic differences among writers from 22 Arab countries? Can a course be representative of Arab women's literary production while focusing on a few works, authors and moments?

In the introduction to his edited volume, *Teaching World Literature*, critic David Damrosch calls not for coverage but for *un*covering "a variety of compelling works from distinctive traditions, through creative combinations and juxtapositions guided by whatever specific themes and issues we wish to raise in a particular course … courses need to be exploratory rather than exhaustive, creating a teachable progression of issues and works rather than striving after some impossible proportional representation." In answer to the question about cultural differences from one Arab society to another, one might consider his suggestion that "an in-depth study of a national tradition can lead far beyond the nation's boundaries, as we follow a writer's multinational literary heritage or look to see how comparable techniques and concerns have been developed by more distant authors" (Damrosch 2009, 9). Although these remarks refer to the teaching of world literature, they apply equally to decisions that professors must make when planning to teach a course on Arab women writers.

What are the politics and ethics of reading Arab women's lives and stories? Identification with a heroine can help to undermine exotic notions of the otherness of Arab women, but it may also lead to a problematic assumption of a "global sisterhood which homogenizes women as a group across classes and cultures, prior to the process of analysis ... and obscures the ways in which Arab writers can themselves engage in orientalist representations of their societies" (Majaj 1992, 7). For Cooppan, the goal is not to convert otherness to sameness, but rather "to stay blocked from that final assimilative moment, at home in the very moment of non-recognition (seeking) difference as much as sameness, a practice that preserves the distinct historical formation and trajectory" (Cooppan 2009, 39).

Gayatri Spivak has proposed "planetarity" as a mode of transnational, transcultural thinking that does not reduce diversity and alterity to the homogeneity of globalization: "Planet-thought opens up to embrace an inexhaustible taxonomy of such names, including but not identical with the whole range of human universals: aboriginal animism as well as the spectral white mythology of post-rational science. If we imagine ourselves as planetary subjects rather than global agents, planetary creatures rather than global entities, alterity remains underived from us; it is not our dialectical negation, it contains us as much as it flings us away" (Spivak 2003, 73). Planetary teaching would decenter the students in their American classroom so that they might learn how to defamiliarize "the familiarity of presumed common humanity" (ibid., 77).

However, if one insists too much on otherness and the importance of staying in the moment of non-recognition, how does one avoid making a feminist literary work that critiques patriarchal norms reinforce negative stereotypes of gender relations in an Arab world said to be oppressive of women? On the other hand, if professors are sensitive to the danger of reinforcing negativity, they may be tempted to explain away and defend difference. In this case, there is another risk, and that is of falling into a kind of cultural relativism that excuses female genital mutilation as a cultural practice. In her article about teaching Arab women writers, Lisa Suhair Majaj discusses the difficulty of challenging "free-floating orientalist 'knowledge' which predetermines popular perceptions of the Middle East, without subverting the critical analysis of Arab societies which writers undertake. While to emphasize the element of feminist critique in Arab women's writing may appear to buttress pervasive stereotypes of Middle Eastern women, to ignore this element distorts Arab women's writing." Can deconstruction of stereotypes "take place simultaneously with the process of construction – of building up a body of knowledge about Arab women which would respond to and challenge these stereotypes" (Majaj 1992, 4, 6)? Answers to these questions may appear in the classroom.

Students must learn to live with contradictions and not try to resolve them. Difference and sameness need to be kept in a fine balance. An ethics of reading texts about and by Arab women will always remain attentive to how local and global issues shape their lives.

Another important concern is how to introduce cultural, social and political information; in other words, how much context should be provided? What is the ideal ratio of primary to secondary texts? Can literary texts be left to tell the story of their culture, its politics and economics, without becoming sociological tools whose sole purpose is to access cultural information? Yet without that information understanding may be compromised and students may slip back into the familiar realm of preconceived knowledge. How to situate the text socio-politically while directing students to the aesthetic of Arab women's oeuvre? Should one pair women's fiction and poetry with that by men in order to address issues of gender in writing? Margaret Higonnet believes that such "dialogic readings can free readers from narrow cultural presuppositions and bring into play more than one kind of gendered interpretation" (Higonnet 2009, 241). Clearly, there are many challenges facing professors and students in a course devoted to Arab women writers. In what follows, I suggest some organizational options and strategies.

Organizational options

1. Diachronic surveys can begin in the pre-Islamic period with Arabian poet al-Khansa', through nineteenth-century Syrian Warda al-Yaziji (Badran and cooke 1990), up to contemporary Arabian novelist Raja' 'Alim and tribal women's oral poetry (al-Ghadeer 2010). Although such a survey would skim the treetops of all countries and genres and might "blur the specificity of cultural and geographical contexts" (Majaj 1992, 5), it would reveal the variety of women's concerns and literary skills across a millennium and a half.
2. Century- or period-specific surveys are now possible, but primarily for the past two centuries. Density of literary production in Syria (which included Lebanon until the early twentieth century) and Egypt during the early period indicates where the level of women's education was highest. Since education for women in the Arabian Peninsula (Saudi Arabia, Yemen, Oman and the Gulf countries) was not fully institutionalized until the late 1960s, it is not surprising that they should be absent from the literature of the earlier period. Tracing the availability of women's writings from 22 Arab countries during the twentieth century is a good indication of who had the power and when.
3. Country-specific courses provide depth and region-specific detail, yet they are limited by the fact that only a few countries have enough women writers to warrant an entire course: Egypt (Booth anthologies, Ashour, El Saadawi, al-Tahawi, Salwa Bakr), Palestine (Khalifa, Liana Badr, Tuqan), Lebanon and Syria

(Idlibi, Khuri, Adnan, Barakat, al-Shaykh, Samman, Yazbek) and the Arabian Peninsula (Akers and Bagader anthologies, ʻAlim, Arebi, al-Ghadeer). While "more attention could be given to the historical specificity of each text, (it) would make it more difficult to discuss thematic and historical connections across national boundaries" (Majaj 1992, 5).

4. Genre is another way to organize a course. To the novel, short story, poetry and memoir have been added the blog and its book or "blook" (Riverbend). The semester might be devoted to one of the genres (including critical works like Zeidan for the novel). Alternatively, the course might be divided into four or five segments, each dedicated to a single genre. There is no shortage now of women's writings that can be used to cover these.
5. Translation may be taken for granted or it may be problematized. Moreover, if there is Arabic fluency among the students, translation can become an organizing principle. According to Lawrence Venuti, "teaching in translation is not the same as raising the issue of translation in the classroom [...] To read a translation simply as the communication of a univocal meaning collapses the translation into the foreign text and conceals the translator's labor of transformation. A translation communicates not so much the foreign text as the translator's interpretation of it, one interpretation among others ... that should be articulated for students, not dismissed as arbitrary or irrelevant or displaced by a competing interpretation." Some instructors – especially if they do not know Arabic – will focus on content and style, even if aware that style has more to do with the work of the translator than of the author. Others who know Arabic might follow Venuti's lead in choosing a single text and its translation to examine how the translator has made the text her own (Venuti 2009, 87, 92, 94).
6. The thematic approach does not raise expectations of coverage and representation, and it enables a comparative approach through cross-national connections:

   a War: Algerian Revolution, 1967, the Lebanese Civil War, the Gulf War, 9/11, the 2003 American involvement in Iraq, the 2011 Arab Spring (Adnan, Riverbend, Yazbek, many films on the Algerian Revolution, the Lebanese Civil War and the Arab Spring (especially Egypt); secondary sources: Accad, cooke, Mehta).
   b Citation, e.g. *A Thousand and One Nights* and discussions of magical realism and the fantastic in women's writings (ʻAlim, Kahf, Samman; secondary sources: Darraj, Gauch).
   c Politics and prison narratives (al-Ghazali, El Bouih, El Saadawi).
   d Islam, about or from the perspective of Muslim women: discussions of veiling (Aboulela, Djebar, al-Ghazali, Kahf, El Saadawi; secondary source: cooke).
   e Life writing: biography and autobiography (Ahmed, Faqir, al-Ghazali, El Saadawi, Tuqan, Golley).

Resources

1. Anthologies:

   a PROTA (Project of Translation from Arabic) volumes of short stories, plays and novel extracts that include many women (Salma Khadra al-Jayyusi series editor)
   b Badran and cooke
   c Akers and Bagader
   d Handal

2. Arabic literature in translation book series at the university presses of American University in Cairo, Syracuse, Columbia and Texas
3. Films by and about Arab women (Women Make Films, ArtEast and Tribecca)
4. Literary criticism (Accad; Arebi; Ashur, Ghazoul and Barakat; cooke; Darraj; Gauch; al-Ghadeer; Majaj; Mehta)
5. Online:

   a *Encyclopedia of Women in Islamic Cultures* (EWIC), with many articles on Arab women: http://sjoseph.ucdavis.edu/ewic/
   b Stories even on Twitter
   c "Maiden Voyages": illustrated diaries of women from Egypt, Jordan and the Palestinian West Bank: www.youtube.com/watch?v=QJrc0JMLkig
   d "Contemporary Arab Women Writers" (includes videos of interviews with writers): www.bu.edu/library/guides/caww/index.html

Appendix: Two course descriptions (thematic and chronological)

1 Muslim women writers

Through fiction, film, autobiography and new media, students will be exposed to the writings of women in Muslim communities in the Arab world, Europe and the United States. During the nineteenth century, the control of women became a battlefield for a major struggle between Muslim men and European colonialists over such issues as veiling and gender segregation. Even when Muslim women spoke out, their voices were marginalized. Today they have become a focus of international concern. Students will consider several key questions: How do Muslim women's voices contest the notion in Asian and African societies that feminism is a Western ideology? What role does Islam play in women's emancipatory discourses? Are women's demands for justice, freedom and equality a recent trend? How have global politics shaped the articulation of Muslim women's rights? What is at stake for Muslims and non-Muslims in highlighting Muslim women's roles and behavior? The course will address major debates surrounding the literary discussion of the veil and the roles of Muslim women in war, marriage, and Islamization.

2 Arab women writers in the twentieth century

This course will explore the emergence of an Arab women's literary tradition over the past century. Although most of the texts were written in Arabic, they come from countries with specific histories and cultures in which the legacies of British and French colonialism still hang heavy. In some cases, Arab women are writing from countries where they have settled after leaving their birthplaces. Some still write in Arabic, others have adopted the language of their place of residence. What difference does language choice make? This literature that comes from several different countries is best understood as international, part of world literature, and it will be studied from a comparative point of view. Most of these writings might be characterized as feminist, yet many refuse both "feminist" and "women" as attributes to describe their work. Why? What does it mean for outsiders to attach their own meanings to actions and texts that their authors refuse? We will discuss the problems that arise when discussing Arab women within a Western frame of reference. Students will be expected to develop a basic understanding of Arab women's self-representations; to learn how to read creative texts critically, to develop analytical skills and to refine research skills.

- Assia Djebar, *Women of Algiers in their Apartments*, trans. Marjolijn de Jager (Charlottesville and London: University Press of Virginia, 1992), pp. 1–52 (WebCT).
- Leila Abouzeid, *The Year of the Elephant.* Moroccan novel about the disempowerment of women activists in the wake of the independence war from France.
- Leila Ahmed, *A Border Passage: From Cairo to America – A Woman's Journey.* Memoir of an Egyptian professor who has taught in the United States for many years.
- Rajaa Alsanea, *Girls of Riyadh.* Controversial Saudi novel about the lives of four young women.
- Radwa Ashur, *Granada.* Contemporary Egyptian novel imagining the period just before the Inquisition and expulsions of Jews and Muslims from Spain.
- Salwa Bakr, *The Golden Chariot.* Egyptian novel about an all-female dystopia.
- Assia Djebar, *Far from Medina.* Algerian novel that reimagines the lives of the first Muslim household, that of the Prophet Muhammad.
- Ulfat Idilbi, *Sabriya: Sabriya* and *Grandfather's Tale.* Novels imagining early twentieth-century domestic life in Syria.
- Alia Mamdouh, *The Loved Ones.* Novel about expatriate Iraqis in Paris and Canada; also dwells on domestic life in wartime Iraq.
- Out al-Kouloub [Qut al-Qulub], *Ramza.* Egyptian novel on early twentieth-century female life.
- Ahdaf Soueif, *The Eye of the Sun.* Egyptian novel (written in English) focusing on a woman writing her dissertation in England and struggling with cultural identity between the "local" community of Egyptians and English society.

- Miral al-Tahawy, *The Tent*. Novel of Egyptian Bedouin life.
- Latifa al-Zayyat, *The Open Door*. Egyptian novel about a young woman's coming of age in the 1940s, and national independence.
- Samar Yazbek, *Woman in the Crossfire*. Syrian memoir about the first months of the 2011 Syrian revolution.

Notes

1 Until the last three or four decades, Arab women writers inside the Arab world were unable to get their voices heard and their writings translated. Ed.

2 The Lebanese Zeinab Fawwaz was the first Arab writer amongst males and females to write a novel, *Husn al-'Awaqib* (1899).

3 Fernea and Bezirgan's *Middle Eastern Muslim Women Speak* was a mixed compendium of short talks, memoir fragments, interviews with illiterate women, literary writings about women by men like Naguib Mahfouz (who would not become Nobel Laureate for over a decade), some poetry and lullabies. The only fiction selection was Ba'albakki's "A Spaceship of Tenderness to the Moon" which earned her fame because of an obscenity trial she underwent for having described her husband's body in loving detail.

4 In 1992 the second edition of Zeidan's *Sources of Women's Literature* added over 160 writers to produce a total of 650 contemporary Arab women writers.

Bibliography

Abdulhadi, Rabab, Evelyn Alsultany and Nadine Naber, eds. 2011. *Arab and Arab American Feminisms: Gender, Violence, and Belonging*. Syracuse, NY: Syracuse University Press.

Aboulela, Leila. 2005. *Minaret: A Novel*. New York: Grove Atlantic.

Accad, Evelyne. 1991. *Sexuality and War: Literary Masks of the Middle East*. New York: New York University Press.

Adnan, Etel. 1980. *Sitt Marie Rose*. Sausalito: Post-Apollo.

Afzal-Khan, Fawzia. 1997. "Introducing a New Course: Muslim Women in Twentieth-Century Literature." *NWSA Journal* 9/1.

Afzal-Khan, Fawzia. 2005. *Shattering the Stereotypes: Muslim Women Speak Out*. Ithaca, NY: Olive Branch Press.

Ahmed, Leila. 1999. *A Border Passage: From Cairo to America – A Woman's Journey*. New York: Farrar, Straus and Giroux.

Akash, Munir and Khaled Mattawa. 1999. *Post Gibran: Anthology of New Arab American Writing*. Bethesda, MD: Kitab Inc. Jusoor Books.

Akers, Deborah and Abubaker Bagader, eds. 1998. *Voices of Change: Short Stories by Saudi Arabian Women Writers*. Boulder, CO: Lynne Rienner.

Akers, Deborah and Abubaker Bagader, eds. 2007. *Oranges in the Sun*. Lynne Rienner Publishers.

al-Ghadeer, Muneera. 2010. *Desert Voices: Bedouin Women's Poetry in Saudi Arabia*. London: I.B. Tauris.

al-Ghazali, Zaynab. 1994. *Return of the Pharaoh: Memoir in Nasser's Prison*. Trans. Mokrane Guezzou. Leicester: Islamic Foundation.

'Alim, Raja. 2005. *My Thousand and One Nights. A Novel of Mecca*. Syracuse University Press.

Al-Radi, Nuha. 2003. *Baghdad Diaries: A Woman's Chronicle of War and Exile*. New York: Vintage Books.

al-Shaykh, Hanan. 1986. *The Story of Zahra*. London: Quartet.

al-Tahawy, Miral. 2002 [1998]. *Blue Aubergine*, trans. Anthony Calderbank. Cairo: American University of Cairo Press.

Amiry, Suad. 2004. *Sharon and my Mother-in-Law: Ramallah Diaries*. New York: Pantheon Books.

Arebi, Saddeka. 1994. *Women and Words in Saudi Arabia: The Politics of Literary Discourse*. New York: Columbia University Press.

Ashur, Radwa, Ferial Jabouri Ghazoul and Hasna Reda-Mekdashi. 2008. *Arab Women Writers: A Critical Reference Guide, 1873–1999*. Cairo: American University in Cairo Press.

Badran, Margot and miriam cooke. 2004 [1990]. *Opening the Gates: A Century of Arab Feminist Writing*. Bloomington: Indiana University Press.

Barakat, Hoda. 1995. *Stone of Laughter*, trans. Sophie Bennett. New York: Interlink Books.

Booth, Marilyn. 2001. *May her Likes Be Multiplied: Biography and Gender Politics in Egypt*. Berkeley: University of California Press.

cooke, miriam. 1987. *War's Other Voices. Women on the Lebanese Civil War*. London: Cambridge University Press.

cooke, miriam. 1997. *Women and the War Story*. Berkeley: University of California Press.

cooke, miriam. 2001. *Women Claim Islam. Creating Islamic Feminism through Literature*. New York: Routledge.

Cooppan, Vilashini. 2009. "The Ethics of World Literature: Reading Others, Reading Otherwise," in David Damrosch, *Teaching World Literature*. New York: Modern Language Association of America.

Damrosch, David. 2009. *Teaching World Literature*. New York: Modern Language Association of America.

Darraj, Susan Muaddi. 2004. *Sheherazade's Legacy: Arab and Arab American Women on Writing*. Westport: Praeger.

Djebar, Assia. 1991 [1987]. *Far from Medina*, trans. Doroty S. Blair. London: Quartet.

El Bouih, Fatna. 2008 [2001]. *Talk of Darkness*, trans. Mustapha Djamal and Susan Slyomovics. Austin: University of Texas Press.

El Saadawi, Nawal. 1983. *Woman at Point Zero*. London: Zed Press.

El Saadawi, Nawal. 1988. *Memoirs from the Women's Prison*, trans. Marilyn Booth. Berkeley: University of California Press.

El Saadawi, Nawal. 1987. *Fall of the Imam*. London: Zed Press.

El Saadawi, Nawal. 1993. *Innocence of the Devil*. Berkeley: University of California Press.

Faqir, Fadia. 1998. *In the House of Silence: Autobiographical Essays by Arab Women Writers*. Reading: Garnet.

Fernea, Elizabeth Warnock and Basima Qattan Bezirgan. 1977. *Middle Eastern Muslim Women Speak*. Austin: University of Texas Press.

Gacemi, Baya. 2006. *I, Nadia, Wife of a Terrorist*, trans. Paul Cote and Constantina Mitchell. Lincoln: Nebraska University Press.

Gauch, Susan. 2007. *Liberating Shahrazad: Feminism, Postcolonialism, and Islam*. Minneapolis: University of Minnesota Press.

Golley, Nawar. 2003. *Reading Arab Women's Autobiographies: Shahrazad Tells her Story*. Austin: Texas University Press.

Golley, Nawar, ed. 2007. *Arab Women's Lives Retold: Exploring Identity through Writing*. Syracuse, NY: Syracuse University Press.

Haddad, Laila. 2010. *Gaza Mom: Palestine, Politics, Parenting, and Everything in Between*. Charlottesville, VA: Just World Books.

Higonnet, Margaret R. 2009. "Weaving Women into World Literature," in David Damrosch, *Teaching World Literature*. New York: Modern Language Association of America.

Kadi, Joanna, ed. 1994. *Food for Our Grandmothers: Writings by Arab-American and Arab Canadian Feminists*. Cambridge, MA: South End Press.

Kahf, Mohja. 2003. *E-mails from Scheherazad*. Gainesville: University Press of Florida.

Khalifa, Sahar. 1976. *Wild Thorns*. London: Interlink.

Khalifa, Sahar. 2005. *The Inheritance*. Cairo: American University in Cairo Press.

Majaj, Lisa Suhair. 1992. "'Female Voices, Feminist Negotiations': An Experience in Teaching Arab Women's Literature." *Association for Middle East Women's Studies Newsletter* 7/3.

Majaj, Lisa Suhair, Paula Sunderman and Therese Saliba. 2002. *Intersections: Gender, Nation and Community in Arab Women's Novels*. Syracuse, NY: Syracuse University Press.

Mehta, Brinda. 2007. *Rituals of Memory in Contemporary Arab Women's Writing*. Syracuse, NY: Syracuse University Press.

Rifaat, Alifa. 1986. *Distant View of a Minaret*. Trans. Denys Johnson-Davies. London: Quartet.

Riverbend. 2005. *Baghdad Burning: Girl Blog from Iraq*. New York: Women's Press.

Samman, Ghada. 1998. *The Square Moon: Supernatural Tales*, trans. Issa Boullata. Fayetteville: The University of Arkansas Press.

Spivak, Gayatri Chakravorty. 2003. *Death of a Discipline*. New York: Columbia University Press.

Tuqan, Fadwa. 1990. *A Mountainous Journey: An Autobiography*, trans. Olive Kenny. St Paul: Graywolf Press.

Venuti, Lawrence. 2009. "Teaching in Translation," in David Damrosch, *Teaching World Literature*. New York: Modern Language Association of America.

Yazbek, Samar. 2012. *Woman in the Crossfire: Diaries of the Syrian Revolution*. London: Haus Publishing.

Zeidan, Joseph. 1995. *Arab Women Novelists: The Formative Years and Beyond*. Albany: State University of New York Press.

Zeidan, Joseph. 1999. *Masadir al-adab al-nisa'i fi al-'alam al-'arabi al-hadith 1800–1996* (Sources of Women's Literature in the Modern Arab World 1800–1996). Beirut: Al-mu'assassa al-'arabiyya lil-dirasat wa al-nashr.

4

TEACHING FRANCOPHONE ALGERIAN WOMEN'S LITERATURE IN A BILINGUAL FRENCH-ENGLISH CONTEXT

Creative voices, dissident texts

Brinda J. Mehta

Francophone Algerian women writers have established their authority in postcolonial literature written in French through a wide array of genres including memoirs, novels, poetry, short stories, testimonials, theater, and autobiographies. Inscribed within a socio-political context, this literature spans the timelines of colonial and postcolonial Algerian history from the French conquest of Algeria in 1830 to the war of independence (1954–62), and the "black decade" of the bloody civil war of the 1990s. While exposing and denouncing the violent historical traumas that have ravaged the country, these writers have also commemorated the courage and resilience of Algerian men, women, and children through the vibrancy of their "torch words" (Djebar 1993, 142) that reveal the trajectories of resistance and oppression in Algerian history. At the same time, the women use literature as a medium to stage creatively their own gendered insurrections against the patriarchal roots of war, marginality, and violence by reframing Algerian historicity from a more gender-sensitive perspective.

This chapter focuses on the importance of teaching francophone Algerian women's writings through a transnational feminist lens in order to appreciate the richness and complexity of francophone Algerian literature to the full. The course is aimed at students who are bilingual in English and French, as it is part of the Letters curriculum in French and Francophone Studies. An Arabic novel in translation is also included to discuss questions of translation and "authenticity." A feminist engagement with these texts is a necessary historical and literary corrective given the fact that Arab women in general "have been left out of history, out of the War Story, out of narratives of emigration and exile, out of the psychical and hermeneutical spaces of religion" (cooke 2001, viii, xxv). Arabic literature for the classroom can remedy a dire situation in which the "Algerian story" in its feminist preoccupations is missing. A syllabus on francophone Algerian women writers can include:

1. Orientalism and false constructions of the gendered Arab Other (Sa'īd, Alloula).
2. Debunking Orientalism and colonial feminism/framing Algerian women's theoretical subjectivity (Badran, Abdulhadi et al., Mohanty, Malti-Douglas, cooke).
3. Reclaiming voice in text (part two) – francophone Algerian women writers Maïssa Bey, Assia Djebar, Leïla Sebbar, Malika Mokeddem, and Faïza Guène.

Orientalizing the Other

The first part of the syllabus (part one) has a general thematic. It begins with Edward Sa'īd's indispensable analysis of *Orientalism*, a text that provides the foundational outline for the course. Sa'īd examines Western constructions of the so-called "Orient" in this groundbreaking book on the synergies between power, knowledge, academic discourse, and Western imperialism. He argues: "Orientalism is a Western style of dominating, restructuring, and having authority over the Orient" (Sa'īd 1978, 3). Students are encouraged to think about the ways in which Orientalism functions as an analytical framework in the Westernized reading of non-Western texts that are situated outside the norms of Western canonicity through marginality, literary chauvinism, and academic racism.

Sa'īd's work is given a "visual" complement and a nuanced gender analysis in Malek Alloula's *Le harem colonial* (*The Colonial Harem*), a text composed of colonial postcards. These visual representations of Arab women frame them within a fixed Orientalized décor of exotification to show how women are doubly marginalized Others in the colonial imaginary, as racialized and sexualized objects. Students are also shown slides of nineteenth-century French Orientalist paintings focusing particularly on Eugène Delacroix's *Women of Algiers in their Apartment*. This painting provides the title for Assia Djebar's collection of short stories written over one century later. If in Delacroix's painting Algerian women are framed within an opulent décor of "Oriental" decadence behind the closed walls of the harem in a drug-induced stupor, Alloula's writings and the Orientalist images prompt students to reflect on the violence behind these mediated images and the imperialist power to control the economy of representation through the machinations of war, conquest, and the subjugation of women.

Western constructions of Arab women found in Orientalist discourses and colonial imagery are further distorted in mainstream "first world" or imperialist feminist readings of non-Western women to expose the collusion between colonization and colonial feminism in the "invention" of "third world" knowledge and historicity. These misrepresentations are "de-Orientalized" through Arab and other non-Western feminist theories related to the decolonization of gender and female subjectivity (Mohanty, Abdulhadi et al., Badran, Malti-Douglas, cooke).

Non-Western feminist decolonizations

A course on francophone Algerian women's writings must necessarily initiate discussions on what constitutes a feminist text in Algerian literature. Algerian author Assia Djebar provides a useful starting point for this discussion. Djebar writes: "What is a feminist novel in Arabic? First of all, it is a voice … a night murmur … an ancient wound finally and gradually opened up to assume its song … We, from the Maghrib … find inspiration at hearing a woman revolt in Arabic. A point for take-off. A combat zone. A restoration of body" (in Badran and cooke 1990, 387).

Djebar makes several important points in her poetic "anti"-definition. First, feminism in the Maghreb or North Africa is not a Western import. It exists "locally" in the form of an ancient wounded voice; this expressivity is like an energetic crescendo that moves from pain to expression through the power of words. Second, Djebar highlights the existence of multiple feminisms that intersect and overlap in the form of converging, divergent, and interstitial "take-off" points. Denying the centrality of any one form of hegemonic or essentialized Arab feminism, Djebar highlights the intersections between personalized and collective forms of feminism expressed by the individual feminine voice that merges with the communal "we, from the Maghreb."

By providing a geographically specific location for this voice, Djebar undermines Western stereotypes of Arab female passivity while outlining the cartography of feminist resistance within and across the Maghreb. This claim is in consonance with the assertions of other Arab feminists like Fedwa Malti-Douglas, who argues that Arab women are the inheritors of a long tradition of feminist consciousness, wherein "gender consciousness is hardly new to Middle Eastern society. Social, cultural, historical and legal questions relating to male-female roles, equality of women, and so forth, have been part and parcel of Arabo-Islamic discourse for centuries" (Malti-Douglas 1995, 16).

As feminist consciousness is not foreign to the Arab-Muslim world, students are thereby reoriented to unlearn presumptions by going against the grain of Western blinders. Three important publications help them in this process. Margot Badran and miriam cooke's insightful introduction to their co-edited anthology, *Opening the Gates: A Century of Arab Feminist Writing*, enlightens students about Arab feminism's interstitial scope found in the analysis of visible and invisible feminism. For example, Badran argues that Arab feminism can be simultaneously discrete and manifest when it transgresses spatial segregations between the public and private spheres. "An analysis of Arab women's discourse allows us to see feminism where we had not previously thought to look" (Badran and cooke 1990, xv, xxxviii). Badran emphasizes the politics of location in the positioning of Arab feminist thought together with a certain politics of reading that is a prerequisite to any formal or informal analysis of Arab women's texts, literary or otherwise.

This introduction is read in tandem with Chandra Mohanty's seminal essay, "Under Western Eyes," a classic text on the decolonization of knowledge and the positioning of non-Western feminist subjectivities. Mohanty (2003, 220) sees the need to "reinvent feminism" by developing "antiracist feminist" (ibid., 2) strategies "anchored in decolonization and committed to an anticapitalist critique" (ibid., 3). Mohanty takes exception to totalizing formulations of the "Third World woman" who is deprived of subjective particularities in mainstream white feminist agendas (ibid., 17). Likening these modalities to a form of (neo-)colonial thought, Mohanty demonstrates how these (neo-)colonial feminisms mirror the capitalist, racist, and classist underpinnings of coloniality.

Rabab Abdulhadi's co-edited anthology, *Arab and Arab American Feminisms: Gender, Violence and Belonging*, takes Mohanty's argument a step further by applying a social justice perspective to Arab feminist engagements with gender, a discursive strategy that "belongs to the tradition of Arab and Arab American knowledge production and further engages in a 'theory in the flesh' or knowledge derived from narrating lived experiences and producing critical lenses through which we see and analyze the social and political world" (Abdulhadi et al. 2011: xxx). The "humanizing" of theory adds further nuance to the corpus of Arab feminism through an engagement "with the flesh," as a de-centered politics of reclaiming. The theoretical engagements with Arab feminism in this anthology provide students with the necessary framework to analyze specific literary texts.

Reclaiming voice in text

This section of the syllabus focuses on specific francophone Algerian women writers and their use of literature as a medium to engage in what I call an "expressive decolonization" in terms of history, culture, nationhood, and the "feminine" condition in Algeria. These writers include Marguerite Fadhma Amrouche, Maïssa Bey, Assia Djebar, Leïla Sebbar, Faïza Guène, Malika Mokeddem, and an arabophone author Ahlam Mosteghanemi.

The section is divided into two modules:

1. French and the problematics of language.
2. Textual analysis:

   a Memoir writing and identity – Marguerite Fadhma Amrouche (*Histoire de ma vie*).

   b War, trauma, and memory in fiction – Maïssa Bey (*Pierre sang papier ou cendre, Nouvelles d'Algérie*), Assia Djebar (*Femmes d'Alger dans leur appartement, L'amour, la fantasia*), Leïla Sebbar (*La Seine était rouge*), Ahlam Mosteghanemi (*Memory in the Flesh – Zakirat al Jassad*).

   c Female rituals of re-membering – Malika Mokeddem (*Les hommes qui marchent*), Assia Djebar (*Femmes d'Alger dans leur appartement*).

   d (Post)colonial *beurettes* in France – writing from the Parisian *banlieue* (housing projects) – Faïza Guène (*Kiffe-kiffe demain*).

Anne Donadey's *Recasting Postcolonialism: Women Writing between Worlds* (2001), Ranjana Khanna's *Algeria Cuts: Women and Representation, 1830 to the Present* (2008), Alison Rice's *Polygraphies: Francophone Women Writing Algeria* (2012), and Jane Hiddleston's *Assia Djebar: Out of Algeria* (2011), frame important questions pertaining to francophone Algerian women writers. What are the patriarchal ideologies that have scarred the face of gender in Algeria? How have women and children in particular paid the price for coloniality and an ambivalent postcolonial anxiety? How have mediated representations of women found in Orientalism, nationalism, and religious traditionalism created impasses in women's lives, and how have women either negotiated or submitted to these aggressions by writing, fighting back or acquiescing? How does writing, as a different kind of weapon, represent a non-violent form of postcolonial feminist dissidence? Can this politicized creative stance provide the necessary transition from the trauma of amnesia to the cathartic effects of anamnesis, as suggested by Anne Donadey (1999)? In other words, can Algeria move beyond traumatic affect to a more fruitful politics of reconciliation? These questions do not necessitate any ideological conclusions that could possibly mirror the dogma of colonial and nationalist ideologies. Instead, they are intended to focus on the ways in which francophone Algerian women writers have exposed and contested all forms of exceptionalism and exclusion.

The syllabus is organized thematically according to author and genre. These genres include memoirs, novels, short stories, and fictionalized autobiographies. A detailed commentary on genre, theme, and author biography provides a template for the selection and analysis of texts. These commentaries are aided by references to an indispensable reference guide, a collection of essays co-edited by Lisa Suhair Majaj, Therese Saliba and Paula Sunderman. Their book, *Intersections: Gender, Nation, and Community in Arab Women's Novels* (2002), establishes the context for contemporary Arab women's writings. Even though the book focuses exclusively on novels, it nevertheless provides the essential framework to situate the literature.

Assia Djebar, Malika Mokeddem, Maïssa Bey, Leïla Sebbar and *beur* writers in France.

In terms of biographical details, the following texts help students to get an intimate appreciation of each writer's life trajectory since it is impossible to separate *Histoire* (History) and *histoire* (personal story) in French. Jane Hiddleston's (2011) monograph on Assia Djebar provides important details on this award-winning writer's life in the introduction. Author biographies help students to understand the synergies between personal stories, "*histoire*," and history, "*Histoire*," through the conflation of nomenclature in French, wherein private and publication narrations are distinguished nominally by a capitalized "H." Students are provided with biographical details of each author to gain some knowledge about the literary trajectories of these writers and their personal struggles at home and in exile.

Djebar's writings encompass the entire expanse of colonial and postcolonial Algerian history. Her repertoire marks a certain progression from the French conquest of Algeria in 1830 to the revolutionary struggles for independence (1958–62), and culminating in the postcolonial angst of a new nation ravaged by the debilitating forces of neo-colonialism, gender marginality, religious revivalism, and socio-economic instability. Djebar underscores the ways in which Algerian women are denied historicity and made exiles in their own land through a colluding colonial and neo-colonial patriarchal gaze that delimits the full expression of voice and subjectivity. These issues are discussed with reference to two texts: *L'amour, la fantasia* and *Femmes d'Alger dans leur apartment.* Jane Hiddleston's *Out of Algeria* (2006), Anne Donadey's earlier study *Recasting Postcolonialism: Women Writing Between Worlds* (2001), Alison Rice's *Polygraphies: Francophone Women Writing Algeria* (2012), and Bouali Kouadri-Mostefaoui's *Lectures de Assia Djebar* (2011) provide valuable bibliographical and academic resources for informed analyses of Djebar's work.

Similar themes and preoccupations are also to be found in the writings of Malika Mokeddem, a doctor by profession and a writer at heart. Two texts provide indispensable details on Mokeddem's life and literary trajectory. These books include Mildred Mortimer's *Maghrebian Mosaic: A Literature in Transition* (2001) and Yolande Helm's *Malika Mokeddem: envers et contre tout* (2000). Mokeddem has won international acclaim for novels such as *Les hommes qui marchent* (1997) and *Le siècle des sauterelles* (1992) set at the very gateway to the great Algerian desert, the home of her nomadic Saharan ancestors, the Doui Menia. Of a mixed-race black African and Arab heritage, Mokeddem's novels highlight the ensuing tensions that result from displaced origins, both in the case of her desert family that was forced to relocate to an urban environment as a result of modernity and its technological encroachments on nomadic spaces, and in her own example as an Algerian immigrant writer in southern France. At the same time, Mokeddem's novels are virulently anti-patriarchal as she offers searing critiques of tribalism, misogyny, religious fundamentalism, and internalized oppression by women. These themes could be explored in novels such as *Mes Hommes* (2005), *L'Interdite* (1993), *Des Rêves et des assassins* (1995), *N'Zid* (2001), and a memoir, *Je dois tout à ton oubli* (2008). Refusing any form of spatial or existential confinement in her life, Mokeddem looks for hybrid spaces that accommodate pluralistic identities and creative reinventions of the self.

In contrast, Maïssa Bey favors a rooted sense of location in the homeland Algeria over the ambiguity of exile. Three works of scholarship provide important insights into this author's life and work in addition to numerous online interviews and YouTube clips. These include Brinda Mehta's award-winning *Dissident Writings of Arab Women: Voices Against Violence* (2014), Alison Rice's study of Algerian women and autobiography in *Polygraphies* (2012), Schahrazede Longou's doctoral dissertation, *Violence et rebellion chez trois romancières de l'Algérie contemporaine* (2009), and Corbin Treacy's article, "Contested Cartographies in Maïssa Bey's *Bleu, blanc, vert*" (2013). Bey's fiction highlights the different levels of psychological exile and physical violence endured specifically by women in an embattled nation. The daughter of an Algerian rebel who was brutally tortured and executed by the French in

February 1957 during the struggle for independence, Bey has used literature as a means of coming to terms with her father's death, while expressing her own sense of unresolved trauma and loss as a result of this violent experience. This painful trajectory is explored in fictionalized form in *Entendez-vous dans les montagnes* (2002). Using a pseudonym instead of her birth name Samia Benameur, Bey adopts an insider/outsider position in her work to demonstrate how the brutality of colonial rule, religious dogma, and patriarchy leads to the corresponding brutalization of women's lives when they are denied speech, ignored, violated, and relegated to the margins of society, as revealed in *Cette fille-là* (2001).

On the other end of the spectrum, Leïla Sebbar's writings reveal the problematic intersections of postcolonial identity and the complex negotiations of a mixed-race Arab/French heritage. The following texts offer in-depth insights into this author's life and literary preoccupations. James Redfield's (2008) interview with Sebbar is an important starting point together with Anne Donadey's *Recasting Postcolonialism* (2001) and Suzanne Gauch's *Liberating Shahrazad: Feminism, Postcolonialism, and Islam* (2006). The daughter of a French mother and an Arab father, Sebbar remains monolingual and writes exclusively in French. At the same time, she contests essentialized categories that limit her to being either a French or francophone author by embracing both positionalities as a part of her identity. Her major fictionalized memoirs and autobiographical works, such as *Je ne parle pas la langue de mon père* (2003), *Journal de mes Algéries en France* (2005), *Parle mon fils, parle à ta mere* (1984) highlight the ambivalence of linguistic, cultural, and historical hybridities, wherein the female body becomes the site of these conflicting affiliations and disaffiliations in Sebbar's work. Her writings provide students with excellent examples of interstitiality, cultural hyphenation, and exilic writing (see also in this volume, Chapter 8).

On the other hand, second- and third-generation Franco-Maghrebi or *beur* women writers born in France to immigrant or first-generation parents question the very idea of French citizenship and reveal their complicated negotiations of their parents' Arab-Muslim heritage. In fictionalized memoirs, autobiographical writings and social texts, (post)colonial *beurettes*, such as Faïza Guène (*Kiffe-kiffe demain*, 2004; *Du rêve pour les oufs*, 2006; *Les gens du Balto*, 2008), Houda Rouane (*Pieds blancs*, 2007), Aïcha Benaïssa (*Née en France: histoire d'une jeune beur*, 1990), Farida Belghoul (*Georgette*, 1986), Farudja Kessas (*Beur's Story*, 1994), Houda Rouane (*Pieds-blancs*, 2008), and Soraya Nini (*Ils disent que je suis une beurette*, 1993), problematize normative ideals of French-ness based on exclusionary paradigms of race, class, gender, religion, and national origin as they confront the limitations of gender within conservative family networks. Alex Hargreaves's (2007, 1997) pioneering work on *beur* identity and fiction provides a useful framework for this literature. Nora Barsali and her co-editors also provide valuable insights into the identity of this community through testimonials and first-person narratives in *Générations Beurs: Français à part entière* (2003). Sylvie Durmelat's *Fictions de l'intégration: du mot "beur" à la politique de la mémoire* (2008), and Dominic Thomas's *Africa and France: Postcolonial Cultures, Migration and Racism* (2013) are also useful references.

In the specific context of francophone Arab women's writing, this literature straddles multiple timelines wherein the past, present, and future merge and disperse in an indeterminate historical continuum termed by Maïssa Bey "une histoire à rebours" (a history in reverse) (Hind 2008, 3). It is thus impossible to isolate each text and confine it to a singular historical time frame. This type of "anti-history" defies colonial timelines and archival documentation through an active reclaiming of historicity from an insider perspective. Bey suggests that history must be read upside down so as to regain its compromised equilibrium in terms of negated perspectives, especially women's voices. Nevertheless, common themes in these writings include the violence of war, exilic negotiations of identity, woman-centered rituals, tropes of memory, preoccupations with language, nationalist exclusions of women revolutionaries, historical omissions and gendered violence, among other topics.

Fictionalized memoirs: Marguerite Fadhma Amrouche

It is helpful to begin the course with the fictionalized memoirs of francophone Algerian women writers. These writings provide the necessary context, scope, and discursive mapping for this literature. This genre dispels any monolithic representations of Algerian women as passive victims of colonial history or as conceptual symbols of nationalist ideology. Students learn to distinguish the nuances between memoir as narrative trope and *mémoire* as memory. They see how the dual connotations of memoir/*mémoire* in French add textual nuance to these works that bridge the gap between narration and the polyphonic ambiguity of memory. Accordingly, students understand how memoir is both a fiction and a medium of re-membering a neglected feminine heritage of intellectual thought, cultural production, historical re-evaluation, and feminist contestation.

The tradition of memoir writing is discussed through Marguerite Fadhma Amrouche's revolutionary text, *Histoire de ma vie* (*A Story/History of My Life*).[1] This memoir's originality lies in its gendering of a traditionally male-centered Western literary narrative form, while giving voice to a distinctly female articulation of colonial history evidenced in the double signification of *histoire* as history and story. The memoir is an indispensable starting point for the teaching of this literature for several reasons. Amrouche's memoir inscribes the personalized "I" within a broader historical context to reveal the intimate links between gender, subjectivity, and the fictionalized creation of the personal, communal, and historical self/selves. This multiple subjectivity is evident in Amrouche's negotiation of her bicultural identity as an Amazigh Muslim woman living under French colonization in Kabylia, a mountainous region of northeastern Algeria, during the early part of the twentieth century. Written from the subaltern point of view of a colonized subject in terms of both gender and history, this memoir reveals the search for exemplarity despite multiple levels of marginalization to provide an enduring "mother text" for future generations of Algerian women writers. More importantly, the memoir highlights the tenacious will to survive truncation as a subaltern caught between colonial and patriarchal disaffiliations, a point that directs students to Amrouche's significant insights.

The language question in Algeria

Before beginning the analysis of the selected primary texts, it is important to discuss the ways in which Amrouche's memoir opens the "language question" for francophone Algerian women writers and their privileged affiliations with *francophonie*, since language choice defines and delimits their work. In their engagements with *francophonie*, these writers negotiate the ambiguity of using the colonizer's language to contest the power-inflected excesses that compromise Algeria's integrity. Students comprehend the impossibility of separating Algerian literature from the politics of language for any meaningful analysis of this literature. Abdelkébir Khatibi's seminal works, *Amour bilingue* (1983) and *Maghreb Pluriel* (1983) are excellent studies both on the problematics of language in the Maghreb and the linguistic ambiguity confronted by francophone Maghrebi writers. Selections from these theoretical discourses are read together with Djebar's novel *L'amour, la fantasia*, in which the postcolonial writer reflects on her own ambiguous use of French as a medium of simultaneous liberation and alienation. Students are encouraged to explore the dialogic connection between Khatibi's theories on bilingualism and Djebar's linguistic ambidexterity to better appreciate the subtleties involved in the process of using the colonial tongue to deconstruct the colonizer's language and worldview through the process of linguistic decolonization in text. Réda Bensmaïa's article "The Phantom Mediators" (1997) is another important source on the politics of language.

The women, and francophone Algerian writers in general, defend their decision to write in French as an explicitly feminist and political act. Moreover, francophone writers insist that the use of French is in keeping with their ideal of supporting a plural Algeria; the women further indigenize French for their de-colonial feminist agendas. The conscious decision to write in French is also an act of open defiance against the indiscriminate assassination of francophone Algerian intellectuals during the black decade of "intellectual cleansing" (Bensmaïa 1997, 86), in which writers and artistes such as Tahar Djaout, Youssef Sebti, Abdelkader Alloula and Lounès Matoub were targeted by religious traditionalists for being an infidel group of secularized francophone elites.

We also discuss the increasing transnational and multilingual scope of Arabic literature since several Arab writers are choosing to write in languages other than Arabic and French as a result of exile and their diasporic locations. We examine the literary intentionality of Arabic literature (written exclusively in Arabic) and Arab literature (written in other languages such as Tamazight, Spanish, Catalan, Italian, and English) to explore the connections between language and Arab identity, while also talking about how linguistic pluralism enables the writers to broaden the richness and diversity of these literatures without compromising their sense of Arab-ness.

Mosteghanemi's novel *Memory in the Flesh* initiates a discussion on what it means to read a text "in translation" without having any proficiency in the target language. We examine the following questions: Does a translated text have an identity of its own or is it a compromised narrative? How do non-Arabic-speaking students and instructors read a translated text responsibly?

War, trauma, and memory

The issue of trauma and its resulting wounds remains a central concern for Algerian women. Cathy Caruth's *Trauma: Explorations in Memory* (1995) and Christiane Chaulet-Achour's *Etats et effets de la violence* (2005) are important references to orient the discussion on writing's association with war, trauma, and memory. Algerian authors are particularly sensitive to the psychological and corporeal wounds inscribed on women's bodies as a result of war, historical fractures, traumatic memory, and patriarchal ideologies, thereby demonstrating how it is impossible to disassociate gender from issues related to conquest and colonization, identity, "modernity," and historical violence.

The module on trauma begins with an analysis of Maïssa Bey's novel *Pierre sang papier ou cendre*. Bey borrows the title of her novel from a poem titled "Liberté" (Freedom) written by French surrealist Paul Eluard during the Nazi occupation of France. Students read Eluard's poem in which a French schoolboy dreams of freedom from tyranny and evokes the devastation wreaked by the enemy on French soil. In a tongue-in-cheek postcolonial repartee, Bey appropriates the title and sentiment of the poem to paint a vivid and disturbing fresco *à la Guernica* of the brutality of 132 years of French colonization in Algeria. Through scenes of bloody warfare, rape, torture, civilian violations, and land annexations, Bey denounces the "fact" of colonization and the hypocritical justifications of the French civilizing mission in Algeria. Through Bey's novel, students realize how the French ideal of civilization is, in fact, a code word for savagery, racism, injustice, and colonial brutality against non-European Others. Students read excerpts from Benjamin Stora's *La guerre des mémoires* (2007) and view Jean-Marie Teno's classic documentary, *L'Afrique je te plumerai* (*Africa, I Will Fleece You*), to understand the perverse ethos of colonization and the subsequent cultural and material ravaging of Africa. The film provides a visual supplement to the novel so that students can better understand the genocidal intent of colonization and its devastating effects in Africa.

The trope of historical trauma is analyzed from another perspective in Assia Djebar's collection of short stories, *Femmes d'Alger dans leur appartement* (1980) translated as *Women of Algiers in their Apartment* (1992). These stories focus on the Algerian war of independence and its impact on women. We revisit Delacroix's painting to juxtapose his immobilized "image" of the women of Algiers with the introspective narratives of Djebar's protagonists who are brought to "life" in writing. Marnia Lazreg's *The Eloquence of Silence: Algerian Women in Question* (1994), an important study on Algerian female revolutionaries, is excellent companion reading to these stories. Djebar's narratives provide students and readers with a poignant example of the fate of many female revolutionaries who were driven to despair and madness as a result of their post-independence displacement and invisibility in

Algerian society. They examine the ways in which Djebar's writings seek reparation for historical injustices against women. Literature endows these forgotten heroines with legitimacy and exposure in text to rectify years of invisibility and negation.

Students view Gillo Pontecorvo's engaging film *La Bataille d'Alger* (*The Battle of Algiers*) for visual effect. They can see how women participated in the war of independence as guerrilla fighters, members of the armed resistance, caregivers and informants, only to be forgotten once independence was gained. The students also read selected interviews with the surviving heroines of the revolution who express their disappointment, anger, frustration, and fears in the post-independence era. These interviews are found in Danièle Amrane-Minne's important book, *Les femmes algériennes dans la guerre* (1991). By combining fiction, film, and testimony (interviews as first-person narratives), students gain a more holistic understanding of the gendered aspects of war and revolution.

In this section, students are also exposed to the feminist writings of Algeria's most prolific arabophone woman writer, Ahlam Mosteghanemi, to highlight francophone and arabophone women writers' common preoccupations in terms of the status and condition of Algerian women. Mosteghanemi's award-winning first novel, *Memory in the Flesh* (Arabic, 1993), is read in translation since the focus of the course is on French-speaking Algerian women writers. We compare and contrast this novel with Djebar's *Women of Algiers in their Apartment* to explore questions of identity, nationalism, gender, memory, and history from different linguistic perspectives.

The link between historical silences and the trauma of memory is also analyzed in Leïla Sebbar's explicitly political novel, *La Seine était rouge* (1999). This novel underscores the silences that have underlined colonial and nationalist history. Sebbar describes one of the most censored events in Franco-Algerian history, an event that took place in Paris on 17 October 1961. Articles by Michel Laronde (2007), Anne Donadey (1996), Mildred Mortimer (2008), Dawn Fulton (2007) and Jonathan Lewis (2012) provide valuable insights into the novel as well as the historical event itself. We examine Laronde's notion of "une histoire forclose" (2007), a history foreclosed by official silencing as well as Donadey's concept of "the Algeria syndrome" (Donadey 1996, 215), a reference to France's refusal to reconcile with its Algerian past. Additional readings from Stora's *La gangrène et l'oubli: mémoire de la guerre d'Algérie* (1991) also help students in their reflections on France's colonial disavowals.

Class discussions are greatly enhanced after students watch Yasmina Ada's documentary on the 17 October massacre, titled *Ici on noie les Algériens* (2011). This documentary includes actual footage from the sites of the massacre, together with the first-person testimonials of survivors, leaders of the National Liberation Front (FLN), French and Algerian intellectuals, human rights activists, and lawyers. We compare the narrative modes of the documentary and the novel to discuss representation, point of view, and the very act of narration. Visual aids greatly assist students in their comprehension of historical events that are not part of their own history.

In Sebbar's novel transnational feminist solidarities demonstrated by the shared resistance of French and Algerian revolutionaries encourage students to see feminism beyond a regional or national focus. They are referred back to Mohanty's (2003) concept of "feminism without borders," and the other essays from this book. Students now understand why the idea of Franco-Algerian solidarity highlighted through the shared war experiences of French and Algerian women is of personal significance for Sebbar; her Franco-Algerian identity reflects the tenuousness of war, violence, and transnationality.

Bey's *Nouvelles d'Algérie* (1998) represents the last text in this section. These short stories pertain to the Algerian civil war of the 1990s. Students engage in word play by examining the double entendre of the title. *Nouvelles d'Algérie* frames a dual problematic in French. The word *nouvelles* refers to short stories as well as to the news; the title thereby reflects the inscription of reality in the fictional through tenuous negotiations between fiction and testimony, already historically framed by Algerian scholars Réda Bensmaïa (1997) and Zahia Salhi (2010).[2]

Female rituals of re-membering

A course on francophone Algerian women writers would be incomplete without a module on the importance of rituals in their writings. This section begins with a general discussion on what constitutes a ritual. Students are then encouraged to talk about a ritual that has personal significance for them. The conversation extends to a conversation on the importance of rituals in a particular community and in society in general, before focusing on the two texts chosen for this section – Assia Djebar's *Femmes d'Alger* and Malika Mokeddem's *Les hommes qui marchent* (1990).

Djebar's narratives are richly layered with the sensorial textures of memory found in female healing rituals. Memory provides the women with a counter-narrative of hope and expressivity in the war against invisibility and disavowal. Brinda Mehta's *Rituals of Memory in Contemporary Arab Women's Writing* (2007), Anastasia Valassopoulos's *Contemporary Arab Women Writers: Cultural Expression in Context* (2007) and Nada Elia's *Trances, Dances and Vociferations* (2000) provide theoretical readings of gender, cultural memory, and rituals in Arab women's writing to supplement the literary texts. These memory-enriched narratives are endowed with a certain corporeality to position the female body as the dual site of oppression and resistance. The rituals cover a range of semantic expressions found in orality, trance, dance, *vocalese, hammam* or Turkish bath culture, and cinematic expressions captured in documentaries, such as Djebar's *La Nouba des femmes du Mont Chenoua* (1979) and *La Zerda et les chants de l'oubli* (1982).

In the context of Djebar's short story, the students understand how the *hammam* can also represent a feminist space; they are reminded of Margot Badran's discussion on visible and invisible feminism highlighted in part one, an essay that makes a case for different kinds of feminism. Discussions also focus on the importance of water in Islam so that the students have a religious and social context for their own reflections on the sanctity of water, rituals of purification, and the primacy of *hammam* culture in Algerian women's literature. They are guided by an earlier work by Abdelwahab Bouhdiba: *La sexualité en Islam* remains a classic in francophone Maghrebi studies today, even though it was written in 1971.

Malika Mokeddem's *Les hommes qui marchent* introduces students to the richness of desert culture. The students understand that the desert does not have an ornamental value in Mokeddem's novel when they compare Orientalist images of the desert found in coffee table books and tourist brochures with Mokeddem's insider perspective. For this author, the desert represents the very source of her identity, cultural and spiritual knowledge, and subjectivity in the face of colonialism. Mokeddem's ancestral and familial affiliations are with the Doui Menia Bedouin of the Sahara, for whom the desert symbolizes the ultimate connection between god, nature, and social space. Students learn how the Bedouin live according to an eco-conscious ethic that predates current debates on eco-living in the Western world. Mokeddem's novel offers them a necessary corrective to Western representations of the desert as a barren wasteland. They are surprised to learn about the ethnic diversity that exists among the Sahara's populations and the richness of desert-based rituals and ceremonies found in oral culture – weaving, pottery, music, dance, storytelling, ancient proverbs, cosmology and cuisine. They view Tunisian director Nacer Khemir's 1984 film, *Les Baliseurs du désert* (*The Wanderers of the Desert*) as a companion piece to *Les hommes qui marchent*. Khemir's film exposes the students to the stunning beauty of the great Sahara and the deep spirituality of its inhabitants. Students are given the opportunity to de-Orientalize their own readings of the desert when they encounter powerful characters like the grandmother figure Zohra in Mokeddem's novel and the eminent "men who walk" in the film.

(Post)colonial *beurettes* in France

The final section of the syllabus focuses on second- and third-generation French writers of Maghrebi descent, popularly referred to as *beurs*, *beurettes* and even post-Beurs (Thomas 2008). The writings of Alec Hargreaves, Sylvie Durmelat, and Nora Barsali help students to understand why these French citizens "with a difference" are marginalized by the French state through assimilation and standardized norms of citizenship. A combination of theory and personal interviews found in Hargreaves and Barsali's work, popular culture, and literature help the students to examine the vexed positionality of *beurs*, Islamophobia in France, and the richness of outer-city or *banlieue* cultural production found in music, art, and cinema.

Kiffe-kiffe demain by Faïza Guène is the chosen novel for this section because it represents the gendered and youth perspective of a teenager who grows up in the housing projects. Two sources help the students in their reading of this work – Dominic Thomas's article, "New Writing for New Times: Faïza Guène, banlieue writing and the post-Beur generation" (2008) and Brinda Mehta's *Dissident Voices of Arab Women: Voices Against Violence* (2014). We discuss the ways in which Guène's explicitly social text exposes and contests the confinement of *beur* children within circumscribed social spaces such as the substandard suburban housing projects; the institutionalized racism they face in disfavored schools; high unemployment and insecure prospects for the future; urban poverty; delinquency; police brutality; the marginalization of immigrant parents; the ambivalent relation to North Africa; alienation within the home and outside; racism toward Arabs and Muslims in France; and the added gendered burdens confronted by women and girls within conservative family structures. At the same time, students also learn how postcolonial French communities of color survive in a supposedly multi-ethnic France.

Particular attention is given to Guène's use of *verlan* or French back slang as a strategy used by *beur* writers to decolonize French from its elitist overtones and to indigenize the language through the infusion of Arabic words and syntax; this fusion leads to the creation of a hybrid street slang. Students marvel at the linguistic creativity of writers like Guène who invent a multi-ethnic French language that is more reflective of France's cultural *métissage* today. Their appreciation of back slang is enhanced by contemporary rap and hip-hop musical selections as an introduction to popular *banlieue* culture.

Concluding reflections

A course on francophone Algerian women writers unravels the diverse textual landscapes used by these women to inscribe their literary and social preoccupations as informed writers, social critics, and impassioned feminists. Students are exposed to the complexity of Arab women's struggles for authority and self-definition; these women confront and attempt to overcome the multiple alienations that govern their lives through the medium of the written word. Students are made aware of multiple forms of feminist resistance and cultural production as they learn to deconstruct patriarchal paradigms of reading through an anti-sexist de-colonial lens. At the same time, they understand the dangers of Orientalist essentialisms that lead to skewed and misinformed readings of these texts. Students learn to become responsible scholars as they incorporate suggestions for responsible scholarship in their own analysis of the primary sources. By the end of the course, they are able to see how these writers refuse passivity and the comfort of victimhood through their calls for social justice and gendered inclusions. It is hoped that this course furthers their appreciation of francophone Algerian women writers and motivates them to pursue further reading upon completion of the semester.

Notes

1 This chapter makes frequent reference to my online submission, "Francophone Algerian Women's Fictionalized Memoirs" in the *Encyclopedia of Women and Islamic Cultures*. General editor Suad Joseph. Leiden, Netherlands: Brill Publishers, Fall 2009.
2 Please consult bibliographical references for Bensmaïa and Salhi.

Bibliography

Abdulhadi, Rabab, Evelyne Alsultany and Nadine Naber, eds. 2011. "Introduction." In *Arab and Arab-American Feminisms: Gender, Violence and Belonging*. Syracuse, New York: Syracuse University Press, xix–xxxix.

Alloula, Malek. 1981. *Le Harem Colonial: Images d'un sous-érotisme*. Genève-Paris: Editions Slatkine. Translated into English from the French by Myrna Godzich and Wlad Godzich, *The Colonial Harem*. Minneapolis: University of Minnesota Press, 1986.

Amrane-Minne, Danièle Djamila. 1991. *Les femmes algériennes dans la guerre*. Paris: Plon.

Amrouche, Fadhma Aïth Mansour. 1968. *Histoire de ma vie*. Paris: François Maspéro. *My Life Story: The Autobiography of a Berber Woman*. Translated into English by Dorothy S. Blair. London: The Women's Press, 1988.

Apter, Emily. 2005. *The Translation Zone: A New Comparative Literature*. Princeton, NJ: Princeton University Press.

Assima, Fériel. 1995. *Une femme à Alger: Chronique d'un désastre*. Paris: Aléa.

Badran, Margot and miriam cooke, eds. 1990. *Opening the Gates: A Century of Arab Feminist Writing*. Bloomington, IN: Indiana University Press.

Barsali, Nora, Xavier Freedland and Anne Marie Vincent, eds. 2003. *Générations Beurs: Français à part entière*. Paris: Autrement.

Belghoul, Farida. 1986. *Georgette!* Paris: Barrault.

Benaïssa, Aïcha. 1990. *Née en France: histoire d'une jeune beur*. Paris: Livre de poche.

Bensmaïa, Réda. 1997. "'The Phantom Mediators' Reflections on the Nature of the Violence in Algeria." Translated by Hassan Melehy. *Diacritics* 27.2 (Summer): 85–97.

Bey, Maïssa. 1998. *Nouvelles d'Algérie*. Paris: Grasset.

Bey, Maïssa. 2001. *Cette fille-là*. Paris: L'Aube.

Bey, Maïssa. 2002. *Entendez-vous dans les montagnes*. Paris: L'Aube.

Bey, Maïssa. 2005. *Surtout ne te retourne pas*. Paris: L'Aube.

Bey, Maïssa. 2007. *Bleu Blanc Vert*. Paris: L'Aube.

Bey, Maïssa. 2008a. *L'une et l'autre*. Paris: L'Aube.

Bey, Maïssa. 2008b. *Pierre sang papier ou cendre*. Paris: L'Aube.

Bouhdiba, Abdelwahab. 1971. *La sexualité en Islam*. Paris: Presses Universitaires de France.

Bouredji, Fella. 2008. *Pierre sang papier cendre* (November 20). www.latribune-online.com/suplements/7887.html (accessed 15 June 2013).

Caruth, Cathy. 1995. *Trauma: Explorations in Memory*. Baltimore, MD: The Johns Hopkins Press.

Chaulet-Achour, Christiane. 2005. *Etats et effets de la violence*. Cergy-Pontoise, France: CRTH.

cooke, miriam. 2001. *Women Claim Islam: Reading Islamic Feminism through Literature*. New York and London: Routledge.

Djebar, Assia. 1957. *La Soif*. Paris: Julliard.

Djebar, Assia. 1958. *Les Impatientes*. Paris: Julliard.

Djebar, Assia. 1962. *Les enfants du nouveau monde*. Paris: Julliard.

Djebar, Assia. 1980. *Femmes d'Alger dans leur appartement*. Paris: Editions des femmes.

Djebar, Assia. 1990. "Introduction to Nawal El Saadawi's *Ferdaous: A Voice from Hell*." Translated by miriam cooke. In *Opening the Gates: A Century of Arab Feminist Writing*," edited by Margot Badran and miriam cooke. Bloomington, IN: Indiana University Press.

Djebar, Assia. 1993. *Fantasia: An Algerian Cavalcade*. Translated from French by Dorothy S. Blair. Portsmouth, NH: Heinemann. *L'amour, la fantasia*. Paris: Livre de poche, 1985.

Djebar, Assia. 1995a. *L'amour, la fantasia*. Paris: Librairie générale française.

Djebar, Assia. 1995b. *Vaste est la prison*. Paris: Albin Michel.

Djebar, Assia. 1996. *Le blanc de l'Algérie*. Paris: Albin Michel.

Djebar, Assia. 2006. *The Tongue's Blood Does Not Run Dry: Algerian Stories*. Translated from the French by Tegan Raleigh. New York: Seven Stories Press. *Oran: langue morte*. Paris: Actes Sud, 1997.

Djebar, Assia. 2007. *Nulle part dans la maison de mon père*. Paris: Fayard.

Donadey, Anne. 1996. "Une certaine idée de la France: The Algeria Syndrome and Struggles over 'French' Identity." In Steve Ungar and Tom Conley, eds, *Identity Papers: Contested Nationhood in Twentieth-Century France*. Minneapolis: University of Minnesota Press, 215–232.

Donadey, Anne. 1999. "Between Amnesia and Anamnesis: Re-membering the Fractures of Colonial History." *Studies in Twentieth-Century Literature* 23.1 (Winter): 111–116.

Donadey, Anne. 2001. *Recasting Postcolonialism: Women Writing Between Worlds*. Portsmouth, NH: Heinemann.

Durmelat, Sylvie. 2008. *Fictions de l'intégration: du mot "beur" à la politique de la mémoire*. Paris: L'Harmattan.

Elia, Nada. 2000. *Trances, Dances and Vociferations: Agency and Resistance in Africana Women's Narratives*. New York: Garland Press.

Elia, Nada. 2002. "The Fourth Language: Subaltern Expression in Djebar's *Fantasia*." In Lisa Suhair Majaj, Paula W. Sunderman and Therese Saliba, eds, *Intersections: Gender, Nation, and Community in Arab Women's Novels*. Syracuse, NY: Syracuse University Press, 183–199.

Fulton, Dawn. 2007. "Elsewhere in Paris: Creolised Geographies in Leïla Sebbar's *La Seine était rouge*." *Culture, Theory and Critique* 48.1: 25–38.

Gauch, Suzanne. 2006. *Liberating Shahrazad: Feminism, Postcolonialism, and Islam*. Minneapolis, MN: University of Minnesota Press.

Geesey, Patricia. 2000. "Violent Days: Algerian Women Writers and the Civil Crisis." *The International Fiction Review* 27.1&2: 48–59.

Guène, Faïza. 2004. *Kiffe-kiffe demain*. Paris: Hachette Littératures.

Guène, Faïza. 2006. *Du rêve pour les oufs*. Paris: Hachette Littératures.

Guène, Faïza. 2008. *Les gens du Balto*. Paris: Hachette Littératures.

Hargreaves, Alec. 1997. *Immigration and Identity in Beur Fiction: Voices from the North African Community in France*. Oxford: Berg Publishers.

Hargreaves, Alec. 2007. *Multi-Ethnic France: Immigration, Politics, Culture and Society*. New York and London: Routledge.

Hargreaves, Alec. 2010. "Third-Generation Algerians in France: Between Genealogy and History." *The French Review* 83.6 (May): 1290–1299.

Helm, Yolande. 2000. *Malika Mokeddem: envers et contre tout*. Paris: L'Harmattan.

Hiddleston, Jane. 2011. *Assia Djebar: Out of Algeria*. Liverpool: Liverpool University Press.

Hind, O. 2008. "Entretien avec l'écrivain Maïssa Bey. Pas de haine … ni de pardon." *L'Expressions: Le Quotidien* (22 May). http://yahia.ksentina.blogspot.com/2008/05/maïssa-bey-pierre-sang-papier-ou-cendre-html (accessed June 17, 2013).

Houari, Leïla. 1986. *Zeida de nulle part*. Paris: L'Harmattan.

Jarmakani, Amira. 2011. "Arab American Feminisms: Mobilizing the Politics of Invisibility." In Rabab Abdulhadi, Evelyn Alsultany and Nadine Naber, eds, *Arab and Arab American Feminisms: Gender, Violence and Belonging*, 229–241.

Kelly, Debra. 2005. *Autobiography and Independence: Selfhood and Creativity in North African Postcolonial Writing in French*. Liverpool: Liverpool University Press.

Kessas, Farudja. 1989. *Beur's Story*. Paris: L'Harmattan.

Khanna, Ranjana. 2008. *Algeria Cuts: Women and Representation, 1830 to the Present*. Stanford, CA: Stanford University Press.

Khatibi, Abdelkébir. 1983a. *Maghreb Pluriel*. Paris: Editions Denoël.

Khatibi, Abdelkébir. 1983b. *Amour bilingue*. Montpellier, France: Fata Morgana.

Kouadri-Mostefaoui, Bouali. 2011. *Lectures de Assia Djebar*. Paris: L'Harmattan.

Laronde, Michel. 2007. "Effets d'Histoire – Représenter L'Histoire coloniale forclose." *International Journal of Francophone Studies* 10: 139–155.

Lazreg, Marnia. 1994. *The Eloquence of Silence: Algerian Women in Question*. New York: Routledge.

Lewis, Jonathan. 2012. "Filling in the Blanks: Memories of 17 October 1961 in Leïla Sebbar's *La Seine était rouge*." *Modern and Contemporary France* 20.3 (August): 307–322.

Longou, Schahrazede. 2009. *Violence et rebellion chez trois romancières de l'Algérie contemporaine (Maïssa Bey, Malika Mokeddem et Leïla Marouane)*. Dissertation. University of Iowa. http://ir.uiowa.edu/etd/401.

Majaj, Lisa Suhair, Therese Saliba and Paula Sunderman, eds. 2002. *Intersections: Gender, Nation, and Community in Arab Women's Novels*. Syracuse, NY: Syracuse University Press.

Malti-Douglas, Fedwa. 1995. *Men, Women and God(s): Nawal El Saadawi and Arab Feminist Poetics*. Berkeley, CA: University of California Press.

Mehta, Brinda. 2007. *Rituals of Memory in Contemporary Arab Women's Writing*. Syracuse, NY: Syracuse University Press.

Mehta, Brinda. 2009. "Francophone Algerian Women's Fictionalized Memoirs." In *Encyclopedia of Women and Islamic Cultures*, gen. ed. Suad Joseph. Leiden, Netherlands: Brill Publishers. www.encquran.brill.nl/entries/encyclopedia-of-women-and-islamic-cultures/representations-memoirs-autobiographies-and-biographies-algeria-francophone-COM_0662 (accessed 17 June 2013).

Mehta, Brinda. 2010. "Negotiating Arab-Muslim Identity, Gender Ideologies, and Contested Citizenship in the Parisian Housing Projects: Reading Faïza Guène's *Kiffe-Kiffe demain*." *Research in African Literatures* 41.2 (Summer): 173–202.

Mehta, Brinda. 2014. *Dissident Writings of Arab Women: Voices Against Violence*. New York and London: Routledge.

Mohanty, Chandra Talpade. 2003. *Feminism Without Borders: Decolonizing Theory, Practicing Solidarity*. Durham, NC: Duke University Press.

Mokeddem, Malika. 1990. *Les hommes qui marchent*. Paris: Ramsay.

Mokeddem, Malika. 1995a. *Des rêves et des assassins*. Paris: Grasset.

Mokeddem, Malika. 1995b. *L'Interdite*. Paris: Livre de poche.

Mokeddem, Malika. 1996. *Le siècle des sauterelles*. Paris: Livre de poche.

Mokeddem, Malika. 2001. *N'Zid*. Paris: Seuil.

Mokeddem, Malika. 2003. *La transe des insoumis*. Paris: Grasset.

Mokeddem, Malika. 2008. *Je dois tout à ton oubli*. Paris: Grasset.

Mortimer, Mildred, ed. 2001. *Maghrebian Mosaic: A Literature in Transition*. Boulder, CO: Lynne Reiner Publishers.

Mortimer, Mildred. 2008. *The Seine Was Red. Paris, October 17: A Novel*. Translated into English from the French. Bloomington, IN: Indiana University Press.

Mosteghanemi, Ahlam. 2003. *Memory in the Flesh*. Translated from the Arabic by Baria Ahmar Sreih. Cairo and New York: The American University in Cairo Press.

Nini, Soraya. 1993. *Ils disent que je suis une beurette*. Paris: Fixot.

Redfield, James Adam. 2008. "Cultural Identity from habitus to au-delà: Leïla Sebbar Encounters Her Algerian Father." *Research in African Literatures* 39.3 (Fall): 51–64.

Rice, Alison. 2012. *Polygraphies: Francophone Women Writing Algeria*. Charlottesville, VA: University of Virginia Press.

Rouane, Houda. 2008. *Pieds-blancs*. Paris: Le Livre de Poche.

Sa'īd, Edward. 1978. *Orientalism*. Harmondsworth: Penguin.

Salhi, Zahia, ed. 2010. "Gender and Violence in Algeria: Women's Resistance against the Islamist Femicide." In *Gender and Diversity in the Middle East and North Africa*. New York and London: Routledge.

Sebbar, Leïla. 1999. *La Seine était rouge*. Paris: Editions Thierry Magnier. 1999.

Sebbar, Leïla and Nancy Houston. 1986. *Lettres parisiennes: autopsie de l'exil*. Paris: Bernard Barrault.

Stora, Benjamin. 1991a. "Women's Writing Between Two Algerian Wars." Translated from the French by Ruthmarie Mitsch. Special issue on Dissident Algeria. Guest Editor Danielle Marx-Scouras. *Research in African Literatures* 30.3 (Fall): 78–92.

Stora, Benjamin. 1991b. *La gangrène et l'oubli: la mémoire de la guerre d'Algérie*. Paris: La Découverte.

Stora, Benjamin. 2007. *La guerre des mémoires: la France face à son passé colonial. Entretiens avec Thierry Leclerc*. Paris: Aube.

Thomas, Dominic. 2008. "New Writing for New Times: Faïza Guène, Banlieue Writing, and the Post-Beur Generation." *Expressions maghrébines* 7.1 (Summer): 33–51.

Thomas, Dominic. 2013. *Africa and France: Postcolonial Cultures, Migration and Racism*. Bloomington: Indiana University Press.

Treacy, Corbin. 2013. "Contested Cartographies in Maïssa Bey's *Bleu, blanc, vert*." *The Journal of North African Studies* 18.3: 402–415.

Valassopoulos, Anastasia. 2007. *Contemporary Arab Women Writers: Cultural Expression in Context*. New York and London: Routledge.

5

APPROACHES TO TEACHING CLASSICAL ARABIC LITERATURE IN ENGLISH TRANSLATION

Jocelyn Sharlet

Along with the call for a world literature mode of reading,[1] contributors to Lawrence Venuti's edited volume on translation remind us that teaching literature in translation involves reading as perpetual translation, and that the best translations are simulacra that diverge from the original and resonate with it.[2] Teaching classical Arabic literature in translation is useful because undergraduates often are not able to reach a level of Arabic at which they can study and enjoy classical Arabic literature in the original format. The study of classical Arabic literature in translation can attract students to the study of Arabic and enrich the program of study for students of other medieval literatures or comparative literature. This chapter outlines a course at the undergraduate level on classical Arabic literature in English translation.

The topics of this course on classical Arabic literature are: pre-Islamic Arabic literature, rulers and other political elites, religion, love, comedy, travel, and fantasy and the supernatural. In addition to suggestions for a course or courses focusing on classical Arabic literature, this organization into topics that may be themes of more general comparative literature or world literature courses is intended to help faculty to integrate classical Arabic literature into the humanities curriculum in a variety of contexts.

David Damrosch explains that world literature "is not an infinite ungraspable canon of works but rather a mode of circulation and of reading; a mode that is as applicable to individual works as to bodies of material."[3] For Damrosch, a text becomes a work of world literature when it circulates beyond the cultural context in which it was produced. Damrosch argues that there is no single way of reading for all texts or even for one text at all times, and that "the variability of a work of world literature is one of its constitutive features and one of its greatest strengths when the work is well presented and read well and its greatest vulnerability when it is mishandled by its newfound foreign friends." When one embraces the variability of a work and reads with skill and respect commensurate with Kwame Appiah's value of cosmopolitanism, one is reading in Damrosch's world literature mode.[4]

A bibliographic base for the course consists of the modern anthologies of translations of classical Arabic literature by Geert Jan Van Gelder, Robert Irwin and Salma Khadra Jayyusi, each of which includes a wide range of material for the topics listed below.[5] Van Gelder's anthology provides the most representative and scholarly coverage of both poetry and prose literature in two chronologically organized sections, with biographies of poets and writers and brief discussion of key topics. Irwin's anthology intersperses selections of poetry or prose writing translated by well-known scholars, and organized in historical periods, with Irwin's own thoughtful commentary. Jayyusi's anthology provides an introduction to literary history and then focuses on narrative literature that is grouped into thematic sections as well as selections from longer prose works. The recent translation in three volumes of one of the major medieval Arabic encyclopedias by Ibn ʿAbd Rabbih can also be considered a core text for this bibliography because it includes material on aspects of each of these topics, and because prosimetrical texts of this kind played a central role in classical Arabic literature.[6]

The translations of entire poems from different periods of classical Arabic literature in the monographs by Suzanne Stetkevych and Raymond Farrin, although this undergraduate course is not designed for the reading of secondary sources, can supplement the limited number of translations that are available.[7] Stetkevych's book discusses the narrative literature that circulated in conjunction with major poems and provides the entire translation as well as the entire Arabic text. Farrin's book introduces each poem with a biography of the poet and then provides translations interspersed with his argument, unfortunately without the Arabic texts, but the book has been translated into Arabic. The availability of the translation along with the Arabic text in both cases will be ideal for students who are studying literature in translation while learning Arabic. The scholarly debates in the books are for scholars and graduate students training in classical Arabic literature to investigate in their survey of secondary literature, but the translations placed in historical context are useful for undergraduates. The bibliography organized by topics consists of titles from classical Arabic literature that might be useful for the teaching of each topic, as well as a few titles from other literatures that are useful for the comparative study of classical Arabic literature.

For background on classical Arabic literature in addition to the introductions, biographies and commentary in the three anthologies mentioned above, instructors can have recourse to Shawqī Ḍayf's multi-volume series on Arabic literature which is available online, the *Cambridge History of Arabic Literature*, and the brief entries in the *Encyclopedia of Arabic Literature*. Instructors who would like to coordinate their teaching and research in classical Arabic literature can also benefit from the more detailed entries in *The Encyclopedia of Islam*, also available online.[8] Sections of several monographs and articles can help instructors teaching classical Arabic literature in translation to gain insights into the aesthetics of classical Arabic literature in its historical context, although the core of this undergraduate course is primary sources.[9]

Readers who follow up on Jayyusi's anthology will recognize her list of topics in this outline: pre-Islamic Arabic literature, rulers and other political elites, religion, love, comedy, travel, and fantasy and the supernatural. Each theme includes a brief discussion and a selection of texts that can be used in addition to the translations found in the anthologies, encyclopedias and monographs mentioned above.

Pre-Islamic Arabic literature

Pre-Islamic poetry and prose literature in Arabic circulated in the Islamic era, in a limited way under the Umayyads (661–750), who were based in Damascus, and in a more extensive way during the more urban and cosmopolitan Abbasid Empire (750–1258), which was based mainly in Baghdad and extended from North Africa into the Middle East and Central Asia.[10] While the long, polythematic poems of the *Mu'allaqāt* which are found in Arberry's translation still enjoy canonical status, the poems on various themes and of varying length of the *Mufaḍḍaliyyāt* which are found in Lyall's translation are probably a more representative selection of pre-Islamic poetic practice. Other translations feature poems from outside these two collections. The Abbasid reconstruction of the honor and warrior values of pre-Islamic tribal society in Arabia provided a counterpoint that helped to define the urban, cosmopolitan, imperial and Islamic culture of the empire. Poems and stories featuring pre-Islamic characters articulate social order through challenges to it in dramatic scenes of vengeance and rebellion, and of community leaders who display self-control in the face of adversity. Some of the volumes in this bibliography include both pre-Islamic- and Islamic-era poetry, which allows instructors to compare and contrast pre-Islamic, provincial, tribal values with the urban, cosmopolitan, mercantile and legal values of early Islamic society.

Rulers and other notable persons

For classical Arabic writers and poets, social order and hierarchy are not a given, they are a contested and dynamic social practice.[11] Did these writers aim to change the political practice or the social hierarchy in their societies? What is the relationship of the writer to the ruler, and what did these writers attempt to do by collecting and juxtaposing selections of prose and poetry? The point of encyclopedic writing, as in the translation of Ibn 'Abd Rabbih mentioned above, is to explore multiple points of view and different angles on a single topic. The genre of medieval prose anthologies shows that the articulation of social order is always partial, incomplete, and in progress, so that it offers insights into the complex intersection of power and cultural production. Historical anecdotes in encyclopedias or in the collections by al-Tanūkhī complement theoretical discussions of politics in works on ethics and political advice, as well as the animal fable by Ibn al-Muqaffa' which was based on a Sanskrit fable, although the Arabic author also added a chapter on justice. Anecdotes of rulers and other elites articulate as a dynamic in which the negotiation of status generates and maintains hierarchy while also displaying shifting relationships.

Poets such as Bashshār, Abū Nuwās and Abū al-'Atāhiyah developed a new and more accessible style of poetry with new approaches to rhetoric and figurative language. These poets helped to define court culture even when they were at odds with political and religious authority: Bashshār played with ideas about ethnicity and orthodoxy, Abū Nuwās led the way in Islamic-era wine, hunting and homoerotic poetry, and Abū al-'Atāhiyah shifted gears from courtly poetry to homiletic poetry which sometimes led to accusations of heresy. Poets who affiliated with the political establishment such as al-Buḥturī, Abū Tammām, Ibn al-Rūmī and al-Mutanabbī referred to pre-Islamic Arabic poetry, Persian culture, theology and philosophy with innovative rhetoric and figurative language, and deployed the new style to articulate and comment on early Islamic political ideology in longer poems. Poets and writers of Andalusia further developed the aesthetics and social practice of classical Arabic literature. These poets demonstrate the importance of challenges to hegemony in the construction of it, since hegemony involves associations with the opposition and the generation of margins at the boundaries of the social order.

Religion

Religion informs or defines a wide range of prose and verse in classical Arabic literature.[12] The values expressed in pre-Islamic Arabic poetry can be compared to and contrasted with the values articulated in the Qur'an. The culture of interpretation in Arabic developed around these two kinds of texts. At the same time, the culture of presenting information in chains of transmission that end in an eyewitness report developed around the collection of sayings of the Prophet and was then applied to the presentation of information in diverse fields including historical anecdotes.

Commentary on or parody of religious ideas and cultural production was just as important for classical Arabic literature as the practices of interpretation and chains of transmission that were shared by the fields of religion and literature. The early poets of the new style, Bashshār, Abū Nuwās and Abū al-'Atāhiyah, circulated ideas about religion in poetry and sometimes parodied orthodoxy along with other forms of authority. The poets affiliated with the establishment contributed to political ideology that was linked to religion.

Some examples of the *maqāmah* genre (see Chapter 15 in this volume), a short text in rhymed prose that is often found in a series, manage to parody the quest for political patronage of poetry as well as religious sermons that help to establish religious authority. This genre, aside from the parody of political and religious authority, was viewed as an important source of literary excellence. Thus the genre can be seen as a literary reception of cultural production that was central for political and religious authority.

Other prose texts also address ideas about religion in an indirect way. Scholars have explored the reception of theological ideas about God's will and human will in prose texts as diverse as al-Tanūkhī's mostly realistic anecdotes and the fantastic stories of the Arabian Nights.[13] Al-Ma'arrī's essay on literary figures in Heaven and Hell (see note 15) also makes use of religious ideas about the afterlife.

The narrative texts by the Brethren of Purity and by Ibn Ṭufayl offer examples of religion and philosophy in literature. Ibn ʻArabī's short mystical verse in the translation by Sells and Ibn al-Fāriḍ's longer mystical poems in the translation by Homerin offer an introduction to mystical religion in literature.

Love

The theme of love in classical Arabic poetry ranges from chaste, unfulfilled desire and erotic love to marriage, and from piety to obscenity.[14] The *nasīb*, an erotic prelude to a longer poem, often explores unresolved loss in heteroerotic love that may be addressed by the social or material fulfillment of the poet's tribal or political affiliations. In Umayyad times (661–750), love poetry and related stories about ʻUdhrī poets such as Majnūn and Jamīl often prioritize chaste love, while the playful love poetry of poets such as ʻUmar b. Abī Rabīʻah depict fulfillment. In addition, Umayyad-era poets such as Jarīr develop the conventional erotic prelude of the longer poem. The *ghazal*, a short independent love poem, may depict a wider range of erotic relationships. Poets like Abū Nuwās expand the range of the *ghazal*, and the poets affiliated with the political establishment continue to develop the reception of conventions of the erotic prelude in longer poems. Poets such as Abū al-ʻAtāhiyah use love language in homiletic poetry, which developed into mystical poetry in the work of poets such as Ibn ʻArabī.

Ibn al-Sāʻī and other writers document the lives of women at court using historical anecdotes and sometimes poetry. The distinction between free and slave status for women is a central feature of court culture. This theme also appears in love manuals such as Ibn Ḥazm's essay, which explores refined manners in erotic relationships with a female or male beloved (see Chapter 16 in this volume).

Comedy

Comic themes play a definitive role in classical Arabic poetry and prose literature.[15] Comic poetry in the pre-Islamic and the earliest Islamic-era Arabic literature was often limited to invective such as that of al-Farazdaq, Jarīr and al-Akhṭal, who lived in Umayyad times and are known for their duels in invective. However, in Umayyad times, in some ʻUdhrī or urban love poetry, and especially in Abbasid times, the range of comic poetry expanded to include themes that parody conventional motifs from the poetic heritage, from love and wine drinking to obscenity and motifs of ordinary life, while invective continued to offer a context for comic poetry (see Chapter 6 in this volume).

Comic anecdotal literature about historical or realistic characters sometimes grows around comic poetry and in other cases appears independently from poetry. The conventions of the manners in courtly settings, and in the ordinary life of more educated or less educated people, left plenty of room in anecdotal literature for comic stories in which the tension that surrounds transgression of manners dissolves into laughter. These stories that play with appearances and identity often portray a world upside down as if it were a temporary escape from social order, and they help to define and diversify social life. However, many scholars have observed that not all provocative behavior portrayed in literature can be assumed to have occurred in social life. Al-Tanūkhī and Ibn ʻAbd Rabbih include anecdotes of this kind.

In addition, one common type of *maqāmah* parodies the use of eloquent language that occurs in sermons and other authoritative religious discourse, and also parodies the practice of composing poetry for patronage. The moral value of lofty language in religious and political discourse is an illusion that is dispelled to reveal the material value of the trickster's effort to win a reward from the audience. The tenth-century writer al-Hamadhānī was considered the founder of the genre, the eleventh-century writer al-Ḥarīrī was considered the best writer in the genre, and it also flourished in the west, in the work of writers such as al-Saraqusṭī (see Chapter 15 in this volume).

The leading ninth-century prose writer al-Jāḥiẓ interrogates social tensions, conflicts, and competing ideologies in his essays and compilations, sometimes with a comic tone. His book about misers parodies the gift exchange system of patronage that played a central role in Islamic culture, and shows that one must either participate in this gift exchange system or remain alienated from society. His book also offers an argument about how to do business, since he shows that wealth must circulate for individual and social prosperity to advance. His wide range of work includes essays that seem to contradict each other and offer multiple points of view about a given topic so that his writing is like a microcosm of the technique found in the classical Arabic encyclopedia.

Travel

The topic of travel is ubiquitous in the other topics that are discussed here, while it is also an important genre of classical Arabic literature.[16] Travel suggests a potential for transformation or at least a new perspective on existing social order and hierarchy. Instructors can find selections in the travelogues of the Moroccan writer Ibn Baṭūṭah and the Andalusian writer Ibn Jubayr whose travels include their pilgrimage, as well as other accounts of China, India and Europe. In *The Book of Strangers: Medieval Arabic Graffiti on the Theme of Nostalgia*, travel in space intersects with distance in time. Travel writing can be explored together with other travel themes in classical Arabic literature such as travel due to love, a quest, a conquest, comic adventures in poetry, or in the *maqāmah*, al-Maʻarrī's essay on heaven and hell, or mystical-philosophical essays.

Fantasy and the supernatural

Arabic literature about fantasy and the supernatural is in some ways marginal to the classical Arabic literature curriculum even as it grows from the heart of classical Arabic literature. Literature of fantasy and the supernatural was looked down on in classical Arabic literature and this view continues to influence the perception of cultural production even though this literature circulates widely. Originality and creativity were understood to inhere in the manner of presentation, interpretation, and the juxtaposition of texts. Nonetheless, a number of texts of this kind developed out of classical Arabic literature on historical characters or through the influence of other literary traditions.[17]

The Arabic epics, unlike their Greek, Latin and Persian counterparts, did not make their way into an authoritative canon. Instead, they grew out of historical anecdotes and related poems and only emerged as extensive legends in the post-classical period. The frametale *The Thousand and One Nights* also did not make it into the canon, but it circulated widely in Arabic and became a modern classic of world literature.[18] Many of the tales include scenes of realistic business such as long-distance trade, the urban market, marriage arrangements, and the traffic in beautiful people and fine things, as well as historical characters. The use of fantasy and the supernatural in these prose texts allows writers and their audience to explore social tensions and conflicts from an indirect angle.

Classical Arabic poets made the real and familiar seem strange and supernatural through their use of rhetoric and imagery. Poets fantasize their depiction of realistic topics such as the natural world, historical individuals, human relationships, social gatherings, the built environment, battles, and the values of manners and morals. Evolving approaches to the fantastic were central to the aesthetics of classical Arabic poetry.

Conclusion

In studying classical Arabic literature, students and instructors need to ask themselves, with David Damrosch, "How has literature been understood in its myriad manifestations over time and across space?"[19] Eloquence and entertainment in classical Arabic literature, as in many pre-modern literatures, were communication strategies to advance arguments about the portrayal of the past, contemporary political issues, social practices, and religious or philosophical beliefs. Classical Arabic literature often plays an instrumental role in defining and commenting on social life, and this literature sometimes challenges social order in playful ways. In the translation anthologies and the translation of Ibn 'Abd Rabbih's encyclopedia, as well as the other translations listed by topic above, teachers and students can gain valuable insights into the aesthetic conventions of classical Arabic literature in their social context.

Notes

(Transliteration as in the English version)

1 Cooppan 2009, 38 and 42.
2 Mehrez 1992, 122; and Johnston 1992, 54.
3 Damrosch 2003, 5.
4 Appiah 2006.
5 Van Gelder 2013; Irwin 2001; and Jayyusi 2010.
6 Ibn Abd Rabbih 2007, 2009, 2011.

7 Stetkevych 2002; and Farrin 2011.
8 Beeston, 1983–2006; Meisami and Starkey 1998; *Encyclopedia of Islam* 2016.
9 Hamori 1975; Kilito 2001; Stetkevych 1993; Bray 2000; Hamori 1981; Szombathy 2014; Bray 2005.
10 Teaching texts for this topic include Arberry 1957; Jones 2011; Polk and Mares 1974; Lyall 1981, 1918, 1921; and Sells 1989.
11 Teaching texts for this topic include Arberry 1967; Beeston 1977; Ibn al-Muqaffa' 2002; Ibn Sa'id 1989; al-Suli 2015; al-Tanukhi 1921–22, 1922; and Tha'alibi 1968. Also see Olivelle 2009, the Sanskrit Pancatantra from which Ibn al-Muqaffa's *Kalīlah and Dimnah* is descended by way of a translation to Pahlavi (Persian).
12 Teaching texts for this topic include Goodman 2003; Homerin 2001; Ibn Hisham 1955; Ibn Kathir 1998; Ikhwan al-Safa' 1978; al-Qur'an 1988; Sells 2000; and Tha'alabi 2002. Also see Jami 1980, an expansion of the story of Joseph into a Persian mystical romance, and Lakhnavi and Bilgrami 2007, an expansion of the historical anecdote about Hamza into an Urdu prose epic based on the Persian version.
13 See al-Musawi 1981, 2009.
14 Teaching texts for this topic include Ibn Hazm 1953; Ibn al-Sa'i 2015; al-Nafzawi 1999; and Robinson 2007. Also see Nizami 1997, an expansion of the Arabic legendary anecdote of Majnun and Layla into a mystical romance in prose translation, and Fuzuli 1970, an Ottoman Turkish version of the romance in verse translation.
15 Teaching texts for this topic include Ibn Butlan 1985; al-Hamadhani 1973; Jahiz 1997, 1980; al-Ma'arri 2013, 2014 (which may have been a model for Dante's *Divine Comedy*); Marzuban 1978; and al-Saraqusti 2002. Also see Alharizi 2003, a collection of Hebrew *maqamas* based on the Arabic genre.
16 Teaching texts for this topic include Ibn Battuta 1972; Ibn Jubayr 1973; and *Two Arabic Travel Books* 2014. Also see al-Isbahani 2000, an Arabic book on graffiti about nostalgia.
17 Teaching texts for this topic include Jayyusi 1996; Haddawy 2008, 1996; Lyons 2010; Norris 1980; Reynolds n.d., online.
18 See Muhsin al-Musawi's (1981) early reading of this phenomenal reception over time since its first translation in French, in *Scheherazade in England*.
19 Damrosch 2009, 3.

Bibliography

Al-Hamadhani, Badi' al-Zaman. *The Maqamat of Badi' al-Zaman al-Hamadhani*, tr. W.J. Prendergast. London: Curzon, 1973.

Alharizi, Judah. *The Book of Tahkemoni*, tr. David Simha Segal. Oxford: Littman Library of Jewish Civilization, 2003.

Al-Isbahani, Abu al-Faraj. *The Book of Strangers: Mediaeval Arabic Graffiti on the Theme of Nostalgia*, tr. Patricia Crone and Shmuel Moreh. Princeton, NJ: Markus Weiner Publishers, 2000.

Al-Ma'arri, Abu al-'Ala'. *The Epistle of Forgiveness Volume One: A Vision of Heaven and Hell*, tr. Geert Van Gelder and Gregor Schoeler. New York: New York University Press, 2013.

Al-Ma'arri, Abu al-'Ala'. *The Epistle of Forgiveness Volume Two: Hypocrites, Heretics and Other Sinners*, tr. Geert Van Gelder and Gregor Schoeler. New York: New York University Press, 2014.

Al-Musawi, Muhsin. *Scheherazade in England*. Washington: Three Continents, 1981.

Al-Musawi, Muhsin. *The Islamic Context of the Thousand and One Nights*. New York: Columbia University Press, 2009.

Al-Nafzawi, 'Umar b. Muhammad. *The Perfumed Garden of Sensual Delight*, tr. Jim Colville. London and New York: Kegan Paul International, 1999.

Al-Saraqusti Ibn al-Ashtarkuwi, Abu al-Tahir Muhammad Ibn Yusuf al-Tamimi. *Al-Maqamat al-luzumiyah*, translated, with a preliminary study by James T. Monroe. Leiden: Brill, 2002.

Al-Suli, Abu Bakr. *The Life and Times of Abu Tammam*, tr. Beatrice Gruendler. New York: New York University Press, 2015.

Al-Tanukhi, al-Muhassin b. 'Ali. *The Table-Talk of a Mesopotamian Judge Being the First Part of al-Nishwar al-Muhadara or Jami' al-Tawarikh of Abu 'Ali al-Muhassin al-Tanukhi*, tr. D.S. Margoliouth. London: Royal Asiatic Society, 1921–22.

Al-Tanukhi, al-Muhassin b. 'Ali. *The Table-Talk of a Mesopotamian Judge*, Parts II and VIII, tr. D.S. Margoliouth. Hyderabad: Islamic Culture Office, ca. 1922.

Appiah, Kwame Anthony. *Cosmopolitanism: Ethics in a World of Strangers*. New York: Norton, 2006.

Arberry, A.J. *The Seven Odes: The First Chapter in Arabic Literature*. New York: Macmillan, 1957.

Arberry, A.J. *Poems of al-Mutanabbi*. London: Cambridge University Press, 1967.

Beeston, A.F.L. *Selections from the poetry of al-Bashshar*, ed. with translations and commentary by A.F.L. Beeston. Cambridge and New York: Cambridge University Press, 1977.

Beeston, A.F.L., ed. *Cambridge History of Arabic Literature*, 6 vols. Cambridge: Cambridge University Press, 1983–2006.

Bray, Julia. "Al-Mu'tasim's 'Bridge of Toil' and Abu Tammam's Amorium Qasida" in *Studies in Islamic and Middle Eastern Texts and Traditions in Memory of Norman Calder*, ed. G.R. Hawting, Alexander Samely and J.A. Mojaddedi. Oxford: Oxford University Press, 2000.

Bray, Julia. "'Abbasid myth and the human act: Ibn 'Abd Rabbih and others," in Philip Kennedy, ed., *On Fiction and Adab in Medieval Arabic Literature*. Wiesbaden: Harrassowitz, 2005. 1–50.

Cooppan, Vilashini. "The ethics of world literature: Reading others, reading otherwise," David Damrosch, ed., *Teaching World Literature*. New York: The MLA Press, 2009.

Damrosch, David. *What is World Literature?* Princeton, NJ: Princeton University Press, 2003.

Damrosch, David. "Introduction: All the World in the Time," in *Teaching World Literature*, ed. David Damrosch. New York: The MLA, 2009. 1–14 at p. 3.

Encyclopedia of Islam, second edition, ed. Wolfhart Heinrichs et al. (Brill Online, 2016) and *Encyclopedia of Islam THREE*, ed. Everett Rowson et al. (Brill Online, 2016).

Farrin, Raymond. *Abundance from the Desert: Classical Arabic Poetry*. Syracuse, NY: Syracuse University Press, 2011.

Fuzuli. *Leyla and Mejnun*, tr. Sofi Huri and Alessio Bombaci. London: Allen and Unwin, 1970.

Goodman, Lenn Evan. *Ibn Tufayl's Hayy b. Yaqzan: A Philosophical Tale*. Chicago, IL: The University of Chicago Press, 2003.

Haddawy, Hussein, tr. *The Arabian Nights* (New Deluxe Edition). With an introduction by Muhsin Mahdi. New York: W.W. Norton and Company, 2008.

Haddawy, Hussein, tr. *The Arabian Nights II: Sindbad and Other Popular Stories*. New York: W.W. Norton and Company, 1996.

Haksar, A.N.D. *Seventy Tales of the Parrot*. NC: Rupa Company, 2009.

Hamori, Andras. *On the Art of Medieval Arabic Literature*. Princeton, NJ: Princeton University Press, 1975.

Hamori, Andras. "Reading al-Mutanabbi's Ode on the Siege of al-Hadath," in *Studia Arabica et Islamica Festschrift for Ihsan 'Abbas on his Sixtieth Birthday*, ed. Wadad Qadi. Beirut: American University of Beirut Press, 1981, pp. 195–208.

Homerin, Th. Emil. *'Umar Ibn al-Farid: Sufi Verse, Saintly Life*. Mahwah, NJ: Paulist Press, 2001.

Ibn Abd Rabbih. *The Unique Necklace*, Vol. 1, tr. Issa Boullata. Reading: Garnet, 2007.

Ibn Abd Rabbih. *The Unique Necklace*, Vol. 2, tr. Issa Boullata. Reading: Garnet, 2009.

Ibn Abd Rabbih. *The Unique Necklace*, Vol. 3, tr. Issa Boullata and Terri DeYoung. Reading: Garnet, 2011.

Ibn Battuta. *The Travels of Ibn Battuta, A.D. 1325–1354*, tr. H.A.R. Gibb. Nendeln: Kraus Reprint, 1972.

Ibn Butlan. *The Physicians' Dinner Party*, tr. Felix Klein-Franke. Wiesbaden: O. Harrassowitz, 1985.

Ibn Hazm. *The Ring of the Dove: A Treatise on the Art and Practice of Arab Love*, tr. A.J. Arberry. London: Luzac, 1953.

Ibn Hisham, 'Abd al-Malik and Muhammad Ibn Ishaq. *The Life of Muhammad*, tr. A. Guillaume. London: Oxford, 1955.

Ibn Jubayr. *The Travels of Ibn Jubayr*, tr. William Wright and M.J. de Goeje. New York: AMS Press, 1973.

Ibn Kathir, Isma'il b. 'Umar. *The Life of the Prophet Muhammad*, tr. Trevor Le Gassick. Reading: Garnet, 1998.

Ibn al-Muqaffa'. *The Fables of Kalilah and Dimnah*, tr. Saleh Sa'adeh Jallad. London: Melisende, 2002.

Ibn Sa'id, 'Ali b. Musa. *The Banners of the Champions: An Anthology of Medieval Arabic Poetry from Andalusia and Beyond*, tr. James A. Bellamy and Patricia Owen Steiner. Madison: Hispanic Center of Medieval Studies, 1989.

Ibn al-Sa'i, *The Consorts of the Caliph*, ed. Shawkat Toorawa, tr. Editors of the Library of Arabic Literature, introduction by Julia Bray. New York: New York University Press, 2015.

Ikhwan al-Safa' (Brethren of Purity), *The Case of the Animals versus Man before the King of the Jinn*, tr. Lenn Goodman and Richard McGregor. Boston, MA: Twayne, 1978.

Irwin, Robert, ed. *Night and Horses and The Desert: An Anthology of Classical Arabic Literature*. New York: Anchor Books, Random House, 2001.

Jahiz, Abu 'Uthman ibn Bahr al-Jahiz. *The Book of Misers*, tr. R.B. Sergeant. Reading: Garnet, 1997.

Jahiz. *The Epistle on Singing Girls of Jahiz*, edited and translated by A.F.L. Beeston. Warminster: Aris and Phillips, 1980.

Jami. *Yusuf and Zulaikha: An Allegorical Romance*, tr. David Pendlebury. London: Octagon Press, 1980. (Persian; cf. "Surat Yusuf" in *Qur'an* and *Lives of the Prophets*.)

Jayyusi, Lena, tr. *The Adventures of Sayf ben Dhi Yazan: An Arab Folk Epic*. Bloomington: Indiana University Press, 1996.

Jayyusi, Salma Khadra, ed. *Classical Arabic Stories: An Anthology*. New York: Columbia University Press, 2010.

Johnston, John. "Translation as Simulacrum," in *Rethinking Translation*, ed. Lawrence Venuti. London: Routledge, 1992.

Jones, Alan. *Early Arabic Poetry: Select Poems*. Reading: Ithaca Press, 2011.

Keller, John Eston, tr. *The Book of the Wiles of Women*. Chapel Hill: University of North Carolina Press, 1956. (Spanish; cf. *Arabian Nights* frametale.)

Kilito, Abdelfattah. *The Author and his Doubles: Essays on Classical Arabic Culture*, tr. from the French by Michael Cooperson with an introduction by Roger Allen. Syracuse, NY: Syracuse University Press, 2001.

Labid. *The Golden Ode*, tr. William Roe Polk and William Mares. Chicago, IL: University of Chicago Press, 1974.

Lakhnavi, Ghalib and Abdullah Bilgrami. *The Adventures of Amir Hamza*, tr. Musharraf Ali Farooqi. New York: Modern Library, 2007. (Urdu; cf. Ibn Hisham, *Life of Muhammad*.)

Lyall, Charles James, tr. *Mufaddaliyyat*. Oxford and New York: Oxford University Press, 1918 and 1921.

Lyall, Charles James. *Translations of Arabic Poetry, Chiefly Pre-Islamic*. Westport, CT: Hyperion, 1981.

Lyons, Malcolm, tr. *The Arabian Nights: Tales of 1,001 Nights*, 3 vols. New York: Penguin Classics, 2010.

Marzuban, Muhammad b. Khalaf. *The Book of the Superiority of Dogs Over Many of Those Who Wear Clothes*, edited and translated by G.R. Smith and M.A.S. Abdel Haleem. Warminster: Aris and Phillips, 1978.

Mehrez, Samia. "Translation and the Postcolonial Experience: The Francophone North African Text," in *Rethinking Translation*, ed. Lawrence Venuti. London: Routledge, 1992.

Meisami, Julie Scott and Paul Starkey, eds. *Encyclopedia of Arabic Literature*, 2 vols. London and New York: Routledge, 1998. 2: 482–484.

Nakhshabi, Ziya al-Din. *Tales of a Parrot*, edited and translated by Muhammed Ahmed Simsar. Cleveland: The Museum, 1978.

Nizami. *The Story of Layla and Majnun*, tr. Rudolf Gelpke, E. Mattin and G. Hill. Last chapter translated by Zia Inayat Khan and Omid Safi. New Lebanon, NH: Omega Publications, 1997.

Norris, H.T. *The Adventures of Antar*. Warminster: Aris and Phillips, 1980.

Olivelle, Patrick, tr. *Pancatantra: The Book of India's Folk Wisdom*. Oxford: Oxford University Press, 2009.

Al-Qur'an: A Contemporary Translation. Translated by Ahmed Ali. Princeton, NJ: Princeton University Press, 1988.

Reynolds, Dwight, translation and transcription, *Sirat Bani Hilal*, n.d., www.siratbanihilal.ucsb.edu/start-0.

Robinson, Cynthia. *Medieval Andalusian Courtly Culture in the Mediterranean: Hadith Bayad wa Riyad*. London and New York: Routledge, 2007.

Sells, Michael Anthony. *Desert Tracings: Six Classical Arabian Odes*. Middletown, CT: Wesleyan University Press, 1989.

Sells, Michael. *Stations of Desire: Love Elegies from Ibn 'Arabi and New Poems*. Jerusalem: Ibis, 2000.

Sheykh-Zada. *The History of the Forty Vezirs*, tr. E.J.W. Gibb. London: George Redway, 1886 and University of Michigan Library Reprints. (Ottoman Turkish; cf. *Arabian Nights* frame tale.)

Stetkevych, Jaroslav. *The Zephyrs of Najd: The Poetics of Nostalgia in the Classical Arabic Nasib*. Chicago, IL: University of Chicago Press, 1993.

Stetkevych, Suzanne Pinckney. *The Poetics of Islamic Legitimacy: Myth, Gender and Ceremony in the Classical Arabic Ode*. Bloomington: Indiana University Press, 2002.

Szombathy, Zoltan. *Mujun: Libertinism in Medieval Muslim Society and Literature*. Gibb Memorial Trust, 2013.

Tha'alibi, 'Abd al-Malik b. Muhammad. *The Lata'if al-Ma'arif of al-Tha'alibi. The Book of Curious and Entertaining Information*, tr. Clifford Edmund Bosworth. Edinburgh: Edinburgh University Press, 1968.

Tha'labi, Ahmad b. Muhammad. *'Ara'is al-Majalis, or: Lives of the Prophets*, tr. William M. Brinner. Leiden: Brill, 2002.

Two Arabic Travel Books: Abu Zayd al-Sirafi, Accounts of China and India, tr. Tim Macintosh Smith and Ibn Fadlan, *Mission to the Volga*, tr. James Montgomery. New York: New York University Press, 2014.

Van Gelder, Geert Jan. *Classical Arabic Literature: A Library of Arabic Literature Anthology*. New York: New York University Press, 2013.

6

CLASSICAL AND MEDIEVAL ARABIC LITERARY DELIGHTS

Towards teaching the humanistic literature of the Arabs

Nizar F. Hermes

Misunderstandings in cultural transactions still persist in our time, especially when some scholars deny the existence of humor in Arabic literature. Such mis-undertandings capture perfectly some of the most challenging problems with which university instructors of Arabic studies have to wrestle. Beyond the contentious, yet regularly offered, courses on Middle Eastern failures – past and present – teaching courses and promulgating themes inspired by and gleaned from the humanistic literary treasures of the Arabs is an urgent necessity. Sad as it is, the remarkably rich and complex literary heritage of the Arabs, to quote Muhsin al-Musawi, "has become the laboratory for one-track investigations of race and gender" (al-Musawi 2007, 266).

In this chapter, I present two teaching projects inspired by the largely neglected premodern humanistic treasures of the Arabs. The first deals with the scarcely taught – in American universities – subject of medieval Arab humor. The second ventures into the fascinating world of Arab-Muslim gastronomical taste, eating/feasting and intimacy. In the course of my discussion, I highlight the cultural benefits and challenges of teaching such courses in the American academy.

Before presenting the two teaching projects, it is worth pointing out that long before the heinous event of 9/11, teaching Arabic literature in American academia was not immune to the largely unsympathetic rhetoric against the Arabs/Muslims and their culture. Pertinent in this context is the late M. al-Nowaihi's study "For a 'Foreign' Audience: The Challenges of Teaching Arabic Literature in the American Academy." With striking forthrightness, the former Princeton lecturer and Columbia professor of Arabic literature offered her personal thoughts on the matter. Focusing mostly on issues related to what she conceived of as (mis)translation, reception, and "canonization" of Arabic literary works in the USA, she lays bare much of the controversy surrounding the teaching of Arabic literature in the American academy in the pre-9/11 era. "The real problem is that in the process of translation and reception," to quote one of her most powerful statements, "texts that are oppositional within their cultures [...] become collaborative with systems of oppression in the adopting culture, validating and legitimizing already held beliefs that, 'those Arabs' mistreat their women, have racist inclinations, violent natures, and so on, and are therefore still very much in need of the civilizing power of Western culture" (al-Nowaihi 2001, 26).

In the post-9/11 era, Roger Allen's "Perspectives on Arabic Teaching and Learning" is an indispensable companion to al-Nowaihi's study. Allen convincingly argues that although teaching Arabic has been perceived as "critical" and "strategic" since World War II, it was immediately after 9/11 that the language of the Arabs dramatically "catapulted ... to the very top of the list of the desideratum of various government agencies" (Allen 2004, 275). Allen provides further glimpses into the intimate relationship between the pedagogical, the political, the cultural, and the historical by suggesting, not without proof, that teaching and learning Arabic since 11 September 2001 have been approached through an ideologically charged epithet: "controversial." As he explains it, "the political and cultural environment within which the Arabic language has been learned and taught in the academies and the institutes of the western world has never been more than unpromising" (ibid., 276). Perhaps in a more straightforward statement, Allen affirms that there is "simply, too much negative baggage involved, both premodern and modern" (ibid., 276).

It should be kept in mind that politicization of academia is neither new, nor peculiar to a specific country or one cultural tradition. In fact, it has existed across the globe at least since the rise of modern academia. In the American context, one can speak volumes of the long chapters of Sovietology or Sinology. The same is very true of the reverse politicization of American studies in the ex-Soviet Union or China during the peak of the Cold War.[1] As much as one is fully convinced that exceptions do always exist, it is not going too far to suggest that in the wake of the heinous attack of 9/11, some academic courses on Arabic-Islamic studies have (un)consciously consolidated a largely demonic image of the Arabs and their culture. This is in most cases the outcome of the predominant interest in and emphasis on essentially controversial topics which quite usually result in "validating and legitimizing already held beliefs" on the Arabs and their culture (al-Nowaihi 2001, 26). This emphasis on controversial topics of Arabic literature and culture comes often at the expense of the lighter, the positive and, I would argue, the hilarious and the entertaining.

Humor in the Arab literary heritage: a course plan for Arabic literature

American universities, especially those that have departments of Middle Eastern studies and comparative literature, should offer more courses on Arab humor, pleasantry, and fun-making. It is mystifying that this amusing chapter of Arabic-Islamic literature and culture is not only among the least taught in the American academy, but largely unstudied by American scholars. The disinterest in Arab humor by American scholars and American universities would probably be justified if studies and courses on Western and non-Western humor were equally neglected, but this is absolutely not the case. In fact, it is all too easy to notice the abundance and popularity of research and classes on (classical) Chinese, Japanese, and (in particular) Jewish humor, as well as ancient, medieval, and early modern Western humor, including the jocular tradition of the Greeks and Romans. This is aside from the plethora of courses on the history and theory of humor from antiquity to modern times, which figure frequently as course offerings in various American departments including comparative literature, philosophy, anthropology, history, and psychology. One would love to believe that the dearth, if not the total lack, of courses on Arab humor is the result of the lack, or even paucity, of humorous literature in Arabic. The paradox, at least in my mind, is that if one explores medieval Arabic literature, one would be astounded by the impressive abundance and intriguing diversity of jocular writing in Arabic.

The Islamic "predilection for humor and gaiety," to use Franz Rosenthal's (1956, 4) phrase, manifested itself in one of the premodern world's richest and most diverse corpora of humorous writing. Indeed, prospective instructors of Arab humor can organize their courses around a fascinating banquet of classical and postclassical jocular texts and poems. In addition to a number of epistles on theosophical and theoretical concepts and issues related to what is mostly referred to as *al-hazl* (pleasantry or jest), the bulk of humorous writing in Arabic includes tales and anecdotes of (and by) misers, spongers, simpletons, duffers, dupes, court jesters, boring persons, beggars, drunkards, greedy persons, buffoons, mad lovers, thieves, Bedouins, religious leaders, teachers, judges, caliphs, funny women, pedant grammarians, arrogant rhetoricians, and even animals. This is in addition to a large number of humorous poems by poet-humorists, who were often famous, but sometimes infamous, jesters, libertines, pranksters, misers, buffoons, and beggars.[2] For instructors interested in comparative approaches, they can rely on both Arabic and modern (non-)Western texts. As a comparativist, I strongly recommend – especially at the graduate level – that instructors explore thoroughly the poetics and politics of humor and laughter in medieval Arabic literature through a number of Western theories of humor which I will briefly introduce, as well as relying on some of the enlightening studies I refer to in the bibliography.

In addition to humorous imprints that can be detected in Quranic, *ḥadīth*, and early hagiographical literature, numerous books of *adab* and *akhbār* are replete with humor, pleasantry, and fun-making.[3] This is not to mention the virtually tens of classical and medieval texts ranging from bulky compendiums and compilations to epistles and treaties which are intensively saturated with humor, jest, playfulness and pleasantry. The enlisting of classical and medieval Arabic jocular texts would hopefully validate my call for more courses and studies on Arab humor in the American academy. Other scholars have argued for the propagation of multicultural humor in the USA. In her appealing study *Humor in Contemporary Native North American Literature*, Eva Gruber has shown that we can better detect and understand "[m]any of the values, ways of knowledge, and world-views of a specific culture" by studying their "humor, what they laugh at, and at which situations and what times laughter arises" (Gruber 2008, 20). Intriguingly – in the context of my discussion of the disinterest in Arab humor in America – she believes that the disregard of "Native humor" in America past and present, is ideologically motivated and has to do with the inherently humanizing nature of humor. "[F]rom an ideological perspective humor may have been absent from early representations of Native people," Gruber writes, "because it is at heart, a sign of shared humanity – and explorers and early settlers had little interest in humanizing the indigenous population" (ibid., 7).

Similarly, Léon Rappaport in his no less informative *Punchlines: The Case for Racial, Ethnic, and Gender Humor*, makes a strong case that "the proper understanding of any culture benefits from examination of its characteristic humor" (Rappaport 2005, 20). Pertinent to my call for more courses and studies on Arab humor in America, is Rappaport's declaration that "perhaps more in North America than elsewhere, humor is seen as a desirable personal and social quality. We admire and reward those who can make us laugh" (ibid., 9). In many aspects, the validity of Rappaport's declaration can be approved by the impressive interest in and incomparable success of Jewish humor, both at the scholarly and the popular level. It is fascinating how Jewish humor has been among the most decisive factors behind dispelling many of most unsavory misconceptions about the Jewish community in the USA. In American academia, through serious research, continuous publications, journals and bulletins, numerous conferences, and regular courses, Jewish humor has taken a superlative position. I think Arab-Americans and instructors of Arabic studies alike, both at the popular and academic levels, have to learn a lot from the success of Jewish humor.

A course on Arab humor would preferably be taught to advanced and/or graduate students who are highly interested in learning the most characteristic elements and idiosyncratic topics of the Arab/Muslim world. If one cannot appreciate the humor of a target culture in which he/she could become an expert – sought for by American media, "think-tanks," and even decision makers – one cannot claim to understand the Arabs and their culture past and present. As noted by Ali (1998, 2), "it would be no exaggeration to say that a true picture of the Arab life and nature is not possible without taking into account the lighter side of these people who had a highly cultivated sense of humor with a remarkable capacity of cracking jokes." In line with Gruber's aforementioned statement on the neglect of native humor in the USA, the disinterest in Arab humor has more to do with the unwillingness to acknowledge this humanizing/humanist tradition than any presumed untranslatability, locality, or humorlessness. After all, it is our role as teachers of comparative literature to "universalize" the local, and, to David Damrosch (2009, 513), "to keep readers alive to cultural difference and to develop illuminating analyses of creative conjunctions of distant works."

The presumed locality, untranslatability and "humorlessness" of Arab humor can be said of other non-national, and even non-regional traditions. Far beyond the ideological tensions, humor can always transcend the cultural, the local, the national, and the racial. After all, to paraphrase and quote Geert Van Gelder's introduction to Rosenthal's *Humor in Early Islam*, one is not claiming that, perhaps quite humorously, Americans will fall on their backs at reading or hearing a premodern Arab jocular anecdote "as caliphs and others regularly do in classical Arabic literature" (Van Gelder 1956, xiv). Propitiously, the epic journey of Jewish humor in the USA is an encouraging sign for Arab humor. On the socio-cultural and literary side, one should not forget to highlight the Arabic influence on Jewish premodern folkloric and jocular writing.[4] After stating that "[t]he Jewish joke, it can be argued, begins with the Qur'an," Hillel Halkin (2006, 47) goes on to note that, "medieval Hebrew literature, a great deal of which was written by Jews living in Muslim lands, was heavily influenced by Arabic models … The comical *iqtibas* reached its peak in an Arabic genre that was once again borrowed by Hebrew writers – namely, the rhymed-prose narrative, known as *maqama* that was highly popular in the Middle Ages" (ibid., 50).

A course on Arab humor, it goes without saying, is both comparatively rewarding and theoretically challenging. Approaching Arabic humorous literature through the prism of a score of intriguing Western theories – especially with graduate students – would provide them with an excellent opportunity to explore comparatively and analyze theoretically one of the world's richest premodern jocular corpora. Of significant theoretical challenge would be testing the applicability of, say, Freud's psychoanalytical theory of humor which he delineated, not without controversy, in his *Der Witz und seine Beziehung zum Unbewussten* (Jokes and their Relations to the Unconscious).[5] This holds especially true of Freud's essentialist definition and linking of humor and laughter to masked sexual and aggressive instincts. In addition to Freud's psychophysical theory of humor, students could also approach the Arabic jocular tradition through other influential Western theorists of humor such as Bergson and Hobbes, who are respectively the main proponents of the "Incongruity and Superiority" theories of humor.[6] Another interesting theory that could be of particular significance is the "Conceptual/Semiotic" theory, which for obvious reasons lends itself as the most applicable of all Western theories of humor to classical and postclassical Arabic humorous tradition. Defining the latter in his insightful *An Anatomy of Humor*, Arthur A. Berger (1998, 4) writes that this theory "argues that humor is best understood as dealing with communication, paradox, play, and the resolution of logical problems." Finally, what some perceive as Islamic objection to laughter and humor should be comparatively approached through exploring possible Greek and Biblical influences.

Food and sexual intimacy: a course plan for Arabic literature

In addition to humor and pleasantry, offering more courses on the rich premodern Arabic writing on food and sexual intimacy can equally shed a much-needed light on the humanistic treasures of the Arabs. Students and instructors alike would be surprised by the punctiliousness Arabs/Muslims lavished on their cooking, eating, and sexual lives. Indeed, as phrased by Paul Fieldhouse in *Food and Nutrition: Customs and Culture*, "eating is not, and never has been, a merely biological activity" (Fieldhouse 1995, 3). Fieldhouse's insightful statement can be extended without reservation to sexual intimacy. "No other fundamental aspect of our behavior as a species except sexuality," Sidney Mintz notes in *Tasting Food, Tasting Freedom: Excursions in to Eating, Culture and the Past*, "is so encumbered by ideas as eating; the entanglements of food with religion, with both belief and sociality, are particularly striking" (Mintz 1996, 8). In spite of the remarkably voluminous corpus of classical and postclassical Arabic gastronomical, culinary, and sexological writing, I have not been able to locate a single American university that offers a course on this fascinatingly humanistic tradition.

For such a course I would suggest the title "*Al-Aṭyabān*, or the Two Delights: Food and Physical Intimacy in Classical Arabic Literature and Culture." Inspired by what Islamically is perceived as legislated worldly delights, this course would venture into the fascinating world of Arab-Islamic pleasure.[7] Early Muslims, within the legal boundaries of their faith, produced a rich literary corpus on gastronomical and carnal pleasures, not only to guide the powerful and the rich, but also to advise the populace, men and women. Quranic and Prophetic narratives will be a major source for exploring these two humanist literary subjects. This is in addition to several classical prose and poetic texts on culinary/gastronomical culture, dietetics, banquets, erotic topics, physical intimacy, aphrodisiacs, sexual education and hygiene, most of which were penned by pious and strict scholars, who would probably be frowned upon as anti-Islamic or at best libertines in the modern Arab-Muslim world. Since Arabs/Muslims are largely depicted as incomprehensibly strict in their diet and dull in their sexuality, one of the main cultural messages of this course would be to enlighten American students that the Arabs enjoy many worldly pleasures – perhaps quite differently – as much as they do.

While a full discussion of the intriguing meaning(s) of *adab* in classical Arabic goes beyond the scope of this chapter, it is important to note that *adab* etymologically and semantically relates to good food offered generously in a sumptuous banquet. *Adab* literally means good manners and unlike the English word literature, it is not solely associated with writing (*kitāba* in Arabic).[8] In other words, not every *kātib* (scribe) is an *adīb* (littérateur or man of letters). To be so, a *kātib* must also educate his/her own *adāb* (manners/etiquettes/behavior) to be an *adīb*, a writer of good manners, education, and culture. More precisely, again at least at the theoretical level, for a person to be able to produce, and hence promulgate, good manners and instruct others in fine cultures and educate them, this person ought first and foremost to be endowed with *adab*: an *adīb* is therefore the person who has good, or even better, perfect manners, fine culture, and high education. Before being an instructor of good manners (i.e. *mu'addib*), one must be an *adīb*. Tellingly enough, the words *adab* and *adīb*, good literature or *belles lettres* and good littérateur, are related to good food, or to be more specific, to good offered food: *ma'duba*, that is a lavishly good banquet. A good Arab *adīb* is after all an Arab in generosity and treating.

A number of scholars are increasingly looking in more depth into this inherently etymological/semantic, but ultimately ontological/cultural, Arabic association between literature and food, between producing great literature and offering great food. "The connection between eating, ethics and literature," Van Gelder tells us in the introduction to *God's Banquet: Food in Classical Arabic Literature*, "is visible symbolically in the apparent etymological link between *adab*, 'literature/good behavior', and *ma'duba* 'meal or banquet for the guest'" (Van Gelder 2000, 3). In addition to their full awareness "of the intricacies of the word, its root, and use, in relation to acquired knowledge and systematic attention to good manners," classical *littérateurs* in al-Musawi's (2007, 291) words, "were aware too of the close connection between the word and the feast where a number of people gather around a banquet table. As a collection of narratives the book is no less inviting than a meaty repast. The feast invites discussion, intimacy, and solidarity, as well as generosity and hosting."

While discussing the varied Arabic sources on humor, I mentioned that classical *adab* and *akhbār* texts are replete with anecdotes of humor, jesting, and frivolity. The same sources – and I should add here other genres, namely the *riḥla* (travel account) – abound also with various culinary and sexual entries. This is in addition to a large corpus of mostly treaties, epistles, and manuals.[9] It is to be said that, impressively and tellingly, several of the treaties, epistles, and manuals on sexual intimacy and *savoir faire*, were penned by, or commonly attributed to, pious and rigid religious scholars. These fascinating sources are widely tabooed and censored in the Arab world. In addition to censorship, manipulative denial on the part of many, if not most, modern and contemporary Muslim religious scholars has turned this rich and impressive corpus into taboo texts. Many others are solely interested in preaching the likes of al-Ghazālī's *Kasr al-Shahwatayn* (Curbing the Two Appetites), the *shahwatān* being a largely negative appellation of food and sex (note here the difference in nomenclature from *al-atyabān* (the two delights). The irony, as will be evidenced in the coming samples, is that most of the authors who did not call for curbing the appetites were as pious as al-Ghazālī and are still widely read and respected. This is certainly the case with the likes of al-Tijānī, al-Nafzāwī, and mainly Ibn Ḥazm and al-Suyūṭī. The latter, with around ten works on sexual intimacy, should be credited with being one of the premodern world's most prolific sexologists.

A digression is necessary here. It is an unfortunate fact that many contemporary Muslim religious scholars jump into denial when even briefly and innocently referring to one of the above books on sexual relations during their lectures on etiquette of marriage or the jurisprudential views of Ibn Ḥazm or al-Suyūṭī: "This is not true. This deviant book or epistle was never written by X, not least because our great imam was too pious to write this type of *fisq* [amorality]." A typical response is to blame the detractors of the presumed author, or as we hear more often, the Orientalist who edited the manuscript, for adding licentious sections or even fabricating the entire book in order to discredit the scholarship and besmear the reputation of this or that scholar. The most nonsensical response I have heard personally came on a Tunisian radio program and relates to al-Suyūṭī's *Nawāḍir al-ayk fī ma'rifat al-nayk* (The Luxuriant Thickets of Sexual Intercourse). Not least because many Tunisians venerate al-Suyūṭī's co-authored Quran exegesis known as *Tafsīr al-Jalālayn* (Tafsir of the two Jalals), found in nearly every Tunisian mosque, a question was put to the sheikh regarding his verdict on al-Suyūṭī's presumably obscene book. "I have no grain of doubt," the sheikh confidently responded, "that the mentioned work was written when our pious scholar was too young to distinguish between truth and falsehood. We have to remember that our ascetic imam expressed regret and repented for writing this 'infamous' book."

To go back to our main topic, and while I do share Professor Van Gelder's (2007, 4) cynicism regarding submerging classical Arabic literature "in the surges of reigning Theorrhoea," a number of anthropological and cultural theories are just tantalizing for classes on Arabic culinary and sexological writing. Towering above the theorists whose work would be comparatively rewarding for the proposed course are Lévi-Strauss's theories of "gustemes" and the "culinary triangle." As he explains it in *Anthropologie structurale* (Structural Anthropology), the gustemes refers to the constituent elements of a particular cooking tradition. These characteristic gustemes of, say, French or English cuisine, can be analyzed through distinguishing "certain structures of opposition and coloration," among which he cites "indigenous" (national) versus "exogenous" (exotic) ingredients (Lévi-Strauss 1974, 86). In the context of the class, instructors could, for example, raise questions such as: What do the "gustemes" of the Arab medieval cuisine tell us about their individual, communal, and international character during the Umayyad and Abbasid periods? Or about the regional differences and similarities between the Maghrib and the Mashriq?

Equally useful in this context is Lévi-Strauss's theory of the "culinary triangle," which he delineated in his essay "Triangle Culinaire" (1965). Briefly stated, cooking is "a truly universal form of human activity" that mirrors language structurally and culturally. In Lévi-Strauss's own words, "the cooking of a society is a language in which it unconsciously translates its structure – or else resigns itself, still unconsciously, to revealing its contradictions" (Lévi-Strauss 1965, 19–29). Like language, cooking contains an unconscious structure which he called the "culinary triangle." In broader terms, this culinary diagram refers to the distinction and association between three types of foods in their relationship to (elaborate) cultural or (non-elaborate) natural transformation: the raw (natural), the cooked (cultural), and the rotten. Related to this is Lévi-Strauss's distinction between three cooking methods: boiling, roasting, and smoking. Such tripartite distinctions can tell us much when it comes to a given society's socio-cultural norms and values: solidarity, hospitality, primitiveness, civilization, and socio-political hierarchies, conveyed through banquets and feasting.

Before concluding, I should note for the benefit of non-specialists and specialists alike that some of the most fascinating texts are available in English translation, which I will cite as an Appendix. Non-specialists are strongly encouraged to incorporate the humanistic heritage of the Arabs in the numerous courses on premodern jocular, culinary and sexological writing, which, as I mentioned earlier, are quite popular in the American academy. As for the specialists whom one hopes will be convinced of offering more courses on lighter topics in classical and medieval Arabic literature, they should expect nothing but success. The enrollment and the evaluation of two courses I taught at Princeton (ARA401/NES708: Classical Arabic Literature I, and ARA402/NES720: Classical Arabic Literature II), demonstrate that the experience is worthwhile. My students, who were primarily senior or graduate students hailing from Near East Studies, Comparative Literature, and Iberian studies, truly enjoyed the texts. In fact, as the courses progressed, their interest and motivation became nothing short of awe-inspiring. To cite an example related to classical texts on humor and food, my students fell in love with al-Khaṭīb al-Baghdādī's *Al-Taṭfīl wa-ḥikāyāt al-ṭufayliyyīn* (Spongers and their Tales). In addition to the anecdotes of Bunān and Ash'ab, the two most (in)famous spongers of premodern Arabic literature, the class was exhilarated by the section on *waṣāya al-ṭufayliyyīn* (wills of spongers), namely the one that reports a dying sponger's will to his attentive son/disciple. At mentioning *al-lawzīnaj* (almond sweet), the dying sponger lost consciousness to alert his son that it was *al-lawzīnaj* that he favored in the elite feasts he used to crash. The students burst into laughter. When they asked me about *al-lawzīnaj*, I informed them that they would find the answers the following week in Ibn Sayyār al-Warrāq (fl. tenth c.), *Kitāb al-ṭabīkh* (Book of Cooked Food). After reading the excerpt on sweets including *al-lawzīnaj*, the students uncovered that this dish was a favorite of the royals and the rich. To my surprise and delight, one of my students presented me with her own version of *al-lawzīnaj*. The class became so attached to the *ṭufayliyyīn* that they decided to set up an email list to inform each other of free meals on campus.[10]

As a general conclusion, one can assert that, in spite of the great efforts of a number of scholars/teachers, there still exists an enormous gap in the curriculum with regard to the humanistic legacy of the Arabs.[11] While one hopes that a more positive context will emerge, it is lamentable that many professors of Arabic literature – including Arabs and Muslims targeting quick academic integration and intellectual conformity – either simply forget or implicitly deny that bridging the cultural gaps between America and the Arab world should be one of their loftiest goals. In many respects, we are still waiting for this age and stage when teaching Arabic will be prompted by, to re-quote Roger Allen (2004, 275), this "kind of enlightened altruism that might lead western learners of Arabic to develop favorable motivations like those that drive, say, learners of Spanish or French." Lest one be misunderstood, I am not in any way calling for a reverse romantic-idealistic approach akin to what Charles Bernheimer (1995, 45) once succinctly described as a "politically correct way of acquiring more or less picturesque information about others whom we don't really want to know." Rather, I mean that Arabists in the USA should do more "to promote significant reflection on cultural relations, translations, dialogue, and debate" (ibid., 45).

If offered more often in American academia, courses and studies on Arab humor, culinary culture, and physical intimacy, could, on the one hand, fill a substantial gap in the teaching of and research on Arab literary humanism, which is vital to challenge the predominantly unpleasant narratives of what al-Hazza and Lucking (2005, 32) have described, not without truth, as "the minority of suspicion." On the other hand, it is time that Arabs and Muslims multiply their efforts to rediscover and cherish their humanistic treasures for their own good and the good of humanity at large. Whereas God and the Prophet Muhammad, as attested by numerous Quranic verses and *ḥadīths*, called upon the believers, males and females, to fully enjoy their sexual lives, many contemporary scholars debate whether it is *ḥalāl* (permitted) or *ḥarām* (prohibited) to engage in physical intimacy for pleasure and not procreation. These scholars seem to ignore lessons they themselves should have learned from the likes of Umm Salama and Umm Sulaym:

> The Prophet used to kiss me while he was fasting. I and the Prophet used to wash ourselves from the same water vessel.
>
> *(Juynboll 2007, 661)*

And:

> Umm Sulaym (the mother of Anas b. Mālik) came to the Prophet and said: "Messenger of God, God wishes that we be truthful about certain matters: when a woman has a nocturnal emission, should she perform a major ritual ablution?" "Yes," the Prophet said, "if she sees the fluid."
>
> *(Juynboll 2007, 201)*

For the sake of scholarly honesty and their own integrity, the least that Muslim scholars should do whenever they refer their students to al-Ghazālī's *Kasr al-Shahwatayn* is, even in passing, draw their attention to al-Suyūṭī's numerous works on *al-aṭyabān*!

Notes

1 Mary Louise Buley-Meissner's article, "Teaching American Literature in China: Learning How Students Read and Respond," deserves some attention in this regard. Buley-Meissner's report on the propagandist nature of teaching American literature in China during the last quarter of the last century evokes much of the political realities of the teaching of Arabic literature in American academia. Very pertinent in this respect is her claim that Chinese students are indoctrinated to focusing on the darker side of the American culture. Instead of appreciating a different culture in a complex society, Chinese students of American literature end up with nearly a dystopian picture of a cruelly capitalist USA, which, as they were made to believe, is the antithesis of their presumably utopian Chinese society and culture.

2 Interchangeably called *al-fukāha, al-du'āba, al-muzāḥ, al-ẓarf* and others. It is to be noted that works of *sukfh* and *mujūn* are largely humorous. See Sinan Antoon, *The Poetics of the Obscene in Premodern Arabic Poetry* (New York: Palgrave, 2014).

3 To cite some examples, one can mention works such as al-Jāḥiẓ (d. 869), *Kitāb al-Bayān wa-al-tabyīn* (Clarity and Clarification); Ibn Qutayba (d. 889), *'Uyūn al-akhbār* (Founts of Information); al-Iṣbahānī (d. 967), *Kitāb al-aghānī* (The Book of Songs); Ibn 'Abd Rabbih (d. 940), *Al-'Iqd al-farīd* (The Unique Necklace); al-Tanūkhī (d. 994), *Nishwār*

al-muḥāḍarah (The Elegant Talk of the Assembly); al-Ḥuṣrī (d. 1022), *Zahr al-ādāb wa-thamar al-albāb* (The Flowers of Instruction and Fruits of the Mind); al-Tawḥīdī (d. 1023), *Kitāb al-Imtā' wa al-mu'ānasa* (Enjoyment and Conviviality); al-Ābī (d. 1039), *Nathr al-durr* (The Scattering of Pearls); al-Tha'ālibī (d. 1039), *Laṭā'if al-ma'ārif* (The Book of Curious and Entertaining Information); al-Nuwayrī (d. 1332), *Nihāyat al-arab fī funūn al-adab* (The Aim of the Intelligent in the Art of Letters); al-Ghuzūlī (d. 1412), *Maṭāli' al-budūr fī manāzil al-surūr* (The Risings of the Full Moons in the Mansions of Joy); and al-Ibshīhī (d. 1464), *al-Mustaṭraf fī kull fann mustaẓraf* (The Most Delighting Items of Every Delicate Topic).

4 S.D. Goitein speaks of a "great Arab-Jewish symbiosis," especially in the pre-modern era.

5 Freud is thought to expand on the older "Relief Theory" propounded by Lord Shaftesbury in "An Essay on the Freedom of Wit and Humor" (1709). This theory argues that humor is essentially related to the release of our nervous energy.

6 The "Superiority Theory" is often traced back to classical Greek philosophers such as Plato and Aristotle. It was, however, adopted and expanded mainly by Thomas Hobbes in *Leviathan*. Briefly stated, this theory argues that humans laugh because they feel themselves superior to others and immune from their misfortunes, failures, deformities and so on. The German word *schadenfreude* is always quoted in this regard. As for the "Incongruity Theory," it was adopted and propounded by many scholars such as Francis Hutcheson, Arthur Schopenhauer, Hegel, Beattie, Kant, and especially Henri Bergson in his "Laughter: An Essay on the Meaning of the Comic" (1900). In a broader sense, this theory argues that humor results from "the perception of something incongruous – something that violates our mental patterns and expectations" (12). For more on the above theories and others, see John Morreall, ed., *The Philosophy of Laughter and Humor* (Albany: State University of New York Press, 1987); N. Caroll, *Humour: A Very Short Introduction* (Oxford: Oxford University Press, 2013); and R. Provine, *Laughter: Scientific Investigation* (Harmondsworth: Penguin, 2000).

7 Numerous classical Arabic sources, namely dictionaries, encyclopedias and compilations, are full of entries discussing what is commonly described as *thunā'iyyāt* (dualities) such as *al-aswadān* (the two black things), *al-aḥmarān* (the two red things), *al-asfarān* (the two yellow things), *al-ajwafān* (the two hollow things), *al-akhbathān* (the two bad things), and many others. Interestingly enough, the sources usually devote much attention and space to *al-aṭyabān* (the two delights) and while mentioning other dual possibilities such as food and drink, or food and sleeping, they tend to concur on associating the world's two most enjoyable delights or pleasures to *al-akl wa al-nikāḥ*: that is food and (legitimate) sex. It is to be noted that in the prophetic tradition, however, the word *al-atyabān* is unanimously associated with *al-tamr* (dates) and *al-laban* (milk). However, there are other ḥadīths that enumerate the Prophet's most enjoyable worldly pleasures in which, even if they do not include food, lawful sex is implied through referring to women. The single most quoted hadith in this regard is "*ḥubbiba ilayyā min dunyākum thalāth: al-'iṭr wa al-nisā*'" [*wa-ju' ilat qurratu 'aynī fī al-ṣalāt*] (I have been made to love three earthly things: women and perfume [but, prayer has been made the apple of my eye).

8 When discussing the intricate meanings of *adab*, scholars usually refer to a saying attributed to Prophet Muhammad: *addabanī rabbī fa aḥsana ta'dībī* (my Lord has educated me and, indeed, he perfected my education).

9 See the Appendix for a selected bibliography of published works on Arab food and sexology.

10 The same enthusiasm and joy are exhibited by my outstanding upper and graduate students at the University of Virginia, ARTR3559/5559: Arabic Literary Delights: Food, Humor, and Erotology.

11 See *Humanism and Religion: A Call for the Renewal of Western Culture* (Oxford: Oxford University Press, 2012); *Humanism in the Renaissance of Islam: The Cultural Revival during the Buyid Age* (Leiden: Brill, 1992); and George Makdisi, *The Rise of Humanism in Classical Islam and the Christian West* (Edinburgh: Edinburgh University Press, 1990).

Bibliography

Al-HazzaT. and Lucking, R. "The Minority of Suspicion: Arab Americans." *Multicultural Review*, 3 (2005): 32–38.

Ali, Abdul. *Arab Legacy to Humour Literature*. New Delhi: M.D. Publications, 1998.

Allen, Roger. "Perspectives on Arabic Teaching and Learning." *The Modern Language Journal*, 2 (2004): 275–278.

Al-Musawi, Mushin. "Abbasid Popular Narrative: the Formation of Readership and Cultural Production." *Journal of Arabic Literature*, 38 (2007): 2661–2292.

Al-Nowaihi, Magda. "For a 'Foreign' Audience: The Challenges of Teaching Arabic Literature in the American Academy." *Middle East Studies Association Bulletin* (2001): 24–27.

Berger, Arthur Asa. *An Anatomy of Humor*. New Brunswick, NJ: Transaction Publishers, 1998.

Bernheimer, Charles. "The Bernheimer Report, 1993: Comparative Literature at the Turn of the Century," *Comparative Literature in the Age of Multiculturalism*, ed. Charles Bernheimer. Baltimore, MD: The Johns Hopkins University Press, 1995, 39–48.

Buley-Meissner, Mary. "Teaching American Literature in China: Learning How Students Read and Respond." *English Education*, 3 (1990): 192–199.

Damrosch, David. "Frames for World Literature," *Grenzen der Literatur: Zu Begriff und Phänomen des Literarischen*. Ed. Simone Winko. Berlin: Walter de Gruyter, 2009, 496–515.

Fieldhouse, Paul. *Food and Nutrition: Customs and Culture*. London: Chapman & Hall, 1995.

Goitein, S.D. *Jews and Arabs: Their Contacts through the Ages*. New York: Schocken Book, 1995.

Gruber, Eva. *Humor in Contemporary Native North American Literature. Reimagining Nativeness*. Rochester, NY: Camden House, 2008.

Halkin, Hillel. "Why Jews Laugh at Themselves," *Commentary Magazine*, 4 (2006): 50.

Juynboll, G.H.A. *Encyclopedia of the Canonical Ḥadīth*. Leiden: Brill, 2007.

Lévi-Strauss, Claude. *Structural Anthropology* (*Anthropologie structurale*, 1961). Trans. Claire Jacobson and Brooke Grundfest Schoepf. New York: Basic Books, 1974.

Lévi-Strauss, Claude. "Triangle Culinaire," *L'Arc* 25 (1965): 19–29.

Mintz, Sidney. *Tasting Food, Tasting Freedom: Excursions in to Eating, Culture and the Past*. Boston, MA: Beacon Press, 1996.

Rappaport, Léon. *Punchlines: The Case for Racial, Ethnic, and Gender Humor*. Westport, CT: Praeger, 2005.

Rosenthal, Franz. *Humor in Early Islam*. Leiden: Brill, 1956.

Van Gelder, Geert. "Introduction," *Humour in Early Islam by Franz Rosenthal*. Leiden: Brill, 1956.

Van Gelder, Geert. *God's Banquet: Food in Classical Arabic Literature*. New York: Columbia University Press, 2000.

Appendix: suggested translated works for the non-specialists

Al-Ābī. *Arabian Wit and Wisdom from Abu Sa'id al-Abi's Kitab Nathr Al-Durar*. Trans. Charles A. Owen. Whitefish: Kessinger Publishing, 2010.

Al-Jāḥiẓ. *Nine Essays of Al-Jahiz*. Trans. W.M. Hutchins, New York: Peter Lang, 1989.

Al-Jāḥiẓ. *Avarice and the Avaricious: Kitab al-Bukhala' by Abu 'Uthman al-Jahiz*. Trans. Jim Colville. London: Kegan Paul International, 1999.

Al-Khaṭīb al-Baghdādī. *Selections from "The Art of Party-Crashing" in Medieval Iraq by al- Khatib al-Baghdadi*. Trans. Emily Selove. Syracuse, NY: Syracuse University Press, 2013.

Al-Nafzāwī. *The Perfumed Garden of Sensual Delight*. Trans. Jim Colville. London: Kegan Paul International, 1999.

Al-Tha'ālibī. *The Laṭā'if al-Ma'ārif of Tha'ālibi: The Book of Curious and Entertaining Information*. Trans. C.E. Bosworth. Edinburgh: Edinburgh University Press, 1968.

Al-Tīfāshī. *Sensual Delights of the Heart. A Tale of Mediaeval Arabic Erotica*. Trans. Daniel L. Newman. London: Saqi Book, 2013.

Anonymous. "The Description of Familiar Foods: Kitāb waṣf al-aṭ'ima al-Mu'tāda," Trans. Charles Perry. *Medieval Arab Cookery*. Ed. Maxime Rodinson *et al.* Devon: Prospect Books, 2001, 273–465.

Ibn 'Arabshāh. *A Literary and Gastronomical Conceit: Mufākharah Adabīyah Ghidhā'īyah: Mufākharat al-Ruzz wa-l-Habb Rummān aw al-Maqāmah al-Simāṭīyah*. Trans. Ibrahim K. Khalil Geries. Wiesbaden: Harrassowitz Verlag, 2002.

Ibn Falītah. *An Intelligent Man's Guide to the Art of Coition*. Trans. Adnan Jarkas and Salah Addin Khawwam. Toronto: Aleppo Publications, 1977.

Ibn Ḥasan al-Ḥajjār. *The Delectable War between Mutton and the Refreshments of the Market-Place*. Trans. Joshua Finke. Blackawton: Prospect Books, 1988.

Ibn Ḥazm. *The Ring of the Dove: A Treatise on the Art and Practice of Arab Love*. Trans. A.J. Arberry. London: Luzac Oriental, 1994.

Ibn Sayyār al-Warrāq. *Annals of the Caliphs' Kitchens: Ibn Sayyār al-Warrāq's Tenth-Century Baghdadi Cookbook*. Trans. Nawal Nasrallah. Leiden: Brill, 2002.

7

LANGUAGE THROUGH LITERATURE

Taoufik Ben Amor

While packing my books recently in preparation to move to a new office, I found a syllabus for an Arabic course offered at Columbia University in the early part of the twentieth century. In addition to reading Ṭaha Ḥusayn's *al-'Ayyām*, Haykal's *Zaynab*, selections from al-Jāḥiẓ, poems by al-Mutanabbī and the *mu'allaqāt*, it required that the students memorize 60 lines of classical poetry. Arabic syllabi have changed a great deal since then, and the Arabic teaching profession has taken many a turn after the advance of proficiency, authenticity, task-based teaching and content-based instruction. That road, however, has not led our students to linguistic and cultural proficiency. Instead, and with the mounting pressure of area studies, we have encountered multiple hurdles, the most prominent of which are the neglect of reading, especially intensive or close reading (Larkin 1995), and demotion of linguistic precision in favor of fluency. Reading literary text has lost ground to skimming media articles. Badawi (2006, xii) laments this situation:

> Materials used for training students tend to be largely drawn from the narrowly defined political type … Such narrowly focused language materials, however, can never furnish the depth, richness, and variety of language necessary for the deep internalizing of the culture. Without a basic dose of literary language … no serious learning of the language can be achieved. It is through the literary genres that learners gain insight into the complexity of the language expression and social phenomena in a single package.

If, as the saying goes, "Arabic is an ocean," then our students are swimming barely on its surface.

Within the framework of content-based instruction (CBI), this chapter argues for using a healthy "dose," to borrow Badawi's term, of literary text at all levels of the language curriculum and proposes ways to remedy the artificial gulf that separates content courses from language classes in most current university programs (Modern Language Association 2006). The chapter begins by examining the status quo and probing for reasons behind our current choices of materials. Subsequently, it examines the versatile ways in which literary genres and their linguistic characteristics lend themselves to helping students achieve linguistic and cultural proficiency. The chapter concludes with a few general principles which illustrate practical ways of designing programs with more literary content.

A canon within the canon

With very few exceptions, such as Frangieh's *Anthology of Arabic Literature, Culture, and Thought from Pre-Islamic Times to the Present* (2004), a survey of past and current Arabic textbooks (Abboud et al. 1983; Allen and Allouche 1986; Alosh 2000, 2005, 2009; Brustad et al. 2004, 2006a, 2007; Younes 1995, 1999) reveals two interesting aspects. First, although the profession has moved toward the use of authentic materials, there is a gradual decrease in the use of literary text. Other than a few songs, poems, and two short stories, the *Al-Kitaab* series, for example, uses very few literary texts compared with newspaper and magazine articles. Few of these texts are the main reading on which vocabulary and grammar are based, and a good number of them, especially excerpts from classical sources, appear as third readings under the rubric of culture. Even the chapter on poetry in part three of the textbook is introduced by a text on poetry, not a poem. The second aspect has to do with the content of such textual choices: whether through the early "self-Orientalizing" choices or the later mainstream depiction of Arab cultures, the authors seem to fulfill the stereotype by portraying Arabs in ways that reinforce issues dominant in American and European mass media: political Islam, human rights, women's issues, censorship, oil, etc. Certainly, Arab cultures portray themselves in a more dynamic, dialectical and complex way. The dominant narratives are often complicated by contending vernacular interpretations, which are often absent from textbooks.

The reasons behind this decrease in the use of literary texts are many. First, while reacting to the old grammar-translation method, an association was made between literary texts, especially classical, with this old-fashioned, inefficient teaching approach. In the vein of characteristic rejection of old methods by new ones, which Abboud (1995) warns about, the baby was thrown out with the bath water, so to speak. Second, most appraisals of current issues and future challenges for the profession (Abboud 1995; Allen 2004; Al-Batal 1995a; Al-Batal and Belnap 2006; Ryding 2006), though not devoid of clairvoyance, emphasize the shift in students' needs and our obligation to respond to them. However, none probes the reasons behind such changes and almost all portray them as a bottom-up surge of new academic and professional demands. Academia has changed, and with it our organization of knowledge, sense of scholarship and how a student will attain it. Our notion of text has expanded beyond the written definition to include other forms of cultural expression and artistic production. It is rather a top-down change, coupled with the political push for area studies and the establishment of regional institutes, professional schools, US government funds and scholarships. Responding to the needs of such professional students does not mean we should gear the entire content of our curricula toward their immediate, and often short-term goals. Very few of these professional Master's degree students reach a functional level of proficiency. Another shift, noticeable in many programs across the United States and abroad, such as the Center for Arabic Studies Abroad (CASA), is that more undergraduate students are studying Arabic. This has an effect on the choice of text, length, and depth of reading, as most of these students still lack the tools essential for critical, analytical literary reading.

Furthermore, the few literary texts selected by teachers, especially at the advanced level, or featured in textbooks, anthologies and readers, even though the last two are not usually designed for classroom instruction, seem to resurface. Irrespective of personal taste, teaching experience, knowledge of literature, national identity, linguistic ease or difficulty, or quality of the content, the selections display a number of biases. First, they have a regional or geographical bias and tend to be Egypt-centric with occasional additions from Syria, Lebanon, Palestine, and seldom from Iraq. The rest of the Arab world is almost completely ignored. In four readers spanning four decades (Rabin 1947; Ziadeh 1964; Brinner and Khouri 1971; Hafez and Cobham 1988), 49 out of the 75 featured authors are from Egypt; the remaining 26 are from Lebanon, Syria, Iraq, Palestine and Jordan. Not even one writer from the Gulf, Sudan or the Maghreb is included. Second, there is a gender bias: only three female authors are included among the 75, and they are featured only in two of these collections. Third, they display a historical or temporal bias. The majority of the works selected even in the most recent literature classes or readers are often two to four decades old. Of course some of these works are established by the canon and are rightfully considered essential reading. However, one should still explore recent and less well-known works. Fourth, these selections show the diaspora bias, or what I would like to call the bent towards the exotic, controversial or that which depicts encounters of the so-called East and West (some like to call it touristic literature). Many examples of such pieces, and some are excellent works, come to mind: Tawfiq al-Ḥakim's *'Uṣfūr min al-sharq*, Ṭayyib Ṣaliḥ's *Mawsim al-hijra 'ilā al-shamāl*, Yaḥyā Haqqī's *Qindīl umm hāshim*, Suhail Idrīs's *al-Ḥayy al-lātīnī*, Bahā' Ṭāhir's *Bil'amsi ḥalumtu bi-ka*, etc. These selections, though they vary in quality and merit, would make an excellent choice for a class on the theme of exile, living abroad, experiencing two cultures or what is called in Arabic *ghurba*. However, it seems striking that the same texts reappear in a wide variety of courses and programs. Given the relative freedom we enjoy in the diaspora, books banned by the rampant censorship in Arab countries gain in luster and attractiveness regardless of their quality, linguistic or pedagogical value. *al-Khubz al-ḥafī*, *al-Ākharūn*, "*Bayt min laḥm*", and even *Mawsim al-hijra* are prime examples of such works. Once again, we end up focusing on certain topics that are valued in our immediate context with little regard for the literary canon in the Arab world and the great array of issues tackled by many authors, and thus create a canon within the canon.

Literary genres and levels of language instruction

The curse and the blessing of the authentic text

Perhaps the most problematic area in the advance of proficiency and CBI is the use of authentic texts, especially at the elementary level. Issues of linguistic difficulty, length and style make these texts very difficult to use with beginners. Some experts (Brustad 2006b) propose writing such texts at the elementary level, while others (Ryding and Stowasser 1997) suggest editing such authentic pieces for length and difficult vocabulary and expressions. Some scholars (Stryker and Leaver 1997a) argue that, regardless of level, the question is not one of ease or difficulty of language and content, but rather of the tasks we set for our students when we ask them to read such texts. In other words, through specific questions or exercises, we guide our students to a partial comprehension of specific aspects or parts of a text. These very texts can be reintroduced at later stages of learning for another level of reading. With the right genres, length, content, and reading tasks, we can use authentic literary texts at all levels of language instruction. Students at the elementary level enjoyed reading some of Darwish's poems, such as "ilā ummī," and Ṣāliḥ's *Muqaddimāt*, while intermediate students coped very well with Kanafānī's *'Ā'id ilā ḥayfā*.

The pedagogical benefits of literary texts

There are innumerable pedagogical benefits to using literary materials in language curricula. These materials are not limited to the written text, but include other input forms and media, such as film, sound recordings, songs, etc. Sometimes combining these forms enhances learning considerably. For example, a poem can be presented as a written text, a recorded recitation by the poet or another reader, and as a song composed by musicians who have put poetry to music. There is indeed a wide repertoire of such compositions spanning centuries of poetry from pre-Islamic times until now.

First, literary texts present language at its best, rich with nuances, connotations, cultural references, and metaphor. This creative use of language offers students ample opportunities to explore these subtleties and shades of meaning in a way that is much broader and deeper than in other forms of writing. The themes of literary pieces often lend themselves very well to exploring specific semantic fields. For example, one of the themes around which Bahā' Ṭāhir's short story "*al-Khuṭūba*" revolves is truth and lying, belief and disbelief, and thus offers the students a great opportunity to explore synonyms and antonyms related to these two important semantic fields. In the same vein, Zakariyya Tāmir's "*Shams Ṣaghīra*" is full of synonyms of happiness, though it is overall a tragic story that ends in a violent death. Most of these words can be found in the text then expanded in class or through an assignment. Furthermore, these literary texts encompass other forms and functions of writing that can be very useful in exposing students to their specific styles and idiomatic expressions. Ṭayyib Ṣāliḥ's "*Risāla ilā Aylīn*", for example, is in the form of a letter in its first part, while Laṭīfa Bāqā's "*Ḥidhā' bidūn ka'b*" takes that of a diary; the first section of Ghassān Kanafānī's "*al-Būma fī ghurfa ba'īda*" is a prime example of a description of a place, Nāfila Ḍhahab's collection *Ḥakāyā al-layl* is a good introduction to popular forms of narration, and Mikha'īl Nu'ayma's "*Mashhadān*" is an excellent sample of a comparison, although the comparison is not direct. This indirect comparison can be equally found in Jubrān's poem, "*Mawākib*" or Ṣāliḥ's short story "*Ḥafnat tamr*," where, after reading these short stories or poems, the students can practice direct comparison and contrast.

Second, literature is rich in cultural content, context, and local flavor. Not only the content of the piece studied, but a biography of the author and a general view of the time the text was composed add to the understanding of the piece and enrich the students' knowledge of the Arab world. In addition, it is important for students of foreign language to develop their literacy in the target language, not only their proficiency. This is particularly true of heritage students, who often are proficient to varying degrees in a dialect but have significant gaps in their cultural knowledge. Indeed, it is not possible to separate linguistic proficiency from cultural literacy, an unfortunate development in the United States where the practice of language teaching has become more of a mechanical and utilitarian task relegated to junior and often unqualified faculty.

Third, reading literature is highly motivational. The motivation to find out how a story develops and ends is intrinsic in the text itself and most readers have a natural curiosity. Reading a short story such as Fu'ād al-Takarlī's "*al-Tannūr*" triggers this internal motivation that students have when reading a narrative. The main character, and narrator, lies and thus keeps changing a crime story, and the reader, like a judge in a court, has to figure out the truth. The discussions that ensue from such a reading happen without any spurring from the teacher, and they become even richer when the students learn that the author was a court judge at a certain point in his life and explore the underlying irony about honor and incest in the story. In addition, students enjoy literary works and often feel that they have accomplished a great deal by completing a literary text, especially a short story or a novel.

Fourth, literature increases the learners' empathy and keeps their affective filter open, which helps undo certain stereotypes, humanizes the other, and makes learning positive. This empathy is essential, especially in light of the recent political implications that Arabic carries. With the US government's "war on terror" and the recent two Gulf wars, Arabic is not only "critical" as the State and Defense Departments categorize it, but also "controversial" (Allen 2004). The attack on

Arabic, especially since 2001, and Middle Eastern Studies in general, has been relentless.[1] As a consequence, teaching Arabic in the United States has become increasingly politicized to the point where teachers hesitate to introduce certain texts, especially works by Palestinian authors, in their courses. It is hard to conceive of a course in modern Arabic literature, or in Arabic in general, that excludes Palestinian authors or avoids the Israeli–Palestinian conflict altogether – both are central in modern Arabic literature.

Fifth, schema theory has shown that students approach reading comprehension with prior knowledge organized into schemata. Students come to foreign language classes with a built-in set of strategies to decode narratives, character relations, and narrative development. Thus, their reading comprehension is not dependent only on the amount of vocabulary and grammar of the foreign language they have acquired, albeit that both need to be significant, but also on their prior knowledge in general.[2] This fact makes pre-reading activities all the more important and fit very well into approaching authentic texts with specific tasks rather than expecting complete comprehension, if that is possible at all. Whether through brainstorming on the general topic of the text, semantic mapping, working on key vocabulary, pre-reading comprehension questions, general discussions, or contextualizing the work by learning about the author and the time of its writing, the students' schemata are triggered for a better comprehension of the text.

Sixth, reading literary texts widens the scope of the students' vocabulary and enhances their incidental learning (Al-Batal 2006). Students are not provided with lists of vocabulary prior to reading the text in order to encourage them to use their abilities to analyze vocabulary and guess meaning from the context and their prior knowledge of the Arabic derivation system of roots and patterns, as well as honing their skills in using dictionaries. This process, though labor-intensive, yields better results in the long run: a more active approach to reading that results in a great deal of incidental vocabulary learned in the process. As students progress in their studies of Arabic, this incidental learning becomes more and more crucial given the great variety in student levels and the impossibility of quantifying what they know. In addition, this process increases the individualization of learning.

Seventh, reading literary texts allows students to see an immediate connection between linguistic form and function in context. Grammar, for example, is no longer a set of theoretical concepts, but an essential tool of expression. This is what Brustad (2006b, 343) aptly calls "applied grammar: grammar put to its proper use in the service of constructing meaning." While reading narratives that depend on a temporal order, students see clearly how these are not possible without mastering tenses. Comparison, as seen for example in a chapter in 'Ashūr's *Faraj* entitled "al-Taw'am," is not possible without certain grammatical devices such as *tamyīz al-muqārana* or *af'al al-tafḍīl*. *Al-maf'ūl al-muṭlaq* is so recurrent in Ṭaha Ḥusayn's *al-'Ayyām* that students realize its stylistic usefulness and versatility. These content courses often integrate language and literature in a very organic way that allows students to learn about both, and move from content to form seamlessly.

Finally, as I will show below, diversity in literary genres offers multiple ways and choices that fit several stages of learning, allows for the work on various skills, and improves students' reading strategies and tools of textual analysis.

Genres at different levels

The variety of genres in modern and classical literature provides us with a wide range of choices of materials to use at different levels. Each genre has a number of intrinsic characteristics that lend themselves well to certain pedagogical applications.

Short stories are ideal reading bites. Although they vary in length, they tend to be concise and focus on one main point. A course built on short stories will have the benefit of diversity in topics, regions, styles, etc. Short stories work well with the upper intermediate and advanced levels.

Novellas are a very effective bridge between reading short stories and novels. Novels are rich in characters, themes and narrative development. A novel read in well-divided and spaced installments offers students an opportunity to deepen their analysis and recycle vocabulary, ideas, themes, and stylistic devices. It also creates suspense and motivates the students to continue reading.

Plays are ideal in role-play and their focus on dialogue. Students can memorize parts and act them. The benefits of such a process in motivating students, improving their pronunciation and reinforcing vocabulary through memorization are immeasurable. Plays, or even short acts, can work at all levels. Also, most plays use *'āmmiyya* and thus are very useful in colloquial courses or in teaching speaking.

Poetry when combined with music in a song is perhaps one of the most efficient ways of teaching language. Poetry is built for memorization and its metaphorical language sensitizes students to style and linguistic and cultural esthetic norms. Lines, stanzas, short poems can be introduced even at the elementary level and often students will remember them for years. Thus, they become a reservoir of vocabulary and expressions, in addition to the literary and cultural significance they carry. Moving from modern to classical poetry offers us the possibility to introduce poems at all levels. Classical poetry, especially a complete *qaṣīda*, is very challenging and should be introduced only at the superior level. Along with poetry, at this level, students can be introduced to the science of *'arūḍ*, prosody.

Classical forms, such as *sīra*, *maqāma*, *ḥikāya* and *akhbār*, can be introduced at the advanced level. They expose the students to the variety of narrative genres used in Arabic literature and can be easily assembled under themes or read as specific genres. Stories from *Alf layla wa layla, Kalīla wa Dimna, al-Bukhalā'* by al-Jāḥiẓ or the *Maqāmāt of Al-Ḥarīrī* are very enjoyable texts to read and can be reasonable in length and difficulty.

Models and parameters of content-based Arabic courses

Literature lends itself well to content-based instruction. CBI rests on three fundamental principles: subject matter core, the use of authentic texts, and appropriateness to the needs of specific students (Stryker and Leaver 1997a). Literary texts can fit well within this theoretical framework: they are theme or content based, authentic, and can be easily selected according to the needs of the students.

Some other methodological parameters are very useful in introducing literary materials or designing content courses.

1 Selecting materials

Though Arabic literature is flexible and diverse in its offerings, it is important to organize content courses along a unifying principle. This unity can be one of theme, genre, author, period or geographical location. Such courses may include the literature of defeat (1967–68), travel literature (1840–1945), war literature in Lebanon or Algeria, women in short stories, women writers, diaspora literature, Europe through Arab eyes, autobiographies, modern poetry in Iraq, etc. Most collections available follow the principle of genre, though few recent anthologies, such as *Kull dhālika al-ṣawt al-jamīl*, which is a selection of short stories by Arab women writers, are based on the gender of authors or region. An eclectic course might fulfill the linguistic objectives of the course, but might lack in cohesiveness and rich content. By focusing the course on a specific genre or, better yet, a specific genre on a specific theme, for example "the Lebanese Civil War through short stories," the students' skill in reading the text and analyzing its content increases with every piece they read. They not only will transfer the knowledge they gained from one story to the next, but will also compare between them in a way that often enriches discussions in class and consequently their grasp of the subject.

2 Sequencing learning tasks

Sequencing these selected materials is equally important. Though progressing in linguistic complexity makes a great deal of sense, alternating between easy and difficult pieces might keep the students challenged and give them respite every now and then. In addition, moving from the modern to the classical, passing through the pre-modern nineteenth and early twentieth centuries, in what I call "reverse gear," seems a sound pedagogical choice. This can be done over the span of several courses and within courses on classical literature. This does not always guarantee a progression from easier to more difficult texts, as individual styles of some authors often vary in complexity regardless of the period in which they lived. Yet, there is an overall progression in style to substantiate such an approach. A course on al-Nahḍa (Arab Renaissance) writings of late nineteenth and early twentieth centuries will prove to be an excellent transition between modern and classical texts. Such a reversed sequence of courses could culminate in reading chapters from *al-Qur'ān* or pre-Islamic poetry.

3 Stages of reading

A practical and efficient way to approach such content classes is the two-stage process: first, students focus on content, then they tackle language. Therefore two readings are carried out in two separate class meetings. The first is an extensive reading guided by a set of comprehension questions; the second is an intensive reading that focuses on the linguistic aspects of the text including vocabulary expansion, grammar in context, and style. Both of these stages are preceded by pre-reading activities to facilitate comprehension and put the literary work in its context. These pre-reading phases involve students' presentations on authors, period of the text, and preparing questions to lead discussions. Students are also assigned post-reading tasks that focus on writing. Thus, class involves not only reading but also a great deal of speaking and writing, which help integrating skills.

4 Individualizing learning

Class activities and assignments in such content-based courses can foster the students' independence, which is the ultimate goal of any language program. By having the students research the authors and historical context of literary works, present and lead discussions in class, they grow confident and conquer their learning anxieties. Besides group readings, each student can be assigned an individual reading project of their choice, granted that it is within the limits of the focus of the course. These individual readings can then become the subject of a class presentation or a final paper. Because students choose what they are interested in, they tend to learn more from such a project.

Conclusion

The versatility of literature, whether in its genres, themes, writers, geographies or historical contexts, can respond to the diverse needs of students. The richness in its imaginative and subjective ways of interpreting and negotiating realities makes it almost immune to categorization. If I were to design a course on the economy of oil and energy in the Middle East, I would make ʻAbd al-Raḥmān Munīf's *Mudun al-milḥ* mandatory reading, Ṣanʻallāh Ibrahim's *al-Lajna* in a political science or a human rights class, Salih's "*Dawmat wad ḥāmid*" and Zifzaf's "*al-Shajara al-muqaddasa*" in a course exploring the issues of modernity and its effects on rural societies. The list goes on.

Notes

1 Columbia Unbecoming and the campaign against the Khalil Gibran International Academy are just two examples of such attacks. For more information, see the coverage in *The New York Magazine*, at http://nymag.com/nymetro/urban/education/features/10868/ and *The New York Times*, at www.nytimes.com/2008/04/28/nyregion/28school.html?_r=1&ref=nyregion&oref=slogin

2 Recent studies suggest that the amount of known vocabulary needs to be very high in order for students to comprehend a text. See N. Schmidt, X. Jiang, and W. Grabe. 2011. "The Percentage of Words Known in a Text and Reading Comprehension," *The Modern Language Journal*, 95 (pp. 26–43).

Bibliography

Abboud, Peter et al. 1971. *Modern Standard Arabic, Intermediate Level* (three volumes). Ann Arbor, Michigan: Department of Near Eastern Studies.

Abboud, Peter et al. 1983. *Elementary Modern Standard Arabic* (two volumes). Cambridge: Cambridge University Press.

Abboud, Peter, et al. 1995. "The teaching of Arabic in the United States: Whence and whither?" In Mahmoud Al-Batal, ed., *The Teaching of Arabic as a Foreign Language: Issues and Directions*. Provo, UT: AATA. 13–33.

Al-Batal, Mahmoud, ed. 1995a. *The Teaching of Arabic as a Foreign Language: Issues and Directions*. Provo, UT: AATA.

Al-Batal, Mahmoud, ed. 1995b. "The Arabic teaching profession: Current realities and future challenges." In Mahmoud Al-Batal, ed., *The Teaching of Arabic as a Foreign Language: Issues and Directions*. Provo, UT: AATA. 1–11.

Al-Batal, Mahmoud, ed. 2006. "Playing with words: Teaching vocabulary in the Arabic curriculum." In Kassem Wahba, Zeinab Taha and Liz England, eds, *Handbook for Arabic Language Teaching Professionals in the 21st Century*. Mahwah, NJ: Lawrence Erlbaum Associates. 331–340.

Al-Batal, Mahmoud, ed. and R. Kirk Belnap. 2006. "The teaching and learning of Arabic in the United States: Realities, needs and future directions." In Kassem Wahba, Zeinab Taha and Liz England, eds, *Handbook for Arabic Language Teaching Professionals in the 21st Century*. Mahwah, NJ: Lawrence Erlbaum Associates. 389–399.

Allen, Roger. 2004. "Perspectives on Arabic teaching and learning." *The Modern Language Journal*, Vol. 88. No. 2 (Summer), pp. 275–278.

Allen, Roger and A. Allouche. 1986. *Li nata'allam al'arabiyya*. Philadelphia, PA: University of Pennsylvania.

Alosh, Mahdi. 2000. *Ahlan wa Sahlan: An Introduction to Modern Standard Arabic*. New Haven, CT: Yale University Press.

Alosh, Mahdi. 2005. *Ahlan wa Sahlan: Functional Modern Standard Arabic for Intermediate Learners*. New Haven, CT: Yale University Press.

Alosh, Mahdi. 2009. *Ahlan wa Sahlan: Functional Modern Standard Arabic for Beginners*. New Haven, CT: Yale University Press.

Al-Warraki, N. Naili and A. Taher Hassanein. 1994. *The Connectors in Modern Standard Arabic*. Cairo: American University in Cairo Press.

Badawi, Al-Sa'īd. 2006. "Arabic for non-native speakers in the 21st century: A shopping list." In Kassem Wahba and Zeinab Taha, eds, *Handbook for Arabic Language Teaching Professionals in the 21st Century*. Mahwah, NJ: Lawrence Erlbaum Associates. ix–xiv.

Brinner, W. and M. Khouri. 1971. *Readings in Modern Arabic Literature*. Leiden: Brill.

Brustad, Kristen et al. 2004. *Al-Kitaab Fii Ta'allum al-'Arabiyya (Part One)*. Second edition. Washington, DC: Georgetown University Press.

Brustad, Kristen et al. 2006a. *Al-Kitaab Fii Ta'allum al-'Arabiyya (Part Two)*. Second edition. Washington, DC: Georgetown University Press.

Brustad, Kristen et al. 2006b. "Reading Fluency in Arabic." In Kassem Wahba, Zeinab Taha and Liz England, eds, *Handbook for Arabic Language Teaching Professionals in the 21st Century*. Mahwah, NJ: Lawrence Erlbaum Associates. 341–352.

Brustad, Kristen et al. 2007. *Al-Kitaab Fii Ta'allum al-'Arabiyya (Part Three)*. Second edition. Washington, DC: Georgetown University Press.

Frangieh, Bassam. 2004. *Anthology of Arabic Literature, Culture, and Thought from Pre-Islamic Times to the Present*. New Haven, CT: Yale University Press.

Hafez, S. and C. Cobham. 1988. *A Reader of Modern Arabic Short Stories*. London: Saqi Books.

Larkin, Margaret. 1995. "The role of close reading in elementary Arabic curriculum." In M. Al-Batal, ed., *The Teaching of Arabic as a Foreign Language: Issues and Directions*. Provo, UT: AATA. 157–173.

Modern Language Association. 2006. *MLA Report*. www.mla.org/Resources/Research/Surveys-Reports-and-Other-Documents/Teaching-Enrollments-and-Programs/Foreign-Languages-and-Higher-Education-New-Structures-for-a-Changed-World.

Rabin, Chaim. 1947. *Arabic Reader*. London: Lund Humphries.

Ryding, Karin. 1995. "Discourse competence in TAFL: Skill levels and choice of language variety in the Arabic classroom." In M. Al-Batal, ed., *The Teaching of Arabic as a Foreign Language: Issues and Directions*. Provo, UT: AATA. 223–231.

Ryding, Karin. 2006. "Teaching Arabic in the United States." In Kassem Wahba, Zeinab Taha and Liz England, eds, *Handbook for Arabic Language Teaching Professionals in the 21st Century*. New Jersey: Lawrence Erlbaum Associates. 13–20.

Ryding, Karin and Barbara Stowasser. 1997. "Text Development for Content-Based Instruction in Arabic." In Steven Stryker and Betty Lou Leaver, eds, *Content-Based Instruction in Foreign Language Teaching: Models and Methods*. Washington, DC: GUP.

Stryker, Steven and Betty Lou Leaver, eds. 1997a. *Content-Based Instruction in Foreign Language Teaching: Models and Methods*. Washington, DC: GUP.

Stryker, Steven and Betty Lou Leaver, eds. 1997b. "Content-based instruction: From theory to practice." In Steven Stryker and Betty Lou Leaver, eds, *Content-Based Instruction in Foreign Language Teaching: Models and Methods*. Washington, DC: GUP. 3–28.

Wahba, Kassem, Zeinab Taha and Liz England, eds. 2006. *Handbook for Arabic Language Teaching Professionals in the 21st Century*. Mahwa, NJ: Lawrence Erlbaum Associates.

Younes, Munther. 1995. *Elementary Arabic: An Integrated Approach*. New Haven, CT: Yale University Press.

Younes, Munther. 1999. *Intermediate Arabic: An Integrated Approach*. New Haven, CT: Yale University Press.

Ziadeh, F. 1964. *A Reader in Modern Literary Arabic*. Princeton, NJ: Princeton University Press.

Ziadeh, F. and R. Winder. 1957. *An Introduction to Modern Arabic*. Princeton, NJ: Princeton University Press.

PART II
Theme

8

LESSONS FROM THE MAGHREB

Hoda El Shakry

In his groundbreaking 1983 work *Maghreb Pluriel*,[1] the late Moroccan novelist and literary critic Abdelkebir Khatibi (1938–2009) theorizes the Maghreb as geopolitically, linguistically and culturally *pluralistic*.[2] He writes, that the "Maghreb should be thought of as a topographic site between the Orient, Occident and Africa that can globalize on its own behalf" (Khatibi 1983, 38–9). He further posits that it is from within this very ontological instability that Maghrebi intellectuals may generate radically new modalities of thinking, being and writing. Khatibi's sentiments are by no means rare in the context of twentieth-century literary and critical thought in the broader region of the Maghreb, which is most commonly understood to include the countries of Algeria, Morocco and Tunisia, and by some accounts, Libya and Mauritania. Thinkers such as 'Abdullāh al-'Arwī (Abdallah Laroui), 'Ali al-Du'aji, Aḥmad al-Madīnī, Maḥmūd al-Mas'adī, Muḥammad Amanṣūr, Tawfiq Bakkar, Muḥammad Barrādah, 'Abdelfattah Kilito, Abdellatif Lâabi, Abdelwahab Meddeb and Sa'īd Yaqṭīne were equally preoccupied with theorizing the *aesthetic* as well as *ethical* dimensions of Maghrebi ethno-linguistic and cultural plurality. Their investigations were both in dialogue with and against the grain of canonical narratives of cultural production in the Arab world. Such accounts either document the unidirectional flow of knowledge from the imperial centers of Western Europe, or they privilege the countries of the Middle East, as is evidenced by the adage: *Cairo writes; Beirut publishes; and Baghdad reads*. While the Cairo-Beirut-Baghdad trajectory certainly resonates with some of the material realities of publishing in the region, it notably elides the Maghreb's extensive theoretical and literary contributions to Arab cultural capital. In so doing, it also neglects to account for many of the subversive networks of intellectual or political exchange staged outside the traditional "East–West" and "North–South" axes.[3] Consequently, the Maghreb and its cultural materials – at once grounded in Arabic, indigenous and vernacular traditions – offer a rich repository of resources for instructors and scholars of Arab/ic literatures.

This essay, on the one hand, critically interrogates the omission of the Maghreb's cultural production and reading publics from the grand narratives of Arab literary history. On the other, it proposes that the ethno-linguistic diversity and unique geopolitics of the Maghreb – situated on the threshold between Europe, sub-Saharan Africa, the Mediterranean and the Middle East – translate into an aesthetic lexicon that is both intellectually and pedagogically germane to the study of Arab/ic literatures. Theoretical as well as literary conceptualizations of a pluralistic or supranational Maghrebi cultural patrimony destabilize orientalist, (neo)colonial and Eurocentric assumptions that continue to haunt the field of Arab/ic literary studies. In what follows, I address these concerns in order to ask: what lessons can the scholar of Arab/ic, comparative, or world literatures learn from the cultural and intellectual history of the Maghreb? Such a question provokes further reflection upon the pedagogical need to address the Maghreb from within its own archives, without circumventing its dynamic historical presence across Arab/ic intellectual traditions. I begin by examining the Maghreb as both an imagined and geopolitical site. I then turn to the disciplinary and institutional problematics that impact the field of Maghrebi Studies. Finally, I address the question of language history, usage and politics in the Maghreb, as well as its significance to the study of comparative and world literatures. Throughout the chapter, I suggest specific authors and texts that may be employed in the classroom for introducing Maghrebi literature and the unique theoretical concerns that it provokes. Following my concluding remarks, I have included an Appendix of Arabophone and Francophone literary and critical works from the Maghreb as a resource for scholars, educators and students of the region.

The other "west"

This investigation contributes to a growing body of work within the field of Arab/ic literary and cultural studies – by such scholars as Michael Allan, Muhsin al-Musawi, Tarek El-Ariss, Elizabeth Holt, Boutheina Khaldi, Mohamed-Salah Omri, Jeffrey Sacks, Samah Selim, Stephen Sheehi and Shaden Tageldin, among others – which seeks to problematize canonical intellectual histories and genealogies of modern Arab/ic cultural production.[4] It is primarily concerned with how the archive of Maghrebi literature and criticism can constructively contribute to the ways in which we define, theorize and most importantly teach Arab/ic literatures. The conceptualization of our field – particularly its linguistic, cultural and geopolitical parameters – fundamentally shapes the choices available to us as scholars and teachers of Arab/ic literature in the United States. This influences not only the regions, historical narratives and texts that become canonized within our discipline, but more crucially, how the corpus of Arab/ic literature and criticism fits within and contributes to the broader theorization and study of comparative or world literatures.

I employ the term Maghreb to designate the countries of Algeria, Morocco and Tunisia, but also to invoke the idea of the Maghreb as an imagined topography.

The "Maghreb" is a site framed by its relational geography vis-à-vis the Arab East or "Mashriq." Etymologically it denotes "the place where the sun sets," from the Arabic root *gh-r-b*, or "to set," while "al-Mashriq" refers to "the place where the sun rises," from the root *sh-r-q*, or "to rise." The term emerged around the seventh century to indicate the western-most territories to be occupied as part of the expansion of the Arabo-Islamic empire, but continues to be used to distinguish the "Middle East" from "North Africa." Its adoption in the French imperial context signals the infamous *TAM* tripartite, employed to codify the countries of Tunisia, Algeria and Morocco under a monolithic colonial entity that sublimated all forms of cultural, ethnic or linguistic difference – not unlike the term *Indochine* in Southeast Asia.[5] The "Maghreb" thus embodies an attempt to unify the region under the rubric of imperial expansion. It also, however, signals a rallying cry against these very hegemonic forces. Calls for unity among the countries of the Maghreb were issued throughout the twentieth century in an attempt to eradicate the French, Italian and Spanish presence in the region. In addition, the Arab Maghreb Union (*Ittiḥād al-Maghrib al-ʿArabī*) was created and ratified by the countries of Algeria, Libya, Morocco, Tunisia and Mauritania in 1989 as a forum for post-independence economic and political alliance.[6] The anti-imperial rhetoric of Maghrebi unity was often mobilized alongside supranational ideologies that relied upon ethno-linguistic, geopolitical or religious forms of identification, such as Pan-Arabism, Pan-Africanism, Pan-Islamism or Third Worldism. These discourses prompted and were promoted by an ethos of intellectual exchange and political affinity not only among the countries of the Maghreb, but also with allies in Sub-Saharan Africa, Asia, Europe and the Americas.

The relationship between the intellectual history of the "Arab East" and Western thought – particularly with respect to the nineteenth-century cultural renaissance known as the *nahḍah* – is a subject that has received significant and thoughtful critical attention in recent years (see Chapter 1 in this volume).[7] However, what happens when we turn to a different "west" – namely the Maghreb? Certainly this would complicate the geopolitical topographies and teleological timelines that undergird such discussions. Maghrebi intellectuals of the early twentieth century engaged with, contested and adapted the ideas that have come to define the Arab *nahḍah* in fascinating and often unacknowledged ways. Moreover, they consciously read themselves as an extension of, and essential to, the creative drive for innovation that marked *nahḍah* discourse.[8] However, beyond a handful of Francophone writers who have been inducted into the French literary annals, there is a palpable absence of cultural artifacts from the contemporary Maghreb featured in canonical Arab/ic literary criticism, intellectual histories, anthologies, and most importantly curricula. This is particularly the case with respect to Arabophone literature and criticism from the region, which is less readily available in English translation.

As I demonstrate in the coming pages, there are a number of lessons that can be gleaned from Maghrebi cultural and intellectual history. Implementing these lessons in our classrooms, however, invites a host of pragmatic concerns – such as which texts are available in the United States, which have been translated into English, and how many remain in print – questions in part addressed by this chapter's Appendix. I am nonetheless concerned with what I believe to be the more critical questions of why it is important to teach Maghrebi literature and criticism in courses on Arab/ic, comparative or world literatures, how we should introduce the intellectual milieu and theoretical preoccupations of modern Maghrebi thinkers, what reading practices texts from the Maghreb foster, and how these practices can contribute to making our students more attentive readers of literature as a medium for refashioning the world. By approaching the Maghreb as a *productively unstable* site, our students can witness complex negotiations of cultural identity being staged alongside dynamic and innovative explorations of literary theory as well as praxis. Tracing this intellectual genealogy across Maghrebi works of fiction and theory reveals how Maghrebi intellectuals continue to challenge monolingual and monolithic conceptualizations of national identity. By this, I mean the geopolitical and institutional attempts to subsume various ethno-linguistic traditions under a singular "national language," in addition to the idea that languages – and their attendant ideological, social and cultural inflections – operate within a closed rather than open semiotic system.

Definitions, demarcations and disciplinarity

One of the challenges within the field of Maghrebi studies emerges from the manner with which departments tend to be structured in the United States and Europe. The "area studies" model – itself emblematic of the orientalist underpinnings of regional scholarship on the Middle East and North Africa – relies upon a regional and/or linguistic orientation that often leaves the Maghreb in a somewhat precarious position.[9] This is especially the case for *Near-Eastern* or *Middle Eastern Studies* departments from which North Africa is technically elided.[10] Even if in name only, this exclusion is symptomatic of larger ideological and geopolitical concerns. The term "Near East" itself emerges from the partitioning of Asia and Africa under British and French imperial expansion – from the name *Proche-Orient* – begging the question, near to whom? While a handful of departments and programs focused on the *Middle East and North Africa* (MENA) have emerged over the years, this has notably been a more common trend amongst nongovernmental organizations and government agencies, rather than academic institutions.[11]

Outside comparative or world literature programs, Francophone literature of the Maghreb is often taught separately from its Arabophone counterparts – a phenomenon not only in universities in the United States and Europe, but also in the Maghreb (Ellis 2007, 6). Similarly, many of the leading professional associations and academic journals in the field highlight the Arabic language or the region of the Middle East in their titles.[12] While this has resulted in a handful of specialized journals and professional associations for the Maghreb and North Africa – such as the *Journal of North African Studies* or the *American Institute for Maghrib Studies* – recent years have also witnessed an increasing crossover between these fields. While a number of departments, professional associations and academic journals have not changed their names, their editorial statements and descriptions indicate more comprehensive coverage of the MENA region. The question remains, however, of how to inclusively structure programs, departments, professional associations and academic periodicals, when nation-states and the discourses and institutions reliant upon them do not adequately account for ethno-linguistic or cultural heterogeneity. These geopolitical realities ultimately impact the kinds of courses that come to meet departmental or general education requirements, subsequently shaping the regions and texts that become canonized in our research and undergraduate teaching, not to mention the training of graduate students.

Exploring precisely how and why the Maghreb does not fit so neatly into existing institutional, disciplinary and professional paradigms, complicates how Arab/ic literature is studied both in our scholarship and our classrooms. It compels us to ask what happens when we displace the Arabic language, or Arab ethnic identity, as primary signifiers for the Middle East and North Africa. To do so alters the parameters of what constitutes the "Arab world," and its shifting topographies of linguistic, religious and ethno-national identity. It calls attention to the designation of Modern Standard Arabic as the official currency of Arab/ic literature, despite the region's historically diverse cultural production in Phoenician, Latin, Turkish, Kabyle, Tamazight, various national and regional dialects, as well as French, Spanish, and English.[13] This is further complicated by the latest trends in diaspora and migrant literature which add Swedish, Portuguese, Italian and German, among other languages, to the list.[14] The corpus of literary and critical works emerging from the Maghreb – particularly across the twentieth century – has already implicitly or explicitly problematized the legitimacy of Arabic as the *lingua franca* of the region. Such texts trouble modern Arab nationhood and identity politics in ways that are theoretically relevant to how we teach, study and conceptualize the field of Arab/ic literature. Moreover, in a political climate in which the signifiers "Arab" and "Islam" have lost any historical or ideological nuance, these distinctions are increasingly important to illustrate in our classrooms.

My own use of the term "Arabophone" as a counterpart to "Francophone" in the context of the Maghreb speaks to these very problematics. It exposes the multitude of languages at play in the region and decenters Arabic as the sole vehicle of Arab ethno-national identity. The term thus renders Arabic a contested locus of identity politics. This opens a window onto other routes and affiliations staged in the region which can be introduced in courses not only on Arab/ic, comparative and world literatures, but also those in the social sciences. This includes the link between North and Sub-Saharan Africa – both of which were subject to Islamic expansion and Anglo-French imperialism – as well as along the Mediterranean coast connecting North Africa with Southern Europe and the Middle East.[15] Third World, anti-colonial, South-South, and internationalist alliances forged with the Maghreb across the twentieth and twenty-first centuries add another supranational dimension to these discussions. The context of the Maghreb further invites us to examine the relationship of different models of colonial occupation to language policy, education, public welfare and civic reform, in addition to various iterations of post-independence national identity. To teach the Maghreb as both a geopolitical entity and an imagined space – what Khatibi describes as "Le Maghreb comme horizon de pensée" (the Maghreb as a horizon of thought) – inevitably destabilizes many of the ethno-national and linguistic categories grafted onto "the Arab world" as a geopolitical and ideological construct.[16] Exposing our students to the complex relations of exchange that exist within neocolonial and neoliberal contexts reveals the subtle ways in which asymmetries of power are confronted, contested and reshaped by cultural materials and their attendant systems of knowledge production, distribution and circulation.

Decolonizing the language question

Borrowing from the critical lexicon of the theorist Mikhail Bakhtin, I propose that the *polyphonic* and *heteroglossic/heterologic* dimensions of Maghrebi cultural production can radically transform how literary scholars conceive of the national as well as epistemological boundaries of languages, texts and their reading practices.[17] Bakhtin invokes the musical concept of *polyphony* to discuss the presence of multiple autonomous voices within a text, while the theories of *heteroglossia* and *heterology* refer to the multiplicity of national languages within one culture, and "the internal heterogeneity of one single natural language," respectively (Zbinden 2006, 69). Bakhtin's theorization of the dialogic coexistence of multiple social voices and types within a given semiotic community – each with their own distinct cultural and ideological inflections – aptly applies to the context of the Maghreb.

If we understand the field of Arab/ic literary studies to be haunted by the specter of imperialism, then one must wonder how the complex colonial dynamics that have marked the region of the Maghreb for centuries have shaped its literary production and reception (Tageldin 2010, 424). In particular, the ambivalent relationship of the indigenous peoples of the Maghreb to Arabic *as a colonial language* in many ways undermines the privileging of European geopolitical as well as cultural imperialism in the Middle East and North Africa. The stringent French colonial policies restricting the use of Arabic in education, government and policy fractured a linguistic landscape where Modern Standard Arabic, in contrast to local dialects, Kabyle and Tamazight, had little traction due to low literacy rates – particularly among women and rural populations. While colonial educational policies varied among the countries of the Maghreb as much as economic and political strategies, Arabic language instruction largely fell under the jurisdiction of Islamic schools. Algeria, as the longest occupied and only settler colony in the region, had the most severe language reforms, with a centralized educational system administered by the Jesuit missionaries *Pères Blancs* and *Soeurs Blanches*.[18] In this context, writing in French was a material reality, rather than a "choice," for most Maghrebi intellectuals who had access to public or private education.

Many authors who emerged from the machinery of French colonial education better equipped to pen their works in French, attempted later in life – largely unsuccessfully – to transition to Arabic. The gifted Algerian novelist and poet Malek Haddad (1927–78), for example, wrote in French until Algeria won its independence. He then infamously took an oath never to write in a language not his own, only to die "by the might of his silence to become a martyr of the Arabic language" (Mosteghanemi 2000: n.p.). Assia Djebar (b. Fatma Zohra Imalayen 1936–2015), who had a prolific career writing Francophone literature and was the first writer from North Africa to be inducted into the illustrious ranks of the *Académie française* as one of their 40 *immortels*, shared a somewhat similar trajectory. After publishing a series of successful novels in French during the 1950s and 1960s, Djebar took a decade-long literary hiatus during which she studied classical Arabic while teaching history, film and literature at the University of Algiers. Her 1985 magnum opus *L'Amour la fantasia* was the belabored product of this period of linguistic reckoning from which French emerged the triumphant language. Other writers were more successful in transitioning from French to Arabic, some even producing bilingual editions or translations of their own work. Mauritanian novelist Moussa Ould Ebnou, for example, published his second novel in both French and Arabic under different titles: *Barzakh* and *Madīnat al-Riyāḥ* (The Windy City), leaving critics baffled as to which edition was the original.[19] The Algerian novelist Rachid Boudjedjra (Rashīd Abū Jadra) similarly switched from French to Arabic in 1981, although he later returned to writing in French. Finally, Kateb Yacine, who wrote his novels in French, was renowned for blending French, Modern Standard Arabic, Algerian dialect, as well as Kabyle and Tamazight in the productions of his popular theater troupe that toured Algeria to an audience of students, workers and farmers.[20]

Writers from the Maghreb, however, have long been navigating this diverse linguistic topography in creative and highly conceptual ways. Francophone novelists, in particular, often negotiate their linguistic ambivalence by adopting a playful approach in their writing. Their works tend to be punctuated by self-conscious meditations on their relationship to French, manipulations of its grammatical dictates, the use of Franco-Arabic neologisms, the mapping of Arabic sentence structure and word order onto French, or simply the inclusion of transliterated words from Arabic without an equivalent translation. This is usually coupled with dense intertextual references that engage the broader Arab/ic canon of classic through modern history, literature, philosophy and the arts. Examples of this writing style can be found across the Maghreb, but particularly in the fiction of Rachid Boudjedra, Driss Chraïbi, Tahar Djaout, Assia Djebar, Malek Haddad, Abdelkebir Khatibi, Abdelwahab Meddeb, Abdelhak Serhane and Kateb Yacine, in addition to the avant-garde poetry of Abdellatif Laâbi, Mohammed Khaïr Eddine and Mostafa Nissaboury. Most of these authors have been translated into English, and their works provide a productively challenging introduction to Maghrebi literature for students of Arab/ic, comparative and world literatures.

While the colonial context of the French language's imposition onto the Maghreb rendered it a fraught vehicle for cultural production, Arabic was by no means neutral. This reality was further exacerbated by French imperial divide-and-conquer strategies that fueled tensions between Francophone, Arabophone and Berberophone populations. Many intellectuals took a staunch stance against the use of the "colonial language" of French in Maghrebi literature. This was particularly the case in Algeria, a settler colony that suffered the region's most aggressive occupation, harshest colonial and cultural assimilationist policies, as well as a protracted and violent eight-year war for independence. Currents of Arab ethno-nationalism subsequently emerged in much of the anti-colonial and decolonizing rhetoric within Algeria.[21] This nationalism relied heavily upon Arabic and Islam as the torchbearers of the nascent post-independence state, as is evidenced by the populist slogan, "Islam is my religion, Arabic is my language, Algeria is my homeland." By way of example, when the Arabophone Algerian novelist al-Ṭāhir Waṭṭār was asked by an interviewer whether the murder of the Francophone novelist Tahar Djaout in 1993 was a loss for Algeria, he infamously replied that it was "a loss for his children, a loss for his wife, and a loss for France" (Waṭṭār n.d.).[22] He further elaborated that "Tahar Djaout was mistaken when he considered the French language to be an Algerian and national language. French, in Algeria, is the language of the administration, the language of the elite [...] This is one form through which French colonialism continues and it is our right to refuse this. It is [in fact] our responsibility to refuse it" (ibid.). Djaout was one of many victims claimed during a targeted attack on Francophone and Berberophone intellectuals and journalists that took place during Algeria's civil war of the 1990s.[23] Waṭṭār's comments thus reveal the deeply entrenched ideological and political stakes of these linguistic, literary and aesthetic questions in the Maghreb – even decades after independence.

While some Maghrebi intellectuals have agreed with Waṭṭār's arguably myopic views on Francophone writing, most Arabophone writers have engaged intertextually with the region's various ethno-linguistic traditions. In addition to French, a number of Arabophone authors integrate Kabyle, Tamazight or local dialects into their poetry, theater and fiction. For example, the novels of the Amazigh Moroccan writer Driss Mesnaoui, who founded the Moroccan Association for Popular Poetry, are formally hybridized in their invocation of the tradition of *Zajal* – oral strophic poetry often delivered in dialect – as well as linguistically in their use of *darija* (Moroccan dialect).[24] While these literary choices might ultimately restrict the readership of these works to a national or in some cases even local audience, they reflect a desire to preserve cultural patrimony while democratizing access to knowledge outside traditional bourgeois-literate circles. Pierre Joris and Habib Tengour's recently published anthology *Poems for the Millennium*, is an invaluable resource for the classroom in this regard. Providing commentary alongside original translations into English, it anthologizes 27 centuries of oral and written poetic traditions from Algeria, Morocco, Libya, Mauritania and Tunisia – spanning early pictograms and rock paintings, through contemporary Maghrebi and diasporic writing. The volume highlights the diverse influences and voices that mark Maghrebi literature by bringing together various languages – such as Tamazight, Phoenician, Latin, Turkish, French and Arabic – in addition to literary, anthropological and historical sources.

The breadth and diversity of Maghrebi literature certainly explains why not only scholars and instructors, but also translators and publishers might shy away from it – as heavily annotated translations are not particularly marketable. Marilyn Booth, one of the most prolific translators of Arabic fiction, has commented on the powerlessness of Arabic translators in the face of commercialized publishing – particularly in the wake of 11 September 2001. In a recent interview she remarked:

> I'm delighted that Arabic literature is more on the international map now, but distressed that what can get published in translation is in some ways more constrained. Publishers want BLING! What many of us want to translate are the intense and beautifully written and consummately constructed but not always easy novels of many writers throughout the Arab world. It is a bit frustrating that certain rather narrow conceptions of "market" – and holdovers of Orientalist concepts of what writers from Arabic-speaking societies should be saying – govern what gets taken.
>
> *(Booth 2016)*[25]

Thus, while Maghrebi literature is not necessarily written with a global or translation audience in mind – as some critics have argued about the work of Orhan Pamuk or Haruki Murakami for example – they are symptomatic of a cultural consciousness that is not bound within a singular ethno-linguistic tradition (Hijiya-Kirschnereit n.d.). Maghrebi literature and criticism should consequently be translated and taught not in spite of, but rather *because of* its supposed recalcitrance. In my experience, while students are certainly challenged by these works, they provide an introduction to the culturally and linguistically heterogeneous world of the Maghreb, while teaching an invaluable lesson in the kinds of reading practices fostered by the discipline of comparative literature.

Algerian novelist Assia Djebar's 1985 *L'Amour la fantasia* (translated into English as *Fantasia: An Algerian Cavalcade*) is an exemplary novel to teach the Maghreb's fraught colonial history and its relationship to language.[26] The work is a polyphonic assemblage that weaves together French archival records and eyewitness accounts of the occupation of Algeria in the 1830s, oral histories recorded in Algerian dialect and Tamazight of women involved in the war of independence from 1954 through 1962, alongside Djebar's personal memories and reflections. Blurring the lines between history and memory, the text's structural creativity troubles students' understandings of the formal category of the novel. It further draws analogies between the violence of Arabization during the Islamic conquest of the seventh century, and the French occupation of the 1830s that decimated approximately one-third of Algeria's population. It does so through references to the indigenous Tuareg, the imposition of the Arabic language by the Banu Hilal tribes, and Ibn Khaldun's graphic accounts of the forced assimilation of the Imazighen (Djebar 1993, 69, 71, 301).[27] Moreover, as a Francophone writer of Amazigh descent, Djebar self-consciously reveals her own personal ambivalences towards both Arabic and French as "colonial languages." I have taught the novel with immense success in general education as well as specialized courses on Arab/ic, Francophone, Maghrebi and comparative literature.

As Djebar's work demonstrates, the ethno-linguistic diversity of the Maghreb has contributed to the production of an intellectually (although not always politically) pluralistic culture. Similarly, Maghrebi supranational rhetoric often invokes both imagined as well as historical models of ethnic, linguistic or religious affiliation. A number of literary invocations of the Ottoman Empire and medieval al-Andalus, for example, have relied upon a nostalgic reimagining of the concept of empire.[28] Arabic literary scholar William Granara argues that Andalusia as a literary topos or chronotope appears across the history of the Arabic novel more than simply as "an 'interfaith utopia,' a cosmopolitan of high culture, religious tolerance, and political ascendency" (Granara 2005, 58). He adds, "the historical consciousness of the 'Andalusian' novel reflects on, explains, and critiques the current state of affairs in the Arab world" (ibid., 57). Similarly, Maghrebi literature and criticism under colonial rule and during decolonization often treated al-Andalus as an alternative to the *mission civilisatrice* underlying French imperial rhetoric. The first Arabophone periodicals in Morocco, for example, emphasized the positive influence that Islamic art, architecture, literature, music, science and philosophy had on Europeans of the Iberian Peninsula (Ellis 2007, 195). Similarly, a number of Tunisian writers and scholars have theorized a transhistorical trans-Mediterranean genealogy, in order to decenter French colonial history (Omri 2005, 288–291).

A fascinating and prolific writer to teach in this regard is Bensalem Himmich, a Moroccan novelist and Islamic philosophy professor at Rabat's Mohammed V University. Himmich's historical novels, which have recently begun to appear in English translation, reanimate early figures of Islamic history in a manner that is socially, culturally and politically prescient to the contemporary Maghreb – not unlike the work of the Lebanese intellectual Jurji Zaydan. His novels: *al-'Allamah* (translated as *The Polymath*) on the fourteenth-century North African historiographer and philosopher Ibn Khaldūn; *Majnūn al-Ḥukm* (translated as *The Theocrat*) on the Fatimid caliph Abu 'Ali Mansur Tāriq al-Ḥākim who ruled Egypt during the tenth century under the adopted name of al-Ḥakim bi 'Amr Allāh (Ruler by God's command); and *Hādhā al-Andalūsī* (translated as *A Muslim Suicide*) on the thirteenth-century Sufi philosopher Ibn Sab'īn from Murcia in al-Andalus, offer a critical introduction to contemporary Arabophone historical fiction from the region.

Lessons in reading

As the above discussion of literary and theoretical materials reveals, Maghrebi intellectual production of the twentieth century offers a diverse cultural tapestry that can be mobilized in the classroom in a variety of fashions. Troubling the categories of form and content, structure and style, as well as language and ideology, these thinkers strove to generate conceptual frameworks for Maghrebi modernity that were part of a supranational community of ideas and imagined geographies encapsulating the Middle East, Sub-Saharan Africa, the Mediterranean and Europe. Moreover, their reflections on and use of the Maghreb's various ethno-linguistic traditions challenge not only the teleology of pre/post/neo-colonial, but more crucially, how we conceive of the relationship between language and national identity. The "lesson" here is thus largely a theoretical one, which seeks to open up avenues of critical inquiry that can be engaged in classrooms of both undergraduate and graduate instruction. Debunking the idea that national literature must be grounded in a singular ethno-linguistic tradition, the introduction of Maghrebi literature and its criticism promotes a pluralistic and polyphonic cultural hermeneutics.

To explore Arab/ic literary pedagogy is to introduce a host of other considerations: from the institutional structuring of academic disciplines and departments, to US geopolitical interests and policies. It invites us to examine how the manner in which we periodize, taxonomize and structure our discipline delimits the formation of literary canons – namely, which texts are read, translated, anthologized and consequently taught. This might cause us to pause on our intellectual, ethical or political obligations as scholars and teachers in a field whose recent growth in the United States is for better or worse bookended by 9/11 and the "Arab Spring." What I hope to highlight here are the questions that many of us in the field should be, and often are, continually asking ourselves about our research, teaching, as well as institutional personas and practices.

In the spirit of offering new pedagogical points of entry into Maghrebi literature and criticism, this chapter has attempted to reroute modern Arab/ic literary history via intellectual discourses and geopolitical networks emerging from the Maghreb. It did so by examining: the Maghreb as a socially imagined space; the influence of (neo)colonial and orientalist epistemologies on the Maghreb's elision from intellectual or cultural histories of the Middle East; and finally, the relationship between ethno-linguistic diversity and Maghrebi conceptualizations of national and supranational identity. I propose that introducing these inquiries into our classrooms – in tandem with the close reading of primary and secondary materials from the Maghreb – exposes our students to a more nuanced understanding of Arab intellectual and cultural history. By approaching works from the Maghreb as semiotically and culturally unstable texts – even in the monolingual context of teaching in translation – one must partake in the kinds of decentered thinking and reading practices invoked by Abdelkebir Khatibi and other Maghrebi intellectuals. The corpus of Maghrebi literature and criticism thus necessitates that students approach it as a perpetually shifting site of confluence, translation, and heterogeneity – an invaluable lesson for the critical reframing of Arab/ic, comparative and world literatures.

Appendix of literary and critical sources of the Maghreb

Arabophone Maghrebi literature

Algeria

Chouaki, Aziz. *The Stars of Algiers*. Trans. Ros Schwartz and Lulu Norman. Minneapolis, MN: Graywolf Press, 2004.
Himmich, Bensalem. *The Polymath*. Trans. Roger Allen. Cairo and New York: American University in Cairo Press, 2004.
Himmich, Bensalem. *The Theocrat*. Trans. Roger Allen. Cairo and New York: American University in Cairo Press, 2009.
Himmich, Bensalem. *A Muslim Suicide*. Trans. Roger Allen. Syracuse, NY: Syracuse University Press, 2011.
Mosteghanemi, Ahlam. *Memory in the Flesh*. Trans. Baria Ahmar Sreih and Peter Clark. Cairo and New York: The American University in Cairo Press, 2000.
Mosteghanemi, Ahlam. *Chaos of the Sense*. Trans. Baria Ahmar Sreih. Cairo and New York: The American University in Cairo Press, 2007.
Mosteghanemi, Ahlam. *The Art of Forgetting*. Trans. Raphael Cohen. Qatar: Bloomsbury Qatar, 2011.
Watar, Tahir. *The Earthquake*. Trans. William Granara. London: Saqi Books, 2000.

Morocco

Berrada, Mohamed. *The Game of Forgetting*. Trans. Issa J. Boullata. London: Interlink Publishing Group, 1998.
Berrada, Mohamed. *The Fugitive Light*. Trans. Issa J. Boullata. Syracuse, NY: Syracuse University Press, 2002.
Choukri, Mohammed. *For Bread Alone*. Trans. Paul Bowles. London: Telegram Books, 2006.

Tunisia

Mosbahi, Hassouna. *A Tunisian Tale*. Trans. Max Weiss. Cairo and New York: The American University in Cairo Press, 2011.
Nasr, Hassan. *Return to Dar Al-Basha*. Trans. William Hutchins. Syracuse, NY: Syracuse University Press, 2006.

Francophone Maghrebi literature

Algeria

Boudjedra, Rachid. *The Repudiation*. Trans. Golda Lambrova. Washington, DC: Three Continents Press, 1995.
Boudjedra, Rachid. *The Obstinate Snail*. Trans. Leon Stephens. Las Cruces, NM: Xenos Books, 2013.

Boudjedra, Rachid. *The Barbary Figs*. Trans. André Naffis-Sahely. London: Haus Publishing, 2013.

Daoud, Kamel. *The Mersault Investigation*. Trans. John Cullen. New York: Other Press, 2015.

Dib, Mohammed. *Who Remembers the Sea*. Trans. Louis Tremaine. Washington, DC: Three Continents Press, 1985.

Dib, Mohammed. *The Savage Night*. Trans. C. Dickson. Lincoln, NE: Bison Books, 2001.

Dib, Mohammed. *At the Café and The Talisman*. Trans. C. Dickson. Charlottesville: University of Virginia Press, 2011.

Djaout, Tahar. *The Watchers*. Trans. Marjolijn de Jager. Minneapolis, MN: Ruminator Books, 2002.

Djaout, Tahar. *The Last Summer of Reason*. Trans. Marjolijn de Jager. Lincoln, NE: Bison Books, 2007.

Djebar, Assia. *Women of Algiers in their Apartments*. Trans. Marjolijn de Jager and Clarissa Zimra. Charlottesville: University of Virginia Press, 1992.

Djebar, Assia. *Fantasia: An Algerian Cavalcade*. Trans. Dorothy S. Blair. Portsmouth, NH: Heinemann, 1993.

Djebar, Assia. *A Sister to Scheherazade*. Trans. Dorothy S. Blair. Portsmouth, NH: Heinemann, 1993.

Djebar, Assia. *Far from Medina: Daughters of Ishmael*. Trans. Dorothy S. Blair. London: Quartet Books, 1994.

Djebar, Assia. *So Vast the Prison*. Trans. Betsy Wing. New York: Seven Stories Press, 1999.

Djebar, Assia. *Algerian White*. Trans. David Kelley and Marjolijn de Jager. New York: Seven Stories Press, 2000.

Djebar, Assia. *Children of the New World*. Trans. Marjojin de Jager. New York: Feminist Press at the City University of New York, 2005.

Djebar, Assia. *The Tongue's Blood Does Not Run Dry*. Trans. Tegan Raleigh. New York: Seven Stories Press, 2006.

Feraoun, Mouloud. *The Poor Man's Son*. Trans. James D. Le Seur. Charlottesville: University of Virginia Press, 2005.

Yacine, Kateb. *Nedjma*. Trans. Richard Howard. Charlottesville: University Press of Virginia, 1991.

Morocco

Ben Jelloun, Tahar. *The Sand Child*. Trans. Alan Sheridan. Baltimore, MD: Johns Hopkins University Press, 2000.

Ben Jelloun, Tahar. *The Sacred Night*. Trans. Alan Sheridan. Baltimore, MD: Johns Hopkins University Press, 2000.

Ben Jelloun, Tahar. *This Blinding Absence of Light*. Trans. Linda Coverdale. New York: Penguin Books, 2006.

Ben Jelloun, Tahar. *Leaving Tangiers*. Trans. Linda Coverdale. New York: Penguin Books, 2009.

Ben Jelloun, *Tahar. A Palace in the Old Village*. Trans. Linda Coverdale. New York: Penguin Books, 2011.

Chraïbi, Driss. *Heirs to the Past*. Trans. Len Ortzen. Portsmouth, NH: Heinemann, 1972.

Chraïbi, Driss. *Flutes of Death*. Trans. Robin A. Roosevelt. Washington, DC: Three Continents Press, 1985.

Chraïbi, Driss. *Mother Spring*. Trans. Hugh A. Harter. Washington, DC: Three Continents Press, 1987.

Chraïbi, Driss. *The Butts*. Trans. Hugh A. Harter. Washington, DC: Three Continents Press, 1987.

Chraïbi, Driss. *Birth at Dawn*. Trans. Anne Woollcombe. Washington, DC: Three Continents Press, 1990.

Chraïbi, Driss. *The Simple Past*. Trans. Hugh A. Harter. Washington, DC: Three Continents Press, 1990.

Chraïbi, Driss. *Inspector Ali*. Trans. Laura McGlashan. Washington, DC: Three Continents Press, 1994.

Chraïbi, Driss. *Mohammed*. Trans. Nadia Benabid. Boulder, CO: Lynne Rienner Publishers, 1998.

Chraïbi, Driss. *Mother Comes of Age*. Trans. Hugh A. Harter. Washington, DC: Three Continents Press, 1998.

Khatibi, Abdelkebir. *Love in Two Languages*. Trans. Richard Howard. Minneapolis: University of Minnesota Press, 1990.

Laâbi, Abdellatif. *The World's Embrace*. Trans. Victor Reinking, Anne George, Edris Makward & Pierre Joris. San Francisco, CA: City Light Books, 2003.

Laâbi, Abdellatif. *The Rule of Barbarism*. Trans. André Nafis-Sahely. New York: Pirogue Collective, 2012.

Laâbi, Abdellatif. *The Bottom of the Jar*. Trans André Naffis-Sahely. New York: Archipelago Books, 2013.

Mimouni, Rachid. *The Ogre's Embrace*. Trans. Shirley Eber. London: Quartet Books, 1994.

Tunisia

Meddeb, Abdelwahab. *Talismano*. Trans. Jane Kuntz. Champaign, IL: Dalkey Archive Press, 2011.

Memmi, Albert. T*he Pillar of Salt*. Trans. Edouard Roditi. Boston, MA: Beacon Press Books, 1992.

Anthologies

Allen, Roger, ed. *Moroccan Folktales*. Syracuse, NY: Syracuse University Press, 2003.

Clark, Peter, ed. *Sardines and Oranges: Short Stories from North Africa*. London: Banipal Books, 2014.

Harrison, Olivia C. and Teresa Villa-Ignacio, eds. *Souffles-Anfas: A Critical Anthology from the Moroccan Journal of Culture and Politics*. Stanford, CA: Stanford University Press, 2016.

Joris, Pierre and Habib Tengour, eds. *Poems for the Millennium, Volume 4: The University of California Book of North African Literature*. Berkeley, CA: University of California Press, 2012.

Critical and historical scholarship on the Maghreb

Abun-Nasr, Jamil M. *A History of the Maghreb in the Muslim Period*. Cambridge: Cambridge University Press, 1987.

Amin, Khalid and Marvin A. *Carlson. The Theatres of Morocco, Algeria and Tunisia Performance Traditions of the Maghreb*. Hampshire: Palgrave Macmillan, 2012.

Anderson, Lisa. *The State and Social Transformation in Tunisia and Libya, 1830–1980*. Princeton, NJ: Princeton University Press, 1986.

Bensmaïa, Réda. *Experimental Nations: Or, the Invention of the Maghreb*. Princeton, NJ: Princeton University Press, 2003.

Berger, Anne-Emmanuelle, ed. *Algeria in Others' Languages*. Ithaca, NY: Cornell University Press, 2002.

Bourqia, Rahma and Susan Gilson Miller, eds. *In the Shadow of the Sultan: Culture, Power and Politics in Morocco*. Cambridge, MA: Harvard University Press, 1999.

Celik, Zeynap, Julia Clancy-Smith and Frances Terpak, eds. *Walls of Algiers: Narratives of the City Through Text and Image*. Los Angeles, CA: Getty Research Institute, 2009.

Clancy-Smith, Julie. *Rebel and Saint: Muslim Notables, Populist Protest, Colonial Encounters: Algeria and Tunisia, 1800–1904*. Berkeley, CA: University of California Press, 1994.

Clancy-Smith, Julie. *Mediterraneans: North Africa and Europe in an Age of Migration, c. 1800–1900*. Berkeley, CA: University of California Press, 2012.

Cox, Debbie. *Politics, Language and Gender in the Algerian Arabic Novel*. London: Edwin Mellon Press, 2002.

Fontaine, Jean. "Arabic Language Tunisian Literature (1956–1990)." *Research in African Literatures* (Summer 1992): 183–193.

Harrison, Olivia C. "Cross-Colonial Poetics: Souffles-Anfas and the Figure of Palestine." *PMLA* 128:2 (March 2013): 353–369.

Harrison, Olivia C. *Transcolonial Maghreb: Imagining Palestine in the Era of Decolonization*. Stanford, CA: Stanford University Press, 2015.

Hayes, Jarrod. *Queer Nations: Marginal Sexualities in the Maghreb*. Chicago, IL: University of Chicago Press, 2000.

Kaye, Jacqueline and Abdelhamid Zoubir. *The Ambiguous Compromise: Language, Literature and National Identity in Algeria and Morocco*. New York: Routledge, 1990.

Laroui, Abdallah. *The Crisis of the Arab Intellectual: Traditionalism or Historicism?* Trans. Diarmid Cammell. Berkeley, CA: University of California Press, 1977.

Laroui, Abdallah. *The History of the Maghreb: An Interpretive Essay*. Princeton, NJ: Princeton Studies on the Near East – ACLA Humanities e-Book, 2008.
McDougall, James. "Myth and Counter-Myth: 'The Berber' as National Signifier in Algerian Historiographies." *Radical History Review* 86 (Spring 2003): 66–88.
McDougall, James. *History and the Culture of Nationalism in Algeria*. Cambridge and New York: Cambridge University Press, 2006.
McDougall, James. "Dream of Exile, Promise of Home: Language, Education and Arabism in Algeria." *International Journal of Middle East Studies* 43 (2011): 251–270.
Mernissi, Fatima. *The Forgotten Queens of Islam*. Minneapolis: University of Minnesota Press, 1995.
Mernissi, Fatima. *Women's Rebellion and Islamic Memory*. London: Zed Books, 1996.
Moore, Lindsey. *Arab, Muslim, Woman: Voice and Vision in Postcolonial Literature and Film*. New York: Routledge, 2008.
Mortimer, Mildred. *Journeys through the French African Novel*. Portsmouth, NH: Heinemann, 1990.
Mortimer, Mildred. *Maghrebian Mosaic: A Literature in Translation*. Boulder, CO: Lynne Reinner Publishers, 2001.
Omri, Mohamed-Salah. "History, Literature, and Settler Colonialism in North Africa." *Modern Language Quarterly* 66:3 (September 2005): 273–298.
Omri, Mohamed-Salah. *Nationalism, Islam and World Literature: Sites of Confluence in the Writings of Mahmud al-Mas'di*. London and New York: Routledge, 2006.
Orlando, Valerie. *Nomadic Voices of Exile: Feminine Identity in Francophone Literature of the Maghreb*. Athens, OH: Ohio University Press, 1999.
Orlando, Valerie. *Francophone Voices of the "New" Morocco in Film and Print: (Re) presenting a Society in Transition*. Hampshire: Palgrave Macmillan, 2009.
Pandolfo, Stefania. *Impasse of the Angels: Scenes from a Moroccan Space of Memory*. Chicago, IL: University of Chicago Press, 1997.
Pennell, C.R. *Morocco Since 1830: A History*. London: Hurst & Company, 1988.
Segalla, Spencer D. *The Moroccan Soul: French Education, Colonial Ethnology, and Muslim Resistance, 1912–1956*. Lincoln, NE: University of Nebraska Press, 2009.
Shepard, Todd. *The Invention of Decolonization: The Algerian War and the Remaking of France*. Ithaca, NY: Cornell University Press, 2006.
Wehrs, Donald. *Islam, Ethics, Revolt: Politics and Piety in Francophone West African and Maghreb Narrative*. London: Lexington Books, 2008.

Online resources:

The Maghrebi Studies site: http://maghrebs.ipower.com/newmaghrebistudies.nitle.org/index.php/maghrebi.html
Arabic Literature (in translation): http://arablit.wordpress.com/
LIMAG: Littérature du Maghreb: www.limag.com
Souffles-Anfas: http://bnm.bnrm.ma:86/ListeVol.aspx?IDC=3 [French] http://bnm.bnrm.ma:86/ListeVol.aspx?IDC=4 [Arabic]

Notes

1 Unless otherwise noted, all translations are my own.
2 For the names of Maghrebi intellectuals I have opted to use the standardized transliterations common within the Maghreb. Otherwise, I will be employing a modified version of the *IJMES* system of transliteration.
3 On how Maghrebi cultural production complicates teleological narratives of decolonization, nationalism, and acculturation within cultural histories of the Middle East and North Africa, see: El Shakry 2017.
4 I am referring in particular to: Allan 2012; al-Musawi 1999, 2002, 2007, 2010, 2015; El-Ariss 2013; Holt 2009; Khaldi 2012; Omri 2006, 2005, 2008; Sacks 2007; Selim 2004a, 2004b, 2011; Sheehi 2000, 2004, 2012; and Tageldin 2011, 2012.
5 Marie-Therèse Ellis makes a parallel point by applying Panivong Norindr's deconstruction of French Indochina as "an elaborate fiction, a modern phantasmatic assemblage" to the use of the term *L'Afrique du Nord* in French colonial periodicals (Ellis 2007, 33).
6 The official website is www.maghrebarabe.org/en/.
7 The *nahḍah* refers to a period of intellectual "awakening," "renewal" or "revival" in Arab cultural production from the late nineteenth through early twentieth centuries, which is said to have followed a long phase of intellectual *inḥiṭaṭ* (decline or degeneration). Recent scholarship has problematized the orientalist epistemologies underlying much of the discourse on the *nahḍah.*
8 Ellis points to the unique topography of cultural exchange in Arabophone periodicals of colonial Morocco, whereby the *Mashriq* was the means through which many intellectuals mediated European thought while circumventing the colonial agent (Ellis 2007, 29).
9 In *Orientalism*, Edward Said argues that the creation of the Orient as an object of analysis and scholarship was part and parcel of broader geopolitical attempts to understand the region in order to control it.
10 A quick survey reveals that the majority of departments in the United States continue to abide by a "Near East" or "Middle East" paradigm. These include: Princeton, Columbia, Cornell, Johns Hopkins, NYU, Berkeley, UCLA, University of Michigan, Yale, University of Chicago, University of Pennsylvania, University of Washington, Indiana University Bloomington, University of Texas, Harvard and Dartmouth, among others.
11 Consider the World Bank, US Department of State, UN Office of the High Commissioner for Human Rights, UN High Commissioner for Refugees, the Organisation for Economic Co-operation and Development (OECD), the Social Science Research Council (SSRC) and Fulbright.
12 Examples include: the *Middle East Studies Association*, *International Journal of Middle East Studies*, *Journal of Arabic Literature*, *Journal of Arabic and Islamic Studies*, *Middle Eastern Studies* and the *Journal of Middle East Women's Studies*, among others.
13 The Kabyle (Iqvayliyen) are a Berberophone ethnic group native to Kabylie in northern Algeria who speak Kabyle. The Imazighen (singular: Amazigh) or "Berbers" are the indigenous populations that inhabited North Africa prior to the Arabo-Islamic conquests of the seventh century. They speak a variety of dialects from the Afro-Asiatic language family including Tamazight. Between the seventh and twelfth centuries, the Imazighen were compelled to disperse throughout various parts of the Sahara. It is estimated that Morocco's Berberophone community is approximately 40% of the population, with Algeria at about 25% (Chaker 2001). In 2001, one study claimed that there were 20,000,000 Tamazight speakers throughout Morocco and Algeria alone (El Aissati). On the history of the Imazighen, particularly in relation to colonial and state attempts to assimilate them, see McDougall 2003.
14 On Arab-Brazilian literature, see Hassan 2011, and Amar 2014. On Swedish-Arab/ic literary exchanges, see the scholarship of Johanna Sellman. Examples of Italian-Arab migrant literature include: Mohamed Bouchane (for a translation of his story "Call Me Ali," see Parati 1999, 43–57), as well as Aziz Bouzidy and Nassera Chohra (see

Lammendola 2013). For an interview with the German-Iraqi writer Abbas Khider on his use of German, see: Khider 2016. Also see: Khalil and Iocca 1995.

15 Mohamed-Salah Omri thoughtfully discusses the Mediterranean as a geopolitical and imagined space in his essay "History, Literature, and Settler Colonialism in North Africa." Also see Clancy-Smith 2012.

16 An earlier version of Khatibi's essay "Pensée-autre," which appears in his collection *Maghreb Pluriel*, was titled "Le Maghreb comme horizon de pensée." For a detailed discussion of this metaphor in Khatibi's work, see Harrison 2013, 365–6.

17 See Bakhtin 1981, 1984. On the translational and theoretical significance of Bakhtin's critical work in the Maghreb, see: El Shakry, 2016.

18 For an overview of French colonial education and language policies, see: Heggoy and Zingg 1976; and Aitsiselmi and Marley 2008. The data referenced by Aitsiselmi and Marley is from Benrabah 1999: 79. On Algeria, see: McDougall 2011; as well as Clancy-Smith 1994. On Morocco, see: Segalla 2009. On Tunisia, see: Anderson 1986.

19 While the French edition was published earlier, it is unclear which was written first. For an analysis of the novel and its linguistic ambiguity, see: Qader 2002.

20 On the different linguistic registers in Kateb Yacine's corpus, see: Salhi 1999.

21 On Arabism in Algeria, see: McDougall 2011, 266.

22 This comment is from an interview that aired in Arabic on the Franco-German station *Arte* in 1994 and over the BBC in the UK. For a more in-depth discussion of al-Ṭāhir Waṭṭār and his views on Arabism and Islamism, please see: El Shakry 2011.

23 Assia Djebar offers a poetic testimony of mourning in her book *Le Blanc de l'Algérie* that recounts the loss of her compatriots during the Algerian civil war. On Djaout, see: Šukys 2007.

24 Alexander E. Elinson's work on Moroccan literature traces the blending of novelistic and poetic genres with the *Maqama* and *Zajal* forms, as well as the use of storytelling, orality and dialect in medieval Andalusian through modern Moroccan literature. See Elinson 2009a, 2013a. Elinson also delivered a paper at the 2013 American Comparative Literature Association's annual meeting in Toronto entitled "Re-telling the Story of Moroccan Resistance in the Novels of Driss Mesnaoui."

25 Arabic scholar and translator Elliot Colla explains that: "About 2 percent of the titles published in the US are translated from other languages. And only 2 percent of this tiny number come from Arabic. Which is to say, for every ten thousand books published in English, about four were translated from Arabic" (Colla n.d.).

26 Moroccan novelist Driss Chraïbi also published a trilogy on the Imazighen that creatively explores the Arabo-Islamic conquest. See: *Une enquête au pays* (Flutes of Death, 1981), *La Mère du Printemps* (Mother Spring, 1982), and *Naissance à l'aube* (Birth at Dawn, 1986).

27 The Tuareg are a nomadic Berberophone population inhabiting the North African Sahara of Niger, Mali, Libya, Algeria and Burkina Faso. As French forces expanded into the central Sahara, a number of violent clashes with the Tuareg resulted in the continued annexation of their territories. On the Tuareg see McDougall 2006, 186–188.

28 See Elinson 2009b.

Bibliography

Aitsiselmi, Farid and Dawn Marley. "The role and status of the French language in North Africa." *Studies in French Applied Linguistics*. Ed. Dalila Ayoun. Amsterdam: John Benjamins Publishing Co., 2008.

Allan, Michael. "How Adab Became Literary: Formalism, Orientalism and the Institutions of World Literature." *Journal of Arabic Literature* 43 (2012): 172–196.

al-Musawi, Muhsin. "The Arabic Literary Heritage: The Development of its Genres and Criticism." *Journal of Arabic Literature* 30:2 (1999): 193–195.

al-Musawi, Muhsin. "Engaging Tradition in Modern Arab Poetics." *Journal of Arabic Literature* 33:2 (2002): 172–210.
al-Musawi, Muhsin. "Engaging Globalization in Modern Arabic Literature: Appropriation and Resistance." *Modern Language Quarterly* 68:2 (2007): 305–329.
al-Musawi, Muhsin. "Beyond the Modernity Complex: 'Abd al-Ḥakīm Qāsim's Re-writing of the Nahḍah Self-narrative." *Journal of Arabic Literature* 41 (2010): 22–45.
al-Musawi, Muhsin. *The Medieval Islamic Republic of Letters: Arabic Knowledge Construction*. Notre Dame, IN: University of Notre Dame Press, 2015.
Amar, Paul, ed. *The Middle East and Brazil: Perspectives on the New Global South*. Bloomington, IN: Indiana University Press, 2014.
Anderson, Lisa. *The State and Social Transformation in Tunisia and Libya, 1830–1980*. Princeton, NJ: Princeton University Press, 1986.
Bakhtin, Mikhail M. *The Dialogic Imagination*. Trans. Caryl Emerson & Michael Holquist. Ed. Michael Holquist. Austin: University of Texas Press, 1981.
Bakhtin, Mikhail M. *Problems of Dostoevsky's Poetics*. Trans. & Ed. Caryl Emerson. Minnesota: The University of Minnesota Press, 1984.
Benrabah, M. *Langue et pouvoir en Algérie: histoire d'un traumatisme linguistique*. Paris: Séguire, 1999.
Booth, Marilyn. "Marilyn Booth on What Should Be Obvious (But Isn't) About Translating Modern Arabic Literature." *Arabic Literature* (in English). Web. 1 June 2016.
Chaker, Salem. "Berber Challenge in Algeria, The State of the Question." *Race, Gender and Class* 8:3 (2001): 135–156.
Chraïbi, Driss. *Flutes of Death*. Trans. Robin A. Roosevelt. Washington, DC: Three Continents Press, 1985.
Chraïbi, Driss. *Mother Spring*. Trans. Hugh A. Harter. Washington, DC: Three Continents Press, 1987.
Chraïbi, Driss. *Birth at Dawn*. Trans. Anne Woollcombe. Washington, DC: Three Continents Press, 1990.
Clancy-Smith, Julia. *Rebel and Saint: Muslim Notables, Populist Protest, Colonial Encounters: Algeria and Tunisia, 1800-1904*. Berkeley, CA: University of California Press, 1994.
Clancy-Smith, Julia. *Mediterraneans: North Africa and Europe in an Age of Migration, c. 1800–1900*. Berkeley, CA: University of California Press, 2012.
Colla, Elliot. "The American Reader Seeking the Arab Other." *Ashraq al-Awsat*. Web. 1 June 2016.
Djebar, Assia. *L'Amour, la fantasia*. Paris: Éditions Albin Michel, 1985.
Djebar, Assia. *Fantasia: An Algerian Cavalcade*. Trans. Dorothy S. Blair. Portsmouth, NH: Heinemann, 1993.
Djebar, Assia. *Le Blanc de l'Algérie*. Paris: Éditions Albin Michel S.A., 1995.
Djebar, Assia. *Algerian White*. New York: Seven Stories Press, 2000.
Ebnou, Moussa Ould. *Barzakh*. Paris: L'Harmattan, 1993.
Ebnou, Moussa Ould. *Madīnat al-Riyāḥ*. Beirut: Dar al Adab, 1996.
El Aissati, Abderrahman. "Ethnic Identity, Language Shift, and the Amazigh Voice in Morocco and Algeria." *Race, Gender and Class* 8:3 (2001): 57–69.
El-Ariss, Tarek. *Trials of Arab Modernity*. New York: Fordham University Press, 2013.
Elinson, Alexander E. "Opening the Circle: Storyteller and Audience in Moroccan Prison Literature." *Middle Eastern Literatures* 12:3 (2009a): 289–303.
Elinson, Alexander E. *Looking Back at al-Andalus: The Poetics of Loss and Nostalgia in Medieval Arabic and Hebrew Literature*. Leiden and Boston, MA: Brill, 2009b.
Elinson, Alexander E. "Darija and Changing Writing Practices in Morocco." *International Journal of Middle East Studies* 45 (2013a): 715–730.

Elinson, Alexander E. "Re-telling the Story of Moroccan Resistance in the Novels of Driss Mesnaoui." American Comparative Literature Association Annual Meeting, Toronto. 5 April 2013b.

Ellis, Marie-Therèse Cecilia. *Empire or Umma: Writing Beyond the Nation in Moroccan Periodicals.* Dissertation. University of California, Berkeley, 2007.

El Shakry, Hoda. "Revolutionary Eschatology: Islam and the End of Time in al-Ṭāhir Waṭṭār's al-Zilzāl." *Journal of Arabic Literature* 42:2–3 (2011): 120–147.

El Shakry, Hoda. "Heteroglossia and the Poetics of the Roman Maghrébin." *Contemporary French and Francophone Studies: SITES* 20.2 (2016): 8–17.

El Shakry, Hoda. "Printed Matter(s): Critical Histories and Perspectives on Tunisian Cultural Journals." *ALIF: A Journal of Comparative Poetics* 37 (2017): 1–29.

Granara, William. "Nostalgia, Arab Nationalism, and the Andalusian Chronotope in the Evolution of the Modern Arabic Novel." *Journal of Arabic Literature* 36:1 (2005): 57–73.

Harrison, Olivia C. "Cross-Colonial Poetics: Souffles-Anfas and the Figure of Palestine." *PMLA* 128:2 (March 2013): 353–369.

Hassan, Waïl. "Al-adab al-'arabi-al-barazili: Mu'allaqat Alberto Mussa wa hiwar al-janub-al-janub." *Alif: Journal of Comparative Poetics* 31 (2011): 215–229.

Heggoy, Alf Andrew and Paul J. Zingg. "French Education in Revolutionary North Africa." *International Journal of Middle Eastern Studies* 7 (1976): 571–678.

Hijiya-Kirschnereit, Irmela. "Orchestrating Translations: The Case of Murakami Haruki." Nippon.com. Web. 1 June 2016.

Himmich, Bensalem. *The Polymath.* Cairo & New York: American University in Cairo Press, 2004.

Himmich, Bensalem. *The Theocrat.* Cairo & New York: American University in Cairo Press, 2009.

Himmich, Bensalem. *A Muslim Suicide.* Syracuse, NY: Syracuse University Press, 2011.

Holt, Elizabeth. "Narrative and the Reading Public in 1870s Beirut." *Journal of Arabic Literature* 40 (2009): 37–70.

Joris, Pierre and Habib Tengour, eds. *Poems for the Millennium. Volume 4: The University of California Book of North African Literature.* Berkeley, CA: University of California Press, 2012.

Khaldi, Boutheina. "Multiple Intellectual Engagements?" *Journal of Arabic Literature* 43 (2012): 197–226.

Khalil, Iman O. and Jeannette Iocca. "Arab-German Literature." *World Literature Today* 69:3 Multiculturalism in Contemporary German Literature (Summer 1995): 521–527.

Khatibi, Abdelkebir. *Maghreb Pluriel.* Paris: Éditions Denoël, 1983.

Khider, Abbas. "German is My New Language." Qantara.de Web. 1 June 2016.

Lammendola, Daniel Julian. *Hybridization and Enunciation in Arab-Italian Migrant Literature.* MA thesis. The Ohio State University, 2013.

McDougall, James. "Myth and Counter-Myth: 'The Berber' as National Signifier in Algerian Historiographies." *Radical History Review* 86 (Spring 2003): 66–88.

McDougall, James. *History and the Culture of Nationalism in Algeria.* Cambridge: Cambridge University Press, 2006.

McDougall, James. "Dream of Exile, Promise of Home: Language, Education and Arabism in Algeria." *International Journal of Middle East Studies* 43 (2011): 251–270.

Mosteghanemi, Ahlam. *Memory in the Flesh.* Trans. Naria Ahmar Sreih & Peter Clark. Cairo & New York: The American University in Cairo Press, 2000.

Omri, Mohamed-Salah. "History, Literature, and Settler Colonialism." *Modern Language Quarterly* 66:3 (September 2005): 273–298.

Omri, Mohamed-Salah. *Nationalism, Islam and World Literature*. New York: Routledge, 2006.
Omri, Mohamed-Salah. "Local Narrative Form and Constructions of the Arabic Novel." *NOVEL: A Forum on Fiction* 41:2/3 (Spring–Summer 2008): 244–263.
Parati, Graziella. *Mediterranean Crossroads: Migration Literature in Italy*. New Jersey: Fairleigh Dickinson University Press, 1999.
Qader, Nasrin. "Fictional Testimonies or Testimonial Fictions: Moussa Ould Ebnou's 'Barzakh'." *Research in African Literatures* 33:3 (Autumn 2002): 14–31.
Sacks, Jeffrey. "Futures of Literature: Inhitat, Adab, and Naqd." *Diacritics* 37.4 (Winter 2007): 32–55.
Said, Edward. *Orientalism*. New York: Random House Inc., 1978.
Salhi, Kamel. *The Politics and Aesthetics of Kateb Yacine: From Francophone Literature to Popular Theater in Algeria and Outside*. New York & Ontario: The Edwin Mellen Press, 1999.
Segalla, Spencer D. *The Moroccan Soul: French Education, Colonial Ethnology, and Muslim Resistance, 1912–1956*. Lincoln: University of Nebraska Press, 2009.
Selim, Samah. *The Novel and the Rural Imaginary in Egypt, 1880–1985*. London: Routledge-Curzon, 2004a.
Selim, Samah. "The Nahda: Popular Fiction and the Politics of Translation." *MIT Electronic Journal of Middle East Studies* 4 (Fall 2004b): 71–89.
Selim, Samah. "Toward a New Literary History." *International Journal of Middle East Studies* 43 (2011): 734–736.
Sellman, Johanna. "Jonas Hassen Khemiri." *Banipal: Magazine of Modern Arab Literature* 41 (Summer 2011): 104–105.
Sellman, Johanna. "The Forests of Exile." *Portal 9 Stories and Critical Writing about the City* (Fall 2014). Web. 1 June 2016.
Sheehi, Stephen. "Inscribing the Arab Self: Butrus al-Bustani and Paradigms of Subjective Reform." *British Journal of the Middle Eastern Studies* 27 (2000): 7–24.
Sheehi, Stephen. *Foundations of Arab Modernity*. Gainesville: University of Florida Press, 2004.
Sheehi, Stephen. "Towards a Critical Theory of al-Nahḍah: Epistemology, Ideology and Capital." *Journal of Arabic Literature* 43 (2012): 269–298.
Šukys, Julija. *Silence is Death: The Life and Work of Tahar Djaout*. Lincoln: University of Nebraska Press, 2007.
Tageldin, Shaden. "One Comparative Literature? 'Birth' of a Discipline in French-Egyptian Translation, 1810–1834." *Comparative Literature Studies* 47:4 (2010): 417–445.
Tageldin, Shaden. *Disarming Words: Empire and the Seductions of Translation in Egypt*. Berkeley, CA: University of California Press, 2011.
Tageldin, Shaden. "Proxidistant Reading: Toward a Critical Pedagogy of the Nahḍah in U.S. Comparative Literary Studies." *Journal of Arabic Literature* 43 (2012): 227–268.
Waṭṭār, al-Ṭāhir. "Interview," www.youtube.com/watch?v=T3RREPoRp0A (accessed 1 June 2016).
Zbinden, Karine. *Bakhtin Between East and West: Cross Cultural Transmission*. London: Legenda – Modern Humanities Research Association and Maney Publishing, 2006.

9

TEACHING HUMOR IN ARABIC LITERATURE AND FILM

Tarek El-Ariss

The Axis of Evil Comedy group is one of the many Arab-American responses to 9/11. Dean Obeidallah, Maysoon Zayid, Ahmed Ahmed, Maz Jobrani, and Aron Kader are among the comedians who appropriated the Bush Administration's "Axis of Evil" in reference to Iran, Iraq and North Korea, in order to subvert it. Like "Black is Beautiful" and the term "queer" mark the inscription of othering, *The Axis of Evil Comedy* group "comes clean" on being Arab, Iranian, Muslim, and evil. In this context, laughing at oneself operates as a strategy of doubling by stepping outside oneself as "oneself" is produced through a public and media discourse that fixes identity. In distancing oneself from this fixed identity, humor unsettles the stereotype, suggesting a multiplicity of selves and a complexity of identities.[1] Humor thus functions as a mode of distancing and creating space for the reader and the viewer to relate to the other at a variety of levels.

Reception theory, from Hans-Robert Jauss to Stuart Hall, has taught us that readers – and viewers – bring their prejudices and personal experiences to the text. The reader's cultural landscape and experiences shape his/her reception of the text and the subject matter. Teaching needs to take into account these relations in order to introduce students to different cultural contexts and aesthetic models. Following 9/11, the attention to these experiences and cultural assumptions became essential for teaching Arabic and Islam in the US. Specifically, strategic use of humor and jest in texts from the Arab and Islamic world was key to unsettle stereotypes, engage a difficult political context, and communicate aesthetic values without reducing texts to mere representations of a culture or a political situation.

I was supposed to meet with my students on 9/11 in order to discuss a documentary on Islamic civilization. The meeting, which was to be held in a classroom in New York City's Greenwich Village, never occurred; it was deferred, the way Derrida uses the concept of *différance* to mean both deferral and difference. The class, a basic introduction to Arabic and Middle Eastern literature and culture, would never be the same again. Like many teachers of this subject matter in the US, I had to adapt and adjust, acknowledge and reposition. While teaching Arabic, Islam, and the Middle East has always been political in the academy, 9/11 forced scholars to rethink curricula and devise new ways to engage this unique event. As a teacher of Arabic and comparative literature, I acknowledge and incorporate the political context yet encourage students to move beyond it, thereby resisting the demand to reduce the literary to the sociological and the political, and the novel or film to a cultural account. At a more fundamental level, my aim is to anchor the study of Arabic literature and culture in the Humanities by connecting it to other literatures, genres, and cultural traditions.

My adaptations and repositioning over a decade and a half of trials led to a syllabus that is constantly negotiating the relation between aesthetics and politics yet always grounded in humanizing the other through engagements with his/her imagination expressed in literature, film, blog, and other art forms.[2] From *One Thousand and One Nights*' shattering of the oppressed Arab woman stereotype, to the gay character in Hanan Al-Shaykh's *Only in London* (2001) who negotiates his sexuality across complex cultural dynamics, my course is in constant dialogue with the pedagogical and political questions that inform the teaching of Arabic literature and culture in the academy.

In this essay, I explore humor's unique ability to mediate the relation between the political and the aesthetic after 9/11. Investigating representations of humor in works engaging war and displacement, I examine the effectiveness of specific texts, namely Ziad Doeuri's film about the Lebanese civil war (1975–90), *West Beirut* (1998); Samuel Shimon's autobiographical narrative about immigration and exile, *An Iraqi in Paris: An Autobiographical Novel* (2005); and Suad Amiry's diaries about life under occupation, *Sharon and My Mother-in-Law: Ramallah Diaries* (2004).[3] Engaging theoretical material from al-Jāḥiẓ to Henri Bergson, I argue that in these diaries and film humor humanizes characters by enabling them to overcome their oppressive political realities through self-deprecation and comedy. In this vein, humor's humanizing function allows students "safely" to enter the text about war and conflict, and read it in relation to literary production from various cultural and historical contexts. My approach explores these works' political contexts while simultaneously investigating their poetics across media and genres.

Humor as pedagogical tool

Humor has always been employed as a pedagogical tool that takes into account questions of reception and psychological disposition. In Arab-Islamic culture, humor is found in scripture, literary texts, and scientific treatises. In his fourteenth-century lexicon, *Lisān al-ʿArab*, Ibn Manẓūr (1988, 62) states that according to Hadith, the Prophet himself was humorous (*fīh duʿābah*) and enjoyed play (*laʿib*). Quoting al-Nuwayrī (d. 1333), Franz Rosenthal writes that the Prophet once "told an old woman that old women were not admitted into Paradise, and when she was greatly upset by his statement, he quoted the Qur'ān 56.35–7/34–6 to the effect that all women in Paradise would be equally young" (Rosenthal 1956, 5–6). In his discussion of authors and characters from the seventh through the tenth centuries, Rosenthal argues that during this period of Islamic history "there existed a pronounced predilection for humor and gaiety which knew few restrictions" (ibid., 4).[4]

Ibn Manẓūr (1988, 62) defines *hazl* or "jest" as *naqīḍ al-jidd* (opposite of earnest). In addition to *hazl*, humor incorporates the meaning of *muzāḥ* and *fukāhah* (joking), *du'ābah* (humor), and *la'ib* (play). Exploring the topos of *hazl* (jest) and *jidd* (earnest) in al-Jāḥiẓ (781–869) but also in al-Ma'arrī (973–1057) and others, Geert Jan Van Gelder argues that it is difficult to separate this complementary structure or define these two terms independently of one another. He writes: "In the case of *jidd* and *hazl* one could notice, for instance, that the former may also mean 'exertion, painstaking' and the latter 'emaciation, leanness', so that it could be said, somewhat jestingly, that too much *jidd* must lead to *hazl*" (Van Gelder 1992, 86).

The need for humor in the serious text is best expressed in al-Jāḥiẓ, the quintessential medieval Arab author and satirist. Van Gelder dwells on al-Jāḥiẓ's *Fil-Jidd wal-hazl* (*In Earnest and in Jest*) and argues that al-Jāḥiẓ's letter to the vizier Ibn al-Zayyāt defends the need for jest, claiming that banning it would be an unequivocal injustice.[5] In *Kitāb al-ḥayawān* (*Book of Animals*), al-Jāḥiẓ discusses jest's didactic role in the acquisition of knowledge:

> If we have bored you with seriousness and sound argumentations … then we will now enliven you by means of some frivolous things, by mentioning witty reasonings and strange argumentations … Now if you are one of those who are easily bored and quickly wearied, this chapter will enliven your heart and relax your strength; then we shall begin with the chapter on pigeons when your fatigue has gone and your energy is renewed.
>
> *(Van Gelder 1992, 100)*

In this passage, al-Jāḥiẓ takes account of the reader's resistance, fatigue, and potential disinterest, structuring his text in such a way as to communicate meaning in the most effective manner. Van Gelder points out that the importance of al-Jāḥiẓ's statement lies precisely in the insistence on alternation and the avoidance of monotony as a way to "enliven" the reader. As he seeks to circumvent the reader's passivity, al-Jāḥiẓ strategically introduces the humorous as complementary to the serious matter at hand. Quoting another passage from *Al-Nisā'* (*The Women*) in al-Jāḥiẓ's *Rasā'il* (*Letters*), Van Gelder relates:

> In literary and educative writings the authors should not insist on pure earnest, unmixed reasonableness, on the bitter truth and arduous thoughts that weary the mind and exhaust one's efforts … There is no harm if the book is adorned with some jest. Although much jesting makes a book foolish, much seriousness makes it heavy-going. A book should contain something to revive the reader's interest and to keep the listener from dozing off.
>
> *(Van Gelder 1992, 100)*

Van Gelder's reading of al-Jāḥiẓ's text identifies the "general public's" short attention span, an apt reference to many students in today's classroom. He points out that al-Jāḥiẓ is keen on holding the attention of the reader at all times, making him/her alert, entertained, as if the value of the book is first and foremost intersubjective, operating in real time. This emphasis transforms al-Jāḥiẓ's model of the book's reception from its exclusive writerly and readerly context to a face-to-face, pedagogic one, which could occur in a classroom setting in order to ensure effective learning.

In taking account of the reader's disposition, al-Jāḥiẓ introduces the question of reception, a key concept for reading and teaching literature today. Humor thus needs to be explored as a framework that takes into account the attention span of the reader/student as al-Jāḥiẓ points out, but also in the context of "foreign" novels, topics, and the "no exit" condition arising from the war text associated with the Arab world after 9/11 especially. Al-Jāḥiẓ's model allows us to frame the function of humor in communicating to students in American classrooms the experience of those who are often dehumanized, stereotyped, or radically othered. In this light, humor chips away at the "foreign" both in reference to the other's experience and as a racial and cultural identity.

Humor as humanizing process

In the Islamicate tradition one finds such legendary tricksters as *Ash'ab*, and the iconic comic character *Juḥa* (or *Djuḥa*), a jester and joker figure, always at the fringe of society, critiquing it, satirizing it, and moving in this way across cultural traditions and historical contexts.[6] Aristotle's *Poetics* traces the origin of comedy to the Megarians in Sicily, whose poets indulged in phallic rituals. He claims that "comedians were so-called not from the revel or komos, but because they toured the villages when expelled from the town" (Aristotle 1996, 6). Given Aristotle's definition, at the origin of comedy lies a structure of exclusion and contempt. Comedy thus denotes a continuous return, a repetition of movement against exile and censorship. In *Jokes and their Relation to the Unconscious* (1905), Freud attributes jokes to the unconscious, operating in similar ways to dreams. He argues that jokes subvert "the critical faculty" (Freud 1960, 128) and "internal inhibitions and repressions" (ibid., 134), by introducing a form of child pleasure and play that has been repressed with adulthood. The space of jokes in Freud is one of subversion and freedom brought about through the suspension of processes of repression.

In *Laughter: An Essay on the Meaning of the Comic* (1900), Henri Bergson discusses humor in relation to such concepts as identification, degradation, aestheticization, and correction. He states that "the comic does not exist outside the pale of what is strictly *human*" (Bergson 1914, 3). According to Bergson, the comic could not be understood in the context of nature, and if that were the case, then it would be the outcome of human projection. As he addresses comedy's various characteristics through readings of La Bruyère, Shakespeare, Molière, and others, Bergson analyzes its aestheticizing function. He writes: "And yet there is something esthetic about it, since the comic comes into being just when society and the individual, freed from the worry of self-preservation, begin to regard themselves as works of art" (ibid., 20). In this formulation, Bergson emphasizes the distance humor enables one to cross in order to transcend a specific social and political reality. Thinking about oneself as a work of art emphasizes one's humanity. This ushers in the category of the *human* as that which prevails over the oppressive political reality that reduces individuals to a state of survival.[7]

Emphasizing the *human*, humor spares characters in the text regression to an archaic state of nature brought about by war and depicted in its literature. To make fun of oneself and of the other in the midst of war is to safeguard one's humanity. Given the aesthetic dimension defined by Bergson, humor characterizes a movement beyond survival, a rebellion against an oppressive reality, thereby making room for readers to enter the text and understand its complexity. Humor in this way allows the reader to sympathize with characters in novels and films about war and displacement, recognizing their humanity and relating to their experiences. Bergson writes:

> The comic character is often one with whom, to begin with, our mind, or rather our body, sympathises. By this is meant that we put ourselves for a very short time in his place, adopt his gestures, words, and actions, and, if amused by anything laughable in him, invite him, in imagination, to share his amusement with us; in fact, we treat him first as a playmate. So, in the laugher we find a "hail-fellow-well-met" spirit – as far, at least, as appearances go – which it would be wrong of us not to take into consideration. In particular, there is in laughter a movement of relaxation.
>
> *(Bergson 1914, 194–195)*

The humorous text thus operates as an invitation to play, a framework that disturbs and unsettles the fixity of conflict and the reduction of those who are caught up in it to "radical" others (or the Other) with whom the reader is unable to identify. From the safety of the American classroom, students of Arabic literature and culture thus enter the text through this invitation, a safe space outside conflict, yet shaped by it. Given this formulation, humor targets the reader's resistance, which is often expressed through forms of cultural projection and the deployment of the stereotype: the oppressed Arab woman, a perennial Middle East conflict, religious fanaticism, and Arab and Muslim masses chanting "death to America." Humor has the potential to engage this resistance and its defensive modality, thereby creating a strategic site of investigation while devising new pedagogical approaches to Arabic literature and culture. Humor mediates the reader's identification without obliterating the text's cultural specificity, thereby preserving its untranslatable elements.

Moreover, the language of humor and its medium – novel, film, or diary – operate in a comparative framework that cuts across cultural traditions. Humor allows students to recognize the humanity of characters in a novel or film, but also to situate the text itself in relation to other representations of humor across cultural and historical frameworks. An intertextuality of humor thus shapes and underlies it in the context of war, conflict, and displacement. This important function transforms the treatment of the text from a window on the social and political reality of war to an engagement with the work of art as such, which could only be revealed through an investigation of its narrative, genre, and various aesthetic elements.

The brothel of Oum Walid

Ziad Doueiri's film, *West Beirut*, tells the story of three teenagers caught up in the violence of the Lebanese civil conflict as they express their fears and desires through play, tricks, and various adventures in their divided city. The film sheds light on the notion of separation between people and regions, examining the kind of humanity that survives in the midst of war, in between and beyond the political and sectarian divisions that gripped Lebanon during the 15-year conflict. Doueiri allegorizes this survival through the brothel of Oum Walid, strategically located in the Zaytouna district – a no man's land between East and West Beirut. Stumbling on it by mistake, the kids find in it a refuge from the barbarism of war. In one particular scene, Tarek and his friends undertake a dangerous crossing to Oum Walid's *bordel*, which operates as a site outside conflict, in Beirut yet outside it. The scene shows the three kids arguing about the danger involved in this crossing. Tarek, the ringleader and trickster, insists that despite sniper fire he will cross with or without his friends. After some back and forth, Tarek finally reveals that he has gotten hold of the "secret code," which is recognized by the sniper who terrorizes city dwellers and prevents them from crossing to the other side. This code is nothing but an item of female underwear (a bra), which the kids brandish as they make their way safely to Oum Walid's brothel. Once there, Tarek and his friends enter Oum Walid's office, addressing her each in turn.

TAREK: Today I found the solution for the Middle East problem: Make Gemayel and Arafat[8] meet right here in Zaytouna …
OMAR: Hello Mrs Oum Walid, I'll have a cup of your coffee with some milk.
MAY: Hi, Mrs Oum Walid.
OUM WALID: Hello? Oum Walid is in deep shit! Someone must have put some strange shit in my bong because I can't see straight. Is this a love house or is this a headache house? Mr Tarek, is this a Friendship Hotel or what? Don't you know what's happening out there?
TAREK: I do, I do. But we have our contacts.
OMAR: We got hold of the secret code.[9]

Initially, Tarek and his friends function as focalizors in Mieke Bal's sense, determining "the relation between the vision and that which is 'seen,' perceived" (Bal 1997, 142). The focalizor, "a specific agent of perception, the holder of the 'point of view'" (ibid., 19), shapes through his/her perception and experience of narrative events that of the viewer or reader. In this sense, the kids accompany the viewer

FIGURE 9.1 *West Beirut* 1

FIGURE 9.2 *West Beirut* 1

on a dangerous yet entertaining trip to the brothel. The crossing into a space outside conflict and the ensuing humor in the back and forth between Oum Walid and the kids, sustain the possibility of the human in the midst of a war-torn city, turned against itself. However, this scene's denouement occurs with the shift of the focalizing perspective to Oum Walid, watching in disbelief the children's arrival and their comic performance. Oum Walid's look and words betray shock and confusion, staging the intersection of the comedic with war's violence and absurdity.

The "secret code" in this scene is key to understanding the relation between humor and war in the classroom context. The secrecy of the code allows the kids to cross a dangerous zone unhurt and thus survive. The logic of desire and play saves the children's lives and leads them safely to Oum Walid's love house. The secret code thus consists of a language that arises in the midst of conflict yet spares the protagonists immanent death as they seek entertainment. The "secret code" is a visual one, visible to the sniper and to the film's viewer, i.e. the student in the classroom context. Understanding this code allows the sniper to spare the kids' lives, and the viewer to recognize their humanity that transcends the mode of survival brought about by conflict. The viewer relates to the kids, shares their secret, "cracks the code" of the humorous scene, and fulfills its humanizing effect. Just like Tarek and his friends, the viewer is afforded a space outside the conflict, outside a structure of identification that would leave the viewer no exit or respite from the dehumanizing violence that consumes those trapped by war. The secret code metaphorically creates a shelter and an oasis, like Oum Walid's brothel, both for the children in the film and for the viewer as well. It also provides a point of entry and exit into and out of the conflict and the texts for the children in the film and for those watching it.

In addition to humanizing the characters in the film and providing them along with the viewer with a safe place to play and pursue their pleasures, humor positions this film in relation to a variety of important literary and visual genres. Tarek's character conjures up the trickster of the *maqāmah* literary genre, which depends on the knowing of the code by one character as a way of tricking others. Originating in the tenth century with the work of Badīʿ al-Zamān al-Hamadhānī (967–1007), the *maqāmah* (plural, *maqāmāt*, assemblies) is a rhymed narrative about a vagrant character engaging in various adventures and tricks in the marketplace.[10] Just like characters in the *maqāmah* manipulate social relations in an urban setting, the kids in *West Beirut* act like "party crashers"[11] by tricking their way into Oum Walid's *bordel*, crossing unhurt beyond divided zones. Their trick provides access to a space outside conflict and from which conflict's violence is critiqued and exposed.

In this film about war in the Middle East, the narrative aligns the *maqāmah* with the picaresque, its European counterpart. In this context, Bergson discusses the role of the obstinate comic figure in European literature, which could be compared to Tarek in the film:

> *A character following up his one idea*, and continually recurring to it in spite of incessant interruptions! The transition seems to take place imperceptibly from the man who will listen to nothing to the one who will see nothing, and from this latter to the one who sees only what he wants to see. A stubborn spirit ends by adjusting things to its own way of thinking, instead of accommodating its thoughts to the things. So every comic character is on the highroad to the above-mentioned illusion, and Don Quixote furnishes us with the general type of comic absurdity.
>
> *(Bergson 1914, 185)*

In this formulation, Don Quixote and Tarek, the war film with picaresque elements, come together to create meaning and frame *West Beirut*'s reception. The work thus operates as a film about war and coming of age which communicates the conflict's horror to the American student yet ushers in the aesthetic dimension, both human and literary, connecting the work to other literary traditions. The *maqāmah* and picaresque elements, staged through the comedic, anchor the film's aesthetic value across genres. The viewer, transported through Tarek's jest to Oum Walid's heaven-like brothel, is introduced to the tragedy of war while simultaneously led to recognize the literary and aesthetic dimension that aligns the film with *Don Quixote* and the *maqāmah*, François Truffaut's *The 400 Blows* and *Huck Finn*.

Saved by Hollywood

The obstinate character in *West Beirut* who arouses sympathy if not identification on the part of the viewer, is also present in the diary of another trickster, Samuel Shimon. Shimon describes in *An Iraqi in Paris* his departure from his village in Iraq and his vagabondage on the streets of Paris. Akin to the picaresque novel, this "autobiographical novel" relates Samuel's encounters through a humorous, stream-of-consciousness narrative. Shimon recounts his beating at the hands of the Syrian *mukhābarāt* (secret police) at one point, and his abduction by a Lebanese militia at the beginning of the civil war at another. Arriving in war-torn Beirut in 1975 and looking for the Assyrian church in the hope of obtaining financial support to travel to the US, Samuel is apprehended in East Beirut. The Phalanges (*Katā'ib*) militia arrests Shimon and condemns him to death as an Iraqi spy. In this scene, Shimon pleads with his executioner, Tony, a French-educated and Gitanes-smoking militiaman holding a gun to his head:

> "I want to make movies. I'm not a spy!" "You terrorist bastard! … What do you know about 'movies', you son of a whore?" "I know everything. I'm not like you and your friends, killing and smoking Gitanes." […] After several moments of silence, Tony said: "Do you know Godard? Do you know someone called Jean-Luc Godard?" I wanted to shake my head to tell him "no" but I did not dare in case it made his handgun go off and fire a bullet into my head, so I said it in a low voice. He asked again: "Haven't you heard of the Nouvelle Vague?" "[N]o," I replied. "Son of a whore," he shouted, "how do you want me to believe that you dream of working in the cinema when you don't know Jean-Luc Godard and haven't heard of the Nouvelle Vague? …" At that moment, I shouted out: "I know everything about John Ford, about John Wayne, about Henry Fonda, James Stewart, Gary Cooper, Maureen O'Hara. I know Katherine Hepburn, I know Roy Rogers the king of cowboys, I know Victor Mature, Ava Gardner, Gregory Peck, Alan Ladd, Vera Miles, Randolph Scott, Clark Gable, D W Griffith … I know Rock Hudson, James Dean, I know Gene Tierney, I know Clint Eastwood, Paul

> Newman, I know Rod Taylor, I know Lee Marvin, Humphrey Bogart, Bob Hope, Errol Flynn, Joan Crawford, I know Dean Martin, I know everything about Montgomery Clift, I know even King Kong and Frankenstein. When I stopped, I heard Tony laughing. I opened my eyes: he had returned his handgun to its place under his belt. "Listen, Cowboy!" he said. "Let it be known that Hollywood cinema is weak compared with the films of the Nouvelle Vague."
>
> *(Shimon 2005, 17–18)*

Samuel's encounter with death in this scene demonstrates that film as an artistic medium transcends conflict and saves the character's life. This dream-like scene stages a humorous *mise en abîme* that brings cinema into the literary text and the literary text into film. In this narrative, Hollywood films specifically save the main character from imminent death. Samuel saves his own life by telling his executioner all that he knows about film, listing its major figures. This telling, like Scheherazade's tales in *One Thousand and One Nights*, functions as a literary text that humanizes the character and spares him execution. Literature, including film in this context, functions as "writing against death," originating in war yet transcending it through the canon of Hollywood cinema. While Samuel's pleading and explanations and his denial of the charge of spying and terrorism fail, on their own, to save his life, literature and film lead him safely outside the conflict, escaping certain death. The humorous encounter thus stages an aesthetic encounter that transforms political conflict into a literary and visual one. The canon of Hollywood cinema in Shimon's work, told in a humorous fashion, humanizes the character in the eyes of his executioner – who acts as a focalizor in this scene – and in the eyes of the reader as well. Just as Tarek's knowledge of the "secret code" in *West Beirut* saves his life, Samuel's knowledge of Hollywood cinema in this scene saves his. Though Tony, the executioner, initially chides Samuel's commercial taste and his ignorance of French avant-garde cinema or Nouvelle Vague, he shares with him the language of film, which allows them both to transcend in this comedic moment ideological and ethnic differences.

Like the obstinate character in Bergson, Samuel sees only his filmmaking regardless of war and conflict. This trickster resumes the sequence of encounters from Iraq to Paris and beyond, in search of opportunities to make and work in film. In this context, the discussion of diaspora and conflict in Shimon's work thus requires a discussion of genres and canons, Hollywood cinema and the Nouvelle Vague. Just as *West Beirut* provides the viewer with a space of identification with the characters as they pursue their desires and pleasures in the midst of war, in Shimon's work the viewer recognizes the humanity of the character and the literariness of his text – the power of his life-saving narrative. As in *West Beirut*, war as an all-consuming reality and its dehumanizing effects and reduction of individuals to a state of survival are both staged and overcome in *An Iraqi in Paris*. This again creates the space for the reader to escape through literature along with Samuel from certain death. The humanizing and aestheticizing function of literature and Hollywood cinema specifically connects this episode to a variety of literary genres, and serves to situate the film at the intersection of war and conflict and their corresponding representation across historical contexts and cultural traditions.

A dog's life

In *Sharon and My Mother-in-Law: Ramallah Diaries*, Suad Amiry offers the quintessential humorous yet tragic account of life under occupation. From relating episodes about faulty gas masks distributed to Palestinians during the first Gulf War (1990) to paranoid reactions to an electric Mecca artwork, offered to her by the teenage neighbor-turned-Israeli collaborator, Amiry describes her daily life in the West Bank. In this impossible situation where she has to jump over fences to save her ailing mother-in-law's life (as she lived next to Arafat's headquarter during the second intifada, in 2000) to driving a dog with an Israeli passport to Jerusalem, *Sharon and My Mother-in-Law* mixes the tragic with the absurd and the comic in order to create an effect that leads students to proclaim at the end of the class, "now we've got it!" in reference to the plight of people living under occupation.

Like Tarek in *West Beirut* and Samuel in *An Iraqi in Paris*, Suad is yet another trickster – rebellious, funny, obstinate, and confrontational – constantly challenging the conditions of war and systematically creating possibilities of movement and play. However, neither Suad nor the work itself could be reduced to the impossibility of life under occupation. Negotiations, tricks, and resistance are constantly at work in the text, sparing the reader a "no exit" scenario often allegorized in the literary genres depicting such conditions.[12]

Many important scenes could be discussed and theorized in this work, but the one with the dog and her driver is certainly among the most poignant and representative of the ways in which humor mediates processes of humanization and aestheticization in this work. Suad's dog, Nura, requires a rabies shot. Suad refuses to take her to Dr Hisham, a nearby Palestinian veterinarian, due to his sexist views on "mongrel bitches." Instead, Suad decides to take Nura to Dr Tamar's animal protection clinic, located in a settled industrial zone on the Ramallah–Jerusalem road. Nura receives the required shots and obtains as a result a Jerusalem ID, a health record issued by the Jerusalem municipality, under the jurisdiction of which the clinic operates. With this ID in hand, Suad, who as a West Bank resident needs a special permit to enter Jerusalem, drives Nura to her newly adopted hometown, going through the Israeli checkpoint while passing for the dog's driver.

> And here was little Nura with a Jerusalem passport.
> "Lucky you baby" …
> "Don't lose it. Take it with you when you travel abroad."
> "You mean the *passport*?" I was just checking.
> "Yes," Dr. Tamar replied.

Both Nura and Dr. Tamar gave me a strange look, as neither of them was that political. It drove me crazy how both took being a Jerusalemite for granted. I walked out, carrying tiny Nura in my left hand and her passport carefully in my right.

"You know what, Nura? This document will get you through the checkpoint into Jerusalem while I and my car need two different permits to get through."

…

It was not long before I decided to make use of Nura's passport.

"Can I see your permit and the car's?" requested the soldier standing at the Jerusalem checkpoint.

"I don't have one, but I'm the driver of this Jerusalem dog," I replied, handing the soldier Nura's passport.

"*Maze* (What)?" asked the soldier, making a funny face.

…

"I am the dog's driver. As you can see, she is from Jerusalem, and she cannot possibly drive the car or go to Jerusalem all by herself."

"And you argh hergh dghiver" he said, rolling his *r*'s in the way that Israelis do when they speak English and dissolving into laughter.

"Yes, somebody has got to be her driver," I laughed back.

The soldier looked closely at me, patted Nura's head, which was still sticking out of the window, handed me her passport and in a loud voice said: "*SA'A* … Go."

I pressed my foot on the accelerator … and to Jerusalem we both flew.

All it takes is a bit of humor, I thought to myself as Nura and I passed the same soldier when we drove back to Ramallah that same afternoon.

(Amiry 2004, 116–117)

Amiry's passage – and the entire work and persona – constitutes a case study in humor. The trickery in her narrative is twofold: She tricks the Israeli veterinarian into getting the shots and the ID, and the soldier at the checkpoint into crossing to Jerusalem. In both cases, the institution of occupation, from the settlement to the checkpoint, are subverted through Suad's tricks and humor. The categories of the human and the animal are unsettled as well through jest in order to expose, at one level, the political context and its "animalizing" of the Palestinians living under occupation, and the aesthetic context, which allows the Palestinian character to devise tactics in order to exploit and displace this animalization. Her act exposes the injustice of denying Palestinians travel and entrance rights while affording them to dogs.

Starting with the position of the animal, understood in its negative association, in this scene Suad humanizes both her and the dog, mediating in this way the reader's understanding of life under occupation. Just like Dr Tamar and Nura (the focalizors) who look at Suad in disbelief when the dog's Jerusalem ID is issued, the students occupy the position of those who go from not realizing the meaning of a

Jerusalem ID and the freedom of movement for a West Bank resident, to "getting it" at the end. In this humorous encounter Suad tricks the students as well, leading them to expose the occupation's absurdity and violence.

In *The Practice of Everyday Life*, Michel de Certeau discusses tactics of resistance as a form of *bricolage* in post-capitalist societies. These tactics bring about localized or micro subversions of hegemonic power structures. Through Clauzwitz and Freud, de Certeau argues that while strategies privilege fixed spatial divisions and group relations, tactics are the instruments of the weak as they invest in creating temporal disruptions. De Certeau writes:

> The art of "pulling tricks" involves a sense of the opportunities afforded by a particular occasion. Through procedures that Freud makes explicit with reference to wit, a tactic boldly juxtaposes diverse elements in order suddenly to produce a flash shedding a different light on the language of a place and to strike the hearer.
>
> *(De Certeau 1988, 37–38)*

Similarly to *West Beirut* and *An Iraqi in Paris*, Amiry's text exposes both the absurdity and the violence of the occupation while devising new ways of resisting it. Amiry's act is one of aesthetic resistance: her tactic consists in creating disruption and suspension of the law – that of the occupation – through humorous interventions. Suad's jest and performance disarm the representative of occupation and secure safe passage to Jerusalem. In this way the text creates an aesthetic space that calls on the reader to identify and critique an oppressive power structure. This opening thus operates as the condition of possibility of the humanizing function of humor, exposing the violence while presenting the reader with a safety net, so to speak, a way to escape, traverse, cross over and cross into another zone as an expression of freedom – freedom of movement, in this case. The narratives of crossing examined in Suad's work and the texts above emphasize the role of humor as something that facilitates, mediates, bridges, goes over, and connects. Political, ideological, and racial divisions are unable to withstand the tricks staged by the various tricksters in order to unsettle their respective models of prohibition and restriction.

Conclusion

While war is presented as a social and political context for the literary and visual works examined in this essay, humor provides the aesthetic dimension from which the humanity of war's victims and survivors emerges. In this context, humor's trajectory, which takes shape through circumvention and camouflage, smuggling and crashing, tricking and decoding, characterizes the process of meaning production at the level of reception. The reader or viewer in this case, engaging these texts from the security of his/her classroom context in the US, is led on a journey of understanding and a mystery of cracking codes and infiltrating prohibited zones. These zones are external and determined by color (green, red, black), but also internal, shaped by associations and stereotypes that emanate from specific cultural and media images and reporting. Humor as a work of exposing and understanding of one's own reality and that of the other thus disrupts and interrogates the reader's associations and preconceived ideas, especially in the context of Arabic and Islam in the US.

Humor goes to the heart of the stereotype's fixity, shattering its construction and opening up meaning in a variety of ways. Specifically, teaching humor constitutes a political move on the one hand, aimed at undermining the association of Arabic and Islam with conflict and violence, and an aesthetic one on the other, aimed at anchoring the study of Arabic literature in the Humanities at large. To put it differently, this chapter addressed the way in which students' interest in Arabic or Islam could be directed in such a way as to open up the Arabic text to the literary and the comparative, the visual and the artistic.

Integrating the teaching of Arabic literature and culture into a larger Humanities framework is a vital process given the critique advanced by Edward Said from *Orientalism* and *Covering Islam* in the late 1970s, and Jack Shaheen's critique of Hollywood's representations of *Reel Bad Arabs*.[13] Given the context of representation and perception of all things Arabic or Islamic in the US, engaging with Arabic cultural production has to take into account the discursive and media construction of the Arab or Muslim. To acknowledge the political context through the emphasis on humor opens the text up to other meanings – aesthetic, cultural, and psychological. The point, therefore, is not to engage the stereotype on its own terms by contesting and refuting its model of representation – Islamic violence, oppression of women, etc. – but to deconstruct and subvert it. Humor thus displaces the political onto the deconstructive reading as such, which takes the reader/viewer off guard, ferrying him/her into a moment of exposure, clarity, self-consciousness, and empathy. The humanizing process in this final tally is multiple, involving viewer and viewed, reader and character, teacher and student. Understanding the other by engaging the literariness of his/her text thus implies an understanding of one's own cultural and historical position – that is, one's own text.

Notes

1 A good example of this strategy could be found in Art Spiegelman's cartoon about the Holocaust, *The Complete Maus: A Survivor's Tale (No 1)*. New York: Pantheon Books, 1996.
2 As Said demonstrated in *Culture and Imperialism*, literature is fundamentally a political enterprise. In Elaine Showalter's words, "the message of the eighties was that literature itself was political" (Showalter 2003, 134).
3 For the diary genre, also see Fadia Basrawi, *Brownies and Kalashnikovs: A Saudi Woman's Memoir of American Arabia and Wartime Beirut*. Berkshire: Garnet Publishing, 2009.
4 For a discussion of humor as a literary and pedagogical tool in religious scholarship, see Devin Stewart, "The Humor of the Scholars: The Autobiography of Niʿmat Allāh al-Jazāʾirī (d. 1112/1701)." *Iranian Studies*, Vol. 22, No. 4 (1989), pp. 47–81.

5 For the full text of al-Jāḥiẓ's letter, see *Nine Essays of al-Jahiz*. Trans. William M. Hutchins. New York: Peter Lang Publishing, 1989. 93–121. For a seventeenth-century comic text, see also Yusuf al-Shirbini, *Brains Confounded by the Ode of Abu Shaduf Expounded*. Trans. Humphrey Davies. Leuven: Peeters Publishers, 2008.
6 See *Tales of Juha: Classic Arab Folk Humor*. Ed. Salma Khadra Jayyusi. Northampton: Interlink Books, 2006.
7 For an excellent article on humor in Palestinian cinema, which aligns Bergson's "humor" with Jacques Rancière's "dissensus" in order to read the aesthetics/politics relation, see Najat Rahman, "'Laughter that Encounters a Void?' Humor, Loss, and the Possibility for Politics in Recent Palestinian Cinema." In *A Companion to Film Comedy*. Eds Andrew Horton and Joanna E. Rapf. Oxford: Blackwell Publishing, 2013.
8 Yasser Arafat and Pierre Gemayel, the warring leaders at the start of the Lebanese conflict.
9 www.youtube.com/watch?v=PZTYq5xFHMY.
10 See "*Maqāma*" in *Encyclopedia of Arabic literature*. Eds Julie Scott Meisami and Paul Starkey. London: Routledge, 1998. Vol. 2. 507–508. The picaresque is thought to have its roots in the *maqāmah*.
11 Salma Khadra Jayyusi, *Classical Arabic Stories: An Anthology*. New York: Columbia University Press, 2010. 24.
12 See Sahar Khalifeh's 1976 novel, *Wild Thorns*. Trans. Trevor LeGassick. New York: Interlink Books, 2000.
13 For a poignant yet humorous documentary on Arab Americans, see the 1996 documentary film, *Benaat Chicago: Growing up Arab and Female in Chicago* (*Daughters of Chicago*). Dirs Jennifer Bing-Canar and Mary Zerkel. Arab Film Distribution, 2003.

Bibliography

Amiry, Suad. *Sharon and My Mother-in-Law: Ramallah Diaries*. New York: Pantheon Books, 2004.

Aristotle. *Poetics*. Trans. Malcolm Heath. London: Penguin Books, 1996.

Bal, Mieke. *Narratology: Introduction to the Theory of Narrative*. Toronto: University of Toronto Press, 1997.

Bergson, Henri. *Laughter: An Essay on the Meaning of the Comic*. Trans. Cloudesley Brereton and Fred Rothwell. 1900. New York: The Macmillan Company, 1914.

De Certeau, Michel. *The Practice of Everyday Life*. Trans. Steven Rendall. Berkeley: University of California Press, 1988.

Freud, Sigmund. *Jokes and their Relation to the Unconscious*. Trans. James Stratchey. 1905. New York: Norton, 1960.

Ibn Manẓūr, Muḥammad ibn Mukarram. *Lisān al-'arab*. Ed. 'Alī Shīrrī, 18 vols. Beirut: Dār Iḥyā' al-Turāth al-'Arabī, 1988. Vol. 15–16.

Khadra Jayyusi, Salma. *Classical Arabic Stories: An Anthology*. New York: Columbia University Press, 2010.

Rosenthal, Franz. *Humor in Early Islam*. Leiden: Brill, 1956.

Shimon, Samuel. *An Iraqi in Paris*. London: Banipal Books, 2005.

Showalter, Elaine. *Teaching Literature*. Oxford: Blackwell, 2003.

Van Gelder, Geert Jan. "Mixture of Jest and Earnest in Classical Arabic Literature." *Journal of Arabic Literature* 23(1992): 83–107.

West Beirut. Dir. Ziad Doueiri. New York Video, 1999. Film.

10

THE ART OF TEACHING ARAB TRAUMAS TRIUMPHANTLY

Hanadi Al-Samman

Recent Arab history is replete with wars, with violent cultural memories of loss and dispossession that are the outcome of British, French, Italian, and Israeli colonialism of the Middle East since the collapse of the Ottoman Empire at the end of World War I in 1918. The average Arab citizen either witnessed firsthand the independence wars from Western mandates in several Arab states (1946–62), the catastrophe of *al-nakba* in Palestine (1948), the tripartite aggression on Egypt during the Suez Crisis (1956), the setback of *al-naksah* (1967), the prolonged 16-year Lebanese Civil War (1975–91), the Israeli invasions of Lebanon (1982, 2006), the American invasion of Iraq during Gulf Wars I (1990–91) and II (2003–11), the unsettling reverberations of the ongoing Arab Spring (2010–17), or experienced these catastrophic events vicariously through a process that Marianne Hirsch and Maria Brown respectively call "postmemory" and "intergenerational trauma" (Hirsch 1997; Brown 1995). To this extent, almost every Arab citizen, man or woman alike, has been scarred by political upheaval and wars' legacies, and has been either an unwilling participant or an innocent victim of their tyranny.

On the literary scene, this extended legacy of pain and displacement explains the explosion of what later came to be known as political literature: *adab al-nakbah* (literature of catastrophe), *adab al-naksah* (literature of defeat, marking the literature produced after the Arabs' defeat in the 1967 Arab–Israeli war), *adab al-ḥarb al-ahlīyyah al-lubnānīyyah* (literature of the Lebanese Civil War, covering the period of 1975 to 1991), and as of late, the literary and digital literature of the Arab Spring and its aftermath. Dealing with historical and personal Arab traumas, this collective literary corpus creates certain challenges for teachers in Western classrooms. While an intrinsic understanding of Arab traumas is a given for local and heritage students, imparting this knowledge to global, non-heritage students calls for an effective, affective pedagogy. There is a need for a strategy that goes beyond the historical facts, the mere *explication de texte*, and into trauma reenactments in real or virtual worlds. The ability both to understand and to embody Arab pain and pleasure is paramount.

Trauma, rememory, and postmemory

Experts define trauma as a sudden and violent event that threatens the life of a person who has experienced or witnessed it, or those in his/her surroundings.[1] Such a traumatic event causes unusual stressors to the conscious mind, to the point that the brain has to resort to several defense mechanisms to protect the affected subject from a total psychological breakdown. These mechanisms involve psychological numbness and dissociation, in which a subject splits off part of itself from the experience, thereby leading to a multiple personality disorder (MPD). Still, the repressed traumatic events have an insidious way of creeping up into the subject's mind through the intrusion of distressing images, dreams and/or fantasies. This leads the affected person to engage further in avoidance mechanisms which, in turn, force the return of these traumatic memories with a vengeance, thereby leading to the subject's hyperarousal (Vees-Gulani 2003, 27). This process applies to individuals who had direct contact with the traumatic event such as first-generation survivors.

Subsequent generations, however, have no direct access to the traumatic site but do experience it indirectly by listening to the ancestors' stories, and constructing an imaginary site from which to re-member and to re-experience traumatic events. "Rememory" is the vehicle for accessing, representing, and reenacting traumatic knowledge as, when recalling the horrors of slavery, Sethe explains to her daughter in Toni Morrison's *Beloved*: "If you go there – you who never was there – if you go there and stand in the place where it was, it will happen again; it will be there for you, waiting for you" (Morrison 1987, 36). Specifically, once "there" what the daughter will experience is a secondhand, intergenerational trauma – one that feminist therapists Maria Root and Laura Brown call "insidious trauma."[2] According to Root, insidious trauma is characterized as "the traumatogenic effects of oppression that are not necessarily overtly violent or threatening to bodily well-being at the given moment but do violence to the soul and spirit" (Brown 1995, 107). Recent mainstream trauma theory, Brown contends, has begun "to recognize that post-traumatic symptoms can be intergenerational." Still it has yet to admit that these symptoms could "spread laterally throughout an oppressed social group" whose membership could mean "a constant lifetime risk of exposure to certain trauma" (Brown 1995, 108).

The act of re-membering, of stitching the painful, absent pieces together, is crucial, then, and evident in the process of postmemory. For, as Hirsch contends, "postmemory characterizes the experience of those who grow up dominated by narratives that preceded their birth, whose own belated stories are evacuated by the stories of the previous generation shaped by traumatic events that can be neither understood nor recreated" (Hirsch 1997, 22). This is certainly the case for contemporary Arab citizens, heirs to the traumatic legacy of colonization, oppression, and authoritarian regimes. How best to convey these intergenerational and lateral traumas to students in the classroom in a way that highlights the processes of rememory and postmemory? How can instructors effect a deeper understanding of Arab traumas – one that challenges students not just to recognize, but also to empathize with the beleaguered Arab masses? The answer lies in an affective pedagogy that follows affect theory's framework, while relying on the manifold facets of real and virtual worlds in its application.

Real and virtual worlds in the lens of affect

Teaching Arab traumas through the lens of affect rather than the mere dissemination of historical knowledge incorporates personal history in a meaningful fashion, thereby paving the way to incorporate collective and personal traumas for a deeper, intrinsic knowledge. Cultivating an affective pedagogy goes beyond contested political ideology and into the universal, globally shared experience of affect, of what Silvan Tomkins calls "affective resonance." In this manner, students will have a tendency to resonate or experience the same affect in response to viewing a display of that affect by another person in real or virtual worlds. Learning about others' traumas by sharing experiences of pain, terror, and emotions of surprise, anger, fear, sadness, disgust, empathy, joy and love, invites students to put aside identitarian, divisive politics and to envision the world with a human-centered lens.

While it is easy to align oneself along political or sectarian ideologies, it is much harder to contest personal hi(stories) backed by live testimonials of individuals who survived national and personal traumas. In teaching courses focusing on Arab history, politics, and the literature of war, historical events would still contextualize the subject matter, and longstanding texts such as Albert Ḥoūrānī's *A History of the Arab Peoples* (1991), Hishām Sharābī's *Neopatriarchy: A Theory of Distorted Change in Arab Society* (1988), and Ḥalīm Barakāt's *The Arab World: Society, Culture, and State* (1993) would offer such framing. However, personal narratives of past traumas would add the materiality of body and voice, hence much-needed relevance and credibility to traumatic recall. In their introduction to an edited collection on *nakba*, Līlā Abū-Lughod and Ahmad Saʿdī highlight the importance of harnessing "the flood of personal memories," of enrolling them to elicit "more of a [public] hearing" (Saʿdī and Abū Lughod 2007, 13).

The process of staging public events such as displaying the Palestinian quilt that represented the 400 destroyed Palestinian villages in 1948, on the National Mall in Washington, DC in 2008, and listening to survivors' stories, who still hold the keys and deeds to their demolished homes, generates an affective resonance capable of connecting others to the trauma of the Palestinian *nakba*. During that particular event, "the names of the villages were read as a bell tolled, and eyewitnesses, or the children of eyewitnesses, spoke about what happened in 1948."[3] In the absence of a museum commemorating *nakba* memories, akin to that of the Holocaust or the African American museums in Washington, DC, teaching Arab traumas through affective resonance brought about by reenactments, digital storytelling, and recitations of personal and cinematic diaries can be an effective pedagogy. Similarly, an interactive museum dedicated to recreating the traumatic experience on a visceral level promotes connectivity with global cultures. Additionally, screening of documentaries such as Emād Burnāṭ's Academy Award-nominated *5 Broken Cameras* (2013) is an effective pedagogical tool geared towards helping students realize that *nakba* is not just a single historical moment, but an ongoing event representing an unparalleled rupture in collective Palestinian memory.

The movie documents the building of the wall, a separation barrier in the occupied West Bank that cuts the village of Bilʿīn in half. It is a cinematic diary that records Bilʿīn residents' non-violent opposition to the wall's construction. The film is shot through five cameras which are eventually destroyed by Israeli Defense Forces. The acquisition of each camera parallels the birth and major milestones of Burnāṭ's youngest child, Gibrīl. Subsequently, the destruction of each camera mirrors the unfulfilled dreams of Palestine's youth generation due to the divisive realities of the wall. Digital and cinematic storytelling personalize the Palestinians' daily strife as they position it on par with the affective, human level. As a result, their current struggle becomes a continuation and a true embodiment of the *nakba* trauma. The combination of real and cinematic rendering of the Palestinian trauma augments the message of canonical literary texts such as Ghassān Kanafānī's *Men in the Sun* (1998), Emīle Habībī's *The Pessoptimist* (2001), and Saʿdallah Wannoūs's *Ḥaflat Samar min Ajl 5 Huzaīrān* (Soirée for 5 June) (1978). An adaptation of such an affective pedagogy facilitates learning through identification with what Heather Love calls a "project of a comparative analysis around social injury and social exclusion" (Love 2011, 187). Still these reenactments or cinematic tools can be greatly enhanced by encouraging students to be immersed in the project of traumatic recall even further by simulating the target environment through the use of the virtual Second Life program – a pedagogical technique capable of bringing the affective experience even closer, to the point of embodiment of others' traumas.

Second Life in the classroom and beyond

Promoting the unique application of Second Life (SL) use in and beyond the classroom, Jeremy Sarachan argues that "while textbooks and films provide linear models or examples of course content, virtual worlds provide 3-D experiential, interactive learning environments" (Sarachan et al. 2013, 76). Since its launch in 2003 by Linden Labs, the SL program has facilitated the creation of virtual worlds "by using easy-to-learn building tools and a basic scripting language" (ibid., 76), and afforded its creators the opportunity to live in parallel worlds that are extensions or repudiations of the real worlds in which they live. The program is capable of linking together its increasing users of 50,000–60,000, grouping their virtual representatives or avatars in islands, private and public spaces, museums and, yes, even universities. The use of SL virtual technology in courses such as English, communication, business, and design has been on the rise, with both students and teachers reporting enhanced connectivity and a rare opportunity to have students play a role in knowledge creation as opposed to their previous role in inactive knowledge consumption.

Second Life benefits from tapping into the increasing Facebook, Twitter, and networking inclination of the millennial generation for an intrinsic, unforgettable learning experience. Students have full control of their constructed, virtual worlds, can benefit from the integration of multimedia within SL (Facebook, YouTube, iMedia) to enhance interpersonal communication with other students and with their teacher. The interactive technology environment forges friendships that transcend the spatial and temporal constraints of the physical world. Hence, students can easily recreate scenes from past personal and national traumas.

Additionally, creating an avatar requires a good deal of planning, learning about the target environment, while simultaneously paying special attention to the "full range of communication modalities of (voice, gesture, body language)" in a way that recognizes the universality of affect (Sarachan et al. 2013, 78). Avatars can boast the freedom of "anonymous or quasi-anonymous identity – with gender, race, personality, possessions, and other personal characteristics kept distinct from real life" (ibid., 79). Consequently, students are encouraged to step out of their comfort zone from the security of their virtual world, without risking their lives or exposure to peer pressure if their true identities were to be discovered. Since accessibility to the wider world community is available to anyone with an Internet connection, "this continuous flow of users and community permits the sharing of ideas, opinions and knowledge that connectivism requires" beyond the classroom (ibid., 79). By utilizing specific techniques such as role-playing and narrative sharing, the program enables individualized avatars to interact within the virtual world of the game, thereby enabling them to transform rigid history into the multiplicity and fluidity of personal history. Consequently, students can interact with each other, with the teacher, and with other students from around the world. In the case of recreating Arab traumatic moments, this feature gives heritage (including diaspora Arabs) and non-heritage students a chance not just to interact, but to experience trauma and to partake in the project of rememory and reconstruction as well.

In an SL course site about Arab traumas, for example, students could reenact the events of *al-nakba*, *al-naksah*, or a live representation of life in the occupied territories with the exclusionary realities of the separation, apartheid wall. They could easily simulate a torture cell in one of the authoritarian regimes that plague the Arab world, experience the barbaric crack-down on demonstrators demanding dignity and freedom in the ongoing Syrian revolution, or stage a live sit-in in the squares of Cairo, *Taḥrīr* (a place where anti-Mubārak and anti-Morsī demonstrators gathered) or *Rābiʿah* (a square where pro-Morsī supporters congregated). Comparable to the ritual reenactments of *Maafa* (Swahili for "Great Disaster" or African Holocaust of Enslavement) in Colonial Williamsburg, in Monticello's Plantation Community Weekends, and on the National Geographic website featuring slave auctions, the "Middle Passage Experience," and the "Underground Railroad Living History," the virtual recreation of Arab traumas can detach these events from official history, and embody them instead in the attachment of personal history. In the case of the National Geographic reenactment of *Maafa*, for example, visitors were directed to a virtual site where they would be given the role of a slave all while listening to a voice telling them, "*You are a slave*. Your body, your time, your very breath belong to a farmer in 1850s Maryland" (Woolfork 2008, 133). They are then presented with a choice whether to accompany Harriet Tubman from Maryland to Canada on her way to freedom, or to stay behind. Involving participants on this personal level activates identification on a deeper, affective level. According to Tomkins, "affects provide a sense of urgency … it makes good things better and bad things worse," thus experiencing them in an SL environment creates a powerful source of "motivation" for political action.

Students are instinctively attuned to make affective connections between unrelated texts in ways that facilitate empathy and coalition building. In one of my courses on modern Arabic literature, at the University of Virginia, featuring texts as varied as Emīle Habībī's *The Secret Life of Saeed: The Pessoptimist* (2001), Ibrāhīm Son'allah's *The Committee* (2001), Naguīb Maḥfoūz's *Midaq Alley* (1991), Abdel-raḥman Munīf's *Cities of Salt* (1989), Hodā Barakāt's *The Stone of Laughter* (1995), Ḥanān al-Shaykh's *Only in London* (2002), Al-Ṭayyīb Ṣaliḥ's *Season of Migration to the North* (1980), and Ghāda Sammān's *The Square Moon* (1998), I was intrigued when students identified "the feeling of being stuck" as a common denominator triggering the trauma of the various characters in question. Each one of these texts lends itself to an SL enactment of the character's dilemma/trauma, and can elicit students' participation via creative projects based on simulations, social media, blogs, international collaboration, and teamwork. Specifically, coalitional politics will be enhanced when a course addressing the Palestinian *nakba* and its aftermath features an SL avatar declaring, "You are a Palestinian. You are prevented from returning to your homeland, separated from the rest of your family by walls and checkpoints, subject to arbitrary arrest, life-long detention, and even death." Activating the power of affective resonance, of aggregating and repurposing the traumatic recall, leads to the exciting possibility of recognizing others' traumas as extensions of our own. Only then can a remembrance of the Jewish Holocaust lead to a deeper understanding and acknowledgement of the Palestinian *nakba*, or the African *Maafa*.

Recently, the power of SL in role-playing, in initiating identification and activism amongst different audiences, was depicted in a documentary, *Scent of a Revolution* (2014), directed by Viola Shafīk. The movie depicts the aftermath of the 25 January 2011 Egyptian revolution by interviewing a Coptic political activist, an Upper Egyptian tax collector, a communist writer, and a female Muslim SL designer. The film asks pertinent questions: "What if you witness a revolution but things get worse? What if your homeland is in ruins and you cannot help it? How do you cope?"[4] Lingering between past and present these four characters display collective grief about an incomplete revolution and a country in ruins. They further express various affects of sadness, anger, frustration, adaptation, and devise different strategies in dealing with their sorrow and the country's political upheaval.

Shafīk explores the possibility of reactivating some of the lost luster of the Egyptian revolution by relying on the potential of postmemory and rememory in constructing a parallel universe that supports the physical, real world. Indeed, this premise plays out extremely well in the case of the female cyberspace designer who, when interviewed, insists that constructing a parallel SL space to envision and to practice the components of the revolution is a must. She maintains that experiencing the revolution within the virtual context of MADA (Arabic for horizon and the new name for this Islamic activist SL site, formerly known as Islam online) allows her "to live the revolution twice."[5] She acknowledges the role SL plays in appeasing the fears and doubts of participants in encouraging them to experience the demonstrations in real life, and in giving them "hope and optimism." With conviction she adds, "[t]he idea of the company is for them [virtual participants] to come to real life in Egypt," and SL provides a venue to interact with others, to practice their right of civil disobedience in the hope of performing it in real life at a later time.[6]

The viewer is then made to experience the simultaneous anxiety and subsequent exhilaration of a secluded Salafī woman as she embarks on joining other political players in the demonstration against Hosnī Mubārak's regime in a virtual *Taḥrīr* Square. With disbelief and appreciation, we witness the avatar representing the Muslim woman interacting with a liberal youth as he assures her of the potential rewards of the revolution. "I am sure that everything will improve, God's willing," his avatar declares. In the real world, there will be little chance for these two characters to meet, let alone discuss their opposing political views. In the SL world, however, they become allies discovering, along the way, their common affection for Egypt and hope for a better future. Unlike the real world, Second Life allows for the interaction of distinct cultures, and students joining the program are not just simply taking classes, but become proficient in "adjust[ing] to a socio-cultural system which is different from their own" (Sarachan et al. 2013, 85). At any given moment in the SL community, a simultaneous process of acculturation (absorbing the new culture) and de-culturation (detachment from the old culture) is taking place and, in the words of Gayatri Spivak, the interactive process of "planetary" dialogue is underway.

The rewards of teaching a class from the standpoint of affect and trauma embodiment lie in the common human elements evoked and resurrected, particularly in the virtual context of SL course sites. In these fluid environments, alternative spaces and discourses intent on changing common misconceptions, challenging prevalent stereotypes and sustaining ongoing dialogues can be the exciting outcome both in physical-virtual classrooms and beyond.

Appendix: sample course descriptions

The following are course descriptions for Arabic literature courses rooted in the findings of trauma and affect theories. Organized around two different thematic traumas – national (Arab wars and political upheaval), and personal (Arab women's physical and literary traumas) – they can be taught with or without an SL component.

Arab national traumas

The Arab world has witnessed vast cultural, economic, and demographic changes, the latest of which are the ongoing Arab Spring revolutions and their aftermath. The advent of European colonialism and the subsequent challenges to pre-existing cultural and religious norms created political upheavals and national traumas extensively reflected in modern Arabic literature. This course will examine the development and the major themes of modern Arabic literature in light of these colonialist and post-colonialist conditions. Through close readings of poetry, short stories, novels, plays, movies, blogs, and blooks (blogs turned into books), we will explore the impact on Arab citizens of several Arab national traumas such as: *al-nakba*, *al-naksah*, the Lebanese Civil War, the Iraqi Gulf War, and the failed project of the Arab Spring. We will examine the different ways in which national traumas were experienced intergenerationally as well as laterally, and how they were manifested in affects of frustration, shame, sadness, anger, madness, laughter, and rebellion. Special attention will be given to modes of rememory and postmemory, and to the re-creation of alternative virtual Second Life universe intent on transforming traumatic memories through fostering a planetary dialogue.

- Primary texts: Maḥmoūd Darwīsh, Nizār Qabbānī, Ghassān Kanafānī, Emīle Habībī, Naguīb Maḥfoūz, Ibrāhīm Son'allah, Abdelraḥman Munīf, Ḥalīm Barakāt, Hodā Barakāt, Tawfīq al-Ḥakīm, Sa'dallah Wannoūs, Ghāda Sammān, Ḥanān al-Shaykh, Nuhā al-Raḍī, Riverbend (2005).
- Secondary texts: Ahmad Sa'dī and Līla Abū-Lughod, Ḥalīm Barakāt, Muḥsin al-Mūsawī, Eyād Houssāmī, Samīra Aghācy, Evelyne Accād, Bassām Haddād, and miriam cooke.
- Films: *The Dupes*, *5 Broken Cameras*, *Scent of a Revolution*.

Trauma in Arab women's writing

This course will explore the representation of trauma in the literature of Arab women writers on the mainland and in the diaspora. We will focus on the modes of traumatic recall, on intergenerational and insidious trauma, and on the processes of postmemory and rememory in women's literature. Special attention will be given to the ways in which Arab women's depiction of trauma differs from that of their male counterparts. Specifically, we will address two cultural traumas evoked by Arab women writers, such as *jāhilīyyah*'s female infanticide (*wa'd al-banāt*) and the erasure of Shahrazād's authorial role as the main narrator of *A Thousand and One Nights*. Unearthing these physical and literary traumas for Arab women's collective memory maps a reconciliatory path where the personal is deconstructed to reconstruct the national anew. By tracing these traumas in autobiography, travel, fantasy, and war genres, these writers highlight the intersections between reality/fantasy, tradition/modernity, and personal/national politics.

- Primary texts: Ghāda al-Sammān, Ḥamīda Na'na', Ḥanān al-Shaykh, Salwā al-Neīmī, Hodā Barakāt, Evelyne Accād, Līānā Badr, and Samar Yazbek.
- Secondary texts: Evelyne Accād, miriam cooke, Brinda Mehta, Hanādī al-Sammān, and Cathy Caruth.
- Film production company: Women Make Movies.

Notes

1 See, for example, Judith Herman, *Trauma and Recovery* (New York: Basic Books, 1992), 33; also see Susanne Vees-Gulani, *Trauma and Guilt: Literature of Wartime Bombing in Germany* (Berlin: W. de Gruyter, 2003), 26–27.
2 See, for example, Laura Brown, "Not Outside the Range: One Feminist Perspective on Psychic Trauma," in *Trauma: Explorations in Memory*, edited by Cathy Caruth (Baltimore, MD: The Johns Hopkins Univ. Press, 1995), 107.
3 See Sylvia Moreno, "Palestinian Quilt Presents a Different View Point" in *The Washington Post*, May 18, 2008. www.washingtonpost.com/wp-dyn/content/article/2008/05/17/AR2008051702471.html
4 *Scent of a Revolution* (2014). Director Viola Shafik. A Viola Shafik Production.
5 Ibid.
6 Ibid.

Bibliography

Accad, Evelyne. 1990. *Sexuality and War: Literary Masks of the Middle East*. New York: New York University Press.

Aghacy, Samira. 2009. *Masculine Identity in the Fiction of the Arab East since 1967*. Syracuse, NY: Syracuse University Press.

Al-Ḥakim, Tawfiq. 1973. *Fate of a Cockroach: Four Plays of Freedom*. Translated by Denys Johnson-Davies. London: Heinemann.

Al-Musawi, Muhsin Jassim. 2003. *The Postcolonial Arabic Novel: Debating Ambivalence*. Leiden: Brill.

Al-Neimi, Salwa. 1994. *Kitāb al-Asrār*. Cairo: Dār al-Thaqāfa al-Jadīdah.

Al-Neimi, Salwa. 1999. *Dhahaba Alladhīna Uḥibbuhum*. Cairo: Dār Sharqīyyāt.

Al-Neimi, Salwa. 2001. *Ajdādī al-Qatalah*. Cairo: Dār Sharqīyyāt.

Al-Neimi, Salwa. 2004. *Innā Ataynāka*. Damascus: Qadmas lil-Nashr wa al-Tawzī'.

Al-Neimi, Salwa. 2007. *Burhān al-'Asal*. Beirut: Rīyyāḍ El-Rayyis Books.

Al-Neimi, Salwa. 2009. *The Proof of the Honey*. Translated by Carol Perkins. New York: Europa Editions.

Al-Radi, Nuha. 2003. *Baghdad Diaries: A Woman's Chronicle of War and Exile*. New York: Vintage.

Al-Samman, Ghada. 1995. *Beirut 75*. Translated by Nancy N. Roberts. Fayetteville: The University of Arkansas Press.

Al-Samman, Ghada. 1998. *The Square Moon: Supernatural Tales*. Translated by Issa J. Boullata. Fayetteville: The University of Arkansas Press.

Al-Samman, Ghada. 1997a. *Al-Riwāyah al-Mustaḥīlah: Fusīfusā' Dimashqīyyah*. Beirut: Manshūrāt Ghādah al-Sammān.

Al-Samman, Ghada. 1997b. *Beirut Nightmares*. Translated by Nancy N. Roberts. London: Quartet Books.

Al-Samman, Ghada. 2003a. *Ra'shat al-Hurrīyyah*. Beirut: Manshūrāt Ghādah al-Sammān.

Al-Samman, Ghada. 2003b. *Sahra Tanakurīyyah lil-Mawtā*. Beirut: Manshūrāt Ghādah al-Sammān.

Al-Samman, Ghada. 2005. *The Night of the Billion*. Translated by Nancy Roberts. Syracuse, NY: Syracuse University Press.

Al-Samman, Hanadi. 2015. *Anxiety of Erasure: Trauma, Authorship, and the Diaspora in Arab Women's Writings*. Syracuse, NY: Syracuse University Press.

al-Shaykh, Hanan. 1994. *The Story of Zahra*. Translated by Peter Ford. New York: Anchor Books.

al-Shaykh, Hanan. 1995. *Beirut Blues: A Novel*. Translated by Catherine Cobham. New York: Anchor Books.

al-Shaykh, Hanan. 2001. *Innahā London yā 'Azīzī*. Beirut: Dār al-Adāb.

al-Shaykh, Hanan. 2002. *Only in London*. Translated by Catherine Cobham. New York: Anchor Books.

al-Shaykh, Hanan. 2005. *Hikāyatī Sharhun Yatūl*. Beīrūt: Dār al-Adāb.

al-Shaykh, Hanan. 2009. *The Locust and the Bird: My Mother's Story*. Translated by Roger Allen. New York: Pantheon Books.

Al-Tayyib, Salih. 1995. *Season of Migration to the North: A Novel*. Translated by Denys Johnson-Davies. Colorado Springs: Three Continents Press.

Badr, Liana. 1994. *The Eye of the Mirror*. Translated by Samira Kawar. London: Garnet Publishing.

Barakat, Halim. 1983. *Days of Dust*. Translated by Trevor Le Gassick. Boulder, CO: Three Continents Press.

Barakat, Halim. 1993. *The Arab World: Society, Culture, and State*. Berkeley: University of California Press.

Barakat, Hoda. 1995. *The Stone of Laughter*. Translated by Sophie Bennett. New York: Interlink Books.

Barakat, Hoda. 2001. *The Tiller of Waters*. Translated by Marilyn Booth. Cairo: The American University in Cairo Press.

Barakat, Hoda. 2004a. *Rasā'il al-Gharībah*. Beirut: Dār al-Nahār.

Barakat, Hoda. 2004b. *Sayyīdī wa-Ḥabībī*. Beirut: Dār al-Nahār.

Barakat, Hoda. 2005. *Disciples of Passion*. Translated by Marilyn Booth. Syracuse, NY: Syracuse University Press.

Brown, Laura. 1995. "Not Outside the Range: One Feminist Perspective on Psychic Trauma." In *Trauma: Explorations in Memory*, edited by Cathy Caruth. Baltimore: The Johns Hopkins University Press.

Caruth, Cathy, ed. 1995. *Trauma: Explorations in Memory*. Baltimore, MD: The Johns Hopkins University Press.

Caruth, Cathy. 1996. *Unclaimed Experience: Trauma, Narrative, and History*. Baltimore, MD: The Johns Hopkins University Press.

cooke, miriam. 1987. *War's Other Voices: Women Writers on the Lebanese Civil War*. Cambridge: Cambridge University Press.

cooke, miriam. 1996. *Women and the War Story*. Berkeley: University of California Press.

Darwish, Mahmoud. 2013. *Unfortunately, It Was Paradise: Selected Poems*. Edited by Sinan Antoon and Amira El-Zein. Translated by Mounir ʿAkish and Carolyn Forché. Berkeley: University of California Press.

The Dupes. 1973. Director Tawfiq Saleh. Damascus: al-Mū'asassah al-ʿAmāh lil-Sīnamā.

5 Broken Cameras. 2013. Directors Emad Burnat and Guy Davidi. Kinolorber.com

Habibi, Emile. 2001. *The Secret Life of Saeed: The Pessoptimist*. Translated by Salma Khadra Jayyusi and Trevor Le Gassick. New York: Interlink Publishing.

Haddad, Bassam, Rosie Bsheer and Zaid Abu-Rish, eds. 2012. *The Dawn of the Arab Uprisings: End of an Older Order?* London: Pluto Press.

Herman, Judith. 1992. *Trauma and Recovery*. New York: Basic Books.

Hirsch, Marianne. 1997. *Family Frames: Photography, Narrative, and Postmemory*. Cambridge: Harvard University Press.

Hourani, Albert. 1991. *A History of the Arab Peoples*. London: Faber and Faber.

Houssami, Eyad. 2012. *Doomed by Hope: Essays on Arab Theatre*. London: Pluto Press.

Ibrahim, Son'allah. 2001. *The Committee*. Translated by Mary Germain and Charlene Constable. Syracuse, NY: Syracuse University Press.

Kanafani, Ghassan. 1998. *Men in the Sun and Other Palestinian Stories*. Translated by Hilary Kilpatrick. Colorado Springs: Three Continents Press.

Love, Heather. 2011. "Queers – This." In *After Sex? On Writing Since Queer Theory*. Durham: Duke University Press.

Mahfouz, Naguib. 1991. *Midaq Alley*. Translated by Trevor Le Gassiek. New York: Anchor.

Mehta, Brinda. 2007. *Rituals of Memory in Contemporary Arab Women's Writing*. Syracuse, NY: Syracuse University Press.

Moreno, Sylvia. 2008. "Palestinian Quilt Presents a Different View Point." *The Washington Post*. May 18. www.washingtonpost.com/wpdyn/content/article/2008/05/17/AR2008051702471.html

Morrison, Toni. 1987. *Beloved*. New York: Plume.

Munif, Abdelrahman. 1989. *Cities of Salt*. Translated by Peter Theroux. New York: Vintage.

Na'na', Hamida. 1995. *The Homeland*. Translated by Martin Asser. Reading: Garnet Publishing.

Qabbani, Nizar. 1996. *On Entering the Sea: the Erotic and Other Poetry of Nizar Qabbai*. Translated by Lena Jayyusi. New York: Interlink Books.

Riverbend. 2005. *Baghdad Burning: Girl Blog from Iraq*. New York: Women's Press.

Sa'di, Ahmad and Lila Abu-Lughod, eds. 2007. *Nakba: Palestine, 1948, and the Claims of Memory*. New York: Columbia University Press.

Sarachan, Jeremy, Nanci Burk, Kenneth Day and Matthew Trevett-Smith. 2013. "Avatars Talking: The Use of Virtual Worlds Within Communication Courses." *Journal of Interactive Learning Research*. 24:1. 75–91.

Scent of a Revolution. 2014. Director Viola Shafik. A Viola Shafīk Production.

Sharabi, Hisham. 1988. *Neopatriarchy: A Theory of Distorted Change in Arab Society*. New York: Oxford University Press.

Spivak, Gayatri Chakravorty. 2003. *Death of a Discipline*. New York: Columbia University Press.

Tomkins, Silvan. 1991. *Affect Imagery Consciousness: The Negative Affects: Anger and Fear*. Vol. 3. New York: Springer.

Vees-Gulani, Susanne. 2003. *Trauma and Guilt: Literature of Wartime Bombing in Germany*. Berlin and New York: W. de Gruyter.

Wannous, Sa'dallah. 1978. *Ḥaflat Samar min Ajl 5 Huzaīrān* [Soirée for 5 June]. Beīrūt: Dār al-Adāb.

Woolfork, Lisa. 2008. *Embodying American Slavery in Contemporary Culture*. Champaign, IL: University of Illinois Press.

Yazbek, Samar. 2011. *A Woman in the Crossfire: Diaries of the Syrian Revolution*. Translated by Max Weiss. London: Haus Publishing.

11

THE URBAN GATEWAY

Teaching the city in modern Arabic literature

Ghenwa Hayek

The literary text has often been allocated a privileged relationship with the city. The modern novel has been inextricably linked to the urban.[1] Raymond Williams argues that "the critically altered relationship between men and things, of which the city was the most evident social and visual embodiment" had also inextricably altered the genre of the novel, so much so that "it does not matter which way we put it: the experience of the city is the fictional method; or the fictional method is the experience of the city."[2] Abdou Maliq Simone has argued that city and text are also ethically linked together: "When diverse peoples, localities and regions intersect, there is a need to narrate the intersection, to define it as an intersection of differences," concluding that "these diversities are already to some extent incorporated into each other, already on the same plane of communicability."[3] What more appropriate form to narrate differences than the literary, particularly the novelistic, whose work is, in effect, to make knowable communities out of seemingly disparate individuals, both to represent and make sense of the "new and complex social order" of modernity?[4] By narrating the "intersection of differences," the urban text "[forces into consciousness] the real and inevitable relationships and connections, the necessary recognitions and avowals of any human society."[5]

To rephrase this in Samia Mehrez's words, narrative literature is a privileged form for talking about cities, "precisely because it allows, through its very form and structure, the representation not only of real material geopolitics and histories, but a complex network of human relations across literary topography as well."[6] If indeed narrative literature is a privileged form for talking about cities, then, in turn, as scholars of literature trained in close reading, we have a privileged role both inside and outside the classroom to make these complex networks visible to our readers, interlocutors, and students. By approaching the novel using the lens of a theoretical approach like cityness, we can begin to untangle these connections without flattening out differences, and to explore the entanglements of such complex social structures as the urban without reduction or over-simplification. As I hope to show in this study, this theoretical framework enables us to revisit and cast light on familiar texts, and examine them in a different critical framework.

In this essay, I will focus on the relationship between cityness and the novel as a paradigm for teaching contemporary Arabic literature in the cultural context of the American academy. While I privilege the novel, I admit the existence of a large body of urban literature outside the novelistic tradition. In this critical and pedagogical reading, I will briefly explain the use of "cityness," and develop my argument that the novel is an especially privileged mode for reflecting upon and producing cityness, as well as making meaning of urban space. Next, I will show how a reading of two canonical novels from the Lebanese civil war focused on the dialectical relationship between literary and spatial practices and understandings can shed new light on canonical texts. Finally, I will briefly discuss the advantages of incorporating this potentially multidisciplinary approach into the classroom.

On cityness

Introducing Abdou Maliq Simone's *City Life from Jakarta to Dakar*, Charles Lambert summarizes cityness as capturing "those elements of city life that cannot be captured, least of all by the organizing categories of modern social science." He adds: "Cityness is about surprises – contradictions that are the source of human enterprise ... the visibility below surface appearances of, yes, terrible human misery but also of people working together in order to live."[7] Moreover, Lambert adds, "cities [...] require multiple ways of talking about and engaging them that do not always seem to easily fit together."[8] Simone's call for new ways to talk about cities is precisely the formal question at the heart of the urban text – in this case, the novel – since its inception; in fact, the most successful urban novels produce and recount precisely the sort of intersections of differences that Simone is concerned about narrating. Polyphonic as they are, novels are inherently concerned with revealing and examining "terrible human misery" – among other things – and they often, as the work of Raymond Williams and his intellectual heirs has revealed, deal with the relations of people working together; in short, literary texts have dealt with the articulation of cityness in its myriad forms. Furthermore, literary texts play a crucial role in writing and capturing the space at the intersection of differences, and forming seemingly unconnected urban individuals into knowable communities.[9] In other words, novels should be a significant voice in the growing dialogue on the global city.[10]

Yet, while literature has often been linked to urban space, and literary criticism has been interested in cities as well as other spatial matters – such as landscape, for example – the body of analytic work about the city, including the Arab city, has often focused on the symbolic or metaphorical representations of urban space and/or landscapes, and less on cities as actual places. On one hand, this is inevitable; after all, literary language *is* metaphorical. However, on the other, the exclusive reliance on metaphor reduces the text's ability to contain the complexities and contradictions that Simone describes as being essential to urban narratives. For example, in her introduction to the canonical anthology *Modern Arabic Poetry*, Salma Khadra Jayyusi uses "the city" as a symbol of what she perceives to be the ills of modernity and tyrannical political rule. She posits that cities are "the center of exploitation and misery, of social injustice and political intrigue," and that poetry largely deals with the "problems of the modern city."[11] Jayyusi places "the symbols of the lost village of innocence, peace and love in tragic opposition to the barren city of corruption and cruelty where love dies and only impotency and cruelty prevail"[12] – a point which reduces or negates the city as a lived space (for more, see Chapter 13 in this volume).

If there is an exception to this rule, it is, in Jayyusi's view, the Palestinian city, for she argues, "the city, like the rest of the land" are "all integral parts of their lost and ever-sought-after dream. It is interesting to note that the symbol of Palestine lost and Palestine regained, of innocence lost and innocence regained, however, is the city."[13] The reductive nature of Jayyusi's approach flattens instead of fleshing out.

While the city has been deployed symbolically in many national and transnational Arab literary traditions, it is also true that readings which emphasize the symbolic and allegorical aspects of urban life suppress or ignore political, social and historical contexts in favor of the abstract or metaphorical meanings of space. In David Harvey's words, "[t]here seems to be a world of difference [between] invocation of space, place and environment (nature) as convenient metaphors on the one hand and integrating them as historical and geographical realities into social and literary theory on the other."[14] For Harvey, the necessity of such work is a matter of theoretical and political consequence, since this "not only has a transformative effect upon the terrain of theory, but also opens up a terrain of political possibilities."[15] One attempt to integrate historical and geographical materiality into literary debate comes from Nirvana Tanoukhi, who argues for a move away from "metaphorical deployments of 'space' toward concrete discussions about the materiality of literary landscapes."[16] This, she suggests, "would enable a more precise formulation of the role of literature, and literary analysis, in the history of the production of space."[17] Furthermore, she argues for the reintegration of a specific historical, political and geographical context into literary analysis: "What better program for a geographically enlarged literary history than to conceptualize the dialectic of lived time and lived space in and around literature – in order to understand the entanglement of literature in the history of the production of space."[18]

Tanoukhi's argument seeks to find a place for the often-marginalized voice of literary production and literary criticism within the disciplines that have traditionally concerned themselves with space: urban studies, policy, economics, but also anthropology, human geography and architecture. In the Arab world, space and place – particularly, in recent years, urban space – have been an especially combustible site of contestations over power, identity, and visibility – one only has to remember the pivotal images of the public city square in cities across the Arab world throughout 2011.

Bringing the city into the classroom

So, how exactly does one go about bringing the city, in all its cityness, into the classroom, and how can one integrate the complex layers of historical and geographical materiality into the teaching of novels, while emphasizing the novel's privileged role in producing images of the city as a site of intersections of gender, class, religions, sexualities, politics, histories and cultures? As an example of how this approach may work in the classroom, I will focus on literary representations of Beirut during the Lebanese civil war. I aim to show how two quasi-canonical texts of the Lebanese civil war (1975–90), Etel Adnan's *Sitt Marie Rose* and, to a lesser extent, Mahmoud Darwish's *Memory for Forgetfulness* (*Ḍhākira lil-Nisyān*) can be read anew with a focus on what Tanoukhi would describe as their "entanglement in the history of the production of space."[19] I have chosen these particular texts as examples because of their quasi-canonicity and ready availability in English translations, and the fact that novels of the Lebanese civil war are taught in a wide-ranging variety of classrooms, and not only in Arabic literature classes.

I initially draw students' attention to ways that metaphor and symbolic language have been deployed to frame the wartime city along gendered lines. In novels such as Adnan's, Beirut is feminized, a city ravaged by patriarchy, "like a great suffering being, too mad, too overcharged, broken now, gutted, and raped like those girls raped by thirty or forty militia men, and are now mad and in asylums because their families, Mediterranean to the end, would rather hide than cure …"[20]

Yet, there is another side to this representation of the city, what miriam cooke refers to as the "whore" side of the victim/whore binary, in which Beirut is represented as a threateningly hypersexual woman.[21] Beirut's sexuality and femininity are depicted as being so dangerous that they have somehow provoked this destiny. In Mahmoud Darwish's prose memoir of the 1982 Israeli siege of Beirut, he speculates on the city's downfall, suggesting it was caused by the fact that "Beirut offers herself to a casual passerby."[22] In *Sitt Marie Rose*, Beirut's destruction is the result of her promiscuity. Beirut, Adnan writes, "was heedless to the point of folly. She gathered the manners and customs, the flaws and vengeance, the guilt and debauchery of the whole world into her own belly. Now she has thrown it all up, and that vomit fills all her spaces."[23] Even in other, less anthropomorphic metaphors, Adnan and Darwish repeat the same point: that the city was torn apart because of its openness. "The city is an electro-magnetic field into which everyone wants to plug himself. It is no longer a place of habitation, but a being which resembles a runaway train," Adnan writes; Darwish describes Beirut as "a global transformer station, that converted every deviation from the norm into a program of action."[24] In much of this writing, then, Beirut is characterized by a stream of superlatives that eventually led to its downfall: the city was too beautiful, too open, too alive, too accepting, these writers seem to suggest, and the price it had to pay was high. Beirut is a central character in these tragic accounts; anthropomorphizing metaphors undergird the key rhetorical images used to represent the imagined city. In *War's Other Voices*, miriam cooke argues that the contradictory and sometimes ambivalent representations of Beirut all co-existed simultaneously, that "writers often addressed this muse, sometimes as a queen, sometimes as a prostitute, sometimes as an ascetic"; in all these representations, Beirut is feminized.[25]

However, I also encourage students to push beyond this, and argue that the relationship between literature and Beirut at war is not merely a reactive, mimetic one, in which the role of the writer is to find a language to express the fragmentation of the nation and the death of the city in symbolic language.[26] The relation is a dialectical one: by writing about the city at war, Darwish, Adnan and other civil war writers also contributed to *producing* a narrative of the city that reinforced its divisions and wartime topography. Much can be learned about Beirut during the war years from these novels, including how literature can become a site of engagement with the political, social and material urban realities of war.

Beirut's urban configuration was irreversibly modified as early as the first ceasefire of 1976.[27] The new logic of divided urban geography could not be overcome by the brief intervals in fighting, and most of the merchants whose shops had been in the center moved their businesses out of the now-desolate area and into the areas controlled by their respective co-religionists. The physical and psychological division of the city into East and West was now complete; in fact, even the traffic was redirected. The changing urban landscape produced its own effects on the city's inhabitants; in many cases, the new reality of division was initially rejected, but eventually became absorbed into the language and practices of everyday life. Under the constraints and rules, the conflict imposed a new understanding of the city, no less so by Beirut's inhabitants, for "space develops its own logic, its own practices which in turn reproduce other spaces. Space propels its inhabitation. It precedes, resists, yields to, and survives those who assume it to be a neutral site for their control."[28] In her account of the Lebanese civil war, Jean Makdisi attests to the imposition and subsequent internalization of a new urban logic onto the cityscape. She points out that whereas the barriers "that divide the city, once entirely artificial, have only partly achieved the intention of those who erected them, there now is a difference between East and West Beirut that never existed before."[29] Makdisi's point recognizes the artificiality of the war-imposed boundary, while acknowledging the potency of intention in actually propagating and enforcing the division between both sides of the city. In fact, urban scholar Maha Yahya actually contends that this division was initially psycho-social and later became physical, "an invisible barrier between the inhabitants of the same city, [that] was rendered visibly present through its scenes of destruction, its snipers and numerous military personnel on either side."[30] Yahya argues that there is a dialectical, rather than causal, relationship between the fragmentary urban space produced by the war and the spatial practices and representations of the city's inhabitants. Yahya states that due to (and during) the war, "[t]he unified image of Beirut is lost in a maze of boundaries carving through it. This destruction is both physical and spatial. It is a physical fragmentation which creates a change in the meaning and perception of boundaries and barriers between different spaces." She explains: "It generates and is generated by a reorganization of Beirut's urban landscape, the use of its spaces, access into and through various territories."[31] It is this dialectical relation between the space of the city and its perceived and constructed meanings that I develop in this section, and attempt to get across in the classroom.

In *Sitt Marie Rose*, the novel's first section, "Time 1: A Million Birds," is narrated by an unnamed, yet domineering, narrator; Beirut slowly, but nevertheless abruptly transforms from the "City" on page 9 to the "city," transitioning from the symbolic to the literal, from the general to the specific, as the war takes hold of Beirut and its inhabitants. Furthermore, as Amal Amireh points out, as the city fragments under the eyes of the narrator, so too does the narrative she is producing, until it is "incoherent and incomplete, offering only a partial view of a fragmented reality."[32] As she realizes this, Adnan's narrator takes recourse in a different kind of language and reproduces a few pages from a newspaper, dealing with war atrocities and murders as "incidents." The novel reproduces the fragmented way in which the city is now comprehended. In a bulleted list, the urban neighborhoods are listed by incident, whether looting, assassination, or arson. The list emerges, mapping out the frontiers of the new city at war: the street near St Joseph Hospital, Ain Remmaneh, Tarik Jdeedeh, Sannine Street, Hammana, Louayzeh, Dekwaneh.[33] However, while it is true that the text of the paper as it is replicated in the novel emphasizes fragmentation, the fragments reconstitute a new whole. Just as the sequence of "incidents" of violence eventually cohered into a "civil war," so too does a new geographical reality of the city begin to take shape. This is an urban geography that is based on the new, wartime geographies, which brought a whole new set of neighborhoods to the forefront of the urban imaginary.

By presenting the new reality of urban division through the mediation of a piece of fragmented newspaper text, the narrator creates a distance between the language of the press and the language of the novel. Yet, just as the text reproduces the fragmentation in the city, it also strives to produce and impose its own vision and articulation of urban space. One of the most striking recurrent images in *Sitt Marie Rose* is the narrator on the balcony of her ninth-floor apartment watching the city below her. Her position gives her a vantage point from which to see the fighters, or the streets emptied of passers-by, or the burning of the port. The balcony, as Amireh suggests, makes her "painfully aware of the limitations of her role as witness," but from her position on a ninth-floor balcony she holds a panoptical gaze, with double vision as voyeur and witness. As Michel de Certeau has pointed out, in every act of voyeurism from above, there is also always "an oblivion and a misunderstanding" of the practices of everyday life.[34] So, while it is true that the narrator inhabits the liminal spaces that place her at a remove from the battles, a closer reading, enabled by the awareness of the multitudinous tensions and contradictions contained in narratives of the urban experience, reveals that Adnan's narrator is very much invested in replicating divisions and in promoting ideological and spatial divides.

In thinking about the divisions of war, I have often found it useful to introduce students to a new concept to the discussion: the issue of geographical scale, which emphasizes how spatial representations are context-specific and, most importantly, are produced through systems of signification that produce meaning, including literature. Geographers make a distinction between physical distance and psychological or conceptual framings of distance in their definition of the term "scale"; certainly, this conceptual framework sheds considerable light on the practices and representations of urban division in these wartime novels. While the *Dictionary of Human Geography* defines scale as "levels of representation, experience and organization of geographical events and processes," it makes a distinction between three kinds of scale: the cartographic, the methodological and the geographical.[35] Expanding upon the third category of geographical scale, it adds, "geographical scale is in no sense natural or given. There is nothing inevitable about global, national or urban scales, for instance. These are specific to certain historical and geographical locations, they change over time, sometimes rapidly sometimes slowly."[36] Moreover, "specific events may embody destructions and reconstructions of various scales at the same time."[37] In short, scale can be used to relate physical space to literary (and other) modes of representation and production of space; as such, it has become of interest to literary scholars, since paying attention to issues of scale can elucidate the relationship between literature and the production of space, and to "the articulation of distance within a particularly spatialized system of social relations."[38]

In both *Sitt Marie Rose* and *Memory for Forgetfulness*, scale is used to emphasize ideological, religious and national difference within Beirut and Lebanon. In both texts, the small physical distance between both sides of Beirut is scaled upwards, the distance exaggerated, such that it appears as large and unbridgeable as the ideological divide between right (East Beirut) and left (West Beirut), and also a symbol in these texts of the divide between global East and West. Commenting on the fragmentation of Beirut, Darwish writes:

> And Beirut herself realized that she wasn't one city, one homeland, or the meeting point of neighboring countries; that the distance between one window and another facing it could be greater than that between us and Washington; and that internecine fighting between one street and another parallel to it could be more intense than that between a Zionist and an Arab nationalist.[39]

By projecting the physical distance between one window and the other onto a complex geopolitical scale, Darwish's imagery exaggerates the divisions of Beirut during war. Darwish further exacerbates the divide between neighboring windows and adjacent streets by comparing it to the especially bitter struggle between Zionism and Arab nationalism; given the context and background for *Memory*, one can hardly read this particular comparison neutrally. In the passage, the urban landscape becomes a symbol for a social and political divide that is insurmountable; the city is too divided to be reconciled.

Similarly, in *Sitt Marie Rose*, one side of the city is placed within a broader geopolitical context that literally distances it from the other side of the city. In the novel, East Beirut is represented as a site of fascist sterility and violence but also as an intrusion, as not belonging to the rest of Beirut. *Sitt Marie Rose* implies that the war is a clash of civilizations between the Westernized eastern Beirutis and the Orientalized western ones. Marie-Rose, *Sitt Marie Rose*'s tragic heroine, sacrificed for transgressing the boundaries between Christian and Muslim, but also for crossing the border and choosing to remain on the other side of the city, explains right before dying that, "this war is a fight between two powers, two powers and two conceptions of the world."[40]

Although controversial, the novel's authorial voice imposes a dominant reading of cultural binaries, which is often conveyed through spatial representation. Lisa Suheir Majaj asserts that "[in the novel], Lebanese identity is predicated upon the establishment of clear boundaries between Christian and Muslim, East and West, Lebanese and Palestinian, 'civilized' and 'primitive' – and upon the implicit relocation of the Christian Lebanese to the 'Western' side of the divide," and that this is established by the strong authorial voice narrating the novel.[41] Despite Amal Amireh's assertion that the polyphonic voices of the novel make Adnan's an "interrogative text," "which therefore refuses the hierarchy of discourses of classic realism, and no authorial or authoritative discourse points to a single position which is the place of the coherence of meaning," I find Majaj's reading more compelling: there *is* an authorial voice, and it certainly imposes a dominant reading of certain binaries, which is often conveyed through spatial representation.[42] Adnan's text detaches East Beirut from its western counterpart, and metaphorically aligns it with Mediterranean – but, more importantly, Christian – Europe, hundreds of miles farther away, suggesting that it does not belong in the Middle East:

> More westernized and efficient in war as in everything, the Christian quarters have a sort of austerity which links them to certain "pieds-noirs" neighborhoods in Nice or Marseilles, or to little towns in Sicily and Greece. The Moslem enclaves still retain the disorder of the Orient which is still the last good in these essentially bastard countries which have no precise culture except for the one that developed from a pell-mell of values in a state of disintegration.[43]

Thus, the Christian areas of Beirut are given a Mediterranean identity, and the Christians are identified with the *pieds-noirs*, signaling that these Christian populations do not belong in this city, just as the French colonial *pieds-noirs* did not belong in Algeria.

Adnan uses this metaphor to emphasize both the historical links between the Christian Lebanese and the French and to exclude the Christian communities of Lebanon from any native authenticity. Furthermore, by describing the "disorder of the Orient" in the Western part of the city as "the last good" that remains in "bastard countries" like Lebanon, Adnan's narrator is clearly setting up an opposition between what she describes as the authentic, disordered Orient in the West of Beirut and the fascist, ordered, westernized East that does not belong in the city, and is the effect of its absorption of other values. While Marie-Rose is punished by the Christians on the Eastern side of the war for being Christian and for crossing over to the other side, in West Beirut Christians are welcome, and "it's a beautiful day on the other side of the city, and the streets, even with bullets flying, are still lively."[44] In contrast to the deaf mute witnesses to her suffering (her students) in East Beirut, whose voices are literally silenced and cannot tell of the murder they have witnessed, in West Beirut, the news of Marie-Rose's kidnapping brings together an improvised community whose voices rise in concern about Marie-Rose's fate: "Telephone calls became more numerous, people went out into the streets to question each other, stunned and carried to the point of rage." Moreover, "[e]veryone knew how horrible this war was, but this woman's capture brought to light a feeling of revolt against the injustice of the war which up till then had been held clenched inside."[45]

The image of community forming together "in the various western quarters, in the sectors allied to the Palestinians" around a shared grief, and a shared love for the alleged "outsider" Lebanese Christian Marie-Rose exacerbates the isolationism, racism, and obsession with purity that Adnan aligns with the eastern side of the city, where no remorse is shown for one of theirs who has crossed over.[46] Adnan's novel often contradicts itself: Marie-Rose and the unnamed narrator frequently criticize the Christian fighters for forgetting that they are Middle Eastern; yet, the novel also seems to ascribe to this division itself through its representation of the spaces of the other side of the city as foreign. Within this contradiction lies the narration of cityness, and the above is the sort of critical reading that it enables. Even in a text dominated by a strong authorial voice, within a novel as dichotomizing and reductive as *Sitt Marie Rose*, reading spatially allows us to see the narration and production of differences. In other words, by mobilizing the strategies and practices of geographical scale in the novel, by writing cityness, Adnan reinforces and produces a geography of difference.

The exaggerated ideological difference between Christian East and Muslim West Beirut in both texts is also represented by another play on spatial metaphor, namely by inverting the older mountain/city binary of early Lebanese nationalism.[47] Where earlier canonical texts idealized the mountain as the site of purity and the placeholder for Lebanese identity, in these narratives the mountain is a metonymy of otherness, and clearly associated with menace and violence; moreover, by emphasizing the spatial distance between city and mountain, the texts also emphasize the exclusionary nature of each narrative. In *Memory*, the mountains are figured as violent and aggressive, and Mahmoud the narrator has to tell himself while making his morning coffee, "[d]on't look at the mountains spitting masses of fire in the direction of your hand. But alas, you can't forget that over there, in Ashrafiya, they're dancing in ecstasy."[48] The mountain and Christian East Beirut are combined in violence, positioned in an elsewhere "over there" that is very far from the actuality and presence of the narrator. Similarly, in *Sitt Marie Rose*, the mountain is associated with the right-wing, isolationist Christian ideology of Marie-Rose's killers, one of whom is her former love interest, Mounir, who thinks of himself as European, because he is Christian, and the priest Bouna (Father) Lias, who urges Marie-Rose to "come back to the community. You'll inhale the aromas of baking bread and of the mountains." The mountains here are contrasted with the death that awaits her if she remains on the "other side."[49] By representing the city as irreconcilably divided into two sides, the narratives continuously reassert this urban division, and reinforce the social divisions of the city and its inhabitants.

In the novels of Darwish and Adnan, the ideological divides of the early war years, between Palestinian left and Lebanese Christian right emerge on the urban landscape and in the text. In *Memory*, Darwish claims Beirut had a different identity from that of Lebanon, and that it was not part of the imagined, folkloric Lebanon sung by Lebanese artists and poets, described in the introduction: "Beirut was excluded because it had ceased to be Lebanon's Beirut. In the sectarian view, Beirut was not Lebanon; it had become Arab and was sung by the Arabs."[50]

These writers, imbricated in the ideological struggle of the time, replicate the divisions of the physical city. In fact, they do more than this: they seem to suggest that the divide is inevitable, a result of the unbridgeable ideological differences of the warring factions. While Darwish's text, to his credit, does attempt some perspective – especially in trying to understand the tension between Palestinians and Lebanese over Lebanon – Adnan's does not. In the words of Elise Salem, the novel is reductive, "heavily ideological, it tends to simplify rather than capture complex Lebanon; and because it is accusative rather than participatory, it is set outside and beyond the Lebanese experience itself."[51]

To some extent both Darwish and Adnan's novels globalize the Lebanese conflict. The first section of Adnan's book compares Lebanon to Syria and Europe; as noted earlier, the Lebanese conflict is often represented as a struggle between global Christianity and Islam, or West and East. Darwish's text, on the other hand, places the city within the framework of the Arab–Israeli conflict. This is one of the reasons why in this chapter I have explicitly chosen to focus on *Memory for Forgetfulness* in part because of its status as a quasi-canonical text in so many modern Arabic literature survey classes, but also because it is a transnational text, and as such, presents a challenge to nationalism of which Darwish himself is well aware. The transnational literary appropriation of Beirut, which was eulogized, drawn, lamented, and represented by a generation of pan-Arab writers and artists, underscores one of the most appealing aspects of teaching a class on cities in literature: that one could break free from the nationalistic constraints of other syllabi and allow students to think of these urban spaces as mixed, heterogeneous, dynamic and creative spaces.

I have focused on Beirut to demonstrate my argument about how literature can participate in debates about the social production of space and also invigorate our teaching of canonical texts, but, of course, such methods would be useful in also thinking about the representation and production of spatial meanings in other cities.[52] Such spatially attentive readings could breathe new meanings into these canonical works, in a field that has, according to Michelle Hartman, become relatively fixed and stable, unwilling to take too many theoretical risks, which in turn "also affects our teaching of these texts – particularly as innovative pedagogy tends to lag behind new theoretical approaches."[53]

Conclusion: sharing cities

At the very beginning of her introduction to *The Literary Atlas of Cairo*, Samia Mehrez describes being flattered when invited to present her work at an interdisciplinary conference, explaining that, "as a scholar of Arabic literature, a field routinely marginalized by the dominant social sciences, I was happy to see that the space for interdisciplinary conversation was both possible and welcome."[54] Then, she adds that "many of the issues raised in the social sciences and in urban studies are in fact represented in literary texts that have provided some of the most eloquent and perceptive readings of urban and social reality and its transformation in a form, language, metaphor, and idiom that are part and parcel of such transformations."[55] It is precisely her interest in the city that enables Mehrez to share her literary approach with other scholars from the social sciences. The city enables her to find a common language and to contribute to a multidisciplinary academic framework, and her scholarly focus on the urban allows her to bring literary debates into new academic fora, to position literature as a privileged interlocutor, alongside the social sciences and urban studies, of the urban experience. Focusing on the city can enable new interdisciplinary networks to be made within and across academic departments which may invigorate teaching, learning and research.

Teaching thematically, through a topic like the city, may enable conversations between colleagues that bridge intellectual divides. In "For a 'Foreign Audience': The Challenges of Teaching Arabic Literature in the American Academy," Magda al-Nowaihi complains of the institutional structures that impede a multi-dimensional, well-rounded scholarly approach to Arabic literature. She describes departments of Middle Eastern studies as:

> A number of individual scholars who have been forcibly lumped together as a matter of convenience for powers that need to look at the countries they focus on as one region. The ghettoization of these departments within the American academy parallels the disenfranchisement of the cultures they represent in the power games on the world arena, and their lack of inner cohesion and solidarity is reminiscent of the sad divisions between the different nation states of the Middle East.[56]

Potentially, by offering a class on an interdisciplinary topic like "the city," one could bring together the disparate scholars that make up a Middle East or Near East Studies department in a collaborative teaching environment: historians, anthropologists, urban scholars and literary scholars could be involved in the design and teaching of such a class. Moreover, by articulating similar challenges as well as national differences, these educators may be able to transcend the nation-centric ghettoization that al-Nowaihi finds problematic in Middle Eastern Studies, but which others have used to critique the project of comparative literature as a whole.

For students, the appeal of a course on the modern city in Arabic literature, I believe, is that it can be truly multidisciplinary; not only could it attract students interested in Arabic literature, or Middle Eastern Studies, but also students who would not be otherwise: those with an interest in urban studies, for example. From the teaching standpoint, it also offers some really exciting opportunities for collaborative and team-teaching initiatives across disciplines. As I see it, thinking about Arabic literature, particularly Arabic literature in translation, from a new pedagogical paradigm will take the focus away from a nation-based, survey-oriented syllabus and bring modern (and even classical) Arabic literature into an engagement not only with itself, but also with other theoretical and cultural frameworks which, in turn, take the field out of the narrow, marginalized frame in which it has found itself.[57] Furthermore, by focusing on the city as the topic of a class, new and interesting connections between various cultures and topics may be made, such as, for example, the city during wartime in literature about Beirut and about Baghdad; the dystopian facts of development in new Cairo and in Saudi Arabia; and life under oppressive circumstances in Tripoli and in Alexandria. By forging new connections between disparate texts, and by designing a syllabus around a flexible, circulating, and ever-increasing body of literature, perhaps one may be able to overcome some of the challenges articulated and identified by other scholars in the field. Furthermore, focusing on space enables literary analysts to engage with different forms of knowledge production – not only with the subject matter of making meaning from words, but also with the intersecting topics that thinking about city space enables: gender, poverty, power, class, ethnicity, migration – all are worthy topics, which can be empowered and produced in a syllabus that focuses attention on these urban intersections without flattening out their meanings and significations.

Notes

1 In the Arab world, recent scholarly attention to the urban in literature can be found in Mehrez 2010; Halim 2013; Aghacy 2015; and Hayek 2014.
2 Williams 1973, 154, 163.
3 Simone 2004, 240.
4 Williams 1973, 155.
5 Ibid.
6 Mehrez 2010, 7.
7 Lambert 2008, x.
8 Ibid., xiii.
9 Any talk of "knowable communities" owes a debt to Raymond Williams, for whom urban novels produced knowable communities by building relationships between strangers within their totalities.
10 Some of the voices in this debate include scholars from geography, anthropology and history: like David Harvey and Neil Smith, and Simone and Saskia Sassen respectively.
11 Jayyusi 1987, 32.
12 Ibid.

13 Ibid., 35.
14 Harvey 1997, 46.
15 Ibid.
16 Tanoukhi 2008, 600.
17 Ibid.
18 Ibid., 613.
19 Ibid. In what follows, I will use Ibrahim Muhawi's translation of Darwish's text.
20 Adnan 1992, 20.
21 cooke 1996, 16.
22 Darwish 1995, 91.
23 Adnan 1992, 20.
24 Adnan 1992, 13; Darwish 1995, 54.
25 cooke 1996, 20.
26 See, for example, Ghandour 1994, Abou El-Naga 2002, as well as miriam cooke's *War's Other Voices*.
27 For discussions of this, see Salibi 1976; and Kassir 2010.
28 Sarkis, "Territorial Claims: Architecture and Post-war Attitudes to the Built Environment," in Khalaf and Khoury 1995, 101–127, p. 104.
29 Makdisi 1989, 76–77.
30 Yahya, "Reconstituting Space: The Aberration of the Urban in Beirut," in Khalaf and Khoury 1995, 128–66, p. 132.
31 Ibid., 128.
32 Amal Amireh, "Bearing Witness: The Politics of Form in Etel Adnan's Sitt Marie Rose," *Middle East Critique*: 251–63, p. 257.
33 Adnan 1992, 22–23.
34 De Certeau 2011, 93
35 "Scale," in Johnston 2000, 724.
36 Ibid., 725.
37 Ibid., 726.
38 Tanoukhi 2008, 605.
39 Darwish and Muhawi 1995, 93.
40 Adnan 1992, 63.
41 Majaj, "Voice, Representation and Resistance," in Majaj and Amireh 2002, 214.
42 Amireh, in Majaj and Amireh 2002, 262.
43 Adnan 1992, 21.
44 Ibid., 85.
45 Ibid., 73.
46 Ibid.
47 For more, see Salem 2003; and Stone 2008.
48 Darwish and Muhawi 1995, 18.
49 Adnan 1992, 64.
50 Darwish and Muhawi 1995, 134.
51 Adnan 1992, 114.
52 Colla 2012, 175–183, p. 177.
53 Hartman 2012, 41.
54 Mehrez 2010, 1.
55 Ibid.
56 Al-Nowaihi 2001.
57 See, for example, al-Nowaihi and Halim's essay in Hassan and Darraj 2012.

Bibliography

Abou El-Naga, Shereen. "Makdisi's War Memoir: Fragments of Self and Place," *Alif: Journal of Comparative Poetics* 22 (2002): 87–106. doi:10.2307/1350051.

Adnan, Etel. *Sitt Marie Rose: A Novel.* Third edn. Sausalito, Calif.: Post-Apollo Press, 1992.

Aghacy, Samira. *Writing Beirut.* Edinburgh: Edinburgh University Press, 2015.

Al-Nowaihi, Magda. "For a 'Foreign Audience': The Challenges of Teaching Arabic Literature in the American Academy," *Middle East Studies Association Bulletin*, 2001. Retrieved from www.mafhoum.com/press2/75C34.htm (accessed 24 February 2012).

Colla, Elliott. "Miramar and Postcolonial Melancholia," in *Approaches to Teaching the Works of Naguib Mahfouz*, ed. by Wail Hassan and Susan Muaddi Darraj. New York: The Modern Language Association of America, 2012. 175–183.

cooke, miriam. *War's Other Voices: Women Writers on the Lebanese Civil War.* Syracuse, NY: Syracuse University Press, 1996.

Darwish, Mahmoud and Ibrahim Muhawi. *Memory for Forgetfulness: August, Beirut, 1982.* Berkeley: University of California Press, 1995.

De Certeau, Michel. *The Practice of Everyday Life*, trans. Steven Rendall. Third edn. Berkeley: University of California Press, 2011.

Ghandour, Sabah. "Foreword," in *The Journey of Little Ghandi*, ed. Elias Khoury, trans. Paula Haydar. Minneapolis: University of Minnesota Press, 1994.

Halim, Hala. *Alexandrian Cosmopolitanism: An Archive.* New York: Fordham University Press, 2013.

Hartman, Michelle. "Teaching Mahfouz as World Literature," in *Approaches to Teaching the Works of Naguib Mahfouz*, ed. by Wail Hassan and Susan Muaddi Darraj. New York: Modern Language Association of America, 2012. 41–52.

Harvey, David. *Justice, Nature and the Geography of Difference.* Hoboken, NJ: Wiley, 1997.

Hassan, Wail and Darraj, Susan Muaddi. *Approaches to Teaching the Works of Naguib Mahfouz.* New York: The Modern Language Association of America, 2012.

Hayek, Ghenwa. *Beirut, Imagining the City: Space and Place in Lebanese Literature.* London and New York: I.B. Tauris, 2014.

Jayyusi, Salma Khadra, ed. *Modern Arabic Poetry: An Anthology.* New York and Oxford: Columbia University Press, 1987.

Johnston, R.J., ed. *The Dictionary of Human Geography.* Fourth edn. Oxford and Malden, MA: Blackwell Publishers, 2000.

Kassir, Samir. *Beirut.* Trans. M.B. DeBevoise. California: University of California Press, 2010.

Khalaf, Samir and Philip S. Khoury, eds. *Recovering Beirut: Urban Design and Post-War Reconstruction.* Leiden and New York: Brill, 1993.

Majaj, Lisa Suhair and Amal Amireh. "Preface," in *Etel Adnan: Critical Essays on the Arab-American Writer and Artist*, ed. by Lisa Suhair Majaj and Amal Amireh. Jefferson, NC: McFarland & Co., 2002. 1–15.

Makdisi, Jean Said. *Beirut Fragments: A War Memoir.* New York: Persea Books, 1989.

Mehrez, Samia, ed. *The Literary Atlas of Cairo.* Cairo and New York: The American University in Cairo Press, 2010.

Salem, Elise. *Constructing Lebanon: A Century of Literary Narratives.* Gainesville: University Press of Florida; London: Eurospan, 2003.

Salibi, Kamal. *Crossroads to Civil War: Lebanon, 1958–1976.* Delmar, NY: Caravan Books, 1976.

Simone, Abdou Maliq. *City Life from Jakarta to Dakar: Movements at the Crossroads.* New York and London: Routledge, 2010.

Simone, Abdou Maliq. *For the City Yet to Come: Changing African Life in Four Cities.* Durham, NC and London: Duke University Press, 2004.

Simone, Abdou Malique. *City Life from Jakarta to Dakar: Movements at the Crossroads.* Abingdon: Routledge, 2008. ix–xiii.

Stone, Christopher Reed. *Popular Culture and Nationalism in Lebanon: The Fairouz and Rahbani Nation*. Abingdon: Routledge, 2008.
Tanoukhi, Nirvana. "The Scale of World Literature," *New Literary History* 39.3 (2008): 599–617. *JSTOR*. Web. 15 April 2010.
Williams, Raymond. *The Country and the City*. New York: Oxford University Press, 1973.

12

TEACHING MAHMOUD DARWISH

Jeffrey Sacks

He taught me the Qur'ān beneath the sweet basil tree
East of the well
We came from Adam and Eve
In the heaven of forgetfulness
Oh grandfather! I'm the last of the living
In the desert. So let's ascend!

(Darwish 2006, 78–81)

1

To teach Mahmoud Darwish is to learn to remain with language and names.[1]

In this chapter I turn to three of Darwish's poems ("First Lessons on a Spanish Guitar," "Like the Nūn in Sūrat al-Raḥmān," and "Who am I Without Exile?"). These poems belong to the corpus of his late lyric poetry – the first two appeared in *Why Did You Leave the Horse Alone?* (Beirut, 1995) and the third in *The Stranger's Bed* (Beirut, 1999) – and yet, I'll argue in what follows that they also interrupt the literary-historiographical investment in temporal periodization. The time of the poem stalls the legibility privileged in reading – and teaching – Darwish. To bring this out, in relation to practices of literary criticism and poetic interpretation, I'll underline that to teach Darwish is to learn to remain with language and names.

Teaching Darwish implies the teaching, reading, and study of his language and writing – it implies his writing becoming an object of study and teaching in the university – but it also occasions one's learning to read the teaching imparted by Mahmoud Darwish. It implies one's learning to read the teaching *of* Mahmoud Darwish, not where Darwish and his poetic writing become an object of study, but where his poetry teaches us. To think about teaching in this way remains urgent, an ethical or pedagogical task, because it disrupts the hierarchical relations between the scholar and the poetic or literary object, between the reader and the poem, between the teacher and poetic writing, and finally, between the teacher and the student.

If language, as Darwish teaches us, is not simply readable, then the relation between the teacher and the student becomes unstable, because the event which mediates that relation – the poem – is not simply itself. Language, in Darwish, does not confirm identity – the identity of the poem with itself, of the reader with the time to which he or she is said to belong, or of the relation between the teacher and the student – but forms an occasion for the interruption of each of these.

In what follows I consider several words in Darwish: the word "teaching," first, and then, and each in relation to the other, "form," "love," "survival," and "binding." What remains decisive in attending to these words, I shall argue, is to linger with Darwish's language in an attention to sound, repetition, reverberation, dissonance, and form. Rather than several of the practices that are privileged in literature studies, comparative and others, and in the pedagogical, literary critical, and public presentation of Darwish – the practices of summary, paraphrase, historical contextualization, the relating of personal or collective biography or experience to poetic writing – what teaching Mahmoud Darwish calls for is a patience that would allow for a slow, interminable, and unfinished reading.

2

To think the relation between poetry and loss takes on an acute intensity in relation to Darwish. Born in Palestine, in the village of Birwe, in 1942, Darwish was expelled, with nearly 1 million other Palestinians, with the colonization of Palestine and the institution of the state of Israel in 1948, and between 1947 and 1949. Returning to Palestine one year later, Darwish declined to leave until 1970, living for extended periods under house arrest.

The institution of a settler-colonial state in Palestine has imposed distinct forms of destruction and violent appropriation.[2] In a collection of prose writing entitled *Journal of Ordinary Grief*, which was first published in 1973, Darwish writes of this violence.

Listen to Darwish: "This is how the Israeli 'homeland' was established: neither by right, nor by history, nor as a result of flight from persecution. By violence alone: We expelled them and inherited them. We burned and razed to the ground. We expelled and negated them," he writes.[3] He continues: "Khirbet Khizeh was not the only place. Palestine in its entirety was translated in this way. The Israeli lives in a home haunted by ghosts, but his devotion to demonstrating his worthiness – and to closing everything that hampers his belonging – makes him deaf and liberates his conscience from asking about the atrocity of the way in which his self was formed."[4]

The foundation of the Israeli state imparts a destruction of life and lives – the historian Walid Khalidi has offered, in a work entitled *All That Remains: The Palestinian Village Occupied and Depopulated by Israel in 1948*, an archive of the over 400 villages destroyed by the state of Israel, through its institution – and this destruction, Darwish underlines, also points to a way of self-formation: the institution of the category "Israeli."[5] "The Israeli," Darwish writes in the passage I have cited here, is given place to through a desire to liberate himself or herself from "asking about the atrocity of the way in which his self was formed."

"The Israeli," Darwish seems to say, is formed through a deafness, a turning away from sound and from language, and through a self-liberation – through a freeing of oneself from a responsibility to think and take responsibility for a violence one has carried out, and which one continues to carry out. This self-formation, in Darwish's rendering, is neither simply active nor passive, but occasions the way in which a subject – the Arabic word Darwish uses is "*dhāt*" – is formed. The words "form" and "formation" intersect in the reading Darwish offers, to imply that the formation of a subject is inseparable from a reflection on – and a practice of – form. This form – the form of an Israeli subject – is given place to through its refusal of a relation to language: it remains deaf. This deafness becomes inverted, it is forcibly exported outwards, onto the land of Palestine and the bodies of Palestinians: "Palestine in its entirety was translated in this way," Darwish writes.

The word "form" is rendered in Arabic as "*shakl*," and it occurs as a verb in the sentence I have translated here: "the way in which his self was formed [*al-ṭariqa allati tashakkalat bihā dhātuhu*]." I underline this passage because it points to the violence occasioned in the colonization of Palestine in 1948, and which continues until our own day. I do so because it opens a reading onto Darwish's poetics. If, in the institution of the Israeli state, temporal coherency is privileged (the past is to be cordoned off into the past, and it is to be understood in historical, and historicist, terms), in Darwish's poetic writing a concern with form disrupts temporal coherency. An attention to metrical patterns and older forms of poetic statement in Arabic is set to work in Darwish's poetic corpus, teaching us, as readers of Darwish, to remain attentive to the discordant, disruptive dimensions of language in his verse.[6]

"There is no moment more/ambiguous than dawn," Darwish writes in a late volume of poetry entitled *Like Almond Flowers or Further* (Beirut, 2005).[7] The ambiguity in the drawing of a distinction between two times – night and day – may be compared to the ambiguity of language, with which Darwish teaches us to remain. What this ambiguity, *iltibās*, occasions is neither a vagueness nor a lack of clarity, but an unsettledness or a displacement, and untimeliness, in relation to language. What is at stake in reading Darwish is, then, not to resolve this ambiguity by translating it into the clarity of discriminating, literary critical prose, but to remain with the difficulty it imparts, where language declines to give place to sense in reading, and where the possibility of reading – of language's giving place to sense – will no longer have been secured in advance.[8]

3

"Love" is a word with which Darwish speaks of this difficulty. Yet love, in Darwish, does not occasion a fusion of the self with another, or, in the field of language, a comprehension of language in the time of its reading. In Darwish, love points to a persisting non-coincidence of language with itself, what Theodor Adorno, through a reading and displacement of G.W.F. Hegel, called an "annulment of all rights": "*Das Geheimness dis Gerechtigkeit in der Liebe ist die Aufhebung des Rechts, auf die Liebe mit sprachloser Gebärde deutet* [The secret of Justice in love is the annulment of all rights, to which love mutely points]."[9] The recuperation of loss and devastation through a formal, temporal culmination, where the losses would be absorbed into a coherency of form, is declined. Mourning, where the past would be left behind, is stalled. In Darwish, one already will have remained with loss – including the loss and destruction of Palestine. The loss of Palestine, then, will never have been final, it will never have been closed into a past or have taken place once and for all, left available for historical interpretation and archival memorialization.

The unfinished quality of destruction is also the quality of what a historical event, in Darwish, is. "The historian is not struck by a fever's/tremor, when he names his victims, nor does he listen/to the guitar's story," Darwish writes in a volume of poetry entitled *Do Not Apologize For What You Have Done* (Beirut, 2004).[10] If history, in its traditional sense and as an academic, archival discipline, privileges the closure of the past, where the past is located on the side of death, the historical, in Darwish, is the quality of something that retains a confounded relation to time.[11] The historical, in Darwish, is what interrupts temporal coherency. Darwish writes of this interruptive quality in relation to sound, what he calls "the guitar's story," and history is, then, not abandoned but is re-designated – it is translated – as a poetic term. Rather than grounding itself in a historical archive – an archive that would derive its legitimacy and epistemic coherency through its designation of the past as having passed – history is what already takes place in relation to more than one loss.

An understanding of history in archival terms (through a historiography) and in developmental terms (as a historicism) has been privileged in the disciplines of literature studies – in the Euro-American languages and in Arabic. This understanding of time is also a pedagogical one, and so to teach Mahmoud Darwish is also to consider Darwish's poetic writing in relation to this understanding. The figure of a subject that is to gain its self-understanding through learning in pedagogy – the figure of the subject that is privileged in the European, Enlightenment ideology and practice of *Bildung*, where one is to cultivate a practice of reason through and as one's growth and development from childhood to adulthood, and through and as a practice and experience of gaining literacy – is the figure privileged in the archival and historicist understandings of history I have underlined. It is a figure we have been taught to read in Friedrich Kittler's *Discourse Networks, 1800/1900*,[12] and which has been proliferated in the Arabic language in what came, in the nineteenth century, to call itself "*nahḍa*" (renaissance) and "*tanwīr*" (enlightenment).[13]

This proliferation is placed in question in what Darwish calls "love." In a poem entitled "Maybe, Because Winter is Late," which appears in *The Stranger's Bed*

(Beirut, 1999), Darwish writes of love in relation to the notes of a guitar. "Perhaps my imagination is more lucid than my reality/and the winds are northerly. I wouldn't love you more/were you not with me/here, now between two icons/ And a guitar that has opened its wound to the moon."[14] The poet stages a question: "What shall we do with yesterday?, you said/while we were heaping the fog upon our tomorrow"; and the guitar responds: "Yesterday will follow us,/I said, as the *nahawand* follows the string."[15] The guitar Darwish calls upon points to the guitar string that appears later in the sequence, just as the string metonymically points back to the guitar, and this interlaced staging is also mirrored in the title of the poem, because that title points to an earlier one, "Rita's Last Winter," published in *Eleven Planets* (Beirut, 1992), which itself gestures earlier still, to "Rita and the Gun," published in *The Nights' End* (Beirut, 1967). What is staged is not so much repetition as citation, and this practice points to an Arabic poetic inheritance, and to a relation to death and loss. In Darwish, the poetic subject does not liberate itself from the past, its own or others, but occurs as an interrupted, persisting relation to what is said to be no longer. One name for this relation, in Darwish, I shall argue, is "love."

I underlined that Darwish was born in Palestine in 1942, and yet birth in Darwish's poetry is a complicated temporal event. Poetic language, as we have seen here, does not regress to a point of origin, but interrupts the origin – for example, a birth – through a practice of citation and repetition. The beginning, in Darwish, then, already comes later, it is already belated, a temporal quality of Darwish's poetry which was underlined by Edward W. Said in an essay published in 1994 alongside an English translation of a selection from Darwish's *Eleven Planets*.

In that essay Said wrote of Darwish in relation to what Adorno called "late style."[16] Said recalls that, "[s]ince Darwish left Beirut in 1982, one of the main topoi in his verse is not just the place and time of ending (for which the various Palestinian exoduses are an all too persistent reference) but what happens *after* the ending, what it is like to live past one's time and place, how survival after the aftermath becomes as esoteric and certainly an exotic situation for the poet and his people," and so, too, has Darwish's verse occasioned a reflection on the interrupted quality of the beginning.[17] The date 1982 points to the Israeli invasion of Lebanon during that year and the massive destruction it imparted, an event which also occasioned the departure of the Palestinian Liberation Organization (PLO) – and of Darwish – from Lebanon during the same year. If poetic statement, in Darwish, takes place "*after* the ending," and after *this* ending, language does not take place as a return to the site of origination, but as a persisting delay or postponement of the end – as in the poetic cycle to which I pointed above.[18]

In Darwish, time – as Said also underlined in the passage I have cited here – is a time of survival, "after the aftermath." The poem, in Darwish, takes place as this aporetical time, where "[u]nintentionally/pebbles become a language or an echo/ and emotions are within every hand's reach/maybe this longing is a way of surviving/and the smell of grass after rain [*rubbamā kāna hādhā al-ḥanīn ṭariqatanā fī al-baqā'/wa rā'iḥat al-'ushb ba'd al-maṭar*]."[19] The survival to which Darwish points translates, in the delicate rendering of Fady Joudah, the word "*baqā'*." *Baqā'* gestures a remaining – a declining to disappear or withdraw, a persistence in the time of "life" after, and with, the colonization and loss of Palestine. The translation of "*baqā'*" as "survival" renders this word in the particular, colonial and colonizing context, which poetry, in Darwish, recalls. What remains in survival is not only one declining the colonizing practice of the Israeli state, but also a declining of its terms. If, in the Israeli state and its ideology, life culminates in and is to be given meaning in death, survival, as Darwish renders it here, disrupts, disorganizes, and displaces these Euro-colonial, and Zionist, terms and the practice they authorize.

4

I have drawn attention thus far to several words – "teaching," "form," "love," and "survival" – in order to approach a reading of the three poems I underlined at the opening of this chapter.

In "First Lessons on a Spanish Guitar" the words I have rendered as "first lessons" are, in Arabic, "*tamārīn ulā*." "*Tamārīn*" are exercises or lessons, a daily or repeated practice. "First Lessons" gesture to a first or a beginning, and they gesture to each of these in relation to a practice and a repeated, disciplined event of rehearsal: exercises or lessons. That poetic statement relates to lessons means that, in Darwish, "first lessons" are never simply left behind. Acts of repetition in the practice of lessons – of performing *tamārīn* – are not left behind in the temporal experience of being or becoming one who practices or composes poetry, but remain in the disjunctive time of poetic statement. It is not that in Darwish the practice of language – and of what takes place with language – is enveloped into the European or Euro-American understanding of language and form privileged in the university, but that his writing offers an instruction in language differently. Poetic statement patiently changes an understanding and practice of what it means to read and do language, where reading becomes an event of dislocation and displacement, and where the one who reads is no longer solicited to understand her or himself through her or his having mastered, formally or otherwise, the object of reading: the poem.

"First Lessons on a Spanish Guitar" may be rendered as follows:[20]

Two guitars
Exchange a *muwashshah*
And tear
With the silk of their desperation
The marble of our absence
From our door
And make the evergreens dance

Two guitars …

A blue eternity carries us
Two clouds sink

Into the sea, near you
Then two waves rise
Over the steps, licking your strides
And set aflame
The salt of the shores in my blood
And migrate
To purple's clouds!

Two guitars …

Water and stone and saffron cry
The wind cries
"our tomorrow is no longer ours …"
A shadow cries behind the hysteria of a horse
Touched by a string, closed in on by the distance
Between the blades and the abyss
So it chooses the arc of vigor

Two guitars …

…

Two guitars …

Only the notes of the *nahawand* will take from you
The Andalus of time and the
Samarkand of time:
A gazelle leaving its funeral procession behind
Flying on the wind of the daisy
Oh love! Oh my ill illness
Enough, enough!
Don't leave your grave
On my mare again
Two guitars will slaughter us here

Two guitars …
Two guitars …

The repetition of the word "two" points to a doubling, which is constitutive for language in Darwish. Arabic renders the words "two guitars" as a single word in the dual. While the English language separates the word "two" from the plural noun "guitars," in Darwish one may not separate the two-ness of the guitars from their rendering in language. Language, in Darwish, and as the novelist and critic Elias Khoury has underlined, in an important and still untranslated essay, is already an event that takes place in the dual.[21] It is not, in Darwish, that in the beginning there was an event of language that was simply or solely itself, but that already the time of language is the time of the self-division of what is said to have been simple. Whatever is said to be one – whatever is said only to be itself – is already two, it is already given place to through a literary-poetic practice of the dual.

In "First Lessons on a Spanish Guitar," a *muwashshah*, an Andalusian poetic form, is exchanged between two guitars. This exchange becomes a way of speaking of poetic language. Exchange does not confirm the two poles of an encounter or of a relation established in language, but dislocates language, teaching us that language points, already, elsewhere. Rising up "[t]o purple's clouds," language does not leave the earthly for the transcendental, but disorganizes the formally secured, temporal grounding of the earthly: the losses endured "[b]etween the blades and the abyss," where "[t]ime breaks up." In Darwish, the breaking up of time is repeated in poetic form.

What Darwish calls "exchange" renders the Arabic word "*tabādul*," a word which shares in and resonates with the word "substitution" ("*badal*" in Arabic may be rendered as "substitution" or "equivalent"). Substitution has been spoken of in vexing terms by the philosopher Emmanuel Lévinas, and Darwish's poem compels attention to them. In Lévinas substitution refers to an ethical relation to alterity, where I am already responsible to and for the other, and for all of the others, where "under accusation by everyone, the responsibility for everyone goes to the point of substitution."[22] "The more I return to myself, the more I divest myself, under the traumatic effect of persecution, of my freedom as a constituted, willful, imperialist subject, the more I discover myself to be responsible; the more just I am, the more guilty I am," Lévinas also writes.[23] However, this "imperialism" is reaffirmed in Lévinas through his privileging of the figure of the Jew and its fraternal relation to Christianity, and through his exclusion of non-Europeans and non-Christians from the Judaeo-Christian fraternity he solicits. What would be at stake would not be to open this fraternity, or the masculinist figure of the brother and the family it privileges, to allow it in its expansiveness benevolently to include others, as Jacques Derrida has underlined in *Politics of Friendship*, but to place in question the relations of fraternal privilege it repeats.[24]

Judith Butler has read Lévinas in relation to his understanding of the ethical, to question his privileging of Jewish singularity as a moment of exemplary chosenness, and to critique the racialist dimensions of Lévinas's thought, where Lévinas spoke of "the countless masses of Asiatic and underdeveloped peoples" external to the fraternal bond between Christians and Jews.[25] This understanding of the ethical is extended by Lévinas to the Palestinians, whose right not to be exterminated at the time of the Sabra and Shatila massacres in 1982 – a right indexed, perhaps, and if minimally, through what Darwish has called "remaining" or "survival" – was spurned by Lévinas. Repudiating his responsibilities, Lévinas failed to hear and respond to the call to which he ought to have been attentive, where Palestinian civilians were placed on the side of a political – rather than an ethical – alterity – and where the massacre of Palestinian civilians elicited, in an interview given during that same year, a disdainful, and if still casual disavowal.[26]

The lessons offered in Darwish, and as his poetic practice, rather than promise a figure of totality or of fraternal belonging, form an occasion for a disjunctive relation of language to time. "This siege will go on," Darwish wrote in 2002, in a text entitled *State of Siege*, at the time of the Israeli siege of the Palestinian town of Jenin, "until we teach our enemies/examples of our *jahili* poetry."[27] It is as if, in this passage, the reflection on form offered in *Journal of Ordinary Grief* is revisited. It is as if Darwish offers to the colonizer a different understanding of form in relation to teaching, where one will have learned, persistently, indefatigably, to remain with something or someone said to belong to the past, if only to the corpus of poetry composed prior to the coming of Islam ("examples of our *jāhilī* poetry").[28]

The time of this remaining – another English word with which one may, and perhaps somewhat more literally, translate the Arabic word "*baqā*'" – is the time of the poem in Darwish. It is a time of remaining with tradition – and with a poetic tradition – and with a destruction and loss of language. It is a time that may not be said simply to end, but which constantly interrupts the closure of time solicited in institutions, and in the colonial and hermeneutic violence of the Israeli state, to give place to a survival that exceeds the time of the present to which the word of the poet is said to belong, and to which the poem is conscripted in reading.

5

> Parting is the silence that divides the voice from its echo.[29]

To speak of "teaching Mahmoud Darwish" is, I shall want to argue, to speak of another sense in which one may understand this phrase (the first being an event wherein Mahmoud Darwish becomes a pedagogical object in the university institution, and the second being one wherein Darwish teaches us, through his poetry, how that poetry is to be read – the teaching *of* Mahmoud Darwish). This third sense is one where poetic statement declines the ideology and practice of *Bildung*, and where poetry occasions a persisting and interruptive relation of language to its hermeneutic and historical appropriation in relation to the state form.

Darwish's poetic text remains, throughout, in tension with such appropriation. Let us consider this tension in "Like the Nūn in Sūrat al-Raḥmān."[30]

> In the olive grove, east
> Of the wells my grandfather withdrew into his abandoned
> Shadow. Mythical grass
> Didn't grow there
> Nor did the lilac's cloud
> Flow through the scene
>
> The land is like cloth woven
> With a needle of sumac in his broken

Dream … My grandfather woke from his sleep
To gather weeds from his orchard
That had been buried beneath the black asphalt …

He taught me the Qur'ān beneath the sweet basil tree
East of the well
We came from Adam and from Eve
In the heaven of forgetfulness.
Oh grandfather! I'm the last of the living
In the desert. So let's ascend!

The sea and the desert that surround his
bare unguarded name
didn't know my grandfather or his children
who stand now around the nūn in Sūrat al-Raḥmān
Oh God … bear witness!

As for him, born of himself
Buried alive, near the fire
In himself
He'll grant the griffin what it needs of
His charred secret after him
To illuminate the temple

In the olive grove, east of the wells
My grandfather withdrew into his abandoned
Shadow. No sun rose over it
No shadow fell across it
And my grandfather is, always, further …

"Like the Nūn in Sūrat al-Raḥmān" is a poem about teaching, and in it teaching is staged in relation to place. "In the olive grove, east/Of the wells my grandfather withdrew into his abandoned/Shadow. Mythical grass/Didn't grow there/Nor did the lilac's cloud/Flow through the scene." But place, in this poem, gives way to places. An articulation of a relation to a specific place and time ("The sea and the desert that surround his/bare unguarded name/didn't know my grandfather or his children/who stand now around the nūn in Sūrat al-Raḥmān/Oh God … bear witness!"), gives way to a writing of distance – and to the word "distance." The English word "further" renders the Arabic word "*ab'ad*," which points both to the noun distance, *bu'd*, and the adjective distant, *ba'īd*. Yet language, like the name of the poet's grandfather, remains "bare" and "unguarded," as if language were a relation to names, and as if, in the writing, poetic statement drew further away from itself – to become, still yet again, something other.

Encrypting a relation to more than one other who has died, this poem about teaching ("He taught me the Qur'ān beneath the sweet basil tree"), also works as a kind of citation. Directing us in its title to the text of the Qur'ān, it is as if the poem repeats the Qur'ānic text it asks us to read ("The All-merciful. He taught the Qur'ān. He created man. He taught him clarity of expression" [*Qur'ān* 55:1–4]).[31] It is this repetition that gives to the poem its relation to time, where language declines its legibility as an autonomous temporal event. The word that renders "teaching" also appears in Darwish's prose work, *Memory for Forgetfulness* (Beirut, 1986). Writing of the Israeli siege and bombardment of Beirut during the summer of 1982, Darwish underscores that, "[a]n intimacy with death has taught us that death is silent. If you hear the sound of the missile it means that you're alive, it means that it has missed you and struck someone else," and this teaching also imparts – and again, not solely – more than one European legacy.[32] The teaching of Darwish in "Like the Nūn in Sūrat al-Raḥmān" – where Darwish is the one who is taught language, and not the object of a pedagogical statement – may not be separated from the one staged in *Memory for Forgetfulness*. Nor may it be separated from the one lodged in *State of Siege*, which I have cited above. The events of violence around which teaching is staged in Darwish – Palestine, 1948; Beirut, 1982; and Jenin, 2002 – also stage teaching in relation to colonial and colonizing legacies and the kind of subject – *dhāt* – that such teaching solicits.

Just as in the opening of "Like the Nūn in Sūrat al-Raḥmān," where place becomes places ("In the olive grove, east of the wells/My grandfather withdrew into his abandoned/Shadow. No sun rose over it/No shadow fell across it/And my grandfather is, always, further …"), so too language, in Darwish, becomes languages. The distance that opens between the poet and his grandfather points to a relation of language to tradition and its loss. It is not, in this poem or elsewhere in Darwish, that the figure of the grandfather is a figure of originarity, a primary or radical source. This point of origination already draws away, it remains, as Darwish writes, and with the ellipses he provides, "always, further …"

It is in relation to the figure of the grandfather, in "Like the Nūn in Sūrat al-Raḥmān," that Darwish is taught the Arabic language: "He taught me the Qur'ān beneath the sweet basil tree." Yet the scene of teaching Darwish stages is not a *Bildungs*-centric scene of language pedagogy, where the poetic subject – or the reader – comes to know herself or himself through an experience of understanding language. The world does not come to make sense through the giving of sense to something else – language – but becomes an event where what is said to be the giving of sense, and of *a* sense, already multiplies, where it is already more than one.

Language, and Darwish being taught to read or recite the Qur'ān, is already given in relation to a dis-coordination of inheritance. Inheritance, in Darwish, is already what Najat Rahman has called a "disorder," where the trajectory of time's movement from the past to the future, from ancestors to progeny, is unsettled.[33] It is not that first Darwish was taught language by his grandfather, and that then he wrote or composed poetry, but that the event of learning to read and recite the Qur'ān already takes place in and through its recollection and repetition in poetic statement. A hierarchy privileging the past as a secure, anterior moment is interrupted, to decline to divide out the past – the event of Darwish having been taught the Qur'ān – from the present, and from the being of the poetic subject which is (dis-)articulated in Darwish's writing.

Language, in Darwish, becomes an event of recitation, where the relation of "I" to another is already a relation to names – to the "bare, unguarded" name of Darwish's grandfather, and to others. Darwish calls this relation "binding," *rabṭ*, and I shall read it, here, and in relation to the words I have underlined thus far ("form," "love," "survival," and "teaching"), in a poem entitled "Who am I without Exile?"

The translation of the poem, offered by Fady Joudah, reads as follows.[34]

A stranger on the riverbank, like the river … water
Binds me to your name. Nothing brings me back from my faraway
To my palm tree: not peace and not war. Nothing
Makes me enter the gospels. Not
A thing … nothing sparkles from the shore of ebb
And flow between the Euphrates and the Nile. Nothing
Makes me descend from the pharaoh's boats. Nothing
Carries me or makes me carry an idea: not longing
And not promise. What will I do? What
Will I do without exile, and a long night
That stares at the water?

Water
Binds me
To your name …
Nothing takes me from the butterflies of my dreams
To my reality: not dust and not fire. What
Will I do without roses from Samarkand? What
Will I do in a theater that burnishes the singers with its lunar
Stones? Our weight has become light like our houses
In the faraway winds. We have become two friends of the strange
Creatures in the clouds … and we are now loosened
From the gravity of identity's land. What will we do … what
will we do without exile, and a long night
that stares at the water?

Water
Binds me
To your name …
There's nothing left of me but you, and nothing left of you
but me, the stranger massaging his stranger's thigh: O
stranger! What will we do with what is left to us
of calm … and of a snooze between two myths?
And nothing carries us: not the road and not the house.
Was this road always like this, from the start,
Or did our dreams find a mare on the hill

Among the Mongol horses and exchange us for it?
And what will we do?
What
Will we do
Without
exile?

Already, from before the beginning, in Darwish, there are two. We have considered this doubling in "First Lessons on a Spanish Guitar" and, differently, in "Like the Nun in Surat al-Rahman," where, in what Darwish calls "teaching," there is already a couple: the poet and his grandfather. In the opening lines of "Who am I Without Exile?," these two are staged as "a stranger" and "me" ("A stranger on the riverbank, like the river … water/Binds me to your name"). The first word in the poem is the word "stranger," suggesting that in the beginning, in Darwish, there is another. "I" in this passage, comes only later: belatedly and after.

I have underlined that in Darwish the origin is already an event of citation and that, like the figure of the grandfather, it remains distant, and persists in growing more distant. Yet in this passage, the first line opens with a noun in the singular, as if that noun preceded being and language – as if it were an origin or a beginning. Holding onto something he is unable to bury or mourn – "a stranger" – the poet, in this word, and in the form of an indefinite noun in the singular, points to "something that remains uninternalizable and objectlike."[35] Poetic utterance is given in this inability – a passivity in relation to time and death. The poet, in Darwish, is not a heroic, autonomous figure, and the poem is not a sovereign statement of linguistic determinacy, but an event given in a stalled, iterated relation to more than one past – and more than one past of language.

I point to this excess because if what "I" am bound to is a stranger – a word that is already an indefinite noun, *gharībun* – it is equally the stranger's name. "A stranger on the riverbank, like the river … water/binds me to your name [*yarbuṭunī bi ismika al-mā'*]." Already, then, the stranger may not be separated from her or his name, and the relation of names to mourning and death. To be given a name is to enter into a relation to legacy, inheritance, and tradition. It is also to remark that with the giving of the name, one is going to die – even as this death ruins the harsh separation of life from death compelled in the European and colonial legacies I have underlined. So, to read the opening lines of this poem is already to read them in relation to language, and in relation to Darwish's writing of his own being taught the Qur'ān. The stranger is not already something or someone distinct from "me," but it or she or he is already something or someone bound up in the event of poetic statement which writes of the stranger and its relation to me. This binding, *rabṭ*, points to more than one event of devastation and loss – a binding and a relation that separates two entities it also – immediately – draws together.

This condition – where "one" already takes place in relation to another, and in relation to a colonizing violence – interrupts an understanding of poetic voice as simply itself. It is not that this anteriority may or ought to be done away with, but that remaining with this interruption is what language, in Darwish, teaches. If Darwish's text teaches us how it may be read – through an attention to form, love, survival, teaching, binding, and others, because in Darwish there is always another, there is always one more – this instruction does not fulfill itself in the reading. The poem leaves us, without certitude, opening the poem to a future – to future readers and doers of language – which Darwish calls, merely, "poetry": yet another name.

6

"Teaching Mahmoud Darwish" is already plural. It is: 1 Darwish becoming an object of study or pedagogical attention in the university; 2 his text teaching us how it may – and perhaps ought – to be read; 3 his text drawing attention to the European – and colonial – ideology and practice of *Bildung* and its relation to reading and to form; and 4 the poetic staging of the poet learning to read or recite the Qur'an. To remain with the non-fulfillment of language in reading – where language is a kind of excess – is a fifth sense in which I wish to offer "teaching Mahmoud Darwish." To read with an ear that remains open to the non-coincidence of language with itself will have been one of the imperatives occasioned in this final sense of teaching – if in a sense that will never have occasioned a finality or an end.

To teach Mahmoud Darwish I have underlined several words ("form," "love," "survival," "teaching," and "binding"), not in order to privilege any one of them, but to suggest that in teaching Mahmoud Darwish language invites or convokes – and, perhaps, stronger, compels – an attention to words and of names. Language, in Darwish, does not privilege a single name, for example the name "Palestine," because such a privileging would subordinate the time of a language to a single word. It would subordinate poetry to a theological understanding of language. So to teach Mahmoud Darwish is to do so without privileging one single word over against the many words – and names – Darwish gives. To teach Mahmoud Darwish is to read the poetry to which he signed his name, while refusing to mute the doubled, discordant, irresolute, and dissonant sound – and sounds – of its names.

One name for this dissonance is "exile." "What/will I do without exile, and a long night/That stares at the water?," Darwish writes. Exile, in the third poem we have considered here, points not only to a condition of expulsion and dispersal from one's homeland, and to the refusal of the Israeli state to allow Palestinian refugees to return following the destruction and occupation of their lands and homes – and with their continued destruction, appropriation, and expropriation – but it also points to what, in Darwish, being and language are. To think a relation to time – to a past and a present, but also to a future – is to think through and with a relation to this event. It is not, in Darwish, that the past is to be left behind – that it is to be securely cordoned off into an archive, staged in a museum, rendered legible through a practice of interpretation, domesticated through its understanding as a historical event that has ceased taking place – but that it persists, confounding the autonomy or sovereignty of a subject of language, to give place to other subjects and other forms and ways of being.

"Nothing brings me back from my faraway/to my palm tree," Darwish also writes in the first stanza of this poem, and this verse points to, and recalls, the distance we underlined when considering Darwish learning to read or recite the Qur'an. The Arabic word rendered as "my faraway" is "*ba'īdī*," my being distant, and it repeats the distance of Darwish's grandfather ("my grandfather is, always, further ... [*wa jaddī, dā'iman, ab'ad* ...]"). This repetition is remarked in the poem we are reading here. Reconciliation is offered neither in longing, *ḥanīn*, nor promise, *wa'd*. This quality of being in exile is, in this poem, not solely empirical ("Was the road always like this, from the start/Or did our dreams find a mare on the hill/Among the Mongol horses and exchange us for it?"), and the decision on the question of whether the condition of being in exile has always been or came to be – following, as Darwish suggests here, the Mongol destruction of Baghdad in 1258 – remains one that is asked without resolution. This irresolution points to the promise Darwish also names. It is a promise remarked in his language, and which opens language, and time, to an eventfulness or a relation, a politics or a poetics, to come.

Already, then, and before the beginning ("Was the road always like this, from the start [*hal kāna hādhā al-ṭarīq kamā huwwa, mundhu al-bidāya*], also, from the beginning" – JS), language, and poetic statement, occur in the fallout of loss. Already, language – and poetic statement – will have lost itself. If poetry will have been called upon to take its place among one or another event of language as words that signify – as words compelled to form themselves according to the controlled, pacified contours of a global, colonial aesthetic – language, in Darwish, declines this call. Language, then, continues to compel and command our attention – an attention which both calls upon and forms the occasion for the responsibility of Darwish's readers. This responsibility does not precede but gives place to who or what "we" are, and it is one to which readers must respond, to which they already will have responded, in teaching Mahmoud Darwish.

Notes

1 Throughout I spell Darwish's name as it is conventionally spelled in English.
2 For a reading of Zionism in these terms see Edward W. Said, *The Question of Palestine* (New York: Vintage, 1979).
3 Mahmoud Darwish, *Yawmiyyāt al-ḥuzn al-'ādi* (*Journal of Ordinary Grief*) (Beirut: Riyāḍ al-Rayyes, 2007), 37.
4 Ibid., 37. Here Darwish points to S. Yizhar's Hebrew-language novel *Khirbet Khizeh*, tr. Nicholas de Lange and Yaacob Dwek (Jerusalem: Ibis Editions, 2008).
5 Walid Khalidi, *All That Remains: The Palestinian Villages Occupied and Depopulated by Israel in 1948* (Beirut: Institute for Palestine Studies, 1992).
6 For a detailed elaboration of modern and modernist Arabic poetics in relation to Arabic meter and prosody, see the foundational work of Salma Khadra Jayyusi, *Trends and Movements in Modern Arabic Poetry*, 2 volumes (Leiden: Brill 1977); and also Muhsin J. al-

Musawi, *Arabic Poetry: Trajectories of Modernity and Tradition* (New York: Routledge, 2006).

7 Mahmoud Darwish, *Ka zahr al-lawzi aw ab'ad* (*Like Almond Flowers or Further*) (Beirut: Riyāḍ al-Rayyes, 2005), 129.

8 I try to offer a reading of form in Darwish, in relation to the problems of reading, in *Iterations of Loss: Mutilation and Aesthetic Form, al-Shidyaq to Darwish* (New York: Fordham University Press, 2015).

9 Theodor Adorno, *Minima Moralia: Reflexionen aus dem beschädigten Leben* (Frankfurt am Main: Suhrkamp Verlag, 1969), 216. Tr. E.F.N. Jephcott as *Minima Moralia: Reflections from Damaged Life* (London: Verso, 1974), 165.

10 Mahmoud Darwish, *La ta'atadhir 'ammā fa'alta* (*Do Not Apologize for What You Have Done*) (Beirut: Riyāḍ al-Rayyes, 2004), 97.

11 I learn here from the reading of the historical pursued in Michel de Certeau, *The Writing of History*, tr. Tom Conley (New York: Columbia University Press, 1992).

12 Friedrich Kittler, *Discourse Networks 1800/1900*, tr. Michael Metteer, with Chris Cullens (Stanford, CA: Stanford University Press, 1990).

13 A standard reference for this period – on which there is an enormous, and growing, literature – is Albert Hourani, *Arabic Thought in the Liberal Age, 1798–1939* (New York: Cambridge University Press, 1983 [1962]).

14 Mahmoud Darwish, *Sarīr al-gharība* (Beirut: Riyāḍ al-Rayyes, 1995), 107. Tr. Fady Joudah in *The Butterfly's Burden* (Port Townsend, WA: Copper Canyon Press, 2007), 79.

15 Darwish, *Sarīr al-gharība*, 107; Tr. Fady Joudah in *The Butterfly's Burden*, 79.

16 Edward W. Said, "On Mahmoud Darwish," *Grand Street 12*, no. 48 (1994): 112–115. And see also Edward W. Said, *On Late Style: Music and Literature Against the Grain* (New York: Vintage, 2006).

17 Edward W. Said, "On Mahmoud Darwish," 115. Emphasis in the original.

18 On the time of poetic utterance in Darwish I learn from Najat Rahman, *Literary Disinheritance: The Writing of Home in the Work of Mahmoud Darwish and Assia Djebar* (Lanham, MD: Lexington Books, 2008), and, most recently, *In the Wake of the Poetic: Palestinian Artists After Darwish* (Syracuse, NY: Syracuse University Press, 2015); and Sinan Antoon, "Returning to the Wind: On Darwish's La Ta'tadhir 'Amma Fa'alta," in *Mahmoud Darwish: Exile's Poet*, ed. Najat Rahman and Hala Khamis Nassar (Northampton, MA: Interlink, 2007), 215–238.

19 Mahmoud Darwish, *Sarīr al-gharība*, 97; *The Butterfly's Burden*, 81.

20 Mahmoud Darwish, *Limādha tarakta al-hiṣān waḥīdan?* (Beirut: Riyāḍ al-Rayyes, 1995), 138–141. Tr. J. Sacks as *Why Did You Leave the Horse Alone?* (New York: Archipelago, 2006), 158–163.

21 Elias Khoury, "Ritā wa shi'iriyyat al-muthannā," *al-Tarīq* (March/April 2001): 126–141.

22 Emmanuel Lévinas, *Autrement qu'être ou au-dela de l'essence* (Paris: Livre de Poche, 1990), 177. Tr. Alphonso Lingis as *Otherwise than Being, Or Beyond Essence* (Pittsburgh, PA: Duquesne University Press, 1991), 112.

23 Lévinas, *Autrement qu'être ou au-dela de l'essence*, 177–178; Tr. Alphonso Lingis as *Otherwise than Being, Or Beyond Essence*, 112.

24 See Jacques Derrida, *Politiques de l'amitié* (Paris: Galilée, 1994). Tr. George Collins as *Politics of Friendship* (London: Verso, 1997).

25 Cited in Judith Butler, *Giving an Account of Oneself* (New York: Fordham University Press, 2004). The passage appears in Emmanuel Lévinas, *Difficile liberté* (Paris: Albin Michel 2006), 216, tr. Seán Hand as *Difficult Freedom* (Baltimore, MD: Johns Hopkins University Press, 1990), 165. And see also the discussion offered by Butler in *Parting Ways: Jewishness and the Critique of Zionism* (New York: Columbia University Press, 2012), 28–68.

26 "The other is the neighbor, who is not necessarily kin, but who can be. And in that sense, if you're for the other, you're for the neighbor. But if your neighbor attacks another neighbor or treats him unjustly, what can you do? Then alterity takes on another character, in alterity we can find an enemy, or at least then we are faced with

the problem of knowing who is right and who is wrong, who is just and who is unjust. There are people who are wrong" (Emmanuel Lévinas, "Israël: éthique et politique," *Nouveaux cahiers* 71 [1982/83], 5. Tr. Jonathan Romney as "Ethics and Politics," in *The Lévinas Reader*, ed. Seán Hand [Oxford and Malden, MA: Blackwell, 1989], 294).

27 Mahmoud Darwish, *Ḥālat ḥiṣār* (*State of Siege*) (Beirut: Riyāḍ al-Rayyes, 2002), 11.

28 For a foundational discussion of this corpus of poetry see Jaroslav Stetkevych, *The Zephyrs of Najd: The Poetics of Nostalgia in the Classical Arabic Nasīb* (Chicago, IL: University of Chicago Press, 1993).

29 Mahmoud Darwish, *Fī ḥadrat al-ghiyāb* (Beirut: Riyad al-Rayyes, 2006), 176.

30 Mahmoud Darwish, *Limādha tarakta al-ḥiṣān waḥīdan?*, 73–75; *Why Did You Leave the Horse Alone?*, 78–81.

31 Consider the translation offered in A.J. Arberry, *The Koran Interpreted* (New York: Macmillan, 1955), 251, which I modify here slightly.

32 Mahmoud Darwish, *al-Dhākira li al-nisyān* (*Memory for Forgetfulness*) (Beirut: Riyāḍ al-Rayyes, 2007), 133–134.

33 Najat Rahman, *Literary Disinheritance*, 111.

34 Mahmoud Darwish, *Sarīr al-gharība*, 112–114; *The Butterfly's Burden*, 88–91.

35 Avital Ronell, *Stupidity* (Urbana and Chicago: University of Illinois Press, 2002), 257.

Bibliography

Adorno, Theodor. *Minima Moralia: Reflexionen aus dem beschädigten Leben*. Frankfurt am Main: Suhrkamp Verlag, 1969. Tr. E.F.N. Jephcott as *Minima Moralia: Reflections from Damaged Life*. London: Verso, 1974.

Al-Musawi, Muhsin J. *Arabic Poetry: Trajectories of Modernity and Tradition*. New York: Routledge, 2006.

Antoon, Sinan. "Returning to the Wind: On Darwish's La Ta'tadhir 'Amma Fa'alta." In *Mahmoud Darwish: Exile's Poet*. Ed. Najat Rahman and Hala Khamis Nassar. Northampton, MA: Interlink, 2007.

Arberry, A.J. *The Koran Interpreted*. New York: Macmillan, 1955.

Butler, Judith. *Giving an Account of Oneself*. New York: Fordham University Press, 2004.

Butler, Judith. *Parting Ways: Jewishness and the Critique of Zionism*. New York: Columbia University Press, 2012.

Darwish, Mahmoud. *Sarīr al-gharība*. Beirut: Riyāḍ al-Rayyes, 1995.

Darwish, Mahmoud. *Limādha tarakta al-hisān wahīdan?*. Beirut: Riyāḍ al-Rayyes, 1995. Tr. J. Sacks as *Why Did You Leave the Horse Alone?* New York: Archipelago, 2006.

Darwish, Mahmoud. *Hālat hisār* (State of Siege). Beirut: Riyāḍ al-Rayyes, 2002.

Darwish, Mahmoud. *La ta'atadhir 'ammā fa'alta* (Do Not Apologize for What You Have Done). Beirut: Riyāḍ al-Rayyes, 2004.

Darwish, Mahmoud. *Ka zahr al-lawzi aw ab'ad* (Like Almond Flowers or Further). Beirut: Riyāḍ al-Rayyes, 2005.

Darwish, Mahmoud. *The Butterfly's Burden*. Tr. Fady Joudah. Port Townsend, Washington: Copper Canyon Press, 2007a.

Darwish, Mahmoud. *al-Dhākira li al-nisyān* (Memory for Forgetfulness). Beirut: Riyāḍ al-Rayyes, 2007b.

Darwish, Mahmoud. *Yawmiyyāt al-huzn al-'ādi* (Journal of Ordinary Grief). Beirut: Riyāḍ al-Rayyes, 2007c.

De Certeau, Michel. *The Writing of History*. Tr. Tom Conley. New York: Columbia University Press, 1992.

Derrida, Jacques. *Politiques de l'amitié*. Paris: Galilée, 1994. Tr. George Collins as *Politics of Friendship*. London: Verso, 1997.

Hourani, Albert. *Arabic Thought in the Liberal Age, 1798–1939*. New York: Cambridge University Press, 1983 [1962].

Khadra Jayyusi, Salma. *Trends and Movements in Modern Arabic Poetry*, 2 volumes. Leiden: Brill, 1977.

Khalidi, Walid. *All That Remains: The Palestinian Villages Occupied and Depopulated by Israel in 1948*. Beirut: Institute for Palestine Studies, 1992.

Khoury, Elias. "Ritā wa shi'iriyyat al-muthannā," *al-Tarīq* (March/April 2001): 126–141.

Kittler, Friedrich. *Discourse Networks 1800/1900*. Tr. Michael Metteer, with Chris Cullens. Stanford: Stanford University Press, 1990.

Lévinas, Emmanuel. "Israël: éthique et politique," *Nouveaux cahiers* 71 (1982/83): 1–8. Tr. Jonathan Romney as "Ethics and Politics." In *The Lévinas Reader*. Ed. Seán Hand. Oxford and Malden, MA: Blackwell, 1989.

Lévinas, Emmanuel. *Autrement qu'être ou au-dela de l'essence*. Paris: Livre de Poche, 1990a. Tr. Alphonso Lingis as *Otherwise than Being, Or Beyond Essence*. Pittsburgh, PA: Duquesne University Press, 1991.

Lévinas, Emmanuel. *Difficile liberté*. Paris: Albin Michel, 2006. Tr. Seán Hand as *Difficult Freedom*. Baltimore, MD: Johns Hopkins University Press, 1990b.

Rahman, Najat. *Literary Disinheritance: The Writing of Home in the Work of Mahmoud Darwish and Assia Djebar*. Lanham, MD: Lexington Books, 2008.

Rahman, Najat. *In the Wake of the Poetic: Palestinian Artists After Darwish*. Syracuse, NY: Syracuse University Press, 2015.

Ronell, Avital. *Stupidity*. Urbana and Chicago: University of Illinois Press, 2002.

Sacks, Jeffrey. *Iterations of Loss: Mutilation and Aesthetic Form, al-Shidyaq to Darwish*. New York: Fordham University Press, 2015.

Said, Edward W. *The Question of Palestine*. New York: Vintage, 1979.

Said, Edward W. "On Mahmoud Darwish," *Grand Street* 12, no. 48 (1994): 112–115.

Said, Edward W. *On Late Style: Music and Literature Against the Grain*. New York: Vintage, 2006.

Stetkevych, Jaroslav. *The Zephyrs of Najd: The Poetics of Nostalgia in the Classical Arabic Nasīb*. Chicago, IL: University of Chicago Press, 1993.

Yizhar, S. *Khirbet Khizeh*. Tr. Nicholas de Lange and Yaacob Dwek. Jerusalem: Ibis Editions, 2008.

13

TEACHING THE MODERNIST ARABIC POEM IN TRANSLATION

Muhsin al-Musawi

Ancient and modern Arabic lyrics can serve neatly to broach Arabic poetry and poetics. Selections from Abū al-Faraj al-Iṣfahānī's *Book of Songs*, along with poems by Maḥmūd Darwīsh, and other modernists can help involve students in heated discussions of the presence of poetry in Arab culture: is it still the archive of the Arabs?[1] Background material including studies of modernism is abundant.[2] Although the modernist movement was largely generated and accelerated by literacy forums and journals run by modernists in contact with European culture, traditional undercurrents continue to operate within patterns of thought and practice. Hence, the passage to modernity has necessarily been fractured and erratic. A classroom may need this context to make sense of difference in style and vision among poets. An overview of this background can serve as preparatory material to modernist poetics, especially when it is framed within a relatively comparative framework of cultural production.[3]

No less problematic are poets' manifestos as declarations of innovation and change. To reflect on the practice of poetry and poetics in view of these manifestos can lead the classroom to further discussions of modernity and its politics. An example is *al-Ghirbāl* (The Sieve, Cairo, 1923) by Mikhā'il Nu'aymah (1889–1988), which has long been recognized as one of the most sustained modern critiques of classical poetics. The book was also the outcome of early meetings in New York among the members of the Pen League, founded by members of the Mahjar School.[4]

Taken together, the Dīwān Group of the 1920s, the Apollo Group of the 1930s, and the Mahjar School managed to be more conversant with the aspirations and concerns of a rising middle class with strong urban aspirations for independence, social welfare, and enfranchisement, along with conspicuous sensitivity to transformation in cultural perception.[5] The bard of these modern groups may often claim these aspirations for himself/herself as a romanticist who also appears in the guise of an alienated artist, as is the case with the Dīwān Group. It is thus left to the continuing role of the neo-classicist, as seen in the output of a poet such as Muḥammad Mahdī al-Jawāhirī (1899–1997) in Iraq, to engage with grand issues that constitute a significant part of the national discourse all over the Arab region, a stand that was equivocally received not only by the Congress for Cultural Freedom,[6] and its journals that devaluate the neo-classicists, but also by aesthetes and socialists who interrogated their role in terms of the static and dynamic as rigorously argued by 'Alī Aḥmad Sa'īd (Adūnīs).[7] These confrontations relate not only to power politics in a Cold War era, but also to concepts of poetry and imagination. That said, the cultural climate in the first half of the last century was strongly colored by anti-colonial struggle. There are always glitches and even complications whenever "modernity" is approached as involving the encounter with Europe, a process that worked dialectically within multiple power struggles for domination and control. In cultural production there are also specifics that accompany change or even generate change. Indeed, Mounah Khouri assigns nineteenth- and early twentieth-century poetry a major role in the reconstruction of identity and selfhood in Egypt.[8] Equally, the case can apply to the rest of the Arabic-speaking region. Hence, it is difficult to assume that the three poetic movements catered to an espousal of a pure aesthetic, devoid of any social or political concerns.

The question of poetic individuation or patching to cope with uncertainty and the unconscious was not in circulation in the first half of the twentieth century, for even the work of the high modernists like T.S. Eliot, Ezra Pound and James Joyce had not as yet reached Arab culture. On the other hand, literary modernity is more of a condition than a privilege. Its setup and accrual through the venues of the press, the academy, the public sphere including assemblies, conferences, and lectures at the turn of the last century, set cultural capital and culture industry in relation to and dialogue with social, economic, and political conditions.

These conditions inform and also determine at times many venues and outcomes that generate a cultural market of authorship, censorship, translation, competition, innovation, and also extensive readership. While these sound too interwoven and complex for a classroom, they may nevertheless help to expand a syllabus in a number of directions that can address one venue or another, including the presence of poetry in national politics which can lead to a contextualization of the literary scene and hence cultural production. With the rising interest in national poetry throughout the twentieth century, political leaders were no less attracted to poets, not necessarily out of admiration as much as out of need to cement emotive links with the masses. The colonizer was no less aware of the power and presence of writers and poets in the makeup of a national consciousness. A British archaeologist, spy, administrator and press secretary for the British colonial administration in Iraq throughout the 1920s, Gertrude Bell (14 July 1868–12 July 1926) censored the poetry of the Iraqi poet Ma'rūf al-Ruṣāfī (1875–1945) for being so outspokenly against the British. In Egypt, Sir Evelyn Baring (1841–1917), Lord Cromer, issued orders against a number of Egyptian intellectuals. All of this attests to the power of poetry and writing, which Khouri has already argued. Such political insights can set the stage for a nuanced engagement with politics and modernity in the Arab world. The *nahḍah*, as a coalesced moment of self- and national awareness may find no better expression than poems by the Egyptians Ḥāfiẓ Ibrāhīm (1872–1932), Aḥmad Shawqī (1868–1932), and the Iraqis al-Ruṣāfī, Jamīl Ṣidqī al-Zahāwī (1863–1936), and many others. This dialogue that brought also an enormous body of appropriations, adaptations, translations and dedications, can help in turning the classroom into a valorized space of comparison and debate.

The modernists

The confrontational precedent of earlier literary movements set the background for the rise of the modernist trend which is usually associated with specific names of poets in the early 1950s. Although defined first as a "free verse" movement (and thus focused solely on metrical concerns), in practice there were a number of directions to the movement in terms of form, artifice, and vision which demonstrate divergence among practitioners and also the unique character of each poetic production. The modernist thrust was partly in dialogue with and also in opposition to the sentimentalism and romantic agony of the Egyptian ʿAlī Maḥmūd Ṭāhā al-Muhandis (1901–49) and his peers in the Arab world who came to prominence before the end of World War II. In other words, prior to the embryonic modernist thrust of the post-World War II era there were poetic modernities alongside a massive neo-classical corpus. That said, the postwar climate was certainly ripe and ready for innovation, not only as an antidote to destruction and human loss, but also as conflation of survivalist autonomies and embryonic national projects of selfhood and phoenix-like regeneration and efflorescence from all the debris and ashes. Innovation in form was no less an escape from prison, an emancipatory proclamation of release from shackles and a rising consciousness of freedom.

The poem in context is not a static moment, but a tick in a series of starts and departures in consciousness and poetic experimentation. Other examples in the history of Arab modernity can build up for a course or syllabus a cultural reservoir, and consolidate a comparative framework that looks upon poems as intersectional and thence intertextual spaces that are loaded with meaning and life, thus turning the classroom into a vibrant climatic environment. Teachers can access some of this cultural vibrancy by viewing episode four (The Power of the Word) in the series *The Arabs: A Living History* by Basim Musallam. This episode was produced by Khālida Saʿīd, herself a noted literary critic, and wife of the important Syro-Lebanese poet Adūnīs. It includes interviews with many noted poets (like Maḥmūd Darwīsh), who perform their works in public settings.

Writers and poets were no less keen to reach and expand their publics in squares, streets, assemblies, and lecture halls. In that they were joined by the press at a time, especially in 1920–80, when those channels and venues were the most viable means of publicity and circulation. Occasionally we come across poets striving to establish a deviationist or innovative trend that requires a manifesto, and even a schema or a set of explanations and rules in order to establish and then canonize through publicity a collective endeavor. These manifestos (and they are many) are not limited to the ones already mentioned, nor are they limited to what the Mahjar poets and writers established early on in the twentieth century in New York, *al-Sā'iḥ* (The Traveler, in 1912), and *al-Funūn* (The Arts, in 1913), whose editors were 'Abd al-Masīḥ Ḥaddād, and Nasīb 'Arīḍa (1887–1940). The 1950s onwards witnessed not only poetic and literary proclamations as editorials, but also small coteries that fought for space in the 1960s. Thus along with *al-Ādāb* (1953), and *Shi'r* (1957) in Beirut, there were *al-Kalimah* in Najaf (1967), *Jālīrī 68* in Cairo,[9] and *Shi'r 69* in Baghdad. These journals had their editorials and *bayānāt* (manifestos), and can be studied as indices of taste, anxiety, unease, and a desire for change. They can constitute an impressive section in any well-defined syllabus.

The modernist consciousness, however, took form in the 1950s, even though the pioneer woman poet, the Iraqi Nāzik al-Malā'ikah (1923–92), and another Iraqi, Badr Shākir al-Sayyāb (1927–64), had both started earlier. Along with 'Abd al-Wahhāb al-Bayātī (1926–99), Buland al-Ḥaydarī (1926–96), and Ḥusayn Mardān (1927–72), we encounter a number of Iraqis who constituted the avant-garde in poetic modernism.[10] This by itself raises questions as to the reasons behind this collective movement in one single region. Poets were so intimately connected to an innovative movement in painting, sculpture and short story writing – a movement in which there is a need to explore the dynamics of change behind this rising and diversified consciousness. Indeed, a classroom focus on this point can bring into discussion issues of aesthetics, politics, history, and other disciplines that may generate an exciting climate of ideas if well guided and researched.

One reason behind the modernist trend in Iraqi poetry, painting, and narrative, for example, could be the impact of war, the coincidental presence of Polish painters as recruits in World War II, relative absence of effective modernity/tradition mediators like the Egyptian doyen of literature Ṭāhā Ḥusayn (1889–1973), and al-'Aqqād who vigorously opposed this experimentation.[11] Another factor relates to the burgeoning of a dynamic and invigorating public space in which the urban Baghdadi cityscape must have played a role. The relatively open uncensored travel of journals and books initiated an active climate of ideas that could circulate through the press and café or assembly readership. Meeting places like the Brazilian and Swiss cafés, bars, bookshops, city libraries, university halls, along with the press gave a modernist poetic movement some power that was disturbing to neo-classicists, especially when these young poets and painters were actively engaged in art design, press layout, and editing literary pages.[12]

At times we tend to overlook the role of individuals in de-territorializing a culturescape. A member of the Dīwān Group, Ibrahim 'Abd al-Qādir al-Māzinī (1889 or 1890–1949), for example, spent years in Baghdad, as did the Egyptian critic and scholar Zakī Mubarak (1892–1952). Certainly with the Palestinian diaspora and enforced exile, the Palestinian poet, intellectual and artist invigorated the milieu and brought into effect significant turns into Arab thought and literature. Both Jabrā Ibrāhīm Jabrā and Maḥmūd Darwīsh, and to a lesser and more controversial degree Tawfīq Ṣāyigh, left noticeable marks in cultural production. In his article,

"The Palestinian Exile as Writer," Jabrā rephrased Arnold Toynbee whom he met in Baghdad in 1957: "He said wherever he went he found Palestinians in leading positions; they were the unacknowledged pace-setters of the Arab world," the "germinators of a new age."[13] Within the modernist movement al-Bayātī spent years in Cairo, Moscow, and later Madrid. These external elements notwithstanding, there must be something indigenous that has imparted something in the Iraqi cultural scene over time, and perhaps since the Sumerian songs, a subject that was touched on by Salma Khadra Jayyusi but still requires further exploration, especially if there is such an interest in the classroom.

More challenging in the Iraqi context in particular is the ideological indoctrination that takes a number of paths and culminates in polarized and contentious forums. As matrices of exchange and initiation and indices of poetic and artistic sensibility, these elements are not meant to underestimate the role of the individual talent, but obviously they beg for a better reading of an Iraqi modernist thrust that was soon to become the most invigorating and controversial literary movement, not only in Iraq but also in Lebanon, Syria and Egypt. Political polarization and ideological difference were not limited to an increasing divide between nationalism and communism or leftism, but also to the rise of existentialist consciousness among the literary elite.[14] Although it was the Iraqi Albert Naṣrī Nādir who offered a pioneering lecture on existentialist philosophy at the College of Arts and Sciences in 1951,[15] we can also cite 1953, the opening editorial in Suhayl Idrīs's immensely influential and widely circulated journal *Al-Ādāb* (published in Beirut) as a notable year for systematic existentialist inroads into poetry and narrative. There were un-indoctrinated "existentialist" probes early on that can be detected in the poetry of Buland al-Ḥaydarī and even in al-Bayātī's first volume, *Abāriq Muhashshamah* (Broken Pitchers), but the existentialist drive, partly espoused by a semi-nationalist journal, took shape alongside the translation and importation of Jean-Paul Sartre and Albert Camus. The tone and existentialist pose of free choice fit the speaking personae in al-Bayātī's "Traveler without Baggage" and al-Ḥaydarī's "Mailman."[16] They also meet the undertones of the Egyptian poet Ṣalāḥ 'Abd al-Ṣabūr (1931–81) in his early poetry. They are even more traceable in the poetry of Nāzik al-Malāi'kah, who turns it into an early feminist search for choice.

However, the most committed leftist among the group and also the most eloquent – with a firm grasp of images and internal poetic music – was al-Sayyāb. He turned against the Communist Party in 1958 and joined the Congress for Cultural Freedom as the correspondent for its journal,[17] *Ḥiwār* (Dialogue), and the indefatigable contributor to an emerging apolitical poetry journal, *Shi'r* (1957) that was edited by Adūnīs (b. 1930) and Yūsuf al-Khāl (1917–87). In a nutshell, the two stages in al-Sayyāb's poetic and personal career place us face to face not only with the politics of the Cold War,[18] but also with the clashes of a laboring modernist poetics. At this Cold War intersection, journals in particular were the sites of heated discussions and experimentation, accusations of theft and plagiarism, and critical proclamations of literary merit or worthlessness. The Iraqi trio was involved in all these, whereas their supporters or enemies pursue a policy of fault-finding as part of focused strategies of defamation and denigration. Finding themselves in these heated debates and bent on establishing a canon against neo-classicist poetics and the politics of genetic and hereditary tradition, poets are bound to develop an acute self-consciousness and a strong penchant for innovation and commitment. Indeed, this intersection can serve as a useful starting point for a syllabus on Cold War Arab poetics.[19]

The modernist poem ultimately negotiates its space, as being both ethnic and local, with a sufficient espousal of the universal image and vision to move elsewhere with little loss in meaning, and possible loss in music, especially in al-Sayyāb's case. His extensive use of Christian symbolism along with some Qur'ānic narrative of ancient tribes and civilizations, endow his poetry with a universal thrust that enables it to pass easily in translation. Thus, the modernist poem has more luck in translation than a neo-classical one that is more focused on rhetoric and rhythm. Hence the modernist poem can be more accommodating for classroom use.

The translated poem

Before drawing on specific characteristics that can ensure marketability for a translated modernist poem, let us also remember that, since the early 1950s, but especially by the end of the 1960s, poets every now and then come up with a metapoem, not necessarily to vindicate a role or case, but also to establish a critical and reading schema for certain audiences. Al-Sayyāb makes use of metapoetics in "The Canticle of the Rain" as a concluding deft but loud prediction whereby the poet appears as both oracle and seer whose voice is no less loaded than the clouds with lightning, thunder and, metonymically, a promise of revolution and change.[20]

From the 1960s generation, both Qāsim Ḥaddād in "The Poets,"[21] and Maḥmūd Darwīsh in "The Birwah Prelude,"[22] for example, practice the technique where self-reflexivity or even impersonal stance strives to sustain control of an otherwise postmodernist poetic that is usually prone to dispersion rather than synthesis. Metapoetics can reclaim the pre-Islamic erotic prelude, to endow it with national overtones that radically transform individuation into nationhood, which al-Sayyāb does in his "Canticle of the Rain." On the other hand, Darwīsh reclaims a prelude from the ruins of memory where a lost childhood in his native but occupied and totally decimated village is reconstructed, triggering a poet's configuration of images and feelings that is poised between memory and poetic resistance through verbal monumentalization. Ḥaddād's "The Poets," in contrast, proclaimed as being a matter-of-fact probing into the birth of a poem, does not convey such intense subjectification.

Emptied of any allegorical or mythical referent or substructure, poems since the 1960s have left behind Eliot's mythical method, something that they had heartily welcomed at one point as suited to the long-anticipated movement of regeneration and resurrection. Side by side with al-Sayyāb's powerful mythos in "Christ after Crucifixion,"[23] there is also in the poem a scathing critique of political and social reality, involving the ruthless exploitation of land and people. Those phenomena had been metonymized in al-Sayyāb's "The Blind Whore," who is exploited, maltreated and damaged. These are the kind of poems from which he will gradually depart, either to address his own personal plight as a forlorn dying soul in intimate and heart-rending confessions to a long-dead mother, or else to pronounce a vituperative and propagandist verdict against the leader of Iraq and the Communist Party and its front organizations.

Although translating al-Sayyāb does some violence to his amazing hold on sound and music, the mythic or allegorical structure in his non-declarative poems emerges powerfully in translation. Al-Bayātī's poetic excursions are many, but his shrewd grasp of the efficacy of the catalogue-like or graphic poem, its visual but also suggestive detail, as well as his selective patching and raids on Lorca, Eliot, Neruda, Hikmet, and Raphael Alberti, establishes a universal plateau that can definitely secure a readership. These poems can serve well in a classroom geared towards comparative and world literatures. Especially in poems that bring together soaring Sufi sentiments and address female symbols of elusive creativity and motion, translation works well – indeed, at times as well as the original.[24] These are captured in his famous Lara poem, "I am Born and Die in my Love," with its Boris Pasternak heroine in *Doctor Zhivago* coalesced with the *femme fatale* archetype and ibn 'Arabī's al-Naẓẓām (The Eye of the Sun). No wonder both al-Bayātī and al-Sayyāb are able to secure a relatively good reception in translation, even better than the suave Lamī'ah 'Abbās 'Imārah, Adūnīs, 'Abd al-Ṣabūr and Amal Dunqul (1940–82), despite their powerful and nuanced poetics. As precursors, al-Sayyāb and al-Bayātī also set the ground for their followers like Sa'dī Yūsuf (b. 1934), Muḥammad Bennīs (b. 1955), Samīḥ al-Qāsim, and Darwīsh, all of whom pursue a number of poetic innovations without giving up their commitment to their language, culture and tradition while finding themselves targets of a proclaimed Cold War policy under the rubric of universalism, abstract art and aesthetic autonomy. These poets and poetics can be coalesced in classroom discussion under the rubric of postmodernism, but with the understanding that their commitment to Arabic language and culture has a strong hold on the structure of the poem which could have suffered fracture in the West.

The poem in the classroom

Modernist Arabic poetry meets the demands of a classroom not as apolitical lyric, with only intrinsic matrices and an ambivalent structure as claimed and practiced by the New Critics, but rather as: 1 reclamation of the traditional register, including images, nomenclature, and thematic concerns to fit into the new; 2 engagement with political reality entailing geographical mapping of land and people in times of deliberate occupation, erosion, deportation and eviction; 3 conversing with and applying popular life, culture and tradition with its folk songs, narratives, troubles, aspirations, colors, and customs; 4 applying what modernity offers by way of collage, bricolage, theatrical divisions, graphic detail, and the language of non-poetic texts or media. Under each of these headings one can cite a large number of poems, but for the sake of this chapter let us focus on an example from each category to see how a poem works in translation and the reasons behind its stance against Cold War politics.

Prior to this exploration, let us also approach two serious implications that make poetry in translation a controversial issue. Are poetry and the lyric in particular translatable? Furthermore, how do we justify the resourcefulness of great poets like Goethe in their East/West poems that strive to capture some shades from each tradition? Or how do we approach poems that are dedicated to Lorca (al-Sayyāb, al-Bayātī, 'Abd al-Ṣabūr, the Sudanese Jīllī 'Abd al-Raḥmān, and Darwīsh) or to Keats (al-Māzinī (d. 1949) and Nāzik al-Malā'ikah), for example?[25] In the ninth century, the polymath and rationalist essayist al-Jāḥiẓ (d. 869) cites poetry and scriptures,[26] i.e. the Qur'ān, as problematic in translation because of inevitable loss in suggestiveness, connotation, figuration, and cadence. Indeed, translation from philosophy or science poses fewer problems simply because of the absence of the above. Apart from this problematic, there are the paratexts, especially dedications. How can we account for these in a classroom discussion?

Insofar as thresholds, preludes, and dedications are concerned, it is already argued by many theorists that each threshold actually penetrates the inside poem, its most elusive structures and claims.[27] A poet dedicates a particular poem because of some fascination with his/her subject, the dedicatee, a fascination and familiarity that amounts to restrained plagiarism. Even when dedicating in proclaimed revulsion against Eliot's conservatism, as al-Bayātī does, the act carries with it more love than hatred: if there is actual revulsion in the dedicatory paratext, it is meant to be seen as a gesture against his rival, al-Sayyāb, as Eliot's outspoken admirer along with Jabrā and others. Al-Bayātī's poetry includes substantial raids on Eliot in style, imagery and method, all of which betray a pervasive familiarity.[28] Notwithstanding their equivocal position in translational configurations, dedications as such, especially when addressed to foreign dedicatees, provide us with subtle inroads into the translatability of poetry. The poet reads and understands the target, i.e. the dedicatee, as a translator, but with a poetic sensibility and subtle delving into an otherwise evasive matrix, mechanism, aesthetic and intimation. A poet working with someone else's verses as a matrix for his own is a translator par excellence, a subtle invader who is too elusive to be fully traced. Whatever traces he/she leaves behind can function as instrumental guides for translators. We can imagine how this intersection can open up discussions and comparisons, among many poems, originals, raids, and imitations.[29]

The medieval writer al-Jāḥiẓ's significant insights on the translation of texts include a closing surmise on the copy industry in the pre-print age. With prodigious insight on source material for translators, he cautions that a current copy might have suffered defilement and distortion by design or out of negligence. A copyist by profession, he is aware of the pitfalls of claiming exactitude. Apart from the ways in which each language is bound to violate the other, al-Jāḥiẓ ranks and categorizes translation according to registers, norms, nature, linguistic density, discipline and the translator's knowledge.[30] The task is almost unmanageable.

Certainly, writers and thinkers have already dwelt on this issue with the rise of modernity. The case of translating Homer elicited some of the most interesting discussions, as Matthew Arnold's many essays demonstrate.[31] However, modernity, in its modernist thrust, is upon us, not only because the rising elite of the late nineteenth and early twentieth centuries felt the urgency of reform through cultural correspondence, importation, appropriation and acculturation, but also because colonial desire has it that the "native" change skin in order to understand and participate in Western cultural hegemony as the basis for economic and political mandates. From the 1950s onwards, Cold War architects established non-governmental organizations like the Franklin Foundation to take care of a widespread translation project that let many American and some European publications, especially of a non-socialist realistic nature, flood the market in the 1950s onwards. Faulkner, T. Williams, T.S. Eliot, and even Camus, for example, are meant to dislodge Russian writing that had carved a popular stream in Arabic through Progress Publishers and other venues.

Poetic reclamations of tradition

Al-Sayyāb draws only elusively and allegorically in the prelude to his "Canticle of the Rain" on the pre-Islamic nostalgic prelude. Canonized in Imru' al-Qays's call on his companions to halt and weep for the memory of a departing lover as signified by the remaining trace or ruin of an abandoned campsite, the erotic prelude, its zephyr of Najd in J. Stetkevych's apt phrase,[32] is reclaimed anew to dwell on one of the most alarming outcomes of modernity: migration, exodus, deportation, and enforced settlements. While poets also resort to the prelude for other reasons, like exile, alienation, nostalgia, etc., it comes anew as an appropriation into a cemented memory-poetics of a momentous human condition that resists erosion and media trivialization. Poetry is not at stake at this juncture: it is there fully up to the occasion of reclamation and authentication. Both are resistance strategies on the level of ethnic, national and cultural identity, and also on the level of poetic autonomy. The poet has to carve a poem from the subtleties of talent, perception and feeling at a moment of looming death. Such is Maḥmūd Darwīsh's "Al-Birwa Prelude" (*Ṭalaliyyat al-Birwah*, 2009),[33] which reclaims his place of birth in 1941, from which he and his family and villagers were evicted by force. Notwithstanding the scant use of the classical pre-Islamic register (horses, rock, encampment, wilderness and abandonment), and its allusion to the multiple meaning of the word *bayt*, meaning in the context of prosody a line of two hemistiches, but otherwise refers to home and displacement, the poem strives to capture the only sustaining vision of a childhood birthplace to which Gaston Bachelard assigns the strongest hold on memory in *The Poetics of Space*.[34] Darwīsh's personae's internalization of a place that is obviously eroded draws on the pre-Islamic nostalgic prelude only as a poetic steeping process for a paradoxical scene where it is eviction rather than choice that triggers a memory of the components of a lost homeland.

Introducing the "Birwah Prelude" in a classroom requires: 1 a brief introduction to the practice in pre-Islamic poetry; 2 some reference to Darwīsh's corpus on memory and absence; 3 reading the poem as a sample of the poetry of paradox that sustains an autonomous text through juxtaposition and tension between two voices and visions – the journalist/tourist and the poet/child. In other words, the poem can collapse ancient and modern poetics, and situate the displacement of individuals, communities, and a people at the center of human calamities and disasters. The political, social, and cultural are brought together subtly to confront all with a situation that the human race has thus far failed to address. If there are specifics to this poem, they relate to its recall of the rural, and hence the popular, and to problematize it as a habitat under occupation. No longer evocative of rustic or idyllic life, it constructs another story, a narrative of enforced displacement and deportation that speaks to us as an unhealed wound.

Engaging the popular

Darwīsh's preludes and songs pertain to a popular tradition, but they differ from the early usage of the pioneers, like 'Abd al-Wahhāb al-Bayātī. The latter was a well-equipped artificer. In making use of popular proverbs, sayings, and images that aspire to cement an emotive link with common people, he comes up with poems of concrete images, juxtaposed structures, and suggestive visual detail. While significantly important as a counter-movement to elitism courted by the Congress for Cultural Freedom (CCF) against realistic representation as a leftist Russian strategy, this populist poetics has not necessarily succeeded in leaving a strong impression. Nevertheless, it is pursued with a nuanced venture into popular life, not through proverbs and popular language that patches the text in al-Bayātī's early poetics, but rather through a dense mapping of the topography of a particular place, Basra in the case of Sa'dī Yūsuf, and a number of locations and cases in the mixed linguistic reservoir of Muẓaffar al-Nawwāb (1934–Feb. 2017). However, al-Bayātī, and other significant poets in Egypt like Ṣalāḥ 'Abd al-Ṣabūr and Amal Dunqul, reach the common person through a register and rhythm of populist communion whereby markets, living conditions, political and human concerns provide the semantic field for a poem. A title for a collection of poems such as *People in my Homeland* by 'Abd al-Ṣabūr speaks for a direction that is not to the taste of Cold War architects. However, al-Bayātī's *Broken Pitchers* (1954) was hailed a year later by no less a critic than Iḥsān 'Abbās in a book that explores modernity through a close reading of the collection. The most obvious use of visual images that are laid out in a procession of rapid scenes is noted by the critic, though with little discomfort. However, knowing that "visual autonomy is the chief aesthetic principle and thus the primary mark of Modernist affiliation," as Noorani rightly notes,[35] we need to look at al-Bayātī's poetics as something carefully wrought in a Cold War era. Rather than giving in to the compelling argument for autonomy as a non-committal pursuit, he lets these successive images nakedly expose a stark reality of exploitation and human degradation. Displacing and replacing classical rhetoric and the whole representational trend, the emphasis on visual stimuli gears poetics towards a scene, for example, in a village market where there are only tattered goods seen and wished for by an impoverished peasant whom the poet's persona perhaps internalizes and quotes:

> The sun, and the lean donkeys and the flies,
> and an old pair of army boots
> passed around, and a peasant staring off into space,
> "At the start of the coming year
> My hands will fill with cash
> And I'll buy these boots."[36]

Although seemingly disconnected, images converge to create the impression of a sordid reality that has to be shocking and disturbing. Romantic representation of some pastoral landscape has disappeared, and the peasant's suffering is visualized through glimpses into a life of destitution. The shift from the spatial to the temporal universalizes the experience in impoverished societies. Hence, while agreeing with Jonathan Crary's reading of an observant modernity, whereby "observation is increasingly a question of equivalent sensations and stimuli that have no reference to a spatial location,"[37] there is in this poem a deliberate effort to augment the reader's sense of discomfort at life in a Third World village market. In other words, al-Bayātī manipulates modernist strategies to address a shocking and disturbing case that exposes the falsity of Western rural/urban binary ethics.

Modernist malaise

Although the Arab poetic scene in the 1950s is rich with experimentation, the Iraqi Kurd Buland al-Ḥaydarī can be credited with the insertion of media bricolage into the scene: his two poems, "The Mailman" and "Twenty Thousand War Casualties" are uniquely suited to the understanding of the presence of media in culture as grasped and articulated in poetry.[38] Collage creates a scenic showcase whereby the poet stands outside the text, observing and documenting while also intruding every now and then in an explanatory parenthetical sentence. The second poem, for instance, narrates the broadcast, the world news in the aftermath of a battle in which the broadcaster (announcer) reads what he is given in a stiff rigid and neutral voice: 20,000 casualties. Divorced of empathy, the broadcaster's voice is trained, like the war itself, to be passionless and cold. The poem exposes the manipulation of media in war situations where embedding is the pervasive practice as a way of debasing human life as war mongers would like it to be.

"The Mailman" is instead concerned with human alienation, for the avowed recipient of the mail is the speaker who is so aware of alienation that he is captured in a poised moment, one of equipoise, between the knock at his door and his response: he is expecting no letter or communication. This same response characterizes al-Bayātī's "A Traveler Without Luggage," where alienation is so bluntly Kafkaesque that one wonders if al-Bayātī is ever as leftist as the left claims him to be in the early 1950s. The poem, already in translation, was written and published in 1954, and it opens and concludes with:

> From nowhere
>
> I have no history, no face, from nowhere
>
> Under the skies in the wailing of the wind I hear it call me: "Come!"

He adds further in the middle of the poem:

> Inside of me a self dies
>
> Like a spider a self dies in me
>
> And on the wall
>
> The light of day
>
> Sucks my years, spits them as blood, the light of day
>
> Absolutely, this day was not made for me
>
> The door has been closed![39]

The full text of the poem can make a good case for the study of a modernist example – not only because it disputes the concept of commitment as a socialist realist pursuit among leftist literati, but also because it directs attention to the ambivalence and uncertainty surrounding such a concept. Divides are erected simply because there are writings that do not fit into autonomy as being synonymous with abstraction, apolitical enunciation that raises no question or disturbs nobody. A poem like this one also opens the gate for further discussions of Kafka's *Metamorphosis*, and the understanding of existentialism or alienation among the literati in that early period. It can certainly lead to a questioning of the aftermath of wars, their impact on people's sensibilities, and their ultimate destruction of selfhood, identities and ethnicities.

The voice, the text and the urban space

One of the significant features and markers of a modernist poetic tradition seems to run opposite to T.S. Eliot's objectification stance, but only seemingly so: self-reflexivity functions as the backbone for a modernist stance. It is a deliberate tool for the manufacture of a schema, a reading manual, as self-awareness betraying a tension between self-aggrandizement and fear, and an indirect engagement with contenders. It builds on the high modernist effort to establish a canon through coteries, journals, little magazines, editorial forums, processes of fraternal promotion aimed at establishing cultural and symbolic capital, and trading on other celebrities through requests for an introduction, a preface or a blurb. Arab poets – though to different degrees – have been no exception to these trends, especially with the rise of social media and other means of media proliferation. Self-reflexivity is another savvy method by which to justify a place or carve another among so many contending voices.[40] The use of masks and alternative personae in the early modernism of the 1950s and 1960s now gives way to this pondering, something which can also be viewed as yet another free market trafficking stratagem: poetry is commoditized like any object and needs further promotion. There is an enormous amount of publication that addresses "poetry" as commodity. It directs attention to this sense of urgency in an open market economy. Poets have to contend for a place in this bustling media hustle. Not all poems or interventions in this direction suit a classroom experience, not only because some lose tangibility and meaning in translation, but also because abstraction often dwindles to univocality while plurivocality brings many interests, voices and concerns together and thence places a poem into a transgeneric order.

Qāsim Ḥaddād's "The Poets" may stand for this transgeneric pattern while Maḥmūd Darwīsh's "A Café, and You with a Newspaper" can serve another purpose, one that unsettles Cold War politics while it substantiates an urban space as chronotopic enough to bring time and space together in politically loaded terms.[41] Qāsim Ḥaddād's "The Poets" empties poetry of referents other than the ones focusing on the process of turning a poem into a creative process that is bound to take form and materialize in people's lives, perception and expectations.[42] The allegedly committed poet lets this piece speak for a larger process that is comprehensive enough to align it with scriptures and narratives that have always been at the back of the mind in human thinking. The celebration is one way of speaking for poetry in poetry, a metapoesis that scrutinizes and plays on the fine thread between vraisemblance and abstraction without an effort to draw on ancient modes or models, a point that instructors can work with in one way or another.[43]

Dating from 2005, but already available in a slightly different translation, Darwīsh's "A Café …" contains most features of his poetics. One can say that it refers to a café without actually offering the reader any spatial particulars. Perhaps it is this dispersion of referents that is in keeping with an ironic sense of solitude, a solitude that is avowedly cherished while it presents a meditating forlorn speaker:

> A café there, and you with a newspaper,
>
> No, you are not by yourself; your glass is half full
>
> the other half filled up by the sun …
>
> From behind the glass, you watch hurried passersby
>
> But you are unseen [a privilege of invisibility: to see but not to be seen]

How free you are, you the forgotten one!
Nobody to see the impression the violin leaves on you,
Nobody stares at your presence or absence
Or scrutinizes your withdrawn diffident foggy look
at a girl …
How free you are in administering your personal business
in this hustle without being watched or read
So do whatever you like with yourself, take off
your shoes or your shirt, if you want,
Your are neglected after all and free in your soaring imagination,
there is no pressing business here for your name
or your face.
You be as you wish … neither friend nor foe watching your memories
So, excuse the one who left you in the café
Because you failed to see her new hairstyle
And the butterflies dancing on her cheek dimples
Also forgive the one who asked for your assassination once
For no reason … other than
you didn't get killed when you bumped into a star …
and wrote thence the first songs with her ink …
A café there, and you with a newspaper,
Forgotten in a corner, with no one bothering your composed mood,
nobody thinking of assassinating you
You are forgotten after all and free in your soaring imagination![44]

The underlying irony only lends more power and effect to the paradoxical structure of the poem, one that brings together a life story of love and war, struggle and poetry, and romanticism and postmodernist indeterminacy. Abstraction is overwhelmed by a presence in the form of absence where only a voice leaves the trace of experience; and that only drives the reader into a similar situation, poised in the same absence. Easy to recover in translation, the poem can open up enough space for queries with respect to memory, imagination, political commitment, the limits and divides of public and private lives, and the expectations of self and others.

The shifts in modernist and postmodernist experimentation can provide a reservoir of translatable poetry for the classroom, especially when a poem lends itself easily to the syntax and linguistic ease of another medium. Al-Bayātī stands foremost in providing a wide canvas of translatable texts. Darwīsh of the 1990s is no less so; others have significant translatable texts that invite careful selection to fit into a classroom while leading the reader or listener to a better understanding of a history and makeup of Arabic poetry as a rich and complex venue for understanding Arab culture. It is indeed as a dynamic in cementing and deepening understanding, identity and national awareness that this poetry competes with other literary forms in cultural production. Combining the testimonial, the confessional, the nostalgic memory, acute politics and Sufi excursions, Arab modern and modernist poems can make a challenging experience in a classroom climate.

Appendix A

Maḥmūd Darwīsh, "The Birwah Prelude"

I step lightly on earth like birds

So as not to wake up the dead[45] and I lock

My sentiment's door to be my other, for I don't feel

I am a rock yearning for a cloud.

Hence I stroll like a tourist or a Western newspaper correspondent

Selecting from this place the blowing wind direction

I choose absence to describe. Absence sits neutral

Around me, and the raven saw how neutral it is.

O companions halt, … let us try the place our way:

Here a certain sky falls

On a rock and makes it bleed to let anemone sprout in spring …

(So where is my song now?) Here is where the gazelle breaks into my window glass to get me to follow it

To the valley (So where is my song now?)

Here where the enchanting morning butterflies carry

the road to my school (So where is my song now?)

Here is the trace where I prepared to fly to my planets a horse (So where is my song now?) I say

to my companions: halt … so as to measure the place

and its barrenness with the pre-Islamic odes that are rich with horses

and departure. For each rhyme there will be erected a camp

And for every line on the way of wind gusts a rhyme …

But I am the son of my first tale. My milk

is yet warm in my mother's breast.

and the crib is rocked by two small birds.

and my father builds my future with his hands

I am not a grown-up to be driven to exile

The tourist says: wait for the pigeon to end its coo

I say: I know her and she knows me; but the message has not reached its destination.

The journalist interrupts my secret song:

Do you see the dairy factory behind that stone pine tree? I say No

I don't see other than the deer in the window

And he says: do you see the modern roads

on the ruins of houses? I say No

I don't see them, I see only the garden below

I see the spider's web. He says:

Dry your tears with a handful of soft grass. I say this other is weeping for the past …

The tourist says: the visit comes to an end, I haven't seen something to photograph other than a ghost

I say: I see absence with components and tools

I touch it and hear it, and it carries me up.

I see the farthest of the faraway skies.

Whenever I die, I wake up, reborn, returning

From absence to absence.

Appendix B

Qāsim Ḥaddād, "The Poets"

Translated by: Khaled Mattawa

Poets draw nature before it prefigures itself
and they invent
and build a hut abandoned by a gang of thugs.
They sing sometimes
and they form a road so water can take the shape of a river.
They instill in mud the memory of the trees.
A bird discovers its colors in the phrases of a poem,
and picks its rare name.
When poets leave sleep behind
the young thugs begin their rampage.
They romp a little
and they throng as if nature is ambushing them.
They storm and they thunder.
And their limbs begin to thin as if the seasons
were all about to start,
as if childhood selected its shapes suddenly,
and eyes
gaze only at the perseverance of nature.
And the young thugs commit their sins
sip by sip
the way poems clash against the triumph of time.
Creatures offer gifts
and take their tempting shapes
as if a tongue made creation.
And people, still startled by their inception,
face the thin ice adorning their mirrors to see

what the poets have done to our feeble dreams.
Poetry maligns speech
and the young thugs commit forgivable sins
the way an infant scratches a breast then weeps to
it the way a text breaks its intentions.
Then the apple of love descends
enamoring a woman with a lost lover,
the way the wolf divulges the myth of the bloody shirt
and the innocent brothers confess their crime
and nature forgives a careless creator then praises him.

Notes

1 See Muhammad Mustfa Badawi, *Critical Introduction to Modern Arabic Poetry* (Cambridge: Cambridge University Press, 1975), 88–90. Also, Salma Khadra Jayyusi, *Trends and Movements in Modern Arabic Poetry* (Leiden: Brill, 1977), 1: 67–72; Muhammad Mustfa Badawi, *Modern Arabic Literature and the West* (London: Ithaca Press for the Board of the Faculty of Oriental Studies, University of Oxford, 1985); Jabra I. Jabra, "Modern Arabic Literature and the West," *Journal of Arabic Literature*, Vol. 2 (1971): 76–91; Muhsin al-Musawi, *Arabic Poetry: Trajectories of Modernity and Tradition* (London: Routledge, 2006), 218–237; Sabry Hafez, "Literary Innovation in Modern Arabic Literature. Schools and Journals," *Quaderni di Studi Arabi*, Vol. 18 (2000): 17–39; and Roger Allen, *The Arabic Literary Heritage* (Cambridge: Cambridge University Press, 1998), 70–82.

2 In Theory, see Matei Calinescu, *Five Faces of Modernity* (Durham, NC: Duke University Press, 1987), 95–97; Giles Scott-Smith, *The Politics of Apolitical Culture* (London and New York: Routledge, 2002); Edward Said, *Culture and Imperialism* (London: Chatto and Windus; Vintage House, 1993), 253–5, 272–3, 378–9; Peter Faulkner, ed. *Modernism* (London: Methuen & Co., 1977); Irving Howe, *Literary Modernism* (Greenwich, CT: Fawcett, 1967); David Lodge, ed., *20th Century Literary Criticism* (London and New York: Longman, 1972). See also George Lukàcs, "The Ideology of Modernism," rpt. in Lodge, pp. 474–87; Stanley Sultan, *Ulysses, The Waste Land, and Modernism* (Port Washington, NY & London: Kennikat Press, 1977); and Joseph Shipley, ed., *Dictionary of World Literary Terms* (London: George Allen & Unwin Ltd., 1970).

3 Muhammad Abd al-Ḥayy, *English Poets in Arabic: The Arab Romantics' Knowledge of English Poetry (1900–1950): A study in comparative literature, with a bibliography of Arabic translations of English and American poetry* (Khartoum: Khartoum University Press, 1980).

4 Andreas Pflitsch writes: "It was to be a decisive evening in the history of modern Arabic literature. In late April 1920 Abd al-Masih Haddad invited a group of Syrian-Lebanese authors to meet at 51, West 10th Street in New York. The meeting led to the birth of al-Rabita al-qalamiyya [the Pen League], an association of writers whose members were to be highly influential in the renewal of Arabic prose. Haddad (1881–1950), originally from Homs in Syria, was the editor of the magazine al-Sa'ih [The Tourist]. There had already been a private meeting at his house the previous week, during which a discussion ensued about the state of contemporary Arabic literature. How, they asked

themselves at this informal gathering, could Syrian authors in New York help to awaken Arabic literature from its stupor – this 'swamp of stagnation and imitation', as Mikhail Naimy (1889–1988), one of those who attended meeting, later described it – and 'revive it, so that it could become a driving force in building the Arab nations'?" See Andreas Pflitsch, "The Circuitous Path of Renewal: The Invention of Modern Arabic Literature during the First World War," *Fikrun wa Fann*, Goethe-Institute. Trans. Charlotte Collins (Nov. 2013). www.goethe.de/ges/phi/prj/ffs/the/a100/en12239384.htm

5 Badawi, *Critical Introduction to Modern Arabic Poetry* ..., 84–114; Jayyusi, *Trends and Movements in Modern Arabic Poetry*, 152–75; and S. Moreh, *Modern Arabic Poetry, 1800–1970*, 66.

6 More on this point, see Frances Stonor Saunder, *Who Paid the Piper? The CIA and the Cultural Cold War* (London: Granta, 1999), 8; Peter Coleman, *The Liberal Conspiracy* (New York: The Free Press, 1989); and Stephen J. Whitfield, *The Culture of the Cold War* (Baltimore, MD: The Johns Hopkins University Press, 1991).

7 Adūnīs, *Al-Thābit wa-al-mutaḥawwil* (The Static and the Dynamic) (Beirut: Al-Saqi, n.d.).

8 Mounah A. Khouri, *Poetry and the Making of Modern Egypt*. Leiden: Brill, 1971.

9 On this journal in an Egyptian context, see Elisabeth Kendall, *Literature, Journalism and the Avant-Garde Intersection in Egypt* (London: Routledge, 2006).

10 For more on Iraqi poets, see Muhsin al-Musawi, *Reading Iraq: Culture and Power in Conflict* (London: I.B. Tauris, 2006).

11 Ibid.; and also *Arabic Poetry: Trajectories*...

12 For recollections of some Baghdadi scenes, especially cafés, hotels, and lecture or exhibition halls in the 1950s, see Jabra I. Jabra, *Princesses' Street*, trans. Issa J. Boullata (Fayetteville: University of Arkansas Press, 2005), 7, 50, 62, 63, 73, 74–75, 80–83.

13 Jabra I. Jabra, "The Palestinian Exile as Writer," *Journal of Palestine Studies*, Vol. 8, No. 2 (Winter, 1979): 77–87, 85.

14 Jabra I. Jabra, "Modern Arabic Literature and the West," *Journal of Arabic Literature*, Vol. 2 (1971): 76–91.

15 Jabra, *Princesses' Street*, 73.

16 For translations, see Mounah A. Khouri and Hamid Algar, trans. and edit. *An Anthology of Modern Arabic Poetry* (Berkeley: University of California Press, 1974), 117–120, and 120–123. The Arabic originals of the poems are placed on facing pages with the translation; also *Modern Arabic Poetry: An Anthology*, ed. Salma Jayyusi (New York: Columbia University Press, 1987).

17 Elizabeth Holt, "'Bread or Freedom': The Conference for Cultural Freedom, the CIA, and the Arabic Literary Journal *Ḥiwār* (1962–67)," *Journal of Arabic Literature* No. 44 (2013): 83–102.

18 Terri De Young, *Placing the Poet: Badr Shakir al-Sayyab and Postcolonial Iraq* (Albany, NY: State University of New York Press, 1998). At the end of chapter 7 (pp. 187–220) she presents the turn in Sayyab's poetry from more traditional political protest to encompass the ideological confrontation between communism and bourgeois exploitation. She also discusses how Sayyāb's contemporary Bayātī adroitly (even more than Sayyāb at this time) incorporates the aesthetic principles of modernism into his work.

19 There is more on this in *Arabic Poetry, Trajectories of Modernity and Tradition*.

20 T. De Young, "A New Reading of Badr Shākir al-Sayyāb's 'Hymn of the Rain'," *Journal of Arabic Literature*, Vol. 24, No. 1 (Mar. 1993): 39–61.

21 Qassim (Bahrain), "Five poems: Stone; The Friends There; Body; Poets; Words from a Young Night," translated by Khaled Mattawa, *Banipal* 3 (October 1998): 48–50.

22 See Appendix A.

23 "Christ after Crucifixion," trans. Basima Bezirgan and Elizabeth Fernea, *Ur* (Jan.–Feb. 1979): 41–43.

24 See Abdul Wahab al-Bayati, *Love, Death, and Exile: Poems*. Translated by Bassam K. Frangieh (Washington, DC: Georgetown University Press, 2004). For a study of Sufism in modern Arabic poetry, see Muhsin al-Musawi,*Islam on the Street* (Lanham, MD: Rowman & Littlefield, 2009), 209–224.

25 Rasheed El-Enany, "Poets and Rebels: Reflections of Lorca in Modern Arabic Poetry," *Third World Quarterly*, Vol. 11, No. 4, Ethnicity in World Politics (Oct. 1989): 252–264. See also Jili ʻAbd al-Rahman, "The Street is shaking O Lorca," translated by Shafik Megally. *Lotus*, Vol. 1, No. 4 (January 1970): 152–153.
26 Abū ʻUthmān al-Jāḥiẓ, *al-Ḥayawān*, ed. ʻAbd al-Salām Hārūn (Cairo, 1938), I: 50–54.
27 See Muhsin al-Musawi, "Dedications as Poetic Intersections," *Journal of Arabic Literature*, XXXI (2000): 1–41.
28 See Muhsin al-Musawi, *Arabic Poetry: Trajectories of Modernity and Tradition*, 218–236.
29 For an example of how another technique denoting influence, *muʻāraḍa*, was appropriated and changed by Arab modernists, see Terri DeYoung, "Muʻarada and Modern Arabic Poetry: Some Examples from the Work of Badr Shakir al-Sayyab," *Edebiyat* (N.S.) Vol. 5 (1994): 217–245.
30 Cited and translated from al-Jāḥiẓ, *Kitāb al-ḥayawān*, ed. Muḥammad ʻAbd al-Salām Hārūn (Beirut: Dār al-Jīl, 1996), I: 75–76; by Hayrettln Yücesoy, "Translation as Self-Consciousness: Ancient Sciences, Antediluvian Wisdom, and the ʻAbbāsid Translation Movement," *Journal of World History*, Vol. 20: No. 4 (2009): 523–557.
31 There are many editions of these lectures: *On Translating Homer: Three Lectures Given at Oxford*, 1861.
32 Jaroslav Stetkevych, *The Zephrs of Najd: The Poetics of Nostalgia in the Classical Arabic Nasīb* (Chicago: Chicago University Press, 1993).
33 Mahmud Darwish, لا أريد لهذه القصيدة أن تنتهي (Beirut: Riyad ar-Rayyes, 2009), 109.
34 For more on this point and the application of Bachelard, see Muhsin al-Musawi, *The Postcolonial Novel: Debating Ambivalence* (Leiden: Brill, 2003, 2005), 283–84.
35 See Yaseen Noorani, 339. "Visual Modernism in the Poetry of ʻAbd al-Wahhāb al-Bayātī," *Journal of Arabic Literature*, Vol. 32, No. 3 (2001): 239–255, 239.
36 Noorani's translation, 241.
37 Qtd. Noorani, 241, from Jonathan Crary, *Techniques of the Observer* (Cambridge: MIT Press, 1990), 24.
38 For a translation of the "Mailman," see Mounah A. Khouri and Hamid Algar, trans. and ed. *An Anthology of Modern Arabic Poetry*, 121.
39 *When the Words Burn*, trans. and ed. by John Mikhail Asfour (Dunvegan, Ont.: Cormorant Books, 1988), 86. Slightly modified.
40 See for more, minus self-reflexivity, Rod Rosenquist, *Modernism, the Market and the Institution of the New* (Cambridge: Cambridge University Press, 2009); and a review by Aaron Rosenberg, "A Spectrum of Modernist Outsiders," *Journal of Modern Literature* Vol. 33, No. 2 (Winter 2010): 149–156.
41 For Darwish's poem on YouTube, *maqha wa anta ma al-jaridah*, at www.youtube.com/watch?v=CpF-ai2g2Zo&feature=relmfu
42 For Qāsim Ḥaddād's 'Poets,' see Khaled Mattawa's translation: www.qhaddad.com/english/poems-d.asp (accessed 8/19/2016).
43 See Appendix B.
44 For a different translation, see Mohammad Shaheen, trans., *Almond Blossoms and Beyond*, by Mahmoud Darwish (Northampton, MA: Interlink, 2009), 7.
45 Allusion to the poet al-Maʻarrī's (d. 1058), "Walk lightly for, so I deem, the soil of this earth is from these bodies."

Bibliography

Abd al-Ḥayy, Muhammad. *English Poets in Arabic: The Arab Romantics' Knowledge of English Poetry (1900–1950): A Study in Comparative Literature, with a Bibliography of Arabic Translations of English and American Poetry*. Khartoum: Khartoum University Press, 1980.

Allen, Allen. *The Arabic Literary Heritage*. Cambridge: Cambridge University Press, 1998.

Al-Musawi, Muhsin. *Arabic Poetry: Trajectories of Modernity and Tradition*. London: Routledge, 2006, 218–237.

Badawi, Muhammad Mustafa. *Critical Introduction to Modern Arabic Poetry*. Cambridge: Cambridge University Press, 1975.

Badawi, Muhammad Mustafa. *Modern Arabic Literature and the West*. London: Ithaca Press for the Board of the Faculty of Oriental Studies, University of Oxford, 1985.

Bayati, Abd al-Wahhab. *Abdul Wahab al-Bayati, Love, Death, and Exile: Poems*. Translated by Bassam K. Frangieh. Washington, DC: Georgetown University Press, 2004.

De Young, Terri. *Placing the Poet: Badr Shakir al-Sayyab and Postcolonial Iraq*. Albany, NY: State University of New York Press, 1998.

Hafez, Sabry. "Literary Innovation in Modern Arabic Literature. Schools and Journals," *Quaderni di Studi Arabi*, Vol. 18 (2000): 17–39.

Khouri, Mounah A. *Poetry and the Making of Modern Egypt*. Leiden: Brill, 1971.

Jabra, I. Jabra. "Modern Arabic Literature and the West," *Journal of Arabic Literature*, Vol. 2 (1971): 76–91.

Jayyusi, Salma Khadra. *Trends and Movements in Modern Arabic Poetry*. Leiden: Brill, 1977.

14

THE POLITICS OF PERCEPTION IN POST-REVOLUTIONARY EGYPTIAN CINEMA

Nathaniel Greenberg

In attempting to dispel some of the inevitable misperceptions of the Middle East one finds in the average American undergraduate classroom, I emphasize neither the "truth" of the Middle East, nor the falsity of American perceptions, but the problem of perception itself. After welcoming students for the day, I ask them to close their books, stand up, and walk outside. I direct them to a specific spot, usually just in front of the entrance to the building and tell them to stand in silence for 60 seconds, to observe what is around them, and then to return to the classroom as a group. Once seated, I ask them to recall what they have seen. Many of the responses are similar: "a girl on a bicycle," "a man with a dog," "a group in the shade." However, there is always variation. Some notice the architecture, others the landscape. Some struggle to recall anything at all. Such is the problem of perception, I posit, that "understanding is never a subjective relation to a given object but to the history of its effect; in other words, understanding belongs to the being of that which is understood," of that which remains once the instance of exposure has passed.[1]

The experiment is a simple one, designed mainly to get students' blood flowing and to create an immediate common experience for the class. However, physical proof of our subjective interventions into the recollection of reality is an important starting point for viewing Egyptian cinema, as it is a tradition that has long held as its central aesthetic ambition realistic interpretations of society. "The cultivation of realism," as film critic Hāshim al-Naḥḥās, wrote, is at once an "enlightened" tradition in Egypt and an explicitly political one, bound to the revolutionary project of liberation in the 1940s and 1950s, and the post-revolutionary projects of social critique. As much as political upheaval heightened the demand for incisive depictions of reality, however, it brought into focus an equally elevated interest in the methodology used for doing so. It is in part for this reason that Egyptian cinema also spawned a vibrant tradition of *auteur* cinema, of filmmakers who are aware of the politics of perception and who have integrated this awareness into the crafting of their visual narratives.[2]

Yūsuf Shāhīn's (Youssef Chahine) short film *Cairo as Seen by Youssef Chahine* (1991) is perhaps the finest example of this latter tradition. I like to use it as a starting point for talking about Egyptian cinema as it speaks to both the need for an accurate accounting of reality in film and the inherent artificiality of such endeavors. Sitting before a group of acting students, Chahine asks them what they would choose to include for a documentary about Cairo to be screened in Paris. "What do you think they expect?" He asks. "Belly-dancers," one responds, "pyramids," "folklore," "sailboats on the Nile," "the souk," or then more soberly: "ecology," "the sandstorms," "the droughts," "the sewers." Chahine responds: "and where is the tragedy in all of this?" "Unemployment," says one student, and another, staring into the camera: "fundamentalism." The film cuts to a shot above the Nile at dawn and Chahine's voice, speaking in French: "*J'aime le Caire*," he says as he sits smoking at his desk. "So profoundly that when asked the question I am at a loss for words." The following 20 minutes, in breathtaking fashion, lead the viewer through Cairo in a way that approximates, presumably, his love of the city, its depth and complexity. On the surface it is an absurd gesture, made all the more evident by the impossible brevity with which he summarizes the vastness. While the narrative he crafts – a brief picaresque tale of an unemployed youth whom he drives from one place to the next in search of work – borrows, in essence, from the tradition of social critique classically embodied by a work like Muḥammad Muwayliḥī's *Ḥadīth ʿĪsā ibn Hishām* (1907),[3] *Cairo as Seen by Chahine* is also a commentary on the power of film in capturing and reorganizing society along ideological lines. The unemployed youth, a college graduate with a degree in English, concludes his day by wandering into a clandestine meeting where a bearded "fundamentalist," whom he earlier identified as a "leftist leader" from the university, belies the evils of the West. "Cut," the director yells, as though emphasizing once again the layered commentary of the piece that aims at dissecting both the social ills plaguing society and the relative crudeness with which such complexity can be reproduced.[4]

This metanarrative quality to Chahine's film can be traced back to the earliest examples of his work. In *al-Bāb al-ḥadīd* (*Cairo Station*, 1958), one of the true masterpieces of Egyptian cinema, the director welcomes the audience to the film with an aerial survey of Cairo's central train terminal. The voice overlay, however, is that of "Madbūlī," a newspaper salesman whose station places him in the heart of the terminal. It is a realistic depiction of the public square, almost neo-realist in its aesthetic (the dock workers and cargo carriers labor beneath the churning steam of giant engines), but Chahine insists on this character-centered point of view. The gesture becomes more pronounced as the central drama of the story unfolds. Madbūlī's assistant, "Qināwī," played by Chahine himself, is a love-starved invalid who develops a fatal obsession for one of the young soda peddlers in the terminal. Midway through the film Chahine takes the viewer into Qināwī's shack behind the tracks where he has cut out and pasted together images of women from magazines. Fragmented and disjointed, the assemblage of images – mainly blonde women in swimwear – reflects his distorted perception of reality. This mediated vision of the world, and its subsequently perverse effects on the feeble-minded Qināwī, is driven home for the audience when he murders a young woman and stores her body in a cargo crate after hearing about a similar act over the radio.

Reel revolutions

Cairo Station was part of a surge in films following the 1952 revolution depicting the machinations of criminal actors. Films like *Rayyā wa Sakīna* (Rayya and Sakina, Ṣalāḥ Abū Sayf, 1953), *Futūwwāt al-Ḥusayniyya* (The Thugs of al-Husayn), Nīyāzī Muṣṭafā, 1954), *al-Waḥsh* (The Monster, Abū Sayf, 1954), and *al-Futūwwa* (The Tough, Abū Sayf, 1957) rendered images of the public sphere in nightmarish fashion.[5] Underground labyrinths and back alleyways within the old cities of Cairo and Alexandria are the predominant settings. Corrupt wholesalers exploit the market. A nefarious gang murders women with impunity. Street thugs do battle for territory. All set before the 1952 revolution and in the waning days of colonialism, these films, based on real events, represented a stark commentary on the perceived lawlessness of the postwar years. However, the narratives were also rife with symbolism drawn from the political atmosphere of the mid-1950s.

In *The Monster*, Ṣalāḥ Abū Sayf, a pioneer of Egyptian realism, depicts the historical events of a criminal gang in Upper Egypt as they invade a small village, transforming it into a horrific theater for their own perverse desires. The gang, referred to as the *ikhwān* (the brothers), appears to enforce a kind of radical *sharī'a*, but the village falls into a state of lawlessness nonetheless. Closely paralleling the military's campaign against the Muslim Brotherhood following the attempted assassination of then Vice-President Jamāl 'Abd al-Nāṣir earlier that year, the film establishes the perverse and hypocritical rule of the "*ikhwān*" as an antecedent to the intervention of the military that finally runs the gang out of town. More telling of the times than the subject matter, however, these films, along with other classics of the time turned the camera towards the public square and depicted a vision of society that for decades had been prohibited.

As film historian Samīr Farīd wrote, the censorship code in Egypt first developed in response to the spread of reports about the 'Urābī uprising, a military officers' revolt against the British- and French-backed Khedive monarchy in 1879. In 1911, the law would be applied to film. Known by 1952 as the Fārūq Code, the censorship laws forbid representations of the country's social underbelly. "Dirt lanes," "poverty," "crowding," and, of course, "political demonstrations" were all prohibited. Egypt had gained a reputation for being lax on the enforcement of the censorship, however, and it was in part for this reason that Cairo and Alexandria continued to attract expatriates from around the Arab world. Artists in Egypt were quite literally in the vanguard. As Farīd writes, periodic additions to the code would often be drafted after the fact of production. The 1947 directives by King Fārūq, for example, appeared only after a string of films during the war years had emerged depicting the struggle for labor rights. All produced by the newly created Studio Miṣr (1935),[6] films like *al-'Azīma* (The Will, Kamāl Salīm, 1939), *al-Sūq al-sawdā'* (Black Market, Kāmal al-Tulamsānī, 1943/47), *al-'Āmil* (The Worker, Aḥmad Kāmal Mursī, 1943), and *al-Muẓāhrāt* (Demonstrations, Manifestations, Kamāl Salīm, 1941), reflected a new form of social consciousness, one that was inherently viewed as threatening by the monarchy.[7]

Although the legislative process behind the Fārūq Code remains murky, the implications of its collapse and the subsequent power of realistic depictions of public life in the march towards revolution are self-evident. As Jean-Paul Sartre wrote, "film, by its very nature, speaks to crowds; it speaks to them about crowds and about their destiny."[8] It provides authority to the everyday man, serving as proof for those opinions born outside the realm of authority. Filmic evidence gives context to indignation and cause to action. The aestheticization of the public sphere in the films of the 1950s signaled a breakdown in the divisions between public and private life, ushering in the prospect of a more engaged citizenry.

That film might be used to delineate, or induce, a kind of political consciousness ignited a deluge of interest, if not investment in the film industry on the part of the revolutionary regime. An inquiry was commissioned into the construction of a Cinema Palace in Cairo designed to seat 10,000 people. Officials aspired to create 100 new theaters annually, each with seating for 300–400 visitors. The program was "far from being completed," but, as film historian Yves Thoraval wrote, many of the efforts made significant headway in expanding viewership. "Cultural caravans" delivered films to remote villages, cine-clubs screened select works of interest. In 1957, the government established the "Supreme Council for the Protection of Arts and Letters" along with the Agency for the Consolidation of Cinema, to channel funds and resources toward domestic production.[9] All part of the process of what would become known as the "Charter on National Action" and that included everything from the construction of the Aswan High Dam, to the retention of "financial institutions, public utilities, transport (excluding taxicabs), industrial concerns, insurance, department stores, large hotels, the media and the press, export-import trade and the marketing of major agricultural crops,"[10] the takeover of Egypt's private film industry represented a major financial boon to the regime. Already, by 1952, film was Egypt's second largest export after cotton, generating some 270 million Egyptian pounds a year, making it the fourth largest film industry in the world. Films screened at the Yugoslavia Film Festival, Cannes, Berlin, the Soviet Union Arab Film Week, and festivals in Uruguay and Argentina.[11] Domestic consumption under-paced that of other film-producing countries its size, however. In 1946, there existed only 285 "regular" theaters, according to Yves Thoraval. Soon following the state's takeover of the industry, 100 additional theaters were constructed, but by 1962, there were still just 15 theaters per 1 million inhabitants. In comparison, Europe, at this time, had on average 160 theaters for every 1 million habitants.[12]

Among those most involved in trying to reverse this trend was the future Nobel laureate in literature, Najīb Maḥfūẓ (Naguib Mahfouz). Already known as a pioneer in the genre of literary realism, Mahfouz quickly became one of the industry's most coveted writers. In addition, Mahfouz took up a number of high-level posts within the revolutionary bureaucracy, first as the chairman of the Cinema Support Organization and later counselor for cinema affairs to the Ministry of Culture. He contributed to a number of the most successful films produced at the time and became a vocal advocate for the use of film as a tool of social enlightenment. He emphasized the import of the cine-clubs established in 1956, and extolled the mission of the Agency for the Consolidation of Cinema to "elevate the artistic level" of filmic production. Writing from his official position as literary advisor to the Cinema Foundation in 1966, Mahfouz argued that cinema could play an important role in the "formation and education" of citizens in a "Socialist-Humanist" state.[13] In a country where illiteracy rates were over 80 percent, the potential for generating social reform through cinema was indeed immense,[14] but this sentiment was also reflective of a prevailing sense among artists at the time that filmmaking in the years prior to the revolution had served as a kind of "opium" for the masses, designed to entertain people at best, and, at worst, to distract them from the concrete reality of the world around them.[15]

Efforts to reverse this trend were hardly flawless. As the renowned filmmaker Ṭawfīq Ṣāleḥ reflected decades later, "realism, in reality, was never really real."[16] Along with the state's increased funding came clear expectations of what films should look like. The alterations to scripts were subtle and often geared more towards diminishing audiences' anticipated reactions, than advancing any clear political agenda. The officer who seduces the youngest daughter of the 'Abd al-Jawād family in *Bayn al-qaṣrayn* (*Palace Walk*, Ḥasan al-Imām, 1964) is rendered in Ottoman, as opposed to British garb, as Mahfouz had written the character in his novel. A New Year's festival is substituted for Purim in Ṣalāḥ Abū Sayf's adaptation of Ihsān 'Abd al-Quddūs *Ana ḥurra* (*I Am Free*, Abū Sayf, 1959). A portrait of the king replaces the name of God in a framed image hanging behind the Purge Committee in the adaptation of Mahfouz's *al-Summān wa-al-Kharīf* (*Autumn Quail*, Ḥusām al-Dīn Muṣṭafā, 1967).[17] In *al-Liṣṣ wa al-kilāb* (*The Thief and the Dogs*, Kamāl al-Shaykh, 1962), based on Mahfouz's brilliant *noir* novel from the year prior, director Kamāl al-Shaykh adds a dreamscape episode where the protagonist finds himself before a kind of ethical tribunal demanding he repent for his crimes. In the novel, the outlaw Sa'īd Mahrān makes no such gesture. His final thought before the police gun him down is complete "indifference." The adaptation of Mahfouz's most biting political critique from the 1960s, *Tharthara fawq al-Nīl* (*Adrift on the Nile*, Kamāl al-Shaykh, 1971) followed a similar pattern. The disenchanted government employee and hashish addict, Anīs, abandons his friends and gives up smoking after the group kills an innocent man during a midnight joyride. The film concludes with Anīs walking the streets, calling out to the people of Egypt to "awake" from their slumber. In Mahfouz's novel, Anīs threatens to turn his friends in, but then smokes himself into oblivion, eventually accepting a laced drink, intended presumably to silence him.

Imposed on the text of the novels is a kind of "horizon of expectations," a reconfiguring of information that insists on organizing the material into a more readily symbolic mode of discourse.[18] Like the king, the Purge Committee in the film *Autumn Quail* is to be read as corrupt. The nation, like Anīs, must be awoken from its slumber. Sa'īd Mahrān, in *The Thief and the Dogs* faces a tribunal because he is guilty of committing crimes. Mahfouz, in his novels, insists on a far more ambiguous, and, in essence, humanistic rendering of his characters, showing them as imperfect and oscillatory actors, often blinded by their own preconceptions of the world. In Ṣalāḥ Abū Sayf's *I am Free*, the free-spirited Amīna, rather than settling into married life after entering the workforce, is sentenced to five years' imprisonment alongside her sweetheart 'Abbās for conspiring against the British-backed government. In the final scene, while still in jail, the two are married, just days before the revolution, on 20 July 1952. It is a complete departure from the novella, but indicative of the desire on the part of the filmmaker to integrate Amīna's story into a greater political aesthetic of national liberation.

Equally significant as the capacity for film to convey ideology by reorganizing and interjecting symbolic material into seemingly realistic stories, the process of scriptwriting entailed a number of formal adjustments that differed dramatically from traditional modes of writing. While the scenarios were often drafted in *fuṣḥā*, or literary Arabic, the dialogue was written in *'āmiyya*, the colloquial. Naguib Mahfouz, who was responsible for over 30 scripts, was so put off by this requirement that he insisted on co-writing his screenplays, deferring the dialogue sections to his collaborators.[19] Voiceover monologues, in the case of Mahfouz's scripts, often assumed a tertiary form, combining literary language with a colloquial pronunciation. Particularly during a film's opening montage, the monologues were accompanied by a literal sequencing of images, which, in turn, created a kind of visual precedent in the drafting of the narrative. Most importantly, however, writing for film demanded the writer enumerate the flow of his narrative in a manner that was wholly unprecedented. In an interview with the Italian filmmaker Anna Albertano, Mahfouz said that writing for film, above all, taught him how to be "brief, how to concentrate things."

> The principal difference between the two [screenplay and novel writing] is that, with a screenplay, time is limited. You count the script in seconds because everything is limited by time, whereas in a novel you can really give the work the length that you desire, it can be long or short according to the subject, but in a film, all films have to be the same length.[20]

French critic André Bazin observed a similar phenomenon among American novelists. While it was difficult to determine, as he wrote, whether the art of Dos Passos or Hemingway preceded the kind of narrative innovations ushered in by the Seventh Art – montage and jump cuts, most notably – "the age of the American novel" reflected a certain vision of the world "informed, no doubt, by the relationship between man and technology (*la civilisation technique*)."[21] The Arab literary boom that would follow the popular development of cinematic aesthetics in Egypt reflected a similar level of technical influence. Writers began turning to film as an exemplary model of storytelling for engaging a modernist project increasingly overwhelmed by the incommunicability of the fast-evolving urban experience. From Mahfouz to Jabrā Ibrahīm Jabrā, al-Ṭayeb Ṣāliḥ, or Nawāl al-Sadāwī, Arabic novelists would produce sharper, slimmer, and more expedient narratives than ever before.

Teaching time

The concentration on time, and how we think and live in time, can be an unusual concept for students, but, as I have suggested here, it is one of the most important in the reading of film. In borrowing from the methodology of the celebrated University of Washington Professor of Russian Film and Literature Willis Konick, I try to make the idea of time experiential. I ask students to demarcate "now" by clapping their hands in unison at the precise moment the second hand falls across the hour. It is an impossibility, of course, and I remind them of Hegel's notion from his introduction to the *Phenomenology of Sprit* that there is, in effect, no "now" ("As soon as I write 'day' it will be night. And as soon as I write 'night' it will be day," etc.).[22] There is, rather, only that which our memories have preserved from the past, that which we imagine for the future, and the immediate next, that which surrounds us. To illustrate the latter way of thinking in time, in essence what the economist Daniel Kahneman describes as "thinking fast," I might conduct a game of "Simon Says," pointing out that in the midst of this game, all minds are focused (mostly) on the next command. To illustrate the former way of thinking in time ("thinking slow"), I might ask them why they are attending college.[23] "To obtain a degree," "to get a job," are the inevitable answers. To which I reply simply "why?" Until it becomes clear that such an imagined future has been engrained in their minds from previous knowledge or past experience. As bizarre as this all might sound, these collective classroom experiences can do wonders in focusing students' attention, which should then quickly be returned to the subject matter at hand – that is, how the technology of film can affect the way we think in time.

This brings me back to the work of Youssef Chahine. In *Cairo Station*, the deranged Qināwī's obsession with the young soda girl is established through just two quick interactions. By the third interaction Qināwī has already begun to plan their future (he wants to take her back to his village) and he proposes to "Hanūma" who dismisses him but is concerned. In the film's most brilliant scene we see Hanūma as she is swept up in dancing and laughing while selling soda to a crowd of passengers. Qināwī approaches from outside the train car and begins to stare at her. The director has brought together, in a single shot, two conflicting frames of mind. Either Hanūma must stop dancing or Qināwī must stop staring for the tension to be resolved. Critics of the film have often read this tension as "sexual,"[24] but tension, as such, needs to be established over time. The depth of Qināwī's obsession cannot be filmed by the camera, which is precisely what

FIGURE 14.1 Hind Rostrom and Youssef Chahine in *Cairo Station*, 1958

renders it so peculiar. We know from his plan to marry her and to return to his village, to his past, that he is a character thinking outside time, and thus, in the context of the film, outside reality. Hanūma, in contrast, is a classic film hero, and appears far more sane, tumbling along from one moment to the next. In this particular scene, Hanūma's fast thinking prevails and the tension is temporarily relieved when she convinces Qināwī to accept a Coke. He drinks it and begins dancing. The power of film in creating conflict through time would henceforth flow easily into literature. A good accompaniment to this film is Mahfouz's novel *The Thief and the Dogs*, where the author creates tension by drafting a character who is obsessed by his past. His self-righteous desire for revenge blinds him to reality, even when it is staring him in the face, in the form of the newspaper accounts that he reads about his illicit exploits. The character's inability to concentrate on the "now" (or the reality of his surroundings) and to stop living in the past forces him to commit a number of errors, including killing the wrong men.[25] There is nothing particularly Arabic or Egyptian about this kind of narrative, but it is indicative of revolutionary aesthetics insofar as the artists, like everyone who has lived through a revolution, are faced with radical new uncertainties, and the desire to hold onto the past can easily become oppressive, if not violent, in the face of change.

The public in squares

Such an aesthetic seems likely to enjoy a renaissance in the Arab world. The veritable tsunami of documented footage generated by the uprisings in Tunisia, Egypt, Libya, Morocco, Yemen, Bahrain, and Syria, can be measured in proportion to the level of shock experienced by those who witnessed the events. Not surprising in this regard, one of the dominant modes of expression to have emerged since the

2011 uprisings began is documentary filmmaking, a genre which, in the Arab context, developed largely in response to the Nasserite-era campaigns of the 1950s to (re)educate citizens through film, as mentioned above. Today the genre has taken on a life of its own. Of the many excellent documentaries following the uprisings of 2011, several lend themselves particularly well to classroom instruction – *Laysa lil-karāma jidrān* (Karama Has No Walls), *al-'Awdah ilā Ḥomṣ* (The Return to Homs), *Biladnā al-rahīb* (Our Terrible Country), and *Anā wa mikhzanī* (My Makhzin and Me), to name just a few. For the sake of brevity I will conclude with a discussion of just one: the much-celebrated 2013 film by the Egyptian documentarian Jīhān Nujaym (Jihane Noujaim): *al-Mīdān* (*The Square*).

Filmed over the course of two and a half years, during and after the fall of Mubārak, *The Square* is at once an excellent documentation of events and a stunning example of a filmmaker deeply entrenched in the art of her medium. Here, as in her previous work, namely the 2004 award-winning documentary *The Control Room*, Noujaim demonstrates that she is well aware of how film can organize and influence our understanding of reality.

The politics of perception are embedded in the film from its opening salvo. Following a still shot of the principal protagonist, Aḥmed, the director splices together an evocative sequence of images: an itinerant youth, riot police surrounded by barbed wire, Mubārak speaking behind a podium. Off camera Aḥmad narrates the history of the revolution, placing himself in the story as a desperately poor youth, selling lemons in the street from the age of eight. The narration is carefully crafted and reflects a picaresque sensibility: Aḥmed is shown roaming and walking while the images of the regime appear fixed and distant; conveyed in phantasmagorical fashion over a television screen, or a YouTube video. His narrative continues as the director films him clicking past horrific images of police torture, the battered head of Khālid Sa'īd whose death would spawn the Facebook page "We Are All Khalid Said," and a recording by the young activist Asmā' Maḥfūẓ, as she calls for protests to commence at Tahrir on 25 January. "I went into

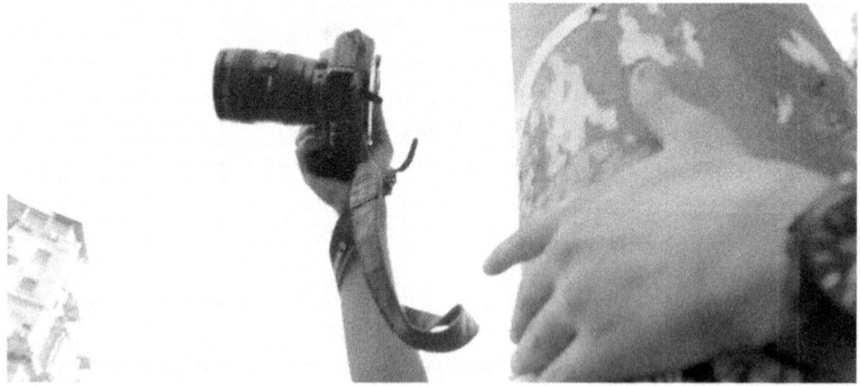

FIGURE 14.2 In Jihane Noujaim's *The Square* (2013) the camera is the subject

the street," he says, the camera accompanying him. As he moves towards a crowd his monologue ends, his reflections interlacing with the sound and image of a present, mirror event. He then introduces the other principal subjects of the film – Majdī, a member of the Muslim Brotherhood, Khālid 'Abd Allah, an expatriate returned home from abroad, 'Āyyda, an activist, and Rāmī 'Aṣām, the "singer of the revolution." Splicing together a continuity of personal reflection, public action and, finally, the introduction of five individuals, Noujaim establishes a clear aesthetic philosophy. Hers is a film that refuses to compromise truth for objectivity, which defends the liberal humanistic ideal that "knowledge and human interest" are inseparable and that any fair accounting of revolution must look into the souls of those who are revolting.[26]

The pragmatic axis at the core of this philosophy hinges on the presence, and power, of personal perception in the acquisition of reality. As the film progresses, this dynamic grows increasingly integral to the story. At one moment Aḥmad suggests that "without cameras there is no revolution." Gathered in a location referred to only as "Pierre's apartment," which sits just above the square, the revolutionaries pour over video footage in search of evidence of the violence witnessed below. Khālid 'Abd Allah (who starred in the film *The Kite Runner*) watches intensely as the number of hits on a video he uploaded to YouTube increases. Overlaid is the voice of an American television journalist describing the uproar generated by the video, this followed by a quick cut to a television broadcast of the Egyptian nightly news which features the head of the Supreme Council of the Armed Forces, General Muḥammad Ḥusayn Ṭanṭāwī, denying emerging footage portraying state violence, which he describes as an attempt to smear the image of the military. Later, Khālid assembles footage to screen before a public audience inside the square. The reactions are powerful and somewhat surprising considering that many of those watching are battle-hardened protesters. However, the effect of the sequence is twofold: it implies both a last-ditch effort on the part of the passionate Khālid who wants the revolution to continue, and, ironically, closure to the revolution itself. Once brought under the auspices of narrative, the revolution requires an ending, just as it required a beginning. Noujaim's *Square*, for better or worse, attempts to close that circle.

By the end, the play of perception in the discourse on reality, as a thematic, has become inseparable from Noujaim's telling of the revolution. A non-linear cut to Pierre's apartment shows Khālid talking with Majdī and his son, shown now for the first time. "Were you at the Presidential Palace?" Khālid asks the boy, referring to one of the anti-Brotherhood rallies staged against then President Muḥammad Morsī. "You were raining down rocks on me and tearing down our tents?" he asks. He shows the boy and his father footage he has assembled on his laptop. The boy is quietly moved to tears. Majdī, the Brotherhood supporter, but friend of the revolutionaries, tells his son in disgust that he can think for himself and that he need not follow the orders of the Brotherhood at all times.

Majdī's admonition to his son becomes part of an unfolding crisis of confidence on his part. Allied by tradition to the Brotherhood, but emotionally tied to the revolutionaries of Pierre's apartment, Majdī is in the midst of an internal revolt. Inside his small apartment, his wife tells the camera that he was just playing revolutionary, wanting to get on camera, to be arrested. He makes his living from the Brotherhood, she exclaims. "But what good has the Morsi Presidency done me?" he says, "I still can't get healthcare." His daughter, presumably overwhelmed by her father's fluctuations, begins to cry. In a subsequent scene Majdī is obliged by Brotherhood orders to attend a sit-in scheduled in opposition to a rally in the square. The interviewer asks if he is not upset to find himself now on the "opposite side" of his friends in Tahrir. "I would never hurt them," he responds. Filmed in brutal honesty, Majdī's story is in many ways the film's most powerful revelation. Imprisoned, harassed, and tortured under the regime as a member of the Brotherhood, it becomes clear just how real the revolution was for him. Beyond narrative his is a quotidian struggle, with no clear resolution in sight, or at least none that can be captured on film. It is a reminder that the revolution will go on, with or without a camera.

Needless to say, it is impossible to conceive of this film having been made before 2011. However, as with the breakthrough that accompanied the 1952 revolution, *The Square* was preceded by several hard-hitting works of realism, most notably Muḥammad Dīb's 2010 *Fīlm 678* and Marwān Ḥāmid's adaptation of the *Yacoubian Building* in 2006.[27] It is difficult to speculate on whether the political turmoil of the Arab Spring will lead to a renaissance in Egyptian filmmaking. The involvement of Khālid 'Abd Allah in *The Square* is reminiscent of the repatriation of filmmakers like Abū Sayf and Youssef Chahine, from France and the United States, respectively, following the 1952 revolution. Though perhaps not at the level it once did, Egypt still produces more films than any other Arab nation, and it is the third largest film-producing country in Africa, after Mauritius and Nigeria.[28]

In viewing some of Egypt's most famous works, students gain an appreciation not only of the tremendous artistry that has shaped Egyptian film over the past century, but the political import of filmmaking in general. Realism, in particular, concentrates students' attention on the synergism of content and form that is always at work in the chronicling of history. The implications of its success stories and the consequences of its failure – made all the more vivid by Egypt's ongoing struggle for democracy – should serve to reinforce for students just how much is at stake in the study of art.

Notes

1 From Hans-Georg Gadamer's *Truth and Method*, xxviii.
2 See Hāshim al-Naḥḥās, "Ṣalāḥ Abū Sayf wa tajdhīr al-wāqi'iyya wa al-tanwīr fī al-sīnimā al-miṣriyya," *Alif: Journal of Comparative Poetics* (1995): 6–21.
3 See Allen and Muwayliḥī 1992.
4 The narrative of youthful drift from unemployment to radicalism has been a stock standard feature in Arabic literature from Mahfouz's *al-Thulāthiyya* (*The Cairo Trilogy*, 1956–1957), to 'Alā' al-Aswānī's *'Imārat Ya'qūbiyān* (*The Yacoubian Building*, 2002). Chahine situates the US invasion of Iraq in 1990 as the Islamist's principal source of anger.

5 Tawfīq Ṣaliḥ's *Darb al-mahabīl* (*Fool's Alley*, 1955), and 'Āṭif Sālim's *al-Nimrawd* (*Nimrod*, 1957) are two more films worth mentioning in this regard. Each, along with most of the films mentioned in this chapter, can be found on YouTube.
6 A rich history in and of itself, Studio Miṣr was created by the then director of Bank Miṣr (Bank of Egypt), Ṭal'at Ḥarb. Once recognizing the earning potential of film, he began touring the major centers of film production in France and Germany. His goal, as Yves Thoraval wrote, was to create a "Hollywood of the Orient" along the Avenue of the Pyramids in Giza. See Thoraval 1975, 18.
7 In Farīd 2002.
8 In "The Situation of the Writer in 1947," available in the collection *"What is Literature?" and Other Essays* (Sartre 1988, 216).
9 See Thoraval 1975, 108; and Qussai Samak, "The Politics of Egyptian Cinema," *Merip Reports* (1977): 12–13.
10 See P.J. Vatikiotis, *Nasser and his Generation* (New York: St Martin's Press, 1978), 213.
11 Hāshim al-Naḥḥās's "The Role of Naguib Mahfouz in the Egyptian Cinema," appeared in Arabic in *al-Hilāl* in 1970; then in translation, *Critical Perspectives on Naguib Mahfouz* (1991), edited by Trevor Le Gassik (Washington, DC: Three Continents Press, 1991), 164.
12 Nevertheless, over 70% of films screened were American (Thoraval 1975, 107–109).
13 Mahfouz, "Anā wa al-sinīma." The article appeared first in the journal *Akhir Sā'a*. It can be found in the collection *Mawsū'at Najīb Maḥfūẓ wa-al-sīnimā, 1947–2000*, edited by Madkūr Thābit and Ibrāhīm Fatḥī (Giza: Akādīmīyat al-Funūn, 2006), 334.
14 See Amin 2000, 39.
15 In 1968, and following the Arab defeat in the Six-Day War, a group calling itself the "New Cinema Collective" articulated this vision of revolutionary cinema in a document they titled *The 1968 Cinema Manifesto*. Qussai Samak provides a translation of part of it in a good short article, "The Politics of Egyptian Cinema," in *The Middle East Research and Information Project* (MERIP) (1977): 12–15. Walter Armbrust discusses the aesthetics of pre-revolutionary and popular Egyptian cinema in *Mass Mediations: New Approaches to Popular Culture in the Middle East and Beyond* (Berkeley: University of California Press, 2000), 292–327.
16 See Tawfīq Ṣāliḥ, "Khawāṭir ḥawl hājis al-Talaqqī fī al-sīnimā [Remarks on Reception Aesthetics in Arab Cinema]," *Alif: Journal of Comparative Poetics* (1995): 85–90.
17 The historical basis for Mahfouz's Purge Committee in *Autumn Quail* is worth iterating. See John Gunther, *Procession* (New York: Harper & Row, 1965), 361–373. The swapping of the king's picture for the name of God in Mahfouz's novel was undoubtedly a controversial gesture, insofar as it appeared to challenge the so-called secularism of the new regime.
18 See Hans R. Jauss, Timothy Bahti and Man P. De, *Toward an Aesthetic of Reception* (Minneapolis: University of Minnesota Press, 1982).
19 Some of those who co-wrote the scripts with Mahfouz – people like Bayram al-Tūnisī and 'Abd al-Raḥman al-Sharqāwī – were major literary figures in their own right.
20 "Nagib Mahfuz, un Nobel Prestato al Cinema," with Anna Albertano is available at Euromedi.org.
21 In Bazin,*Qu'est-ce que le cinéma?* (Paris: Éditions du Cerf, 1958), 14–16.
22 This basic summary of Hegel's theory of the "Now" comes from Jean Wahl's 1929 *Vers le concrete* (Paris: Vrin, 2004), 29.
23 Daniel Kahneman, *Thinking, Fast and Slow* (New York: Farrar, Straus and Giroux, 2011).
24 Cf. Samak, 13; and two essays from the excellent collection *Arab Cinematics: Toward the New and the Alternative*, ed. Ferial J. Ghazoul (Cairo, Egypt: American University in Cairo Press, 1995): Raymond Baker's "Combative Cultural Politics: Film Art and Political Spaces in Egypt" (6–38); and Maureen Kiernan's "Cultural Hegemony and National Film Language: Youssef Chahine" (130–153).
25 Qināwī too kills the wrong woman in *Cairo Station*.

26 I borrow this phrase, and the idea, from Jürgen Habermas's *Knowledge and Human Interests* (Boston, MA: Beacon Press, 1971).

27 Both of these films engaged as their topics existent social crises, public sexual violence in the case of *Film 678*, which is named after a notorious bus route in Cairo, and Islamic radicalization in *The Yacoubian Building*.

28 Nigeria is the second largest film-producing nation after India and ahead of the United States, with 997 feature films produced in 2011. Egypt produced 28 films in 2011. See the 2013 UNESCO report "Emerging Markets and the Digitalization of the Film Industry," available at www.uis.unesco.org/culture/Documents/IP14-2013-cinema-survey-analysis-en.pdf.

Bibliography

Albertano, Anna. "Nagib Mahfuz, un Nobel Prestato al Cinema." *Euromedi.org*. www.euromedi.org/home/azioni/pubblicazioni/artedanza/salah/ALBERT1.PDF

Allen, Roger and Muḥammad Muwayliḥī. *A Period of Time*. Reading: Ithaca, 1992.

al-Naḥḥās, Hashīm. "Dawr Najīb Miḥfūẓ fī-al-Sīnimā al-Miṣriyya." *al-Hilāl* 1.2 (1970): 182–191.

Amin, Galal. *Whatever Happened to the Egyptians?: Changes in Egyptian Society from 1950 to the Present*. Cairo: American University in Cairo Press, 2000.

Bazin, André. "Death Every Afternoon," Trans. Mark A. Cohen. *Rites of Realism: Essays on Corporeal Cinema*. Ed. Ivone Margulies. Durham, NC: Duke University Press, 2003.

Farīd, Samīr. *Tārīkh al-raqābah 'alā al-sīnimā fī Miṣr* (The History of Film Censorship in Egypt). Cairo: al-Maktab al-Miṣrī li-Tawzī' al-Maṭbū'āt, 2002.

Gadamer, Hans-Georg. *Truth and Method*. New York: Seabury Press, 1975.

Gordon, Joel. *Revolutionary Melodrama: Popular Film and Civic Identity in Nasser's Egypt*. Chicago, IL: Middle East Documentation Center, 2002.

Rancière, Jacques. *The Politics of Aesthetics: The Distribution of the Sensible*. London: Continuum, 2004.

Sartre, Jean-Paul. *"What is Literature?" and Other Essays*. Cambridge, MA: Harvard University Press, 1988.

Thābit, Madkūr, and Ibrāhīm Fatḥī. *Mawsū'at Najīb Maḥfūẓ wa-al-sīnimā, 1947–2000*. Giza: Akādīmīyat al-Funūn, 2006.

Thoraval, Yves. *Regards sur le cinéma Égyptien*. Beyrouth: Darl el-Machreq, 1975.

PART III
Text

15

TEACHING THE *MAQÂMÂT* IN TRANSLATION

Roger Allen

I might begin this chapter by posing the question, "teaching the *maqâmât* in translation to whom?" I should make it clear, in view of what now follows, that I have assumed that since we are talking about the use of translated texts here, the answer to that question is to undergraduates; in my own case, either those taking a course in Arabic literary history, or else, on a broader scale, those taking a world narratives class through the Program in Comparative Literature.

A second question might well be: why would anyone wish to contemplate the idea of teaching the *maqâmât* in translation to such a cohort? After all, they surely represent one of the acmes of stylistic virtuosity in the entire Arabic literary canon and thus must be considered, along with the best of its poetry, as more than partially untranslatable (to cite a Walter Benjamin term in the negative) – an opinion that al-Jâḥiẓ expounded with reference to the translation of poetry many centuries ago. An initial response on my part might be to point out that my first published work was a study and translation of Muḥammad al-Muwayliḥî's renowned narrative text, *Ḥadîth 'Isâ ibn Hishâm*, first known as a series of newspaper articles (1898–1902) and later in its book form (1907), reprinted many times since and mostly recently in a parallel-text edition.[1] I might thus be seen as perhaps defending a cause initiated in my youth, but in our current context I would prefer to place my rationale into a broader frame of reference, that of the presentation to students in the context of the Arabic literary heritage of "narrative" and the admittedly slippery term of "fiction," along with the twin notions of modernity and generic transformation.

The *maqâmah* emerges, it would appear, as a "modern" genre in the tenth century CE, in the sense that, as the result of a process of generic development, it inserts itself into a literary tradition in which certain genres and themes are already well established. Al-Hamadhânî (d. 1008) succeeds in bringing together a number of separate strands and trends in the process of presenting what appears to be a "new" mode of writing. Among those strands I would mention most obviously the increasing predilection for elaboration of language, typified by the compositions of the court of al-Ṣâḥib ibn 'Abbâd at Rayy (some of whose members are duly recorded and indeed excoriated in Abû Ḥayyân al-Tawḥîdî's renowned work, *Kitâb mathâlib al-wazîrayn*) and the resort to the long-revered style of *saj'* (rhyming and cadenced discourse), an overwhelming presence in the text of the Qur'ân itself.[2] Second, there is the existence of a system of guilds in the society of the time, a reflection of which are those known as the "Banû Sâsân," the beggar guilds described in detail for us by Edmund Bosworth along with the specific "*maqâmât Sâsâniyyah*" in which their hierarchies and activities are depicted.[3] Third, there is the entire realm of fiction and its ironic underpinnings. Many studies have appeared in recent times that consider both the precedents to al-Hamadhânî's oeuvre and its fictional characteristics, but that is too large a topic to take on here. I would merely conclude this introduction by suggesting that if the works of Aḥmad Fâris al-Shidyâq and Muḥammad al-Muwayliḥî, not to mention 'Â'ishah al-Taymûriyyah, Ḥâfiz Ibrâhîm, Bayram al-Tûnisî and 'Abd al-Salâm al-'Ujaylî, are to be considered contributions to modern Arabic literature in one way or another, and if indeed Emil Ḥabîbî's classic post-1967 gesture, *Al-Waqâ'i al-gharîbah f-ikhtifâ' Sa'îd Abî al-naḥs al-mutashâ'il* (1972–74), is to be included in a list of the great works of modern Arabic fiction, then the *maqâmah* or its vestiges continue to exert an "anxiety of influence" on contemporary writing in Arabic.[4]

Maqâmât and translation

Let me now specify precisely what aspects of the term and genre "*maqâmah*" I wish to consider in the context of the current investigation, namely the feasibility of teaching some of them through translation. It is fairly obvious, I would suggest, bearing in mind the primary feature of the original texts to which I have just drawn attention, that the stylistic aspect, the characteristics of *saj'*, cannot be conveyed in such a pedagogical situation, except through the feeble medium of description. We do have available, of course, a couple of truly virtuoso pieces of translation into English that attempt to replicate some of the stylistic features of the original: there are, first, Nicholson's versions of the Sâwah and Damascus *maqâmât* of al-Ḥarîrî, and then the more recent and equally virtuosic translation into English "rhyming prose" by Geert Jan van Gelder of the "Yâqûtiyyah" and "Miskiyyah" *maqâmât* of Jalâl al-dîn al-Suyûtî (and, if we are to include the above-mentioned work of al-Shidyâq within our purview, then we need to mention the equally virtuosic translation of Humphrey Davies). I myself have used the Nicholson translation in class in order to illustrate at least one aspect of the phenomenon of Arabic *saj'*, but, in spite of the existence of such unique exercises in translation, I trust that I am not disparaging our potential readership in suggesting that references such as those to "toil and teen" and "pleasure's tourney" (to be found in Nicholson's renderings) are likely to be almost as alien as the verbal pyrotechnics of the original – this, I fully realize, being acknowledged as part of its generic purpose within the source culture.[5]

Here I must note that one of the things that I find most amusing in using older translations of the *maqâmât* (or, at least, those currently available of al-Hamadhânî and al-Ḥarîrî) is that students are thereby exposed in a maximal fashion to what I will term the literature of orientalist footnotes, which, in this case as with William Wright's famous English version of Caspari's Arabic grammar, seem to anticipate, indeed require, a knowledge of a variety of languages. Being myself an ex-Classicist, I have often wondered what it is about the process of acquiring an advanced reading competence in Latin that is supposed to equip one to deal with the more extravagant exercises in classical pornography or what is considered less than decent, as with Suetonius and Petronius, for example.[6] In the case of the translation of al-Ḥarîrî's *maqâmât*, for example, are we not grateful to have a footnote on the Damascus *maqâmah* in which the Arabic phrase "*uff wa-tuff*" is explained as "*sordes aurium*" and "*sordes unguium*," quite apart from the generous references to the poetry of Horace and Anacreon duly cited in their original languages?

I also have to admit that in making this decision about matters of style as a criterion, I am in effect precisely reflecting the criticism that my Moroccan colleague, 'Abd al-Fattah Kilito, makes about *maqâmât* criticism in his path-breaking study (originally his doctoral thesis) on this genre: namely that Western scholarly concern has tended to concentrate on those examples of the genre that are more "user-friendly" in Western narrative terms and that are only partially representative of the genre and its changing generic purposes within its own cultural environment and the course of its generic development. Al-Hamadhânî composes some amusing anecdotes, as it were, and then al-Ḥarîrî comes along and changes (read "ruins") everything.[7] While acknowledging that this scholarly reaction may well have been the case, I would respond to the current context by saying that we are discussing here the use within a pedagogical frame of reference of examples of the *maqâmah* genre translated into English, the aim being presumably to introduce this typical and intrinsically Arabic genre to readers as being representative of one example of the multi-faceted Arabic literary heritage in narrative form. Certainly I would suggest that a partial response to this issue involves making a selection of *maqâmât* from those available in English translation that will be more reflective of the variety of contexts, scenarios, and even genres that are available.

However, if in our current pedagogical context we do indeed leave the virtuosic aspect of style in the *maqâmât* aside and its attempted replication or explanation in English translations and commentaries on them, then what remains for the would-be teacher? What is left is, I would submit, still a potentially rich mixture, available for analysis on the basis of both its narrative modes and the social and cultural contexts that it portrays. However, before I proceed to a further investigation of such possibilities, let me provide a listing of the authors and texts that, to the best of my knowledge at least, represent the potential repertoire of Arabic *maqâmât* in English translation from which one can or might select specific examples for analysis:

1. Al-Hamadhânî:

   a tr. W.J. Prendergast [1915], London: Curzon, 1973.[8]
   b "Al-Maqama al-Madiriyya," tr. Bernard Lewis, in *Islam* Vol. II, New York: Harper & Row, 1974.

2. Al-Harîrî:

   a tr. Theodore Preston [1850], Farnborough, England: Gregg International, 1971.
   b tr. Thomas Chenery & Francis Steingass [1867], Farnborough, England: Gregg International, 1969.
   c tr. R.A. Nicholson, see note 5.

3. Al-Saraqustî ibn al-Astarkûwî, *Al-Maqâmât al-Luzûmiyyah*, tr. James T. Monroe, Leiden: E.J. Brill, 2002.[9]
4. Al-Suyûtî:

   a tr. Geert Jan van Gelder, "Four Perfumes of Arabia: A Translation of al-Suyuti's *al-Maqâma al-miskiyya*," *Res Orientales*, 11 (1999), pp. 203–212 (special issue "Parfums d'orient," ed. Rika Gyselen).
   b tr. Geert Jan van Gelder, "Precious Stones, Precious Words: al-Suyûtî's *al-Maqâma al-yâqûtiyya*, translated and annotated," in Arnoud Vrolijk and Jan P. Hogendijk (eds), *O ye Gentlemen: Arabic Studies on Science and Literary Culture in Honour of Remke Kruk*, Leiden: Brill, 2007, pp. 313–332.

5. Al-Muwaylihî, see note 1.[10]

Alongside the texts themselves, in their translated versions, there is now a growing repertoire of studies of the genre in English, and in both book and article form. I shall append a selected list of such works at the conclusion of this chapter.

Teaching the *maqâmât*

Having thus identified the potential repertoire, we face the question as to which of them to choose for teaching purposes, and more specifically for reading and interpretation. Here, of course, we are helped by the fact that each example of the genre constitutes a separate narrative unit and thus allows for the selection of samples on the basis of a number of possible criteria. We might, for example, subdivide the possible modes of analysis into three parts: first, what the *maqâmât* talk about; second, how they perform that function; and third, how those two aspects may be read and interpreted. In what follows I will endeavor to allude to each of these aspects in discussing my selection, but, in a pedagogical context, I personally prefer to insert an additional dimension of a historical nature, in that, given attitudes towards the lengthy period that I will term "pre-modern" and the vigorous prevalence of the *maqâmah* genre in particular within that lengthy era, it seems to me to be important to demonstrate the continuing influence that what I have elsewhere termed the "*maqâmah* spirit" has had right up to the contemporary period.[11] This latter approach is now much assisted by studies of the genre and its development in English by, among others, Jaakko Hameen-Anttila and Devin Stewart.[12] I will immediately admit that the availability of translations is by no means ideal in any attempt to fulfill that goal, but I nevertheless think it is worth the try.

To start then with al-Hamadhânî. It will surprise no one, I suspect, if my first choice is the "Maḍîriyyah," named after a famous and much desired meat dish. The wonderful portrait that it offers of the most crass of bourgeois values invites a comparison – and often in my own case a parallel reading – with the disarmingly similar scenario to be found in the Feast of Trimalchio section of the *Satyricon* by Petronius (d. *c.* 66 CE). Abû al-Fatḥ is subjected to a non-stop description of everything inside the merchant's house, not excluding the toilet and utterly inappropriate comments about his wife. To these features I would add, from a narrative perspective, that the action in this *maqâmah* only involves Abû al-Fatḥ al-Iskandarî; after the initial formulaic introduction, "*ḥaddathanâ 'Îsâ ibn Hishâm qâla*," the narrator disappears. The reverse is the case in the "Baghdâdiyya" *maqâmah* that I will discuss briefly below.

If the "Maḍîriyyah" *maqâmah* deals with a topic and adopts a narrative approach much favored throughout the ages, then the "Asadiyyah" may perhaps be seen as more specific in terms of its cultural references since it involves, at least by implication, a desert journey. For that reason it might well be twinned with the "Damascus" *maqâmah* of al-Ḥarîrî. As is the case more often than not, it is the al-Hamadhânî example that is more filled with events. It can be readily divided into two parts: in the first the group sets out from Ḥimṣ, but encounters the lion of the title that kills a heroic young member of the troupe; in the second part they traverse the desert, but encounter a beauteous young man who initially serves 'Îsâ ibn Hishâm before tricking the entire group, tying them up, and abusing them. 'Îsâ ibn Hishâm manages to stick a knife into him, whereupon they repair to a nearby town where they encounter Abû al-Fatḥ al-Iskandarî, who has otherwise been uninvolved in the narrative. In al-Ḥarîrî's example, by contrast, a great deal of time is spent in the search for a guide to lead the caravan across the desert from Damascus to Iraq and in learning the lengthy talisman that their guide – Abû Zayd, needless to say – teaches them. The journey itself is covered relatively quickly, and the rest of the *maqâmah* consists of an altercation between the narrator and Abû Zayd, who launches into a lengthy ode in which he endeavors to explain his apparently contradictory, not to say hypocritical behavior, one that shifts from a surface piety to riotous living.

Remaining with al-Hamadhânî for a moment longer, another relatively lengthy narrative is the "Saymariyyah" *maqâmah*, a wonderful tale of sweet revenge, based on an actual cultural figure, Abû al-'Anbas al-Saymarî (d. *c.* 888). After being snubbed by his guests at a dinner party he has been hosting, the second narrator – al-Saymarî – recounts how he travels, earns money, and returns to Baghdad.

Inviting his guests a second time, he turns the tables on all of them by getting them all drunk and then shaving off their beards. Apart from its overall narrative plot involving insult avenged, this *maqâmah* presents an interesting picture of the *majlis* culture of the times, something that is explored in further and more specific detail in the "Shi'riyyah [Poetry]" and "Jâḥiẓiyyah" *maqâmât* devoted to poetry and prose writing, respectively.

Several other examples of the *maqâmah* share with the "Asadiyyah" the structural feature of being dividable into two segments, and at least two of them introduce another element into the narrative mix, namely humor or indeed farce. My particular favorite in this category is the "Ḥulwâniyyah," where in the first part the head of a returning Ḥâjj is subjected to all kinds of abuse in a public bath before the entire scene degenerates into a wonderful parody of legal procedure: when 'Îsâ ibn Hishâm is cross-examined as to the ownership of his head and responds that it is indeed his own, the information is deemed irrelevant to the case at point. The second half involves a truly wonderful example of malapropisms, although I have often found it necessary to explain to student readers the humor to be found in the assumption that an inhabitant of Qum has to be a Sunni. The same kind of farcical situation is to be found in the bipartite "Mawṣiliyyah" where both 'Îsâ ibn Hishâm and Abû al-Fatḥ are involved in some nasty chicanery, failing to revive a dead man in the first part and to divert water from a village in part two. One wonders whether Yûsuf Idrîs was bearing the final scene in mind – with the two rogues fleeing as the village is prostrate in prayer and unable to move – when he wrote his story, "A Kân Lâ Budd yâ Lîlî an Tuḍî' al-Nûr?"[13] Student readers can enjoy the similar piece of trickery in the "Baghdâdiyyah" *maqâmah*, this time involving only 'Îsâ ibn Hishâm, as noted above. As James Monroe has noted in his study of al-Hamadhânî's *maqâmât*, the moral of the tale would seem to be: never accept a free meal from someone who cannot get your name straight.[14]

While many scholars have drawn attention to the picaresque qualities that mark some examples of the *maqâmât*, not least those that involve skullduggery of one kind or another, the aspect of travel and place is normally more implicit than explicit, in spite of the specific names of places that often make up the title of the *maqâmah* in question (even al-Hamadhânî's "Asadiyyah," for example, is said to involve the Syrian city of Ḥimṣ). Even so, both al-Hamadhânî and al-Ḥarîrî hail from the Eastern regions of the Islamic dominions, and their choice of place names as titles reflect the fact (with al-Ḥarîrî virtually moving farther afield than al-Hamadhânî while still remaining essentially in the Mashriq).

By contrast, as we now turn to al-Saraqustî and his remarkable *al-Maqâmât al-Luzûmiyyah*, we encounter a much broader geographical perspective, stretching from the Maghrib itself, via the Middle East, all the way to China. As several of the scholars already mentioned have noted, al-Saraqustî is clearly bent on imitating, if not besting, al-Ḥarîrî, the repute of whose *maqâmât* must have led to their rapid dissemination across the Islamic world. The very title of the collection links their composition to the challenges taken up earlier by Abû al-'Alâ' al-Ma'arrî in his *Al-Luzûmiyyât*: a clear relish for complex exercises in verbal elaboration, in al-Saraqustî's case involving elaborate rhyme schemes, uses of the same grapheme in every word in the text, and so on.[15] In the context of teaching the *maqâmah* in translation, James Monroe has courageously taken up the transfer of these challenges along with a commentary, so we can offer a further example of the "Ḥarîrian" model with a Maghribî twist by discussing al-Saraqustî's 41st ("Barbariyyah") *maqâmah*.[16]

By this stage, the pattern of naming established by al-Hamadhânî in his *maqâmât* seems to have become firmly established: from his 'Îsâ ibn Hishâm and Abû al-Fatḥ al-Iskandarî and al-Ḥarîrî's al-Ḥârith ibn Hammâm and Abû Zayd al-Sarûjî we now encounter al-Ṣâ'ib ibn-Tammâm and his rogue counterpart, Abû Ḥabîb al-Sadûsî (and the tradition is to continue into the modern period, where al-Muwayliḥî revives the name of al-Hamadhânî's narrator, while Bayram al-Tûnisî takes things to farcical lengths with his Sa'rân ibn Falsân and al-'Âjiz ibn 'Imyân). Curiously perhaps, bearing in mind the fact that this al-Saraqustî lives in Spain, he has his narrator be on the African side of the Straits aspiring to cross into Spain – specifically in Tangier, "whence I could survey the portals of the Frankish lands," as James Monroe's excellent translation has it.[17] Even more curiously, at least initially, al-Ṣâ'ib ibn-Tammâm encounters a group of people whom we would now call Amazîgh, although in the context of this *maqâmah* it is appropriate to term them Berbers, not only because of the original title, "al-Barbariyyah," but also because the narrative presents an extremely negative portrait of a group of "people like cattle and ostriches, and humans like wolves or hyenas, whose speech I could not understand, and with whose minds my own did not agree." In this *maqâmah* the characteristic recognition moment comes relatively early in that al-Ṣâ'ib encounters his colleague, the heavily disguised Abû Ḥabîb who, it seems, can converse in both an unidentified "foreign tongue" and Tamazikht (Berber), and who proclaims loudly his immaculate Arab peninsular origins. Both men are well entertained, fed and watered by their hosts, who are still disparaged: they "kicked up their heels in an outlandish dance, neighing and howling. What pleased them did not please me ..."[18] Monroe's discussion of the implications of this narrative focuses on the ironic intent of this and many other *maqâmât* narratives. After all, one has to assume that Abû al-Fatḥ's verses at the conclusion of al-Hamadhânî's "Mawṣiliyyah" *maqâmah* demand such an interpretation:

> How marvelous was the stupidity of people,
> Which I took advantage of with ease!
> I received from them full measure of good,
> While I weighed out to them nought but fraud and falsehood.[19]

In the case of the "Barbariyyah" *maqâmah*, we are perhaps supposed to chuckle – at least – at the pomposity of a claim to pure Arab descent in thirteenth-century Spain, while at the same time acknowledging, as Monroe does, the distinct possibility that a message concerning the corruption of Arab values and the potency of Amazigh ones may also be part of the ironic message. Beyond all this, one might also suggest that this example of a Maghribî *maqâmah* may provide a pre-modern example of the extent of Arabic-based culture that is still in need of emphasis within the modern period and the study of Arabic literary texts.

The name of Ibn Ṣayqal al-Jazarî (d. 1301) and his *Al-Maqâmât al-Zayniyyah* are also frequently mentioned in this post-Ḥarîrî connection, but they are of such linguistic complexity that no one thus far has ventured to translate them or indeed to analyze them critically. With regard to translation, the same holds true, unfortunately, with regard to al-Qalqashandî (d. 1418) and his *maqâmah*, although we do have an excellent study of it in English by Muhsin al-Musawi. As al-Musawi makes clear, al-Qalqashandî is well aware of the developing tradition into which his own offering is to be placed, making complimentary references to his august predecessors, al-Hamadhânî and al-Ḥarîrî, but he also points to the ways in which this particular *maqâmah* displays an awareness of the original generic purpose and structure of the genre and the ways in which it is being gradually transformed.[20]

That process of transformation is to appear even more clearly in the contributions of the next composer of *maqâmât* in our chronological survey, the renowned polygraph, Jalâl al-dîn al-Suyûṭî (d. 1516), two of whose *maqâmât* have been translated by van Gelder. In fact, al-Suyûṭî suits my current purpose admirably in that, in addition to being a major figure in the much-neglected period of Arabic literary culture between 1200 and 1800, he sits almost exactly half way between the emergence of the *maqâmah* genre and its so-called "revival" at the hands of a number of eighteenth- and nineteenth-century littérateurs. There is perhaps an irony to be found in the fact that, as van Gelder notes in his commentaries on the two *maqâmât* of al-Suyûṭî that he has translated, two of the primary commentators on the genre and its development, Kilito and Hameen-Anttila, choose to criticize al-Suyûṭî's use of the term "*maqâmah*" to describe his particular contributions, as though the model established initially by al-Hamadhânî and later elaborated by al-Ḥarîrî and his imitators was somehow supposed to remain fixed in its generic purpose and stylistic features for all time. As van Gelder notes, al-Suyûṭî's *maqâmât* resemble far more the genre of *munâẓarah adabiyyah* (literary debate) whereby the relative merits of a variety of differing positions or entities would be argued by their proponents. Al-Suyûṭî proceeds to use the genre in extremely creative ways. Because of the format whereby various examples of a particular category argue their respective merits, he particularly favors a concentration on number. His most famous (or most commonly cited) *maqâmah* is the "Miskiyyah," during which four perfumes discuss their various merits along with poetic citations to underline those qualities. As van Gelder notes, but with considerable skepticism, it has been suggested that this *maqâmah* is a parodic representation of four Mamluk contestants for the Sultan's position following the death of Qa'it Bey.[21] However, the number seven seems a special favorite of al-Suyûṭî: vegetables in the "Zumurrudiyyah," nuts in the "Fustuqiyyah," and fruits in the "Tuffâḥiyyah."

Following al-Suyûṭî, of course, we enter what has long been regarded as Arabic literary history's "slough of despond." That, however, is also a period during which, it would appear, the generic characteristics of the *maqâmah* blended well with the esthetics of the period and thus guaranteed its continuity.[22] Bearing the translated repertoire in mind, we might pause briefly at Peter Gran's version of Ḥasan al-'Attâr's (d. 1835) "*Maqâmah fî dukhûl al-Faransâwiyyîn li-al-diyâr al-Misriyyah*,"[23] and pass regretfully by Nâṣîf al-Yâzijî's neo-classical imitation of al-Ḥarîrî (to whom he pays tribute) in his *Majma' al-Baḥrayn*, and even more regretfully by Aḥmad Fâris al-Shidyâq's pioneering narrative, *Al-Sâq 'alâ al-Sâq fîmâ huwa al-Fâryâq*, to arrive finally at Muḥammad al-Muwayliḥî's (d. 1930) *Ḥadîth 'Îsâ ibn Hishâm*.

Al-Muwayliḥî's work is, of course, not specifically in the *maqâmah* form, and indeed the version of it that was heavily revised for publication in book form (1907) succeeds in eradicating some of the characteristic features that clearly tie its original version to its forebear.[24] Obviously, the revival of the name of al-Hamadhânî's participant narrator is intended to serve such a purpose, but the format of the currently available text obscures the fact that each original article published in the newspaper, *Miṣbâḥ al-Sharq* – many of which were later combined into lengthy chapters in the book – began with a passage of elaborate *saj'*. Thus, to the readers of the original texts in newspaper article form, the linkage to the stylistic feature of the *maqâmah* tradition was clearly indicated by its initial position within each episode, whereas now some of the more elaborate passages of description find themselves embedded in chapters that are a blend of passages of *saj'* and lengthy passages of al-Muwayliḥî's admittedly lofty prose style.

Both al-Shidyâq's and al-Muwayliḥî's works acknowledge a clear debt to the pre-modern tradition of the *maqâmah* and its developmental phases, but in one crucial way al-Muwayliḥî breaks away, by writing a sequence of episodes in which the action is sequentially linked. I would hasten to add that a good deal of reordering and editing was necessary before the original newspaper articles were to be arranged in the convincing sequence in which they have since appeared in the book form of the work, but even then it is relatively easy to identify moments when the linkages are weak, almost to the point of non-existence. Even the most popular segments of the narrative, those involving the country *'umdah* who comes to the rapidly Westernizing city of Cairo in search of wine, women and song, reflect the "classical" narrative modes of the *maqâmah* by using the same set of characters (and indeed with 'Îsâ ibn Hishâm and the Pâshâ being very much in the background), and by being situated in separate locations that might be reorganized into a different sequence with little or no impact on the narrative. With all these traits and qualities in mind, I would select from among the many possibilities those episodes that serve to illustrate the variety of narrative techniques that al-Muwayliḥî employs, not least his penchant for sarcasm and parody and his considerable erudition. The opening segment ("Al-'Ibrah"), with its several invocations of Abû al-'Alâ' al-Ma'arrî's verses, would be one, added to which would be the wonderfully detailed and sarcastic opening description of the visit to the records office ("Al-Daftarkhâne al-Shar'iyyah"), the elaborate description of a wedding celebration, and the initial episode in which the *'umdah* meets in the newly refurbished Ezbekiyya Gardens the two Egyptian companions who will eagerly escort him around Cairo's nightlife and spend large amounts of his money.

Conclusion

During the course of this rapid survey I have alluded at several points to particular modes of analysis that might be applied to the *maqâmah* genre in general and to particular examples of it from different periods. The specific examples that I have selected have aimed to represent different periods in the genre's development but also to show that, apart from the continuing emphasis on the virtuoso use of language, there is a great deal of variety in both content and purpose. Other selections, for example, could easily concentrate on those examples that constitute narratives, where characters, incidents and structural sequence can all be analyzed: the role of humor and parody, for example, and the frequent resort to an unfamiliar situation into which a moment of recognition is inserted as a concluding strategy.

In the more specific context of Arabic literature and its heritage, the *maqâmah* can be shown to be serving a crucial bridge function, a textual genre that develops and thrives throughout the lengthy period of centuries, the esthetics of which have apparently been seen as so alien to our own traditions of interpretation. Its introduction into our curricula – albeit in translation – can thus continue a process whereby we may view the literary heritage of the Arabs as a series of continuities rather than breaks.

Notes

1 Muḥammad al-Muwayliḥî, *What 'Isa ibn Hisham Told Us* (Library of Arabic Literature) 2 vols, New York: New York University Press, 2015.
2 See Devin Stewart, "Saj' in the Qur'an: Prosody and Structure," *Journal of Arabic Literature* Vol. XXI no. 2 (Sept. 1990): 101–139.
3 Clifford Edmund Bosworth, *The Medieval Islamic Underworld*, 2 vols, Leiden: E.J. Brill, 1976. The various specialties practiced by such groups are rehearsed in detail in al-Hamadhânî's "Ruṣafah" *maqâmah*.
4 I had discussed some of these issues elsewhere: "Literary History and Generic Change: The Example of the Maqama," in *Studies in Honour of Clifford Edmund Bosworth. 1. Hunter of the East*, Leiden: E.J. Brill, 1999, pp. 3–14; and *The Arabic Novel: An historical and critical introduction*, 2nd edn, Syracuse, NY: Syracuse University Press, pp. 209–22.
5 See R.A. Nicholson, *Eastern Poetry and Prose*, Cambridge: Cambridge University Press, 1922, pp. 116–24; and Geert Jan van Gelder, "Precious Stones, Precious Words: al-Suyûtî's *al-Maqâma al-yâqûtiyya*, translated and annotated," in Arnoud Vrolijk and Jan P. Hogendijk (eds), *O ye Gentlemen: Arabic Studies on Science and Literary Culture in Honour of Remke Kruk*, Leiden: Brill, 2007, pp. 313–32. For al-Shidyâq, see *Leg Over Leg*, 4 vols (Library of Arabic Literature), New York: New York University Press, 2013.
6 In the Loeb Classical Library's edition of those two authors, for example, the more obscene passages are left in their original Latin versions within the text of the English translation.
7 Abd al-Fattah Kilito, *Les séances*, Paris: Sindbad, 1983.
8 For the sake of completeness, I need to point out that I have recently translated into English five of the *maqâmât* of al-Hamadhânî (those of Baghdad, Balkh, Mawṣil, Ḥulwân, and Asad) and one of al-Ḥarîrî (Damascus) for an anthology of pre-modern Arabic prose edited by Salma Jayyusi: *Classical Arabic Stories: An Anthology*, New York: Columbia University Press, 2010, pp. 358–73.

9 Both Rina Drory and Devin Stewart call him Abû Ṭâhir al-Ashtarkûnî (or al-Ishtarkûnî [from Estercuel]) al-Saraqustî (d. 1143). See "The *Maqâma*," in *The Cambridge History of Arabic Literature: The Literature of al-Andalus*, ed. Maria Rosa Menocal, Raymond P. Scheindlin and Michael Sells, 2000, pp. 194–5; and Devin Stewart, "The *Maqâma*," in *The Cambridge History of Arabic Literature: The Post Classical Period*, ed. Roger Allen and D.S. Richards, Cambridge: Cambridge University Press, 2006, pp. 151–2.

10 As is the case with the *maqâmât* that are included within Aḥmad Fâris al-Shidyâq's renowned 19th-century masterpiece, *Al-Sâq 'Alâ al-Sâq fî-mâ Huwa al-Fâryâq* (1855), I am quite prepared to acknowledge that Al-Muwayliḥî's work pays tribute to the pre-modern tradition of the *maqâmah* (not least through its title), but is not, strictly speaking a "*maqâmah.*"

11 See Roger Allen, "Literary History and Generic Change: The Example of the *Maqâmah*," in *Studies in Honour of Clifford Edmund Bosworth: 1. Hunter of the East*, Leiden: E.J. Brill, 1999, pp. 3–14.

12 Jaakko Hameen Anttila, *Maqama: A History of a Genre*, Wiesbaden: Harrassowitz, 2002; Devin Stewart, "The *maqâma*," in *Cambridge History of Arabic Literature: The Post-Classical Period*, ed. Roger Allen and D.S. Richards, Cambridge: Cambridge University Press, 2006, pp. 145–58. As part of an ongoing research project, Devin Stewart has discovered a very large number of authors of *maqâmât* in what we might term the "post-Ḥarîrî" period.

13 Yûsuf Idrîs, "A Kân lâ budd yâ Lîlî an Tudî' al-Nûr?" in *Bayt min lahm*, Cairo: n.p., n.d., pp. 15–35.

14 James Monroe, *The Art of Badī' al-Zamān al-Hamadhānī as Picaresque Narrative*, Beirut: American University of Beirut, 1983, pp. 141–2.

15 See Monroe's translation, and also Devin Stewart, "The *maqâma*," in *Cambridge History of Arabic Literature: The Post-Classical Period*, pp. 151–2.

16 Monroe, *Al-Maqâmât al-Luzûmiyyah*, 418.

17 Monroe, *Al-Maqâmât al-Luzûmiyyah*, 418.

18 Ibid., 421.

19 Al-Hamadhânî, *Maqâmât*, tr. W.J. Prendergast, 88.

20 Muhsin Jassim al-Musawi, "Vindicating a Profession or a Personal Career? Al-Qalqashandi's *Maqamah* in Context," *Mamluk Studies Review* Vol. 7 no. 1 (Jan. 2003), 111–135. See also C.E. Bosworth, "A *Maqâma* on Secretaryship: Al-Qalqashandî's *Al-Kawâkib al-Durrîya fi al-Manâqib al-Badriyya*," *Bulletin of the School of Oriental and African Studies* Vol. 27 (1964): 291–98.

21 This "Miskiyyah" *maqâmah* is translated and discussed by Van Gelder in his article "Four Perfumes of Arabia: A Translation of al-Suyuti's *al-Maqama al-miskiyya*," *Res Orientales*, 11 (1999), pp. 203–12 (special issue: "Parfums d'orient," ed. Rika Gyselen).

22 That this period (roughly the 16th–18th centuries) was not as infertile as the literary-historical record might claim is now generously illustrated by *Essays in Arabic Literary Biography Vol. 2: 1350–1850*, ed. Joseph E. Lowry and Devin J. Stewart, Wiesbaden: Harrassowitz, 2009.

23 See Peter Gran, *The Islamic Roots of Capitalism: Egypt 1760–1840*, Austin: University of Texas Press, 1979, pp. 189–91; and Peter Gran, "Hasan al-'Attâr," in *Essays in Arabic literary Biography Vol. 2: 1350–1850*, pp. 56–68.

24 That duly noted, my recent parallel-text edition of the work (see note 1 above) is entirely based on the original newspaper articles and thus restores all the omitted materials.

Bibliography

Abu-Haidar, Jareer, "Maqamat Literature and the Picaresque Novel," *Journal of Arabic Literature* V (1974): 1–10.

Allen, Roger, "Literary History and Generic Change: The Example of the Maqama," in *Studies in Honour of Clifford Edmund Bosworth. 1. Hunter of the East*, Leiden: E.J. Brill, 1999. 3–14.

Al-Musawi, Muhsin Jassim, "Vindicating a Profession or a Personal Career? Al-Qalqashandî's Maqâmah in Context," *Mamluk Studies Review* Vol. 7 no. 1 (Jan. 2003).

Al-Shidyâq, Aḥmad Fâris, *Leg Over Leg*, 4 vols. (Library of Arabic Literature), New York: New York University Press, 2013.

Beaumont, Daniel, "The Trickster and Rhetoric in the Maqamat," *Edebiyat* Vol. 5 no. 1 (1994): 1–14.

Beeston, A.F.L., "The Genesis of the Maqamat Genre," *Journal of Arabic Literature* II (1971): 1–12.

Beeston, A.F.L., "The Role of Parallelism in Arabic Prose," in *Arabic Literature to the End of the Umayyad Period Cambridge History of Arabic Literature Vol. 1*, Cambridge: Cambridge University Press, 1983. 180–185.

Bosworth, C. Edmund, *The Medieval Islamic Underworld: The Banu Sasan in Arabic Society and Literature*, Leiden: E.J. Brill, 1976.

Cachia, Pierre, "The Narrative Genres," in *An Overview of Modern Arabic Literature Islamic Surveys 17*, Edinburgh: University of Edinburgh Press, 1990. 104–122.

Classical Arabic Stories: An Anthology, ed. Salma Jayyusi, New York: Columbia University Press, 2010. 358–373.

Hameen-Anttila, Jaakko, *Maqama: A History of a Genre*, Wiesbaden: Harrassowitz, 2002.

Katsumata, Naoya, "The Style of the Maqama: Arabic, Persian, Hebrew, Syriac," *Middle Eastern Literatures* Vol. 5 no. 2 (July 2002): 117–138.

Kilito, Abd al-Fattah, "Le genre 'Seance': une introduction," in *Studia Islamica* XLIII (1976): 25 ff.

Kilito, Abd al-Fattah, *Les séances*, Paris: Sindbad, 1983.

Kilito, Abd al-Fattah, *Al-Ghâ'ib: dirâsah fî maqâmah li-al-Harîrî*, Casablanca: Dâr Tubqâl li-al-Nashr, 1987.

Malti-Douglas, Fedwa, "Maqâmât and Adab: 'Al-Maqâma al-Madîriyya' of Al-Hamadhânî," *Journal of the American Oriental Society* Vol. 105 no. 2 (April–June 1985): 247–258.

Mattock, J.N., "The Early History of the Maqâma," *Journal of Arabic Literature* XV (1984): 1–18.

Monroe, James T., *The Art of Badî' az-Zamân al-Hamadhânî as Picaresque Narrative*, Beirut: Center for Arab and Middle East Studies, American University in Beirut, 1983.

Monroe, James T., "Al-Saraqustî, ibn al-Ashtarkûwî: Andalusî Lexicographer, Poet, and Author of al-Maqâmât al-Luzûmîya," pt. 1: *Journal of Arabic Literature* Vol. XXVII no. 1 (March 1997): 1–37; pt. 2: *Journal of Arabic Literature* Vol. 29 no. 2 (July 1998): 31–58.

Nemah, H., "Andalusian maqâmât," *Journal of Arabic Literature* V (1974): 83–92.

Ouyang, Wen-chin, "The Maqâmât of al-Hamadhânî and al-Harîrî," in *Great Literature of the Eastern World*, ed. Ian P. McGreal, London: Harper-Collins, 1996. 488–495.

Van Gelder, Geert Jan, "Four Perfumes of Arabia: A Translation of al-Suyûtî's Al-Maqâma al-miskiyya," *Res Orientales* XI (1998): 203–212.

Van Gelder, Geert Jan, "Rhyme in Maqâmât: Or Too Many Exceptions Do Not Prove a Rule," *Journal of Semitic Studies* Vol. 44 no. 1 (1999): 75–82.

Van Gelder, Geert Jan, "Precious Stones, Precious Words: Al-Suyūtī's Al-Maqâma al-Yāqūtiyya," in *O Ye Gentlemen: Arabic Studies on Science and Literary Culture in Honour of Remke Kruk*, Leiden: E.J. Brill, 2007. 313–332.

16

IBN HAZM

Friendship, love and the quest for justice

Terri DeYoung

Al-Andalus (Muslim Spain) – though conquered in 711 CE – was a part of the Islamic world that was slow to develop its own distinctive culture. The greatest literary patron of the tenth century, the Buwayhid vizier (chief minister) al-Ṣāḥib ibn ʻAbbād (938–95) famously dismissed the encyclopedic masterpiece of the Andalusian courtier Ibn ʻAbd Rabbih (860–940) *Al-ʻIqd al-farīd* (*The Unique Necklace*) as "our own goods brought back home to us" when he encountered the work in Baghdad.[1] However, when, in the next century, Andalusian culture and society did attain its own discrete voice, it quickly became extraordinarily sophisticated and innovative, widely admired in the rest of the Islamic world.[2]

The catalyst for this change was at least in part due to the efforts of two remarkable friends: Ibn Ḥazm (994–1065)[3] and Ibn Shuhayd (992–1035),[4] both of whom overcame long odds to produce – each individually – a body of work that would inspire and challenge Muslim intellectuals for centuries. Ibn Hazm even wrote an entire treatise in his youth devoted to summarizing the excellence of Andalusian scholarship: *Risāla fī faḍl al-Andalus* (Treatise on the Merit of Andalus).[5] This was a reply – requested by one of his close friends – to a letter, addressed to the latter, in which a Tunisian scholar had belittled the accomplishments of Andalusians. Throughout the *Risāla*, Ibn Hazm constantly singles out his compatriots for praise, even at one point going so far as to compare them, in their lack of recognition, to Jesus, "the prophet without honor in his own country."[6] Clearly, the reputation for inferiority Andalusians still encountered at the beginning of the eleventh century stung Ibn Hazm to the quick. Two hundred years later such a defense would hardly have been deemed necessary.

In the twentieth century, through extensive translations of their works into European languages, both Ibn Hazm and Ibn Shuhayd gained new admirers among scholars in the West.[7] The rough edges found in both their personalities, however, have also meant that some have found them difficult subjects to deal with fully in conventional academic settings.[8] So their works have not found the broad recognition one might otherwise expect, given their creativity. Nevertheless the very idiosyncrasy and individuality that gave rise to these negative judgments also means that their work can be especially useful in class settings as springboards for engaging in worthwhile discussion about the relationship between ideas and personality in intellectual discourse. Should *what* someone says (the quality of their arguments) be judged by *who* they are and how they act in other contexts? Obviously a person's beliefs and opinions change over his or her lifetime. When someone renders a particular opinion at one juncture in their lives (especially when it is repugnant to contemporary mores) should this be irrevocably attached to any consideration of their whole body of work? Ibn Hazm (and Ibn Shuhayd) are particularly engaging subjects for such inquiries in a classroom setting.

I have taught about Ibn Hazm in two courses. They both focus more on writing and class discussion as tools for reflective engagement with the subject matter than introductory or gateway courses, but they do not ask the students to produce original research, as graduate-level seminars would. The first of these courses is on the Arab/Islamic ethical tradition and uses the work of Ibn Hazm as a philosopher and theologian to explore some of the later trends in the development of a truly Islamic ethical tradition. Ibn Hazm serves very well as an example in this course, because his ideas (though not necessarily adopted later into the mainstream) represent original and genuine efforts to synthesize the various strands of ethical thought (ancient Greek/Aristotelian, Arabian tribal and Islamic) that were familiar to intellectuals of his time. The other course (syllabus included here) I have been teaching for far longer and treats of Ibn Hazm (along with Ibn Shuhayd) in a broader context, as early leading intellectuals and literary figures who see themselves as first and foremost Andalusians (although the equals of any counterparts from the East).

Although my treatment of Ibn Hazm in either of these courses has been constrained by the strictures of the ten-week quarter system in which I must teach, I am looking forward to the opportunity in the future to perhaps treat his work in a more wholistic fashion. The following represents one possible scenario for so proceeding.[9] As one of his most recent biographers in English has said, "[h]is life was in many respects a microcosm of the life of al-Andalus, sharing some of its splendor and much of its tragedy."[10]

Ibn Hazm had been, in his twenties through his forties, a major player in some of those dynastic intrigues and had found himself in prison more than once. This phase of political activism in his life came to an end, however, when Hishām al-Mu'tadd (d. 1031), the last serious claimant to the Umayyad throne, was ignominiously defeated before the gates of Cordoba and driven away. Ibn Hazm had been in Hisham's entourage, probably one of his main political advisors, and himself barely escaped with his life to the east, finally resurfacing on the island of Majorca, where he established himself as a philosopher and religious scholar of some note.[11] Sometime after 1048, however, he returned to western Iberia and took up residence for a while in Seville.

The disintegration of political unity in the caliphate during the course of the eleventh century was accompanied by a cultural maturation of dimensions unmatched anywhere else in Europe or the Muslim lands of the day. Al-Andalus, despite its political chaos, went from a peripheral satellite of the civilization surrounding it to a major player in the intellectual life of the Mediterranean. Significant advances in science, philosophy (including the fields of logic and ethics), literature, and religious studies were made by Andalusians in the eleventh through fourteenth centuries. In many cases, these developments were anticipated by Ibn Hazm's writings. So, though his political ambitions were frustrated, early and often, his intellectual legacy was very real.

While still a young man, during a lull in the almost constant political upheavals that enmeshed him until he was in his thirties, Ibn Hazm composed a small treatise on the nature of love called *Ṭawq al-ḥamāma* (*The Dove's Neck-Ring*).[12] This seemingly light-hearted work survived almost by accident in a single manuscript copy that was purchased by the Dutch ambassador of the day, Levinus Warner (*c.* 1618–65) sometime during the 22 years (1644–65) he lived in Istanbul.[13] It gives an almost unique insight[14] into the elegant, sophisticated world where Ibn Hazm grew up, which vanished so abruptly in 1009 when fighting broke out in Cordoba.

In one sense, then, *The Dove's Neck-Ring* can be usefully read as a powerfully nostalgic homage to the world and people Ibn Hazm had lost. Later in life he would deny any debilitating effect on his powers of reasoning of such disturbing elegiac emotions,[15] but at this early stage, when the pain was still fresh, things may very well have been quite different. Certainly, in his book, he brings the past vividly back to life, as he adheres consistently to the technique of using personal experience as the touchstone for measuring the reliability of the generalizations about the nature of love circulating in the society of his day.

For example, the historians may tell us that the walls of Cordoba were pierced by seven gates, and that the western one, called the "Gate of the Perfumers," opening out onto a bridge (originally built by the Romans), eventually led travelers through a series of gardens to the high road heading for Seville. They may also say that the area around the gate became a meeting place for the young women of the city who flocked there to sample the merchants' wares and meet their would-be lovers.[16] However, only Ibn Hazm could transform such spare description into a meditation on the truthfulness of the principle that love can emerge at the first sight of the beloved which he movingly captures through his incorporation of the poet Yūsuf Ibn Hārūn's story of "Love at First Sight" for Khalwa.[17]

In the story, a dialogic exchange between the lovers quickly displaces the authoritativeness of a single, third-person voice (the author's) articulating the principle that love can, indeed, be precipitated by a single glance (rather than being the product of long familiarity), and describing its effects. The indeterminacy of the love experience (its ambiguity and instability), enhanced by the vividness of the dialogic form is further underscored by the disappearance of Khalwa (in Arabic, her name means "seclusion, withdrawal") from the environs of the Perfumers' Gate in the anecdote, and in the mention of Yūsuf Ibn Hārūn's long (though ultimately fruitful) search for her, Ibn Hazm's delicate artistic control of the text can scarcely be matched in contemporary writing. His vivid reconstruction of the interaction between the lovers through a constructed dialogue makes passion (love) and reason (speech) equal participants in the creation of this reality.[18] Nevertheless, Khalwa is not Petrarch's beloved, Laura, who never speaks in the Italian poet's famous sonnets and essentially exists solely as an inspiration for the loquacious lover. Khalwa, in contrast, constructs her lover's reality, which he must operate within and cannot change.

The course I teach on Hispano-Arabic literature involves developing the students' sympathy for, and understanding of, a tradition of behavior and literary effort (using the term *adab* in both its commonly accepted modern senses) – centered on love and unfulfillable desire – that is often very foreign to their experience, though not necessarily difficult to understand once they have engaged with it. I have found Ibn Hazm's short chapters on falling in love (such as the one analyzed above) as springboards for student presentations in the class. Since these chapters often rely on dialogue as a means for presenting their point of view (or can be easily adapted to such a method), I have asked the students to follow Ibn Hazm's lead in preparing their own review of his arguments about "falling in love from a description," or "falling in love while asleep." This allows them to internalize Ibn Hazm's method and argument while engaging a kinesthetic sensibility[19] that is all too often absent from the typical college classroom: especially so in a class that focuses (as so many Arabic literature courses must necessarily do) on acquainting students with a cascade of new – and generally unfamiliar – information.

On a more theoretical note, Ibn Hazm's continual resort to a sort of privileged empiricism in *The Dove's Neck-Ring* distinguishes it from his later legal and religious writings, which tend to emphasize the authority of textuality and assert that absolute truthfulness is to be found only in the Divine word. This could certainly be approached as an opportunity to include Ibn Hazm's mature work (though it is difficult to find modern, reliable translations into English) in a course on Islamic theology, law or religious practice, especially in a historical context. Certainly his support of the Ẓāhirī *madhhab* (school) of law in the face of the Malikī approach common in Andalus deserves thorough consideration in any review of the development of Islamic law. Ignác Goldziher's groundbreaking study of this *madhhab*[20] can still be remarkably helpful in this regard.

Ibn Hazm's last book, however, returns to the somewhat skeptical attitude, grounded in a personal vision, characteristic of *The Dove's Neck-Ring*.[21] It is a work on ethics,[22] and draws on the framework of values articulated centuries before in Aristotle's famous treatise on the subject, *The Nicomachean Ethics*.[23] In this work, Aristotle sketched the outlines of a system leading to correct behavior (and ultimately happiness) based on the cultivation of certain character traits, one that had become conventional in Greek thought even before his time. At its center lie the four "virtues": wisdom, courage, temperance and justice. To these four traditional Greek virtues, Aristotle would add a fifth, friendship, which he considered most important of all. The framework of "virtue ethics," based on Aristotle's pioneering work, dominated the philosophical discussions of ethics in Europe and the Islamic world until the threshold of modern times. Even when other ethical systems were proposed, the *Nicomachean Ethics* formed the background on which they were constructed.

Aristotle's treatise was translated into Arabic at a relatively early date,[24] and gave rise to several treatments of ethics by Muslim authors, of which probably the most famous is Miskawayh's (c. 932–1030) *Tahdhīb al-akhlāq* (*The Refinement of Character*).[25] The precepts of Aristotle's ethical thought (including his treatment of the four virtues) even find their way into what is undeniably the most influential religious guidebook of the age, *Iḥyā' 'ulūm al-dīn* by al-Ghazālī (1058–1111).[26] Approximately a century before Miskawayh, the Baghdadi scholar Qudāma ibn Ja'far (c. 873 or 874–948)[27] had written a guide to Arabic literary criticism, *Naqd al-shi'r*, which uses the Aristotelian virtues as the backbone for its discussion of Arabic panegyric. Qudāma, much influenced in general by Aristotle's doctrines, denied that any legitimate panegyric of a ruler could be written if it used any but Aristotle's virtues (or some combination thereof) as its basis.[28] His position generated endless debate in medieval Arabic rhetorical criticism as to its legitimacy as a criterion for successful panegyric. Notable entries in the controversy include the work of Qudāma's contemporary Abū al-Qāsim al-Āmidī (d. 987) – who categorically disagreed with him, holding him up to considerable ridicule – and the more nuanced treatments of their successors in the two succeeding centuries, Ibn Sinān Al-Khafājī (1031–74)[29] and Ibn Rashīq al-Qayrawānī (1000–63 or 1071).[30]

Ibn Hazm initially conforms more rigorously to the mainstream philosophical and religious path trodden by Miskawayh and al-Ghazālī and their successors. He frames ethics as a question of morality and theology rather than pursue directly its application to literature.[31] However, the approach to the subject he adopts gradually reveals he has his own special concerns that guide his approach to outlining a system of ethical values. Unlike his predecessors (who drew most heavily upon Aristotle for their inspiration), Ibn Hazm does not say that human happiness is the goal to be achieved by the cultivation of ethical virtues.[32] On the contrary, he takes the minimalist (and in some ways opposed) position that the goal of a human being should be "to be free from anxiety" and avoid pain.[33] In this we can perhaps see a legacy of his own early experiences: the death of his family members, the destruction of his family home and the thwarting of his political ambitions.

Ibn Hazm's specific interest in ethics late in his life may also have been the fruit of the disastrous outcome of his residence in Seville following his departure from Majorca in 1048. After only a short time there, he ran afoul of the ruler of Seville, 'Abbād al-Mu'tadid (d. 1069), and his books were publicly burned. He was then forced to leave for his family estate in Mante Lisham, high in the mountains, where he spent the rest of his life in virtual seclusion.[34] He left a poem about the experience:

> If you burn the sheets of paper, you will not burn what the sheets of paper contain, for that is in my heart,
>
> It goes with me wherever my riding camels alight, dismounting when I do, and they will be buried in my grave,
>
> Spare me from burning the parchment and paper and speak of knowledge so that the people will see who [really] knows,
>
> And if not, then let them return to the libraries as a beginning and how often there are veils before what you might seek concerning God.[35]

He begins by minimizing the effect that the destruction of his books will have on the impact his beliefs and opinions can have, either before or after his death (lines 1 and 2). This would seem, at first, to be a fairly standard variant of the universalist argument against considering censorship important often favored among early modern writers and philosophers: that knowledge (and truth) resides within the human mind, and writings – however important or persuasive – are merely the record of that thought and can always be reproduced if they are destroyed. This argument gives primacy to knowledge and its independent existence (hence the universalist label) – and likewise to human rationality – while merely bowing cursorily to the idea that knowledge has a divine source (for Muslims, in God and the Qur'anic text) – that dimension then becoming what constitutes its importance. Truth from that source exists in a veiled form, and humanity's eternal task, for Ibn Hazm, would seem to be to use the tools of humanist, rationalist learning to discover that truth. Philosophical speculation could always be considered a vital part of that quest.

Perhaps that is why Ibn Hazm never bothered to correct the statement he made in one of his relatively early religious works, the comparative history of religions known as *Kitāb al-fiṣal* (or, as some scholars transcribe it: *Al-fiṣal fī al-milal wa-al-ahwā' wa-al-niḥal* (Book of Distinctions Concerning Religions, Sects, and Denominations)):

> The truth [represented by] philosophy – its meanings, its fruit, and the goal intended by learning it – is nothing but the reform of the soul. You can use it [=philosophy] in this world for its virtues and as a good path to follow, leading safely to the hereafter, as well as [a source of] good policy in matters domestic and social. This itself is nothing other than the goal of the religious law (*al-sharī'a*), not differing in any way from what is found among scholars of philosophy.[36]

The contrast between Ibn Hazm's attitude, as expressed here, and that of some of his contemporary religious scholars is rather breathtaking. Many of those individuals condemned philosophy in all of its branches (logic, ethics, and (meta)physics) absolutely. As Zakarīyā Ibrāhīm has noted, they believed that "philosophy was an evil, logic is the gateway to philosophy and the gateway to an evil is an evil. So logic was therefore also evil."[37] Perhaps it can be said, as George Hourani emphasized in his analysis of the passage, that Ibn Hazm was only endorsing philosophy pursued as a utilitarian "practical" activity, following Aristotle's own definition in the *Nicomachean Ethics* (1099a1–5). Nevertheless, that Ibn Hazm equates it in this very passage to religious law (God-given wisdom) would seem to argue that he saw philosophy as something more than merely a practical exercise of only limited use that could be easily dispensed with.

It would be difficult to imagine such an argument about the value of philosophy centralized in Ibn Hazm's middle, textualist (Ẓāhirī) and rigorously Islamist period. Ibn Hazm never rejected his earlier statement out of hand, but he never again articulated his support of philosophy so resolutely. Zakariya Ibrahim also makes a pertinent argument when he connects the relative silence about philosophy in the middle phase of Ibn Hazm's life to a controversy he engaged in with the theologian Abū al-Walīd al-Bājī, "who had set himself up as an enemy of logic,"[38] and had issued a *fatwā* (advisory religious decree) stating that no good Muslim should study philosophy, except as a preliminary to writing about its power to corrupt people's minds. It was not long after this controversy began that Ibn Hazm left Majorca, his residence for nearly 30 years, along with several of his students.

On the other hand, the great Aristotelian philosopher of the next century, Ibn Rushd (1126–98), represented the counter-trend, in continuing to support the idea that philosophy and religious belief could be reconciled. This idea forms the backbone of one of his major works, his refutation of al-Ghazali's *Tahāfut al-falāsifa* (*The Incoherence of the Philosophers*).[39] Ibn Rushd, who appears to have been influenced by Ibn Hazm's work, and mentions him with respect in his own works, articulated for future generations the notion that the best practitioners of philosophy saw the acceptance of the religious practices of their time as a necessary and beneficial step in their own philosophical education, not contradicting it in any way.

Clearly, however, the last period of Ibn Hazm's life needs to be examined more carefully to discover if there are continuities between his immediately preceding writings and the products of the final phase of his thought, as exemplified in the poem about the burning of his books in Seville, and his ethical treatise. Perhaps the final phase in the development of his thought represents more of a return to the empiricism of his youth (and *The Dove's Neck-Ring*) than it does the constitution of a coda to his arguments and analysis of *sharī'a* legal textuality in a Ẓahiri context as found in his *magnum opus* produced on Majorca, *Kitāb al-iḥkām li-uṣūl al-aḥkām* (Book of the Establishment of the Roots of Legal Decisions). These later works appear, as mentioned earlier, to give pride of place to the importance of knowledge, but Ibn Hazm no longer seems to be satisfied with the argument that to know principles and precepts will bring us closer to the Divine and ultimate truth (a position he had held in his religious tracts). Now he comes closer to what – in a European context – would be a very Hobbesian argument: that the only thing that will save humanity from a life of constant war, one that is "solitary, poore, nasty, brutish and short,"[40] is a more nuanced attention to the construction of a mode of social interaction that will cause individuals to believe their needs will be met and not disregarded.[41]

In this framework of speculation about knowing and its importance to determining a rational basis for ethical behavior, it may not be surprising that during his last exile, at his family home following his expulsion from Seville, Ibn Hazm turns to the subject of ethics and composes his *Kitāb al-akhlāq wa-al-siyar* (*The Pursuit of Virtue*). As was mentioned earlier, this treatment of ethics demonstrates a particularly individualistic cast in its analysis in comparison to other Arab treatises on ethics which shadow much more closely the *Nicomachean Ethics*. Ibn Hazm does, however, follow the norm of philosophers in his age and adopt the essentially Aristotelian framework of the four virtues: wisdom, courage, temperance and justice.[42] He even lauds, intermittently, the fifth Aristotelian virtue of friendship, which – for Aristotle – obviated the cultivation of the other four, especially justice. If one could truly cultivate friendship at its highest (most disinterested) level, and understand it completely, making it second nature, then concern with the implementation of justice becomes unnecessary.[43] Despite the fact that Ibn Hazm never explicitly includes friendship in his catalogue of basic virtues, he reminisces about specific friends and friendship more generally in *Pursuit*, as in the following:

> For a long time I have been thinking about death. I had certain dear friends, as closely bound to me by the bonds of affection as the soul is bound to the body. After they died, some of them appeared to me in dreams. Others did not. While one of the latter was alive, we had each promised to visit the other in a dream after we had died, if at all possible. But I have not seen him at all since he preceded me into the other world. I do not know whether he has forgotten or been engaged.[44]

It is tempting (though there is no proof) to see Ibn Hazm's unnamed friend as Ibn Shuhayd. The latter's death preceded his friend's by more than 30 years, and Ibn Hazm officiated at his burial, braving the dangers of war-torn Cordoba to do so.

Whether or not Ibn Shuhayd was the source of Ibn Hazm's reference is less important than how the relationship of the two friends is portrayed in the paragraph above. Their friendship is notable for its mutability and, especially, for a lack of communication between the two that starts with the death of one of them. In this, the relationship is closer to Aristotle's lesser friendships, "of utility," that wax and wane according to circumstances.[45] Ibn Hazm's essentially jaded and pessimistic attitude toward the power of friendship to add something positive to human experience carries over into his general advice about friendship:

> Anyone who criticizes you cares about your friendship. Anyone who makes light of your faults cares nothing about you.
>
> Criticizing a friend is like melting an ingot: it will either become refined or it will disappear …

> Do not try to be friends with those who scorn you. You will gain nothing from it but deception and shame.[46]

Even when he is asserting the value of friendship – as when he speaks about criticism by a friend as a constructive thing – Ibn Hazm frames his argument in negative terms. Friends "criticize" – they do not support or praise each other (in fact to do so, for Ibn Hazm, is to be a false friend). Besides the very question of how stable and permanent such friendships can be, to discriminate between friends who "criticize" you and those who "scorn" you would, in addition, seem to be a very difficult thing. Yet Ibn Hazm gives us no guidelines for fulfilling this task. So we are left with a very strong impression that friendship is less of a value upon which to build a system of ethics than it might appear at first glance, at least in Ibn Hazm's treatise. In this – as we saw in Ibn Hazm's articulation of a purpose (*telos*) for human life – there is a very strong similarity to Hobbes's theory of human behavior as articulated in *Leviathan*. If humanity's natural state is one of competition and war (not Adam's life in paradise), it is no surprise that friendship plays a very small role in Hobbes's universe. In fact, the case can easily be made that "Hobbes's political thought contains a sustained attack on friendship,"[47] which makes him the precursor of the interest (or lack thereof) in friendship on the part of many modern theorists. For all these thinkers, friendship too easily degenerates into patronage relationships that have no controls (like an imperative for justice) external to them. Ibn Hazm does not explicitly take such a stand, but his emphasis on the mutability of friendship and its tendency to devolve into a relationship of utility certainly points in that direction.

If friendship – cultivated as a virtue – is inadequate, in Ibn Hazm's opinion, as a basis for a coherent system of ethics, then what might be the alternative? Consistent with the earlier interest in love presented in *The Dove's Neck-Ring* (and more generally the conflation of friendship with love in the Arabic philosophical tradition),[48] Ibn Hazm then devotes an entire chapter in *The Pursuit of Virtue* to the topic of love, and the possibility of employing it within an ethical framework. In the beginning, he celebrates the power of love as attractive and unifying, but very quickly (by the end of the first paragraph) he begins to dwell upon the darker side of the emotion:

> Thus love can take different forms: we have seen men die broken-hearted because of their sons exactly as a lover may have his heart broken by his loved one. We have heard of a man who burnt with such fear of God, with such love, that he died of it. We know that a man can be as jealous of his prince and of his friend as of his wife[,] as jealous of them as a lover is of his mistress.[49]

In the course of the chapter – despite his earlier fascination with the emotion (and its fulfillment)[50] – Ibn Hazm decides that love is too closely associated with the idea of "lacking something," and therefore it can too easily become an infinite longing or desire, as obsession that can never be assuaged:

> There are five stages in the growth of love: the first is to think someone pleasant, that is, someone thinks of someone else as being nice or is charmed by their character. This is part of making friends. Then there is admiration; that is the desire to be near the person one admires. Then there is close friendship when you miss the other one terribly when they are absent [...] Then there is amorous affection when you are completely obsessed with the loved one. In the special vocabulary of love this is called *'ishq*, "the slavery of love." Finally there is passion, when one can no longer sleep, eat or drink. This can make you ill to the point of delirium and even death. Beyond this there is absolutely no place where love ends.[51]

The movement from disinterested admiration to rank obsession in Ibn Hazm's hierarchy of love shows that love could not – no more than friendship could – be an adequate anchor for a productive society. Those subjected to it find it has no limits, nothing to control it and they cannot function in their everyday lives. Since love generates care and a continual dissatisfaction – even more than friendship – it could hardly become the focus of a system whose purpose, according to Ibn Hazm, should be "the dispelling of care and anxiety."

So, in the next chapter, Ibn Hazm returns to the more traditional virtues initially described in the *Nicomachean Ethics* (wisdom, courage, temperance and justice), this time summarizing them in a short poem (the only time he uses poetry in the *Pursuit*):

> The reins which control all the virtues are justice, intelligence, generosity and strength.
> The other virtues are composed of these four. Anyone who possesses them is at the head of his people.
> Likewise it is in the head that one finds the qualities of good sense that enable one to resolve all difficulties.[52]

As he does elsewhere, Ibn Hazm uses different vocabulary items for the virtues than is customary in Arabic philosophy. The one term that remains the same, however, is "justice" (*al-'adl*), suggesting its importance to Ibn Hazm. This is further underscored by the placement of the term as first on the list. However, justice, for all those who have dealt with it, is a term notoriously difficult to define. Plato, in *The Republic*, book 1 (131), is caught by the inadequacies of the traditional Greek definition of justice as: "the art that gives back benefits to friends and hurts to enemies," or, in other words, gives individuals what they are due, good or bad. He has Thrasymachus, Socrates's interlocutor, propose another definition: "I declare justice is nothing but the advantage of the stronger" (137). Socrates then spends a great deal of the remainder of *The Republic* arguing that justice is not a pretext for taking advantage of others, but a good thing because those who practice it are individuals of integrity. Otherwise it is not true justice. He also uses an argument in support of the practice of true justice (which anticipates, to a certain degree, Hobbes positing a natural state of war): that if a group faces an outside threat, they would be wise to act justly to one another, because just treatment of members of the group is the only insurance that they will cooperate with one another against an attack (book 1, 151). A political system where justice is ensured (everyone receives what is due to him or her) will create a society of which people want to be a part.

Ibn Hazm articulates something similar (though not identical to these ancient Greek philosophers) in the place where he makes the most sustained case for justice as a pivotal virtue:

> Justice is a fortress in which all who are frightened take refuge. In fact, if a tyrant feels oppressed, does he not call for justice and scorn and condemn injustice? But you never see the opposite, someone condemning justice. Therefore a man who is equitable by nature can rest at peace in this impregnable fortress.[53]

It is clear that this perfectly just society is not one that Ibn Hazm himself ever experienced. However, the ideal, for him, remained powerful and persuasive. He sought to become someone who was familiar with equity and fairness, and this goal appealed to him even more than friendship or love at the end of his life.[54] Unfortunately it will probably never be possible to determine how his compatriots or their immediate descendants reacted to his ideas, or whether they even saw them. His book on ethics appears to have been lost for many centuries and only resurfaced in the late nineteenth century. Like *The Dove's Neck-Ring*, a unique copy was found by accident in a library in Istanbul.[55] Thus the perception of intellectual history often hangs on a slender thread. To explore the implications of this proposition is what I hope to do in any future opportunities I (and my students) have to engage with Ibn Hazm's work. What I have found most helpful hitherto[56] is to have the students discuss – and especially compare and contrast, comment and reflect on (in writing) – Ibn Hazm's observations on justice in *The Pursuit of Virtue* and Hobbes's pivotal chapter xiii, "Of the Natural Condition of Mankind, as Concerning their Felicity and Misery."

Notes

1 In the context of Ibn 'Abd Rabbih's work, see the "Introduction" to his translation of *Al-'Iqd al-farīd* (*The Unique Necklace*) written by Issa J. Boullata: vol. 1 (London: Garnet Publishing, 2006), xvi.

2 Two recent films provide good overviews of the history and intellectual impact of the Andalusians: *Cities of Light: The Rise and Fall of Islamic Spain* (sponsored by the United States Public Broadcasting System in 2007) and *When the Moors Ruled in Europe* (sponsored by British Channel Four Television in 2005).

3 The most recent biographical introduction to Ibn Hazm's life and work in English can be found in the essay by Terri DeYoung, "Abū Muḥammad Ibn Ḥazm," in *Essays in Arabic Literary Biography: 925–1350*, vol. 1, ed. Terri DeYoung and Mary St. Germain (Wiesbaden: Harrassowitz Verlag, 2011), 150–67. A similarly informative essay, focusing

more on Ibn Hazm as a philosopher and religious thinker, is Eric Ormsby, "Ibn Hazm," in *The Literature of al-Andalus*, ed. Maria Rosa Menocal, Raymond P. Scheindlin and Michael Sells (Cambridge: Cambridge University Press, 2000), 237–51. Absolutely indispensable for tracing the details of Ibn Hazm's long and complex career, as well as the general intellectual trajectory of his life is Anwar Chejne's book-length biography *Ibn Hazm* (Chicago, IL: Kazi Publications, 1982).

4 Ibn Shuhayd, although less prolific than his friend, has attracted attention because of the boldness and creativity of his major literary work, *Risālat al-Tawābi' wa-al-Zawābi'* (*The Treatise of Familiar Spirits and Demons*), trans. with an intro. by James T. Monroe (Berkeley: University of California Press, 1971). The most recent assessment of his career is also contained in an essay by Terri DeYoung, "Abū 'Āmir Ibn Shuhayd," in *Essays in Arabic Literary Biography: 925–1350*, vol. 1, ed. Terri DeYoung and Mary St. Germain (Wiesbaden: Harrassowitz Verlag, 2011), 189–203. James Dickie's article, "Ibn Shuhayd: A Biographical and Critical Introduction," *Al-Andalus* 29 (1964): 243–310, provides a thorough and detailed outline of his life. Absolutely essential is James Monroe's introduction to his translation of the *Risala*.

5 Aḥmad ibn Muḥammad al-Maqqarī, *Nafḥ al-Ṭīb*, vol. 3, ed. Ihsan 'Abbas (Beirut: Dār Ṣādir, 1968), 156–79.

6 Maqqarī, 167.

7 See A.J. Arberry's translation, *The Ring of the Dove* (London: Luzac, 1953). This translation is also available at www.muslimphilosophy.com/hazm/dove/index.html. A systematic comparison between this work and *De Amore* (*On Love*) by the scholastically trained clergyman Andreas Capellanus (fl. second half of the 12th century) has yet to be done. Similarly, now that an excellent translation into English of Ibn Shuhayd's *magnum opus*, *The Treatise of Familiar Spirits and Demons*, exists, it should be a priority to examine the work from the viewpoint of its literary influence. The translation itself is prefaced by an important introduction placing Ibn Shuhayd's work in its historical, philosophical and literary context. It also painstakingly reconstructs (pp. 14–17) the probable date for the composition of the *Treatise*, indicating that it was almost certainly an influence on *Risālat al-Ghufrān* (Epistle of Forgiveness) by Eastern poet Abū al-'Alā al-Ma'arrī' (973–1058) and raises the likelihood that it may have influenced *The Divine Comedy* by the Italian poet Dante, which similarly takes as its subject the author's journey to the heavens and his encounters with figures famous from his literary tradition. This latter hypothesis, though often referenced, has not been systematically examined since the publication by Miguel Asín Palacios and Harold Sunderland of *Islam and the Divine Comedy* (New York: E.P. Dutton, 1926).

8 For Ibn Hazm, a case in point is the treatise he composed as a reply to Samuel Ibn al-Naghrīla (a Hebrew scholar and vizier working for Badīs (1038–73), the Granadan ruler of the time). Ibn al-Naghrila (993–1056) had written about certain contradictions he believed he had found in the Qur'anic text. The introduction to Ibn Hazm's treatise certainly contains some very objectionable generalizations about Jews that had no foundation in truth and contrast very strikingly with Ibn Shuhayd's contemporary portrait admiring the erudition, work ethic and quick mind of a Jewish student of his who outshines all of his other (Muslim) pupils (quoted in Ibn Bassam 1975, 1/1:233–36 and partially translated into English by Monroe, 45–46, fn.123).

9 An excellent and concise general history (in English) of the disintegration of the Umayyad caliphate can be found in Mahmoud Makki, "The Political History of al-Andalus (92/771–897/1492)," in *The Legacy of Muslim Spain*, vol. 1, ed. Salma Khadra Jayyusi (Leiden: E.J. Brill, 1994). See also David Wasserstein, *The Rise and Fall of the Party-Kings: Politics and Society in Islamic Spain 1002–1086* (Princeton, NJ: Princeton University Press, 1985). Students can also benefit from reading Hugh Kennedy's synoptic history *Muslim Spain and Portugal: A Political History of al-Andalus* (London: Longman, 1996), which integrates the most recent scholarship in a very readable format.

10 Chejne, 20.

11 For full biographical details, see DeYoung, "Ibn Hazm," 161–62.

12 Arberry's translation has recently been made available on www.muslimphilosophy.com

13 Al-Ṭāhir Aḥmad Makkī, "Introduction" to Ibn Hazm al-Andalus, *Ṭawq al-hamāma*, ed. with an intro. by Al-Ṭāhir Aḥmad Makkī (Cairo: Dār al-Ma'ārif, 1977), 3.

14 The exception would be several long letters composed by Ibn Shuhayd. If Ibn Shuhayd wrote any letters to Ibn Hazm, they have been lost, but over the years Ibn Shuhayd wrote letters to several of his friends and patrons who had escaped the fall of Cordoba and taken refuge in the eastern part of al-Andalus. The most intimate were written to al-Mu'taman, the grandson of Ibn Shuhayd's father's patron al-Mansur. These letters contain detailed and poignant reminiscences of palace life in the waning years of the caliphate. They are preserved in Ibn Bassam 1.1:193–208. Detailed summaries of the content of these letters in English may be found in DeYoung, "Ibn Shuhayd," 190–191, and James Dickie, 251–252.

15 Toward the end of his commentary on Aristotle's set of logical treatises (the *Organon*), probably first begun in the mid-1030s, Ibn Hazm recounts an incident where he was able to solve a particularly difficult question about logic while he was imprisoned and kept confined in a dungeon by one of his political enemies, the Umayyad al-Mustakfī, father of the princess Wallāda (d. 1091), the famous beloved of the poet Ibn Zaydūn (1003–1070). Then he suddenly utters as an aside: "We would never have composed this book of ours, or many of our books, without having been exiled (*mugharrab*), sent far from our homeland (*al-waṭan*), our family or our children, fearing in our souls tyranny and enmity" (*Al-Taqrīb li-ḥadd al-manṭiq*, ed. 'Abd al-Ḥaqq ibn Mulāḥiqī al-Turkmānī (Beirut: Dār Ibn Hazm, 2007), 610). Clearly, Ibn Hazm is asserting here that exile and fear should properly sharpen one's intellect and reasoning abilities, not compromise them.

16 See Makki's edition of the *Tawq*, 41.

17 Ibn Hazm, *Tawq*, ed. Makki, 41–42. Translation is mine. A useful text for comparison, especially as to style, can be found in Ibn Shuhayd's description of his trip to the royal palace, Ibn Bassam, 1/1:195–96.

18 The modern philosopher John Passmore's observation is apt here: "it is at once clear that reason and passion cannot in any way interact with one another. Passion cannot stir reason into action because reason cannot act" (*Philosophical Reasoning* (London: Duckworth, 1961), 45). In this passage, in a nutshell, is articulated why Yusuf (reason) and Khalwa's (passion) encounter is ultimately unproductive. Yusuf does not demonstrate any power over words (and is reduced to silence), words being the medium through which passion and reason might find a way to interact.

19 "Kinesthetic" learning, or "learning by doing" is an increasingly important component of many epistemological approaches to the classroom. For a discussion of how this learning preference can be used effectively to engage students with material that is perceived as unengaging or otherwise difficult, see Rita Dunn and Shirley Griggs, *Multiculturalism and Learning Style* (Westport, CT: Praeger, 1995), 20–21. As Dunn and Griggs (like many others) have noted, kinesthetic learning dominates, especially at younger ages, and less often addressed, especially in traditional learning environments, than other learning styles (pp. 7–8).

20 Ignác Goldziher, *Die Zahiriten, ihr Lehrsystem und ihre Geschichte*, skillfully translated into English and edited by Wolfgang Behn as *The Zahiris: Their Doctrine and Their History* (Leiden: E.J. Brill, 1971). The newest edition has a useful introduction by Camilla Adang, herself an important scholar in the field of Zahirism.

21 I have found modeling – for students – how I proceed in my own research an effective technique in teaching. The following is based on that technique, since I am currently involved in studying the development of Islamic ethics down to modern times, as well as the relationship ethics has had to Arabic rhetoric and the presentation of character in Arabic literary works.

22 Ibn Hazm, *Kitāb al-akhlāq wa-al-siyar fī mudāwāt al-nufūs* (English translation *The Pursuit of Virtue*).

23 Recent English translations of Aristotle's *Nichomachean Ethics* are Terence Irwin's (Indianapolis/Cambridge: Hackett Publishing 1999), 2nd edn, and Sarah Broadie and Christopher Rowe's (Oxford: Oxford University Press, 2002).

24 A translation into Arabic of the last four books of the *Nicomachean Ethics* (dated 1232) was discovered in 1951–52 in the Qarawiyin Library in Fez, Morocco by A.J. Arberry. Shortly thereafter the manuscript of the first six books was also found. See D.M. Dunlop, "The Nicomachean Ethics in Arabic Books I-VI," *Oriens* 15 (1962): 18–34.

25 The author, Abū 'Alī Aḥmad ibn Muḥammad Miskawayh, is sometimes (mistakenly) referred to as "Ibn Miskawayh." An accessible English translation of the Arabic is Ibn Miskawayh, *The Refinement of Character*, trans. Constantine Zurayk (Chicago: Kazi Publications, 2002).

26 For an English translation of the sections of the *Ihya'* dealing with ethics (including an extremely valuable introduction that details the Aristotelian influence on them), see T.J. Winter's translation of books 22 and 23: Al-Ghazali, *On Disciplining the Soul Kitāb Riyādat al-nafs & on Breaking the Two Desires Kitāb Kasr al-shahwtayn*, trans. with an introduction and notes by T.J. Winter (Cambridge: The Islamic Texts Society, 1995), esp. pp. 22–23. For a broader analysis of the place of ethics in Ghazali's thought, see Mohamed Ahmed Sherif, *Ghazali's Theory of Virtue* (Albany: SUNY Press, 1975). For an extremely suggestive reading of the Platonic (and mystical) aspects of Ghazali's discourse on ethical issues, see Ebrahim Moosa, *Ghazali and the Poetics of the Imagination* (Chapel Hill: University of North Carolina Press, 2005), especially 229–232. Moosa's contention, that "Ghazali's ethical project strongly veered toward the formation of a responsible ethical subject" (229), can be profitably contrasted with Ibn Hazm's more socially oriented construction.

27 For background on Qudāma and an outline of his important works, including *Naqd al-shi'r*, see Ali Hussein, "Qudāmah ibn Ja'far," *Essays in Arabic Literary Biography 925–1350*, ed. Terri DeYoung and Mary St. Germain (Wiesbaden: Harrassowitz Verlag, 2011), 285–98.

28 See Qudāma ibn Ja'far, *Kitāb naqd al-shi'r*, ed. Seeger Bonebakker (Leiden: E.J. Brill, 1956), 29, where he says: "It is necessary, on the basis of appropriate analogy, for poets to praise men according to these characteristics [wisdom, courage, justice and temperance], and no others."

29 See Abū Muḥammad 'Abd Allāh Ibn Sinān al-Khafājī (c. 979–1069), *Sirr al-Faṣāḥa* (Cairo: Maṭba'at Muḥammad 'Alī, 1969), 256–57, where he says: "Qudama … has expressed the belief that praise for goodness and beauty, or criticism on account of ugliness, is neither true praise nor blame, and everyone who praises or criticizes for such things is mistaken." While al-Khafaji ends up short of endorsing Amidi's critique of Qudāma in its entirety, he does not, on the other hand, support Qudāma's point of view, and seems to prefer to leave judgment up to the individual poet.

30 Ibn Rashīq clearly wants to split the difference between Qudāma and Amidī when he says that "it is best to describe the patron only in terms of the Aristotelian virtues, but other qualities [appearance, skill at arms, etc.] may be brought into the poem" (*Al-'Umda fī sinā'at al-shi'r*, vol. 2, ed. al-Nabawi 'Abd al-Wāḥid Sha'lān (Cairo: Maktabat al-Khanjī, 2000), 807. Ibn Rashīq's views on the art of rhetoric in poetry were widely influential and his opinion counted for a great deal in subsequent generations, though it is debatable whether or not his work influenced his contemporary Ibn Hazm, or that Ibn Hazm even knew of it.

31 Although it should be noted that he adopts the same procedure for combining the four basic virtues into "compound" ones (*Pursuit* 165f., especially in the poem) that was first articulated as a principle by Qudāma, 31.

32 The canonical explanation of Aristotle's principal that "virtue promotes happiness" and that happiness is the goal (*telos*) of human endeavor (*eudaimonism*) would now have to be that found in Terence Irwin's *The Development of Ethics: A Historical and Critical Study*, vol. 1 (Oxford: Oxford University Press, 2007), 116–17, which usefully contrasts Plato's and Aristotle's views on this subject. Stephen Halliwell also provides a useful definition

of Aristotle's *eudaimonia* (from a more literary perspective) in *Aristotle's Poetics* (London: Duckworth, 1986), 203.

33 *The Pursuit of Virtue*, 122. The Arabic original is *ṭard al-hamm* (Makki, 87). As will be discussed more fully later, one can see in this a marked similarity to the notion of a *telos* for human beings as a governing principle for their actions – what inclines them most strongly to peaceful pursuits – as propounded by Thomas Hobbes (1588–1679) in "the fear of death" and the avoidance of it (see *Leviathan*, xiii, 14, ed. Edwin Curley (Indianapolis: Hackett Publishing, 1994), 78; xxvii 19–54 (pp. 196–203) is also instructive in this regard). Perhaps Hobbes's similarly negative view of life and its purpose can be found in the fact that Hobbes, like Ibn Hazm, lived much of his middle life amidst the travails of a particularly brutal and unnecessary war (in his case the English Civil War, 1642–51), and he became well acquainted with its irrationality and horror. For the effect of the Civil War on Hobbes's political thought, see Irwin 2:101–02, and Jerome Schneewind, *The Invention of Autonomy* (Cambridge: Cambridge University Press, 1998), 83.

34 Chejne, 30.

35 The Arabic text of the poem can be found in Ibn Bassam 1/1:171.

36 Ibn Hazm, *Kitāb al-Fiṣal wa-al-ahwā' wa-al-niḥal*, 75. The relevant passage is translated and analyzed in George Hourani, "Reason and Revelation in Ibn Hazm's Ethical Thought," *Islamic Philosophical Theology*, ed. Parviz Morewedge (Albany: State University of New York Press, 1979), 152. A more general assessment of the relationship between Ibn Hazm's education and the philosophy of his time can be found in Chejne, *Ibn Hazm*, 152–54.

37 Zakarīyā Ibrāhīm, *Ibn Hazm al-andalusī: al-mufakkir, al-zāhirī al-mawsū'ī* (Cairo: Maktabat Misr, 1966), 104.

38 Ibrahim, 105.

39 Several translations of Averroes's refutation, *The Incoherence of the Incoherence* (including the entire searchable text of the 1954 E.J.W. Gibb memorial volume produced by Simon van den Bergh) are available through the "Ibn Rushd page" on muslimphilosop hy.com

40 Thomas Hobbes, ed. Curley, *Leviathan*, xiii, 9 (p. 76).

41 Irwin, 2:117–18. Here, Irwin calls attention to the crucial emphasis on the achievement of peace (and the end of the natural state of war) in Hobbes's thinking. That the spread of justice (through law) will enhance peace by removing grounds for war is implicit in Hobbes's own statement (from *Leviathan*, ed. Curley, xiii, 13, p. 78). The restoration of justice, fairness and the law is what Hobbes aims for in his depiction of how his commonwealth should be run.

42 He says: "The virtues have four roots which form all virtue. They are: fairness or justice (*al-'adl*), intelligence (*al-fahm*), courage (*al-najda*) and generosity (*al-jūd*)" (*Pursuit*, 168, and *Kitab al-Akhlaq*, Makki, 186).

43 Aristotle, *Nicomachean Ethics* 1155a25–29 (Book 8, p. 209): "there is no need for rules of justice, between people who are friends, whereas if they are just, they still need friendship – and of what is just, the most just is what belongs to friendship."

44 *Pursuit*, 138 (122 in Makki's Arabic edition).

45 Aristotle, *NE*, 1157a 15–20 (p. 212 of the Broadie and Rowe translation). Miskawayh's much more developed ranking and hierarchy of friends and their qualities (pp. 125–135) is also relevant for evaluating Ibn Hazm's treatment of the subject.

46 *Pursuit*, 147 (143 in Makki's Arabic edition).

47 The topic sentence of Travis Smith's essay, "Hobbes on Getting By with Little Help from Friends," in *Friendship and Politics: Essays in Political Thought*, ed. John von Heyking and Richard Avramenko (Notre Dame, IN: Notre Dame University Press, 2008), 214–47. Nor is this surprising, given Hobbes's consistent hostility to Aristotle.

48 See Miskawayh's Fifth Discourse, which is entitled "Love and Friendship," and begins with a definition of love that calls it, despite its varieties, "the remedy for all deficiencies" (*Refinement*, 123).

49 *Pursuit*, 157.

50 See *The Dove's Neck-Ring*, chapter 18, "On Union" for such an idealistic portrayal of love as enhanced by fulfillment.
51 Ibn Hazm, *Pursuit*, 161.
52 Ibn Hazm, *Pursuit*, 166.
53 Ibn Hazm, *Pursuit*, 186.
54 Interestingly, Hobbes seems to have developed a similar regard for justice, as indispensable to the principle of self-defense as he proceeded through *Leviathan*. See Richard Tuck's analysis of chapter xv in "Hobbes's Moral Philosophy," *The Cambridge Companion to Hobbes*, ed. Tom Sorell (Cambridge: Cambridge University Press, 1996), 186–87.
55 Muhammad Abu Layla, "Introduction," *The Pursuit of Virtue*, 103.
56 Primarily in the class I have developed on Islamic ethics.

Bibliography

Aristotle. *Nichomachean Ethics*. Translated by Terence Irwin. 2nd edition. Indianapolis and Cambridge: Hackett Publishing, 1999.

Aristotle. *Nichomachean Ethics*. Translated, with an introduction and notes by Sarah Broadie and Christopher Rowe. Oxford: Oxford University Press, 2002.

Chejne, Anwar. *Ibn Hazm*. Chicago, IL: Kazi Publications, 1982.

Deacon, Rowan, *Wildfire Television. When the Moors Ruled in Europe*. Silver Spring, MD: Acorn Media, 2005.

Gardner, Robert, Carrie Gardner and Sam Mercurio. *Cities of Light: The Rise and Fall of Islamic Spain*. Potomac Falls, VA: Unity Productions Foundation.; Gardner Films, Inc., 2006.

Goldziher, Ignaz. *The Zahiris: Their Doctrine and their History* (*Die Zahiriten, ihr Lehrsystem und ihre Geschichte*). Translated and edited by Wolfgang Behn, with an introduction by Camilla Adang. Leiden: E.J. Brill, 1971.

Halliwell, Stephen. *Aristotle's Poetics*. London: Duckworth, 1986.

Hobbes, Thomas. *Leviathan*. Edited by Edwin Curley. Indianapolis: Hackett Publishing, 1994.

Hourani, George. "Reason and Revelation in Ibn Hazm's Ethical Thought," in *Islamic Philosophical Theology*, edited by Parviz Morewedge. Albany: State University of New York Press, 1979.

Ibn Ḥazm, Abū Muḥammad. *The Ring of the Dove* (*Ṭawq al-ḥamāma*). Translated, with an introduction by A.J. Arberry, London: Luzac, 1953.

Ibn Ḥazm, Abū Muḥammad. *Al-Taqrīb li-ḥadd al-manṭiq*. Ed. ʻAbd al-Ḥaqq ibn Mulāḥiqī al-Turkmānī. Beirut: Dār Ibn Ḥazm, 2007.

Ibn Ḥazm, Abū Muḥammad. *Ṭawq al-hamāma*. Edited, with an introduction by Al-Ṭāhir Aḥmad Makkī. Cairo: Dār al-Maʻārif, 1977.

Makki, Mahmoud. "The Political History of al-Andalus (92/771–897/1492)," in *The Legacy of Muslim Spain*. Vol. 1, pp. 3–87. Edited by Salma Khadra Jayyusi. Leiden: E.J. Brill, 1994.

Miskawayh (Ibn Miskawayh), Abū ʻAlī Aḥmad ibn Muḥammad. *The Refinement of Character* (*Tahdhīb al-Akhlāq*). Translated, with an introduction and notes by Constantine Zurayk. Chicago, IL: Kazi Publications, 2002.

Ormsby, Eric. "Ibn Hazm," in *The Literature of al-Andalus*, 237–251. Edited with an introduction by Maria Rosa Menocal, Raymond P. Scheindlin and Michael Sells. Cambridge: Cambridge University Press, 2000.

Passmore, John. *Philosophical Reasoning*. London: Duckworth, 1961.

Schneewind, Jerome. *The Invention of Autonomy*. Cambridge: Cambridge University Press, 1998.

Sherif, Mohamed Ahmed. *Ghazali's Theory of Virtue*. Albany: SUNY Press, 1975.

Smith, Travis. "Hobbes on Getting By with Little Help from Friends," in *Friendship and Politics: Essays in Political Thought*, 214–247. Edited by John von Heyking and Richard Avramenko. Notre Dame, IN: Notre Dame University Press, 2008.

Tuck, Richard. "Hobbes's Moral Philosophy," in *The Cambridge Companion to Hobbes*. Edited by Tom Sorell. Cambridge: Cambridge University Press, 1996.

Wasserstein, David. *The Rise and Fall of the Party-Kings: Politics and Society in Islamic Spain 1002–1086*. Princeton, NJ: Princeton University Press, 1985.

17

THE STORY OF ZAHRA AND ITS CRITICS

Feminism and agency at war

Elizabeth M. Holt

For the first time, about three-quarters of the way through Ḥanān al-Shaykh's *Ḥikāyat Zahrah* (*The Story of Zahra*) – and so several months into the civil war ravaging Beirut in 1975 – Zahra climbs the stairs of an abandoned apartment building to the landing where the neighborhood sniper passes his afternoons, and the two have sex. The passage reads:

> His voice moved closer, and with it his body. I could smell the heavy scent of his perspiration. He put a hand on my breast and then removed it as I went on peering hard at his features in the half-light. He must have begun to undo his trousers with one hand as he started to knead my shoulder with the other.
>
> Then, in one move, he pounced on me and pushed me on to the stairs. He lifted my dress to the waist. He spread out his body on mine without even taking off my knickers. He did not seem to mind that he made my back and side hurt, and though I twisted about with discomfort, he paid no attention. He came quickly, shuddering briefly in his spasm of pleasure. Then he stood up, wiped himself off at his trouser opening and began to do up the buttons. At that point I got up too, aware of the hurt in my back and side and rubbing my limbs where the bones ached.[1]

This scene has had a curious critical afterlife in English, providing a relief of how female Arab characters are read through vectors of victimhood and pleasure under the gaze of Western imperialism.

Global feminism's often-teleological theories of women's agency underwrite how we read Arab women's writing. This chapter is intended for use in the classroom, to be read by students and their teachers in courses on women's writing, the Arabic novel, war literature, translation, and American feminism; and invites students and teachers to take *The Story of Zahra* as an opportunity for closer reading. I argue that a focus on this stairwell scene's changing critical afterlife can help students understand their own responses to the text, and in turn the stakes of several decades of feminist debate in the West as it encounters Arabic literature. *The Story of Zahra* offers a case study in which the hesitations of a piece of fiction both warn against the imposition of a reader's politics of feminism, and yet seem persistently also to stage those very critical tendencies.

An influential and pioneering feminist reading of women's writing of the Lebanese civil war, miriam cooke's *War's Other Voices* (1987), inspired many of the critics who would read the stairwell scene after her. cooke interprets the stairwell encounter as one in which Zahra "decided to go where no one had dared … There she met the sniper, Sami, who raped her."[2] cooke revises this reading slightly in 1995, describing Zahra as "crazy and alienated," stating that she "decided to enter the fray" and so pays a visit to the sniper, who "rapes her."[3] Roger Allen makes a similar argument in *The Arabic Novel*, adjudicating that "their first encounter constitutes a rape,"[4] while a number of other prominent critics have followed in this reading. In 1990, Evelyn Accad, and in the years to follow Muhsin al-Musawi as well as historian Samir Khalaf, would all read this scene as rape in influential books addressing contemporary Arabic literature in Lebanon.[5]

By these readings, Zahra is a victim. However, she is also "mesmerized" by the sniper, as Rana Kabbani has it in her 1988 review of the English translation of *The Story of Zahra*, figuring Zahra as a 30-year-old woman with a "habit as pernicious as any addiction" of "sleep walk[ing] up to the rooftop … in order to offer him her body."[6] cooke and Kabbani, when they describe Zahra as "crazy" or "mesmerized," do not attend to *why* Zahra climbs those stairs to the sniper's perch. Kabbani cites instead Zahra's "passivity," seeing Zahra as "a victim of her circumstances," one in which she "does not take pleasure."[7] Kabbani ends the review essay "long[ing] for a different sort of heroine to emerge … one who is less a passive victim." We understand from Kabbani that in *The Story of Zahra*, Zahra does not "transform her destiny through her own actions."[8] Charles Larson in a 1991 article entitled "The Fiction of Hanan al-Shaykh, Reluctant Feminist," seems to concur with the readings of cooke, Kabbani, and others, describing Zahra as "directionless" and "little more than [a] victim," visiting the sniper each afternoon "for reasons that initially make little sense to her."[9] Victimized, pleasureless, "ever controlled by the people around her,"[10] in this stairwell encounter, one that ultimately bears deeply on both the end of Zahra's life as well as that of *The Story of Zahra*, the tragic character of Zahra the victim leaves in her critical wake an aporia of agency.

By the mid-1990s, feminism's take on Zahra in the stairwell would dramatically shift. Replacing a "crazy," "mesmerized" Zahra with one of political and erotic agency. As a historical register of critical responses, the stairwell scene yields something of a paradox. No longer legible as "crazy and alienated," critics such as Joseph Zeidan in his 1995 *Arab Women Novelists* write of a Zahra who "experiences her first real sexual pleasure with Sami, the sniper,"[11] focusing on a scene of orgasm and its part in "Zahra's plans." Here we encounter a deeply agentic Zahra: she "brings about their relationship and she remains in control of it for most of the story after this point [...] Zahra and the sniper are equals in this relationship, and they are in a war zone [...] It is the only time she has ever been in a position of power over her body and sexual activity."[12] "In control," "in a position of power," Zeidan reads Zahra as she climbs the familiar stairs to the sniper's perch as not a sleepwalking addict or a crazy, alienated rape victim, but as the sniper's "equal," a woman with "power over her body and sexual activity." In 2001, Ann Marie Adams goes further: it is with the sniper that Zahra felt "ecstasy for the first time."[13] Samira Aghacy, also writing that year, sees wartime Beirut as "giv [ing Zahra] license to do as she pleases," and reads her initial afternoon with the sniper as "the first time in her life that she has had an orgasm."[14] Bouthaina Shaaban's recent book, *Voices Revealed: Arab Women Novelists, 1898–2000,* despite its intellectual indebtedness to cooke, breaks with her reading of this scene, hewing closer to Aghacy and others and seeing this as "the first time in her life she feels really alive, as the sniper is the first man to awaken her passion."[15]

A reading of victimhood in the late 1980s and early 1990s is – as the century nears its end, as critics read Zahra's encounter with the sniper as one driven by Zahra's agency – resisting both war and received notions of women's action. Aghacy for her part is careful to point out that Zahra's visits with the sniper are not only a moment of intense pleasure for Zahra, but also "a willed attempt on Zahra's part at subverting an imposed social order."[16] Desire is for Aghacy "a revolutionary act": "an articulate, erotic, and individualistic self is constructed that is strongly opposed to and in conflict with patriarchal constructions of femininity."[17] Kabbani's 1988 wish that Zahra be a different kind of heroine, "less a passive victim," able instead to "transform her destiny through her own actions," seems to have been answered by critics like Aghacy, Shaaban, Adams, and Zeidan, reading an agentic, rebellious protagonist who – the scandal of it – takes her pleasure through her politics with the neighborhood sniper in the late fall afternoons of 1975 Beirut.

These paradoxically opposed readings of *The Story of Zahra* – both those that render Zahra a victim of repeated rapes, and those that see a defiant embrace of ecstasy in a stairwell – read Zahra, as Aghacy puts it, "in conflict with patriarchal constructions of femininity." The patriarchy is either raping her, or she is acting against it and in the name of freedom. Many a student, in my experience, shares this predisposition for reading both *The Story of Zahra,* and Arab women's writing more generally, against a backdrop of oppressive Arab patriarchy. Marilyn Booth, reviewing Accad's 1990 *Sexuality and War: Literary Masks of the Middle East*, notes Accad's sense of her academic work as an extension of "nonviolent resistance buttressed by reordered notions of sexuality, notions she feels are crucial for building a lasting peace in Lebanon."[18] Accad and others offer critiques of Arab women's writing and the lives of their mostly female protagonists as a form of resistance, seeing in the violence of civil war Beirut a feminist opportunity to theorize "gendered differentiation" through the "ways sexuality is inscribed in Arab cultures and women's struggles to free themselves of received expectations."[19] Literary criticism, for Accad, cooke and many other readers of Arab women's writing, is a way to do feminist politics, to oppose the patriarchal order, whether Zahra is read through a prism of victimhood or agentic pleasure.

How it is possible to sustain such radically divergent readings of Zahra is something *The Story of Zahra* itself has already staged, with significant bearing on the American classroom. The first part of the novel is set in the months leading up to the war, as Zahra moves between her past and present, and between Beirut, a village in South Lebanon, and a community of Lebanese expatriates in an African village. The difficulty of interpreting what motivates Zahra structures the first-person narrative in Book One as it cycles from Zahra, to Hashem (her uncle), to Majed (briefly her husband in Africa), and back to Zahra, with each shift in voice marked by chapter breaks. Readers soon discover that with each new narrator, the question of why Zahra acts as she does remains both pressing and difficult for any of the characters, including Zahra, to answer.

Nevertheless, they try. When Zahra collapses and is hospitalized in Africa, Majed relates: "Zahra was suffering from a minor shock, [Hashem] told me, at being separated from her family, and for this she was undergoing treatment. It made me laugh up my sleeve. I never tried to tell Hashem the true reason for her disturbance as I saw it."[20] Majed maintains rather that the reason for Zahra's condition is that she is "a liar, frightened of her own shame, and making a pretense of her remorse and regret."[21] These men are interpreting Zahra's actions, narrating what motivates her when she will not. The Arabic is more explicit than the English's "shame," directing us to a *faḍīḥah*,[22] a publicly scandalous and scandalizing act, by which Majed means the loss of Zahra's virginity prior to their marriage agreement.[23] Here too, Zahra is either crazy, or she is a rebellious pleasure-seeker courting *faḍīḥah*.

Majed reveals his diagnosis of Zahra during a conversation with Hashem to which Zahra is a silent witness, if also the first-person narrator. Though Majed begins the conversation, "With Zahra's permission, I have to make certain matters clear," the text moves immediately to Majed's account without any accession by Zahra.[24] Upon hearing of this alleged *faḍīḥah*, Hashem immediately dismisses the idea that it could be the root of Zahra's condition, telling Majed that "the question of whether or not [Zahra] was a virgin was beside the point."[25] The diagnosis centering on *faḍīḥah* is revoked, however, only to shift the parameters of diagnosis to make space for yet another interpretation of Zahra's state. Hashem, sure now that Zahra must be in love, tells Zahra to let him help her marry her former lover. Writing over Zahra's serial silence, Majed and Hashem construct a chain of narratives explaining Zahra's condition; they both interpret and critique. Voiceless, Zahra silently asks herself in the midst of her uncle's questioning: "what chance did I have of making him see things otherwise? … How could I express it in simple terms and say that this was something which really had nothing to do with me – that, from beginning to end, I had been a mere spectator (*shāhidah*)?"[26] A spectator, a witness, Zahra silently attends the narration of herself: The Story of Zahra.

It is not fear that keeps her from speaking, though the reader of the English translation – the one most frequently taught in the American classroom – might not know that, as two lines in the Arabic that get close to explaining Zahra's actions are missing from Peter Theroux's translation, done in cooperation with Hanan al-Shaykh: "*Lā urīdu an ataḥauwala ilā imra'ah ukhrā. Urīdu an akūna al-mar'ah allatī ta'rifuhā wa-urīdu an atruka Afrīqiyyā*": "I do not want to change into another woman. I want to be the woman that you know and I want to leave Africa."[27] Following the Arabic, there is the suggestion of a causal relationship between Zahra's silence, her inability to tell her uncle what she is feeling, and her remaining *al-mar'ah allatī ta'rifuhā*, the woman he, and we, know. Silence is presented by Zahra in her first-person Arabic narrative as constitutive of the image others have of her *and* of who she wants to be, extending to our image and knowledge of Zahra as well as we read *The Story of Zahra*.

Attentive to this silence, Saba Ghandour points readers to how Zahra becomes the object of narration, an effect that plays on the double sense of the title in both Arabic and English: the story *of* Zahra. Rather than finding in Zahra a teller of her own tale, Ghandour reads characters such as Hashem and Majed as discursively "construct[ing]" Zahra "as a speechless entity, a woman 'who cannot object to anything,'"[28] showing how Zahra is "made into an object or an entity that is constantly 'spoken for.'"[29] It is Zahra's own silence that enables the paradoxical interpretations of Zahra by Majed and Hashem. Here, we can read *The Story of Zahra* as a novel that warns against the hazards of interpretation, but does so through its textuality, insisting on close(r) reading in order to approach the significant stakes at work in the act of interpretation.

Zahra's objectification as docile subject – in an Arab women writers classroom, perhaps reminiscent of the Delacroix tableau on the cover of Assia Djebar's *Femmes d'Alger dans leur appartement* and the essay on the Orientalist gaze it contains – has a long imperial history. In 2003, Anastasia Valassopoulos read *The Story of Zahra* alongside al-Shaykh's later *Beirut Blues* and Mai Ghoussoub's *Leaving Beirut*, charting a literary and critical tradition of "silencing … the Middle Eastern woman through the persistence of the Orientalist fantasy,"[30] a gesture that Valassopoulos sees repeated by cooke and Accad in the tendency of "both critics [to] pay little attention to Zahra's actual words."[31] Valassopoulos redirects her reader in an effort to "piece together a logic underlying the apparent confusion and disorientation attributed to Zahra."[32]

When in 1995 cooke writes of a "crazy, alienated" Zahra, that same sentence ends reading her as a victim-cum-"combatant," a role she is figured as hysterically maintaining through successive rapes by the sniper. Valassopoulos reads instead a nexus of pleasure, desire, and masochism in a time of war, offered in response to what she terms a "re-Orientalization" of Arab women by literary critics, whereby "they are re-interpreted to an audience that cannot accept, and presumably cannot be persuaded to accept, an autonomous Arab woman … rather than posit Zahra as the agent of her actions, she is presented as a victim of war and of her mental faculties."[33]

In an effort to attend to the text itself, to the "actual words" on the page, Valassopoulos takes Zahra for neither a repeat rape victim nor a political combatant, but rather an "autonomous Arab woman." While she condemns readings in which "female protagonists are denied a sexual experience by their critics and made to carry the burden of political foresight,"[34] the Zahra that Valassopoulos reads still rages against the Arab patriarchy. Loosed from political burden, martyrdom, and victimhood, Valassopoulos celebrates Zahra's "freedom": "Zahra's visits to the sniper symbolize her ability to be free from regulatory norms that restrict her movements otherwise."[35] Valassopoulos, though well aware that "it can be dangerous to propose a living feminism that can only flourish in the context of the destruction of ethical and social norms," nevertheless maintains that "normal society is deadening for women."[36] Mobilizing for a reading of Zahra that rejects not only victimhood and political burden, but also "regulatory norms that restrict" women, Valassopoulos plots Zahra on a feminist telos of liberation and freedom, this time through the pleasure of sexual experience.

These readings cohere around a Zahra who sets out one Beirut afternoon in 1975 to shock the lone and stoic, almost archetypal figure of the neighborhood sniper, joining many of my students in registering their alarm. In her work on Lebanese women writers, Aghacy argues that "the city [of Beirut] has represented a liberating experience for women generally since the 1960s," and that beginning in the 1960s "the rigid taboos and traditions inherited and represented by the nuclear family, the father, as well as by the rural setting" were being superseded. Beginning in 1975, however, the matter of taboos and norms becomes more complicated, and this "liberating urban experience … became inextricably bound up with the war experience."[37] The taboo-breaking literary tactics of Beirut's women writers during the 1960s, represented by works such as Laylā Ba'albakī's erotic 1963 short story "*Safīnat ḥanān ilā al-qamr*" ("Spaceship of Tenderness to the Moon") and its explicit engagement of female arousal and pleasure, are deployed by Zahra in the midst of civil war in order to shock her audience, the sniper. Zahra is looking to stage a *faḍīḥah*; as readers, we are reading acts of performance, interpretation, reception. Norms have collapsed into a state of civil war, and with them "the rigid taboos and traditions inherited and represented by the nuclear family, the father," and indeed, by Lebanese women's writing of the 1960s. Through Zahra's encounter in the stairwell, shock though it might its readers into a paradox of interpretation – Is she crazy? Was she raped? Is this a political plan? Private erotics? – in the "actual words" of the text, the paradox rests in her work to reinstate norms through *faḍīḥah*, a contravention of taboo that can only take place if those norms and taboos are legible, if the patriarchy (or even the feminists) are still maintaining some sort of order.

Having once seen the sniper while hanging out her aunt's wash, Zahra is vexed by the sniper's image in the newspaper: "I tried to wipe the image clean and think how should I act. Should I throw a hand-grenade at him? Should I learn to use a gun and aim it at his heart?"[38] Zahra becomes obsessed with the sniper and with finding a way to act:

> A strange idea took place in my mind. I wondered what could possibly divert the sniper from aiming his rifle and startle him to the point where he might

> open his mouth instead? Perhaps a troupe of dancers would do it? Perhaps a gypsy with a performing monkey? Or perhaps a naked woman, passing across his field of fire? Maybe if such a sight crossed his vision he would pause for just one moment and wonder whether the world has indeed gone mad in the midst of this war.[39]

The Arabic makes the project more explicit, asking if such a shocking sight might lead the sniper to wonder "*hal janna huwa bi-qanṣihi li-l-abriyā'?*," "had he gone crazy in his sniping of the innocent?"[40]

Zahra returns one afternoon to her Aunt Najiba's apartment, her aunt having left Beirut for their village in the south, to see if she might be able to "possibly divert the sniper from aiming his rifle." Walking out onto the balcony wearing only a few towels, Zahra begins to hang these towels on the line, disrobing to become the "naked woman" of her "strange idea." When the sniper sees her and asks, "what is the young lady doing there?,"[41] Zahra hastily grabs a towel and runs inside, later reflecting on the relative success of her foray out on the balcony as she thinks, "I had got him to look at me as a man would look at a woman in peacetime."[42] A few lines later she adds, "I should have asked him to lay down his arms."[43] Zahra's afternoon encounters in the stairwell are an extension of her will to break the war frame so that the sniper might look at Zahra "as a man would look at a woman in peacetime."

Yet, however daring Zahra's pursuit of the sniper is, however much pleasure she in the end derives from their afternoons together, and however many ineffective birth control pills she takes while sleeping with him, Zahra's ultimate aim – to get the sniper to look at her "as a man would look at a woman in peacetime" – is one that sits uneasily with the model of rebellious agency championed by successive generations of feminist literary critics. "How a man looks at a woman in peacetime" is not what feminist critics read for: Valassopoulos reads for an "autonomous Arab woman," who for Aghacy would be "strongly opposed to and in conflict with patriarchal constructions of femininity," Kabbani "long[s] for a different sort of heroine to emerge," and Accad's literary criticism is part of a project of "non-violent resistance buttressed by reordered notions of sexuality." Zahra, though, wants to be liberated from the war frame not into a transcendent feminist freedom, but rather to a state where the sniper is not a sniper, but a man who would look at her as he would a woman in peacetime. To the extent that Zahra is agentic, she is not raging against the patriarchy; what she is resisting is the collapse of the gendered status quo.

Read against Zahra's normative gender roles of peacetime Beirut, the critical tendency to register shock at Zahra's encounter with the sniper, to read it as anything from rape to ecstatic rapture, is where we can approach the horizon of the normative giving way to the taboo. Saba Mahmood challenges her readers to "problematize … the universality of the desire – central for liberal and progressive thought, and presupposed by the concept of resistance it authorizes – to be free from relations of subordination and, for women, from structures of male domination."[44]

The readerly assumption of a "desire … to be free from relations of subordination" reads Zahra into a state of resistance that *The Story of Zahra* itself resists.

Zahra is, rather, invoking norms through her provocation of both the neighborhood's sniper and her audience. Zahra can only elicit a sense of shock and scandal from the sniper if there are patriarchal norms to contravene, and her project cannot succeed unless it goes beyond their afternoon encounters and establishes a more enduring relationship that "inhabits" patriarchal norms: "Could I say I had been able to save anyone, even in those moments when we met and had intercourse? But I couldn't even consider these to hold a reprieve of death for anyone. My visits only replaced his siestas."[45] A reprieve for Zahra, and in turn for wartime Beirut, would begin with a wedding.

Zahra dreams of a lasting peace; she is looking for an end to both the inner and the outer turmoil, and she locates salvation in the sniper, whom she wants to look at her as he would "a woman in peacetime." When we turn away from a progressive feminism as critical frame to consider the words on the page, we find a pregnant Zahra who is neither a victim of the sniper's repeated rapes, nor longing for a radical new feminist agency of politics and/or pleasure, but instead willing into wartime Beirut the normative gender roles of peacetime in the city. Confessing to the sniper that she is too far along in her pregnancy to abort, the sniper momentarily fulfills this fantasy, promising Zahra that he will visit her home the next day with his family. For Zahra, "[i]t seems as if the war has suddenly come to a stop with his promise that we will marry. Everything seems normal."[46] Zahra has no illusions about peacetime, given what she has witnessed at the foot of her mother and her lover's bed, at the feet of her belt-wielding father in the kitchen, in the back room of a factory in Beirut, and in her marriage bed in Africa. Indeed, she has never even experienced sexual pleasure in peacetime. Yet faced with life in civil war Beirut, it is the "normal" of "how a man looks at a woman in peacetime" for which she longs, however untraditional her means of getting there.

The Story of Zahra is not looking for women's liberation, even if critics and our students might be. In a 2005 interview, Hanan al-Shaykh objects to being read as a feminist writer: "I'm not talking about women's liberation. I'm a novelist and I want to meet my artistic ends. People in the Arab world, but especially in the West, try to portray me as a feminist writer defending Arab women; they pigeonhole me."[47] Elizabeth McKee, writing in 1996, testifies that this has been a source of enduring frustration not only for al-Shaykh, but others as well: "Several Arab women writers that I know (including Laylā Ba'albakī, Ḥanān al-Shaykh and Emily Nasrallah), have expressed their irritation at the way in which Western feminist critics have appropriated their works and manipulated their contents to serve a feminist agenda."[48] Reading *The Story of Zahra* as part of a project of "women's liberation" and "a feminist agenda" reads Zahra as either a victim or a resistor to the patriarchy. This chapter invites a reading that would attend rather to the quiet narrative aporia surrounding a reticent Zahra, the challenge her will to be "look[ed] at [as] a woman in peacetime" presents to liberal feminist literary criticism in English, and what that all might have to do with the narrative conditions of war in Arabic.

Notes

1 al-Shaykh 1994, 148–49.
2 cooke 1988, 55.
3 cooke 1995, 189.
4 Allen 1995, 241.
5 See cooke 1988; Accad 1990; Khalaf 2002; and al-Musawi 2003.
6 Kabbani 1988, 340.
7 Ibid.
8 Ibid., 341.
9 Larson 1991, 14.
10 Ibid., 15.
11 Zeidan 1995, 211–12.
12 Ibid., 216.
13 Adams 2001, 205.
14 Aghacy 2001, 508. See also Aghacy's reading of Zahra in *Masculine Identities in the Fiction of the Arab East since 1967*, and my review: Holt 2012.
15 Shaaban 2009, 123.
16 Aghacy 2001, 508.
17 Ibid., 509.
18 Booth 1991, 18.
19 Ibid., 18.
20 al-Shaykh 1988, 90.
21 Ibid., 89.
22 Ibid., 105.
23 My thinking on *faḍīḥah* here is indebted to Tarek El-Ariss's discussion in *Trials of Arab Modernity*.
24 al-Shaykh 1988, 112.
25 Ibid.
26 Ibid., 114.
27 Ibid., 134 (my translation).
28 Ghandour 2002, 239.
29 Ibid., 240.
30 Valassopoulos 2003, 183.
31 Ibid., 185.
32 Ibid., 187.
33 Ibid., 186.
34 Ibid., 187.
35 Ibid., 194.
36 Ibid., 190.
37 Aghacy 2001, 504.
38 al-Shaykh 1988, 156.
39 Ibid., 157.
40 Ibid., 185 (my translation).
41 Ibid., 158.
42 Ibid., 159.
43 Ibid., 160.
44 Mahmood 2004, 10.
45 al-Shaykh 1988, 160.
46 Ibid., 212.
47 al-Shaykh 2005, 16.
48 McKee 1996, 133.

Bibliography

Accad, Evelyn. *Sexuality and War: Literary Masks of the Middle East*. New York: New York University Press, 1990.

Accad, Evelyn. "Arab Women's Literary Inscriptions: A Note and Extended Biography," *College Literature* 22:1 Third World Women's Inscriptions (February 1995).

Adams, Ann Marie. "Writing Self, Writing Nation: Imagined Geographies in the Fiction of Hanan al-Shaykh," *Tulsa Studies in Women's Literature* 20:2 (Fall 2001): 201–216.

Adnan, Etel. *Sitt Marie Rose: A Novel*. Sausalito, CA: Post-Apollo Press, 1982. (Translated from *Sitt Marie Rose*. Paris: des femmes, 1977.)

Aghacy, Samira. "Lebanese Women's Fiction: Urban Identity and the Tyranny of the Past," *International Journal of Middle Eastern Studies* 33:4 (November 2001).

Aghacy, Samira. *Masculine Identities in the Fiction of the Arab East since 1967*. Syracuse, NY: Syracuse University Press, 2009.

Ahmed, Leila. "Western Ethnocentrism and Perceptions of the Harem," *Feminist Issues* (Fall 1982): 521–534.

Ahmed, Leila. "Arab Culture and Writing Women's Bodies," *Feminist Issues* (Spring 1989): 41–55.

Allen, Roger. *The Arabic Novel: An Historical and Critical Introduction*. New York: Syracuse University Press, 1995 (1982).

al-Musawi, Muhsin J. *The Post-colonial Arabic Novel*. Boston: Brill, 2003.

al-Shaykh, Ḥanān. *Ḥikāyat Zahrah*. Beirut: Dār al-Ādāb, 1988. (First published in Arabic in 1980 in Beirut by Dār al-Nahār.)

al-Shaykh, Hanan. *The Story of Zahra*. New York: Anchor Books, 1994.

al-Shaykh, Hanan. "War and Writing," *New Perspective Quarterly* 22:3 (Summer 2005).

Ba'albakī, Laylā. "Safīnat ḥanān ilā al-qamr," *Ḥiwār* 1:4 (May/June 1963).

Best, Stephen and Sharon Marcus. "Surface Reading: An Introduction," *Representations* 108:1 (2009).

Booth, Marilyn. "Crossing the Demarcation Line," *The Women's Review of Books* VIII:8 (May 1991).

Chedid, Andrée. *The Return to Beirut*. London: Serpent's Tail, 1989. (Translated from *La maison sans racines*. Paris: Flammarion, 1985.)

cooke, miriam. *War's Other Voices: Women Writers on the Lebanese Civil War*. Cambridge: Cambridge University Press, 1988.

cooke, miriam. "Death and Desire in Iraqi War Literature," in Allen, Roger, Hilary Kilpatrick and Ed de Moor, eds. *Love and Sexuality in Modern Arabic Literature*. London: Saqi Books, 1995.

cooke, miriam. "Gender and September 11: A Roundtable: Saving Brown Women," *Signs* 28:1 (Autumn 2002): 468–470.

Djebar, Assia. *Femmes d'Alger dans leur appartement*. Paris: Éditions des femmes, 1980.

El-Ariss, Tarek. *Trials of Arab Modernity*. New York: Fordham University Press, 2013.

Fayad, Mona. "Reinscribing Identity: Nation and Community in Arab Women's Writing," *College Literature* 22:1 Third World Women's Inscriptions (February 1995).

Ferguson, Frances. "Rape and the Rise of the Novel," *Representations* 0:20 (Autumn 1987).

Ghandour, Sabah. "Hanan al-Shaykh's *Hikayat Zahra*: A Counter-Narrative and a Counter-History," in Majaj, Lisa Suhair, Paula W. Sunderman, and Therese Saliba, eds. *Intersections: Gender, Nation, and Community in Arab Women's Novels*. Syracuse, NY: Syracuse University Press, 2002.

Harlow, Barbara. *Resistance Literature*. New York: Methuen, 1987.

Hartman, Michelle. *Native Tongue, Stranger Talk: The French and Arabic Linguistic Landscapes of Lebanon*. Syracuse, NY: Syracuse University Press, 2014.

Hayek, Ghenwa. *Beirut, Imagining the City: Space and Place in Lebanese Literature*. London: I.B. Tauris, 2014.

Holt, Elizabeth M. "Review of *Masculine Identities in the Fiction of the Arab East since 1967*, by Samira Aghacy," *Middle Eastern Literatures* 15:1 (2012).

Ibrāhīm, Ṣāliḥ. *al-Jins wa-l-zawāj fī adab Ḥanān al-Shaykh* (Sex and Marriage in the Literature of Ḥanān al-Shaykh). Beirut: al-Jāmi'ah al-Lubnāniyyah al-Amīrkiyyah, 1997.

Kabbani, Rana. "Fatal Passivity: Women in Arabic Fiction," *Third World Quarterly* 10:1 Succession in the South (January 1988).

Khalaf, Samir. *Civil and Uncivil Violence in Lebanon: A History of the Internationalization of Communal Conflict*. New York: Columbia University Press, 2002.

Larson, Charles R. "The Fiction of Hanan Al-Shaykh, Reluctant Feminist," *World Literature Today* 65:1 (Winter 1991).

Layoun, Mary. "Translation, Cultural Transgression and Tribute, and Leaden Feet," in Dingwaney, Anurdha and Carol Maier, eds. *Between Languages and Cultures: Translation and Cross-Cultural Texts*. Pittsburgh: University of Pittsburgh Press, 1995.

Mahmood, Saba. *Politics of Piety*. Princeton, NJ: Princeton University Press, 2004.

Mahmood, Saba. "Feminism, Democracy, and Empire: Islam and the War on Terror," in Joan Wallach Scott, ed. *Women's Studies on the Edge*. Durham, NC: Duke University Press, 2008.

Majaj, Lisa Suhair, Paula W. Sunderman and Therese Saliba, eds. "Introduction," in *Intersections: Gender, Nation, and Community in Arab Women's Novels*. Syracuse, NY: Syracuse University Press, 2002.

Makdisi, Jean Said. "The Mythology of Modernity: Women and Democracy in Lebanon," in Mai Yamani, ed. *Feminism and Islam: Legal and Literary Perspectives*. New York: NYU Press, 1996.

Marcus, Sharon. "Fighting Bodies, Fighting Words," in *Feminists Theorize the Political*. Judith Butler and Joan W. Scott, eds. New York: Routledge, 1992.

McKee, Elizabeth. "The Political Agendas and Textual Strategies of Levantine Women Writers," in Mai Yamani, ed. *Feminism and Islam: Legal and Literary Perspectives*. New York: NYU Press, 1996.

Rooney, Ellen. "Criticism and the Subject of Sexual Violence," *Modern Language Notes* 98, no. 5 (December 1983).

Said, Edward. *Orientalism*. New York: Vintage, 1979.

Salem, Elise. *Constructing Lebanon: A Century of Literary Narratives*. Miami: University Press of Florida, 2003.

Shaaban, Bouthaina. *Voices Revealed: Arab Women Novelists, 1898–2000*. Boulder, CO: Lynne Rienner Publishers, 2009.

Spivak, Gayatri Chakravorty. "Can the Subaltern Speak?" in *Marxism and the Interpretation of Cultures*, eds. C. Nelson and L. Grossberg. Urbana: University of Illinois Press, 1988, 271–316.

Valassopoulos, Anastasia. "The Legacy of *Orientalism* in Middle Eastern Feminism," *Thamyris/Intersecting* no. 10 (2003): 183–199.

Zeidan, Joseph T. *Arab Women Novelists: The Formative Years and Beyond*. New York: State University of New York Press, 1995.

18

THE ARABIC FRAMETALE AND TWO EUROPEAN OFFSPRING

James T. Monroe

Introduction

During my years of teaching in the Department of Comparative Literature, at the University of California, Berkeley, I devised a one-semester, undergraduate, upper division course, which I would like to describe on this occasion.

According to the rules of that department, upper division courses were required to include literatures in three different languages, of which the students were expected to be able to read at least two in the original. For my reading list I chose works in Arabic, Old Spanish, and Middle English, while providing my students with both texts and translations in all three languages. As a result of my prior readings on the graduate level, I settled on the subject of the frametale, as it was developed in Arabic literature, and adopted by some European writers. To illustrate the points I made, I included in my reading list works such as *The 1001 Nights*, *The Book of Kalīla wa-Dimna*, and *The Maqāmāt* of al-Hamadhānī and al-Saraquṣṭī, on the Arabic side. On the European side I included the Spanish *Libro de buen amor* by Juan Ruiz, Archpriest of Hita, along with Geoffrey Chaucer's *Canterbury Tales*. Other European works belonging to the frametale genre could also have been included, such as Petrus Alfonsi's *Disciplina Clericalis*, Don Juan Manuel's *Conde Lucanor*, Boccaccio's *Decameron*, or Marguerite de Navarre's *Heptameron*, but, out of respect for the principle of *non multa, sed multum*, I decided to restrict my coverage to the works mentioned above, as I attempted to broaden my students' horizons, by taking them on a literary journey to the East. In what follows, let me go into some detail in describing the conclusions I came to in the course.

The 1001 Nights

In his *Murūj al-Dhahab*, composed in Egypt in the year 332/943 the Shī'ī historian al-Mas'ūdī tells us that there was a Pahlavi work about a king, his vizier, the latter's daughter and her slave, named Shīrāzād and Dīnāzād, respectively. This work had been translated into Arabic with the title of *Alf Khurāfa* (A Thousand Fantastic Tales).[1] This statement is confirmed by the Shī'ī bookseller from Baghdad, Ibn al-Nadīm, who, in his *Fihrist*, completed in the year 377/987, adds that the basis for the title of the book of *A Thousand Fantastic Tales* was that a king used to marry a woman, spend a night with her, and kill her the next day. Then he married a concubine of royal blood called Shahrāzād, who would begin telling him a story, but interrupt her narrative at the end of the night, which encouraged the king to spare her for 1,000 nights. During this time she bore him a son, and informed him of the trick she had played upon him. The king appreciated her intelligence, and spared her. He had a head of his household named Dīnār Zād who was in league with Shahrāzād in this matter. Ibn al-Nadīm adds that although the stories contained in the book were spread out over 1,000 nights, they amounted to fewer than 200 tales, and dismisses it as "a coarse book, without warmth in the telling."[2]

As if to confirm the accounts of al-Mas'ūdī and Ibn al-Nadīm, in 1949 Nadia Abbott published a manuscript fragment containing the very beginning of a work entitled *Alf Layla* (A Thousand Nights), found in the Oriental Institute of the University of Chicago (No. 17618). According to Professor Abbott this text represents a fragment from the earliest known extant Arabic book, dating from the first quarter of the ninth century. In it, we are offered the beginning of the familiar tale, in which the two female protagonists are called by what seem to have been their original names as found in al-Mas'ūdī, that is to say, Dīnāzād and Shīrāzād.[3]

Modern scholarship has thus established that a Pahlavi work was translated into Arabic in the late eighth or early ninth century with the title of *Alf Khurāfa*. The title was first changed to *Alf Layla*, and eventually came to be known as *Alf Layla wa-Layla* (A Thousand and One Nights). As the centuries went by, more stories were added to the collection, leading scholars to suggest that there are three major strata to the work as it appears today: 1 an ancient group of stories of Indo-Persian origin; 2 a later group that is of Iraqī ('Abbāsid) provenance; and 3 a group that is of Egyptian (Fāṭimid, Mamlūk, and Ottoman) inspiration.

According to one very persuasive theory, proposed by Ferial Jabouri Ghazoul,[4] *The 1001 Nights* is not merely a collection of tales randomly and inorganically brought together. Instead, the Chinese-box-like structure of the work, in which characters within tales tell further tales, all harking back to Shahrāzād in the frametale, is organized to make one major point: she is telling tales to King Shahriyār not merely to gain one further day of life, but also to cure the king of his destructive case of misogyny. To this end, the tales she tells him are ones in which women often play exemplary and inspiring, when not heroic, roles. Let me offer three examples, in further support of her arguments.[5]

1. "Sindbad the Sailor and Sindbad the Porter." The Sindbad group consists of seven tales in which Sindbad the Sailor narrates seven adventures he underwent in the course of his travels. For our purpose, it is important to note that women interact with him in only two tales. In each of these, be it noted, Sindbad marries. As a result of the first marriage, in the fourth and central tale, he is buried alive *underground* and almost dies. However, even if the death of his first wife has exposed him to mortal danger, it cannot be argued that she is at fault, insofar as her death was unintentional. In contrast, in the seventh and last story, Sindbad is transported *high up into the sky*, while his second wife warns him of the danger inherent in living among demons, and urges him to leave the city, thus saving his life. Shahrāzād is, therefore, invoking, for the benefit of King Shahriyār, the example of two good women, living within wicked or barbarous societies, despite which they have managed to cope with adverse circumstances not of their own making. Shahrāzād is only doing so in order to undermine the king's prejudice against women, while she herself is a good woman who has volunteered to marry the king in order to save the daughters of the kingdom, thereby putting her own life at risk. She is, in other words, a person of heroic stature.
2. "The Lady and the Bear" and "The Princess and the Ape." In these two parallel stories, seemingly of Mamlūk origin, and dealing with the theme of feminine bestiality, one woman refuses to repent for her sins, and is killed, whereas the other does so, and is reintegrated into society. Again, Shahrāzād's message to her king is clear: not all women are necessarily evil by nature.
3. "The Seven Viziers." According to al-Mas'ūdī, this collection, originally known as the *Book of Sindibad*, was translated from Sanskrit into Pahlavi. Subsequently, other versions appear in innumerable languages, including Hebrew, Greek, Latin, French, Spanish, and English. An Arabic version was incorporated into *The 1001 Nights* as "The Seven Viziers."[6] Interestingly enough, most versions of the collection provide us with a similar ending: the wicked concubine in the frametale is put to death, usually by incineration. For example, in the Spanish version, *Sendebar*, or *Libro de los engannos y asayamientos de las mujeres*, she is roasted in a red-hot cauldron.[7] However, in the version that made its way into *The 1001 Nights*, the prince whom the concubine has attempted to destroy is inclined to mercy, and merely banishes her from the kingdom that she has put at such risk by plotting the death of its heir apparent. The moral of the story is that even a wicked woman deserves clemency, not death. Nor do the stories told by the concubine and the seven viziers to illustrate the innate wickedness of the opposite sex really support the thesis being defended. A case in point is the tale of "The Young Woman and her Five Lovers," told by the sixth vizier to illustrate the wickedness of women. The point of the story is that a young woman who is abandoned by her husband can hardly be considered wicked for taking a lover, especially one to whom she proves faithful, despite the fact that five men, four of whom are officials of the kingdom, abuse their positions of power by

attempting to seduce her. Instead, she has used the wiles of women to save herself and her lover. Note here that the point is not whether or not women are wily (they certainly are so portrayed in *The 1001 Nights*), but the purpose to which they put their wiles. This lady is, in other words, a virtuous woman, as is Shahrāzād, who is, all along, tricking King Shahriyār in order to cure him.

Here, let us note that *The 1001 Nights*, in their Arabic form at least, are clearly informed by the theology of the Ash'arī school which, in turn, upholds a belief in the omnipotence of God, and teaches that human beings live under the constraints of Predestination, as a result of which they are not responsible for their own acts, of which the evil ones they commit may be pardoned by the divinity if the individual sinner repents, even if he should only do so on his deathbed. The principle by which God judges one's acts according to their intention is everywhere to be found in *The 1001 Nights*. Even King Shahriyār himself is operating under the good intention of ridding his kingdom of wickedness, thereby upholding the famous rule of "commanding good and forbidding evil," the implementation of which is expected of all righteous rulers. He just happens to be seriously misguided (if not mad), and going about matters in a disastrously wrong way. As a result, rather than being punished, providence sends him a wily woman who teaches him how to follow the right path. This woman too, though wily, is using her wiles for a good and noble cause, namely that of saving the daughters of the kingdom. As a result, both she and the king are ultimately rewarded with a life of happiness together. Everywhere in *The 1001 Nights*, the workings of an enlightened form of providence are to be observed and, since Ash'arī theology was adopted into the Sunnī confession of Islam, we may conclude that this collection of stories, in all its surviving Arabic versions, is basically a Sunnī-inspired work.

The Book of Kalīla wa-Dimna

The *Book of Kalīla wa-Dimna* is an Arabic version of a Sanskrit work known as the *Panchatantra*, an Oriental frametale collection of animal fables probably compiled before AD 500, and possibly derived from Buddhist sources.[8] The *Panchatantra* was first translated into Pahlavi during the reign of the Sassanian King Chosroes I (r. AD 531–579), by a Persian doctor named Burzoe, after which that text, now lost, was retranslated, first into ancient Syriac by a Christian monk named Būd, in the sixth century AD,[9] and then, once again, directly from the Pahlavi into Arabic by 'Abdallāh ibn al-Muqaffa' (fl. *ca.* 102/720–*ca.* 139/756), who was a descendant of a distinguished Persian family, and who served the early 'Abbāsid caliphs.[10]

Ibn al-Muqaffa''s version constitutes the first work of classical Arabic prose fiction. Its Arabic is characterized by a number of loan translations and grammatical lapses of the sort that a Persian speaker might make, as may be attested by the oldest manuscript of the work to have survived. Subsequent scribes gradually corrected these mistakes and touched up the work until it acquired the reputation of being a stylistic model for Arabic prose. The modifications in the text made over the course of centuries were such, however, that little may have survived of Ibn al-Muqaffa''s original wording.[11]

A major problem that arises in studying *The Book of Kalīla wa-Dimna* is that we do not possess the text of the original version of the *Panchatantra* on the one hand, nor of its Arabic descendant on the other, while its Pahlavi intermediary has been lost. Despite these lacunae in transmission, a comparison of the extant Sanskrit versions on one end of the translation line, with the Syriac and Arabic versions (both of which translate the lost Pahlavi text independently of one another) on the other end of that line can, up to a certain point, help us reconstruct, *grosso modo*, what was and what was not included in the lost Pahlavi version. In turn, such a comparison strongly suggests that Ibn al-Muqaffa' added certain passages, and even entire chapters of his own, to the work, as a result of which the Arabic version is less a faithful translation of the Pahlavi text than it is a somewhat free adaptation of the latter. What, then, were the underlying principles guiding the modifications Ibn al-Muqaffa' introduced into his original?

Concerning this question it is probably not entirely insignificant that, as modern scholarship has proven, Ibn al-Muqaffa' was, for the greater part of his brief life, not a Muslim, but a Manichaean.[12] Moreover, his formative years were spent in the Iraqī city of Basra, where he came to be deeply influenced by the Mu'tazilī school of Islamic theology.[13] Concerning the first point, it has been shown that among his many other works, Ibn al-Muqaffa' also composed, in Arabic, a parody or imitation of the *Qur'ān*, a holy text that Islamic dogma holds to be inimitable.[14] Ibn al-Muqaffa''s imitation, which has not survived, was, therefore, considered blasphemous by Muslim scholars. A Shī'ī *imām* of the Zaydī sect, named al-Qāsim ibn Ibrāhīm, who lived a century after Ibn al-Muqaffa', composed a refutation of the latter's parody, and this work has survived.[15] In it, the author cites numerous passages from the original imitation, with the express purpose of refuting each one of them point by point. From these passages it becomes clear that the guiding principles of Ibn al-Muqaffa''s belief system were those espoused by the Manichaeans. We thus have two ideologies that may have been influential in Ibn al-Muqaffa''s thought, namely those of the Manichaean religion and those of the Mu'tazilī theological school of Islam. What are the areas of coincidence between the two systems and could their tenets have determined the modifications Ibn al-Muqaffa' introduced into the Pahlavi original when he adapted it into Arabic?

Since these tenets are of some relevance to *The Book of Kalīla wa-Dimna*, it is only appropriate to offer a brief summary of Manichaean beliefs, as follows:

(A) Chinese handbook of that religion states:

(B) Everyone who wishes to join the sect must know that Light and Darkness are principles, each in their own right and that their natures are completely distinct. If he does not perceive this how will he be able to practice the religion? Next he must be enlightened on the "Three Moments": (1) The Former Time, (2) The Present Time, (3) The Future Time.

The work then describes the significant events that take place in these periods:

- In the Former Time, there are yet no heavens or earths, there exists only Light and Darkness. The nature of Light is wisdom; that of Darkness is folly. In all their motion and rest they are completely opposed to each other.
- In the Present Time, Darkness invades Light and gives rein to its passions to chase [the Light] away. Light in turn enters Darkness and is deputed with pledges to push back this "Great Calamity." It [i.e. the Light] detests its departure from its original body and pleads to leave the "fiery abode." One must therefore wear out the [physical] body in order to save the [luminous] nature [?]. This is what the holy doctrine explicitly states and if the truth is fashioned from falsehood, who would dare listen to the commandments? One must therefore be critical and search for the cause of deliverance.
- In the Future Time, the things which we teach and preach on come to an end and truth and falsehood return to their roots. Light once more belongs to the Great Light and Darkness returns to the Ultimate Darkness. The Two Principles return to their normal state and give up and return to each other [what they have received from each other].[16]
- In sum, Light and Darkness, along with Good and Evil, Justice and Injustice, Spirit and Matter were, in the Former Time, separate from one another. In the Present Time, they have commingled, whereas in the Future Time they will return to their previous state of purity and perfection. In other words, there is a struggle between Good and Evil in the present, but Good will prevail in the future, implying that Justice is preordained and prescribed for mankind.

The theological system of the Mu'tazila rests upon the affirmation that God is primarily just and, from this basic principle, all else is derived. Since God is just, He has promised to reward the righteous and to punish the wicked on the Day of Judgment and, as Mu'tazilīs put it, "He will not change His mind." This being the case, it would be unjust on the part of God to coerce human beings into committing evil, only to punish them for so doing. As a result, and in keeping with His justice, God grants human beings Free Will in the area of moral decisions.

Unfortunately for the Mu'tazila, of those passages in the Qur'ān referring to the issue of Free Will as opposed to Predestination, the majority of them favor the doctrine of Predestination, which was adopted by the rival Islamic theological school of the Ash'arīya. This being the case, the Mu'tazila developed a method for interpreting the sacred text allegorically (*ta'wīl*). This method was based on recognition of the fact that language is ambiguous. Thus, if a key word in the sacred text had more than one meaning, this might allow the interpreter to find a hidden or esoteric (*bāṭin*) sense to the text, in support of an interpretation favorable to the doctrine of Free Will, even though the surface or exoteric meaning (*ẓāhir*) might appear to favor the doctrine of Predestination.[17] This practice even led to the writing of a genre of manuals on the double meanings of words, destined for usage by Qur'ānic interpreters.[18] It was further assumed by Mu'tazilī scholars that the hidden meaning of the text was the only true one, whereas the surface meaning was patently false. Therefore, the act of reading a text involved penetrating beyond its surface in order to get to the *bāṭin* of things. In turn, this way of reading influenced Ibn al-Muqaffa' who, as we have seen, was in close contact with the Mu'tazilī school of thought for, in the prologue to *The Book of Kalīla wa-Dimna*, he states:

> It is imperative that the reader of *Kalilah and Dimnah* should grasp the meaning beyond the text … frustration awaits anyone who reads this book of fables without comprehending both the apparent and the implicit ideas within … the book of fables, *Kalilah and Dimnah*, is not written for entertainment only … the reader should therefore spend time on understanding every fable and every word in the book … [he/she] should therefore spend careful and tireless time on understanding it … similarly, people who miss the point of this book and do not comprehend its deeper meanings, but are satisfied with the superficial, are like the ignorant fisherman … there are insights intended for the royalty, the gentry, and common folk as well … and there is wisdom here ultimately and exclusively meant only for philosophers.[19]

We are thus justified in concluding that the Manichaean belief in the preordained triumph of Light, Good and, with them, Justice, and the Mu'tazilī doctrine of Free Will have been combined in the mind of Ibn al-Muqaffa'. This may be confirmed by a brief analysis of *The Book of Kalīla wa-Dimna* itself. The first chapter of that work, "The Fable of the Lion and the Bull," contains a story about how no one can escape his preordained fate. It should not escape one's attention that the merchant's companion, who tells him this story has, on the surface, done so to justify the bull's alleged death, but on a deeper level, the real reason he tells it is to conceal his own dereliction of duty and to give credence to a blatant lie, namely that the bull is dead. Therefore, the fatalistic argument offered by the companion is false. Be it further noted that the man in the framed story is thrice spared his fate: first he is saved from the maw of a ferocious wolf, then from a river in which he is about to drown, and finally from a thieving gang of murderers. He only dies, according to some versions, when, unlike the villager who took the trouble of rescuing him from drowning in the river, he fails to take any action to rescue the merchant who is about to be murdered by the robbers. Thus, the true implication of the story is that rather than being ruled by a blind fate, the universe is controlled by a just Providence that rewards good deeds and punishes evil ones.

"The Fable of the Lion and the Bull" is the story of how the bull, abandoned by his master, as well as the latter's companion, finally extricates himself from the mud in which he is trapped, and enters the realm of a lion-king, who befriends him and appoints him to be his second-in-command as well as his intimate companion. A jackal named Dimna, who aspires to those very same royal favors, yet who has been pre-empted by the bull, consequently becomes jealous of the latter's standing at court, and slanders him before the lion by telling the monarch that the bull is plotting to overthrow him in order to rule in his stead. Conversely, Dimna informs the bull that the lion is plotting to kill and devour the bull. By getting rid of the bull, Dimna hopes he will be able to replace him as the lion's favorite. The lion and bull are both easily hoodwinked by the scheming jackal, whose words they foolishly take at face value (i.e. without subjecting them to critical analysis through the application of allegorical interpretation). This is amply illustrated by a story told by Dimna to Kalīla as proof of the fact that he will effectively bring about the bull's death. In this story, the animals are not very intelligent for, if matters had been left as they were, those same animals would at least have had the chance of escaping from the predatory lion. Instead, they have traded in their chance for survival, slim though it may have been, for voluntary slaughter on a systematic, daily basis, by means of a pact according to which there is no longer any chance of their escape. That is to say, they have entered into an agreement that is hardly in their best interest since they have merely exchanged one form of fate (the chance that the lion might catch them) for another (the chance that they might be designated by lot to be the lion's lunch). In fact, the agreement favors the lion, who is now guaranteed to get a free lunch every day. The lion too, is a fool, for in mistaking a reflection of himself and the cunning hare, in the water of the cistern, for his purported rival and his purloined lunch, he has confused appearance with reality or, to put it differently, he has failed to interpret matters correctly, as a result of which he dies.

In what is possibly the most ironic story in the entire first chapter of the book, Dimna, in attempting to arouse the suspicions of the bull in order to pit him against the lion, warns the bull that the lion's evil advisors are attempting to persuade him to kill and devour the bull. Upon hearing this news, the bull declares that no one may escape his preordained fate and, in essence, relates a tale that foretells his own downfall. In this instance too, the camel in that tale dies because he fails to perceive the underlying deception being perpetrated against him; in other words, like the lion in the framing story, he is unable to read between the lines to get at the truth. Furthermore, the story of the hapless camel is being told by the equally hapless bull in justification of the latter's belief that he will not be able to escape his fate, now that the lion has turned against him. In contrast, the intelligent reader is being invited by the author to see through the cunning jackal's deception in ways that cannot be perceived by the foolish bull. As a result, that reader interprets the text correctly, and realizes that the true reason why the bull dies is that he fails to see through Dimna's ruse, and not because fate has decreed his death. In other words, the reader is being advised to adopt the technique of allegorical interpretation.

The tragic flaw of the above animals lies, then, in their inability to penetrate beyond surface appearances and thereby grasp the truth. Put differently, they misinterpret the signs placed before them. Eventually, the lion kills and devours the bull, and there the first chapter ends, with the triumph of Dimna's evil deeds over the good but ineffective intentions of the lion and the bull.

Dimna has a brother named Kalīla who is fully aware, and strongly disapproves of, Dimna's devious plotting to get rid of the bull. Being a carnivore with a conscience, Kalīla spends most of his time repeatedly upbraiding Dimna for the latter's evil actions and intentions but, until the very end, even as the bull is being killed and devoured by the lion, Kalīla does nothing to prevent Dimna from pursuing his devious schemes; instead, he merely preaches to him. Kalīla is, therefore, all words and no action. At this juncture it should be noted that it was precisely the Mu'tazila who first formulated a guideline for human conduct that was to become an imperative for all Islamic monarchs. According to this imperative, the monarchs were required to "command good and forbid evil" (*al-amr bi-l-ma'rūf wa-l-nahy 'an al-munkar*).[20] In the case of the two jackals, however, Dimna perpetrates evil and prevents good, whereas Kalīla promotes good but fails to prevent evil. Both are, then, at fault and, as such, both are literary villains.

In the extant Sanskrit versions, as well as the Syriac translation, the story of the lion and the bull ends with the death of the bull, killed by the lion as a direct result of Dimna's devious machinations. Therefore, we have some grounds to suspect that the lost, intermediary Pahlavi version ended in more or less the same way. One may further speculate that a Sanskrit author with an Indian conception of the human soul, based on the doctrine of metempsychosis, would have expected the intelligent reader to assume that the evil jackals' punishment for their sins would be postponed until their next life, at which time their souls would be incarnated in an even lower form of existence, in accordance with Indian beliefs. For Ibn al-Muqaffa', however, justice needed to be meted out in this world if the foolish lion-king were to be saved through his good deeds, in accordance with the Mu'tazilī doctrine of a just God and, conversely, if Good were to triumph over Evil, according to the doctrine of the Manichaeans, whose beliefs he espoused. Therefore, it must have been Ibn al-Muqaffa' himself who composed and added to the book an entire second chapter entitled "The Fable of the Investigation of Dimna," for that chapter is not found in either the Sanskrit or the ancient Syriac versions, and was thus probably not in the Paḥlavi text being translated by Ibn al-Muqaffa'.[21]

It should also be noted that the relationship between the lion-king and his mother, the lioness in chapter 2, is a close, if inverted, parallel to the relationship between the jackal Dimna and his brother Kalīla in chapter 1. In each instance we are presented with two characters who are close blood relatives, and in each case one of these relatives offers advice to the other, who refuses to take it: Kalīla offers his brother good advice, whereas the lioness offers her son bad advice: although she has heard (but only on the authority of one witness, this being contrary to Islamic justice, in which a minimum of two witnesses are required for conviction) that Dimna is guilty, she wishes to see him condemned and executed without a fair trial. Thus, Kalīla promotes good, but fails to prevent evil, whereas the lioness promotes evil, but fails to prevent good. In sum, they both mean well, but go about matters in the wrong way, and here, in a Mu'tazilī-inspired work, it should be noted that at least one of the characters, namely Kalīla, is *not* rewarded for his good intentions (on the basis of which acts are judged in the Sunnī tradition). These two examples thus underscore the fact that the lion-king has learned from his mistakes, and has now become an exemplary ruler. To such an extent is this so, that he will not even take advice from someone as close to him as his own mother, should that advice be bad. In contrast, Dimna never learns from his mistakes, and thus dies. Hence, by offering the reader the example of a ruler who learns from his mistakes, the work functions as a true mirror for princes.

In sum, the Arabic translator/adaptor has modified his Pahlavi original to provide the reader with the portrait of a righteous monarch who, having learned from the initial mistake he made by allowing himself to be manipulated into unjustly killing the bull, now embodies the Islamic ideal of the just ruler who commands good and forbids evil and can, as a consequence, aspire to Paradise in the next world, according to the Islamic principles of the Mu'tazila, as much as he can contribute to the war against Darkness, Evil, and Injustice in the Present Time of the Manichaeans. By illustrating the triumph of Good over Evil and portraying a king who learns the true nature of Justice, which he then proceeds to uphold, the author has adapted a Buddhist work to the belief system of the Manichaeans and to the theology of the Mu'tazila.[22] Needless to say, this is an extraordinary instance of religious and cultural hybridization.

The Maqāmāt

As we have pointed out, Mu'tazilī theology upholds a belief in the justice of God, and teaches that human beings consequently enjoy Free Will, and are thus responsible for all their acts, which will be scrupulously rewarded or irrevocably punished by the divinity. They will, then, be judged on the basis of their acts, and not on that of their intentions. This theological doctrine came to be adopted by the Shī'ī confession of Islam. As we shall see, this is of some importance to our understanding of the *maqāma.*

The *maqāma,* insofar as it is a genre, was invented by Badī' al-Zamān al-Hamadhānī (358/969–398/1008). Time and again, in this genre, the anti-heroic protagonist argues that because times are difficult, he must obtain money from his victims by dishonest means, adding sentiments such as "Don't blame me; blame the times." Such a justification for dishonesty suggests that, in his own view, the protagonist is not responsible for his acts, but that all blame for them should, instead, be placed on time, fate, and ultimately on God, by Whom all earthly events are predestined. The anti-hero of the *maqāma* genre is thus a believer in Predestination, and yet, clever rhetorician that he is, he uses this belief perversely, as a justification for his misconduct. In the meantime, the text itself is at some pains to deconstruct his argument, by showing us that it is based on false logic and, in many cases, on false facts – that is to say, on outright lies. The protagonist is thus an unreliable narrator and, as such, he espouses an 'Ash'arī version of morality that is being subjected to critical scrutiny from a Mu'tazilī theological perspective.

For example, in his "*Maqāma* 26 (The Exhortation)," al-Hamadhānī has his protagonist appear in a street of the Iraqī city of Basra, when he is an old man, and where he is preaching a sermon in which he exhorts his listeners to repent before it is too late. The sermon is, however, based on Mu'tazilī principles and relies heavily on Šī'ī authorities, according to which, a deathbed repentance is a futile act. Since the preacher himself is now old, it becomes clear that, according to the very doctrine he is promoting, and which constitutes the theological basis for his sermon, his words, moving though they may seem, are hardly applicable to his own situation. Therefore, we must conclude that the preacher is being presented as a man who does not practice what he preaches. Put differently, he is a hypocrite, and his sermon is no more than a ruse designed to extract monetary donations from a crowd of gullible sympathizers, which is exactly what he proceeds to do immediately after concluding it.[23]

The Book of Good Love

Two recent studies promise to shed new light on the identity of Juan Ruiz, Archpriest of Hita, the enigmatic author of that masterpiece of fourteenth-century Spanish literature known today as *El libro de buen amor* (The Book of Good Love).[24] According to these studies, there was a certain Juan Ruiz de Cisneros (1295/6–1351/2), whose father, a Castilian nobleman named Arias González, was captured by the Muslims of Granada, possibly at the Christian defeat of Moclín in 1280, and was probably taken to the town of Alcalá la Real (then known as Alcalá de Benzaide) in that kingdom.[25] There, he spent some 25 years in captivity.

We are told, in an official dispensation issued by Pope John XXII in AD 1321, that because Arias González was a bachelor, the king of Granada bestowed a virgin Christian slave-girl upon him. It is more likely, however, that the boy's mother, far from being a Christian, was instead a Muslim, and that Arias González apostatized in order to be conjoined with her. She bore Arias González six sons, of whom the second was named Juan Ruiz.

The boy was brought up in Islamic territory, where he lived until the age of nine or ten, at which time the generous king (who would have been Muḥammad II [r. 671/1273–701/1302]), freed Arias González and his sons, who then moved back to Castile in 1305. There, Juan Ruiz grew up, eventually became Archpriest of Hita, and was sent, by the Roman See, on a three-year stint to Avignon, in Provence. Juan Ruiz would thus have been old enough, when he left Granada, to have learned the colloquial register of the Arabic language, as a native speaker, from his mother, her relatives, and the inhabitants of the kingdom in general. He would also have been old enough to learn the rudiments of Islam, in which religion he may well have been brought up. In addition to the above, his stay in Provence would have familiarized him with those tenets of courtly love that he was, in later years, to turn so mischievously on their heads in his *Libro de buen amor* (*LBA*). In sum, the *LBA* was probably written by a convert from Islam to Christianity, who had a more than passing familiarity with various aspects of Arabic culture; a familiarity that manifests itself on numerous occasions within the work itself.

The *LBA* is a masterpiece of Spanish literature in which Juan Ruiz, Archpriest of Hita, narrates in the first person singular, his endless attempts at seducing women, in none of which he succeeds, with the exception of two nuns who die immediately after their lapse from celibacy. In this sense, and like the *maqāma*, we have episodic tales of trickery, but unlike the *maqāma*, the trickster inevitably fails in most of his attempts at seduction. One of the major challenges in the study of the *LBA* lies in the fact that most Romanists who have devoted their efforts to examining that work, while they have been able to come up with numerous sources clearly derived from the Western tradition, at the same time have been largely at a loss when it comes to identifying a Western genre, or group of genres, within which the *LBA* may be convincingly included. In contrast, students of medieval Arabic and Hebrew literature are immediately able to recognize that here we are dealing with a Semitic genre, or rather, a group of genres that have been innovatively combined.

Insofar as the *LBA*'s episodic structure, chronicling the adventures of a trickster, is concerned, we can at once point to the Arabic *maqāma* genre.[26] Insofar as that trickster is a striking failure in his attempts at roguery, we can point to the Andalusī *zajal* tradition, particularly as we know it from the poetry of Ibn Quzmān (d. 555/1160).[27] Finally, insofar as the narrative constitutes a frame that includes subordinate, framed narratives within it, we can point to that rich Oriental frametale genre that was introduced to the Iberian Peninsula via works such as *The Book of Kalīla wa-Dimna*, which had been translated directly from Arabic into Castilian by order of the future Alfonso X the Learned, in the year AD 1251 of the Julian calendar, while Alfonso was still heir apparent to the throne of Castile. In this respect, it is irrelevant that many of the stories and episodes included in the *LBA* have Western sources. To argue the contrary would be to commit the serious mistake of confusing a work's structure and genre with its materials and their sources. Here, the concept of a hybrid work, in which the structure is patterned after Eastern genres, whereas its materials are derived from the Western tradition, may be of some help.

In his prologue to the *LBA*, and like Ibn al-Muqaffa', along with several *maqāma* authors before him, Juan Ruiz warns the reader that his book should not be understood literally, but that it should, instead, be read for its esoteric sense. Following the precedent set for Arabic literature by the Mu'tazilīs, he makes a further distinction between the intelligent and the ignorant reader. This distinction became central to the thought of the great Andalusī philosopher Ibn Rushd (=Averroes, 520/1126–595/1198). According to Ibn Rushd, there is only one truth, but that truth is perceived and understood differently by three different mindsets, namely that of the (rational) philosophers, the (dialectical) theologians, and the (rhetorical) masses. Ibn Rushd maintained that a *philosophical* understanding of truth, based on reason alone, was superior to a *dialectical* understanding of truth, based on revealed texts, that is to say, on faith. Finally, both these forms of understanding were superior to the *literal* or *rhetorical* understanding of truth prevalent among the ignorant masses. This was so because words, being ambivalent, needed to be interpreted correctly.[28]

Unlike the case of Saint Augustine's *Confessions*, to which the *LBA* has sometimes been compared, and in which the seducer boasts of his *successful* conquests, the resounding *failure* in the Archpriest's attempts at seduction has a striking precedent in the *zajal* poetry of Ibn Quzmān. The vast majority of Ibn Quzmān's *zajals* are, in appearance, panegyric in nature, while at the same time the poet often ridicules his patrons by placing his praise in the mouth of a literary persona who is presented as a ritual clown or buffoon. By so doing, the poet manages to be devastating in criticizing his patrons, while at the same time not offending their sensibility. In several typical examples of this strategy the panegyric is subverted, and the patron is indirectly mocked. In one of these, specifically "Zajal 20," the reader/listener is even left wondering where the poet's wife was on the night he was sneaking his neighbor's wife into their marriage bed. Was she, too, out for the night, in the arms of another man and, if so, did the poet know that this was the case and, consequently, that the coast would be clear for him to bring another woman into his home? If so, the poet is, at very least, a wittol![29]

Whereas in the *maqāma*, a victim, who is the first-person narrator, tells us how he has been tricked by an individual who is not the narrator, in the *LBA* the opposite occurs: a would-be trickster confesses to us, in the first person, how he has failed in his attempts at tricking a victim, exactly as occurs in the poetry of Ibn Quzmān.

The fact that the would-be seducer of the *LBA* is a priest must also be placed within its historical context: just a century before the composition of the *LBA*, the Roman Catholic Church had finally succeeded in imposing ecclesiastical celibacy on its clergy. If we apply to the *LBA* Ibn Rushd's method of perceiving the truth, we may conclude that the dialectical interpretation of the work, based on faith, is that the text is showing us a bad priest who is breaking the rules of the Church. On this level, then, the text is teaching us by negative example; it is indirectly exhorting priests to follow the rule of celibacy. On a higher, philosophical level, and in many different ways, the text is arguing instead that sex and the priestly condition are hardly incompatible. This being the case, the *LBA* offers a strong critique of the doctrine of ecclesiastical celibacy, while in so doing, it makes use of various Arabic literary and philosophical approaches and techniques.

The Canterbury Tales

In his *Canterbury Tales*, Chaucer (*ca.* AD 1340–1400) brings together some 29 characters from all walks of life, plus his own *persona*, and has them tell stories on their way to the shrine of Saint Thomas à Becket in Canterbury.[30] The framing context is, therefore, that of a holy pilgrimage. Unlike his predecessors, Chaucer goes to great lengths in describing his characters. For example, we know nothing about the personal appearance of Shahrāzād, and are only told that she is a wise woman; in other words, she is a stereotype. In contrast, we are told that Chaucer's Miller has a red beard, and that he even has a wart on his nose from which red hairs protrude.[31] We are, therefore, at the pre-dawn hour of Renaissance portraiture. The character of the individual pilgrims is also developed and, in each case, the character of the teller is, in one way or another, related to the tale being told, thus providing a new form of unity to the work. For example, the Knight is the very embodiment of the medieval courtly ideal: he is both brave and gentle, and has fought some 15 wars, mostly against the Muslim "infidel," in defense of Christianity. He is also pious, and has just returned from his latest battle, only to go on a holy pilgrimage, as an act of faith. However, he has done so in such haste that he has not even had time to change his clothes, as a result of which they are still *besmottered* ("stained") with the rust of his armor. Yet this same "very gentle, perfect Knight" tells a tale about some "knights" of Greek antiquity (note here that the medieval mind viewed the past as essentially similar to the present) who are neither pious nor just. King Theseus, who is one of these knights, is a hothead who imposes an arbitrary form of justice on his subjects, in a world ruled over by unjust, deceptive, and unreliable gods, the point here being that such an unjust pagan world is being rejected by our pious medieval Knight, and should also be rejected by his Christian contemporaries, the readers/listeners.

After the Knight's tale is concluded, and in keeping with those hierarchical ideas dominant in feudal society, it would have been the Monk's turn to speak, but the red-bearded Miller, who is drunk, rudely interrupts the former, in order to tell an obscene fabliau about an elderly carpenter who was cuckolded by his 18-year-old wife. This offends the Reeve, a dishonest man, who steals from the young master whose estate he oversees, and who also happens to have begun his career as a carpenter. Out of sheer revenge, the Reeve tells a tale about how a Miller was cuckolded by two students from Cambridge, who managed to sleep both with his wife and his daughter. Note that this tale, inspired by the sentiment of revenge, and containing further acts of revenge within it, is being told on the occasion of a holy pilgrimage, despite the fact that revenge is an entirely inappropriate sentiment in the context of a religion that recommends turning the other cheek in forgiveness of one's enemies. According to the medieval belief in the four humors, and their influence on the human temperament, the Miller is characterized as a sanguine personality or, as we would say today, he is an extrovert: he is stout and portly, he bashes down doors with his head, he is a drunkard, he rudely interrupts those who are his superiors on the social scale, and he rides at the head of the procession of pilgrims, loudly playing a bagpipe. In contrast, the Reeve is a choleric, introverted, personality: he is lean, he is sober, he is overly sensitive, he holds a pointless grudge against an unintended slight, and he rides at the end of the procession, brooding in silence.

Finally, let us consider the case of the Wife of Bath: she is an older woman who has had five legitimate husbands (apart from other unspecified company in her youth). Three of these husbands she considers to have been good, whereas two were bad. The three good ones were old and rich, they allowed her to take control of the marriage, and they died leaving her all their money. In contrast, the two bad ones were younger than she (one of them was 20 when she was 40), they attempted to control her, and one of them even boxed her in one ear, leaving her deaf. The Wife of Bath tells a story about a young man whom an ugly old hag tricks into marrying her. It turns out, however, that the hag (who is really a fairy) has magic powers that allow her to appear youthful to her young husband alone, whereas to everyone else she appears to be a decrepit old woman. The young man surrenders control of everything to her, and they live happily ever after. Not only is this tale a fantasy on the part of its teller, the Wife of Bath who, in her middle years, dreams of future young husbands and lovers she will be able to control, but it should also be noted that in the story she tells, King Arthur effectively hands over control of the young rapist's punishment to his own wife, Queen Guinevere, who in turn finds a way to pardon him for the crime of rape. We are further told that the Wife of Bath has been on pilgrimages to some of the major Christian shrines in Europe and elsewhere, including Santiago de Compostela in Galicia. She does so wearing a "gay scarlet gown," whenever her husband is away, it is implied, in order to find new lovers. Nor should we fail to note that, as she speaks, she is on a pilgrimage, gaily dressed and, no doubt, looking for a sixth husband, if not another lover.

In this way, Chaucer has used the frametale to explore new possibilities. In the *Canterbury Tales*, the characters are portrayed, on a human level, as possessing all the foibles and defects of ordinary human beings, even if some of them, such as the Wife of Bath, are perhaps more human than others. In Chaucer's masterpiece, the character and appearance of each storyteller is, in one way or another, related to the story he or she tells.

Conclusion

In sum, *The 1001 Nights*, originally translated into Arabic from Middle Persian, acquired an Islamic, and specifically Ash'arī and Sunnī ideological underpinning while, remarkably, many of the stories added in later centuries continued to uphold the principle that not all women are necessarily wicked by nature, but that each woman should instead be judged individually, according to her intentions, not her gender.

In contrast to *The 1001 Nights*, the *Book of Kalīla wa-Dimna*, which was also translated from a Pahlavi intermediary, in this case going back to a known Sanskrit original, conveys a mixed Manichaean and Mu'tazilī ideology. The *Maqāmāt*, invented by al-Hamadhānī, in turn represent a critique of Ash'arī beliefs and Sunnī practices from a Mu'tazilī and Shī'ī ideological perspective.

From Arabic, these three works became influential, directly or indirectly, on a host of European frametale collections, among them, that of Juan Ruiz in Castile, who used the genre to criticize the recently introduced Catholic requirement of clerical celibacy, and Geoffrey Chaucer in England, who, by portraying both virtuous knights and sinful scoundrels, all in the process of telling tales about all-too-human characters, was able to uphold certain basic Christian values. In this way, a genre traceable all the way back to Buddhist India, Manichaean Persia, and Arab Islam, was introduced to Western civilization, within which it inspired the creation of several medieval literary masterpieces, of which echoes have resounded down the ages, one of the most recent being that of the Chilean author Isabel Allende's two novels, *Eva Luna*[32] and *Cuentos de Eva Luna*.[33]

For the larger cultural context within which the medieval Arabic and Spanish works studied above are to be found, the English-speaking student is advised to consult standard works on Arabic and Spanish history and literature respectively. In particular, the following are recommended:

Arabic

Gibb, Hamilton Alexander Rosskeen, *Mohammedanism: An Historical Survey* (New York: Oxford University Press, 1962).

Gibb, Hamilton Alexander Rosskeen, *Arabic Literature: An Introduction* (Oxford: Clarendon Press, 1963).

Hitti, Phillip K., *History of the Arabs* (London: Macmillan, 1937).

Nicholson, Reynold Alleyne, *A Literary History of the Arabs* (London: Cambridge University Press, 1969).

Spanish

Castro, Americo, *The Spaniards, an Introduction to their History* (Berkeley: University of California Press, 1971).

Gies, David T. (ed.) *The Cambridge History of Spanish Literature* (Cambridge and New York: Cambridge University Press, 2004).

Notes

1 See Charles Barbier de Meynard (ed.), and A. Pavet de Courteille (trans.), *al-Mas'ūdī, Les prairies d'or* (Paris: Imprimerie Impériale, 1865), reprint of the Arabic text, revised by Charles Pellat, *Murūj al-dhahab* (Beirut: Manshūrāt al-Jāmi'at al-Lubnānīya, 1965–79), 7 vols, vol. 2, p. 406, parag. 1416.

2 See Bayard Dodge (trans.), *The Fihrist of al-Nadīm: A Tenth-Century Survey of Muslim Culture* (New York and London: Columbia University Press, 1970), 2 vols, vol. 2, pp. 713–714.

3 See "A Ninth-Century Fragment of the 'Thousand Nights': New Light on the Early History of the Arabian Nights," *Journal of Near Eastern Studies*, vol. 8 (1949), pp. 129–164.

4 See *The Arabian Nights: A Structural Analysis* (Cairo: National Commission for UNESCO, 1980). Also Mia Irene Gerhardt, *The Art of Storytelling: A Literary Study of the Thousand and One Nights* (Leiden: Brill, 1963); Tzvetan Todorov, *The Poetics of Prose*, trans. Richard Howard (Ithaca, NY: Cornell University Press, 1977); Robert Irwin, *The Arabian Nights: A Companion* (London: Tauris, 2005); and Muhsin al-Musawi, *The Islamic Context of the Thousand and One Nights* (New York: Columbia University Press, 2009).

5 For the Arabic texts of the stories from *The 1001 Nights* discussed here, I have consulted five major editions: 1 Shaykh Aḥmad ibn Muḥammad Shirwānī al-Yamānī (ed.), *The Arabian Nights Entertainments in the Original Arabic: Published under the Patronage of the College of Fort William* (Calcutta: Pereira, 1814–18), 2 vols (=Calcutta I); 2 C. Maximilian Habicht and Heinrich L. Fleischer (eds), *Tausend und Eine Nacht Arabisch: Nach einer Handschrift aus Tunis* (Breslau: J. Max & Comp., 1825–43), 12 vols (=Breslau); 3 Shaykh Muḥammad Qiṭṭaṭ (ed.), *Alf Layla wa-layla* (Cairo: Būlāq, 1833), 2 vols (=Būlāq I); 4 W.H. Macnaghten (ed.), *The Alif Laila or Book of the Thousand Nights and One Night, Commonly Known as "Arabian Nights' Entertainments": Now, for the First Time, Published Complete in the Original Arabic, from an Egyptian Manuscript Brought to India by the Late Major Turner Macan, Editor of the Shah-Nameh* (Calcutta: Baptist Mission Press, 1839–42) (=Calcutta II); 5 Muhsin Mahdi (ed.), *The Thousand and One Nights (Alf Layla wa-Layla)*

from the Earliest Known Sources (Leiden: E.J. Brill, 1984), 2 vols. I have also consulted the English translations of: 1 John Payne, *The Book of the Thousand Nights and One Night: Now First Completely Done into English Prose, from the Original Arabic* (London: Villon Society, 1882–89), 9 vols; 2 Edward William Lane, *"The Thousand and One Nights" Commonly Called in England "The Arabian Nights' Entertainments"* (London: Charles Knight & Co., 1839–41), 4 vols; 3 Richard F. Burton, *A Plain and Literal Translation of the Arabian Nights Entertainments, now Entitled The Book of the Thousand Nights and a Night* (Benares-London: Kamashastra Society, 1885), 10 vols, *Supplemental Nights* (1886–88), 6 vols; 4 Husain Haddawy, *The Arabian Nights: Based on the Text of the Fourteenth-Century Syrian Manuscript Edited by Muhsin Mahdi* (New York and London: W.W. Norton & Company, 1990). As a translation suitable for classroom usage, I have relied upon N.J. Dawood, *Tales from the Thousand and One Nights* (London: Penguin Books, 1973).

6 See Charles Pellat, ed. cit. vol. 1, p. 90, parag. 167, vol. 2, p. 406, parag. 1416; J.P. Guillaume, "Sindbād al-ḥakīm (Syntipas)," *The Encyclopaedia of Islam: New Edition* (Leiden: E.J. Brill, 1978), vol. 9, p. 640, cols. a–b (henceforward abbreviated *E.I. 2*); Bonnie Diane Irwin Lotfizadeh, *The Book of Sindibad and the Seven Sages of Rome: Perspectives on the Frame and Its Relationship to the Interpolated Tales in the Persian, Arabic, Latin, and Spanish Versions* (PhD dissertation in Comparative Literature, University of California, Berkeley, 1991). Although al-Mas'ūdī's attribution of the *Book of Sindibad* to a Sanskrit original is the most widely accepted hypothesis of its origin, this attribution is questioned by some scholars, on the grounds that no Sanskrit text is known to have existed. See the discussion in Irwin Lotfizadeh, p. 7.

7 "E el rey mandola quemar en una caldera en seco." See John Esten Keller (ed.), *El libro de los engaños*, Textos Antiguos Españoles, I (Valencia: Castalia, 1959), p. 64. The Greek version is more merciful: her head shaved and her face covered with ashes, the concubine is to be mounted on an ass, backwards, and paraded throughout the entire city, accompanied by two heralds, one going ahead of her, and the other following behind, while both loudly proclaim her attempted crime for all to hear. See Alfred Eberhard (ed.), *Fabulae Romanenses Graece Conscripta, Vol. Prius quo Continentur De Syntipa et de Aesopo Narrationes Fabulosae Partim Ineditae* (Leipzig: B.G. Teubner, 1872), p. 117, l. 17-p. 118, l. 5; p. 181, l. 14-p. 182, l. 4. It is a great pleasure to thank my friend and colleague, the Hellenist Christopher Simon, for kindly identifying and translating the Greek passage for me.

8 See C. Brockelmann, "Kalīla wa-Dimna," *E.I. 2*, vol. 4, pp. 503–506, at p. 503, col. a. For two English translations of the Sanskrit text, see Arthur W. Ryder, *The Panchatantra* (Chicago, IL: The University of Chicago Press, 1925, repr. 1964); Patrick Olivelle, *Pañcatantra: The Book of India's Folk Wisdom* (Oxford: Oxford University Press, 1997). According to Olivelle (p. xii), current scholarly consensus places the composition of the original Sanskrit text around AD 300. See also, Ibrahim Abdallah S. Dawood, *The Panchatantra, Kalilah wa-Dimnah, and The Morall Philosophie of Doni: A Comparative Study* (PhD dissertation in Comparative Literature, University of Indiana, 1983).

9 See *E.I. 2,* loc. cit.; William Wright, *A Short History of Syriac Literature* (London: Adam and Charles Black, 1894), pp. 123–241. For an edition and German translation of the Syriac text, see Gustav Bickell, *Kalilag wa-Damanag: die alte syrische Version des indischen Furstenspiegels (Bidpai's Fabeln): ubersetzt im sechsten Jahrhundert nach dem Pehlevi Text: syrischer Text herausgegeben nach den einzigen Handschrift und ins Deutsche ubersetzt; mit einer ausfuhrlichen historischen Einleitung von Theodor Benfey und Erganzungen von Th. Noldeke, I. Low und L. Blumenthal* (Amsterdam: Philo Press, 1982).

10 For the numerous Arabic editions, see *E.I. 2*, op. cit., p. 503, col. b–p. 504. col. a. For the biography of Ibn al-Muqaffa', see Francesco Gabrieli, "Ibn al-Muḳaffa'," *E. I. 2*, vol. 3, pp. 883–885. See also, Francesco Gabrieli, "L'opera di Ibn al-Muqaffa'," *Rivista degli studi orientali*, vol. 13:3 (1932), pp. 197–247; P. Kraus, "Zu Ibn al-Muqaffa'," *Rivista degli studi orientali*, vol. 14:1 (1933), pp. 1–20; Carlo Alfonso Nallino, "Noterelle su Ibn al-Muqaffa' e suo figlio," *Rivista degli studi orientali*, vol. 14:2 (1933), pp. 130–134; Dominique Sourdel, "La biographie d'Ibn al-Muqaffa' d'après les sources anciennes," *Arabica*, 1 (1958), pp. 307–323.

11 See ʻAbd al-Wahhāb ʻAzzām (ed.), *Kalīlah wa-Dimnah* (Beirut: Dār al-Shurūq, 1973). This edition is based on the oldest known MS, which is located in the Aya Sofia Library of Istanbul. It was copied in 617/1221, around five centuries after the death of Ibn al-Muqaffaʻ. On the Persian grammatical and syntactic constructions affecting its Arabic, see pp. 20–21. On pp. 14–20 the editor discusses the relative merits of the other major scholarly editions of the Arabic text.

12 See Michelangelo Guidi, *La lotta tra l'Islam e il Manicheismo: un libro di Ibn al-Muqaffaʻ contro il Corano confutato da al-Qāsim B. Ibrāhīm. Testo arabo pubblicato con introduzione, versione italiana e note* (Rome: R. Accademia Nazionale dei Lincei, 1927). At least two stories in *Kalila wa-Dimna*, namely those of "The Merchant and the Jeweller," and "The Three Fish" are of Manichaean origin. For these stories, see Saleh Saʻadeh Jallad (trans.), *The Fables of Kalilah and Dimnah: Adapted and Translated from the Sanskrit through the Pahlavi into Arabic by ʻAbdullah ibn al-Muqaffaʻ AD 750* (London: Melisende, 2002), pp. 71, 98. For their Manichaean prototypes, see W.B. Henning, "Sogdian Tales," *Bulletin of the School of Oriental and African Studies (University of London)*, vol. 21 (1943–46), pp. 466–487, at. pp. 466–468 and p. 471. Of "The Merchant and the Jeweller," Henning comments that it "formed part of a *kephalaion*, ... in other words ... it was supposed that Mani had narrated the story to his disciples. This is presumably a fiction (it is mostly so with *kephalaia* literature, Coptic or Turkestanian), but not necessarily so. For the story is known only from Burzōi's preface to *Kalila wa Dimna*, hence it is quite likely Persian, and not Indian by origin."

13 See F. Gabrieli, "Ibn al-Muḳaffaʻ."

14 See Michelangelo Guidi, op. cit.

15 See Michelangelo Guidi, ibid. See also, Josef van Ess, "Some Fragments of the *Muʻāradat al-Qurʻān* Attributed to Ibn al-Muqaffaʻ," in Wadād al-Qāḍī (ed.), *Studia Arabica et Islamica: Festschrift for Iḥsān ʻAbbās* (Beirut: American University of Beirut, 1981), pp. 151–163.

16 Apud Samuel N.C. Lieu, *Manichaeism in the Later Roman Empire and Medieval China: A Historical Survey* (Manchester: Manchester University Press, 1985), p. 8. For further studies on Manichaeism see F.C. Burkitt, *The Religion of the Manichees: Donnellan Lectures for 1924* (Cambridge: The Cambridge University Press, 1925); Geo Widengren, *Mani and Manichaeanism* (New York: Holt, Rinehart and Winston, 1965); A.V.W. Jackson, *Researches in Manichaeanism with Special Reference to the Turfan Fragments* (New York: AMS Press, 1965).

17 On the doctrines of the Muʻtazila in general, see D. Gimaret, "Muʻtazila," *E.I. 2*, vol. 7, pp. 783–793; William Montgomery Watt, *Free Will and Predestination in Early Islam* (London: Luzac, 1948).

18 See James T. Monroe (trans.), *Al-Maqāmāt al-Luzūmīyah by Abū l-ṭāhir Muḥammad ibn Yūsuf al-Tamīmī al-Saraqusṭī ibn al-Ashtarkūwī* (d. 538/1143), *(Translated with a Preliminary Study)*, Studies in Arabic Literature, vol. 22 (Leiden: E.J. Brill, 2002), pp. 36–41.

19 Saleh Saʻadeh Jallad, op. cit., pp. 29–30, 34–36.

20 See D. Gimaret, "Muʻtazila," p. 787, col. a.

21 Further support for this hypothesis may be found in the fact that a Greek translation of the work was made for the Byzantine Emperor Alexios I Comnenos (r. 1081–1127) by Symeon Seth, ca. 1080. This translation was made directly from the Arabic of Ibn al-Muqaffaʻ rather than the Syriac of Būd (see Hélène Condylis-Bassoukos, *Stéphanitès kai Ichnélatès, traduction grecque (XIè siècle) du livre Kalīla wa-Dimna d'Ibn al-Muqaffaʻ (VIIIè siècle). Étude lexicologique et littéraire*, Académie Royale de Belgique: Classe des Lettres, Fonds René Draguet, vol. 11 (Louvain: Aedibus Peeters, 1997), p. XIV: "C'est la traduction la plus ancienne du texte arabe en langue européene." See also, Carl Brockelmann, op. cit. p. 506, who indicates that the Greek translation was made directly from an Arabic source early enough to be free from later additions. This translation, which is older than the oldest extant Arabic MS of the text (copied in 1221), already contains a version of the added chapter on the trial of Dimna that is not found in the independent Syriac translation. See also, Vittorio Puntoni, *Stephanites kai Ichnelates*, Società Asiatica Italiana (Florence: Successori Le Monnier, 1889), vol. 2, pp. 134–154; Lars-Olof Sjöberg, *Stephanites und Ichnelates:*

Überlieferungsgeschichte und Text, Acta Universitatis Upsaliensis, Studia Graeca Upsaliensia (Stockholm: Almqvist & Wiksell, 1962), vol. 2, pp. 191–200.

22 This raises another, more complicated issue, which I shall not attempt to deal with here, namely the extent to which the rise of Mu'tazilism may possibly have been influenced by pre-existing Manichaean principles and beliefs.

23 For a further discussion of al-Hamadhānī, see James T. Monroe, *The Art of Badī' az-Zamān al-Hamadhānī as Picaresque Narrative* (Beirut: American University of Beirut, 1983). For the Arabic text, see Muḥammad 'Abduh (ed.), *Badī' al-Zamān al-Hamadhānī, Maqāmāt* (Cairo: Mu'assasat Aḫbār al-Yawm), repr. 1988. For an English translation, see, W.J. Prendergast (trans.), *The Maqámát of Badí' al-Zamán al-Hamadhání* (London: Luzac and Co., 1915), repr. (London and Dublin: Curzon Press, 1973). For a previously unknown and recently discovered *maqāma*, possibly by our author, see, Bilal W. Orfali and Maurice A. Pomerantz, "A Lost *Maqāma* of Badī' az-Zamān al-Hamadhānī?," *Arabica*, vol. 60 (2013), pp. 245–271. For the Arabic text of al-ḥarīrī, see his *Maqāmāt* (Beirut: Dār ṣadir, 1965). For an English translation, see, Thomas Chenery and F. Steingass, *The Assemblies of al-ḥarīrī* (Williams and Norgate, 1867–98), 2 vols. For the Arabic text of al-Saraqusṭī, see, Ibrāhīm Badr Aḥmad ḍayf (ed.), *al-Maqāmāt al-luzūmīya li-l-Saraqusṭī* (Alexandria: al-ḥay'a al-Miṣrīya al-'Āmma li-l-Kitāb, 1982); ḥasan al-Warağlī (ed.), *al-Maqāmāt al luzūmīya: ta'līf Abī l-ṭāhir Muḥammad ibn Yūsuf al-Tamīmī, al-Saraqusṭī* (Rabat: Maṭābi' Manshurāt 'Ukāẓ, 1995). For an English translation, see James T. Monroe, *Al-Maqāmāt al-Luzūmīyah.*

24 Emilio Sáez and José Trench, "Juan Ruiz de Cisneros (1295/1296–1351/1352) autor del *Buen amor*," *Actas del I Congreso Internacional sobre el Arcipreste de Hita*, ed. M. Criado de Val (Barcelona: S.E.R.E.S.A., 1973), pp. 365–368; Francisco Márquez-Villanueva, "La nueva biografía de Juan Ruiz," in William Mejías López (ed.), *Morada de la palabra: homenaje a Luce y Mercedes López-Baralt* (San Juan: Editorial de la Universidad de Puerto Rico, 2002), 2 vols, vol. 1, pp. 33–51. For a more detailed discussion of the question of Arabic influences on Juan Ruiz, see James T. Monroe, "Arabic Literary Elements in the Structure of the *Libro de buen amor*," *Al-Qanṭara*, vol. 32:1–2 (2011), pp. 27–70; 307–332.

25 Cf. the remark, "fija, mucho vos saluda vno que es de alcalá ..." ("Daughter, one who is from Alcalá sends you many greetings"), *LBA*, v. 1510a. See, Juan Ruiz, *The Book of Good Love* (ed. and trans. Elizabeth Drayson Macdonald) (London: J.M. Dent; Vermont: Charles E. Tuttle, 1999).

26 Discussed in Francisco Fernández y González, "Influencia de las lenguas y letras orientales en la cultura de los pueblos de la península ibérica," *Discursos leídos ante la Real Academia Española* (Madrid: Maestre, 1894); María Rosa Lida de Malkiel, *Two Spanish Masterpieces: The "Book of Good Love" and "The Celestina,"* Illinois Studies in Language and Literature, vol. 49 (Urbana: The University of Illinois Press, 1961), pp. 1–50.

27 On whom, see, James T. Monroe, *The Mischievous Muse: Extant Poetry and Prose of Ibn Quzmān of Córdoba (d. AH 555/AD 1160) (Edition, Translation, and Notes, Along with an Analysis of Selected Poems)* (Leiden: E.J. Brill, in press).

28 On this point, see Léon Gauthier (ed. and trans.), *Ibn Rochd (Averroès): Traité decisive (Façl el-maqâl) sur l'accord de la religion et de la philosophie, suivi de L'appendice (Dhamīma)*, 3rd edn. (Algiers: Carbonel, 1948); George F. Hourani (ed.), *Ibn Rushd (Averroes): Kitāb Faṣl al-Maqāl, with its Appendix (ḍamīma) and an Extract from Kitāb al-Kashf 'an Manāhij al-Adilla* (Brill: Leiden, 1959).

29 For a detailed analysis, see, James T. Monroe, "The Mystery of the Missing Mantle: The Poet as Wittol? (Ibn Quzmān's *Zajal 20*)," *Journal of Arabic Literature*, vol. 37:1 (2006), pp. 1–45.

30 See, A.C. Cawley (ed.), *Geoffrey Chaucer, Canterbury Tales* (London, Melbourne and Toronto: J. M. Dent; New York: E.P. Dutton, Everyman, 1978); Joseph Glaser (trans.), *The Canterbury Tales in Modern Verse* (Indianapolis, IN and Cambridge: Hackett Publishing Company, Inc., 2005).

31 Note that, according to universal popular belief, red hair was a sign of dishonesty and unreliability, and that millers, this one included, were proverbial for cheating their customers.

32 Barcelona: Plaza y Janés, 1987.

33 Barcelona: Plaza y Janés, 1989.

Bibliography

Abbott, Nadia, "A Ninth-Century Fragment of the 'Thousand Nights': New Light on the Early History of the Arabian Nights," *Journal of Near Eastern Studies*, vol. 8 (1949): 129–164.

al-Ḥarīrī, *Maqāmāt*, Beirut: Dār ṣadir, 1965.

Allende, Isabel, *Eva Luna*, Barcelona: Plaza y Janés, 1987.

al-Waraġlī, Ḥasan (ed.), *al-Maqāmāt al luzūmīya: ta'līf Abī l-ṭāhir Muḥammad ibn Yūsuf al-Tamīmī, al-Saraqusṭī*, Rabat: Maṭābi' Manshurāt 'Ukāẓ, 1995.

al-Yamānī, Shaykh Aḥmad ibn Muḥammad Shirwānī (ed.), *The Arabian Nights Entertainments in the Original Arabic: Published under the Patronage of the College of Fort William*, Calcutta: Pereira, 1814–18, 2 vols. (=Calcutta I).

Armistead, Samuel G., James T. Monroe, and Joseph H. Silverman, "Was Calixto's Grandmother a Nymphomaniac Mamlūk Princess? (A Footnote on "Lo de tu abuela con el Ximio" [La Celestina, Acto 1])," *eHumanista* 14 (2010): 1–23.

Barbier de Meynard, Charles (ed.), A. Pavet de Courteille (trans.), *al-Mas'ūdī, Les prairies d'or*, Paris: Imprimerie Impériale, 1865.

Burton, Richard F. (trans.), *A Plain and Literal Translation of the Arabian Nights Entertainments, now Entitled The Book of the Thousand Nights and a Night*, Benares and London: Kamashastra Society, 1885, 10 vols, *Supplemental Nights* 1886–88, 6 vols.

Castro, Americo, *The Spaniards, an Introduction to their History*, Berkeley: University of California Press, 1971.

Cawley, A.C. (ed.), *Geoffrey Chaucer, Canterbury Tales*, London, Melbourne and Toronto: J.M. Dent; New York: E.P. Dutton, Everyman, 1978.

Chenery, Thomas, and F. Steingass (trans.), *The Assemblies of al-Ḥarīrī*, Williams and Norgate, 1867–98, 2 vols.

Dawood, N.J. (trans.), *Tales from the Thousand and One Nights*, London: Penguin Books, 1973.

Dodge, Bayard (trans.), *The Fihrist of al-Nadīm: A Tenth-Century Survey of Muslim Culture*, New York-London: Columbia University Press, 1970, 2 vols.

Drayson Macdonald, Elizabeth (ed. and trans.), *Juan Ruiz, The Book of Good Love*, London: J.M. Dent; Vermont: Charles E. Tuttle, 1999.

Eberhard, Alfred (ed.), *Fabulae Romanenses Graece Conscripta, Vol. Prius quo Continentur De Syntipa et de Aesopo Narrationes Fabulosae Partim Ineditae*, Leipzig: B.G. Teubner, 1872.

Fernández y González, Francisco, "Influencia de las lenguas y letras orientales en la cultura de los pueblos de la península ibérica," in *Discursos leídos ante la Real Academia Española*, Madrid: Maestre, 1894.

Gabrieli, Francesco, "Ibn al-Muḳaffa'," *E. I.* 2, vol. 3: 883–885.

Gabrieli, Francesco, "L'opera di Ibn al-Muqaffa'," *Rivista degli studi orientali*, vol. 13:3 (1932): 197–247.

Gerhardt, Mia Irene, *The Art of Storytelling: A Literary Study of The Thousand and One Nights*, Leiden: Brill, 1963.

Gies, David T. (ed.), *The Cambridge History of Spanish Literature*, Cambridge and New York: Cambridge University Press, 2004.

Glaser, Joseph (trans.), *The Canterbury Tales in Modern Verse*, Indianapolis and Cambridge: Hackett Publishing Company, Inc., 2005.

Guidi, Michelangelo, *La lotta tra l'Islam e il Manicheismo: un libro di Ibn al-Muqaffa' contro il Corano confutato da al-Qāsim B. Ibrāhīm. Testo arabo pubblicato con introduzione, versione italiana e note*, Rome: R. Accademia Nazionale dei Lincei, 1927.

Guillaume, J.P., "Sindbād al-ḥakīm (Syntipas)," *E.I.* 2, 1978, vol. 9: 640, cols. a–b.

Habicht, C. Maximilian and Heinrich L. Fleischer (eds), *Tausend und Eine Nacht Arabisch: Nach einer Handschrift aus Tunis*, Breslau: J. Max & Comp., 1825–43, 12 vols. (=Breslau).

Haddawy, Husain (trans.), *The Arabian Nights: Based on the Text of the Fourteenth-Century Syrian Manuscript Edited by Muhsin Mahdi*, New York and London: W.W. Norton & Company, 1990.

Henning, W.B., "Sogdian Tales," *Bulletin of the School of Oriental and African Studies (University of London)*, vol. 21 (1943–46): 466–487.

Hitti, Phillip K., *History of the Arabs*, London: Macmillan, 1937.

Hourani, George F. (ed.), *Ibn Rushd (Averroes): Kitāb Faṣl al-Maqāl, with its Appendix (ḍamīma) and an Extract from Kitāb al-Kashf 'an Manāhij al-Adilla*, Brill: Leiden, 1959.

Irwin, Robert, *The Arabian Nights: A Companion*, London: Tauris, 2005.

Irwin Lotfizadeh, Bonnie Diane, *The Book of Sindibad and the Seven Sages of Rome: Perspectives on the Frame and its Relationship to the Interpolated Tales in the Persian, Arabic, Latin, and Spanish Versions* (PhD dissertation in Comparative Literature, University of California, Berkeley, 1991.

Jackson, A.V.W., *Researches in Manichaeanism with Special Reference to the Turfan Fragments*, New York: AMS Press, 1965.

Jallad, Saleh Sa'adeh (trans.), *The Fables of Kalilah and Dimnah: Adapted and Translated from the Sanskrit through the Pahlavi into Arabic by 'Abdullah ibn al-Muqaffa' AD 750*, London: Melisende, 2002.

Keller, John Esten (ed.), *El libro de los engaños*, Textos Antiguos Españoles, I, Valencia: Castalia, 1959.

Kraus, P., "Zu Ibn al-Muqaffa'," *Rivista degli studi orientali*, vol. 14:1 (1933): 1–20.

Lane, Edward William (trans.), *The Thousand and One Nights' Commonly Called in England "The Arabian Nights' Entertainments"*, London: Charles Knight & Co., 1839–41, 4 vols.

Lida de Malkiel, María Rosa, *Two Spanish Masterpieces: The "Book of Good Love" and "The Celestina,"* Illinois Studies in Language and Literature, vol. 49, Urbana: The University of Illinois Press, 1961.

Lieu, Samuel N.C., *Manichaeism in the Later Roman Empire and Medieval China: A Historical Survey*, Manchester: Manchester University Press, 1985.

Macnaghten, W.H. (ed.), *The Alif Laila or Book of the Thousand Nights and One Night, Commonly Known as "Arabian Nights' Entertainments": Now, for the First Time, Published Complete in The Original Arabic, From an Egyptian Manuscript Brought to India by the Late Major Turner Macan, Editor of the Shah-Nameh*, Calcutta: Baptist Mission Press, 1839–42, (=Calcutta II).

Mahdi, Muhsin (ed.), *The Thousand and One Nights (Alf Layla wa-Layla) from the Earliest Known Sources*, Leiden: E.J. Brill, 1984, 2 vols.

Márquez-Villanueva, Francisco, "La nueva biografía de Juan Ruiz," in William Mejías López (ed.), *Morada de la palabra: homenaje a Luce y Mercedes López-Baralt*, San Juan: Editorial de la Universidad de Puerto Rico, 2002, 2 vols, vol. 1, pp. 33–51.

Monroe, James T., *The Art of Badī' az-Zamān al-Hamaḏānī as Picaresque Narrative*, Beirut: American University of Beirut, 1983.

Monroe, James T. (trans.), *Al-Maqāmāt al-Luzūmīyah by Abū l-ṭāhir Muḥammad ibn Yūsuf al-Tamīmī al-Saraqusṭī ibn al-Aštarkūwī (d. 538/1143)*, (Translated with a Preliminary Study), Studies in Arabic Literature, vol. 22, Leiden, Boston, MA and Koln: Brill, 2002.

Monroe, James T., "Improvised Invective in Hispano-Arabic Poetry and Ibn Quzmān's 'Zajal 87' (When Blond Meets Blonde)," in *Voicing the Moment: Improvised Oral Poetry and Basque Tradition*, ed. Samuel G. Armistead and Joseba Zulaika, Center for Basque Studies, 3 (Reno: University of Nevada, 2005, pp. 135–159.

Monroe, James T., "The Mystery of the Missing Mantle: The Poet as Wittol? (Ibn Quzmān's Zajal 20)," *Journal of Arabic Literature*, vol. 35:1 (2006): 1–45.

Monroe, James T., "Arabic Literary Elements in the Structure of the Libro de buen amor," *Al-Qanṭara*, vol. 32:1–2 (2011): 27–70, 307–332.

Monroe, James T., *The Mischievous Muse: Extant Poetry and Prose of Ibn Quzmān of Córdoba (d. AH 555/AD 1160), (Edition, Translation, and Notes, Along with an Analysis of Selected Poems)*, Leiden: E.J. Brill, in press).

Monroe, James T. and Mark F. Pettigrew, "The Decline of Courtly Patronage and the Appearance of New Genres in Arabic Literature: The Case of the Zajal, the Maqāma, and the Shadow Play," *Journal of Arabic Literature*, vol. 34 (2003): 138–177.

Nallino, Carlo Alfonso, "Noterelle su Ibn al-Muqaffa' e suo figlio," *Rivista degli studi orientali*, vol. 14:2 (1933): 130–134.

Nicholson, Reynold Alleyne, *A Literary History of the Arabs*, London: Cambridge University Press, 1969.

Olivelle, Patrick (trans.), *Pañcatantra: The Book of India's Folk Wisdom*, Oxford: Oxford University Press, 1997.

Orfali, Bilal W. and Maurice A. Pomerantz, "A Lost Maqāma of Badī' az-Zamān al-Hamadhānī?," *Arabica*, vol. 60 (2013): 245–271.

Payne, John (trans.), *The Book of the Thousand Nights and One Night: Now First Completely Done into English Prose, from the Original Arabic*, London: Villon Society, 1882–1889, 9 vols.

Pellat, Charles (ed.), *al-Mas'ūdī, Murūj al-Ḏahab*, Beirut: Manshūrāt al-Jāmi'at al-Lubnānīya, 1965–1979, 7 vols.

Prendergast, W.J. (trans.), *The Maqámát of Badí' al-Zamán al-Hamadhání*, London: Luzac and Co., 1915, repr. London and Dublin: Curzon Press, 1973.

Puntoni, Vittorio (ed.), *Stephanites kai Ichnelates*, Società Asiatica Italiana (Florence: Successori Le Monnier, 1889, 2 vols.

Qiṭṭaṭ, Shayḫ Muḥammad (ed.), *Alf Layla wa-layla*, Cairo: Būlāq, 1833, 2 vols (= Būlāq I).

Ryder, Arthur W. (trans.), *The Panchatantra*, Chicago, IL: The University of Chicago Press, 1925, repr. 1964.

Sáez, Emilio and José Trench, "Juan Ruiz de Cisneros (1295/1296–1351/1352) autor del Buen amor," in *Actas del I Congreso Internacional sobre el Arcipreste de Hita*, ed. M. Criado de Val (Barcelona: S.E.R.E.S.A., 1973, pp. 365–368.

Sjöberg, Lars-Olaf (ed.), *Stephanites und Ichnelates: Uberlieferungsgeschichte und Text*, Acta Universitatis Upsaliensis, Studia Graeca Upsaliensia (Stockholm: Almqvist & Wiksell, 1962, 2 vols.

Sourdel, Dominique, "La biographie d'Ibn al-Muqaffa' d'après les sources anciennes," *Arabica*, 1 (1958): 307–323.

Todorov, Tzvetan, *The Poetics of Prose*, trans. Richard Howard, Ithaca, NY: Cornell University Press, 1977.

van Ess, Josef, "Some Fragments of the Mu'āradat al-Qur'ān Attributed to Ibn al-Muqaffa'," in Wadād al-Qāḍī (ed.), *Studia Arabica et Islamica: Festschrift for Iḥsān 'Abbās*, Beirut: American University of Beirut, 1981, pp. 151–163.

Watt, William Montgomery, *Free Will and Predestination in Early Islam*, London: Luzac, 1948.

Widengren, Geo, *Mani and Manichaeanism*, New York: Holt, Rinehart and Winston, 1965.

Wright, William, *A Short History of Syriac Literature*, London: Adam and Charles Black, 1894.

19

TEACHING THE *ARABIAN NIGHTS*

Muhsin al-Musawi

There are perhaps a very few texts that can occupy a full semester or even an academic year like the *Thousand and One Nights* (better known as the *Arabian Nights*, hereafter *AN*). Its warm reception in Europe and later the US, and the rest of the world, its history of translation, its narrative richness, fecundity of images, and stylistic variations and techniques, and also its thematic patterns offer themselves easily to syllabus planning and designing. However, to speak or write about teaching the *Thousand and One Nights* may sound so belated that it raises a question of a different kind: why has the issue remained unaddressed for so long? The tales were seldom accorded any attention in academia throughout the twentieth century, and writing about them was almost an incongruity, if not a weird anomaly. Scholarly interest lasted for a few decades, but it increasingly dropped by the second half of the twentieth century.[1] Indeed, although my dissertation on the *Arabian Nights* at Dalhousie University (1978) was passed with distinction by a committee that included Richard Altick, Malcolm Ross, D.V. Varma, and the eminent Orientalist Wilfred Cantwell Smith, not many were ready then to concede to my argument to place the *AN* at the center of European literary theory and popular taste. Nevertheless, it drew some attention and substantial reviews when published as *Scheherazade in England* (1981).[2] The French celebration in 2004 of Antoine Galland's (1646–1715) first translation of an available text drew significant responsiveness to that venture that once took Europe by surprise, and indeed caught the attention not only of the common public but also of prominent writers, poets, and journalists.[3] Unless we keep in mind the actual reception, role, and considerable popularity of the *AN* in Europe, we may fail to gauge the need for further studies of the *AN* as one of the few books with an abiding impact,[4] an impact that deserves the engagement of a classroom.

Galland's *Les Mille et une Nuits: Contes Arabes*, has kept the title of the original, but added "Arabian tales" as a subtitle to reach out to specific audiences. The simultaneous anonymous Grub Street translation in English (1704–06) played the title differently and made it perhaps the most popular commodity in book publishing throughout the eighteenth and nineteenth centuries. Indeed, all over Europe there were many reprints, so-called "complete editions," "new translations," and "careful editions," which, according to the American Orientalist Duncan Black MacDonald, "should make a weighty chapter in the history of the great publishing humbug."[5] Playing on "nights" and "entertainments," the translator and publisher forged a new discourse that would fit well in the Orientalization process. As argued in *Scheherazade in England* (1981), the English translation was able to sustain a realistic touch throughout that drew more reviewers, essayists, editors and readers. It appealed to melodramatists and fiction writers and became one of the most widely circulated books. *The Times* of London of 5 April 1825 (no. 12619) described the translation as "a work to which our melodramatists are deeply indebted." Much earlier, on 6 January 1723, the thrice-weekly *London News* serialized these tales over three years in "four hundred and forty-five installments." Other magazines and journals carried out similar projects, while still others, like Harrison's *The Novelist's Magazine* published the *AN* in full in 1785.[6] Hence, the question with respect to what edition to suggest for the classroom now leads us back to the controversy over centuries: do we speak of a core or a late concoction and redaction? Perhaps, the argument below offers some answers.

The British translator distanced the tales from a French perspective, neutralizing their politics through an appeal to "entertainment," and struck hard at the classical critique of fiction. By underscoring entertainment, he unwittingly sides with a handful of Arab medievalists who disputed the belletrists' downgrading of whatever falls outside their elevated domain of fine writing. A new transactional activity took place in both cultures, the French and the British, whereby audiences, proprietors, including translators and publishers, along with reviewers and editors, launched their projects into a growing market. Other questions relating to original authorship receded into the background as the specific concern of some Orientalists or antiquarians. Transactions that took the *Thousand and One Nights* as a commodity were no less complicated and profit-driven than any popular product, but their cultural politic operated as well on other levels of enterprise, fashion, and aesthetics. A response by such a poet and critic as Samuel Taylor Coleridge takes form within these two processes, for example: a subjectification process whereby a romantic understanding of vision and imagination drove him to identify with the supernatural and the wonderful, and an objectification mode that sat well in the growing discursive battling with neo-classical rational reasoning. With Coleridge's reading and response in mind, along with the responses of other Romantics, we have something worth pursuing in relation to comparative poetics for the classroom.

The fourteenth-century manuscript

The story of Galland's partial manuscript of *Contes Arabes*, is itself a story of suspense, excitement, forgery, and make-believe. The partial manuscript consists of the tales that were considered the core, which is no more than the only extant version which Galland brought from Aleppo. It consists of the frametale, the story of King Shahrayar and his brother, and the embedded tales within like the Ox and the Ass, which provide a balanced view of human desire, beyond gender demarcations. The second story is that of "The Merchant and the Genie," with three tales that branch out from there, and lead back from the natural supernatural to other variations on the theme of desire beyond class and social borders, including royal barriers, and on the power of magic in transgressions of this kind. However, human reason and ingenuity are highly recognized in this tale and the next, "The Fisherman and the Genie," with its four embedded stories. With the steady elevation of the human and the natural, the fourth tale, "The Porter and the Three Ladies of Baghdad" with its six stories, including those of the *qalandaris* (dervishes) consolidates the proximity and, indeed, the bond between the natural and the supernatural before letting the other tales in the sequence retain the real with its mundane factuality in the fifth tale, "The Three Apples," or with its rapture, art and love in the sixth one, "The Two Viziers," usually listed as "The Story of Badr al-Din Hasan," which allows coincidence to function strongly in an otherwise powerful realistic and historical tale. It prepares the reader for tale number seven, "The Story of the Hunchback," with its 11 stories of urban life, where a realistic strain brings together different professions from the marketplace, the urban sector and its professional physicians. Perhaps numbers eight and nine, "Ali b. Bakkar and Shams al-Nahar," and "Nur al-Din Hasan and Anis al-Jalis" come at the right moment, to give the tales a high dose of passion, music, and humor. Thus, they invaded Paris and London, and enthralled no less than the British Poet Laureate Alfred, Lord Tennyson (1809–92) who blended them in his famous contribution to the aesthetics and romanticism of poetry in an otherwise increasingly utilitarian culture: "Recollections of the Arabian Nights" (1830). The core of the tales concludes with the story of "Jullanar of the Sea," which appeared in the Harvard fourteenth-century manuscript, avowedly the same one that Galland produced in 1704–07.[7] This is a core that fits the classroom.

Tales that do not belong to the established core of Galland's fourteenth-century manuscript could have been traceable to a different manuscript tradition. Some of these, like "The Story of the Sleeper Awakened," were found in other manuscripts of a later date, but some of the most popular ones, like "Aladdin of the Wonderful Lamp," "The Story of the Blind Man Baba Abdalla," and "Ali Baba and the Forty Thieves," remained a challenge to translators and scholars for some time.[8] Galland was, after all, as keen as his readers to comply with the literal meaning of "one thousand nights and one" that comprises the original title, ignoring for the time being its metaphorical application as an unlimited number. Along with scattered tales from variegated sources he had to rely on Hanna Diyab, a Syrian Christian from Aleppo who joined him in Paris, 1704–17, inscribing tales that had no original other than the live authority of the storyteller. In other words, Galland could make an interesting classroom case for the study of imperial and individual enterprise, a kind of Robinson Crusoe in a textual terrain.

The translator as producer

At this juncture, there is a need to acquaint the student with Galland's career as translator, and producer of texts. After all, it was his version that evoked so much response, imitation, and search for origins, duplication, and adaptation for the theater. Although coming two centuries later, the American Orientalist and theology scholar Duncan Black MacDonald devoted no less than 60 years of his career to search for Galland's original manuscript, its vogue among scholars and readers, and its challenge to Orientalist scholarship.

The renowned traveler, anthropologist, translator and critic Richard F. Burton (1821–90) was unconcerned with establishing a genealogical exploration of the *Arabian Nights* and its linguistic transformations in translation; nor was MacDonald. Only Jorge Luis Borges came up in 1935 with a studied reading of "The Translators of *The Thousand and One Nights*,"[9] where he largely draws a number of uncontested conclusions. Thus, he writes that by including tales other than the ones in his fourteenth-century manuscript, "Galland established the canon, incorporating stories that time would render indispensable and that the translators to come his enemies would not dare omit." This canon can work nicely in a classroom where issues of canonicity can be raised. Burton drew comparisons with the versions submitted by first translators, as the eminent Victorian Edward William Lane (1801–78) did after spending five years in Egypt, coming up with the second significant translation in 1838–41, a translation that spoke to a Victorian middle class and learned society. Its power lies in the extensive notes and realistic detail that spoke to an age that valued a seemingly realistic image of the East. In Borges's neat conclusion each translator "annihilated" a predecessor. "Lane translated against Galland, Burton against Lane; to understand Burton we must understand this hostile dynasty."[10] However, if I tried in 1977–81 to deal with translations in English as indices of taste, readership, and also politics of a masochistic bourgeoisie in the heyday of empire, it is time to go even beyond what I researched in the footsteps of the eminent Richard Altick's *The English Common Reader*, and engage more with the whole culture industry, which MacDonald aptly describes as the great "publishing humbug."[11] In a classroom, I shall interrogate these as contexts, matrices and informing material conditions constituting a cultural script and impacting or responding to a translation as another index in cultural production. Each newly claimed translation has a readership, and indeed a very significant one, as publishers' registries, writers' response, readership and publication data convey. We need to keep in mind that in England, in particular, the *Arabian Nights' Entertainments* (1704–06), as its anonymous Grub Street translator baptized it, was next only to the Bible in popularity and vogue.[12]

A translation venture in a classroom

With the publication of Galland's original Arabic, Harvard's fourteenth-century Syrian manuscript,[13] minus the tales narrated in person by the Maronite Hanna

Diyab, we can speak of a primal text and also assess Galland and his detractors in specific terms related to standards of translatability. Although the Arab scholars in the heyday of an imperial Islamic order in the ninth century came up with nuanced and sophisticated theories of translation, nineteenth-century European explorations, especially during colonial planetary reach, showed no less sophistication in the hands of George Meredith, Matthew Arnold, and F.W. Newman. The polymath and highly rationalist ninth-century Arab thinker Abū 'Uthmān al-Jaḥiẓ (d. 868), differentiates transference from transformation and translation. As long as a lexical register fails to accommodate philosophical terms or resists conceptualizations pertaining to divinity, you "transfer." However, Indian mathematics and other sciences can be translated word for word and sense for sense. The pre-Islamic (Sassanid) Persian knowledge undergoes "transformation" in the process. All in all, an Arabization takes place to fit foreign knowledge into an Arab/Islamic cultural script.[14] If Matthew Arnold disputes F.W. Newman's claim to recapture Homer's environs in their syntactical idiosyncrasy and semantic fields,[15] George Meredith admonishes translators to recapitulate the spirit and mood of the Arab in order to claim fidelity and faithfulness.[16] With his discerning insight, Meredith was unwilling to subscribe to the ongoing discussion of translating the Arab and the Orient in the age of empire, an age that acts on the Other as another commodity for a cultural Crystal Palace (1851).[17] Galland's venture culminates a long and well-sustained competition between contending colonial powers to transfer and translate manuscripts, especially from the Levant and Egypt. Indeed, G.J. Toomer's painstaking cataloguing and reading of this movement leaves us sufficient space to question and analyze the means, methods, and horizons in this translation movement.[18]

As the Enlightenment philosophers of seventeenth- and eighteenth-century Europe were not alien to the movement, and as the rising publishing industry heavily invested in its constitution and makeup, we have every reason to take this movement seriously as no less essential to the empire than its commercial and military pursuits. In both England and France, royal orders were definite with regard to the importation of manuscripts from the Levant.[19] Desire in an age of empire has its rhetoric which in sum conveys the longing and ultimate will to raid the Other.

Daniel Defoe's canonical *Robinson Crusoe* (1719), which was contemporaneous with Galland's translation, speaks for an imperial unconscious to inhabit, domesticate, and possess an uninhabited island, an island for containing and impacting people and space.[20] Defoe perhaps de-philosophized the Andalusian Abu Bakr ibn Tufayl's protagonist Hayy ibn Yaqzan (Alive Son of Awake) to fit into Locke's and Hume's *homo sapiens*. What we get in Defoe's novel is the idea of a colony begging for a white colonizer to resurrect its potential for survival and fruition. The master is the one to lead the native through, like the future native elites in nineteenth-century colonies. However, the savage/civilized paradigm needs modification, for eighteenth-century rationalists knew that the Levant and North Africa could not fit into that. Their three-century translation movement simply refutes it. Hence, technical and scientific achievement emerges as the new paradigm. The emphasis is laid on scientific advancement as the rationale to invade and therefore "civilize" the Other, a point which the speaker in Shaykh Ḥassan al-'Aṭṭār's "Maqāmah" does not shy from celebrating.[21] The colonial logic highlights this paradigm as the much-needed move into a Europeanized, post-mercantile stage. No wonder the sage Imlac in Samuel Johnson's (1709–84) *Rasselas* (published in 1759) has to invoke colonial invasion as the only way towards that leap and thence the civilization of Ethiopia and the African coast. Equating power with knowledge and wisdom, Johnson's sage has to argue as follows: "They [Western nations] are more powerful, Sir, than we … because they are wiser, knowledge always predominates over ignorance, as man governs the other animals."[22] Although there is always an ironic twist in Johnson's writings, he subscribes in *Rasselas* to an eighteenth-century colonial paradigm, whereby knowledge as reached and applied in the West inevitably has to dominate other nations and cultures.

Galland's translation in context

Is Galland's fourteenth-century Syrian manuscript another uninhabited land, a land without people that has to undergo domination? Galland's *Contes Arabes* is without an author, or a copyist who can tell us when and where it is transcribed. An orphan disclaimed by Arab classicists, the text is open to the interested bidder who may at his discretion share adoption with the Maronite Hanna Diyab. Taking hold of the matter as his property now, Galland proved assiduous. He was no mere dabbler in Arabic and should have known how storytelling denies single authorship. He has to remedy the situation, not through Huet's theory of an Eastern origin for fiction, but through a number of strategies that cover black holes in a disputed and even doubtful genealogy of the incorporated tales, and also respond to and even generate the urgent need to grant the new commodity a place of honor in a culture that prides itself on some *belles-lettres* and elegant manners. In other words, as much as Defoe's island invites being turned into a white habitat, so does the manuscript in hand: it needs to secure the right entry into French culture. This textual terrain has many political and literary implications, and it is up to the course designer to address this comparison between two texts, a novel, and a translation that appeared at the same time.

Entry into the French milieu

Galland dedicates the book to Madame la Marquise d'O, dame du Palais de Mme la Duchesse de Bourgogne.[23] While the dedication opts to secure a place for the new production among aristocracy and upper classes, it implies some editorial trimming to ensure that status. He was silent with respect to the Arab belletrists' low opinion of the tales. The transactional nature of the dedication carves out a line of decorum that cannot be reduced to distortion; but for a classroom, it remains important as a stepping stone to draw a comparative sketch within the receiving milieu in particular. There are no serious discrepancies between the manuscript and the translation apart from the prerequisites of "decorum" that touch on finesse, women, and the mention of God and other religious expressions.[24] Decorum for Galland means occasional stylistic modifications and alterations that nevertheless make a considerable portion. Hence, Borges is right in saying: "Word for word, Galland's version is the most poorly written of them all, the least faithful, and the weakest, but it was the most widely read."[25] For two centuries, it was the most widely read, not only among the youth of France and England, as Walter Bagehot would like us to believe in his neo-classist reading in 1859, but also among notables, scholars and writers.[26] Galland was shrewd enough to pacify readers through paratextual material: a dedication, a preface, and a third advertisement that suppresses "night breaks."

However, I take the issue of advertisement further; indeed, as far as placing it into a double-bind problematic that situates the advertisement within the body of translation as an informing narrative strategy. As a paratextual threshold, the forewarning announcement plays on the text as a subtext that requires tightening and refinement within the rules of fidelity to the "genius and character" of the original or its inventiveness and manners. While the original has already done away with the opening sisters' formula, the advertisement is not only superfluous and meaningless, but also an affront to the reader of an original manuscript. The advertisement must then be a contrivance, an artificial device to make the translator's presence felt and needed as the master of the show in this profitable enterprise that obviously won him the attention of the "learned."

The other side of the problematic is even more challenging. These are called "advertisements" in the age of a nascent print industry. They fight for publicity and space in an early open market economy. The print industry, the rise of journalism, commercial enterprise abroad, and competition with other European nations are all aspects of this economy and its theoretical base. Translation as such is not a passing "fine arts" fulfillment. It is a commercial transaction carried out for the sake of the learned public who paid for it in terms of material and symbolic capital. As the long dedication shows, Galland thinks of his translation as symbolic payment in exchange for favors, but he derives symbolic and material profit through this association with the nobility. The venture proved so popular and highly esteemed that he felt obliged to engage further with the manuscript dealer, Paul Lucas, who brought with him from Aleppo (February 1709) the storyteller Hanna Diyab. With an incomplete manuscript and Hanna Diyab's handwritten supplement that covered volumes 10–12, we understand the reasons behind Galland's unrequired emphasis on issues of "propriety and taste" and "the circumspection required by the refinement of our language and our age," an excuse which Muhsin Mahdi found unwarranted and only justified as laziness.[27] It is not laziness, however. Galland's "word-for-word" translation is a commodity that happened to establish its presence in an early open market economy, and carve its own cultural inroads among the learned and the rising middle-class publics. Even if there were no serious transgressions, Galland was obliged to revise some phrases to make his translation saleable to the nobility and the learned.

However, these advertisements that weave themselves through the translation also address issues of fashion and expectations. They indeed made the text conversant with the majority of the reading public. In *Scheherazade in England* (1981) there is a detailed analysis of critical, literary and popular taste that appeared over two centuries in periodicals, glosses, commentaries, articles, chapters, rejoinders, along with prefaces to oriental tales and imitations. These display also multiple sides of an active cultural life in an age of social transformation and colonial expansion, a cultural life that was behind the minor liberties Galland took with the original and the large ones that involved interpolation from other sources.[28]

Galland's translation can be understood better in terms of context when set against the major translations that follow. Lane's translation, 1838–41, sets translatability in sharp relief. Only against the Victorian translation can we understand strategies of translation as necessarily and inevitably informed by what Michel Foucault considers the "episteme in which knowledge has its conditions of possibility."[29] The post-Enlightenment configurations in the construction of knowledge have a decisive empirical turn that enforces not only utilitarian values, but also and along with them an opaque narrative, a realistic detail and a thick documentary record, as the case is in Edward William Lane's edition. It is not enough to accept Galland's appeal to the increasing interest in other nations and cultures. There Galland writes, "[a]ll the Orientals, Persians, Tartars and Indians are characterized … and appear as they are, from the sovereign down to persons of the humblest condition."[30] Early in the nineteenth century, the poet and critic James Henry Leigh Hunt (1784–1859) would stretch this to allow for other possibilities and horizons where desire answers to the attending social mobility in an industrial age. Life is a macrocosmic stock exchange and Galland's translation is another ground where will and desire, fortune and misfortune are unlimited. The Romantic "interior infinite" makes up the landscape that is boundless in opportunity and promise.[31]

This infinitude has to be itemized, systematized and organized according to capitalist decrees. The distribution of labor, economies and human conduct pass through other mediations to which Lane was responsive. These conditions, and not only his sojourn in Cairo for five years, were the ones that made his translation a work for "the parlor table," a center for "placid reading and chaste conversation," in Borges's words.[32] In line with an early twentieth-century critique of this probity, Borges adds: "neither the high Egyptian nights nor the black and opulent coffee with cardamom seed nor the frequent literary discussions with the Doctors of the Law nor the venerable muslin turban nor the meals eaten with his fingers made him forget his British reticence and the delicate central solitude of the masters of the earth."[33] Borges explains Lane's strategy of documentation and authentication in philological, lexicographic and socio-theological terms. On the level of language, "Lane justifies his interpretation of each problematic word."[34] He substantiates his critiques of Lane's philological enquiry with further notes, for Lane "furnishes editions and page numbers … [and] accumulates a chaos of clarifications which, in organized form, make up a separate volume." Even the philological side is not a choice. It is imposed as part of the "conditions of possibility." At a certain time in French culture when decorum was *a priori*, Galland was able to carry out the "literal mode" of translation which was championed more than a century later by F.W. Newman and a few others against Matthew Arnold, who discounts peculiarities as historically improvable. Lane's translation fits in neither mode, for he retains and suppresses peculiarities as he likes, using a footnoting apparatus to help out in sustaining a sense of authenticity. The emerging texts are no mere translations, for they are translations that respond to a milieu, its tastes and demands. At this juncture, there is material for the classroom to draw connections and meanings.

In exploring the condition of possibility that constitutes an epistemic turn, we find a disparity between Lane's highly claimed sojourn in Cairo and the very noticeable and marked subscription to a Victorian culture.[35] It is not only utility that decides a translation and the translator's strategies, but also a powerful middle-class ethos that imposes its checks and balances on every transaction. Borges further explores the language of sex and the sanitized European transference:

> Galland corrects occasional indelicacies because he believes them to be in bad taste. Lane seeks them out and persecutes them like an inquisitor. His probity makes no pact with silence: he prefers an alarmed chorus of notes in a cramped supplementary volume.[36]

These are the major translations, for the rest, including John Payne's and Burton's voluminous one, build on them to bring into the canon tales from other sources which constitute no sustainable manuscript tradition.[37] Indeed, Muhsin Mahdi's salvage of Galland's manuscript can help us to excavate the canon in its entirety, not as a philological enquiry, though this can be helpful, but primarily through a text that leads us out of the maze of oral tradition. Written down as a text for professional storytellers and their trainees, the text is less hospitable to mutilation or addition. The text can serve copyists, booksellers and readers. It is a much desired commodity in urban cities and their social fringes. Translatability becomes an affordable enterprise for a translator who may reap interest, financial and symbolic, even though he can claim a better taste than what popular tales convey. Interest holds sway; otherwise why should Galland have undergone the project and be desperate to have it grow into 12 volumes?

However, translation is not the acted-on object; it also emerges as an actor in its own right, deciding modes of reception and impacting ways of perception. In Galland's version, decorum allows larger possibilities to infiltrate the reading social strata, implicating writers and essayists in an activity that reached into Europe and impelled Grub Street hack translators in England to impart the merchandise in their language. Conversely, Lane's learned production with its heavy documentation alienates the common public, distances the text from this readership and reserves it for the pursuit of scholars, middle-class drawing rooms and the functionaries of the empire. Lane's translation is a Victorian production that proved the caliber of an eminent Orientalist in consolidating a growing imperial archive of the Arab East. In this configuration in time and in relation to the empire and the East, Lane's translation and notes set the tone for a differentiated grid of knowledge in France and England. Documentation and anthropological and ethnographic apparatus define at this point the grand imperial claims of full mastery on its colonies. If Lane's contentment was also that of the empire, as shown in the Crystal Palace exhibition, Galland's harping on light entertainment and delicacy addresses a dying aristocracy, but a rising middle-class readership. Hence, he ends up with some discontent rather than with an imperial grandeur.

Muhsin Mahdi quotes from Galland's private correspondence an entry in his journal in which he laments wasting his time on a project, which was meant for "frivolous court and society women."[38] Mahdi perhaps fell into the same trap. The grand and grave professor of Islamic philosophy made a sharp turn in his career with the resurrection of Galland's manuscript. He might have been projecting Galland's lament into his own career, a self-elegy and premonition that the *AN* brings on its enthusiasts. It is an elegy that nevertheless always grants them a second life in an enduring human engagement with storytelling.

The twentieth century: how different?

Richard F. Burton's notorious translation, edition, and redaction was no less significant in terms of annotation and heavy apparatus than his "Terminal Essay," which is larger in size than a usual monograph. Burton's virtue lies somewhere else: he demonstrates a wide knowledge, more than any before him including the sagacious and reticent Edward William Lane. Burton rewrites stories, crowded them with "circumstantial detail and physiological traits" that make up his vast reservoir of reading and experience,[39] but he also shocked the late Victorians, and enraged a society that had accommodated Galland's version and found in Lane's edition solace, comfort, and knowledge of some East.[40]

Few from among twentieth-century critics or scholars showed zeal equivalent to eighteenth- and nineteenth-century responses when Europe was taken by surprise at the introduction of a book of so much variety, richness, and appeal. However, twentieth-century littérateurs like Tzevtan Todorov, Jorge Luis Borges, and John Barth found something else that met their theoretical or literary expectations. Their perspectives are in line with their own theories of fiction.[41] If academia made use of these perspectives it was only as part of interest in theory, an interest that grew stupendously after 1968, but was also prepared for by the vogue of structuralist poetics after World War II and the commencement of the Cold War. From the classroom lyric that was the occupation of New Critics to post-Vladimir Yakovlevich Propp's readings of narrative morphologies, there was a line of critical thought that was also a reaction and response to hard-core Stalinist ideology and state. In later periods, and especially after the birth of new alliances in reaction to Nazi, capitalist or socialist ideologies, systems of thought witnessed revisionist readings. Indeed, the *Thousand and One Nights* still serves as a potential index of taste in theory, after it was also an index of popular taste in the eighteenth and nineteenth centuries.[42] Significantly it was used in feminist theorizations on women's roles, but it made its way to cinematic productions, proved usable in theoretical discourses on aesthetics, and was easily manipulated in media images to consolidate racist and politically motivated divides against Arabs and Muslims, who are usually portrayed as static, violent and traditional societies.[43]

In 2004, we have lectures, conferences, special issues of journals, and books on the *Thousand and One Nights*. The very celebration of Antoine Galland's translation of the tales, *Les Mille et une Nuits: Contes Arabes*, 300 years after that groundbreaking enterprise, has led to conference papers, books, readers, encyclopedias, and more courses in academia. Some new university branches overseas jumped on the occasion as a publicity venue, calling for papers and holding grand conferences on the *Thousand and One Nights*. What is worth noticing, however, is the fact that most of these efforts are enlisted under the rubric of the *Arabian Nights*, not the *Thousand and One Nights*. Catering to the familiarity of their audiences with that Anglicized title is only one concession, among many, to an assimilationist drive that rests on interest and value transaction.[44] The move should not be seen outside the context of global-reach programs, and the thriving category of world literature which used to exclude Arabic literature, and even the *Thousand and One Nights*, from its curricula.

In world literature: a comparative sketch before and after

The upsurge of *Arabian Nights* in the post-world war periods coincides with structuralist and post-structuralist tendencies, but this could not be gauged in its entirety as part of the climate of ideas without seeing it in context of the 1960s and the growing dissatisfaction with closed systems of thought, ideology, and institutionalized academia. It was no coincidence for our purpose here, for example, that Ferial Ghazoul got involved in the structural analysis of the *AN* when T. Todorov was at Columbia University in the 1970s. Binary structures, narrative units, semiotics, systems, and relations negate coincidence, and prioritize construction as a structural activity, based on selection and relation. This activity undermines not only the "new critical" devotion to the lyric to bring forth narrative motifs and agents (actants), but also traditional inquiry. The method and perspective open up possibilities as a series of generative openings through embedding, choice and selection in the vast horizon of possibility. The *AN* is exemplary as we notice in Todorov's study of the *Fantastic* and the *Poetics of Prose* where he picks on intricate interstices, the ones where the wonderful, the uncanny and supernatural have their full play, or when narrative men make up life in loquacity.[45]

Henceforth, emphasis was laid on readability of translations, propriety for the study of the fantastic, and somehow relevance and validity for narratology. In other words, the *Arabian Nights* was still read until the end of the 1970s as a Western commodity, a usable hybrid to explain attitudes and positions, a margin to authenticate a body of texts or theories, and an Appendix that can be conducive towards forming a thesis without burdening users with any other accountability. Randomly classified under oriental works in eighteenth-century Europe, before the definite application of the term to Southeast Asia, the book elicits imitations under other rubrics and epithets like Tartar, Persian, Indian, and Turkish. Apart from some elitist celebratory critiques or grudging remarks, which have already been studied in *Scheherazade in England* (1981),[46] publishers and shrewd specialists in the contours of literary taste used the book also for utilitarian, moral, and sheer entertainment purposes,[47] connecting it with whatever body of literature struck the redactor as important. Behind these there is, however, what Roland Barthes discerns in the writings of no less a cynic than Voltaire.[48] Building on an inventory of compartmentalization that also relied heavily on Galland's translation and on earlier Jesuit and medieval images of the "Mohammedan Arab, the Turk, the Chinese, the Siamese, and, most prestigious of all, the Persian," Voltaire, like his contemporaries, used the available "veritable rhetoric of exoticism, a kind of digest whose figures are so well formed and so well known," whereby "the oriental is not the object, the term of genuine consideration, but simply a cipher, a convenient sign of communication," as Roland Barthes succinctly explains.[49] The nations themselves "are for Voltaire … forms, mobile signs, without actual content, humanity at zero degrees (Centigrade), which one nimbly grasps in order to signify … oneself."[50]

Critics and writers rely on a legacy of appropriation that made its definite statements about lands and texts as its own belongings. The prominent explicator of literary taste in England, Robert Chambers, wrote in the second half of the nineteenth century that the tales were "amongst similar things of our own which constitute the national literary inheritance."[51] Chambers was right, however, because translations are also appropriations that cater more to the taste and needs of their audiences rather than those of their originators. This commodity transaction has two sides, for it demonstrates how these translations can be a weighty chapter in a national literature. A survey of English or French literature in the eighteenth and nineteenth centuries can tell us as much. On the other hand, its actual exclusion from literary history signifies the other side of colonialism, for the colonized, like the appropriated, belongs to a proprietor who has the power not only to claim the property but also to negate its identity or significations. Thus while the *Athenaeum* reviewer wrote in 1838 that translations, imitations and reviews "must form no uninteresting chapter in any comprehensive history of modern literature,"[52] there is no significant mention of this breathtaking phenomenon in the cultural history of Europe. If there is any mention, it is reserved for the translator, the proprietor and hero of such enterprise.

This exordium intends to map out reception trajectories including the critical history of taste which may prepare us for the less arduous issue of designing syllabi and planning viable means of meeting the premises of Robert Chambers and situating thereby the *Arabian Nights* – otherwise *Thousand and One Nights* – among the "things of our own which constitute the national literary inheritance," while exploiting to the utmost the positive gains in cultural studies and postcolonial theories. The book as such has to appear not only as a landmark in literary and cultural history, but also as a base for theoretical thinking. Thus, a study of reception, for instance, can work nicely, not only within programs in world literature, comparative studies, and Middle Eastern offerings, but also in courses designed for other departments like political science, history, sociology and other social sciences. The receptions in Europe over three centuries invite historical, economic, societal, cultural, pure literary or media studies. Receptions include a study of common readership, the press, publishing and culture industry. These will lead to a better knowledge of the genealogies of colonialism and also the genealogy of knowledge and institutions in Europe and America, for example. As a fecund source and index of culture industry, the history of translations, imitations, adaptations, abridgements, periodical criticism and melodramatic production, evolves as a handy inventory whose equal is rare.

The acute lover of books, the poet and essayist Leigh Hunt, upon reviewing six new editions of the *Thousand and One Nights* for the *London and Westminster Review* in October 1839, wrote that it is "the most popular book in the world."[53] Years later, in 1875, another sharp critic and literary essayist, James Mew, stipulates: "No deciduous laurel is this book, from the leaves of which greedy Time steals gradually away the beauty and the verdure. As it once drew us, it still draws out children from the playground, and in the chimney corner its glittering conceits still carry consolation to old age."[54] Decades later, other cultures showed also varied responses that are worth taking into account to investigate points of agreement and departure. Taken as a British legacy, and indeed with gusto, the British carried and exported the tales wherever they made new colonies and achieved more colonial expansion. It was used for teaching Arabic to their personnel in India in the early decades of the nineteenth century, and the gesture should not be read lightly, for to inculcate a language through a text could never happen in British thought had not the *Arabian Nights* been taken as a British commodity. Macaulay's guidelines for education in India can tell us as much.[55] On the other hand, the fact that references, images and epithets from the book have invaded authors' production offers us another index, not only of national or imperial tastes, but also of a process of appropriation that builds on the empowering digestion of other cultures. A cursory survey of writings throughout Europe will demonstrate that this proliferation is paradoxically an imposition of limits on other cultures, an occupation of a sort that forces its own terms in understanding or negating Others.[56]

In keeping with the early stipulation that appearance and reception also fluctuate and vary in different times, places, and under changing circumstances and cultural milieux, it is also worthwhile to study the frametale, not only in terms of aesthetic proclamations of life as imitative of art, or art as provider for life, but also in its availability to feminist theories. The focus on Scheherazade/Shahrayar syndrome has already been manipulated by the Brontës Emily and Charlotte in *Wuthering Heights* and *Jane Eyre*, respectively, where Heathcliff and Rochester duplicate a Byronic version of the frametale protagonists and where Rochester admits to being conquered and mastered by Jane. However, "Shahrazad Feminist," a phrase coined perhaps by Fadwa Multi-Douglas, has evolved since then not only as heroine in a third wave feminism, free from male discourse and powerful enough to launch her challenge to male hegemony,[57] but also as an adept in postcolonial theory where there is a visible struggle for selfhood.[58]

Other scholars, especially folklorists, find other syndromes that cut across the tales as structural patterns, like the brother-sister, and the father-daughter. According to the explicators of these syndromes, these orient the *AN* in a large and expansive folklorist and popular narrativity.[59] The attention to the frametale is a twentieth-century distinction. Writers and critics have not been concerned with other storytelling clusters of interconnected tales as much as they have been concerned with embedding narrative, typology, and death/life equation between dullness and eloquence. Each category can be broken into many subdivisions. The celebration of life versus impending death is a major narrative dynamic which Edward William Lane, and concomitant with his philological training, takes as attestation of the Arab disposition to eloquence.[60]

European aesthetes find something else, however, for there is not only that sense of abandon and unrestraint, but also and along with it the struggle against rigidity, absolutism, and the polymorphous presence in discourses of power which Michel Foucault genealogizes in *The History of Sexuality*.[61] An articulation of this celebration of art takes place later, in such articles as the one on the "Everlasting Nights" by G.K. Chesterton in his *Spice of Life and Other Essays*.[62] There Chesterton concludes: "Never in any other book, perhaps, has such a splendid tribute been offered to the pride and omnipotence of art." This premise may lead others, like Michel Foucault, to use it partially to buttress or debunk the shifting position of authorship and the agency of the author. After expounding on the relationship between "writing with death," as "the theme and pretext of Arabian narratives," he concludes: "Scheherazade's narrative is an effort, renewed each night, to keep death outside the circle of life."[63] Foucault would like to assert the metamorphosis of warding off death into an obsession in Western thought, but Scheherazade's role can grow beyond this whenever Scheherazade becomes merely unmapped agency, a device of convenience that can easily lead to a study of the art itself, as Todorov does in the *Poetics of Prose* and *Fantastic* where he partially builds his narratology, especially on "narrative men,"[64] and the triple subdivisions of fantastic poetics, already mentioned.[65]

Many will try also to see how the art itself recognizes its power through forcing ifrits, demons, and kings to surrender to the power of storytelling and accept it as full or piecemeal ransom for one's endangered life.[66] Embedding then acquires more narrative significance and assumes ongoing conceptualization, not as mere containment of scattered tales or else an imposition of a system on otherwise disparate elements. Narrative generates and auto-invests in its own power and doubles it through consistent recognition. The master narrator plans not only to save her life but also to devise an art that is preemptive of all means and manifestations of brutal control. This said, we must not think in complacent terms of a storyteller who is keen on an opportunist gain, for notwithstanding the fact that storytelling is a commodity that needs promotion, it cannot gain much without symbolic, paradigmatic and syntagmatic functions.[67] Although Todorov's few insights into structural patterns sit well in current theories of narrative and thence promote the study of the *Arabian Nights*,[68] it is good to remember that many other studies of structures and semiotics in the collection have not fared well because of lack of linguistic preparation to engage with layered levels of meaning or flippant colloquial antics.[69] Not knowing the nuances of language daily use and under different circumstances and in different times and locations may not lead to a thorough reading of the threadlike horizontal concatenations that have to meet or cross vertical axes which Barthes, for one, holds as basic to the story and the syntax of character and discourse.[70]

The storyteller insists, for example, on descriptions of young men or women as in the "Story of the Porter and the Three Ladies of Baghdad," the "Story of Ali b. Bakkar and the Slave-Girl Shams al-Nahar," and the "Story of the Slave-Girl Anis al-Jalis and Nur al-Din Ali ibn Khaqan," elaborating on their physical and moral properties. This seemingly parasitic dallying will soon explain how two people fall in love with each other, and how even demons are ready to recognize this beauty and consequentially use it as the reason behind their intervention in human affairs. This seemingly residual part, with its poetry and physical descriptions, lays the ground not only for homoerotics, evoked by such elaborate description of boys like Nur al-Din Ali,[71] but also for the many faces and doubles of authorship. The king's buffoon in the steward's cluster, as well as the barber's brothers, and along with the physician Duban, play on the limits of life and death, narrative and negation, and center and periphery. They continue a process of documentation and erasure, presence and absence, power and loss, and open up the tales for further analysis, exploration, and also joy.

The "Tailor's Tale: The Lame Young Man from Baghdad and the Barber" tells as much. Never can a narrator claim more. The artist as a common man has emerged in full, manipulating every discourse and every ruse to his/her own advantage, but paying tribute nevertheless to the arch narrator who allows him some space to parody and challenge her refinement and elegance. The barber's role is not merely an extension of the master narrator Scheherazade: he is the parodist par excellence who competes with her not only in claiming diversified and comprehensive knowledge, but also in building embedded narratives that rely on tribal solidarity or, to apply Michel Foucault's term, "sexuality of alliance," whereby all is kept within the family. There he presides as master of ceremonies. He carries parody further however, exhausts its limits, and turns it into a travesty. Everything is changed into masquerade and grotesquery. Even the royal center where the royal family presides is turned upside down. He assumes Scheherazade's roles, whereas his implicated objects are emptied of grandeur or power. There are no defeated or conquered Shahrayars, but war casualities where his curiosity and nosiness hunts them down, leaving them disabled and forlorn. If the idealized city drives his brothers outside its gates as unwanted, troublesome, or unfit, it is his job to manipulate his knowledge and narrative skill to turn the wheel of fortune against the moneyed classes that sustain a system which he negates by other means. He looks upon his human casualities as unworthy of the wealth left for them, as mere squanderers whom he has to expose, but with faith in his right to bring them under control. He is the unwanted paterfamilias. If they try to outsmart him and run to the end of the world, he is there nevertheless, exasperating them to the utmost, and making them see him as their fate.

A study of narrative art and the underpinnings of a theoretical base for narratology can make a weighty chapter in any European literary history. An entire liberal arts curriculum can be devised in terms of technique, semiotics, semantics, painting, cuisine and culinary arts, language, knowledge, travelogue and topography. As I have shown in "Nonverbal Narratives," there is so much in the least conspicuous narrative units.[72] There is more, however, because the tales play also on the limits of the real. With patience and prudence, one can develop a whole sequence of courses devoted to the *Thousand and One Nights.* Its reservoir of animal tales, concepts of transgender beauty, and the presence or absence of limits and transgressions, can lead the discussion further and place it at the center of social sciences.

The acute and perhaps most erudite and delicate British romanticist Leigh Hunt is worth citing in this instance. After elaborating on the general characteristics of infinitude that will be termed as "interior infinite" by Bakhtin – in a different context and outside the domain of these tales and without even the slightest reference to them[73] – Leigh Hunt comes across this rich repertoire in the *Thousand and One Nights* and finds it useful to acquaint his readers with his thoughts. He explains:

> Hope and imagination have their fair play, as well as the rest of us. There is action heroical, and passion too: people can suffer, as well as enjoy, for love; you have bravery, luxury, fortitude, self-devotion, comedy as good as Moliere's, tragedy, Easter[n] manners, the wonderful that is in a commonplace, and the verisimilitude that is in the wonderful calendars, cadis, robbers, enchanted palaces, paintings full of color and drapery, warmth for the senses, desert in arms and exercises to keep it manly, cautions to the rich, and hope for the miserable.[74]

This surmise opens up more horizons that are relevant not only to reading, enjoying or understanding the *Thousand and One Nights*, for both the "interior infinite" and the exterior or the topographical, the realistic and the theological, for example, also rest on and along a number of axes which may force us again to enlist what has already been hinted at or cursorily studied, like issues of sexuality, gender in general, race, religion and class. These may also bring us back to an engagement with a European corpus of readings that has already claimed the *AN* as its property without giving due attention to the elements that make up its Indo-Persian, and Arabic/Islamic formation.[75] In other words, we need also to make use of this corpus but with a more rigorous approach to contexts that have helped the burgeoning of this formation in its own terms. To continue applying a one-sided critique, notwithstanding its richness and diversity, is also dysfunctional. It distances the product from its producers and cuts off its richness from its tributaries of meaning.[76] Recent receptions of the text in Japan, India, China, Western Africa, North Africa, South Africa, and Latin Americas demonstrate serious differences in understanding, use and imitation. These may also suggest how earlier periods and societies may have received the tales or contributed to their outcome and formation.

While arguing for a study of the tales as they are, or as narratives in an Islamic context, I must mention the effort of the late Suhayr Qalamawi who was a pioneer in reading the *Thousand and Nights* in this vein in her doctoral dissertation supervised by Ṭāhā Ḥusayn in the 1930s.[77] The direction is important not only because of its validity for the stipulation of this intervention, but also because it reorients the theories about the framing of the collection as imposed by her supervisor Ṭāhā Ḥusayn and the eminent playwright and novelist Tawfīq al-Ḥakīm. After all, both Ḥusayn and al-Hakim came up with a number of narrative variations on the frametale, as I explained in my book in Arabic, on *The Arabic Novel: Its Initiation and Growth* (1986/1988).[78] In a cultural dependency and partial involvement in a subservient transactional activity that took cognizance of the image of Scheherazade as exported by the European and French aesthetes in particular, they both emphasized the frametale to the exclusion of the collection as a whole. In their joint narrative *Al-Qaṣr al-Masḥūr* (The Enchanted Palace), Scheherazade and Shahrayar are let out of the frame to exercise their power on the writers, who became culprits in trapping the royal figures in a stereotyped juncture. The latter is a genuine addition to European manipulation to be sure, but it builds its argument on an aesthetic proposition of art for art's sake that also bypasses the cultural and societal implications of a collection that generates its powerful storytelling through other layers of meaning and contention. Cycles and clusters of tales and narrative units assume some dynamism through their dialectical chains of relation, refutation or corroboration. In an early work, I have also drawn attention to this issue as a prototype for another joint narrative by both Jabrā Ibrāhīm Jabrā and ʻAbd al-Raḥmān Munīf in their *ʻĀlam bilā khara'iṭ* (Unchartered World).[79]

Earlier interest, signified by al-Ḥakīm and Ṭāhā Ḥusayn, gave way in the second half of the twentieth century, especially after 1967 as a defining point, to a different turn whereby the *Arabian Nights* becomes a space for an oblique critique of corrupt politics, as in Najīb Maḥfūẓ's *Layālī Alf Laylah* (translated as *Arabian Nights and Days*).[80] In theater, it fared even better, especially at the hands of the late Egyptian playwright Alfred Faraj, in his *ʻAlī Janāḥ al-Tibrīzī and his Slave Quffah.*[81]

The most important point is that we are constantly dealing with an open book that creates its own open horizons, including its contextual premises. No one syllabus can cover its material, and in what follows I can draw a number of course titles that can serve as guidelines for courses. Both titles (*Thousand and One Nights* and *Arabian Nights*) are used:

- Scheherazade as a Travelling Trope: The Multi-Faced Receptions of the *Arabian Nights* across Cultures
- The *Arabian Nights*: narrative and narratological approaches

- The Islamic specifics in the *Thousand and One Nights*
- Translating the *Arabian Nights*: texts as sites for cultural dynamics and power relations
- *The Arabian Nights*: an introductory course
- Narrative techniques in the *Arabian Nights*
- The *Arabian Nights*: a global commodity?
- Sex and gender in the *Arabian Nights*
- Social life in the *Thousand and One Nights*
- Politics of silence in the *Thousand and One Nights*
- Speech as gain in the *Arabian Nights*
- Economic transactions and deals: the outcomes of Scheherazade's tales
- The celebration of pleasure in the *Arabian Nights*
- The *Thousand and One Nights* in world literature
- The *Thousand and One Nights* as world literature
- Women of the *Arabian Nights*
- The *Thousand and One Nights* in Arabic literature

Notes

1 For a discussion, see Muhsin al-Musawi, "The Growth of Scholarly Interest in the Arabian Nights," *Muslim World* (Hartford, CT) LXX (1981): 196–212.
2 Reviews by D.P. Varma, *Canadian Review of Comparative Literature* 10 (1983): 443–45; Mahmoud Manzalaoui, *Yearbook of English Studies* 16 (1986): 334–35; M. Youssef, *International Journal of Middle East Studies* 15, no. 03 (August 1983): 390–391; Issa Peters, "Scheherazade in England: A Study of Nineteenth-Century English Criticism," *MESA Bulletin* (1982): 23–24.
3 See Muhsin al-Musawi, *Scheherazade in England* (Washington, DC: Three Continents Press, 1981).
4 For a survey of the first reception, see Christopher Knipp, "The Arabian Nights in England: Galland's Translation and its Successors," *Journal of Arabic Literature* V (1974): 44–54; Robert Erwin, *The Arabian Nights: A Companion* (London: Allen Lane/Penguin, 1994); Muhsin al-Musawi, "Introduction," Barnes and Noble Edition of the *Arabian Nights* (New York: Barnes and Noble, 2007), xv–xxxviii. See also Dwight Reynolds, "A Thousand and One Nights: A history of the text and its reception," in *Arabic Literature in the Post-Classical Period*, eds Roger Allen and D.S. Richards (Cambridge: Cambridge University Press, 2008), pp. 270–291.
5 D.B. MacDonald, "On Translating the 'Arabian Nights'," Pt. I, *The Nation* LXXI, no. 1835 (Aug. 30, 1900): 167–68, 167; cited in *Scheherazade in England*, 11.
6 Ibid., 59.
7 See Husain Haddawy, trans., *The Arabian Nights*, based on the text of the fourteenth-century Syrian manuscript. Edited by Muhsin Mahdi (New York and London: W.W. Norton, 1990).
8 For a study of the manuscript tradition, see Richard F. Burton, "Terminal Essay," *Book of the Thousand Nights and a Night*. Vol. 10 (London: Burton Club for Private Subscribers Only, n.d.); and "Biography of the Book and its Reviewers Reviewed," *Supplemental Nights*. Vol. 6 (London: Burton Club for Private Subscribers only); D.B. MacDonald, "A Bibliographical and Literary Study of the First Appearance of the 'Arabian Nights' in Europe," *Library Quarterly* II, no. 4 (Oct. 1932): 387–420. For a full bibliographic listing

of bibliographical material until 1981, see Muhsin al-Musawi, *Scheherazade in England*, 147–188.

9 See Jorge Luis Borges, "The Translators of *The Thousand and One Nights*," in *Selected Non-Fiction*, ed. Eliot Weinberger, trans. Esther Allen (New York and London: Penguin, 1999), 92–110; also, Jorge Luis Borges, "The Thousand and One Nights," trans. Eliot Weinberger, *The Georgian Review* (Fall 1984): 564–574.

10 See Jorge Luis Borges, "The Translators of *The Thousand and One Nights*," in *Selected Non-Fiction*, 92–110, 92.

11 "On Translating the 'Arabian Nights'," Pt. I, *The Nation* LXXI, no. 1835 (Aug. 30, 1900): 167; cited in *Scheherazade in England*, 11.

12 See *Scheherazade in England*, 10, 13, 26–27, 29–30, 42–5, 72–5, 81–85.

13 *The Thousand and One Nights = Alf Layla wa-Layla*: Arabic text edited with introduction and notes by Muhsin Mahdi; from the earliest known sources (Leiden: Brill, 1984), 2 vols: 1. Arabic Text; 2. Critical Apparatus.

14 For more on this point see, Muhsin al-Musawi, "The Republic of Letters: Arab Modernity?" *The Cambridge Journal of Postcolonial Literary Inquiry* (November 2014): 1–16, 4. DOI: 10.1017/pli.2014.21, published online: 12 November 2014; also cited and translated from al-Jāḥiẓ, Kitāb al-ḥayawān, ed. Muḥammad 'Abd al-Salām Hārūn (Beirut: Dār al-Jīl, 1996), I: 75–76; by Hayrettİn Yücesoy, "Translation as Self-Consciousness: Ancient Sciences, Antediluvian Wisdom, and the 'Abbāsid Translation Movement," *Journal of World History* 20, no. 4 (2009): 523–557.

15 Matthew Arnold, *On Translating Homer*: Three Lectures Given at Oxford (1961); reproduced: *Essays by Matthew Arnold: Including Essays in Criticism*, 1865, *On Translating Homer* (with F.W. Newman's Reply), and *Five Other Essays Now for the First Time Collected* (Oxford: Oxford University Press, 1914), eBook.

16 Quoted in al-Musawi, *Scheherazade in England*, 97–98.

17 Meant as an empire on display, the Crystal Palace exhibition assorted all achievements and artifacts from the colonies along with the metropolis industrial products.

18 See G.L. Toomer, *Eastern Wisdom and Learning: The Study of Arabic in Seventeenth-Century England* (Oxford: Clarendon Press, 1996).

19 As a king's letter of 15 February 1634 indicates, the British need for acquisition of manuscripts was not confined to the humanistic side, but also because, "there is a great deal of learning that very fit and necessary to be known, that is written in Arabike, and there is a great defect in both our Universities." The association between translation from Arabic and imperial interest is made clear: "for the knowledge of those parts, [is of] … some accommodation to trade," says a draft of Laud's letter, as the king's envoy and Oxford University President. Quoted in Toomer, p. 108, 109. See Muhsin al-Musawi, *Anglo-Orient* (Tunis: Centre de Publication Universitaire, 2000), 32.

20 See among the latest on this topic, Mahmud Baroud, *The Shipwrecked Sailor in Arabic and Western Literature: Ibn Tufayl and his Influence on European Writers* (London: Philip Wilson Publishers/I.B. Tauris & Co., 2012).

21 For a partial translation, see Peter Gran, "Hasan al-'Aṭṭār," in *Essays in Arabic Literary Biography, 1350–1850* (Wiesbaden: Harrassowitz Verlag, 2009), 56–68; and "Maqāmah fī dukhūl al-Faransāwiyīn li- 'l-Diyār al-Miṣriyyah," trans. as "The Maqāmat al-'Aṭṭār," in *Islamic Roots of Capitalism: Egypt, 1760–1840*, 2nd rev. ed. (Syracuse, NY: Syracuse University Press, 1998), Appendix I, 189–91. A full translation of another version is in progress. Hādhihī al-Maqāmāt al-Suyūṭiyah, by Suyūṭī (1445–1505), where Ḥasan al-'Aṭṭār's (1776–1834) is included (Cairo: Ṣāliḥ al-Yāfī, 1859).

22 *The History of Rasselas Prince of Abbisinia*. Ed. with an introduction by G. Tillotson and B. Jenkins (Oxford: Oxford University Press, 1977), chap. 11, p. 30.

23 Marie Anne de la Vergne Guilleragues (1657–1737), the wife of Marquis d'O; her father was the Ambassador of France (d. 1685).

24 Antoine Galland, *Arabian Nights' Entertainments*. Trans. 4 vols (London: Longman, 1783), I, ix.

25 "Translators of *The Thousand and One Nights*," 92.

26 Walter Bagehot, "The People of the Arabian Nights," IX (July 1859): 44–71. See my discussion in *Scheherazade in England*, 102–110, 134–36.
27 Muhsin Mahdi, 34.
28 Muhsin Mahdi, p. 35.
29 *The Order of Things* (New York: Random House – Vintage Books, 1994), xxii.
30 Qt. Muhsin Mahdi, 21.
31 For his reviews of Galland and Lane, see Muhsin al-Musawi, *Scheherazade in England*, 81–85. Infinite interior is used by Mikhail Bakhtin, *Rabelais and his World*, trans. Helene Iswolsky (Indiana, Bloomington: Indiana University Press, rpt. 1984), p. 44.
32 "The Translators of the Thousand and One Nights," 94.
33 Ibid.
34 Ibid., 95.
35 See Muhsin al-Musawi, *Scheherazade in England*, 91–7, 121–29.
36 "The Translators of the Thousand and One Nights," 94.
37 For a summary of this manuscript tradition, see Muhsin al-Musawi, "The History of the Book," Barnes and Noble Edition of the *Arabian Nights*, 655–664.
38 Muhsin Mahdi, 37.
39 Borges, 101.
40 For a study of responses, see Muhsin al-Musawi, *Scheherazade in England*, 115–146; and Richard F. Burton, "Biography of the Book and its Reviewers Reviewed," *Supplemental Nights*. Vol. 6 (London: Burton Club for Private Subscribers only).
41 See also Muhsin al-Musawi, *The Postcolonial Arabic Novel* (Leiden: Brill, 2003) for a review and assessment of use of Todorov and John Barth. See also his *Anglo-Orient: Easterners in Textual Camps* (Tunis: University Publication Center, 2000), especially the chapters on Arabian Nightism and Orientalism.
42 Ghazoul's "A Structural Analysis of the Arabian Nights," co-supervised by Edward Said and T. Todorov was updated and revised under another title: see Ferial Ghazoul J., *Nocturnal Poetics: The Arabian Nights in Comparative Context* (Cairo: The American University in Cairo Press, 1996). For bibliographic record of scholarship, see *Scheherazade in England*, pp. 147–188.
43 See Jack Shaheen, *Reel Bad Arabs: How Hollywood Vilifies a People* (New York: Olive Branch Press, 2001); *The TV Arab* (Bowling Green, Ohio: Bowling Green State University Popular Press, 1984); and *Arab and Muslim Stereotyping in American Popular Culture* (Washington, DC: Center for Muslim-Christian Understanding, History and International Affairs, Edmund A. Walsh School of Foreign Service, Georgetown University, 1997).
44 See the discussion in *Anglo-Orient*, pp. 18, 62–64, 60–61, 69–70, 107, 115–117, 166–167, 313; and *The Islamic Context of the Thousand and One Nights* (New York: Columbia University Press, 2009).
45 Tzvetan Todorov, *The Fantastic: A Structural Approach to a Literary Genre*, trans. Richard Howard (Ithaca, NY: Cornell University Press, 1975); *Poetics of Prose*, trans. Richard Howard (London: Blackwell Publishers, 1977).
46 See especially 9–142.
47 Ibid., 9–36.
48 Roland Barthes, "The Last Happy Writer," in *A Barthes Reader*, ed. Susan Sontag (New York: Barnes Noble, 2009), 127–136, at 130–131.
49 Roland Barthes, "The Last Happy Writer," 131.
50 Ibid.
51 See Muhsin al-Musawi, *Scheherazade in England*, 38; cited from his article, "What English Literature Gives Us?" in Alexander Ireland's edition of *Book Lover's Enchiridion: Thoughts on the Solace and Companionship of Books* (London: Simpkin, Marshall, 1883), 287.
52 Review of Edward William Lane's translation, no. 572 (October 13, 1838), 737. Cited in *Scheherazade in England*, 37.
53 Leigh Hunt, "New Translations of the Arabian Nights," *London and Westminster Review*, XXXIII (Oct. 1839), 101–37. Cited in *Scheherazade in England*, 42.

54 Ibid., 42. James Mew, "The Arabian Nights," *Cornhill Magazine* XXXII (Dec. 1875): 711–32, 712.

55 See Syed Mahood, *History of English Education in India, 1781–1893: Extracts from Parliamentary Papers, Official Reports*, etc. (Calcutta: Baptist Mission Press, 1895), 268–270.

56 On the amount of allusions in writings see, for example, M.C. Annan, "The Arabian Nights in Victorian Literature," unpublished PhD, Northwestern University, 1945.

57 See Fadwa Multi-Douglas, "Shahrazad Feminist," 40–55pp. In Richard Hovannisian, Georges Sabagh, eds, *The Thousand and One Nights in Arabic Literature and Society* (Cambridge: Cambridge University Press, 1997). See also Muhsin al-Musawi, *The Postcolonial Arabic Novel*, 1–115.

58 See among the latest studies, Silvia Nagy-Zekmi, "Images of Scheherazade: Representations of the Postcolonial Female Subject," *Journal of Gender Studies* 12/3(2003): 171–180.

59 See Hasan El-Shamy, "A Motif Index of Alf Laylah wa Laylah: Its Relevance to the Study of Culture, Society, the Individual, and Character Transmutation," *Journal of Arabic Literature* XXXVI:3 (2005): 235–268; and "Siblings in the Arabian Nights," *Journal of Fairy-Tale Studies*. Special Issue: *The Arabian Nights: Past and Present*, guest editor Ulrich Marzolph, Vol. 18:2 (2004): 170–186.

60 Qt. from Edward William Lane, *The Thousand and One Nights, Commonly Called, in England the Arabian Nights' Entertainments* (London: Charles Knight, 1839–1841) 1: 63, n.18, in Muhsin al-Musawi, *The Islamic Context of the Thousand and One Nights*, 24.

61 See Michel Foucault, *The History of Sexuality* (New York: Random House – Vintage editions, 1990), 18.

62 G.K. Chesterton, *The Spice of Life and other Essays*, ed. Dorothy Collins (Beaconsfield: Darwen Finlayson, 1964), 58–60.

63 Michel Foucault, "What is an Author?" in *Foucault's Reader*, ed. Paul Rabinow (New York: Pantheon Books, 1984), 102.

64 Tzvetan Todorov, *The Poetics of Prose*. Tran. Richard Howard (Oxford: Basil Blackwell, 1971), 67–79.

65 Tzvetan Todorov, *The Fantastic*. Tran. Richard Howard (Ithaca, NY: Cornell University Press, 1973, 1975), 40–77, 107–110, 113–116, 164–167. More noticeable is the tendency among publishers and editors to draw on the *Arabian Nights* treasury for more money: thus a recent Norton edition, for example, is based on the same translator's version which was republished many times by the publisher, but this time with an apparatus of criticism of an already published material, including Todorov's critical insights. See *The Arabian Nights: Norton Critical Editions*, translated by Husain Haddawy. Edited by Daniel Heller-Roazen (New York: Norton, 1990).

66 See for example, David Pinault, *Story-Telling Techniques in the Arabian Nights* (Leiden: Brill, 1992), pp. 16–30. Pinault does discuss "story-telling techniques" here, but he does not speak specifically about how these techniques are used in a power dynamic.

67 Although Roland Barthes uses these as relations of the sign and the system of signification, it is worthwhile applying them to functions that he treats succinctly in "Introduction to the Structural Analysis of Narratives"; see *A Barthes Reader*, 212–249. The symbolic builds on an interior relation, like any symbol, whereas the other two have an exterior one. The paradigmatic becomes evident in opposition or difference, whereas the second builds on association or neighboring. See "The Imagination of the Sign," ibid. 179–184, at 179–180.

68 See for example Andras Hamori's neat use of approaches to narrative, "The Magian and the Whore: Readings of Qamar al-Zaman," in *1001 Nights: Critical Essays and Annotated Bibliography, Mundus Arabicus* 3 (Cambridge, MA: Mahjar, 1985), pp. 25–40; and *On the Art of Medieval Arabic Literature* (Princeton: Princeton University Press, 1974).

69 Although I prepared a complete, yet unpublished, bibliography other scholars came up later with some bibliographies: see Ulrich Marzolph ABC bibliography. See *The Arabian Nights Bibliography*, compiled by Ulrich Marzolph (last updated November 28, 2013) www.user.gwdg.de/~enzmaer/arabiannights-engl-elektr.html

70 See *Roland Barthes: A Reader*, 218–219.
71 See in Haddawy's translation (Norton, 1990), pp. 347–349.
72 Muhsin al-Musawi, "Scheherazade's Nonverbal Narratives," *Journal of Arabic Literature* 36, no. 3, *The Thousand and One Nights* (2005): 338–362.
73 See Mikhail Bakhtin, *Rabelais and his World* (Bloomington, IN: Indiana University Press, 1984), 44. See Also Muhsin al-Musawi, *Anglo-Orient* (Tunis: Centre de Publication Universitaire, 2000), 27.
74 *Leigh Hunt's London Journal* 1. no. 30 (October 22, 1834): 233–37, at 233.
75 "The Changing Value of 'Alf Laylah wa Laylah' for Nineteenth-Century Arabic, Persian, and English Readerships," *Journal of Arabic Literature* 36, no. 3 (2005): 269–287.
76 See Muhsin al-Musawi, *The Islamic Context of the Thousand and One Nights.*
77 Published as *Alf Laylah wa-Laylah* (Cairo: Dār al-Ma'ārif, 1941; reprint 1966).
78 Muḥsin al-Musawī, *Al-Riwāyah al-'Arabiyyah: al-nash'ah wa al-taḥawwul* [The Arabic Novel: Its Initiation and Growth] (Baghdad: Al-Taḥrīr, 1986; Beirut: al-Ādāb, 1988; Cairo: Al-Hay'ah al-Miṣriyyah).
79 See al-Musawī, *Al-Riwāyah al-'Arabiyyah.*
80 For more see Muhsin al-Musawi, *The Postcolonial Arabic Novel: Debating Ambivalence*, 375–388; and *Islam on the Street* (Lanham, MD: Rowman & Littlefield, 2009), 72–87.
81 Translated into English by Rasheed el-Enany and Charles Doria as "'Ali Jannah al-Tabrizi and his Servant Quffa," in *Modern Arabic Drama: An anthology*, ed. Salma Jayyusi and Roger Allen (Bloomington: Indiana University Press, 2005), 305–51.

Bibliography

Selected bibliography of articles in English

Abbott, Nabia. "A Ninth-Century Fragment of the 'Thousand Nights': New Light on the Early History of the Arabian Nights." *The Arabian Nights Reader*. Ed. Ulrich Marzolph. Detroit, MI: Wayne State University Press, 2006.

Ahmed, Syed Jamil. "Transcultural Mutation of The Thousand and One Nights and its Contemporary Relevance." *Dhaka University Studies* 54.1(1997): 1–77.

Alderson, Brian. "Scheherazade in the Nursery." *The Arabian Nights in English Literature*. Ed. Peter L. Caracciolo. New York: St Martin's Press, 1988. 81–94.

Allen, Roger. "An Analysis of the 'Tale of the Three Apples' from The Thousand and One Nights." *Logos Islamikos: Studia Islamica in Honorem Georgii Michaelis Wickens; Pontifical Inst. of Medieval Studies*. Ed. Roger M. Savory and Dionisius A. Agius. Toronto: Papers in Mediaeval Studies, 1984. 51–60.

Al-Musawi, Muhsin Jassim. "The Arabian Nights in Eighteenth Century English Criticism." *The Muslim World* 67(1977): 12–32.

Al-Musawi, Muhsin Jassim. "The Growth of Scholarly Interest in the Arabian Nights." *The Muslim World* 70(1980): 196–212.

Al-Musawi, Muhsin Jassim. "The Taming of the Sultan: A Study of Scheherazade Motif in Jane Eyre." *Adab al-Rafidian* 17(1988): 59–81.

Al-Musawi, Muhsin Jassim. "The 'Mansion' and the 'Rubbish Mounds': The Thousand and One Nights as Popular Literature." *Journal of Arabic Literature* 35,2(2004): 329–367.

Al-Musawi, Muhsin Jassim. "The Growth of Scholarly Interest in the Arabian Nights." *The Arabian Nights Reader*. Ed. Ulrich Marzolph. Detroit, MI: Wayne State University Press, 2006. 1–20.

Bodine, J. Jermain. "Magic Carpet to Islam: Duncan Black MacDonald and the Arabian Nights." *The Muslim World* 67(1977): 1–10.

Bonebakker, Seger A. "Some Medieval Views on Fantastic Stories." *Quaderni di studi arabi* 10(1992): 21–43.

Borges, Jorge Luis. "The Thousand and One Nights." *The Georgia Review* 38,3(1984): 564–574.

Brockway, Duncan. "The Macdonald Collection of Arabian Nights: A Bibliography." *The Muslim World* 61(1971): 256–266.

Clinton, Jerome W. "Madness and Cure in the 1001 Nights." *Studia Islamica* 61(1985): 107–125.

el-Shamy, Hasan. "Oral Traditional Tales and the Thousand Nights and a Night: The Demographic Factor." Ed. Morten Nøjaard. *The Telling of Stories: Approaches to a Traditional Craft.* Odense: Odense University Press, 1990.

el-Shamy, Hasan. "A Motif Index for Alf Layla wa-layla [The Thousand Nights and a Night]." *Minpaku Anthropology Newsletter* 15(2002): 5–7.

Furtado, Antonio L. "The Arabian Nights: Yet Another Source of the Grail Stories?" *Quondam et Futurus: A Journal of Arthurian Interpretations* 1.3(1991): 25–40.

Graham, Victor E. "Marcel Proust and the Mille et une Nuits." *Canadian Review of Comparative Literature* 1(1974): 89–96.

Heath, Peter. "Romance as Genre in 'The Thousand and One Nights': Part II." *Journal of Arabic Literature* 19,1(1988): 1–26.

Heath, Peter. "Romance as Genre in The Thousand and One Nights." Ulrich Marzolph, ed. *The Arabian Nights Reader.* Detroit, MI: Wayne State University Press, 2006. 170–225.

Horovitz, Josef. "The Origins of the 'Arabian Nights'." *Islamic Culture* 1(1927): 36–57.

Irwin, Bonnie D. "Narrative in the Decameron and the Thousand and One Nights." *Approaches to Teaching Boccaccio's Decameron.* Ed. James McGregor. New York: Modern Language Association of America, 2000. 21–30

Keyser, James M.B. "1001 Nights: A Famous Etiquette Book." *Edebiyât* 3(1978): 11–22.

Knipp, C. "The Arabian Nights in England: Galland's Translation and its Successors." *Journal of Arabic Literature* 5(1974): 44–54.

Kobayashi, Kazune. "The Illustration of the Old Man of the Sea and the Story of Sindbad the Sailor: Its Iconography and Legendary Background." Ed. Tetsuo Nishio. *Cultural Exchange in the Arab World.* Osaka: National Museum of Ethnology, 2001. 101–118.

Kruk, Remke. "Warrior Women in Arabic Popular Romance: Qannâsa bint Muzâhim and other Valiant Ladies." *Journal of Arabic Literature* 24(1933): 213–230.

Lane-Poole, Stanley. "The Arabian Nights." *Edinburgh Review* 164(1886): 166–199.

Leeuwen, Richard van. "Translating the Thousand and One Nights." *Différée, ignorée, altérée: Les mécomptes de la traduction.* Ed. W. Lenschen. Lausanne: Centre de traduction littéraire, 1995. 125–135.

MacDonald, Duncan B. "On Translating the Arabian Nights." *Nation* 71.6(1900): 167–168, 185–186.

MacDonald, Duncan B. "Story of the Fisherman and the Jinni, transcribed from Galland's MS. of the 'Thousand and One Nights'." *Orientalische Studien, Theodor Nöldeke zum siebzigsten Geburtstag,* 1(1906): 357–383.

MacDonald, Duncan B. "Maximilian Habicht and his Recension of the Thousand and One Nights." *Journal of the Royal Asiatic Society* (1909): 685–704.

MacDonald, Duncan B. "'Ali Baba and the Forty Thieves' in Arabic from a Bodleian Ms." *Journal of the Royal Asiatic Society* (1910): 327–386.

MacDonald, Duncan B. "Further notes on 'Ali Baba and the Forty Thieves'." *Journal of the Royal Asiatic Society* (1913): 219–221.

MacDonald, Duncan B. "A Missing MS. of the Arabian Nights." *Journal of the Royal Asiatic Society* (1913): 432.

MacDonald, Duncan B. "From the Arabian Nights to Spirit." *Moslem World* 9(1919): 336–348.

MacDonald, Duncan B. "A Preliminary Classification of Some Mss. of the Arabian Nights." *A Volume of Oriental Studies: Presented to Edward G. Browne on his 60th Birthday*. Eds. Thomas W. Arnold and Reynold A. Nicholson. Cambridge: University Press, 1922. 304–321.

MacDonald, Duncan B. "The Earlier History of the Arabian Nights." *Journal of the Royal Asiatic Society* (1924): 353–397.

MacDonald, Duncan B. "A Bibliographical and Literary Study of the First Appearance of the Arabian Nights in Europe." *Library Quarterly* 2(1932): 387–420.

Macleod, Dianne Sachko. "The Politics of Vision: Disney, Aladdin, and the Gulf War." *The Emperor's Old Groove: Decolonizing Disney's Magic Kingdom*. Ed. Brend Ayers. New York: Peter Lang, 2003. 179–192.

Mahdi, Muhsin. "Remarks on the 1001 Nights." *Interpretation* 3(1973): 157–168.

Mahdi, Muhsin. "Exemplary Tales in the 1001 Nights." *The 1001 Nights: Critical Essays and Annotated Bibliography*. Eds. Campbell et al. Cambridge, MA: Dar Mahjar, 1985. 1–24.

Mahdi, Muhsin. "From History to Fiction: The Tale Told by the King's Steward in the 1001 Nights." *Oral Tradition* 4(1989): 65–79.

Mahdi, Muhsin. "The Sources of Galland's Nuits." *International Journal of Islamic and Arabic Studies* 10,1(1993): 13–26.

Mahdi, Muhsin. "From History to Fiction: The Tale Told by the King's Steward in The Thousand and One Nights." *The Thousand and One Nights in Arabic Literature and Society*. Ed. Richard G. Hovannisian and Georges Sabagh. Cambridge: Cambridge University Press, 1997. 8–105.

Marzolph, Ulrich. "The Story of Abū al-Ḥasan the Wag in the Tübingen Manuscript of the Romance of ʻUmar ibn al-Nuʻmān and Related Texts." *Journal of Arabic Literature* 45 (2014): 316–348.

Mottahedeh, Roy P. "'Aja'ib in The Thousand and One Nights." *The Thousand and One Nights in Arabic Literature and Society*. Ed. by Richard C. Hovannisian and Georges Sabagh. Cambridge: Cambridge University Press, 2006. 29–39.

Moussa-Mahmoud, Fatma. "A Manuscript Translation of the Arabian Nights in the Beckford Papers." *Journal of Arabic Literature* 7(1976): 7–23.

Moussa-Mahmoud, Fatma, 'English Travellers and the Arabian Nights.' *The Arabian Nights in English Literature: Studies in the Reception of The Thousand and One Nights into British Culture*. Ed. Peter L. Caracciolo. New York: St Martin's Press, 1988. 95–110.

Murphy, Christopher M. "A Brief Look at Illustrated Translations of the Arabian Nights." *The 1001 Nights: Critical Essays and Annotated Bibliography*. Ed. Kay Hardy Campbell et al. Cambridge, MA: Dar Majhar, 1985. 86–100.

Naddaf, Sandra. "Magic Time: Narrative Repetition in the Thousand and One Nights." *The 1001 Nights: Critical Essays and Annotated Bibliography*. Ed. Kay Hardy Campbell et al. Cambridge, MA: Dar Majhar, 1985. 41–57.

Ouyang, Wen-chin. "Romancing the Epic: 'Umar al-Nu'man' as Narrative of Empowerment'." *Arabic and Middle Eastern Literatures* 3(2000): 5–18.

Pannewick, Friedericke. "The Hakawātī in Contemporary Arabic Theatre: The Re-emergence of an Old Pattern of Communication." *Myths, Historical Archetypes and Symbolic Figures in Arabic Literature*. Ed. Angelika Neuwirth et al. Beirut: Deutsche Morgenländische Gesellschaft, 1999. 337–348.

Perho, Irmeli. "The Arabian Nights as a Source for Daily Life in the Mamluk Period." *Studia Orientalia* 85(1999): 139–162.

Perry, Ben E. "The Origin of the Book of Sinbad." *Fabula* 3(1960a): 1–94.

Perry, Ben E. "Some Traces of Lost Medieval Story-Book." *Humanoria: Essays in Literature, Folklore, Bibliography, Honouring Archer Taylor*. Ed. Wayland D. Hand and Gustave O. Arlt. Locust Valley: Augustin, 1960b. 150–160.

Pinault, David. "Bulaq, Macnaghten, and the New Leiden Edition Compared: Notes on Storytelling Technique from the Thousand and One Nights." *Journal of Semitic Studies* 32 (1987): 125–157.

Pinault, David. "Story-Telling Techniques in the Arabian Nights." *International Journal of Middle East Studies* 26, 2(May 1994): 358–360.

Popper, William. "Data for Dating a Tale in the Thousand and One Nights." *Journal of the Royal Asiatic Society* (1926): 1–14.

Poremba, Daphne. "A Story from the Thousand and One Nights in Five Versions: The Sexual and Social Discourse in Comparative Context." *Jamâ'a* 2,1(1998): 9–28.

Reeve, Henry. "The Arabian Nights." *Edinburgh Review* 164(1886): 166–197.

Rehatsek, Edward. "A Few Analogies in the 'Thousand and One Nights' and in Latin Authors." *Journal of the Bombay Branch of the Royal Asiatic Society* 14(1880): 74–85.

Reynolds, Dwight. "A Thousand and One Nights: A History of the Text and its Reception." *Arabic Literature in the Post-Classical Period*, eds. Roger Allen and D.S. Richards. Cambridge: Cambridge University Press, 2008. 270–291.

Rosenthal, Melinda M. "An Admirable and Ridiculous Hero: Some Notes on the Bedouin in Medieval Arabic Belles Lettres, on a Chapter of Adab by al-Râghib al-Ishfânî, and on a Literary Model in which Admiration and Mockery Coexist." *Poetics Today* 10(1989): 471–492.

Rosenthal, Melinda M. "Burton's Literary Uroburos: The Arabian Nights as Self-Reflexive Narrative." *Pacific Coast Philology* 25(1990 Nov.): 116–125.

Sallis, Eva. "Sheherazade/Shahrazâd: Rereading the Frame Tale of the 1001 Nights." *Arabic and Middle Eastern Literatures* 1,2(1998): 153–167.

Schacker-Mill, Jennifer. "Otherness and Otherworldliness: Edward W. Lane's Ethnographic Treatment of The Arabian Nights." *Journal of American Folklore* 113/448(2000): 164–184.

Segert, Stanislav. "Ancient Near Eastern Traditions in The Thousand and One Nights." *The Thousand and One Nights in Arabic Literature and Society*. Ed. Richard G. Hovannisian and Georges Sabagh. Cambridge: Cambridge University Press, 1997. 106–113.

Shaw, Sheila. "Early English Language Editions of the Arabian Nights." *Muslim World* 49 (1959): 232–238.

Shaw, Sheila. "The Rape of Gulliver: Case Study of a Source." *Publications of the Modern Language Association of America* 90(1975): 62–68.

Talmon, Adi. "Tawaddud – The Story of a Majlis." *The Majlis: Interreligious Encounters in Medieval Islam*. Ed. Hava Lazarus-Yafeh et al. Wiesbaden: Harrassowitz, 1999. 120–127.

Todorov, Tzvetan. "Narrative-Men." *The Arabian Nights Reader*. Ed. Ulrich Marzolph. Detroit, MI: Wayne State University Press, 2006. 226–238.

AFTERWORD

Teaching Arabic literature, Columbia University, May 2010

Jaroslav Stetkevych

Such a promise, of magic in clarity, when approaching Arabic literature, is as enticingly irresponsible as it is also true on its deepest levels of critical intuition. Starting with the almost iconic image/*figura* of the Arabic language, we remain awestruck by the structural clarity of its morphology. The verbal and nominal obviousness of the logic of the inner working of all its elements create the effect of clarity and transparency unobtainable in, or irretrievable by, other languages. On that logical and *ishtiqāq*-analogical level alone, it is nothing other than "*mubīn*" – a phenomenon of "clarity."

Expanding from this linguistic "wonder of clarity" to the super-structure, or bridge on which the Arabic language seems to have taken its first steps into realms of aesthetics – that is into literature, which is into poetry – there emerged, harnessing that language's pure "logic," the further step, or claim for "clarity," as transparent as its analogical clarity of *ishtiqāq*, the inborn – let us not have any doubt about it – chain-circular harness (its own system of clarity of logic) of the specifically Arabic prosody – *'arūḍ*.

A perfect, that is, "clear" literary beginning was thus to be obtained within a perfect, "clear," language. Everything would appear perfectly "clear," needing no further "clarification," were it not for the requirement of (and for) understanding. Because together with these basic clarities, there were also all those other autochthonies of the Arabic language: the expressions of its own speaking self. Specifically, to mention only one such proffering, there was the extant and "existing" ruling and overruling form and structure: the poem-*qaṣīdah*. In the circle of autochthonous perfections, transparencies and clarities, the *qaṣīdah* enjoyed an associative existence of moot acceptance, of enthusiasm tapering off into tolerance, or a final, insincere-for-unmotivated rejection. Everything about it, however, for uncomfortably long critically intellectually unobservant generations, remained "clear," in deep hermeneutical exclusion.

Arabic literature has reached us, or we have been drawn to it, by the "magic" of its autochthony – or its selective autochthonies. The clarity of the ordered word, especially in its analogical *ishtiqāq* geometry; the rhythm of its prosodic challenges and promises of unknown harmonies, achievable, it seemed, only in struggles against odds of alien, to us aggressively disturbing, cacophonous counter-sounds and counter-rhythms and claims to harmonies to be extracted out of unison. These requirements and cultural-anthropological impositions reached us when we were still culturally open-minded and open-hearted, when romanticism was still spawning on the receptive soil of idealism, when we did not yet want to know all the cultural truth, and when we thought ourselves amply rewarded with the knowledge of only such things that would "harmonize" with what was already ours – things that enriched, that is, "expanded us" without our responsibility, before Rilke's requirement: *Du mußt dein Leben ändern*. Such would have been our lives as philologist-scholars or even historian-scholars, enwrapped in "cold" realities of the culture of pre-literary understanding. Our horizons would be those of the abstract possibilities of analogies and linguistic geometry. They would be what we could obtain with surprising ease – the literary derivative of the poetic word in form and act. Their domain and their imposition upon the critic – and even the scholar – was, however, something quite different.

Here we have to shift to talking of the Arabic *qaṣīdah* as that linguistic culture's "universal poem."

Just as it was conceivable – and certainly acceptable – that the ground-laying two former levels of literary cognition and inquiry of the Arabic language (as poetic language) were, or would be, taken over – let us put it this way – by hands and minds of philological hard science. The actual literary-critical and literary-analytical enterprise, however, ought never to have become a bailiwick in philological hard science's hands and minds, even if such was once the position of Ḍiyā' al-Dīn Ibn al-Athīr (early thirteenth century]. This, however, never truly escaped from the Arabic claims for philology's (*al-Lughah*) literary-critical primary authority, excepting, perhaps, or precisely, that rare case of Ḍiyā' al-Dīn Ibn al-Athīr, who categorically disenfranchised cold philological sciences, especially cold philologists.

"Extramurally," that is, outside the Arab "owners" of the philological-critical pre-emptive posture in "academia" – at first of European, and presently even of American orientalism – the claim for authoritative apportionment of critical regency still hesitates to forsake the old position of primacy of voice, even if this is done with the pretense of some form of deference to the primary possessors of the Arabic poetic-critical stance. Such a pose of deference, however, lacks sincerity for being self-defensive and abdicating. The pivots of identity and the lines, or circles, of circumspection of Arabic creativity within the inerasable autochthony of its first pristineness, alas, all this has been there from the beginning, it would seem, and it is still "there," as it is already "here." How little has changed, or is changing? Where is the "legacy of the primacy"?

Here we are, very much like the select group I remember of almost 50 years ago from a lecture (of mine) at Oxford's St Antony's College. The language is the same, the problems, the challenges are the same; at least one of those faces then present is still here and the same. However, something has changed, or is changing – now not in a gothic renaissance cocoon of old legacies of authority, but still so far back in its own past, so parochially part of that past. Now no longer alone, in New York, at Columbia University, under new aegis and with stronger, clearer purpose – I hope!

INDEX

For Product Safety Concerns and Information please contact our EU representative GPSR@taylorandfrancis.com
Taylor & Francis Verlag GmbH, Kaufingerstraße 24, 80331 München, Germany

www.ingramcontent.com/pod-product-compliance
Lightning Source LLC
Chambersburg PA
CBHW071753110726
47908CB00006B/1792

* 9 7 8 1 1 3 8 2 1 1 9 7 1 *